Cybersecurity Policies and Strategies for Cyberwarfare Prevention

Jean-Loup Richet
University of Nantes, France

A volume in the Advances in Digital Crime, Forensics, and Cyber Terrorism (ADCFCT) Book Series

An Imprint of IGI Global

Managing Director:	Lindsay Johnston
Managing Editor:	Austin DeMarco
Director of Intellectual Property & Contracts:	Jan Travers
Acquisitions Editor:	Kayla Wolfe
Production Editor:	Christina Henning
Development Editor:	Brandon Carbaugh
Cover Design:	Jason Mull

Published in the United States of America by
Information Science Reference (an imprint of IGI Global)
701 E. Chocolate Avenue
Hershey PA, USA 17033
Tel: 717-533-8845
Fax: 717-533-8661
E-mail: cust@igi-global.com
Web site: http://www.igi-global.com

Library of Congress Cataloging-in-Publication Data

Cybersecurity policies and strategies for cyberwarfare prevention / Jean-Loup Richet, editor.
     pages cm
  Includes bibliographical references and index.
   ISBN 978-1-4666-8456-0 (hardcover) -- ISBN 978-1-4666-8457-7 (ebook) 1. Cyberterrorism--Prevention. 2. Cyber intelligence (Computer security) 3. Cyberspace operations (Military science) 4. Computer crimes--Prevention. I. Richet, Jean-Loup, 1988-
   HV6773.15.C97C923 2015
   364.4--dc23
                              2015009640

This book is published in the IGI Global book series Advances in Digital Crime, Forensics, and Cyber Terrorism (ADCF-CT) (ISSN: 2327-0381; eISSN: 2327-0373)

British Cataloguing in Publication Data
A Cataloguing in Publication record for this book is available from the British Library.

For electronic access to this publication, please contact: eresources@igi-global.com.

Advances in Digital Crime, Forensics, and Cyber Terrorism (ADCFCT) Book Series

ISSN: 2327-0381
EISSN: 2327-0373

MISSION

The digital revolution has allowed for greater global connectivity and has improved the way we share and present information. With this new ease of communication and access also come many new challenges and threats as cyber crime and digital perpetrators are constantly developing new ways to attack systems and gain access to private information.

The **Advances in Digital Crime, Forensics, and Cyber Terrorism (ADCFCT) Book Series** seeks to publish the latest research in diverse fields pertaining to crime, warfare, terrorism and forensics in the digital sphere. By advancing research available in these fields, the **ADCFCT** aims to present researchers, academicians, and students with the most current available knowledge and assist security and law enforcement professionals with a better understanding of the current tools, applications, and methodologies being implemented and discussed in the field.

COVERAGE

- Database Forensics
- Identity Theft
- Watermarking
- Mobile Device Forensics
- Computer virology
- Network Forensics
- Criminology
- Malware
- Digital Surveillance
- Vulnerability

IGI Global is currently accepting manuscripts for publication within this series. To submit a proposal for a volume in this series, please contact our Acquisition Editors at Acquisitions@igi-global.com or visit: http://www.igi-global.com/publish/.

Titles in this Series

For a list of additional titles in this series, please visit: www.igi-global.com

New Threats and Countermeasures in Digital Crime and Cyber Terrorism
Maurice Dawson (University of Missouri–St. Louis, USA) and Marwan Omar (Nawroz University, Iraq)
Information Science Reference • copyright 2015 • 369pp • H/C (ISBN: 9781466683457) • US $200.00 (our price)

Handbook of Research on Digital Crime, Cyberspace Security, and Information Assurance
Maria Manuela Cruz-Cunha (Polytechnic Institute of Cavado and Ave, Portugal) and Irene Maria Portela (Polytechnic Institute of Cávado and Ave, Portugal)
Information Science Reference • copyright 2015 • 602pp • H/C (ISBN: 9781466663244) • US $385.00 (our price)

The Psychology of Cyber Crime Concepts and Principles
Gráinne Kirwan (Dun Laoghaire Institute of Art, Design and Technology, Ireland) and Andrew Power (Dun Laoghaire Institute of Art, Design and Technology, Ireland)
Information Science Reference • copyright 2012 • 372pp • H/C (ISBN: 9781613503508) • US $195.00 (our price)

Cyber Crime and the Victimization of Women Laws, Rights and Regulations
Debarati Halder (Centre for Cyber Victim Counselling (CCVC), India) and K. Jaishankar (Manonmaniam Sundaranar University, India)
Information Science Reference • copyright 2012 • 264pp • H/C (ISBN: 9781609608309) • US $195.00 (our price)

Digital Forensics for the Health Sciences Applications in Practice and Research
Andriani Daskalaki (Max Planck Institute for Molecular Genetics, Germany)
Medical Information Science Reference • copyright 2011 • 418pp • H/C (ISBN: 9781609604837) • US $245.00 (our price)

Cyber Security, Cyber Crime and Cyber Forensics Applications and Perspectives
Raghu Santanam (Arizona State University, USA) M. Sethumadhavan (Amrita University, India) and Mohit Virendra (Brocade Communications Systems, USA)
Information Science Reference • copyright 2011 • 296pp • H/C (ISBN: 9781609601232) • US $180.00 (our price)

Handbook of Research on Computational Forensics, Digital Crime, and Investigation Methods and Solutions
Chang-Tsun Li (University of Warwick, UK)
Information Science Reference • copyright 2010 • 620pp • H/C (ISBN: 9781605668369) • US $295.00 (our price)

Homeland Security Preparedness and Information Systems Strategies for Managing Public Policy
Christopher G. Reddick (University of Texas at San Antonio, USA)
Information Science Reference • copyright 2010 • 274pp • H/C (ISBN: 9781605668345) • US $180.00 (our price)

DISSEMINATOR OF KNOWLEDGE

www.igi-global.com

701 E. Chocolate Ave., Hershey, PA 17033
Order online at www.igi-global.com or call 717-533-8845 x100
To place a standing order for titles released in this series, contact: cust@igi-global.com
Mon-Fri 8:00 am - 5:00 pm (est) or fax 24 hours a day 717-533-8661

Editorial Advisory Board

Table of Contents

Section 3
National Issues, Strategies and Policies

Section 4
Concluding Remarks and Reflections on the Essence of Cyberwarfare

Detailed Table of Contents

Section 1
Introduction to Cybersecurity and Cyberwarfare Principles

Increasing global dependence on cyberspace, rapidly and continuously changing technology, sustained vulnerabilities, and advanced persistent threats are driving an increasing societal risk of attack in cyberspace. Assuring a broad range of infrastructure critical for a well-functioning society is essential in a broad range of areas including but not limited to communications, transportation, and commerce. Based on an engagement with government, industry, and academia, and building upon prior research in computer security principles, this chapter articulates a set of enduring cybersecurity principles that can serve as a focusing framework to improve trust and assurance of systems considering requirements, architecture and design, and operations and maintenance. This chapter first outlines the threat and its consequence, describes prior research in cybersecurity principles, and then outlines a set of succinct and actionable cybersecurity principles.

The term cyber warfare is becoming increasingly common in mainstream media, on the political stage and in military circles. To many it will appear as if the world has been caught unaware by the rise of cyber warfare and its impact on global society. In reality, research on cyber warfare in the form it is known today dates back to the 1980s. This chapter presents cyber warfare from the perspective of the research community. It highlights current research into eight distinct areas of cyber warfare, and examines the arguments, agreements and disagreements between various authors in each field. The chapter is organised into sections, with each section providing background and analysis into a particular area.

Chapter 3

Clement Guitton, King's College London, UK

Attribution, finding the identity of actors behind an attack, is of primary importance to be able to classify an attack as a criminal act, an act of war, or an act of terrorism. But attribution is difficult. Many experts and analysts have explained this difficulty with technical arguments. This chapter seeks to bring nuances to such arguments closely analysing how attribution functions. It brings a focus on political factors constraining attribution, and on specifically three ones: standards of evidence, time, and private companies. It makes three main arguments. Firstly, standards of evidence are only secondary to the political will to attribute an attack. Secondly, time cannot only be reduced; the context surrounding attribution is as much important. Thirdly, companies' important role in attribution also gives ground for accused party to easily undermine their claims. The chapter concludes with opening up the debate on the usefulness of meta-data for attribution.

Section 2
Cybersecurity at Stake: Monitoring Threats, Managing Risks and Defensive Measures

Chapter 4

Claude Fachkha, Concordia University, Canada

Adversaries are abusing Internet security and privacy services to execute cyber attacks. To cope with these threats, network operators utilize various security tools and techniques to monitor the cyber space. An efficient way to infer Internet threat activities is to collect information from trap-based monitoring sensors. As such, this chapter primarily defines the cyberspace trap-based monitoring systems and their taxonomies. Moreover, it presents the state-of-the-art in terms of research contributions and techniques, tools and technologies. Furthermore, it identifies gaps in terms of science and technology. Additionally, it presents some case studies and practical approaches corresponding to large-scale cyber monitoring systems such as Nicter. We further present some related security policies and legal issues for network monitoring. This chapter provides an overview on Internet monitoring and offers a guideline for readers to help them understand the concepts of observing, detecting and analyzing cyber attacks through computer network traps.

Chapter 5

Neila Rjaibi, Department of Computer science, Institut Supérieur de Gestion de Tunis (ISG), Tunisia
Latifa Ben Arfa Rabai, Department of Computer science, Institut Supérieur de Gestion de Tunis (ISG), Tunisia

This chapter presents the security concepts terminologies (threat, risk, security risk management, security risk management process, security threat model) and present the state of the art of security risk management models, compare and discuss strengths and weaknesses of such models. Then it presents the Mean Failure Cost (MFC) model for quantifying security threats as a rigorous measure of cyber security, and as a cascade of linear models in order to estimate the system security using the loss of a given stakeholders as a result of security breakdown. Finally it presents an overview of the applicability of the MFC measure to e-systems. In the conclusion, the chapter criticizes the MFC Cyber Security Measure and presents an overview of different perspectives.

Chapter 6

Dr. Raymond J. Curts, George Mason University, USA
Dr. Douglas E. Campbell, Syneca Research Group, USA

Systems engineering is the branch of engineering concerned with the development of large and complex systems, where a system is understood to be an assembly or combination of interrelated elements or parts working together toward a common objective. Past experience has shown that formal systems engineering methodologies have not always been successfully applied to large and complex cybersecurity systems. These complex systems have become commonplace when applying cyberstrategies in cybersecurity operations. The ability to build, operate and maintain such systems is crucial to the effectiveness of cybersecurity operations. Most importantly, a cyberstrategy program must surround these systems on a global scale across multiple inter-related platforms. In this chapter, the authors demonstrate why a systems engineering approach is best suited for large and complex information systems used in cybersecurity, as well as the overall cyberstrategies that must also reside over these systems.

Chapter 7

Filipe Caldeira, University of Coimbra and Polytechnic Institute of Viseu, Portugal
Tiago Cruz, University of Coimbra, Portugal
Paulo Simões, University of Coimbra, Portugal
Edmundo Monteiro, University of Coimbra, Portugal

Critical Infrastructures (CIs) such as power distribution are referred to as "Critical" as, in case of failure, the impact on society and economy can be enormous. CIs are exposed to a growing number of threats. ICT security plays a major role in CI protection and risk prevention for single and interconnected CIs were cascading effects might occur. This chapter addresses CI Protection discussing MICIE Project main results, along with the mechanisms that manage the degree of confidence assigned to risk alerts allowing improving the resilience of CIs when faced with inaccurate/inconsistent alerts. The CockpitCI project is also presented, aiming to improve the resilience and dependability of CIs through automatic detection of cyber-threats and the sharing of real-time information about attacks among CIs. CockpitCI addresses one MICIE's shortcoming by adding SCADA-oriented security detection capabilities, providing input for risk prediction models and assessment of the operational status of the Industrial Control Systems.

Chapter 8

Cameron S. D. Brown, Australian National University, Australia

This chapter examines legal and technical issues that arise when considering strategic retaliatory countermeasures to cyber-attacks. Implications connected with endorsing techniques of active defense for nation-states are viewed alongside challenges faced by private entities. Proactive avenues for tackling cyber-security threats are evaluated and shortcomings within the international system of governance are analyzed. Retributive justice as a legal and philosophical concept is viewed through the lens of customary international law pertaining to use of force and self-defense. Difficulties in adapting rules governing kinetic warfare to instances of cyber-conflict are elucidated. The danger of executing counterstrikes for private entities is explained with reference to cross-border dilemmas, conflict of laws, and risks stemming from civil, criminal, and also administrative liability. Protocols for safeguarding anonymity are observed and the problem of attribution is illustrated. Costs and benefits associated with adopting methods of active defense are presented and solutions to avoid accountability failure are recommended.

Section 3
National Issues, Strategies and Policies

Chapter 9

Cyberspace is at once an area of immense cooperation and a no-holds barred arena for competition. Difficulties in creating a stable environment in cyberspace stem from differing national perceptions regarding the freedom of the Internet, application of international law and problems associated with attribution. Information space has no borders and no recognized rules of engagement or internationally accepted regulatory mechanisms. State parties, freelancers, criminals and terrorists all consider cyber operations beyond the pale of international jurisdiction. Some agreements have emerged concerning cybercrime but cyber warfare remains outside binding legal obligations. In the absence of a consensus on treaty obligations, it is a good idea to begin by constructing credible confidence building measures (CBMs) in information space between rival states. The prospects of an unintentional war as a consequence of a cyber-attack can spell disaster for South Asia. This paper discusses a range of CBMs that can be created between India and Pakistan in cyber space to control malicious cyber behavior and avert an inadvertent war. It advocates cyber cooperation instead of cyber warfare.

Chapter 10

Cyber attacks launched by individuals and/or supported by nation states have increased due to the prevalence of information technologies at critical infrastructure of the states. In this chapter, such attacks and consecutive impacts are visited. In connection with this issue, evolution of cyber threats from annoying malware to serious weapons is studied by examples; hence, precautions against such threats are visited and usage of anti-malware applications as prevalent precautions is assessed within the scope. Selected information security standards and strategies of selected states and precautions for cyber security of Turkey are studied. Our findings underline that educated citizens and companies along with public institutions should cooperate to provide a nationwide cyber security. Consequently, it is defended that governments should play an affective role to protect, educate, and guide governmental and private companies and citizens on the cyber security by promoting the cyber security topic in the successive national development plans.

Chapter 11

States and non-states actors in the Middle East are totally aware about the strategic importance of cyberspace. They all use it in the conflicts where they are involved in order to improve, for example, their communication, propaganda or intelligence operations. Nevertheless, all these actors have different capabilities in the cyber field. This article sums up how Middle East governments are developing those offensive capabilities and how cyber has changed the way States handle the threat that they are facing. In the other hand, it analyzes how non-states actors are using cyber tools and what kind of targets they are reaching or they want to reach in the near future.

Chapter 12

In November 2013 a series of protests in the Ukraine resulted in a change of government, which was followed by a pro-Russian incursion of Crimea in 2014 and an attempted breakaway by Eastern Ukraine. During this crisis information warfare tactics were used extensively, from propaganda and misinformation to cyber-attacks. The chapter discusses these information warfare activities based on reports, social media activity, and secondary data. The time period of interest is up to mid-May 2014, however subsequent major events are considered. An 'ideal' information warfare campaign and possible future repercussions of the conflict are discussed. The information warfare campaigns are discussed in relation to cyber-strategies. The impact of the cyber-strategies of the two nations involved and lessons learned will be discussed.

Section 4
Concluding Remarks and Reflections on the Essence of Cyberwarfare

This chapter examines Islamist cyberpropaganda case studies live in 2014, namely Al Qaeda, Islamic State, Boko Haram and Al Shabaab. The authors define cyberpropganda as the exploitation of the generative characteristics of online interaction for the production and reproduction of propaganda. The cross-case analysis identifies key messages and themes, how cyberpropaganda is generated and spread, and how it is made attractive to those who may act on it. In the discussion that follows implications for the policy-maker are identified and addressed. These include whether to tackle symptoms or causes of the problems and whether to treat the problems as essentially global or local. The final issue is how the counter-propagandist can make themselves heard.

The international system now depends on cyberspace, a global 'substrate' of massive, complex, insecurely designed networks providing systemic advantages to masses of predators and adversaries. States today face an unprecedented spectrum of 'cybered conflict' between peace and war with growing existential implications. Their piecemeal searches for defensible jurisdictions are creating a rising Cyber Westphalian world crisscrossed with gateways, holes, national cyber forces, and often partial, uncoordinated, or vague strategies. Over time, the world will have robust, midlevel, and poor cyber powers, with the first tier coercing the others and dominating the rules of exchange. Democratic civil societies are not guaranteed to be robust. For acceptable future societal well-being in a deceptive and opaque cybered world, decision-makers need a systemic approach based on the logic of complex socio-technical-economic systems (STES) to create the systemic resilience and disruption capacities across shareable (across allies/sectors) secure architectures essential to becoming a robust cyber power, which is the focus of this chapter.

This chapter seeks to define the term "cyberinsecurity" as the intersection of human fears and errors with user behaviour in a digital setting. Examining links between psychology and human-computer interaction, the author explores several case studies set against the context of cyber-authoritarianism in Asian countries and argues that any attempts to address or advance studies in cybersecurity and cyberwarfare must be grounded in a solid foundation of current social science theory.

Preface

The non-profit Privacy Rights Clearinghouse (PRC) maintains an ongoing chronology of significant data breaches in its efforts to raise awareness about consumer privacy issues. During 2011 alone, PRC reported 535 breaches compromising millions of records. The top six worst data breaches were criminal attacks on Sony, which compromised data related to its PlayStation Network and Qriocity music service operations in 101.6 records; the attacks on cloud based email provider Epsilon that breached between 50 to 60 million emails (which means as many as 250 million were affected in some way); the theft of nine servers from Health Net containing personal information on more than 1.9 million policy holders; the data breach at Sutter Physician Services and Sutter Medical Foundation that compromised the personal data of more than 3.3 million patients; the theft of backup tapes from Science Applications International Corporation (SAIC) containing healthcare patient data on 5.1 million active and retired members of the armed services and their families; and finally, the State of Texas Comptroller's Office, where thieves accessed 2 to 3.5 million records from three different state agencies, including the Teach Retirement Center, the Texas Workforce Commission and the Employees Retirement System of Texas (Schwartz, 2011). In the age of the Internet, cybersecurity will necessarily remain a vital concern.

On July 26, 2012, the United States Senate passed a procedural motion to begin debate on what is known as the Cybersecurity Act of 2012. The most controversial component of the bill addressed information sharing between private entities and governments, with the intention to prevent unwanted cybersecurity threats. The legislation is only the most recent attempt by U.S. legislators to either control certain aspects of private cyberspace or to address various elements of cybersecurity. Cybersecurity has also taken center stage at the international level, with such efforts as the United Nations World Summit on the Information Society in 2003 and 2005, the annual Information Security Summits conducted by Asian World Summit, and the International Telecommunication Union (ITU) with its 2010 Plenipotentiary Conference and its 2012 World Conference on International Telecommunications. In 2007, the ITU also launched the Global Cybersecurity Agenda, a general framework for potential international coordination of efforts to address the technical and social aspects of cybersecurity.

Cybersecurity has grown tremendously over the past decade as private industry, public administration, commerce, and communication gained greater online presence. The discipline intersects a number of fields including information systems, computer science, criminology, economics, management, and political science, among others. Cybersecurity also represents a productive, but costly industry in the global economy. In contrast to traditional crime, cybercrime has the possibility to directly affect very large groups of individuals and businesses. In the cybersecurity literature, potential extra effects beyond those directly affected exist and are known as network effects (Gandal, 2006, p. 79).

This book presents a multi-faceted lens on Cybersecurity Policies and Strategies for Cyberwarfare Prevention. Such a review is a necessary step in the process of creating a cumulative culture for the continued growth of any field of research (Webster and Watson, 2002) and can make a substantial contribution when it reveals new avenues of research, frameworks, and operating theories (Rowe, 2012). This is especially relevant in the field of information systems, where cybersecurity is a subdomain that crosses the boundaries of multiple fields. The purpose of this book is to examine the current knowledge in the field and provide an accurate and current reference point from which further development may take place.

This book aim to provide a needed perspective on emerging policies, doctrines, strategies in cyberwarfare and cybersecurity. It highlights a structural framework within which to organize present cybersecurity and cyberwarfare literature, as well as a historical snapshot of its main analytical strands and related policy positions. The book intends to highlight the different dimensions of cybersecurity policies and economics, and collect different perspectives on cyberwarfare.

Given the sophistication of cybercriminals and their advantageous positions as attackers in cybersecurity, it is expected that future research will target modeling and prevention of attacks as well as mitigating the consequences of breaches and attacks when they do occur.

Furthermore, online transactions have become indispensable for public administration. This means that criminal networks will target these transactions for breach and fraudulent activities, and will continue to innovate in ways to infiltrate security systems. These innovations must be matched by academic and industry researchers in a cyber arms race of sorts so that they are not always one step behind criminal networks. A development spearheaded by some governments is to enforce cybersecurity standards as they apply to privately-run electric grids (Wright, 2012; Zhang, 2011). Since public infrastructure is vulnerable and poses wide economic and safety risks to societies, such standards may prove to be useful in the development of cost-effective and innovative information security products.

Future work in modeling attack and defense, especially that based on Varian's (2004), suggests that information security is best optimized by companies when software developers hire fewer but more skilled programmers, use many testers, and acquire security architects with the greatest expertise. Since this early work, analytical research has further captured and defined externalities present in information security investment decisions whereby security level is a public good while defensive costs are private. Future research on attack and defense will continue to develop models of security hardening that takes into account costs and benefits. As these models are refined based on emerging attack data, organizations can tailor their information security hardening to their particular needs.

As Internet and communication technologies continue to change and evolve, cybersecurity and cyberwarfare will remain a vital area of research.

Regardless of the research avenue and particular focus in cybersecurity, future research will focus on the social, political, technical, and economic challenges that are considered when making security investment decisions. Wider policies on information security rely on sound information and empirical research evidence, which will prompt many industry individuals, legislators, and politicians to stay ahead of the curve in anticipating the impact of security breaches and attacks. Ultimately, a coordination of effort among researchers, private industry, consumers, and other intermediaries is necessary in navigating the complex, interrelated world of cybersecurity.

ORGANISATION OF THE BOOK

The book is organized into three sections and fifteen chapters. A brief description of each of the chapters follows:

Section 1 – Introduction to Cybersecurity and Cyberwarfare principles

Chapter 1 - *Toward Principles of Cyberspace Security*. This chapter outlines a set of cybersecurity principles that aim to identify strategies to assure operations in contested environments in the face of increased dependence, complexity and vulnerability.

Chapter 2 - *Cyber Warfare: The State of the Art*. This chapter provides a concise overview of cyberwarfare topics (in its politics, social, legal and technical dimensions.

Chapter 3 – *Attribution*. This chapter highlights that attribution is not only technical and brings a focus on political factors constraining attribution.

Section 2 – Cybersecurity at stake: monitoring threats, managing risks and defensive measures

Chapter 4 - *Security Monitoring of the Cyber Space*. This chapter defines the cyberspace trap-based monitoring systems, and presents the state-of-the-art in terms of techniques, tools and technologies.

Chapter 5 - *The Rigorous Security Risk Management Model: State of the Art*. This chapter presents the security concepts terminologies and present the state of the art of security risk management models.

Chapter 6 - *Cybersecurity Requires a Clear Systems Engineering Approach as a Basis for Cyberstrategy*. This chapter demonstrate why a systems engineering approach is best suited for large and complex cybersecurity information systems.

Chapter 7 - *Towards protecting critical infrastructures*. This chapter addresses Critical Infrastructure Protection (CIP) paying particular attention to the risk alert exchange among Critical Infrastructures.

Chapter 8 - *Cyber-attacks, retaliation and risk: Legal and technical implications for nation-states and private entities*. This chapter examines key legal and technical issues that arise when an adversary considers strategic retaliatory countermeasures in response to a cyber-attack.

Section 3 – National Issues, strategies and policies

Chapter 9 - *Developing Confidence Building Measures (CBMs) in Cyberspace between Pakistan and India*. This chapter outlines the usefulness of CBMs in preventing wars and facilitating conflict resolution.

Chapter 10 - *Cyber Attacks and preliminary steps in cyber security in national protection*. This chapter study cyberwarfare prevention in the context of Turkey cybersecurity strategy.

Chapter 11 - *Conflict in the cyberspace, the case of the middle east*. This chapter highlights the various cyber strategies in the Middle East Area.

Chapter 12 - *Information Warfare in the 2013-2014 Ukraine Crisis*. This chapter focuses on information warfare tactics used in times of crisis.

Section 4 – Concluding remarks and Reflections on the essence of cyberwarfare

Chapter 13- *The Islamist Cyberpropaganda Threat and Its Counter-Terrorism Policy Implications*. This chapter examines four Islamist cyberpropaganda cases studies, and outlines recommendations for counter-terrorism policy.

Chapter 14- *Thinking Systemically about Security and Resilience in an Era of Cybered Conflict*. This chapter argue that cybered conflicts cannot be resolved by military or intelligence organizations. Rather, it emphasizes that cybersecurity will require systemic thinking that enlists the full range of government and private organizations.

Chapter 15- *Cyberinsecurity and Cyberwarfare: the Case for Social Science and Philosophical Approaches. Reflections from Asia*. This chapter draw attention to the social grounding of cyberspace and the need to employ traditional social science and philosophy to examine cyberspatial politics.

Jean-Loup Richet
University of Nantes, France

REFERENCES

Gandal, N. (2008) "An Introduction to Key Themes in the Economics of Cyber Security", in Janczewski, L. and A.M. Colarik (eds.) (2008) Cyber warfare and cyber terrorism. Hershey: Information Science Reference.

Rowe, F. (2012). Toward a Richer Diversity of Genres in Information Systems Research: New Categorization and Guidelines. *European Journal of Information Systems, 21*(5), 469–478. doi:10.1057/ejis.2012.38

Schwartz, E. (2011, December 23) "The Biggest Data Breaches of 2011", *techsecuritytoday*. Retrieved from (Current November 19, 2012).

Varian, H. (2004) "System Reliability and Free-Riding", in Camp, L.J. and S. Lewis (eds.) Economics of Information Security, Volume 12 of Advances in Information Security Kluwer Academic Publishers, pp. 1-15. doi:10.1007/1-4020-8090-5_1

Webster, J., & Watson, R. (2002). Analyzing the Past to Prepare for the Future: Writing a Literature Review [), pp iii-xiii.]. *Management Information Systems Quarterly, 26*, 2.

Wright, K. (2012). Cybersecurity roundtable: The enemy is unknown. *Electric Light and Power, 90*(2), 28–31.

Zhang, Z. (2011). NERC's Cybersecurity Standards for the Electric Grid: Fulfilling its Reliability Day Job and Moonlighting as a Cybersecurity Model. *Environmental Practice, 13*(3), 250–264. doi:10.1017/S1466046611000275

Acknowledgment

I would like to acknowledge the help of all the people involved in this project and, more specifically, to the authors and Editorial Advisory Board members that took part in the review process. Without their support, this book would not have become a reality.

First, I would like to thank each one of the authors for their contributions, time and expertise to this book. This book aim to provide a needed perspective on emerging policies, doctrines, strategies in cyberwarfare and cybersecurity – I hope it will become a praised coursebook and a future reference for lecturers in cybersecurity or cyberwarfare.

Second, I wish to acknowledge the valuable contributions of the reviewers regarding the improvement of quality, coherence, and content presentation of chapters. Most of the Editorial Advisory Board members served as referees; we highly appreciate their task.

Jean-Loup Richet
University of Nantes, France

Section 1
Introduction to Cybersecurity and Cyberwarfare Principles

Chapter 1
Toward Principles of Cyberspace Security

Mark T. Maybury
The MITRE Corporation, USA

ABSTRACT

Increasing global dependence on cyberspace, rapidly and continuously changing technology, sustained vulnerabilities, and advanced persistent threats are driving an increasing societal risk of attack in cyberspace. Assuring a broad range of infrastructure critical for a well-functioning society is essential in a broad range of areas including but not limited to communications, transportation, and commerce. Based on an engagement with government, industry, and academia, and building upon prior research in computer security principles, this chapter articulates a set of enduring cybersecurity principles that can serve as a focusing framework to improve trust and assurance of systems considering requirements, architecture and design, and operations and maintenance. This chapter first outlines the threat and its consequence, describes prior research in cybersecurity principles, and then outlines a set of succinct and actionable cybersecurity principles.

CONTESTED CYBERSPACE ENVIRONMENT

Increasing cyberspace threats, vulnerabilities, and dependencies are driving a rapid escalation of enterprise cybersecurity risk and consequences. Figure 1 quantitatively illustrates a number of strategic trends that characterize the cyberspace domain. For example, static malware signatures are expected to increase from just less than three million today to over 200 million by 2025. At the same time, fiscal constraints will limit resources to counter these threats and drive increased autonomy. By 2025 there will be an estimated 5.5 billion people online using 25 million applications, engaging in billions of interactions per day, and creating 50 zetabytes (trillion gigabytes) of data. While supercomputers will be able to sustain operations at the 10 Exaflops level, time will remain a precious resource given the speed of attacks and velocity of threat evolution. Integrated circuits will continue to shrink to around 8-10 nanometers. Unfavorably, the United States will experience a limited future supply of domestic graduates in computer science (e.g., 3,800 doctoral graduates per year by 2025 in contrast to China's 8,500).

DOI: 10.4018/978-1-4666-8456-0.ch001

Figure 1. Strategic trends 1999-2025

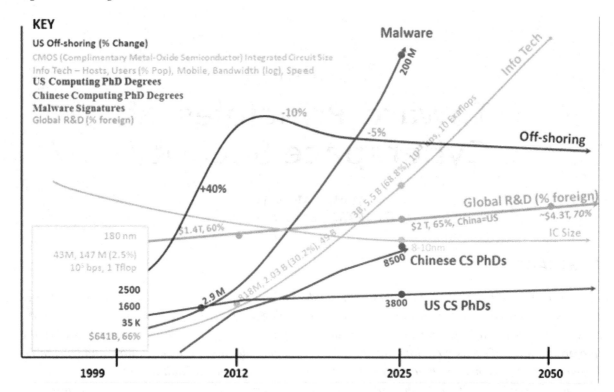

One key opportunity will be steady growth in the $1.4 trillion in global R&D investments. The foreign portion of this investment will grow from 60% to over 70% which will mean both increased technical threats and opportunity originating from overseas.

Another problematic trend is along the economic dimension. The 2013 Cost of Cyber Crime Study sponsored by Hewlett-Packard found there were over one hundred successful cyber attacks per company (an infiltration of a company's core networks or enterprise systems) requiring on average 32 days to resolve each incident and costing each company on average $11.6M in 2013 (Ponemon, 2013), a 78% increase since their first study four years ago. The 2013 Global Report on the Cost of Cyber Crime found similar trends in Australia, Germany, Japan and the United Kingdom. Aberdeen Group (Brink, 2010) estimates that a software security incident costs on average $300k per event. Gorman (2013) estimates annual U.S. cybercrime costs at $100 billion. Beyond direct cost, financial damages of cyber-attacks are now beginning to potentially be existential for companies. For example, an empirical analysis of the impact of software vulnerability announcements on stock price (Telang & Wattal, 2007) found that a vendor loses around 0.6% value in stock price when a vulnerability is reported and that the first day of a vulnerability announcement resulted in an $860M average market value loss. These trends underscore the increasing sophistication, frequency, and damage of cybercrime on a global scale.

INCREASINGLY CONSEQUENTIAL THREATS

The growth in software systems size, complexity, and external dependencies implies increasing future consequences of software failure. This is evident across modern machines from robots to automobiles to

Figure 2. Capability growth in software in fighter jets

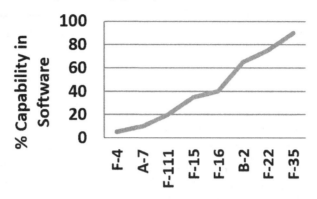

aircraft. For example, Figure 2 illustrates the growth in how functionality dependent upon software grew from only five percent in Vietnam era F-4 fighter to over ninety percent in today's Joint Strike Fighter (F-35), a combat system with over nine million lines of code embedded on the platform.

This growing software complexity and dependency is occurring simultaneously with increases in vulnerability, offensive capability, and the challenge of attack attribution. Deputy Security of Defense Lynn (2010, 2011) noted the inability to identify attacks in cyberspace means that "cold war deterrence models do not apply to cyberspace." He describes a worrisome example:

In 2008, the U.S. Department of Defense suffered a significant compromise of its classified military computer networks. It began when an infected flash drive was inserted into a U.S. military laptop at a base in the Middle East. The flash drive's malicious computer code, placed there by a foreign intelligence agency, uploaded itself onto a network run by the U.S. Central Command. That code spread undetected on both classified and unclassified systems, establishing what amounted to a digital beachhead, from which data could be transferred to servers under foreign control. It was a network administrator's worst fear: a rogue program operating silently, poised to deliver operational plans into the hands of an unknown adversary.

As evidenced by the appearance of worms such as Stuxnet and platforms such as Flame, not only the Internet but also cyber physical systems (e.g., power grids, communication systems, transportation systems) are facing increasing virtual and physical risks. Implants embedded in humans include hardware and software and, not unexpectedly, hacking biomedical devices (insulin pumps) was recently demonstrated at Black Hat (Basu, 2013).

Cyberspace operations against Air Force systems, networks and platforms are deliberate and unrelenting. The global ability to rapidly and accurately attribute detected offensive cyberspace operations (OCO) remains immature, increasing risk and a potentially destabilizing factor. According to the Director of National Intelligence, "innovation in functionality is outpacing innovation in security and neither the public nor private sector has been successful at fully implementing existing best practices" (Clapper, 2012). Thus, an area of great concern is the Air Force's ability to maintain rapid and accurate detection of foreign OCO in a contested and congested cyberspace domain.

Figure 3. illustrates the cyber kill chain (Richard & Sain, 2012) describing the typical sequence of actions that occur in a cyber campaign. Note any particular attack does not need to follow this idealized chain in a strictly linear fashion. Reconnaissance of a cyber target and weaponization of an attack

Figure 3. Cyber attack chain

capability precede the delivery and exploitation of the weapon, followed by command and control of the implant and/or platform upon which the cyber payload lives, followed by execution (e.g., targeted information access or activation of a compromised hardware or software asset, including possible exfiltration of data) and then maintenance of the implant to support future asset exploitation. Cyber adversaries employ a range of methods of attack ranging from direct attacks (e.g., distributed denial of service, social engineering to acquire or escalate privileges), malicious insiders, or supply chain attacks.

RESPONSE

Given the serious nature of the threat, the US government has imposed mandatory cybersecurity standards on large sectors of the economy. Section 10 of a February 2013 Executive Order requires all agencies with responsibility for regulating the security of critical infrastructure to start a process of developing mandatory cybersecurity requirements based on the National Institute of Standards and Technology (NIST) cybersecurity framework (NIST, 2014). Associated DOD regulations include (1) a requirement to "adequately safeguard" IT systems, (2) a requirement to report cyber incidents, and (3) a new rule on mitigating supply chain risks (such as from malware embedded in components of weapon systems) (Blanchard, 2014). These rules aimed to safeguard unclassified technical information (UCTI) and associated systems will be incorporated in all new DOD solicitations and contracts. We can expect the Federal Acquisition Regulation Council to issue a FAR provision on cybersecurity, likely mirroring the DoD regulation. The term "Adequate security" is defined as "protective measures that are commensurate with the consequences and probability of loss, misuse, or unauthorized access to, or modification of information." The regulation specifies that, at a minimum, adequate security requires that the IT systems on which UCTI transits or is stored must comply with specified security standards in NIST Special Publication (SP) 800–53.

Another important step was the Department of Defense initiated in 2012 (97 FCR 486, 5/15/12) a voluntary Defense Industrial Base (DIB) Cyber Security/Information Assurance (CS/IA) information sharing program between DoD and eligible DIB companies. When eligible DIB companies sign a Framework Agreement (FA), the program shares US government threat information with those companies who in turn report cyber incident information with the government regarding network intrusions that could compromise DoD programs and missions.

While these approaches promise to mitigate risk, the rapid pace of change, increasing complexity and dependencies, and heightened threats argue for a need for a deeper approach including more attention to fundamentals of cyberspace security. Happily, well-motivated designs can mitigate the risk from such threats. This chapter describes a set of principles that can be applied to mitigate cyber security risks and build upon the previously published principles in Air Force Cyber Vision 2025 (Donley & Maybury 2012, Maybury et al., 2012).

PRIOR RESEARCH IN COMPUTER SECURITY PRINCIPLES

Saltzer and Schroeder's (1974) review nine design principles for the protection of information in computer systems from unauthorized use or modification. These include economy of mechanism (simple and small to ease inspection), fail-safe defaults (access decisions are based on permissions not exclusion, where default situation is lack of access (Glaser, Couleur & Oliver, 1965; Glaser, 1967)), complete mediation (a system-wide authorization of any access or authority request), open design (Baran, 1964) to enable review (decoupling protection mechanisms from protection keys enabling review by many), separation of privilege (Needham, 1972) with protections that require two keys to unlock (as in a safety deposit box), least privilege, least common mechanism (minimize the amount of mechanism common to more than one user and depended on by all users), and psychological acceptability (transparency/understandability and ease of use). In addition they suggest considering work factor (resources required for an attack) and compromise recording to detect loss and trigger information modification for protection. In related work, Glaser (1967) cites security principles of compartmentalization (functional separation to limit loss in case of breach), and auditing (e.g., operating system instrumentation). The CISSP identifies principles of information security as the confidentiality, integrity, and availability of information. Confidentiality means that secret information is accessible only to those who are authorized, integrity that information is trustworthy, complete, and correct and availability that access to it is not inappropriately denied. CISSP further identifies universal security principles including least privilege, defense in depth, minimization, compartmentalization, simplicity, fail securely, secure the weakest link, use choke points, leverage unpredictability, and segregation of duties. It also recommends performing cost-benefit analysis. Bodeau and Graubart (2013) details principles for and mechanisms to anticipate, withstand, recover, and evolve from attacks. It articulates cyber resiliency methods which include many of the above as well as adaptive response, analytic monitoring, coordinated defense, deception, diversity, dynamism/non-persistence, substantiated integrity and unpredictability.

ENDURING CYBERSPACE SECURITY PRINCIPLES TO ASSURE MISSIONS

Table 1. captures the primary outcome of detailed analysis of past efforts such as those referenced above in addition to extensive outreach to national cyberspace experts, including over one hundred inputs to a public request for information. This resulted in the articulation of a group of enduring concepts that have been employed to mitigate cyber risks across public, private, and non-profit organizations, in some cases over the past several decades. Each principle captured in Table 1 includes a description of the driving requirement for that principle, how it can be employed in information system architecture and design, and how it can be realized in operations and maintenance.

Least Privilege. For example, by adhering to the principle of least privilege, users only receive permissions necessary to accomplish their mission. This can be encapsulated in an architecture by eliminating unnecessary privilege to users, software, or hardware or by designing in discretionary access control. During design, developer privilege can be limited by allowing only the use of pre-approved software or services. Least privilege can be supported in hardware, for example, using the ring architecture of the Pentium chip to limit access or functionality. In operations, actively managing user privileges, whitelisting, or using containers to limit functionality can also implement least privilege. Least privilege reduces

Table 1. Cybersecurity Principles

Principle	Requirements	Architecture and Design	Operations and Maintenance
Least Privilege	Provide only necessary permissions or authority	Limit access – architect/design out privilege, discretionary access control	Limit escalation of privilege, white list, employ containment
Separation	Require distribution of authority	Distribute permissions in architecture/ design	Segment authority/permissions, peer review, two person rule
Non-Interference	Representation and transparency of operations to enable coordinated action. Eliminate unnecessary dependencies.	Enable components, connections, and operations to co-exist or block on multiple levels of abstraction. Reduce inter-dependencies	Coordination and synchronization of operations (e.g., via mission planning)
Minimization	Limit capability to essential requirements	Limit attack surface by limiting capabilities and limiting dependencies	Limit operations to meeting essential needs
Simplification	Allow only necessary complexity	Avoid complex design and unnecessary (functional or technical) complexity. Employ open standards (interfaces/ controls) and loose coupling.	Least complex operations
Awareness	Situational awareness of vulnerabilities, threats, dependencies, consequences. Key to enable priorities for investment and defensive measures	Architect open and transparent systems. Design in cyber sensors, correlation and fusion. Use approved infrastructure with predictable behaviors to enable anomaly detection.	Understand crown jewels and vulnerabilities. Maintain deep knowledge of threat. Employ sensors. Triangulate multiple sources. Train for vigilance and sense making.
Agility	Provide early detection and responsiveness	Architect/design in agility (e.g., flexibility/ maneuver), speed (responsiveness), modularity, and evolvability	Train and maintain for fitness/ readiness, speed of action
Resilience	Ensure robustness via redundancy, diversity, reserve, and other approaches (e.g., evolution to overcome vulnerability and/or threat)	Architecture and design for redundancy and re-constitution. Design for and enable diversity and evolution and dependency management (e.g., open standards, loose couplers). Maintain out of band channel and "war time" reserve.	Rapidly reconstitute. Promote diversity in operations. Evolve operations.
Affordability	Balance cost of defense with risk of loss of confidentiality, integrity and availability. Balance cost of offense with expected benefits and assess in relation to alternative means (e.g., kinetic actions). Focus and prioritize based on criticality, mission key dependencies.	Design cost effective systems across the life cycle (e.g., design, implementation, operation) emphasizing open architectures, standards, reuse, rapid evolution.	Seek methods for efficient operations and maintenance (e.g., competition, autonomy, outsourcing); Prioritize and focus on critical threats and vulnerabilities which have most significant consequences.
Optimization	Optimize balancing offense/defense, human creativity and machine intelligence, cost/benefit	Architect/design effective mix of defense/offense, human and machine. Automate wherever possible.	Pursue O&M methods which balance needs
Asymmetry	Maximize adversary cost/risk/ uncertainty; maximize friendly benefit/assurance/ efficiency	Balance architectural complexity with cost/complexity imposition. Employ diversity and adaptiveness.	Foster cyber hygiene (e.g., encrypting data at rest/in motion, effective identity management, passwords); Ensure chain of custody; Actively defend; Employ cost and risk imposing O&M (e.g., deception, randomness, unpredictability, adaptive response)

the opportunity for unintentional missteps or intentional mischief. For example, the Akamai's global network for caching has never suffered an availability loss because it employs least privilege from policy to architecture to operations.

Separation/Balance of Power. By distributing authority, employing peer review, or using two person rules, checks on power can be used to help maintain positive control, helping counter malicious insiders or outsiders. Balance of power is related to the fundamental principle of separation or segregation of duties from the Orange Book (OB).

Non-Interference. The principle of non-interference expresses the need to minimize unnecessary interdependencies and for the assured separation of security levels as well as requiring that one operator not thwart the actions of another, achievable through careful coordination and synchronization of loosely coupled but mutually enabling action. This is essential, for example, when coordinating defense across joint, interagency, public-private, and international networks.

Minimization and Simplification. Minimization of attack surfaces by pursuing solutions that do only necessary functions (not more), limiting dependencies, or providing only essential services can help reduce potential avenues of attack and/or vulnerabilities. Simplifying systems (e.g., standard architectural interfaces, avoiding complexity, limiting developers to pre-approved code) can reduce cost and risk. Simplification and minimization and the ability to replace compromised components are consistent with the principle of "modularity" within Trusted Computing Base (TCB).

Awareness and Agility. System resilience and survivability can be enhanced by readiness, improved intelligence and situational awareness, faster responsiveness, flexibility and ability in reacting to a threat (cyberspace maneuver), and rapid evolution as threats and opportunities advance. MITRE's framework for cyber resiliency (Bodeau and Graubart, 2013) provides detailed resiliency goals, objectives, and techniques.

Resilience. Disruption can be either a sudden or a sustained event and may be natural or manmade (e.g., internal failure or external attack). Since attacks often cannot be avoided and sophisticated adversaries successfully penetrate defenses, resilience can be enhanced by including redundancy, alternate (e.g., wartime) modes, diversity of components, active defenses, and rapid reconstitution following a catastrophic attack. Resilience enables systems to repel, absorb, and/or recover from attacks. Resilience can be enhanced through hardening, reduction of attack surfaces, critical mission segregation, and attack containment. Autonomous compromise detection and repair (self-healing) and adaptation to and evolution from changing environments and threats can enhance survival.

Affordability. Defenders must balance costs and benefits. Open architectures, standards, reuse, and rapid evolution can also help mitigate costs of architectures and designs. Efficient operations and maintenance via appetite suppression (i.e., focusing and limiting requirements and associated efforts), competition, and autonomy can free significant resources.

Optimization. Some of the most successful organizations are able to integrate and optimize across defense and offense and tap into the appropriate mix of automation and human intelligence to allow them to properly balance between confidence in distributed operations and the need for detailed, centralized control.

Asymmetry. Some of the best organizations leverage limited talent, treasure, and time, by focusing on maximizing the benefits of their cyber posture (cost savings, efficiencies, and effectiveness) while maximizing costs to the adversary (resources, risks, uncertainty) and/or denying them benefits, thus deterring attacks.

IMPROVE CYBER PRACTICES IN ARCHITECTURE, ACQUISITION, AND TEST

In addition to these principles, a number of recommended practices were identified in the *Cyber Vision 2025* study. For example, systems should design-in redundancy, diversity, and roots of trust to enhance resilience. Architectures should employ open standards and loose couplers between major elements (e.g., data exchange standards) to avoid the brittleness of customized and direct connections. Fractionating (i.e., physically and logically decomposing and distributing) capabilities and authorities can increase survivability and reduce the likelihood of privilege escalation by requiring more coordinated and visible attack and allowing concentration of protection on true crown jewels. Finally, incentivizing good cyber hygiene reduces a significant number of vulnerabilities. For example, encrypting data at rest/in motion and ensuring chain of custody reduces information loss risks.

In addition, cyber acquisition can be improved by demanding clear/focused requirements, early/continual user/test involvement, early prototyping and rapid cycles for evolution, modular/open standards, and model driven architectures. Finally, focusing efforts on the acquisition, development and proper engagement of highly experienced cyberspace experts can help mitigate challenges.

Agility and Resilience

Survivability in a contested cyberspace will demand an effective mix of redundancy, diversity, and fractionation (i.e., distributed functionality). System risk can be minimized by reduction of attack surfaces, segregation of critical mission systems, and attack containment. This can be enhanced by autonomous compromise detection and repair (self-healing) and real-time response to threats. And advancing from signature based cyber sensors to behavior based detection can enhance attack detection. Finally, active defense demands rapid cyber maneuver enabled by dynamic, randomizable, reconfigurable architectures.

In cyber warfare, as in traditional maneuver warfare, speed and agility matter most. In order for AF missions to avoid, fight through, and recover from attacks, AF cyber architectures must be agile and resilient at many levels. Transforming the Air Force cyber infrastructure from its current static configuration to a dynamic architecture enabling diversity will raise the level of difficulty for adversaries to conduct attacks as well as make the infrastructure more adaptive and resilient. Table 2 summarizes a roadmap for agile operations and resilient defense. The full CV25 study includes similar roadmaps for each theme area (assurance and empowerment, agility and resilience, human-machine optimization, and foundations of trust) in each mission area (air, space, cyber, C2, ISR).

Table 2. Agility and Resilience

Area	Thread	Near (F12-FY15)	Mid (FY16-20)	Far (FY21-25)
Enhance Agility & Resilience	Resilience	• Real-time encryption at 10Gbits (F) • Secure mobile platforms (F)	• Embedded anti-tamper pwr (F) • Red team automation (F)	• Anticipatory defense(L) • Autonomic anti-tamper (L) • Self-Healing Networks (F)
	Agility	Morphable architectures (L)	Protected root of trust for cyber C2 (L)	Agile virtual machine replacement (L)
	Cloud	• Virtualization for C2 (L) • Cloud services (W)	• Formal logic (W) • Resilient services (F)	Composable architectures (F)

Resilience can be improved in several ways. In the near term, S&T can drive high (line) speed encryption down to a minimal cost that is acceptable to almost all applications. In the midterm, unique anti-tamper protections can be derived from nanotechnology advances including the potential for perpetually powered portions of chips that encapsulate a root of trust. Near-term work must be done to secure mobile platforms and thin out functionality that can be moved to more secure servers in cloud environments where redundancy can enhance resilience. Finally, military-grade hardware and software can be selectively mixed with COTS technology to greatly reduce vulnerability surfaces and increase the difficulty of devising successful attacks.

Agility can be similarly improved at several levels. Beyond present capabilities to quickly hop network IP addresses, instruction set morphing at sub second rates to stay within adversary command and control loops will reach Technology Readiness Level (TRL) 6 demonstration, as will agility in network configurations and routing policies. By 2017, Cyber C2 promulgation will be built upon these foundations. The emergence of cloud computing will be an important contributor to resilience and agility as well as affordability. Near term, key services will be moved to the (private vs. public) cloud and shifted over to the use of managed information. Low level operating systems will be strengthened by applying formal methods to their construction as a key contribution to the resilience and trust of security in, for example, cloud environments. Later, with increasing security, clouds will afford the opportunity to move mission applications amongst a multiplicity of virtual machines to create a moving target to attackers at a layer above the traditional application layer. In much of the cloud S&T, the AF will be a fast follower, expecting to adopt, adapt, or augment the work of others.

CONCLUSION

Nearly all of major systems of modern society (communications, transportation, commerce, energy, financial, health care) are dependent upon cyberspace which is under increasing attack. Given limited time, treasure, and talent, it is essential to maximally leverage knowledge, capabilities, and investments in a range of communities to improve foundations of trust and enhance agility and resilience, to assure societal services. This chapter outlines a set of cybersecurity principles that aim to identify strategies to assure operations in contested environments in the face of increased dependence, complexity and vulnerability.

SUMMARY/KEY INSIGHTS

- Modern societal systems such as communications, financial, transportation and medical are increasingly complex and large scale software systems
- Increasingly aggressive cyber threat actors (evidenced by exponential growth of malware signatures), limited global supply of computing expertise, and financial pressures for affordability and global supply chains pose increasing challenges for assuring systems
- Employing enduring assurance principles such as least privilege, minimization, and resilience increases adversary costs (resources, risks, uncertainty) and denies adversaries benefits, thus deterring attacks.

- Advances in cyber agility and resilience through redundancy, diversity, decomposition and distribution of capabilities and authorities can reduce the risk of catastrophic failure in the face of a cyber attack.
- Cyber situational awareness requires not only network and critical infrastructure awareness but also mapping threats, vulnerabilities and consequences to missions and the information, networks, systems and services they rely upon.

ACKNOWLEDGEMENT

This effort was initiated and builds on a foundation of cyber security research led by Air Force chief scientists and operators from across the United States Air Force, sister services and other national agencies. In addition it has benefited from detailed technical comments from Richard Graubart, Harriet Goldman, Vipin Swarup, Rich Pietravalle, Deb Bodeau, Keith Ibarguen and Nick Multari.

REFERENCES

Baran, P. (1964). Security, secrecy, and tamper-free considerations. *Distributed Communications*, No. 9.

Basu, E. (2013). Hacking Insulin Pumps and Other Medical Devices from Black Hat. *Forbes.com.* Retrieved from www.forbes.com/sites/ericbasu/2013/08/03/hacking-insulin-pumps-and-other-medical-devices-reality-not-fiction

Blanchard, C. (2014, January 27). Promises to be Another Banner Year for Cybersecurity. *Aerospace & Defense Law,* 360.

Bodeau, D., & Graubart, R. (2011, September). Cyber Resiliency Engineering Framework, Version 1.0. *mitre.org.* Retrieved from http://www.mitre.org/sites/default/files/publications/pr-14-4035-cyber-resiliency-engineering-aid-techniques.pdf

Bodeau, D., & Graubart, R. (2013). Cyber Resiliency Assessment: Enabling Architectural Improvement. *mitre.org.* Retrieved from www.mitre.org/sites/default/files/pdf/12_3795.pdf

Brink, D. (2010, October 7). *Quantifying Business Value of Application Security: Cost Avoidance, Cost Savings.* Retrieved from http://blogs.aberdeen.com/it-security/quantifying-business-value-of-application-security-cost-avoidance-cost-savings/

Certification of Information Systems Security Principles (n. d.). Retrieved from http://mhprofessional.com/downloads/products/0072254238/0072254238_ch01.pdf

Clapper, J. R. (2012, February 2). Unclassified Statement for the Record on the Worldwide Threat Assessment of the United States Intelligence Community for the House Permanent Select Committee on Intelligence.

Department of Defense Strategy for Operating in Cyberspace. (2011, July). *U.S. Department of Defense.* http://www.defense.gov/news/d20110714cyber.pdf

DOD announces the expansion of Defense Industrial Base (DIB) Voluntary Cyber Security Information Sharing Assurance. (2012, May 11). *U.S. Department of Defense (CS/IA)*. [Press Release]. Retrieved from http://www.defense.gov/releases/release.aspx?releaseid=15266

Fight Cyber Crime infographic. (2013, October). Ponemon Institute. Retrieved from www.hp.com/hpinfo/newsroom/press/2013/309_ponemon.jpg

Framework for Improving Critical Infrastructure Cybersecurity, Version 1.0. (2014, February 12). *National Institute of Standards and Technology*. Retrieved from http://www.nist.gov/cyberframework/upload/cybersecurity-framework-021214.pdf

Glaser, E. L. (1967, April 18-20). A brief description of privacy measures in the multics operating system. In Proceedings of the *Spring Joint Computer Conference (AFIPS '67)*. New York, NY, USA. (pp.303-304). doi:10.1145/1465482.1465529

Glaser, E. L., Couleur, J. F., & Oliver, G. A. (1965, November 30-December 1). System design of a computer for time sharing applications. In Proceedings of the Fall Joint Computer Conference (AFIPS '65). ACM, New York, NY, USA. (pp. 197-202). doi:10.1145/1463891.1463913

Gorman, S. (2013, July 22). Annual U.S. Cybercrime Costs Estimated at $100 Billion. *Wall Street Journal*. Retrieved from http://online.wsj.com/news/articles/SB10001424127887324328904578621880966242990

Jabbour, K. & Muccio, S. (2011, Summer). The Science of Mission Assurance. *Journal of Strategic Security*, IV(2), pp. 61-74.

Joint Publication JP 3-12 Cyberspace Operations Final Coordination. (2012, April 10).

King, S. (2011, November 8). Office of Secretary of Defense Research and Engineering's Cyber S&T Priority Steering Council Research Roadmap. Proceedings of *National Defense Industrial Association Disruptive Technologies Conference*. 8 November 2011.

Lukasik, S. (2011, September). Protecting Users of the Cyber Commons. *Communications of the ACM*, *54*(9), 54–61. doi:10.1145/1995376.1995393

Lynn, W. J. (2010, September/October). Defending a New Domain. *The Pentagon's Cyberstrategy*.

Lynn, W. J. (2011, September). One Year Later. *The Pentagon's Cyberstrategy*.

Maybury, M. (2012, December 13). Air Force Cyber Vision 2025. United States Air Force Cyberspace S&T Vision 2012-2025. *USAF Office of the Chief Scientist*. Retrieved from http://www.defenseinnovationmarketplace.mil/resources/cyber/cybervision2025.pdf

Maybury, M. (2013, August 1). Global Horizons. *Armed Forces Journal*. Retrieved from http://www.armedforcesjournal.com/global-horizons/

Needham, R. (1972). Protection systems and protection implementations. In FJCC, AFIPS Conf. Proc., Vol. 41, pt. 1, pp. 571-578.

Report of the Defense Science Board Task Force on High Performance Microchip Supply. (2005, February). *DTIC* Report ADA435563. Retrieved from http://www.dtic.mil/docs/citations/ADA435563

Richard, M., & Sain, J. J. (2012, October 14). Security Intelligence: Attacking the Cyber Kill Chain. *SansDfir*. Retrieved from http://digital-forensics.sans.org/blog/2009/10/14/security-intelligence-attacking-the-kill-chain

Robertson, J. (2013, July 23). Medical device hackers find government ally to pressure industry. *Bloomberg.com*. Retrieved from http://www.bloomberg.com/news/articles/2013-07-22/medical-device-hackers-find-government-ally-to-pressure-industry

Saltzer, J. H., & Schroeder, M. (1973, October). The Protection of Information in Computer Systems. Fourth ACM Symposium on Operating System Principles. In *Communications of the ACM 17*, (1974, July 7). Retrieved from web.mit.edu/Saltzer/www/publications/protection/

Telang, R., & Wattal, S. (2007, August). An Empirical Analysis of the Impact of Software Vulnerability Announcements on Firm Stock Price. *IEEE Transactions on Software Engineering*, *33*(8), 544–557. Retrieved from www.heinz.cmu.edu/~rtelang/tse_published.pdf. doi:10.1109/TSE.2007.70712

Trusted Computing Base. (2015, May 16). *Wikimedia.org*. Retrieved from en.wikipedia.org/wiki/Trusted_computing_base

Vautrinot, S. (2012, July 25). *Improving Military Capabilities for Cyber Operations*. [Statement to the House Armed Services Committee Subcommittee].

KEY TERMS AND DEFINITIONS

Agility: Nimbleness and adaptability (e.g., dynamic architectures such as IP hopping).

Cyberspace Situational Awareness (CSA): The requisite current and predictive knowledge of the cyberspace environment and the operational environment upon which cyber operations depend - including physical, virtual, and human domains - as well as associated threats, vulnerabilities, and dependencies - as well as all factors, activities, and events of friendly and adversary cyber forces across the spectrum of conflict.

Deception: Those measures designed to mislead by manipulation, distortion, or falsification of evidence to induce the adversary to react in a manner prejudicial to the adversary's interests.

Insider Threat: A person, known or suspected, who uses their authorized access to facilities, systems, equipment, information or infrastructure to damage, disrupt operations, commit espionage on behalf of a extenal entit.

Mission Assurance (cyberspace): Measures required to accomplish essential objectives of missions in a contested environment. Mission assurance entails prioritizing mission essential functions, mapping mission dependence on cyberspace, identifying vulnerabilities, and mitigating risk of known vulnerabilities.

Resilience: The ability to avoid (or deflect or absorb), survive, and recover from disruption.

Chapter 2
Cyber Warfare:
The State of the Art

Michael Robinson
Airbus Group Innovations, UK

Kevin Jones
Airbus Group Innovations, UK

Helge Janicke
De Montfort University, UK

ABSTRACT

The term cyber warfare is becoming increasingly common in mainstream media, on the political stage and in military circles. To many it will appear as if the world has been caught unaware by the rise of cyber warfare and its impact on global society. In reality, research on cyber warfare in the form it is known today dates back to the 1980s. This chapter presents cyber warfare from the perspective of the research community. It highlights current research into eight distinct areas of cyber warfare, and examines the arguments, agreements and disagreements between various authors in each field. The chapter is organised into sections, with each section providing background and analysis into a particular area.

1. INTRODUCTION

The United States Department of Defense defines cyber warfare as "an armed conflict conducted in whole or part by cyber means" (Giles & Hagestad, 2013). This short and simple definition of the term can arguably obscure the fact that the topic of cyber warfare is a complex and multi-dimensional one. Looking beneath the surface of cyber warfare, issues of politics, social, legal and technical dimensions present problems that the cyber warfare research community has been working to address.

The aim of this chapter is to look beyond the surface and dig into these complexities, providing an insight into the research problems they present. Due to the scale of the research landscape, the scope of the chapter is designed to provide a concise overview of each topic, without being an exhaustive com-

DOI: 10.4018/978-1-4666-8456-0.ch002

pilation of all research. In this regard, the chapter should be considered as an introduction to the state of the art and as a resource from which further research can be launched.

Eight significant cyber warfare topics are presented, along with discussion of the views and contrasting arguments of researchers within each. A visual representation of how the topic of cyber warfare is constructed is shown in Figure 1.

2. ETHICS OF CYBER WARFARE

Any activity that has the potential to cause harm is subject to ethical considerations and cyber warfare is no exception. Responsible practitioners of cyber warfare wish to act in an ethical manner, just as they do in traditional, kinetic warfare. Irresponsible practitioners may not have the same internal drive to act ethically, but the ability to concretely identify actions that violate agreed ethical guidelines is essential in highlighting wrong doing on the international stage and holding perpetrators responsible.

There is currently no set of ethical guidelines for cyber warfare, which has led to a number of researchers performing work into how such guidelines could be created and what they may consist of.

2.1 Background: The Ethics of Traditional Warfare

Traditional warfare is guided by a set of principles known as just war theory (Taddeo, 2012). Just war theory sets out the criteria for answering two questions:

- *Jus ad bellum*: When is the use of warfare ethically justified?
- *Jus in bello*: How does one conduct warfare ethically?

Figure 1. Eight dimensions of cyber warfare research

2.1.1 Jus Ad Bellum

Just war theory dictates that resorting to warfare is only ethically justifiable if the following conditions are true:

- There is a just cause (i.e. protecting innocent life, correcting a public evil)
- It is a last resort
- It is declared by a proper authority
- It has the right intention (to achieve the just cause only)
- There is a reasonable chance of succeeding in the intention
- It is proportionate (the expected results of the warfare outweigh the expected harm)

2.1.2 Jus in Bello

With regards to how warfare should be conducted, the following principles apply:

- Discrimination: Ensuring attacks only harm legitimate targets
- Proportionality: Attacks should not cause excessive harm beyond what is needed to achieve an objective.

2.2 Applying Just War Theory to Cyber Warfare

Taddeo (2012) has approached the problem of forming ethical guidelines for cyber warfare by examining how Just War Theory can be applied to warfare in the cyber domain. She argues that with kinetic warfare being a violent and bloody activity, the principle of last resort makes sense. However, since cyber warfare does not involve physical harm and violence the principle of last resort is less justified. Using this reasoning, she puts forward the argument that it may be ethically justified to resort to cyber warfare early in a conflict. In doing so, a just cause may be achieved without the risk of physical harm associated with kinetic warfare.

Although this is an appealing concept, it must be remembered that cyber warfare cannot automatically be considered to be free of physical harm. Attacks on critical infrastructure such as transport networks or water treatment plants may cause physical harm to populations, if not via immediate effects then by unpredictable secondary effects, which violate the principles of discrimination and proportionality. With this in mind, caution must be used before discarding the principle of last resort. Taddeo acknowledges this issue, giving an example of a virus which causes an aircraft to crash.

Taddeo proposes that a new set of principles would be helpful in defining the ethics of cyber warfare. She puts forward the idea of an Infosphere, which is a representation of the health of all informational entities (living, non-living, real and virtual). She states that by using the concept of an Infosphere, the ethics of cyber warfare can be considered by the effect that an act in cyberspace would have on all entities inside of it. Using this concept, she proposes new principles that would constitute ethically justified cyber warfare:

1. Cyber war ought to be waged only against those entities that endanger or disrupt the wellbeing of the Infosphere.
2. Cyber war ought to be waged to preserve the well-being of the Infosphere.
3. Cyber war ought not to be waged to promote the well-being of the Infosphere.

Looking at these principles, it is clear that Taddeo is proposing that cyber warfare is only justified to maintain the well-being of the Infosphere and return it to its previous state after it is damaged. Cyber warfare which intends to improve the well-being beyond its current state is not ethically justified. Questions must be asked about the practicality of these principles however. If a state begins to censor information about a controversial artist, has the well-being of the Infosphere been damaged? If so, is cyber warfare then ethically justified to undo that damage? Caution must be used in this scenario, since initiating cyber warfare to undo this wrong to the artist and their creations may escalate into further conflict and even kinetic warfare.

Lin et al. (2012) have also examined the principles of Just War Theory and present the following questions that need to be answered before it can be usefully applied to the cyber domain:

- Aggression: what kind of cyber attack counts as aggression worthy of a military response?
- Discrimination: is it possible to be precise enough with cyber attacks that collateral damage is avoided?
- Proportionality: What kinds of responses are proportionate for particular cyber attacks?
- Attribution: There is a moral obligation to be correct in assigning blame for an attack. Can this be done in the cyber domain?

These four questions help in the application of Just War Theory to cyber warfare, however in addition the issue of perfidy in cyber warfare needs to be addressed in order to identify clear similarities between kinetic and cyber warfare with respect to ethical considerations.

2.3 The Perfidy Issue

Lin et al. (2012) raise the ethical issue of perfidy in cyber warfare. The Geneva Protocol (International Committee of the Red Cross, 1977) defines perfidy as:

"Acts inviting the confidence of an adversary to lead him to believe that he is entitled to, or is obliged to accord, protection under the rules of international law applicable in armed conflict, with intent to betray that confidence." (International Committee of the Red Cross, 1977).

Put more simply, perfidy is the act of deceiving your enemy into believing you are a protected entity and using that belief to gain a military advantage. Dressing soldiers as civilians to pass across enemy lines and then attack from behind is one example of perfidy.

Lin et al. (2012) state that perfidious attacks are much easier to perform in the cyber domain, and that this ease of committing perfidy is a danger that must be addressed by ethical research. Rowe (2010) shares this concern and highlights an example of hiding a cyber attack inside of civilian traffic. In traditional warfare, it would be ethically wrong to hide soldiers amongst civilian activity; doesn't the same reasoning apply to cyber warfare?

It can be argued that there are reasons why perfidy in cyber space is not as ethically wrong as in the kinetic world. It must be remembered that the intent of the perfidy rule is to ensure that truly protected entities enjoy continued protection without distrust or suspicion. Once a force begins to distrust protected groups, their safety is brought into question. This is a valid concern in the kinetic world, since a lack of trust could lead to physical harm being inflicted on the protected group. In the cyber domain however, a lack of trust in protected entities has much less serious consequences. If civilian internet traffic becomes distrusted, forces may begin to inspect it more carefully or drop it entirely. This may result in civilians being unable to access internet services. Although such services are arguably important, it is a much less grave consequence than being under threat of physical harm. It can also be argued that perfidious-like attacks are unavoidable in cyber warfare. Attacks must pass through the same infrastructure as civilian traffic and cyber attacks are not specially marked as such.

Guidance on perfidy in cyber warfare is provided by NATO in the Tallinn Manual (Schmitt, 2013). It makes two points with regards to how participants in cyber warfare should conduct themselves to avoid breaching perfidy rules:

1. Combatants are not obliged to mark websites, IP addresses or other information technology facilities that are used for military purposes. But making such entities appear to have civilian status with a view to deceiving the enemy in order to kill or injure is perfidious.
2. Concealing the origin of an attack is not perfidious, but inviting the enemy to conclude that the originator is a protected person is perfidious.

Looking at these points, it seems that the Tallinn Manual is in agreement that perfidious-like attacks are unavoidable, but retains the principle that intentionally disguising your infrastructure as protected is a perfidious activity.

2.4 Looking to the Future

The issue of ethics in cyber warfare is one that remains a problem for researchers. There are currently no widely adopted ethical guidelines relating to resorting to and conducting cyber warfare. Rowe (2010) has stated that those carrying out cyber warfare will not require a physical courage, but instead a moral courage to conduct their activities in a way that is right without the guidance of established ethical codes. Dipert (2010) supports this view, stating that "cyber warfare appears to be almost entirely unaddressed by the traditional morality and laws of war." (Dipert, 2010).

The formulation of an accepted set of ethics for cyber warfare is essential, as it is a prerequisite for other significant achievements such as formulating laws. Without knowing what is ethically right and wrong, the process of creating a set of laws to enforce those morally right choices cannot begin. Despite this observation, efforts to translate existing laws into the cyber domain have been ongoing. In the following chapter we are discuss some of these efforts.

3. LEGALITY OF CYBER WARFARE

The human race has such a long history of warfare that we find ourselves today with an established set of laws that are generally accepted and enforceable (DiMeglio et al., 2012). The UN Charter, Geneva

Convention and its additional protocols all proscribing what is considered legal and illegal in the international community's eyes.

With the arrival of new types of warfare, legal scholars have worked to adapt these laws. The development of biological and chemical, as well as nuclear weapons have all triggered the formulation of laws which complement and sit alongside existing ones. Cyber warfare is no exception, and the arrival of cyber as a domain of war has triggered a race to formulate a set of laws that regulate how it is conducted on the international stage.

Arguably the most successful and significant attempt to date has been the publication of the Tallinn Manual (Schmitt, 2013). The Manual, written by an international group of experts and published by NATO, is not a legally binding document but is a comprehensive set of 95 rules governing cyber warfare. A discussion of every rule given in the manual is not feasible for this chapter, but an overview of its approach to the problem can be given.

3.1 The Tallinn Manual

The Tallinn Manual (Schmitt, 2013) has examined existing law on traditional warfare and has attempted to translate the major legal issues into the cyber domain. To give an understanding of how the manual approaches the issue, rule 44 has been picked out for examination.

Rule 44 concerns cyber booby traps, and discusses the legality of using such methods in cyber warfare. The group of experts explain how the basis for the rule is the Mines Protocol and Amended Mines Protocol (International Committee of the Red Cross, 1996). They discuss whether the existing law on the use of booby traps can be applied to a cyber equivalent, explaining their thought process and any disagreements between the group members. They set out four conditions that must be met in order for an attack to be classed as a cyber booby trap and therefore considered illegal. To illustrate their decision on the issue, they present an example scenario that would be deemed in violation of the rule. The manual continues to follow this methodology of rule, basis, discussion and example for each of the 95 rules, allowing the reader to follow their logic and understand the reasoning behind each decision.

The manual is a comprehensive and logical approach towards translating existing laws into the cyber domain but it does have some limitations which must be kept in mind when using it as a resource. Firstly, many of the rules inside of the manual demonstrate that the group of experts rarely reach a unanimous agreement on the topic at hand. A handful take position X, while another take position Y, giving some rules a lack of a definitive answer. An example of this is in the manual's discussion over the use of force. Rule 11 attempts to define when a use of force has occurred in the cyber domain, but the experts are forced to conclude that it is subjective. A nation seeking to prove that it has been a victim of a use of force in the cyber domain will not find an answer inside of the Tallinn Manual.

A second limitation of the manual is that only Canadian, German, British and American military manuals have been consulted in the formulation of the 95 rules. This bias towards western military thinking potentially limits the effectiveness of the rules, especially when they are attempting to regulate what is naturally a global issue. Despite these limitations, the manual is a positive step towards formulating a set of laws for cyber warfare and the manual has been found to generally be in agreement with the US position on how the laws should be interpreted (Schmitt, 2012).

3.2 An Alternative Approach

The process followed by the Tallinn Manual could arguably be compared to a brute force approach. The experts took the existing laws of kinetic warfare and one by one attempted to force them to apply to the cyber domain, even in cases where extreme difficulty was found in doing so.

Rauscher and Korotkov (2011) have argued that cyber warfare is so different to kinetic warfare that a different approach is required. They suggest that before attempting to translate the existing laws, the process of conversion needs to be made easier by taking a number of steps:

1. Detangle Protected Entities in Cyberspace: Separating civilian and military systems.
2. Apply the Distinctive Geneva Emblem Concept in Cyberspace: Marking protected zones, e.g. medical systems.
3. Recognise New Non-State Actor and Netizen Power Stature: Recognising that non state actors may be involved in cyber warfare.
4. Consider the Geneva Protocol Principles for Cyber Weaponry: Understanding cyber weapons as different from kinetic weapons
5. Examine a Third, 'Other-Than-War' Mode: Classifying cyber warfare as something different, avoiding the need to adapt existing rules.

Some of these suggestions by Rauscher and Korotkov (2011) are challenging to achieve from multiple perspectives. Detangling civilian and military systems is a technical challenge but also a social one, in that organisations will require an incentive to do so. Other suggestions such as considering protocols for cyber weaponry imply that the problem of formulating laws for cyber warfare won't be solved until other complex issues are addressed. Nevertheless, the alternative approach presented by Rauscher and Korotkov (2011) provides a good example of how the task of creating a set of laws for cyber warfare could be approached differently to the method used by the Tallinn Manual.

In summary, it is essential that nations engaging in cyber warfare have an understanding of how to act legally, both to avoid unnecessary suffering of civilians and to avoid accusations of war crimes. As demonstrated, the ongoing research is focusing on not just what the laws should be, but also what methodology is best in trying to convert the established laws to apply in the cyber domain. Until such a process is complete, it is difficult to disagree with authors such as Foltz (2012), who states that "nations should be prepared to conduct cyber warfare under ambiguous guidelines and legal grey areas for the foreseeable future."

4. DEFENCE AND DETERRENCE

The question of how to defend oneself and deter attacks arises alongside every new domain of warfare. The arrival of armoured vehicles led to the development of tank traps and anti-tank mines. The arrival of air warfare led to the development of anti-aircraft weaponry. For every new domain of war, nations seek to build defences and deterrents.

The arrival of the cyber domain is no different and nations will be asking these very same questions:

1. How do we defend ourselves in the cyber domain?
2. How can we deter someone from attacking us in the cyber domain?

4.1 Defence

Saydjari (2004) has looked at the issue of defence in the cyber domain and has put forward the idea of a comprehensive defence system which consists of six elements. These are shown in Table 1.

While Saydjari offers a comprehensive list of six elements, it arguably misses a seventh which we have included in italics. The element of exercises, represents the view that a defence system requires testing and rehearsal to ensure that each element operates well.

The issue of defining what a cyber defence system should consist of is only one challenge facing researchers in this area. Once an effective system has been identified, the challenge of how to actually build and implement it presents itself. Should this be a government led endeavour or should individuals and organisations be taking the lead?

4.1.1 Top-Down vs. Bottom-Up Defence

There is disagreement within the research community on the best approach to building an effective cyber defence system. Authors such as Saydjari (2008) argue that the best defence requires a top down approach. He suggests that a government led, concentrated national effort with support from the U.S. President is the best approach. Clarke & Knake (2010) support the view that cyber defence is something that governments should be taking the lead on, arguing that asking civilians to protect themselves is akin to asking them to install anti-aircraft guns at their offices.

There is however another view which argues that cyber defence should be built using a bottom-up approach. Fernandez Vazquez et al. (2012) support this view, suggesting that information sharing between organisations is an effective way of bolstering the cyber defence of the nation. To this end, they have examined why information sharing schemes have failed in the past and present suggestions on how future schemes could be improved. O'Connell (2012) also supports the idea of bottom-up cyber defence,

Table 1. Saydjari's elements of cyber defence

Defence Element	Description
Sensors and exploitation	The eyes of the defence system – determining attack capability, plans and actions of enemies.
Situational awareness	Transforming sensed data into a useful decision aid
Defensive mechanisms	Technological measures to counter attacks: e.g. Firewalls.
Command and control	Making and executing decisions in an orchestrated manner.
Strategies and tactics	A knowledge of what decision is best in a particular situation
Science and engineering	Developing new and improved defences to keep ahead of the enemy
Exercises	*Rehearsal of procedures to identify weaknesses and find improvements*

stating that many attacks against a nation could be made more difficult if the general population practiced what she terms "good cyber hygiene".

The answer to which method is best may be neither. A combination of top-down and bottom-up will likely prove to be the best defence, as can be seen with the United States' approach to terrorism defence. While the intelligence services work to gather intelligence and act at a high level, individual citizens are encouraged to play their part with the "See Something, Say Something" campaign ("If you see something," 2014).

4.1.2 Early Warning Systems

A significant aspect of cyber defence is the creation of effective early warning systems. Early warning in traditional warfare is arguably simple in comparison to cyber warfare. The mass movement of ships and troops can be observed by satellite and spy plane, giving advance warning that an adversary is preparing an attack and what that attack may consist of. In the cyber domain however, the signs of preparation for cyber attack are much less understood.

Golling and Stelte (2010) have suggested that a cyber early warning system should be able to answer the following questions:

- Is a Cyber War taking place right now/about to begin?
- Who is attacking?
- What is the target?
- What kind of attack methods are being used?

The problem of developing an effective early warning system is one that will benefit from research in other areas of cyber security. Research into attack prediction, intrusion detection and network monitoring will all provide useful contributions in formulating future cyber early warning systems. There is also some overlap to other areas discussed in this chapter. For example, determining who is attacking is discussed in detail in the attribution section, and also the ethical issues section.

Although it is tempting to think of all the technical solutions, Sharma et al. (2010) point out that a cyber early warning system must consider more than just technical indicators. They state that social, political, economic and cultural events can all be used as indicator of an impending cyber attack. Moran (2012) agrees with this view and has suggested that four stages occur before a politically motivated cyber attack, which can be used as indicators for a cyber early warning system. These stages are shown in Figure 2.

While caution must be used in assuming that all politically motivated attacks will follow this order of events, Moran's model provides an example of how cyber warning systems should be approached in future. By combining information and understanding from multiple disciplines, nations will be able

Figure 2. Moran's (2012) four stages of a politically motivated cyber attack

Latent Tensions   Cyber Recon   Initiating Event   Cyber Mobilization   Cyber Attack

to create systems that use all available information to best provide the earliest possible warning of an impending attack.

4.3 Deterrence

Despite the concern over how to construct effective cyber defences, it is arguably more desirable to convince an enemy to not even attempt a cyber attack in the first place. This goal has led to research and discussion into how the concept of cyber deterrence may best be approached. Libicki (2009) has defined cyber deterrence as "a capability in cyberspace to do unto others what others may want to do unto us." This definition suggests that cyber deterrence is limited to threatening a cyber attack in retaliation for any cyber attacks inflicted upon a nation. However, it is arguably an unnecessarily restrictive definition in that the threat of a kinetic response should not be entirely ruled out when considering effective deterrents, at least until laws concerning cyber warfare have been formulated.

Libicki (2009) has highlighted how deterrence has proven useful in situations such as the Cold War, but that the concept of cyber deterrence faces some unique obstacles, as shown in Table 2:

Aside from these obstacles, Libicki (2009) notes a bigger problem with the concept of cyber deterrence. He argues that the success of nuclear deterrence lay in the fact that a nuclear retaliatory response would result in the crippling of a nation. He suggests that a cyber retaliatory response would not be so grave, and would actually reveal how weak the retaliation was. He therefore concludes that a cyber deterrent is only effective if it is not used.

It must be noted however that nuclear deterrence also suffered from a similar problem. While each superpower threatened nuclear retaliation, it was never a certainty that such a thing would occur. Therefore, it can be argued that perceived, rather than actual threat is what makes all kinds of deterrent valuable to nations.

The view that cyber deterrence will not work is not shared by all researchers in the area. Alperovitch (2011) and Hare (2012) are more optimistic about the value of cyber deterrence, and disagree with the view that the threatened retaliation must be a cyber attack. They suggest that nations could be deterred from launching cyber attacks by declaring red lines, which if crossed would lead to hostile political positioning on the international stage. However, as events in Syria have shown (Cohen 2013), leaders

Table 2. Libicki's (2009) obstacles to cyber deterrence

Obstacle	Description
Attribution	If the attacker remains anonymous, there is little fear of retaliation.
Failure to recognise risks	An attacker may underestimate the ability of those they attack to inflict harm in retaliation
Repeatability	Cyber attacks can be single/limited use. Once used in retaliation, it may provide no future deterrence
Setting Thresholds	It is unclear what actions in cyber space are worthy of a retaliatory response
Escalation	Caution must be used to not escalate a minor cyber event into a major kinetic event
Cyber Dependence	If a nation has very little cyber infrastructure of its own, a cyber response serves as very little deterrent.

should be cautious of setting red lines, since a response will be expected once they are crossed. They also argue that conclusive attribution of an attack is not necessary, and that reasonable suspicion is all that is needed to initiate such a response.

Sterner (2012) has taken an alternative approach to the issue, and puts forward the idea that cyber deterrence is incorrectly being looked at in the nuclear "all or nothing" sense. Rather than threatening a catastrophic response at a defined threshold, Sterner argues that nations should consider using what he calls "active-deterrence". According to Sterner, this involves using combinations of threats and retaliatory attacks to dynamically manage a situation while encouraging the attacker to stop. In this respect, Sterner suggests that instead of being the last line of defence, active cyber deterrence should be just one tool in a nation's cyber defence toolbox.

The issue of whether cyber deterrence can be a useful tool and what it should involve is an ongoing problem facing cyber warfare researchers. As with other challenges discussed in this chapter, advancements in others areas such as attribution and the formulation of legal guidelines may help to shape how deterrence is carried out in the future and how effective it can be.

5. CONCEPTUALISING CYBER WARFARE

While other topics discussed in this chapter are relatively narrow in scope, the topic of conceptualising cyber warfare is one that enjoys a broad scope and attempts to present new and unique ways of thinking about cyber warfare.

Tibbs (2013) presents the conceptual idea that cyber warfare can be seen as a game. He suggests that anyone using an internet connected device is a player in this game, but that states wield the most power. Each player in the game can take different positions on the cyber game board, and this position affects how they act in cyber space and who their adversaries are. Players are free to move around to different squares, with the ultimate goal being to gain an advantage over other players. A visual representation of the cyber game board can be seen in Box 1.

Tibbs' game board is a novel way of considering the idea of cyber warfare, but others such as Libicki (2012) have put forward the idea that cyber should not even be considered a domain of war, since it is a man-made creation in comparison to other domains which are all natural. It can be counter argued

Box 1. Tibbs' (2013) cyber game board

	Connection Physical Data Handling Domain	Computation Virtual Interactivity Domain	Cognition Knowledge and Meaning Domain
Cooperation Integrative Social Power (Infopolitik)	Open source hardware (e.g. mesh networks)	Open source code, social software (e.g. Linux, Github)	Shared knowledge and narrative (e.g. Wikipedia)
Co-Option Economic Exchange Power	Dominate hardware market (e.g. Cisco, Huawei)	Dominate software market (e.g. Microsoft, Apple)	Knowledge services, marketing, PR, advertising, spin
Coercion Destructive Hard Power (Realpolitik)	Kinetic attack on information infrastructure	Malware attack, IP theft (e.g. Stuxnet)	Threats, disinformation, psyops

however, that it is up to those who practice warfare to decide on such things, and the US Department of Defence has stated that cyber warfare is a domain of war (United States Department of Defense, 2013). Others such as Gartzke (2013) agree that cyber is a domain of war, but that its importance in future conflicts is being over exaggerated. He compares cyber warfare to the use of artillery: While clearly useful, it alone cannot win wars and is just one tool of many that are needed to achieve meaningful gains in war.

6. NATIONAL APPROACHES

This research strand of cyber warfare is concerned with examining how the practitioners of warfare are approaching the subject. With cyber being a relatively new type of warfare, nations are faced with constructing doctrines and approaches that provide an insight into military thinking and the possible shape of future cyber conflict.

6.1 Finding Similarities

Perhaps the easiest task when looking at national approaches to cyber warfare is to highlight similarities. The most immediate similarity to note is that the major powers are alert to the fact that cyber warfare is a significant issue that they need to prepare for. Publications from the United States military have referred to cyber as an operational domain in which it must organise, train and equip (United States Department of Defense, 2011). Similar statements highlighting recognition of cyber's importance to future military operations can be found in Chinese and Russian documentation (Billo & Chang, 2004). Looking further, Chinese and American military doctrine both make similar calls for government and civilians to work together to secure cyber space (Thomas, 2011).

Finding similarities in doctrine is a useful task, since it shows where nations are in agreement and potentially begins to define how cyber warfare should be conducted simply by setting a precedent. An arguably more interesting endeavour however, is to locate, examine and consider the reasons for differences in approaches.

6.2 Comparing Differences

Thomas (2009) has highlighted one such difference in approaches to cyber warfare. He shows that Russia and China have a significant focus on the concept of using cognitive attacks, while the United States does not. Russia in particular uses cognitive attacks as a central theme, aiming to understand the enemy's thought process and then intentionally presenting certain actions to exploit that understanding. By manipulating the decisions made by the enemy, those using a cognitive attack can generate situations favourable to themselves. Billo & Chang (2004) agree with this observation, stating that China has a heavy focus on the psychological aspects of cyber warfare, whereas the U.S. appears to focus more on the technological, network attack aspects.

Billo & Chang (2004) suggest that the reason for these differences can be traced to a national mindset of how war should be conducted. He highlights how Chinese cyber doctrine contains numerous references to Sun Tzu, setting out traditional principles such as subduing an enemy without battle. It can therefore be argued that psychological aspects have always played a role in Chinese warfare, making it unsurprising that it also appears in cyber warfare doctrine.

It must also be noted that national approaches to cyber warfare appear somewhat linked to negative experiences that a nation has faced in the past. For example, Billo & Chang (2004) state that one of Russia's significant fears about cyber warfare is that it will become engaged in a cyber arms race that it cannot win. Looking at this fear, it is difficult to deny that memories of the Cold War may be influencing Russia's cyber warfare doctrine. Similarly, U.S. military leadership has repeatedly expressed concern over becoming the victim of a "Digital Pearl Harbor" (Parrish, 2013). Looking at these concerns expressed by nations, it is clear that history is playing some part in the construction of modern cyber warfare doctrines.

6.3 Words of Caution

When considering national approaches to cyber warfare, it must be remembered that the issue is fundamentally one of national security. With this in mind, it cannot be assumed that nations are automatically willing to publicise the full truth on their respective approaches. Further to this, it can be argued that nations have an incentive to distribute misinformation in order to portray a certain appearance to potential adversaries. In the face of evidence suggesting that nations are aware of and employ elements of cognitive warfare, it is prudent to keep these words of caution in mind when looking at this research area.

Nevertheless, researchers such as Thomas (2009) and Billo & Chang (2004) have provided some useful work on comparing and contrasting national approaches to cyber warfare. As the topic of cyber warfare matures, states will continue to refine and enhance their doctrines and continued research in this area will be required.

7. Cyber Weapons

The concept of a weapon in the kinetic world is well understood. The Oxford English Dictionary (2014) gives two definitions:

1.   A thing designed or used for inflicting bodily harm or physical damage.
2.   A means of gaining an advantage or defending oneself in a conflict or contest.

When it comes to the cyber domain however, the task of defining and describing cyber weapons has been a challenge that researchers have been working to overcome. Looking at the first definition offered by the dictionary, the requirements to inflict bodily harm or physical damage do not seem applicable to the cyber domain. A piece of malware designed to steal data does not inflict either.

The second definition at first seems more suitable, since cyber weapons arguably do aim to provide an advantage in a conflict. But the emphasis on being a "means" suggests that the second definition refers to methods and tactics used rather than distinct items that can be activated.

Arimatsu (2012) has examined existing definitions of weapons and concludes that they are unsuitable for defining cyber weapons. She highlights how cyber weapons have a dual use aspect – a tool such as a network sniffer has perfectly legitimate and peaceful uses, but can quite easily be used in cyber warfare for harmful purposes. It must be noted that this is not an issue unique to cyber warfare however. A knife in the hands of a chef is a tool. The same knife in the hands of someone with harmful intent becomes a weapon. She argues that to solve the definition problem regarding cyber weapons, it is essential that capability and intent are examined together. Therefore, a piece of code only becomes a cyber weapon when it has both the capability and intent to cause harm.

7.1 Controlling Cyber Weapons

Denning (2000) has stated that with well-established controls on the production, use and trade of traditional weapons, the question of whether the same controls could be applied to cyber weapons is one that should be asked. She argues that having such controls would bring a number of advantages including a reduction in cyber attacks and an easing of international tensions regarding cyber warfare. According to Denning, there are obstacles in the way of enacting such controls:

- Enforcement Difficulties
- Reaching international agreement
- Defining acceptable limits of activity
- Impact on free speech
- Hampers a nation's ability to retaliate to attacks

Looking at these obstacles, they appear to be primarily political ones that can only be solved by political discussion. With concern over cyber warfare high, it may become the case that such discussions occur before unrestricted cyber weapons become a significant problem. However, history shows that intensive efforts to control harmful new types of weapons tend to occur after demonstrations of their use (Organisation for the Prohibition of Chemical Weapons, 2014).

Arimatsu (2012) has examined the various types of treaty that may be useful in controlling cyber weapons. She concludes that the only valid type of treaty is one that restricts the use of specific types of cyber weapon. For example, those which do not discriminate between civilian and military targets, or which cause disproportionate damage could be banned and their use made illegal.

In agreement with Denning, Arimatsu states that the biggest problem with such a treaty is the task of enforcement. Kinetic weapons such as chemical or nuclear warheads are difficult to hide, and can be located with the use of weapon inspection teams to highlight when a treaty has been violated. Cyber weapons are much easier to hide. Data can be encrypted and stored on a tiny device, or even uploaded to the cloud. Locating cyber weapons that are hidden in this manner would be an almost impossible task. In addition, the dual aspect nature of cyber weapons only adds to the problem. A national leader would have trouble convincing the world that a cache of chemical weapons had a peaceful use, but a collection of computer equipment and software can easily be explained as legitimate. As Denning has suggested, it would also be a challenge to define acceptable limits and highlight a specific cyber weapon that crosses them. At what point does a cyber weapon become indiscriminate, or disproportionate? Does it cause these effects upon every use, or do the effects vary? These questions highlight another problem: the measuring of cyber weapon effects.

The problem of measuring cyber weapon effects is compounded by additional issues. Rowe (2010) points out that cyber weapons are unavoidably unpredictable in their effects. Network configurations, software and hardware can all influence the effect a cyber weapon has. This influence is not minor, the changing of a rule in a firewall could transform a cyber weapon from being catastrophic to having no effect whatsoever. Caution must be used however, in that it would be incorrect to say that weapon unpredictability is unique to cyber warfare. Kinetic weapons can also be unpredictable in that bombs may not detonate and rifles may jam. The difference arguably lies in the source of the change in behaviour. A failure of a kinetic weapon can be said to lie solely with the weapon itself. The triggering mechanism on the bomb failed: a product of minor defects in the production process. Being a piece of code that is replicated exactly, cyber weapons do not have production defects. The unpredictability of cyber weapons therefore can only come from external factors.

Another barrier to measurement is that of damage assessment. Rowe (2010) has examined this issue and highlights how damage from a kinetic weapon is relatively easy to assess: A ship has been sunk, or an airstrip rendered unusable. In comparison, the damage inflicted by a cyber weapon is more difficult to determine. It may not be clear that an attack has even occurred. If the attack is detected, it is a challenge to determine what systems it has impacted, what its effects were and whether it is ongoing or a one off payload. The negative effects of a cyber weapon may be subtle and continue to cause an impact long into the future and even post conflict. In this regard, Rowe (2010) compares cyber weapons to land mines.

While authors such as Denning (2000) and Arimatsu (2012) have contributed work regarding controlling the production and use of cyber weapons, there is another aspect to cyber weapon control that has received research attention: the control of automated cyber weapons.

Tyugu (2012) has contributed to this area by studying command and control issues with both automated cyber attack and defence systems. He warns that the more intelligent cyber weapons become, the harder they will be control and that effective control must be a high priority throughout the design of such future weapons. In particular, Tyugu identifies four potential problems with automated cyber weapons:

1. Misunderstanding of a command - Protocols used between automated agents not verified well enough, leading to incorrect decisions being reached by an agent.
2. Misunderstanding of a situation – An agent reaching an incorrect conclusion about the situation it is observing.
3. Unexpected emotions – A false alarm urgently triggering an incorrect severe action, comparable to the human emotion of panic.
4. Undesirable coalitions – Advanced artificial intelligence may decide to form coalitions and make collective decisions which escape human control.

Tyugu's concern over automated cyber weapons is not unwarranted, with governments increasingly showing an interest in automating cyber defences (UK Ministry of Defence, 2014) and other authors such as Caton (2013) sharing his concerns.

As with many of the other issues regarding cyber warfare, the problem of controlling cyber weapons is arguably best approached from a multi-disciplinary perspective. Setting limits on the levels of automation, mandating a requirement for kill-switches, and defining what types of effects are undesirable are all issues that are best approached by combining legal, political, military and technical expertise.

8. CONDUCTING CYBER WARFARE

The arrival of a new domain of war always triggers a race between nations to determine the most effect methods for operating inside of it. With the arrival of flight, the air domain was opened up for military exploitation and a race to develop an understanding of its unique characteristics and implications for warfare began. Today, that process is very mature: air forces around the world have well defined operating procedures and training for conducting air warfare in an efficient manner. The arrival of cyber as a domain of war is no different. Research is underway which aims to define the characteristics of cyberspace and the implications those characteristics have on warfighting.

8.1 Applying Existing Principles

Liles et al. (2012) have approached this topic by examining the existing principles of warfare used by the US Army (Table 3) and discussing how each one could be applied to cyber warfare.

Liles et al. (2012) argue that the objective principle can be applied easily: cyber attacks used for military purposes will have an objective in mind, and the use of attacks without an objective would be difficult to justify. They suggest that applying the offensive principle to the cyber domain will be difficult, since the lines between offense and defence are blurred in the cyber domain. However, this point must be challenged since cyber teams often run red vs blue exercises, where the offense and defence roles are well defined. Further to this, the offensive principle could arguably be applied to the cyber domain in the form of constantly seeking new zero day exploits and probing adversaries for weaknesses.

Liles et al. (2012) claim that the mass principle is also challenging to apply to cyber, since an event such as a distributed denial of service attack requires little mass but has great effect. Again, this argument can be challenged since it depends on how mass is defined in the cyber domain. If mass is considered as CPU cycles, then a botnet of hundreds of thousands of machines is a considerable mass that is leveraged against the enemy during a denial of service attack.

Examining the maneuver principle, they conclude that maneuvering in the cyber domain can be achieved by simply making quick decisions. It can be argued that a better translation of this principle would be a cyber attack team swiftly moving between systems and staying ahead of defenders. In this respect, swift movement in cyber space is placing the defenders into a disadvantageous position.

Liles et al. (2012) suggest that the unity of command can be easily translated into cyber warfare, since the use of IT automatically boosts command and control. This view must be challenged however, since it cannot be assumed that the use of IT automatically makes command and control easier. It can be argued that the cyber domain makes command and control more difficult: attacks and counter attacks can be launched within milliseconds, and as discussed in the section on cyber weapons, the effects of attacks may be difficult to determine. Therefore, it can be argued that the increased pace of warfare, lack of situational awareness and the use of automated systems can lead to a loss of command and control ability.

Table 3. US Army's principles of warfare

Principle	Description
Objective	Every military act should have a defined and attainable objective
Offensive	Seize, retain, and exploit the initiative
Mass	Focus the effects of combat power at the decisive place and time
Economy of Force	Allocate minimum essential combat power to secondary efforts
Maneuver	Place enemies into a disadvantageous position through the flexible application of combat power
Unity of Command	Ensure unity of effort under one responsible commander
Security	Never permit the enemy to acquire an unexpected advantage
Surprise	Strike the enemy at a time or place or in a manner for which he is unprepared
Simplicity	Plans and orders should be clear and concise

Regarding the security principle, Liles et al. (2012) suggest that avoiding unexpected advantages in the cyber domain is difficult: even if perfectly secure, an insider attack may still present an unexpected advantage for an opponent. In light of the cyber domain being difficult to perfectly secure, this principle could be adapted. Instead of demanding that security never be compromised, it should be applied with the aim of minimising the impact of unexpected breaches in security. Therefore, the principle of security in the cyber domain could focus on demanding defence in depth, rigorous monitoring and on having well-rehearsed response plans in place.

With respect to the surprise principle, Liles et al. (2012) suggest that cyber attacks should be targeted where they are least expected. However, surprise arguably also includes using cyber weapons that can remain stealthy. Securing covert backdoors into systems and using sleeper malware are all actions that support the principle of surprise.

Applying simplicity to cyber warfare, they claim that there is nothing simpler than the one or zero of binary. While this is true, it can be argued that the purpose of this principle is to ensure plans and orders are simple enough to be carried out as intended. In the cyber domain, this can translate to ensuring that orders are clear and concise, such as denying a particular service to an enemy for x number of hours.

8.2 Alternative Approaches

Parks and Duggan (2011) have also examined the existing principles used by the US Army, but have taken a different approach to the problem by suggesting a set of new principles that are unique to cyber warfare.

Lack of Physical Limitations

Traditional warfare is subject to physical limitations such as terrain, borders and distance. Parks and Duggan (2011) suggest that these physical limitations do not exist in cyber warfare, allowing attacks to launch from anywhere with equal impact.

While it is true that there are less physical obstacles to launching attacks, it can be argued that physical limitations still exist. Just as a missile must fly through the air, a cyber attack must pass along a communication medium, be that a physical cable or a wireless network. It can even be argued that physical limitations are more severe in cyber warfare: how do you attack a system if the network cable is unplugged? In the case of delivering malware via USB, physical limitations also still apply in getting the USB to the required USB port.

Where a lack of physical limitations is more convincing is in the production of cyber weapons. Traditional weapons require both materials and time to produce - cyber weapons do not have these same requirements, and can be replicated quickly and cheaply. Parks and Duggan (2011) give the example of the Low Orbit Ion Cannon, a cyber weapon which was freely available to download online.

Kinetic Effects

The aim of cyber warfare is to cause kinetic effects. This can be physical damage or a cognitive attack to influence an enemy's decision. An attack which has no kinetic effect cannot be considered cyber warfare. Caution must be used when using terms like kinetic effect however. If a nation performs a cyber attack and steals military plans, but they turn out to be outdated plans, has cyber warfare occurred or not? There was arguably no kinetic effect because the plans were outdated. Similarly, if a key logger is installed onto a military system but no actionable intelligence is gained, has cyber warfare occurred?

When looking at the idea of kinetic effects, it is arguably more suitable to state that a kinetic *intent* is required, rather than an actual effect. Requiring intent covers cases where it is questionable if an act resulted in an effect or not.

Stealth

In kinetic warfare, stealth involves performing actions whilst remaining unseen by the enemy. This can involve the use of technology such as camouflage or anti-radar measures. Parks and Duggan argue that in the cyber domain, stealth is centred on hiding amongst legitimate traffic.

It must be counter argued that stealth can also be seen as similar in both domains. Both require an attacker to blend into their surroundings. While a soldier will wear camouflage suitable to the surrounding environment, a cyber attack will attempt to look similar to surrounding traffic so that it goes unnoticed. In both domains, the goal is to not stand out amongst the environment.

Mutability and Inconsistency

The cyber domain is unpredictable: while a bullet will fly a predictable path, a cyber attack may never act the same way twice. However, it is debatable whether mutability and inconsistency are unique to the cyber domain. Minor imperfections on individual bullets and human factors in aiming mean that a bullet is never entirely predictable. Therefore, inconsistency and mutability are arguably not unique to cyber warfare.

Identity and Privileges

The goal of a cyber attacker is to assume the identity of someone who holds the level of access to achieve an objective. Exploit code achieves root access; social engineering gathers passwords for privileged users. This contrasts with traditional warfare, whereby assuming identities is likely to be considered a war crime. It is difficult to argue against this point, since gaining access to privileged accounts is a major aspect of cyber warfare. It does however ignore some other aspects such as distributed denial of service attacks.

Dual Use

Cyber weapons are dual use, having both harmful and peaceful uses. This is unlike kinetic warfare, where the weapons are single use. This principle correctly identifies that cyber weapons are dual use, but the idea that dual use is unique to cyber warfare can be challenged. Kinetic weapons have dual uses also: hunting, competitive sports and even for celebration. Therefore, it can be argued that the dual use principle is not unique to cyber weapons.

Infrastructure Control

A significant part of cyber warfare is infrastructure control. With traffic having to pass through hardware controlled by various third parties, gaining control over as much infrastructure as possible provides advantages to combatants. This principle has merit, since having direct control over devices gives advantages to defenders (better situational awareness and the ability to block traffic) and attackers (large bot nets allowing greater impact from attacks). However, it must be argued that the principle is not unique

Table 4. Laprise's (2006) comparison of naval and cyber principles

Strategic Principle	Maritime Example	Cyberspace Example
Decisive Battle	Fleet Battle	None (due to inability to cause irreparable harm)
Siege	Blockade	Denial of Service Attack
Area Control	Aircraft Carrier Defence	Webmaster Vigilance
Area Denial	Aerial Patrol and Surveillance	Compromised Website
Commerce Warfare	Submarine Warfare	Hacking

to cyber warfare. Kinetic forces will also seek to control infrastructure. Bridges, ports and airfields are all infrastructure that militaries will desire direct control over to better serve their needs.

Information as Operational Environment

Kinetic warfare requires the physical environment to be transformed into information that commanders can make decisions with. In cyber warfare the environment is already information, and no conversion is required. This principle is debatable however, since the network to be used in cyber warfare is still made up of physically existing equipment, and the targets of attacks may be physical, such as power plants or factories. In this regard, it cannot be assumed that no conversion from physical measurement to information will be required.

As has been demonstrated by examining both Liles et al.'s (2012) and Parks and Duggan's (2011) work, the task of applying existing principles or creating a new set is a challenging one. Laprise (2006) has taken on the challenge using another method, by comparing cyber warfare to naval warfare and looking for similarities that could help translate existing concepts. The results of his comparisons are shown in Table 4.

Laprise states that all of the strategic principles have identifiable comparisons in the cyber domain, except for decisive battle. While operating systems may be wiped, there is no permanent physical damage to the hardware and therefore cyber warfare alone cannot win a war. This is in agreement with authors such as Gartzke (2013), who argue that cyber warfare must operate alongside kinetic warfare to have any decisive result.

There are imaginable situations where cyber warfare could inflict a decisive blow. As ships become increasingly reliant on technology, sleeper malware could in theory disable all weapon systems on an entire fleet simultaneously. As Gartzke and Laprise point out however, such a disabling is futile without the threat of a kinetic force to take advantage of it.

The topic of identifying effective principles of cyber warfare is a challenging one. This section has examined a number of approaches taken by researchers in the field, and identified problems with each approach. It must be concluded that no effective set of cyber warfare principles currently exist. It is unclear if future research can address this issue, or if it is a challenge that can only be addressed through experience of cyber warfare. The first air combat pilots did not have the luxury of well-defined principles to guide their actions; they were developed based on the experiences of air warfare pioneers. In this regard, the emergence of effective cyber warfare principles may rely on the experiences of cyber warfare pioneers.

9. ATTRIBUTION

The problem of attribution is one that is common to all aspects of cyber security, not just cyber warfare. The use of botnets, stepping stones, VPNs, and free wireless access points results in the ability to launch attacks and perform harmful actions whilst remaining unidentified.

9.1 Attribution is Difficult

Wheeler and Larsen (2003) have looked at the issue of attribution in depth and have concluded that there are generally seventeen methods by which it could be achieved in the cyber domain. However, most of these methods rely on the concept of prepositioning either trust or technology. For organisations to share information and trace the attack backwards, an element of trust needs to exist between those organisations. Trying to build this trust after an event is difficult – language barriers, differing cultures, worries over commercial data and privacy issues may hamper any attempt to work together and locate an attacker. Similarly, technological solutions such as logging are not useful unless they were already prepositioned before the attack began. Wheeler and Larsen suggest that the prepositioning problem could be overcome by the adoption of industry standards. A legally approved, standardised set of tools that provides information about the source of an attack would remove the need for trustful relationships by having the technology prepositioned by default in network devices.

However, authors such as Boebert (2010) remind us that even with these standards, technical attribution alone is not useful. An IP address cannot be held responsible for a cyber attack. The owner of said machine can claim it was stolen, used by a visitor or taken over by malware and used remotely. None of those defences are implausible in today's world of cyber crime. He therefore argues that technical attribution needs to be converted into human attribution: proving that a human being performed action A at time B. This is a much more difficult task, and is one that the research community continues to work on.

9.2 Is it Necessary?

Attribution is undoubtedly a problem facing cyber security, and some insist that it is also a problem for cyber warfare. Wheeler and Larsen (2003) argue that attribution is an essential element of cyber warfare, claiming that: "As with conventional warfare, a good offense is often the strongest defense. However, many offensive techniques, such as computer network attack, legal action (e.g., arrests and lawsuits), and kinetic energy attacks, can only be deployed if the source of the attack can be attributed with high confidence". Dever & Dever (2013) agree with this view, stating that cyber defence models "rely heavily upon the advancement of technological capability to assist with the ever vexing issue of attribution." Friesen (2009) concurs, stating that the inability to attribute a cyber attack stands in the way of regulating cyber warfare.

However, authors such as Hare (2012) have put forward the argument that attribution is not as important in cyber warfare as some suggest. Hare argues that lacking absolute attribution of a cyber attack will not prevent a nation from responding. He suggests that international politics is dynamic enough to allow for retaliation without conclusive proof. An example given is of a nation taking a political stance that negatively affects the interests of the suspected attacking nation. As long as the suspected attacker realises that this hostile political positioning is in response to the cyber attack, the victim has effectively responded to the attack without conclusive attribution.

Looking at this field of research, it must be concluded that attribution is clearly important both in cyber security and in cyber warfare. However, as Hare (2012) has argued, it is debateable whether attribution is as much of an obstacle as some suggest. Research in the area continues, with work regarding the issue being performed from a variety of angles, including specifically in the area of critical national infrastructure (Nicholson, 2013).

10. CONCLUSION

In this chapter, we have given a survey of the contemporary research problems that cyber warfare presents. We have described some of the works in each area and contrasted the arguments presented by a selection of authors.

While progress is being made across the board, it must be concluded that the majority of challenges cannot be resolved by a singular approach. Technical minds alone cannot solve the issue of creating a set of cyber warfare laws. This must be approached by a team of legal, military and technical minds. The Tallinn Manual is a good example of this approach, and shows promise for the creation of future laws. To achieve further progress, the same approach must be applied to other areas such as cyber weapons, attribution and defence.

REFERENCES

Alperovitch, D. (2011).Towards establishment of cyberspace deterrence strategy. In *Proceedings of the 3rd International Conference on Cyber Conflict (ICCC)*, Tallinn:IEEE.

Arimatsu, L. (2012). A treaty for governing cyber-weapons: Potential benefits and practical limitations. In *Proceedings of the 4th International Conference on Cyber Conflict (CYCON)*. Tallinn:IEEE.

Billo, C., & Chang, W. (2004). *Cyber warfare an analysis of the means and motivations of selected nation states*. Retrieved from http://www.ists.dartmouth.edu/docs/cyberwarfare.pdf

Boebert, W. E. (2010). A Survey of Challenges in Attribution. In *Proceedings of a Workshop on Deterring Cyberattacks: Informing Strategies and Developing Options for U.S. Policy*. Washington, DC: The National Academies Press.

Caton, J. (2013). Exploring the prudent limits of automated cyber attack. In *Proceedings of the 5th International Conference on Cyber Conflict (CYCON)*, Tallinn:IEEE.

Clarke, R. A., & Knake, R. (2010). *Cyber War: The Next Threat to National Security and What to Do About It*. New York, NY: HarperCollins.

Cohen, T. (2013, September 5). Obama: It's the world's 'red line' on Syria; Senate panel backs military strike plan. *CNN*. Retrieved from http://edition.cnn.com/2013/09/04/politics/us-syria/

Denning, D. E. (2000). Reflections on cyberweapons controls. *Computer Security Journal, 16*(4), 43–53.

If you see something, say something. (2014). *Department of Homeland Security*. Retrieved from http://www.dhs.gov/see-something-say-something

Dever, J., & Dever, J. (2013). Cyberwarfare: Attribution, Preemption, and National Self Defense. *Journal of Law and Cyber Warfare, 2*(1), 25–66.

DiMeglio, R. P., Condrom, S. M., Bishop, O. B., Musselman, G. S., Lindquist, T. L., & Gillman, A. D. …Stigall, D.E. (2012). Law of Armed Conflict Deskbook. Johnson, W.J., & Gillman, A.D. (Eds.). US Army: Virginia.

Dipert, R. R. (2010). The Ethics of Cyberwarfare. *Journal of Military Ethics, 9*(4), 384–410. doi:10.1 080/15027570.2010.536404

Fernandez Vazquez, D., Pastor Acosta, O., Brown, S., Reid, E., & Spirito, C. (2012). Conceptual framework for cyber defense information sharing within trust relationships. In *Proceedings of the 4h International Conference on Cyber Conflict (CYCON)*, Tallinn:IEEE.

Friesen, T. L. (2009). Resolving tomorrow's conflicts today: How new developments within the U.N. Security Council can be used to combat cyberwarfare. *Naval Law Review, 58*, 89–127.

Gartzke, E. (2013). The myth of cyberwar: Bringing war in cyberspace back down to earth. *International Security, 38*(2), 41–73. doi:10.1162/ISEC_a_00136

Giles, K., & Hagestad, W. (2013). Divided by a common language: Cyber definitions in Chinese, Russian and English. In *Proceedings of the 5th International Conference on Cyber Conflict (CYCON)*, Tallinn:IEEE.

Golling, M., & Stelte, B. (2011). Requirements for a future EWS – cyber defence in the internet of the future. In *Proceedings of the 3rd International Conference on Cyber Conflict (ICCC)*, Tallinn:IEEE.

Hare, F. (2012). The significance of attribution to cyberspace coercion: A political perspective. In *Proceedings of the 4h International Conference on Cyber Conflict (CYCON)*, Tallinn:IEEE.

International Committee of the Red Cross. (1977). *Protocol Additional to the Geneva Conventions of 12 August 1949, and relating to the Protection of Victims of International Armed Conflicts (Protocol I).*

International Committee of the Red Cross. (1996, May 3). *Protocol on Prohibitions or Restrictions on the Use of Mines, Booby-Traps and Other Devices.*

Laprise, J. (2006). Cyber-warfare seen through a mariner's spyglass. *Technology and Society Magazine, IEEE, 25*(3), 26–33. doi:10.1109/MTAS.2006.1700019

Libicki, M. C. (2009). *Cyberdeterrence and Cyberwar.* Santa Monica, CA: RAND Corporation.

Libicki, M.C. (2012). Cyberspace is not a warfighting domain. *I/S: A Journal of Law and Policy for the Information Society, 8*(2), 325–340.

Liles, S., Rogers, M., Dietz, J., & Larson, D. (2012). Applying traditional military principles to cyber warfare. In *Proceedings of the 4h International Conference on Cyber Conflict (CYCON)*, Tallinn:IEEE.

Lin, P., Allhoff, F., & Rowe, N. C. (2012). War 2.0: Cyberweapons and ethics. *Communications of the ACM, 55*(3), 24–26. doi:10.1145/2093548.2093558

Moran, N. (2012). A Cyber Early Warning Model. In J. Carr (Ed.), Inside Cyber Warfare (179-189). O'Reilly Media Inc.: Sebastopol, CA.

Nicholson, A., Janicke, H., & Watson, T. (2013). An initial investigation into attribution in SCADA systems. In *Proceedings of the 1st International Symposium for ICS & SCADA Cyber Security Research*. Leicester, UK: BCS.

O'Connell, M. E. (2012). Cyber security without cyber war. *Journal of Conflict and Security Law, 17*(2), 187–209. doi:10.1093/jcsl/krs017

Organisation for the Prohibition of Chemical Weapons. (2014). *Chemical Weapons Convention: Genesis and Historical Development*. Retrieved May 14, 2015, from http://www.opcw.org/chemical-weapons-convention/genesis-and-historical-development

Parks, R., & Duggan, D. (2011). Principles of cyberwarfare. *Security Privacy, IEEE, 9*(5), 30–35. doi:10.1109/MSP.2011.138

Parrish, K. (2013, February 6). Panetta warns cyber threat growing quickly. *American Forces Press Service*. Retrieved from http://www.defense.gov/news/newsarticle.aspx?id=119214

Rauscher, K. F., & Korotkov, A. (2011). *Working towards rules for governing cyber conflict*. New York: The East-West Institute.

Rowe, N. (2010). The ethics of cyberweapons in warfare. *International Journal of Cyber Ethics, 1*(1), 20–31.

Saydjari, O. S. (2004). Cyber defense: Art to science. *Communications of the ACM, 47*(3), 52–57. doi:10.1145/971617.971645

Saydjari, O. S. (2008). Structuring for strategic cyber defense: A cyber Manhattan project blueprint. In *Proceedings of Computer Security Applications Conference (ACSAC)*, Anaheim, CA:IEEE. doi:10.1109/ACSAC.2008.53

Schmitt, M. N. (2012). International law in cyberspace: The Koh speech and Tallinn Manual juxtaposed. *Harvard International Law Journal, 54*, 13–37.

Schmitt, M. N. (Ed.). (2013). *The Tallinn Manual on the international law applicable to cyber warfare*. Cambridge: Cambridge University Press. doi:10.1017/CBO9781139169288

Sterner, E. (2011, Spring). Retaliatory deterrence in cyberspace. *Strategic Studies Quarterly,* 62–80.

Taddeo, M. (2012). An analysis for a just cyber warfare. In *Proceedings of the 4h International Conference on Cyber Conflict (CYCON)*, Tallinn: IEEE.

Thomas, T. L. (2011). Nation-state Cyber Strategies: Examples from China and Russia. In F.D. Kramer, S.H. Starr, L.K. Wentz (Eds.), Cyberpower and National Security (465-488). National Defense University Press: Washington, D.C.

Tibbs, H. (2013). *The Global Cyber Game*. London: Defence Academy of the United Kingdom.

UK Ministry of Defence. (2014). Automating cyber defence responses. Retrieved from https://www.gov.uk/government/publications/cde-themed-competition-automation-of-cyber-defence-responses

United States Department of Defense. (2011). *Department of Defense strategy for operating in cyberspace*. Retrieved from http://www.defense.gov/news/d20110714cyber.pdf

United States Department of Defense. (2013). *Air-sea battle*. Retrieved http://www.defense.gov/pubs/ASB-ConceptImplementation-Summary-May-2013.pdf

Wheeler, D. A., & Larsen, G. N. (2003). Techniques for cyber attack attribution. Retrieved from http://www.dtic.mil/cgi-bin/GetTRDoc?AD=ADA468859

KEY TERMS AND DEFINITIONS

Cyber Attack: An act conducted in cyberspace which could reasonably be expected to cause harm.

Cyber Defence: Measures taken to reduce exposure to and mitigate impact from cyber attacks.

Cyber Deterrence: Measures taken to prevent an adversary from launching cyber attacks.

Cyber Early Warning System: A system to give warning of incoming cyber attacks before their harmful effect occurs.

Cyber War: A war in which only cyber warfare is used.

Cyber Warfare: The use of cyber attacks with a warfare-like intent.

Cyber Weapon: Code which has the capability to cause harm, used with harmful intent.

Chapter 3
Attribution

Clement Guitton
King's College London, UK

ABSTRACT

Attribution, finding the identity of actors behind an attack, is of primary importance to be able to classify an attack as a criminal act, an act of war, or an act of terrorism. But attribution is difficult. Many experts and analysts have explained this difficulty with technical arguments. This chapter seeks to bring nuances to such arguments closely analysing how attribution functions. It brings a focus on political factors constraining attribution, and on specifically three ones: standards of evidence, time, and private companies. It makes three main arguments. Firstly, standards of evidence are only secondary to the political will to attribute an attack. Secondly, time cannot only be reduced; the context surrounding attribution is as much important. Thirdly, companies' important role in attribution also gives ground for accused party to easily undermine their claims. The chapter concludes with opening up the debate on the usefulness of meta-data for attribution.

INTRODUCTION

Attribution, the process of finding out the chain of actors involved in a cyber attacks is important for three distinct reasons. The first one is rather technical, and concerns the model of thinking about security in terms of a 'parameter' to defend (Gady, 2010). To defend information systems against cyber attacks, the model advises to integrate technical solutions such as firewalls or intrusion detection systems. Such techniques were particularly well suited against the mass outbreak of viruses that propagated in the years 2000s, but today's attacks look a lot different. They are targeted and the perpetrators are well resourced to develop attacks evading such measures. Hence, the rationale behind attribution is that instead of focusing on technical solutions to thwart the attack, finding the perpetrator of attacks allows the victim to then take a series of measure against the instigators. These series of measures can range from merely shaming the actors, to diplomatic actions, to incapacitating the instigators by jailing them for instance, if they are criminals.

A second argument for focusing on attribution follows directly from the first one. By ensuring that one has the capacity to attribute attacks, it is possible that the capacity will deter other actors from launching similar attacks. Fearful of the consequences attackers could face, and assuming that the attackers fol-

DOI: 10.4018/978-1-4666-8456-0.ch003

low a strictly rational decision-making thought process, the likeliness that the victim will find them can outweigh the benefits of launching an attack in the first place and deter them from proceeding further. Unfortunately, deterrence is not so straightforward, and the empirical record proving that attribution can be effective in deterring attacks is rather mixed, in a criminal and international relation context (Guitton, 2012). The case of the Mandiant report offers a sharp reminder of this difficulty. Mandiant, a cyber security company, published a report denunciating the Chinese military as instigators of attacks on 141 US companies in February 2013. High officials used the report to confront China on this issue. Following publication, the attacks stopped but only for two months before resuming with the exact same modus operandi (Sanger & Perlroth, 2013).

Lastly, a third argument for focusing on attribution is that it allows the distinction between what types of response is the most appropriate to a cyber attack. If a state is behind a cyber attack, the measures taken are entirely different than if a criminal individual is. Attribution involves making the distinction between different types of actors, and to know which further processes will be engaged as a result of the cyber attack.

Attribution is therefore an important aspect for tackling cyber threats, and needs careful attention from students of cyber security. Unfortunately, attribution is also difficult and raises many different questions. What makes attribution difficult? How do different actors go about achieving attribution? What are the policy and strategic implications of striking an 'appropriate' balance for attribution between being anonymous online and being secure?

A common quick answer to these questions is that attribution is difficult because of the way the Internet is engineered. But this answer is misleading and highly insufficient for anyone looking closely at attribution. This chapter starts, firstly, by delving into the current debate on attribution and shows that much of the current debate approaches the difficulty of carrying out attribution as lying in technical elements. Secondly, the chapter continues with refuting those claims and breaks down the constraints for attribution into three main ones: the standards of evidence, the time required for carrying out the process, and the role of private companies. Thirdly and lastly, the chapter analyses the relevance of meta-data collection by intelligence services and law enforcement agencies for attribution and the far ranging ripple effects that the debate on attribution has on privacy, anonymity and Internet governance.

Background: Current Approach to Attribution

The current debate in academic and policy circles on attribution is heavily technically oriented. It assumes that attribution is technical, and that it requires as such technical solutions. This is only partly correct.

To traceback the origin of an attack, be it from a denial of service attack or from a malware, it seems *a priori* useful to know the genuine IP address from which the attack originates. Attackers can easily forge the IP addresses of the traffic they send, and can also route it via several computers they already control to make the victims believe it originated from a specific location. Both of these aspects make it difficult to trace back traffic to its real origin, and has led prominent figure, such as Mike McConnell, former director of the NSA, to state that 'we need to reengineer the Internet to make attribution more manageable' (McConnell, 2010). Many other policy makers have embraced this view, including the former directors at the FBI Shawn Henry and Steven Chabinsky (Chabinsky, 2013; Kaplan, 2012). Christopher Painter, the State Department Coordinator for Cyber Issues, similarly stated in a briefing: 'One of the problems in cyberspace is attribution. It's difficult because of the way the internet is constructed' (US Department of State, 2011).

Following this assessment, the different official and non-official strategies the United States put into place sought to foster the development of techniques in order to achieve attribution. Starting with the official ones, attribution is mentioned only once in the US 'Blueprint for a secure cyber future' published in 2011, and it refers to the innovation of technology for attribution (US Department of Homeland Security, 2011, p. 21). Other policy documents, such as the 2009 Cyberspace Policy Review (The White House, 2009) and the 2011 Department of Defense Cyberspace Policy Report (US Department of Defense, 2011) have similarly supported technical solutions for attribution. The Cybersecurity Act, a yet-to-pass Bill supposed to enhance the protection of critical infrastructure in the US, also mentioned attribution only to support the research of technology to solve the problem ("Cybersecurity Act of 2012," 2012).

What do these technical solutions look like? The academic literature can offer a first brief overview. Before delving into it, it is also relevant to note that the same assumptions permeate the academic literature. The professor of philosophy Christopher Eberle even bluntly put it: 'attribution is a "technical" problem, to be resolved by those with the relevant computer and forensic skills' (Eberle, 2013, p. 57). The developments have been of two types. On the one hand, they have sought to increase the quantity and quality of forensic data one can retrieve to identify instigators. This involved suggestions very close to McConnell's statement about servers logging all packets (Wheeler & Larsen, 2003), or that servers would only accept authenticated packets (Hunker, Gates, & Bishop, 2011). Both techniques would involve important changes to the structure of the Internet, without guaranteeing that attribution would be easier. On the other hand, recent research has focused on trying to maximise the collectable information in the after-math of an attack, organise it and process it in order to extract as much useful data as possible (Caltagirone, Pendergast, & Betz, 2013; Nguyen, 2013; Parker, Devost, Sach, Shaw, & Stroz, 2004). This is particularly useful to detect when instigators attack a second time, which is increasingly the case. Although the techniques may not yield a name, they can better inform on how to protect the information system (Thonnard, 2010; Thonnard, Mees, & Dacier, 2010). Noticeably, it is also possible to apply these frameworks more specifically to certain attacks, such as attacks against industrial control servers (Nicholson, Janicke, & Watson, 2013) or even spamming (Nguyen, 2013).

Other technical solutions implemented by the United States have come out from the recent leaks by the former NSA contractor Edward Snowden and which concerns the capture and analysis of huge batch of data. The extent of the NSA programmes is such that it allegedly covers 75% of all communication traffic passing through US infrastructures, which constitutes an important backbone for worldwide traffic (Valentino-Devries & Gorman, 2013). The capture of data comes from domestic telecommunications companies such as Verizon, but it also emerged that the NSA targeted foreign telecommunications providers such as in Brazil (BBC News, 2013) and Belgium (Reuters, 2013). The British signal intelligence agency, with whom the NSA shares extensive intelligence, also uses similar techniques, for instance with the tapping of undersea fibre-optic cables to gather all traffic possible (MacAskill, Borger, Hopkins, Davies, & Ball, 2013). Once they have collected the data, the NSA uses data processing tools such as XKeyscore, which the NSA describes as being to gather 'nearly everything a typical user does on the internet'(Greenwald, 2013).

The mere existence of these programmes does not guarantee that the United States used them for attribution. Different officials and senators vehemently defended the surveillance programmes on the ground that they actually served to foil terrorist plots – not cyber attacks. But do their uses not extend beyond? Once law enforcement agencies are in possession of potentially useful data, it can be difficult to refuse them access to it. Despite the claims that it was solely used for terrorism related cases, on July 8, 2013, the *New York Times* reported that the surveillance programmes also played a role to pursue suspects of cyber attacks (Lichtblau, 2013). A NSA spokeswoman confirmed that the NSA's 'activities are centred on counterterrorism, counter-proliferation and cybersecurity', with a purpose on foreign intelligence (Risen & Poitras, 2013a). In addition, a NSA programme called 'Follow the money trail' included the fight against cyber crime (Poitras, Rosenbach, & Stark, 2013). Such a use of resources to find instigators of attacks match a 2012 classified strategic document about the NSA's goals for the next year. The document read: 'defeating the cybersecurity practices of adversaries in order to acquire the data the agency needs from "anyone, anytime, anywhere"' (Risen & Poitras, 2013b). Also, in a 2014 speech about changes to signal intelligence practices, President Obama reiterated this goal and the role of intelligence to achieve them. 'We cannot prevent terrorist attacks or cyber threats without some capability to penetrate digital communications', he said (Obama, 2014).

Yet the picture is still not so clear and needs to be nuanced. Despite these claims, it is in fact difficult to know if the NSA actually passes on the information to law enforcement agencies for the identification and arrest of criminals. Since 9/11, there has been an increased amount of data being shared between law enforcement agencies and intelligence services. However, the *New York Times* acknowledged in 2013 that many requests to the NSA by other law enforcement agencies to have access to the collected data had in fact been rejected. The requests did not meet the criteria, set in the law or in the form of policy directives, for exchanging information: to be able to show 'links to terrorism or foreign intelligence' (Lichtblau & Schmidt, 2013). Many cyber attacks the FBI deals with may classify only difficultly under the label of 'terrorism' as they are mostly non-violent, and do not even fall under foreign intelligence (e.g., sabotage operations routed through proxies in the United States would not *a priori* meet the requirements) (Lichtblau & Schmidt, 2013). The extent of the use of the data collected by the NSA by other law enforcement agency is hence very difficult to assess. But noteworthy, the US Drug Enforcement Administration was able for six years to access the NSA's database of phone logs – an apparently common practice in the course of investigating drug dealers (Shane & Moynihan, 2013). It does not take a great stretch of mind to imagine that the same technique could be used to track instigators of cyber attacks, especially the instigators of criminal cyber attacks. Giving credit to this stretch of mind is the recent case where hackers managed to steal the credit card details of 40 million people – a case not very different to the many credit card frauds that happen every month except in terms of scale (Perlroth, 2013a). But this time the *New York Times* reported that the '*Secret Service* and Justice Department continue to investigate' [emphasis added] (Perlroth, 2013b). It is unclear which secret service specifically is investigating the breach, but the theft of credit card records quite clearly does not reach the level of the terrorism threat. And yet, they are very likely to use very similar techniques, as the one exposed above.

They are several issues with the current heavily technically centred approach to attribution. Firstly, technical data can only badly inform on sponsors of attacks, and especially on state sponsorship. They can be well suited for finding out the names of people involved, but can only tell one side of the story. If an attack originates from one particular country, as an IP address would show, if the attackers invested considerable resources in the attack to make it 'sophisticated' (Guitton & Korzak, 2013), and even if the entities targeted are only political, then it is not possibly to infer that a state sponsored the attack. These constitute only circumstantial elements that need not only to be substituted by solid evidence, but also by a solid framework of analysis. The use of such criteria is probably a reflection of the frustration of not being able to achieve attribution immediately and with a high level of confidence. But keeping high standard of proof does not make it impossible to attribute attacks either. Solid evidence can come from whistle-blowers, or from documents showing that a government ordered an attack for instance. The attribution of the only known state-sponsored malware that successfully caused physical damage,

Stuxnet, occurred notably this way. Confirmation that the United States and Israel were behind Stuxnet emerged as anonymous whistle-blowers talked to the *New York Times* journalist David Sanger (Sanger, 2012). Edward Snowden also later confirmed the sources (Der Spiegel, 2013). These elements are non-technical, but still played a preponderant role, which cannot be easily dismissed.

Secondly, and following this line of thinking, attribution is in a few cases the reflection of a particular decision by the political class to render the claims public. Attribution is then a careful consideration of the benefits and costs which are associated with pointing the fingers publicly at an attacker, and potentially even framing the attacker as an 'enemy' or as a threat to national security. In many cases, governments may refuse to engage another state on the topic because it would not benefit the interest of the state to do so at this particular time (e.g., if both states are about to sign an important trade deal). The decision can be deferred to the highest level of the political hierarchy. As Francis Maude, British Minister for the Cabinet Office, pointed out in a hearing in the House of Commons in June 2012, 'if something looked like it could be a sovereign attack', the judgement of deciding sponsorship 'would clearly be for the Prime Minister' to make (*Defence and Cyber Security*, 2012). Attribution is therefore political (Guitton, 2014), and is a political decision. This is also the case for criminal cases. An activity is criminal because it breaches the law; laws are the outcome of a political process that reflects prevailing norms and powers in a society (Heywood, 2004, p. 122). An emphasis on attribution as being technical dismisses these important political aspects.

Thirdly, in the context of crime and not sponsors specifically, a focus on technical data tends to dismiss other traditional method of investigation. The investigation of cyber attacks may have a few specific elements to it, but it is not completely unique either. For example, following a bomb explosion in a major city, it is also not apparent from the very start whether a state or any other group sponsored the attack. The police and other services need to start investigating using only what they have at hands, which can be very little information. In the case of cyber attacks, instead of focusing only on technical elements, the police can also use many other more traditional investigation techniques, such as using informants, infiltrating deviant groups, and above all, fostering partnership with other countries to facilitate the exchange of information. This last point is an important constraint for attribution repeatedly mentioned by various members of law enforcement agencies. In the past, attribution also largely improved due to better cooperation between various judicial entities than due to better technology. Yet, instead of focusing on improving bureaucratic process, policy makers have at repeated times preferred to emphasise the development of techniques for attribution. Focusing the debate on techniques seems to make it logical that improving attribution cannot come without investing in technical solutions (e.g., increasing the storage and access to meta-data in order to better follow the trace of packets, or a re-engineering of the Internet). These solutions are more privacy intrusive than the aforementioned and more traditional investigation techniques. In addition, as the last part of this chapter will cover, they are not necessarily associated with better rates for identifying actors.

CONSTRAINTS OF THE ATTRIBUTION PROCESSES

The Attribution Processes

If considering only technical constraint to attribution is misleading, what are then the other important constraints for attribution? The rest of the chapter will delve specifically into three of them: standards of proof, time, and the role of companies. Each of these constraints subtly differs in function on the context in which they are present. Mainly, attribution of cyber attacks can be separated into two non-mutually exclusive different processes: one process closer to the judicial process for purely criminal cases, and one process closer to the executive branch of power for cases that raise to the level of national threat (Guitton, 2013).

The actors involved in these two processes differ, from law enforcement agencies to intelligence services, and their goals as well. There is a sharp distinction between the very well established chain of judicial steps required to go through to convict an individual in a domestic court, and the process behind the identification and the retaliation against enemies of the state, which happens outside the setting of a court mainly within governmental institutions. One is focused on individuals; the other is broader and can concentrate on state and non-state actors alike.

One of the direct consequences of a case being regarded as a threat to national security is that the means to investigate becomes completely different. Most law enforcement agencies, such as the FBI, are accountable entities, which operate under public light. They need to constantly ensure that they collect evidence in a legal fashion in order to be able to present them in front of a court. But within the national security context, the higher stakes involve a readiness to trade accountability for using more invasive means to collect intelligence. The main goal is to discover who the enemies and their sponsors are, not to hold a public and fair trial against them. Against this backdrop of potential high political stakes involved, investigators and government officials show a readiness to resort to extraordinary and less accountable investigative means mainly provided by intelligence services, especially when it comes to using technical forensics.

However, this leads to considering a certain paradox. More resources are deployed to investigate cyber attacks regarded as national security threats, as they are framed in terms of finding an 'enemy of the state' than for criminal attacks. Consequently, it is easier to make a first guess about who this enemy is, but it is also harder to conclusively prove it. Conclusively proving the identity of a criminal attacker on the other hand once investigators have a first genuine track to follow is much easier.

There is therefore an evident conflict between the different standards of proof that are applied for attribution in these two contexts. In fact, there are conflicts of standards even within the set of criminal cases.

Standards of Proof

From March 1994, a hacker going by the handle Kuji was using his dial-up connection to browse text documents on different servers in the United States. At one point, he found a file containing several passwords and usernames to connect into military networks, including at the NASA (the Goddard Space Flight Centre) and a US Air Force Base at Wright Patterson. In parallel, another hacker, DataStream Cowboy, was doing similar activities on similar networks. By guessing a password, he managed to gain a low level entry access into a US Air Force base near New York, the Griffiss Air Force. Investigators at the base started looking closely into the attack. They were able to note the handle used by the hackers, and in April 1994, an informant came forward giving the police a tip on what DataStream Cowboy's telephone number for his own bulletin board was, effectively giving them the identity of the individual. DataStream Cowboy was a British teenager, 16 at the time, named Richard Pryce. On 21 March 1997, the Court condemned Richard Pryce on twelve charges and fined him the small amount of $1,200 for the twelve charges brought against him (Fresco, 1997).

Meanwhile the police also found who Kuji was: Mathew Bevan, aged 21 when arrested in 1996 (Bevan, 1997). When arrested, Bevan asked the officer how they found him, who answered: 'it's someone we both know'. Jokingly, Bevan asked further: 'My dad?', to which the officer responded: 'No, someone else' (Bevan, 2012). The identity of this person remains unknown. Bevan admitted hacking into NASA computers, and computers of the US Air Force at Wright Patterson (Williams, 1999). Pryce's sentencing influenced greatly Bevan's one by setting a precedent. The number of charges against Bevan was not as high. There were only five of them, putting the maximal sentence to around $500. On top of that, as the trail of evidence was scant, the Court would hence have had to pay for US officials to fly over to the UK to present evidence. From the United States' standpoint, the trial was worth it. US officials estimated the damage to be at around $500,000. Furthermore, Special agent Jim Christy working for Air Force Office of Special Investigations allegedly referred to Bevan as 'nearly start[ing] a third world war', while another American Air force commander allegedly called Bevan 'the single biggest threat to world security since Adolf Hitler'. But despite these comments, the UK Court dropped the case on 22 November 1997 for financial reasons (Ryan, 2005): the cost of the trial exceeding by far the maximal sentence. The court said that that 'it was not in the public interest to pursue the case, which was expected to last three months and involve witnessing being flown from the United States to give evidence' (Agence France Presse, 1997).

Although no court condemned Bevan for his misdeed, it seems reasonable to attribute the attacks to him, especially as he confessed to several of the breaches. This discrepancy between outcomes raises the question of the role of the court, especially as Bevan's case is not isolated. Other famous cases where attribution occurs without a court confirming it include the incident behind the 'Love Bug' malware in 2000 (Mydans, 2000) or with the British national Gary McKinnon ("Gary McKinnon v. Government of the USA," 2007). Therefore, the relevance of courts' judgements is disputable for attribution when heeding how attribution and court proceedings differ.

Decision by a court comes down to distinguishing between two options: guilty, or non-guilty of the charge. Attribution, however, is a lot more nuanced, and comes with various degrees. Attribution is not binary, and cases have more outcomes than only being attributed or not attributed. As already mentioned, attribution is a process. It is not a one time off problem that necessitates only one solution. Depending on the time and context, the certainty required to consider the process as completed may necessitate a high level of proof; at other times, it may not. Further, the process evolves as more and more information is gathered, linked together by various entities, weighed, judged, and publicly claimed until being, sometimes, consensually accepted as genuinely true beyond the point of any contention.

The attribution of the now infamous Stuxnet, which targeted the Iranian nuclear power plant at Natanz is a perfect example of this constantly evolving process where many different actors and opinions come together. As soon as Stuxnet's existence came out in June 2010, experts had suspicions of US and Israeli involvement in the operation (Broad, Markoff, & Sanger., 2011; Halliday, 2010). Two years later, these suspicions were first confirmed as a journalist at the New York Times, David Sanger, had access to confidential sources confirming in details the operation (Sanger, 2012). The Obama's administration, in what could be seen as a confirmation of the veracity of the claim, started legal proceedings to find the leakers who talked to Sanger and there were suspicions that former General James Cartwright was actually the main leaker (The Guardian, 2013). A year later, Edward Snowden confirmed the revelations to the German magazine Der Spiegel (Appelbaum, 2013). Neither the United States nor Israel has acknowledged being the author of Stuxnet. But attribution has come clearer and clearer has the process has moved along. Far from knowing with great certainty from the beginning who the authors were, achieving attribution has therefore necessitated going through some steps. With time, attribution has evolved, and in this case, the evidence came to strengthen the hypothesis.

As Stuxnet illustrates, attribution occurred without the involvement of any court. Courts' role in attribution is hence not only disputable for criminal cases, but as well for cases rising to the level of national security. In this latter context, several legal experts have already recognised the applicability of international law to cyber attacks (International Group of Experts, 2013), although a very active on-going debate is still taking place discussing whether cyber attacks can amount to the use of force or to armed attacks (Goldsmith, 2013a; Koh, 2012; Rubin, Fraser, & Smith, 1995; Schmitt, 1998; Waxman, 2011). A further point of contention about the role of courts in the attribution of state sponsored cyber attacks concerns more specifically the setting of standards that they have to use to consider an actor guilty. Courts and states do not have to follow just one standard to attribute an attack. Instead, the standard chosen will be entirely dependent on political will, and adapted to fit the political will. In other words, if a government choses to frame a certain country as the guilty party, it may hype up the importance of certain pieces of 'evidence' – mostly circumstantial in all likeliness – while downplaying the uncertainty surrounding the attribution process. Similarly, international courts are also subject to 'some measure of politics' and are not the objective hand of justice that they can sometimes be portrayed to be (Koskenniemi, 1990, p. 5).

Two points illustrate this malleability. Firstly, the lack of scrutiny in the media for the evidence really behind attribution means that it is possible for officials or representatives to be misleading. In most cases, no definitive proof, or even scant proof, has emerged about any state's involvement in cyber attacks. Yet statements by US Representative Michael Rogers (Rogers, 2014) or Senator Lieberman ("Newsmakers with Senator Joe Lieberman," 2012) about the involvement of Iran and China were for instance clearly echoed and without nuance in various newspapers, including the prestigious and thorough-fact-checking New York Times (Hider, 2012; Perlroth, Sanger, & Schmidt, 2013; Shanker & Sanger, 2013). This comes in sharp contrast with the identification of authors of other high stake incidents, such as the August 2013 chemical attack in Syria, where scrutiny was the rule (Black & Sample, 2013).

Secondly, many analysts use several criteria to make the case that an attack is state sponsored. The use of criteria facilitates the manipulation of the case to fit a pre-conception of the enemy in order to further realise a political agenda. The use of a framework based on criteria – such as 'sophistication' (Guitton & Korzak, 2013) – by intelligence analysts can help this manipulation. The framework represents the use of a low standard of evidence in sharp contrast with showing involvement 'beyond reasonable doubt'. It easily leads to the misinterpretation of information heavily influenced by expectations, an effect famously known in intelligence circle and called 'perseveration' (Aldrich, 2010, p. 388). Sophistication is only one criterion amongst a few used by cyber security analysts to circumvent evidence and focus instead on circumstantial non-conclusive evidence. In fact, many experts commonly use six criteria to attribute attacks to states: the geo-political context, the political character of the victim, the apparent origin of the attacker, the sophistication of an attack, the scale of the attack, and the beneficiaries of the attack. These criteria should not constitute anything more than forming a first hint for starting to compare different hypotheses (Heuer, 1999), although they are more often than not taken as conclusive.

It is tempting to think that the low standards of evidence used in certain cases stem from the lack of time policy makers can have before reacting to an incident. The two, time and evidence, seem *a priori* to exist as a trade-off: the more time investigators have, the more evidence they can find. For instance, in the case of Mathew Bevan, his arrest came three years after his attacks, a very long and rather uncommon time. For criminal cases, investigators can theoretically take this time (in practice, they also need to move onto the next case quickly enough if they cannot actually find any evidence). But in the national security context, it seems, quick reaction is often warranted in order for retaliatory measures to be meaningful if it were to take place.

Time

The high speed at which cyber attacks are conducted have led many analysts to think that it warrants a similarly rapid reaction. Richard Clarke, the former White House official author of the seminal book 'Cyber War' noted:

As the board [Pentagon's Defense Science Board] noted, cyberattacks can occur very quickly and without warning, requiring rapid decision-making by those responsible for protecting our country (Clarke & Andreasen, 2013).

Similarly, Jody Prescott, a senior fellow at the US prestigious military academy West Point noted that '[w]ith cyber operations conceivably moving at near light speed, commanders in cyber warfare will likely need to rely extensively upon autonomous decision-making processes (ADPs) to be effective' (Prescott, 2013). Prescott went on to even suggest several methods that would in the end short-circuit the political decision-making process and act autonomously to decide whether to retaliate. Admittedly, a decision about the response, and hence about attributing the cyber attacks needs to be taken by the government in place rapidly. But how rapidly?

Time is indisputably one of the big constraints for attribution. Shawn Henry, former Executive Assistant Director at the FBI, bluntly stated it: 'It [attribution] takes time. There is no simple fix' (Jackson, 2012). *The Business Insider*, likewise, noted that 'the high degree of anonymity of digital interactions makes identifying an attacker a time-consuming, if not impossible, task' (Masters, 2011). Phil Meek, Associate General Counsel of the US Air Force, remarked that many factors make attribution 'much more time consuming that you may normally have in an armed conflict scenario' (*China's Views of Sovereignty and Methods of Access Conrol*, 2008). Susan Brenner, a lawyer expert in questions of cyber security, also stated that attribution 'can be difficult and time-consuming' (Brenner, 2007, p. 420).

What makes attribution time consuming is mainly due to the necessity to deal with the issuing of warrants domestically, or with law enforcement agencies in another country in order to obtain information (Brenner, 2007, p. 420). 'The formal methods used to obtain assistance can take months or even years when digital evidence is fragile and can disappear by the time the investigators obtain the assistance they need', explains Brenner (2007, p. 420). The issue of having to deal with foreign bureaucracies to be able to produce a chain of evidence is especially relevant for the indictment of criminals and when law enforcement agencies use 'formal' channels. For instance, on 10 May 2007, Estonia issued a formal request to Russia by using the 'mutual legal assistance treaty' they had with the country in order to exchange information concerning the distributed denial of service attacks the country underwent. The response by Russia, a refusal, came a year later (Tikk & Kaska, 2010). Even for a refusal to come in, the process took quite a long time.

The time investigations required is hence long especially in comparison with the high speed usually associated with cyber attacks (cyber attacks are, however, not always as fast – Stuxnet took probably from a few days to a few months to effectively and stealthily destroy the Iranians nuclear centrifuges).

But the fact that attribution is time-consuming in a criminal context is nothing unusual: it is very easily comparable to the investigations of other types of crime or attacks, which easily fit within this timeframe. Murders are never instantly identified, although their crime can last only a very short amount of time. It can take less than a second for a bullet to reach another human being, and months to find who fired the weapon. Likewise, for incidents of national security, the length of investigation to identify sponsors could be described as 'time-consuming'. It took a couple of months to find the sponsors of 9/11, and even after a few months, there still remains large doubts on the sponsors of chemical attacks that took place in August 2013 in Syria for instance (Joint Intelligence Organisation, 2013; Lewis & Williams, 2013; The White House, 2013b).

The problem of time is hence not unique to cyber attacks only. But under the assumption that it is, many overly technical solutions have been suggested to improve attribution, with even US officials exhorting companies to play a role in fulfilling the demand to shorten attribution times. Steve Chabinsky, Deputy Assistant Director of the Cyber Division at the FBI, told an audience at a 2012 conference on cyber conflict that 'the owners and operators of an electric power grid in which all of the workers are cleared wants to have perfect attribution of who's on the system at any given time' (Chabinsky, 2012). He then continued his presentation saying:

Right now, no systems, or very few systems, are designed to provide assurance and attribution. There are markets that are begging to be filled right now for these types of capabilities – that we really could sell globally if we're the ones here in this country that produce that – that are not being fulfilled (Chabinsky, 2012).

On the same panel than Chabinsky was CrowdStrike's president, Shawn Henry, also former director at the FBI. As the president of CrowdStrike, one of the few companies marketing itself as a pioneer and leader in the field of attribution, Henry immediately recognised the market opportunity it represented. Just a year following Chabinsky's remark, CrowdStrike released a new product directly aimed at filling that gap: the CrowdStrike Falcon Platform. When presenting the new product, CrowdStrike's chief executive officer, George Kurtz, reiterated that the company is 'shifting the discussion from defending against malware to defending against the adversary' (Wireless News, 2013). According to the company's presentation of the product, the Platform could 'provides damage assessment and attacker attribution', while 'detect[ing] zero-day threats and prevent[ing] damage from targeted attacks in real time' (Wireless News, 2013).

For any proponent of extremely short attribution time, 'real time attribution' technology seems to be the most appropriate solutions. Real time attribution will, however, never be able to show indications as to who the sponsors of an attack are. It is difficult to see how a technology alone could solve this issue. On top of that, there are two other major problems with discussing technology to greatly reduce attribution time: it does not match the historical record, and it dismisses the context. Technology for 'real time attribution' is not in accordance with the assessment that the reason for high attribution times is due to slow bureaucratic processes (e.g., issuing of warrants, or request of information). Historically, attribution times have been primarily reduced thanks to smoother judicial procedures – not to new technology. In 1986, it took a year to follow the trace of hackers in US military networks through several routers in the United States all the way to Germany (Stoll, 1989). Three factors impeded the identification of the hackers at the time: the difficulty to obtain warrants to track down the telephone line, the lack of criminal law in Germany, and the lack of retention of traffic data. Already solving some them, ten years later, it took only half the time to identify a similar hacker operating from Argentina (Power, 2000). And in 2000s, the police even identified the authors of malware within the matters of days (Brandt, 2005; Farqhar, 2003; Mydans, 2000; Verton & Brandt, 2012). In all these cases, the short time frame for attribution was mainly due to functioning legal systems, an analysis shared by Christopher M. Painter, Coordinator for Cyber Issues, at the U.S. State Department:

There was a ministerial meeting back in 1999 where this was pushed as a major agenda item that countries need to have better laws, better capabilities. Of the three legs of the stool you have to have good capacity to fight these crimes – law enforcement and others. You had to have good laws in place. And you have to have the ability to cooperate internationally (Chabinsky, 2012).

The second issue with technologically centred discussions to reduce time concerns context. Attribution is a political statement made public, especially when it involves an attacker who the authorities frame as an enemy of the state. This means that a political decision must be taken whether to attribute an attack, and that this decision can by no means be rendered automatic. However, discussions of 'real time attribution', or more in general of reducing attribution time, inherently hold the assumptions that attribution is automatic and that it is somehow possible to short circuit this political decision process. Yet state actions have inherently high stakes. Attribution claims may sometimes not be beneficial for the state to make, and furthermore, no state would want to retaliate against the wrong enemy. This implies that they would certainly prefer carrying out a diligent assessment of the situation before taking any actions, including attributing the attack. As the element of who an attack benefits can be misleading, and as the attacker can hide under a false-flag to trigger a specific response, carefully considering the identity of the attacker is far more sensible than simply seeking to attribute and retaliate as fast as possible, 'in real time' (Libicki, 2009, p. 44). With higher stakes comes a sense of responsibility that attribution needs to be correct and which cannot be traded for a shorter time-response.

Reducing time for attribution is important, but should not be over-emphasised either. Noticeably, the relevance of attribution does not decrease because it only comes years later. Mandiant's report on China mentioned in the introduction came following attacks that the Chinese military had perpetrated four years ago. But that did not take any value off the report, which still sparked high-level discussions between the United States and China. The same is true with Stuxnet. Stuxnet probably started spreading around 2005, was discovered in June 2010, and Sanger's story unravelling the involvement of the United States and Israel only came in June 2012. The time between the discovery of the breach and its attribution is hence nothing close to 'real time', but nonetheless still highly relevant.

Reliance on technology for reduction in attribution time is misguided. There is still, however, room for improvement, regarding judicial procedures. It is still very difficult for investigators to juggle with the different requirements in terms of standard of proof that exist in different jurisdictions, especially as the investigation of almost any criminal case of cyber attacks always spans a certain number of countries. Even within the European Union, where a law from 2000 but operational since 2005 is supposed to make the exchange of criminal information easier between police forces, the procedure remain tedious, formal, and take time as it 'often require judicial authorization' (Brown & Korff, 2009, p. 125). The time spent by investigators obtaining warrants points towards the need for a more unified framework to deal with many of these issues distributed throughout the judicial process. By simplifying legal processes, and potentially by lowering the standards of evidence required to shut down infrastructures used in illicit activities to support cyber attacks, attribution time can still amply be reduced. A few countries of the

'Anglo sphere' representing the Five Eyes (the US, UK, Canada, New Zealand and Australia) have subsequently started discussions in 2011 to harmonize their laws on top of the 2001 Budapest Convention by including a response to state sponsored attacks, and to foster their exchange of information on cyber attacks (Levin & Goodrick, 2013, p. 133). The outcome of such discussions should lead to increased capacity for identifying authors of cyber attacks.

Private Companies

The last constraint this chapter delves into may not appear as such from the start. Private companies have always worked closely with law enforcement agencies to reduce criminal activities threatening their clients. Their work in a criminal context is a welcome help to law enforcement, and constitutes the bulk of the cyber security company's work. It is not very 'spectacular' and concerns mostly disruptions of botnets, or forensic analysis of cyber criminals making much money off fraud. But over the past few years, a dimension of the work of cyber security companies has received increasing media attention: the detection of large state sponsored operations, and at times, the naming of these attacking states in reports. This work in a national security context, still rather the exception than the norm, is more problematic, as it can easily attract criticisms undermining their claims.

Pointing out the fingers to state actors is never easy: it requires having strong evidence of sponsorship, and also requires making judgement calls about how to interpret the evidence (Guitton, 2014). Judgement calls are by definition fallible and open to criticism. In addition to these already important barriers to attribution come three further issues specific to the work of private companies: companies' informal ties with government agencies as many former officials work for them; the timing at which reports are published in support of a government's policies; and their seeming reluctance to name states as instigators, even though their reports can sometimes strongly hint at who they think stands behind it. These three points often constitute naysayers' core arguments as they seek to refute the companies' attribution claims.

Firstly, many companies recruit former state officials, and more in particularly former members of the intelligence community. This is part of a common trend started in the 1990s with the outsourcing of the work of intelligence services (Shorrock, 2008). In itself, it is rather a positive development, as it allows a certain synergy between the companies and the community: the companies can informally run their conclusions to former colleagues who can confirm whether they reach similar ones. But it also unfortunately gives sticks to the accused to beat the accuser. The company Mandiant is a case in point. At the time Mandiant published the report, Kevin Mandia, its chief executive officer, still carried a top-secret clearance (Easton, 2013, p. 83), as he had worked as a cyber crime investigator for the US military. Mandia hired several people with such a similar background at various hierarchical positions within the company ("Mandiant Hires Travis Reese," 2006; Easton, 2013, p. 85). When the report came out, the Chinese media did not fail to notice that and doubt the sincerity of the claims on the mere basis that the interests of the company were vetted, or at least, non-transparent. The *Global Times* wrote that Mandia's background 'raise[s] doubts over the motives of the revelation' (Jinghao & Wuning, 2013). It further pointed out that even the *Associated Press*, a Western press agency, had also noted Mandiant's 'obvious commercial interest in releasing the information' (Flaherty, 2013).

Secondly, the timing can give raise to much suspicion. Continuing with the example for the Mandiant report, the report could have gone unnoticed considering the number of reports that various organisations publish daily. But it came at a very specific moment, which probably gave it momentum. From October

2012, a series of attacks targeted journalists working for the *New York Times*. Investigators already believed early in their investigations that the attackers had ties with the Chinese government. A few months later, on 1 February 2013, and importantly, two weeks before the publication of Mandiant's report, the Associated Press reported that the US administration was preparing a report 'to better understand and analyze the persistency of cyberattacks against America which come from China' (Osborne, 2013). The report came out a couple of days later, stayed confidential, but it leaked out that it mentioned China as carrying out vast espionage operations via cyber attacks (Nakashima, 2013b). Then, on 10 February, a report from the different US intelligence agencies was released. Although confidential, its conclusions were leaked to different media outlets. *The Washington Post* wrote:

The National Intelligence Estimate identifies China as the country most aggressively seeking to penetrate the computer systems of American businesses and institutions to gain access to data that could be used for economic gain (Nakashima, 2013a).

Following the intelligence report, on 12 February, the White House issued an executive order on cybersecurity to strengthen the exchange of information between private and public organisations ("Improving Critical Infrastructure Cybersecurity," 2013). The executive order came as the Congress had repeatedly failed to pass any legislation on cyber security, despite recurring calls by the White House to do so. The same day, President Barack Obama gave his annual State of the Union address in which he made a veiled reference to Chinese espionage operations. He insisted that 'now, we know hackers steal people's identities and infiltrate private emails. We know foreign countries and companies swipe our corporate secrets' (Obama, 2013). And two days after the release of the Mandiant's report, on 20 February, the White House released a new strategy to combat the theft of intellectual property, identifying China as a 'persistent collector' (The White House, 2013a). Therefore, from an analysis of the timing, it is very tempting – but wrong – to assimilate sequence of events with causality. There may have been slight coordination with the White House, but the opacity gives in any case enough material for naysayers who wish to undermine the report.

Thirdly, cyber security companies understandably want to be extremely cautious of the claims they make, as they risk their reputation when they do so. But the caution can at times border the ridicule, leaving room for questioning about the companies policies. For instance, Kaspersky Lab, a Russian company with headquarters in the United Kingdom, repeatedly stated it was not interested in who carried out attacks (Rashid, 2012; RT, 2012). Many of its report, however, give enough pointers that consistently build towards considering just one entity as being behind an attack. For instance, when looking at Duqu, a spying malware, Kaspersky Lab stated that its sophistication meant it came from a state (Kamluk, 2011), and that the working hours of people login onto the command-and-control server corresponded to Jerusalem's working time, and to people respecting the Sabbath (Perlroth, 2012). This is a clear wink-wink that Kaspersky is hinting at the state of Israel, although it does not say so. The reluctance to name actors gives ground, even if unfounded, to arouse the public's suspicion on how a company would react if it were to learn about a state sponsored attack: would it really go public? As many companies face fierce competition for lucrative contracts with intelligence services and the military, they could feel pressured to give in to request by security services to help by keeping their findings secret as an extraordinary measure and in order to maintain sound relations with them (Dourado, 2013).

The model of companies attributing attacks has advantages for the companies and more importantly for state actors. Companies come under the spotlight for their reports, and act as authoritative actors on the international scene. This also means that the companies draw criticisms especially from the accused state, which can be detrimental for its business with that particular state. On the other hand, for state actors, the ambiguity of their relation with companies, even if untrue, can be a blessing. For example, it can limit the escalation conflict between states, as states do not accuse each other directly. A state being accused of misbehaviour by a company can simply choose not to respond to it – a dismissal that would be much harder to do if the accusation came directly from a state actor. Also, it allows attribution to take place despite the limited evidence that can exist against a party. Furthermore, the formulation of a judgement, which is publicly published, allows for a public debate to take place. The public can question the evidence and question the conclusion of reports. This contributes in making the attribution process less secret, which would be the case if only intelligence services were dealing with it. It also contributes in making attribution rest on more sound evidence and conclusions.

FUTURE RESEARCH DIRECTIONS AND CONCLUSION

The chapter has highlighted that attribution is not only technical and has delved more specifically into a few of the rather political constraints it faces. The key conclusions were threefold: standards of proof are easily malleable and depend on the political will to frame a specific actor; time is reducible by improving judicial procedures but no improvement can ever guarantee automated attribution, as it greatly disregard political decisions that are unavoidable; private companies can play in reshaping the inter-state political agenda, but one that is also subject to easy criticism. This conclusion leads to considering directions for future research that further seeks to move the debate around attribution beyond its technical compass. More specifically, one key issue needs important focus in the coming years: the role of meta-data, and its usefulness.

A lot of attention on the role of meta-data has come following the revelations by Edward Snowden that the United States was involved in collecting and storing important quantity of such data. The thinking that a lot of data is indeed crucial for attribution runs deep in the US intelligence community. Keith Alexander, the former director of the NSA, reportedly told government officials that he 'can't defend the country' until he is 'into all the networks' (Goldsmith, 2013b). The acquisition of all data by intelligence services may not be so much warranted. Many studies seem *a priori* to indicate the contrary.

Empirical evidence from Czech Republic rather suggests that having 'too much' communication data can hinder investigations. In 2011, the constitutional court of Czech Republic declared unconstitutional the data retention law transposing the European Union directive on data retention. Subsequently, the police could not use communications data as they had been used to. But what could have caused a hindrance to solve cases did not show up in the statistics. The clearance rate increased from 37.55% to 38.54% between 2010 and 2011 (UN Watched, 2012). The argument explaining such an increasing appears to be that the more information the police obtain, the more they have to wade through it and the more difficult and complex the task becomes. More generally, the researcher Ian Brown noted that 'data retention could raise the crime clearance rate by 0.002% at best' (Brown, 2010, p. 107). By augmenting tremendously the amount of data available to them, the increase in complexity also implied that it made it more difficult to find the relevant information, if it was even there.

In more layman terms, Keith's argument is that 'you need the haystack to find the needle' (Gellman & Soltani, 2013). But the answer to that is also that 'if you are looking for a needle in a haystack, it doesn't help to throw more hay on the stack' (Brown & Korff, 2009, p. p.125). Another study also undermines

Keith's statement. The New America Foundation looked at 225 cases of terrorism and found that the bulk collection of metadata had 'had no discernible impact on preventing acts of terrorism' (Bergen, Sterman, Schneider, & Cahall, 2014; Nakashima, 2014). The Foundation found that in most cases, conventional investigative techniques helped initiate the investigation into the cases, a similar conclusion reached by a White House panel appointed the previous month (Clarke, Morell, Stone, Sunstein, & Swire, 2013; Nakashima & Soltani, 2013). These studies put into the question the necessity of collecting metadata not only for the attribution of cyber attacks, but for wider criminal and terrorism related cases too.

Policies associated with attribution have important consequences on civil liberties. It is therefore important to understand attribution and its constraints correctly in order to take policy decisions that are not misinformed. Decisions taken on how to shape the attribution processes will further impact the way issues of privacy, surveillance and Internet governance will evolve, and more generally, the role of communications in everyone's life. Such a core issue to society therefore requires much attention from policy makers and academics, as much as from practitioners.

REFERENCES

Aldrich, R. J. (2010). *GCHQ*. London: HarperPress.

Bergen, P., Sterman, D., Schneider, E., & Cahall, B. (2014). *Do NSA's Bulk Surveillance Programs Stop Terrorists?* Washington, DC: New America Foundation.

Bevan, M. (1997). History. Retrieved from http://www.kujimedia.com/articles/

Bevan, M. (2012, November 9). [Details about information leading to the arrest].

Black, I., & Sample, I. (2013, August 29). UK report on chemical attack in Syria adds nothing to informed speculation. *The Guardian*. Retrieved from http://www.theguardian.com/world/2013/aug/29/uk-report-chemical-attack-syria

Brandt, A. (2005, May 5). Stupid hacker tricks, part two: The folly of youth. *InfoWorld Daily News*.

Brenner, S. W. (2007). At Light Speed: Attribution and Response to Cybercrime/Terrorism/Warfare. *The Journal of Criminal Law & Criminology*, *97*(2), 379–476.

Broad, W. J., Markoff, J., & Sanger, D. E. (2011, January 15). Israeli Test on Worm Called Crucial in Iran Nuclear Dela. *The New York Times*.

Brown, I. (2010). Communications Data Retention in an Evolving Internet. *International Journal of Law and Information Technology*, *19*(2), 95–109. doi:10.1093/ijlit/eaq016

Brown, I., & Korff, D. (2009). Terrorism and the Proportionality of Internet Surveillance. *European Journal of Criminology*, *6*(2), 119–135. doi:10.1177/1477370808100541

Case dropped against hacker accused with breaking into USAF computers. (1997, November 22). *Agence France Presse*.

Chabinsky, S., Henry, S., & Painter, C. (2012, May 16). Lessons from Our Cyber Past: The First Cyber Cops. *Atlantic Council*. Retrieved from http://www.atlanticcouncil.org/index.php?option=com_content& view=article&id=9693:lessons-from-our-cyber-past-the-first-cyber-cops&catid=8:events&Itemid=101

Mandiant Hires Travis Reese as Vice President of Federal Services. (2006, April 25). *Business Wire*.

US allies Mexico, Chile and Brazil seek spying answers. (2013, July 11). *BBC News*.

Newsmakers with Senator Joe Lieberman. (2012, September 21). *C-Span*. Retrieved from http://www.c-spanvideo.org/program/JoeLiebe

Appelbaum, J., & Poitras, L. (2013). "Als Zielobject markiert": Der Enthüller Edward Snowden über die geheime Macht der NSA [Mark as Target: The whistleblower Edward Snowden about the secret power of the NSA]. *Der Spiegel, 28,* 22-24.

Caltagirone, S., Pendergast, A., & Betz, C. (2013). *The Diamond Model of Intrusion Analysis*. Arlington, VA: Threat Connect. (pp. 1–61).

Chabinsky, S. (2013). *Cyber Warfare*. Paper presented at *the American Center for Democracy*. http://www.youtube.com/watch?v=Uiz2R_f1Lxo

China's Views of Sovereignty and Methods of Access Control, (2008).

Clarke, R. A., & Andreasen, S. (2013, June 15). Cyberwar's threat does not justify a new policy of nuclear deterrence. *The Washington Post*. Retrieved from http://js.washingtonpost.com/opinions/cyberwars-threat-does-not-justify-a-new-policy-of-nuclear-deterrence/2013/06/14/91c01bb6-d50e-11e2-a73e-826d299ff459_story.html

Clarke, R. A., Morell, M. J., Stone, G. R., Sunstein, C. R., & Swire, P. (2013). *Liberty and Security in a Changing World: Report and Recommendations of The President's Review Group on Intelligence and Communications Technologies*. Washington, DC: The White House.

Cybersecurity Act of 2012. (2012). U.S. Congress.

Defence and Cyber Security. (2012).

Dourado, E. (2013, October 10). Put trust back in the Internet. *The New York Times*.

Easton, N. (2013, July 22). The CEO Who Caught the Chinese Spies Red-Handed. *Fortune, 168,* 80–88.

Eberle, C. J. (2013). Just War and Cyberwar. *Journal of Military Ethics, 12*(1), 54–67. doi:10.1080/15027570.2013.782638

Flaherty, A. (2013, February 20). A look at Mandiant, allegations on China hacking. *The Associated Press*.

Fresco, A. (1997, March 22). Schoolboy hacker was 'No 1 threat' to US security. *The Times*.

Gady, F.-S. (2010, November 25). The Cyber Fortress Mentality. *Foreign Policy Journal*.

Gary McKinnon v. Government of the USA, No. EWHC 762 (High Court of Justice Queen's Bench Division 2007).

Gellman, B., & Soltani, A. (2013, October 14). NSA collects millions of e-mail address books globally. *The Washington Post*. Retrieved from http://www.washingtonpost.com/world/national-security/nsa-collects-millions-of-e-mail-address-books-globally/2013/10/14/8e58b5be-34f9-11e3-80c6-7e6dd8d22d8f_story.html

Goldsmith, J. (2013a). How Cyber Changes the Laws of War. *European Journal of International Law*, *24*(1), 129–138. doi:10.1093/ejil/cht004

Goldsmith, J. (2013b, October 10). We Need an Invasive NSA. *New Republic*. Retrieved from http://www.newrepublic.com/article/115002/invasive-nsa-will-protect-us-cyber-attacks?utm_content=bufferc47b9&utm_source=buffer&utm_medium=twitter&utm_campaign=Buffer

Greenwald, G. (2013, July 31). XKeyscore: NSA tool collects nearly everything a user does on the internet. *The Guardian*. Retrieved from http://www.theguardian.com/world/2013/jul/31/nsa-top-secret-program-online-data

Guitton, C. (2012). Criminals and Cyber Attacks: The Missing Link Between Attribution and Deterrence. *International Journal of Cyber Criminology*, *6*(2), 1030–1043.

Guitton, C. (2013, 11-12 July). *Modelling Attribution*. Paper presented at the *12th European Conference on Information Warfare and Security*, Jyväskylä.

Guitton, C. (2014). (Forthcoming). Attribution of Cyber Attacks and Its Reliance on Judgement Calls. *Security Dialogue*.

Guitton, C., & Korzak, E. (2013). The Sophistication Criterion for Attribution. *The RUSI Journal, 158*(4).

Halliday, J. (2010, September 24). Stuxnet worm is the work of a national government agency. *The Guardian*.

Heuer, R. J. (1999). *Psychology of Intelligence Analysis*. Washington, D.C.: Centre for the Study of Intelligence.

Heywood, A. (2004). *Political theory: an introduction*. New York: Palgrave Mcmillan.

Hider, J. (2012, May 29). Iran attacked by Israeli computer virus. *The Times*.

Hunker, J., Gates, C., & Bishop, M. (2011). *Attribution Requirements for Next Generation Internets*. Paper presented at the *International Conference on Technologies for Homeland Security*, Waltham.

Improving Critical Infrastructure Cybersecurity. (2013The White House.

International Group of Experts. (2013). *Tallinn Manual on the International Law Applicable to Cyber Warfare*. Cambridge: Cambridge University Press.

Jackson, W. (2012, April 19). Former FBI cyber cop: Hunt the hacker, not the hack, *Government Computer News*.

Jinghao, Y., & Wuning, D. (2013, February 21). Regular cyber attacks from US: China. *Global Times*. Retrieved from http://www.globaltimes.cn/content/763142.shtml

Joint Intelligence Organisation. (2013). *JIC assessment of 27 August on Reported Chemical Weapons use in Damascus London.* Cabinet Office.

Kamluk, V. (2011, November 30). The Mystery of Duqu: Part Six (The Command and Control servers), *SecureList.* Retrieved from http://www.securelist.com/en/blog/625/The_Mystery_of_Duqu_Part_Six_The_Command_and_Control_servers

Kaplan, D. (2012). *Offensive line: Fighting back against hackers. SC Magazine.*

Koh, H. H. (2012). *International Law in Cyberspace.* Paper presented at the *USCYBERCOM Inter-Agency Legal Conference*, Fort Meade, Maryland.

Koskenniemi, M. (1990). The Politics of International Law. *Journal of International Law, 1*, 5–32.

Levin, A., & Goodrick, P. (2013). From cybercrime to cyberwar? The international policy shift and its implications for Canada. *Canadian Foreign Policy Journal, 19*(2), 127–143. doi:10.1080/11926422.2013.805150

Lewis, P., & Williams, H. (2013, September 19). Syria under Scrutiny: Chemical Weapons Inspections, *Expert Comment.* Retrieved from http://www.chathamhouse.org/media/comment/view/194267

Libicki, M. C. (2009). *Cyberdeterrence and Cyberwar.* Santa Monica, CA: RAND.

Lichtblau, E. (2013, July 6). In Secret, Court Vastly Broadens Powers of N.S.A. *The New York Times.* Retrieved from http://www.nytimes.com/2013/07/07/us/in-secret-court-vastly-broadens-powers-of-nsa.html?_r=0

Lichtblau, E., & Schmidt, M. S. (2013, August 3). Other Agencies Clamor for Data N.S.A. Compiles, *The New York Times.* Retrieved from http://www.nytimes.com/2013/08/04/us/other-agencies-clamor-for-data-nsa-compiles.html?pagewanted=all

MacAskill, E., Borger, J., Hopkins, N., Davies, N., & Ball, J. (2013, June 21). GCHQ taps fibre-optic cables for secret access to world's communications. *The Guardian.* Retrieved from http://www.guardian.co.uk/uk/2013/jun/21/gchq-cables-secret-world-communications-nsa

Masters, J. (2011, May 24). Here's How The U.S. Plans To Plug The Holes In Its Cybersecurity Policy. *The Business Insider.*

McConnell, M. (2010, February 28). Mike McConnell on how to win the cyber-war we're losing. *The Washington Post.* Retrieved from http://www.washingtonpost.com/wp-dyn/content/article/2010/02/25/AR2010022502493.html

Mydans, S. (2000, May 11). Student Sought In Virus Case In Philippines. *The New York Times.* Retrieved from http://www.nytimes.com/2000/05/11/business/student-sought-in-virus-case-in-philippines.html?ref=oneldeguzman

Nakashima, E. (2013a, February 11). Cyber-spying said to target U.S. business. *The Washington Post.*

Nakashima, E. (2013b, February 11). U.S. said to be target of massive cyber-espionage campaign. *The Washington Post*. Retrieved from http://www.washingtonpost.com/world/national-security/us-said-to-be-target-of-massive-cyber-espionage-campaign/2013/02/10/7b4687d8-6fc1-11e2-aa58-243de81040ba_story.html?hpid=z1

Nakashima, E. (2014, January 12). NSA phone record collection does little to prevent terrorist attacks, group says. *The Washington Post*. Retrieved from http://www.washingtonpost.com/world/national-security/nsa-phone-record-collection-does-little-to-prevent-terrorist-attacks-group-says/2014/01/12/8aa860aa-77dd-11e3-8963-b4b654bcc9b2_story.html

Nakashima, E., & Soltani, A. (2013, December 18). Panel urges new curbs on surveillance by U.S. *The Washington Post*. Retrieved from http://www.washingtonpost.com/world/national-security/nsa-shouldnt-keep-phone-database-review-board-recommends/2013/12/18/f44fe7c0-67fd-11e3-a0b9-249bbb34602c_story.html

Nguyen, V. (2013). Attribution of Spear Phishing Attacks: A Literature Survey (C. a. E. W. Division, Trans.). Edinburgh, South Australia: Australian Government.

Nicholson, A., Janicke, H., & Watson, T. (2013). *An Initial Investigation into Attribution in SCADA Systems*. Paper presented at *the International Symposium for ICS & SCADA Cyber Security Research*, Leicester.

Obama, B. (2013, February 12). Remarks by the President in the State of the Union Address. *The White House*. Retrieved from http://www.whitehouse.gov/the-press-office/2013/02/12/remarks-president-state-union-address

Obama, B. (2014, January 17). Remarks by the President on Review of Signals Intelligence. *The White House*. Retrieved from http://www.whitehouse.gov/the-press-office/2014/01/17/remarks-president-review-signals-intelligence

Osborne, C. (2013, February 1). US government debates action over alleged Chinese cyberattacks. *ZDNet*. Retrieved from http://www.zdnet.com/us-government-debates-action-over-alleged-chinese-cyberattacks-7000010679/

Parker, T., Devost, M. G., Sach, M. H., Shaw, E., & Stroz, E. (2004). *Cyber Adversary Characterisation*. Rockland: Syngress Publishing.

Perlroth, N. (2012, May 30). Researchers Find Clues in Malware, *The New York Times*. Retrieved from http://www.nytimes.com/2012/05/31/technology/researchers-link-flame-virus-to-stuxnet-and-duqu.html?_r=1&ref=world

Perlroth, N. (2013a, December 19). Target Struck in the Cat-and-Mouse Game of Credit Theft. *The New York Times*. Retrieved from http://www.nytimes.com/2013/12/20/technology/target-stolen-shopper-data.html?src=me&ref=general&_r=0

Perlroth, N. (2013b, December 27). Target's Nightmare Goes On: Encrypted PIN Data Stolen, *The New York Times*. Retrieved from http://bits.blogs.nytimes.com/2013/12/27/targets-nightmare-goes-on-encrypted-pin-data-stolen/?ref=technology

Perlroth, N., Sanger, D. E., & Schmidt, M. S. (2013, March 3). As Hacking Against U.S. Rises, Experts Try to Pin Down Motive. *The New York Times*. Retrieved from http://www.nytimes.com/2013/03/04/us/us-weighs-risks-and-motives-of-hacking-by-china-or-iran.html?_r=0

Poitras, L., Rosenbach, M., & Stark, H. (2013, September 16). Follow the Money': NSA Monitors Financial World. *Der Spiegel*. Retrieved from http://www.spiegel.de/international/world/how-the-nsa-spies-on-international-bank-transactions-a-922430.html

Power, R. (2000, October 30). Joy Riders: Mischief That Leads to Mayhem. *informIT*. Retrieved from http://www.informit.com/articles/article.aspx?p=19603&seqNum=3

Prescott, J. M. (2013). *Autonomous Decision-Making Processes and the Responsible Cyber Commander*. Paper presented at the *5th International Conference on Cyber Conflict*, Tallinn. doi:10.2139/ssrn.2283767

Rashid, F. Y. (2012, November 21). Eugene Kaspersky: Definition Of 'Cyberwar' In Flux, Threat Of Cyber Weapons Underestimated. *SecurityWeek*. Retrieved from http://www.securityweek.com/eugene-kaspersky-definition-cyberwar-flux-threat-cyber-weapons-underestimated

Reuters. (2013, September 16). Belgium investigates suspected cyber spying by foreign state. *Reuters*. Retrieved from http://www.reuters.com/article/2013/09/16/us-usa-security-belgium-idUSBRE-98F0A320130916)

Risen, J., & Poitras, L. (2013a, September 28). N.S.A. Gathers Data on Social Connections of U.S. Citizens. *The New York Times*. Retrieved from http://www.nytimes.com/2013/09/29/us/nsa-examines-social-networks-of-us-citizens.html?hp&_r=0

Risen, J., & Poitras, L. (2013b, November 22). N.S.A. Report Outlined Goals for More Power. *The New York Times*. Retrieved from http://www.nytimes.com/2013/11/23/us/politics/nsa-report-outlined-goals-for-more-power.html?ref=international-home&_r=0

Rogers, M. (2014). *Rebooting Trust? Freedom vs. Security in Cyberspace*. Paper presented at the *Munich Security Conference*, Munich.

RT. (2012, 16 October). Global cyber war: New Flame-linked malware detected, *RT*. Retrieved from http://rt.com/news/mini-flame-malware-kaspersky-519/

Rubin, H., Fraser, L., & Smith, M. (1995). US and International Law Aspects of the Internet: Fitting Square Pegs Into Round Holes. *International Journal of Law and Information Technology*, *3*(2), 117–143. doi:10.1093/ijlit/3.2.117

Ryan, M. (2005, June 8). The 'spider's web' of hacking, *BBC News*. Retrieved from http://news.bbc.co.uk/1/hi/uk/4072938.stm

Sanger, D. E. (2012, June 1). Obama Order Sped Up Wave of Cyberattacks Against Iran. *The New York Times*. Retrieved from http://www.nytimes.com/2012/06/01/world/middleeast/obama-ordered-wave-of-cyberattacks-against-iran.html?pagewanted=all

Sanger, D. E., & Perlroth, N. (2013, May 19). Chinese Hackers Resume Attacks on U.S. Targets. *The New York Times*. Retrieved from http://www.nytimes.com/2013/05/20/world/asia/chinese-hackers-resume-attacks-on-us-targets.html?hp&_r=0

Schmitt, M. N. (1998). Computer Network Attack and the Use of Force in International Law: Thoughts on a Normative Framework. *Columbia Journal of Transnational Law, 37.*

Shane, S., & Moynihan, C. (2013, September 1). Drug Agents Use Vast Phone Trove, Eclipsing N.S.A.'s. *The New York Times.*

Shanker, T., & Sanger, D. E. (2013, June 8). U.S. Helps Allies Trying to Battle Iranian Hackers. *The New York Times.* Retrieved from http://www.nytimes.com/2013/06/09/world/middleeast/us-helps-allies-trying-to-battle-iranian-hackers.html?pagewanted=1&_r=2

Shorrock, T. (2008). *Spies for Hire: The Secret World of Intelligence Outsourcing.* New York: Simon and Schuster.

Stoll, C. (1989). *The cuckoo's egg: tracking a spy through the maze of computer espionage.* New York: Doubleday.

The Guardian. (2013, June 28). Former US general James Cartwright named in Stuxnet leak inquiry. *The Guardian.* Retrieved from http://www.guardian.co.uk/world/2013/jun/28/general-cartwright-investigated-stuxnet-leak?CMP=twt_gu

The White House. (2009). *Cyberspace Policy Review.* Washington, D.C.

The White House. (2013a). *Administration Strategy on Mitigating the Theft of U.S. Trade Secrets* Washington, DC: The White House. (pp. 141).

The White House. (2013b, August 30). Government Assessment of the Syrian Government's Use of Chemical Weapons on August 21, 2013. *The White House.*

Thonnard, O. (2010). *Vers un regroupement multicritères comme outil d'aide à l'attribution d'attaque dans le cyber-espace. (PhD).* Paris: Ecole Nationale Supérieure des Télécommunications.

Thonnard, O., Mees, W., & Dacier, M. (2010). On a Multi-criteria Clustering Approach for Attack Attribution. *ACM Special Interest Group on Knowledge Discovery and Data Mining Explorations, 12*(1), 11–21.

Tikk, E., & Kaska, K. (2010). *Legal Cooperation to Investigate Cyber Incidents: Estonian Case Study and Lessons.* Paper presented at the 9th European Conference on Information Warfare and Security, Thessaloniki.

United Stated of America v. Jeffrey Lee Parson, No. 03-457M (United States District Court, Western District of Washington 2003).

Tschechien: Neuer Anlauf zur Wiedereinführung der Vorratsdatenspeicherung [Czech Republic: New attempt to reintroduce the data retention]. (2012). *U.N. Watched.* Retrieved from https://http://www.unwatched.org/EDRigram_10.11_Tschechien_Neuer_Anlauf_zur_Wiedereinfuehrung_der_Vorratsdatenspeicherung?pk_campaign=edri&pk_kwd=20120606

Blueprint for a Secure Cyber Future. (2011US Department of Homeland Security Washington, DC: US Department of Homeland Security. (pp. 50).

*Department of Defense Cyberspace Policy Report: A Report to Congress Pursuant to the National Defense Authorization Act for Fiscal Year 2011*US Department of Defense. (2011). Washington, D.C.: Department of Defense.

Cybersecurity Update (2011, October 18). US Department of State. Retrieved from http://fpc.state.gov/175773.htm

Valentino-Devries, J., & Gorman, S. (2013, August 20). What You Need to Know on New Details of NSA Spying, *The Wall Street Journal*. Retrieved from http://online.wsj.com/news/articles/SB1000142 4127887324108204579025222244858490

Verton, D., & Brandt, A. (2012). Biography of a Worm. *PC World*. Retrieved from http://pcworld.about.net/magazine/2211p115id117808.htm

Waxman, M. C. (2011). Cyber-Attacks and the Use of Force: Back to the Future of Article 2(4). *Yale Journal of International Law*, *36*(2), 421–459.

Wheeler, D. A., & Larsen, G. N. (2003). *Techniques for Cyber Attack Attribution*. Alexandria, Virginia: Institute for Defense Analyses.

Williams, M. (1999). Hacker Discovers Antigravity File in Military Computer. Retrieved from http://www.bibliotecapleyades.net/ciencia/secret_projects/project159.htm

Wireless News. (2013, June 29). CrowdStrike Unveils Big Data Active Defense Platform. *Wireless News*.

ADDITIONAL READING

Brenner, J. (2011). *America the Vulnerable*. New York: The Penguin Press.

Brenner, S. W. (2009). *Cyber Threats: The Emerging Fault Lines of the Nation State*. Oxford: Oxford Scholarship Online. doi:10.1093/acprof:oso/9780195385014.001.0001

Brenner, S. W. (2013). Cyber-threats and the Limits of Bureaucratic Control. *Minnesota Journal of Law, Science, and Technology*, *14*, 137–258.

Brenner, S. W., & Schwerha, J. J. (2002). Transnatinoal evidence gathering and local prosecution of international cybercrime. *The John Marshall Journal of Computer & Information Law*, *20*, 347–396.

Clark, D. D., & Landau, S. (2010). *Untangling Attribution*. Paper presented at the Workshop on Deterring CyberAttacks: Informing Strategies and Developing Options for U.S. Policy, Washington, DC.

Clayton, R. (2005). *Anonymity and traceability in cyberspace. (PhD)* (p. 653). Cambridge: University of Cambridge.

Crump, C. (2003). Data Retention: Privacy, Anonymity, and Accountability Online. *Stanford Law Review*, *56*(1), 191–229.

Daugherty, W. J. (2004). *Executive Secrets: Covert action and the presidency*. Lexington: The University Press of Kentucky.

Decker, D. K. (2011). *Before the First Bomb Goes Off: Developing Nuclear Attribution Standards and Policies*. Cambridge, MA: Harvard Kennedy School.

Deibert, R., & Crete-Nishihata, M. (2011). Blurred Boundaries: Probing the Ethics of Cyberspace Research. *Review of Policy Research, 28*(5), 531–537. doi:10.1111/j.1541-1338.2011.00521.x

Deibert, R., Palfrey, J., Rohonzinski, R., & Zittrain, J. (2012). Access Contested: Toward the Fourth Phase of Cyberspace Controls. In R. Deibert, J. Palfrey, R. Rohonzinski, & J. Zittrain (Eds.), *Access Contested: Security, Identity, and Resistance in Asian Cyberspace*. Cambridge, MA: MIT Press.

Deibert, R., & Rohonzinski, R. (2012). Contesting Cyberspace and the Coming Crisis of Authority. In R. Deibert, J. Palfrey, R. Rohonzinski, & J. Zittrain (Eds.), *Access Contested: Security, Identity, and Resistance in Asian Cyberspace*. Cambridge, MA: MIT Press.

Deibert, R. J., Rohozinski, R., & Crete-Nishihata, M. (2013). Cyclones in cyberspace: Information shaping and denial in the 2008 Russia – Georgia war. *Security Dialogue, 43*(3), 3–24.

Demchak, C. C. (2011). *Wars of disruption and resilience*. Athens, London: The University of Georgia Press.

Diffie, W., & Landau, S. (2010). *Privacy on the Line: The Politics of Wiretapping and Encryption. San Bruno*. MIT Press.

Gibbs, J. P. (1985). Deterrence Theory and Research *Nebraska Symposium on Motivation: The Law as a Behavioral Instrument* (Vol. 33). Lincoln: University of Nebraska Press.

Godson, R. (2001). *Dirty Tricks or Trump Cards: US Covert Actions & Counterintelligence*. New Brunswick: Transaction Publishers.

Healey, J. (2012). *Beyond Attribution: Seeking National Responsibility for Cyber Attacks* (pp. 1–7). Washington, DC: Atlantic Council.

Healey, J. (2013). A Fierce Domain: Conflict in Cyberspace, 1986 to 2012. Washington, DC: CCSA; The Atlantic Council.

Levy, S. (2001). *Crypto: How the Code Rebels Beat the Government Saving Privacy in the Digital Age*. New York: Penguin Books.

Libicki, M. (2012a). Cyberspace Is Not a Warfighting Domain. *A Journal of Law and Policy for the Information Society, 8*(2), 325-340.

Libicki, M. (2012b). The Specter of Non-Obvious Warfare. *Strategic Studies Quarterly, Fall*, 88-101.

MacKinnon, R. (2012). Corporate Accountability in Networked Asia. In R. Deibert, J. Palfrey, R. Rohonzinski, & J. Zittrain (Eds.), *Access Contested: Security, Identity, and Resistance in Asian Cyberspace* (pp. 195–216). Cambridge, MA: MIT Press.

Nissenbaum, H. (2010). *Privacy in Context: Technology, Policy, and the Integrity of Social Life*. Stanford, California: Stanford Law Books.

Rid, T. (2013). *Cyber War Will Not Take Place. London*. Hurst: Company.

Untangling Attribution: Moving to Accountability in Cyberspace, United States House of Representatives, 2nd Session Sess. 12 (2010).

Villeneuve, N., & Crete-Nishihata, M. (2012). Control and Resistance: Attacks on Burmese Opposition Media. In R. Deibert, J. Palfrey, R. Rohonzinski, & J. Zittrain (Eds.), *Access Contested: Security, Identity, and Resistance in Asian Cyberspace*. Cambridge, MA: MIT Press.

KEY TERMS AND DEFINITIONS

Attribution: The process through which the chain of entities involved in a cyber attack is identified.

Cyber Attack: The intentional breach of at least one of the five components of an information system, namely confidentiality, integrity, availability, authenticity and non-repudiation.

Intelligence Services: A state organ devoted to the protection of national security as defined by a government and whose programmes are partially non-public, although they usually fall under the scrutiny of a congressional committee. The programmes involve notably the collection, organisation and mining of data to identify threats and their potential authors. The chapter draws a sharp distinction between these services and law enforcement agencies that operate in the public light and with the aim of bringing testable evidence in a court against attackers.

Malware: A piece of code launching a cyber attack.

Meta-Data: All data about a communication other than its content (e.g., sender and recipient, time and date of the communication).

Political (Sphere): The activities encompassing the expression of a group's will to power. The chapter restricted the understanding of the political sphere to those activities only carried out by a representative of the state.

State Actor: The recognised representatives of a state, which have the authority to act on its behalf. This includes most notably accredited officials, governmental organisations (e.g., law enforcement agencies and intelligence services), and more directly, members of the government.

Technical (Sphere): The activities encompassing the automatic recording or processing of data by a system.

Section 2
Cybersecurity at Stake:
Monitoring Threats, Managing Risks and Defensive Measures

Chapter 4
Security Monitoring of the Cyber Space

Claude Fachkha
Concordia University, Canada

ABSTRACT

Adversaries are abusing Internet security and privacy services to execute cyber attacks. To cope with these threats, network operators utilize various security tools and techniques to monitor the cyber space. An efficient way to infer Internet threat activities is to collect information from trap-based monitoring sensors. As such, this chapter primarily defines the cyberspace trap-based monitoring systems and their taxonomies. Moreover, it presents the state-of-the-art in terms of research contributions and techniques, tools and technologies. Furthermore, it identifies gaps in terms of science and technology. Additionally, it presents some case studies and practical approaches corresponding to large-scale cyber monitoring systems such as Nicter. We further present some related security policies and legal issues for network monitoring. This chapter provides an overview on Internet monitoring and offers a guideline for readers to help them understand the concepts of observing, detecting and analyzing cyber attacks through computer network traps.

1. INTRODUCTION

As of 2014, the Internet, the network of networks, provides information sharing and communication systems to more than 7 billion users (Internet Word Stats, 2014). This number is dramatically increasing as humans are becoming more dependent on social media/networks, mobiles, telecommunication, gaming, dating websites in addition to various cloud services and facilities. This increase rises the size of information sharing and hence created the term Big Data. This term has become the focus, the challenge and the exclamation mark for Internet Service Providers (ISPs), organizations, law enforcements and government agencies. For example, the questions are how to handle such large amount of information? How to analyze the traffic and how to secure and control such big data?

In regard to privacy, security and control, this cyberspace challenge takes an appeal of a continuous conflict due to the fact that computer attack tools and techniques are becoming more intelligently

DOI: 10.4018/978-1-4666-8456-0.ch004

designed and hackers are capable of launching worldwide impacting attacks for various reasons such as large-scale Denial-of-Service (CloudFlare, 2014), cyber-terrorism, information theft, hate crimes, defamation, bullying, identity theft and fraud. For instance, the Flame code, the most complex malware ever found, is a new generation of malware discovered in 2012 that aims to target nuclear power plants machines (Nakashima, Miller, and Tate, 2012). This obviously open the door of a new cyber war impacting the whole world including critical physical infrastructure such as power plants, nuclear, and more. Furthermore, the existence of widely available encryption and anonymizing techniques makes the surveillance and the investigation of cyber attacks much harder problem. In this context, the availability of relevant cyber threat collecting and monitoring systems is of paramount importance.

In this content, we attempt in this chapter to find answers to the following questions:

- How do we investigate large-scale cyber events?
- What is the state of the art of cyber security monitoring systems?
- Who has the capability to monitor the cyberspace?
- What are the privacy and security policies behind security analysis and deployment?

Answering the above questions can help security operators to understand the objectives of network monitoring technologies, their corresponding pros and cons, their deployments, their traffic analysis processes, their embedded threats, the difference among them as well as their research gaps. Moreover, the readers can have an overview on the security policies and legal issues that mostly unknown for network operators and even adversaries.

The rest of this chapter is organized as follows. Section II presents the background information on various network monitoring concepts and cyber threats. Section III provides the state of the art of trap-based monitoring tools. Section IV discusses the security policies and legal issues in network monitoring. Section V presents the trend and the future research directions. Finally, Section V summaries and concludes with a discussion on the monitoring systems and research.

2. BACKGROUND

This section provides an overview on the major elements of this chapter, namely, the trap-based monitoring systems and their embedded cyber threats.

2.1 Trap-Based Cyber Security Monitoring Systems

The Internet involves several telecommunication elements and machines such as servers/clients, network infrastructure (routers, switches, etc.), services (email, web, etc.) and databases, among many others. One way to monitor the information sharing among these devices is to build network management tools based on SNMP services (Stallings, 1998). In addition to managing the Internet, several security monitoring systems exist online. These methods run over various network layers such as physical, network and application as well as covers various areas such as storage, access control, etc. Trap-based monitoring sensors are systems that aim to trap adversaries online. The purpose is to collect insights on the attack traces and activities such as probing/scanning for vulnerable services, worm propagation, malware downloads and other command-and-control activities such as executing Distributed Denial of Service

Figure 1. Basic Monitoring Systems using Trap Sensors

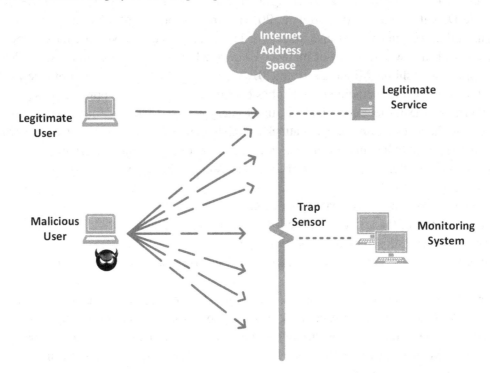

(DDoS) cyber attacks using Botnet (Freiling, Holz, & Wicherski, 2005). Figure 1 depicts a basic concept of trap-based sensor and monitoring on the Internet.

As shown in figure 1, a trap monitoring sensor is deployed on the Internet address space to attract malicious users. In some cases, these trap sensors run on unused but routable IP address, hence, all traffic destined to them is considered suspicious and therefore requires further investigation. The trap attracts adversaries by running vulnerable services. As shown in figure 1, once these attackers connect to the sensors, all the malicious traffic is forwarded from the sensor to the monitoring systems for further analysis. In the rest of this chapter, we discuss the state of the arts of these monitoring systems, their deployments, their embedded threats as well as their pros and cons.

2.2 Trap-Based Embedded Cyber Threats

Several cyber threats exist on the Internet, we define below the major threats that can be found through the analysis of sensor-based monitoring systems.

Scanning/Probing: Scanning, also known as reconnaissance activities, is the first step in a cyber attack life cycle. Adversaries run scanning activities to infer vulnerabilities on the Internet. Once a machine is found vulnerable, the attacker attempts to control or infect this host based on the inferred vulnerability. For instance, an attacker check for vulnerabilities in remote access services first before trying to access remotely and take control. Scanning various in natures, strategies and approaches. Moreover, several scanning techniques exists such as stealthy, sweep, open and half open scans, among others (Allman, Paxson, & Terrell, 2007).

Botnet: Botnet can be used as a platform for adversaries. It is designed to command and control compromised machines. Hence, it aims to provide a powerful tool for hackers distribute and amplify their attacks. A typical botnet consists of three major elements, a bot master, command-and-control (C&C) hosts and bots/zombies of compromised machines. A bot master controls an army of bots through C&Cs. For instance, a bot master can order all bots to flood (send extensively) large number of requests to one single victim to exhaust or/and deny its resources. Further, a bot master can send spams on the Internet through his botnet infrastructure. Several botnet infrastructure exists such centralized (IRC-based) and decentralized (P2P-based) (Dagon, Gu, Lee, & Lee, 2007).

Distributed Denial of Service (DDoS): DDoS attacks are characterized by an explicit attempt to prevent the legitimate use of a service. DDoS attacks employ multiple attacking entities (e.g., compromised

Machines/bots) to achieve their intended aim which mainly targets depleting bandwidth and host resources (e.g., CPU usage). In general, botnet is an impeccable tool to execute DDoS attacks with high impact (Mirkovic, Dietrich, Dittrich, & Reiher, 2004).

Distributed Reflection Denial of Service (DRDoS): DRDoS attacks are special type of DDoS. A reflection, also known as amplification attack, is a well known practice of a DDoS, in which malicious users abuse open resolvers (e.g., DNS servers) to bombard a victim with reply traffic (Fachkha, Bou-Harb, & Debbabi, 2014). The technique consists of an invader directing a lookup query to an open server having the source IP spoofed to be the victim's address. Subsequently, all server amplified responses will be sent to the targeted victim. In general, malicious users will request domains that cover a large zone to increase the amplification factor (Fachkha, Bou-Harb, & Debbabi, 2015).

Exploit: Exploit is a software or a sequence of commands that tackles bugs, glitches or/and vulnerabilities in computer system for the purpose of executing malicious acts such as gaining control, accessing root privileges, compromising and infecting exposed machines (Wang, Guo, Simon, & Zugenmaier, 2004).

Malware: Malware is a piece of code designed to perform malicious activities. Malware comes with various types such as viruses, worms, trojans, etc. Each of these types has different features and families. Some of these features can include propagation and replication. For instance, worms are known to have self-propagating activities. Malware can damage computer services in many ways like in compromising machines, stealing information, taking control, corrupting system files, exhausting resources, etc. (Skoudis, 2004).

3. Trap-Based Cyber Monitoring Systems

In this section, we provide a state-of-art study on the main trap-based monitoring systems. The purpose of this section is to offer the reader a guideline on monitoring systems, namely, darknet, IP gray space, honeypot, greynet, honeytokens, etc. Therefore, we aim to answer the following questions: How do we investigate large-scale cyber events? What is the state of the art of cyber security monitoring systems?

3.1 Darknet

Darknet, also known as network telescopes (Moore, 2003), Internet background radiation or blackhole, is a chunk of Internet address space running on unused but routable IP addresses. Therefore, all traffic destined to them is more likely suspicious. To the best of our knowledge, darknet research and analysis started in the beginning of the 1990th when Bellovin leveraged the unused address space to uncover malicious activities (Bellovin, 1992). Few years later, darknet research and analysis started to become more attractive for researchers. At that time, darknet was found as a good source to collect security insights online. Some of the projects include the analysis of Internet threat through darknet (Fachkha, Bou-Harb, Boukhtouta, Dinh, Iqbal, & Debbabi, 2012) such as DDoS (Moore, 2006), DRDoS (Fachkha et al., 2014), worms (Moore, & Shannon, 2002), scanning (Bou-Harb, Debbabi, & Assi, 2013) as well as misconfiguration (Bailey, Cooke, Jahanian, Myrick, & Sinha, 2006).

3.1.1 Darknet Deployment

This section represents an overview of darknet deployment. The first step in darknet technique is to deploy a sensor monitoring system. Therefore, understanding the network architecture is a most. Thus, a careful configuration must be done on the dynamic host server or the upstream router to forward unreachable packets to the darknet sensors. Two major elements must be done for this deployment setup, namely, the storage and network requirements and the deployment techniques. First, it is critical to identify the exact storage and network requirements for a darknet system. In order to collect darknet data, *PCAP* and *Netflow* formats are the most suitable for this network traffic. The amount of darknet packets received are based on the placement of the sensors, the size of the monitored IPs and the configuration setup. In terms of placement, previous studies has shown that the traffic collected by two different but equally sized darknet is not the same. In terms of size of the darknet and network requirements, a study has shown that a small /24 sensor has approximately a rate of 9 packets per second, while a /16 sensor receives 75 packets per second, and a large /8 monitor receives over 5000 packets per second (Bailey et al., 2006). Second, in terms of deployment techniques, there are mainly three major darknet deployment approaches: i) the first is to simply send Address Resolution Protocol (ARP) replies for each dark address to the router. This technique, although it is simple, it works well when the darknet addresses are well known and are limited in size. When the unused addresses reach thousands or million, the monitoring activity becomes less efficient; ii) the second approach is considered more scalable and link a static range of IP address block to the monitor. This is a simple approach but it needs the dark address block to be specifically separated for analysis; iii) the third approach is done by forwarding all non-configured packets to the sensor. It is like forwarding all unused packets of an organization network to the sensor. The above mentioned methodologies deal with unused and reachable dark addresses. However, to capture unused and non-reachable packets, RFC 1918 (Groot, Rekhter, Karrenberg, Lear, 1996) specifies some IP ranges that fit in this category. We refer the reader to (Bailey et al., 2006) for more information regarding these techniques and how to implement them.

3.1.2 Darknet Data

In terms of protocols, TCP packets are the most common traffic found on darknet, UDP packets are the second and ICMP packets are the third (Pang, Yegneswaran, Barford, Paxson, & Peterson, 2004; Wustrow, Karir, Bailey, Jahanian, & Huston, 2010). Moreover, in terms of threat types, the majority of the inferred traffic consists of scanning and worms activities (Pang et al., 2004; Wustrow et al., 2010), backscatter traffic from DDoS victims (Moore et al., 2006) whereas the minority consists of misconfiguration of network devices such as routers. Concerning scanning and worm scenarios, the attack aims to scan or probe the Internet address space looking for gathering information (e.g., vulnerabilities in services) or infecting machines (e.g., downloading a malware), etc.. In regard to backscatter traffic scenario, the adversary sends a flood of requests signed by the IP address (spoofed) to the victim. Subsequently, the victim replies to the flood by sending backscattered (reply) packets to the sensors. In this scenario, the assumption is that the attacker chooses a spoofed IP address that belongs to the monitored darknet space. In another DDoS cases, the attacker flood the Internet with requests spoofed by the address of the victim. Hence, all open services (e.g., DNS resolver) found online will reply to the victim with amplified replies (Fachkha et al., 2014). For all aforementioned cases, while generating these malicious activities, some of this traffic might reach the darknet sensor and hence become available for IT investigators. Subsequently, security operators can study the traffic (e.g., analyze the speed and impact of the attack) and understand the malicious strategy that are being used on the Internet. This exercise might help in detecting, preventing, mitigating and even attributing cyber attacks.

3.1.3 Darknet: Pros and Cons

Since darknet monitors solely unused address space, the major advantage of this approach is the security aspect on the monitor side. In other word, only uni-directional traffic (towards darknet sensor) is captured on the darknet. Recall that, unused address space do not communicate, and hence darknet is called passive monitoring. The security advantage of this approach is that darknet sensors are safe and not threaten by the attack. Further, darknet deployment is considered easy to deploy since it is passive (run in a listening mode) and do not require interaction with the adversary. On the other hand, the major disadvantage of darknet is the collection of data. Since there is no interaction with the adversary, investigators will not detect the complete attack scenario but only the first stage of it. For example, IT analysts can infer the scanning attempt for vulnerability but cannot save the malware (e.g., the executable) used while using this scanning attack. Therefore, compared to other monitoring systems, information gathered on darknet is considered low.

3.2 IP Gray Space

These addresses refer to devices that are not assigned to any host throughout a given time period (e.g. 1 hour, 1 day). In concept, IP gray space is very similar to darknet. The only difference is that IP gray space addresses are unused for a limited time only, whereas darknet addresses are permanently unused. Unlike darknet analysis techniques which can potentially be evaded, IP gray space might be harder to detect by an attacker since they are active and operating as a regular machine at some periods of time. The aim of this experiment is to confuse the adversaries while they are trying to gain some information from the targeted address space. For instance, after a successful compromising a machine that is running in active mode, the adversaries try to control the victim using a C&C. However, since this active machine might switch to inactive mode, the security operators might trick the attackers (e.g., botmaster) and infer their malicious next-step activities. Obviously, the assumption is that adversaries do still believe that the compromised machine is still under their control (Jin, Zhang, Xu, Cao, Sahu, 2007; Jin, Simon, Xu, Zhang, & Kumar, 2007).

3.2.1 IP Gray Space Deployment

As mentioned above, IP gray space addresses have mainly two status, namely, active and inactive. The analysis of IP gray space is done when the addresses are in passive (inactive mode). Therefore, in order to deploy IP gray space, you need a setup similar to darknet deployment in Section 3.1.1 when the addresses are in the inactive mode. However, when the addresses switches to active mode, the setup is switch to a regular active hosts online. Another way to deploy IP gray space, is simply disconnect an active machine for a limited period of time and sniff all incoming packets destined to its addresses. In literature, there is no detailed guideline to follow on deploying IP gray space network. For further information on IP gray space, we refer the reader to (Jin et al., 2007).

3.2.2 IP Gray Space Data

Since IP gray space is darknet for a specific period of time or has both active and inactive modes, collected inactive traffic can be darknet data (DDoS, scanning, misconfiguration) plus active traffic (Botnet C&C, malware) data. Therefore, assuming the IP gray space deployment is correctly done, analyzing its space can be more relevant and insightful than examining darknet data. For example, since darknet monitor only unused IP addresses (in passive/inactive mode), it is unlikely to find on its sensors interactive activities such as botnet/malware communication. In contrary, IP gray space monitoring can infer these communication as its addresses can run in active mode for a certain period of time.

3.2.3 IP Gray Space: Pros and Cons

Obviously, IP gray space monitoring holds the disadvantages and advantages of darknet while running in passive mode. However, while running in active mode, the IP gray space might have the following pros and cons. Regarding the advantages, as mentioned before, more data will be collected such as malware/botnet communication and hence more insights can be inferred. Regarding the disadvantages, running in active mode will provide adversaries with capabilities of attacking monitoring servers (sensors). Therefore, the deployment of IP gray space requires more attention and has more challenges than deploying darknet.

3.3 Honeypot

This is a computer system, mostly connected to the Internet that is configured to trap attackers. Honeypots are similar in nature to darknet with more specific goals. Honeypots, in general, require more resources than darknet since the aim is to interact with the adversary. There are 3 major types of honeypots, namely low, medium and high interactive honeypots. Types are differentiated based on their interactivity level with the initiator of the communication. On one hand, a low-interactive honeypot, is a simple solution configured to interact with the intruder at a basic level by emulating services (e.g., send *ECHO Reply* message to an *ECHO Ping Request*). Further, a medium-interactive honeypot is similar to low-interactive one but with further interactions and more emulated services for more data capturing and analysis (e.g., reply *SYN ACK* to a *SYN* request). On the other hand, a high interactive honeypot is a computer system that do not emulate some services. Instead, it runs a complete vulnerable or non-patched operating system and applications such as an OS version on a virtual machine. Note that a collection of honeypots form a honeynet (Spitzner, 2003).

3.3.1 Honeypot Deployment

Similar to other monitoring systems, honeypot deployment depends on several factors such as the location of the sensor, configuration of the sensor, and most importantly, the type of the sensor (low, medium, high). First, a major factor in honeypot deployment is choosing the location. A good practice exercise recommends installing several honeypot in separate locations and separate from the production system to prevent liability issues (Lilien, Kamal, Bhuse, & Gupta, 2006). The more distributed are the sensors, the better are the extracted insights and the vision. Second, configuring a honeypot changes based on the need of the analysts. For instance, setting up a highly-interactive honeypot with capabilities to detect botnet is less challenging than deploying a low-interactive honeypot to monitor solely scanning activities. In any case, the deployment of low-interactive honeypot is close to darknet deployment whereas deploying high-interactive honeypot must be done in a way to emulate the operation of a regular machine. Therefore, a practical way to deploy high-interactive honeypot is to run the trap on a virtual machine (VM) (Mokube, & Adams, 2007) and run this service in a safe environment. A practical honeypot deployment is found in (Provos, 2004).

3.3.2 Honeypot Data

Honeypot is probably the best source for collecting security information due to the fact that these sensors can save the complete (bi-directional) communication or session with the adversary. Therefore, through honeypot, traces can track all attack stages such as scanning/probing for vulnerabilities, exploits, P2P and C&C communications, malware download activities, storing executable malicious codes, drop locations, etc. Several researchers investigate honeypot and extract various useful information on adversaries operation and strategies. For more information on honeypot data collection we refer the reader to (Spitzner, 2003; Provos, & Holz, 2007).

3.3.3 Honeypot: Pros and Cons

Honeypots, similar to any other trap-based monitoring system, have their own pros and cons. In terms of advantages, despite the fact that honeypot deployment is more complex than passive monitoring systems such as darknet, however, the technology today made implementing and running a honeypot a simple and flexible monitoring system. Most importantly, honeypots capture various security information regarding adversaries methodologies and techniques. The honeypot stored information is larger and more insightful than the darknet ones. In terms of the disadvantages, honeypots, since they interact with adversaries, this make this operation challenging. For instance, security operators must be very careful to avoid being detected by the hacker and/or get infected or/and become compromised. If the attackers discover any suspicious monitoring services, they might block the traced communication or even send irrelevant information to confuse investigators. Therefore, deploying the honeypot sensor might require more attention than other trap-based sensors such as darknet where monitoring do not require interaction with the adversary (Mokube et al., 2007).

3.4 Greynet

This network is sparsely populated with darknet inactive addresses interspersed with active IP addresses. In other word, greynet uses both darknet (passive) and honeypots (active) on the same monitoring space during the same period of time. The purpose is to make the monitored IP block more attractive trap for the attacker. For example, a range of IPs that have both darknet and other active sensors running some fake services (e.g., reply to *ICMP ECHO* requests) might trick the attackers and have them think that the whole range of IPs in this monitored block is an appropriate organization target.

3.4.1 Greynet Deployment

Obviously, since greynet is an address space containing both darknet and honeypot, this means that deploying a greynet require deploying both darknet and honeypot. Therefore, deploying greynet is considered the most complex among all aforementioned trap-based monitoring systems. For instance, security analyst must distinguish between the passive and active monitoring traces and check for a possible link among them; at first, attackers might probe unused addresses (passive host) looking for vulnerable services and at second, the same or even other attackers might target a honeypot (active host) while searching for an active bot. This scenario might confuse investigators while collecting and interpreting this case to infer the pattern and the link among traces, if any. Research in this area is still required, for more information on greynet, we refer the reader to (Harrop, & Armitage, 2005).

3.4.2 Greynet Data

Through Greynet, researchers and security operators can benefit from the fact that darknet and honeypot traces can be trapped. Therefore, in terms of passive monitoring, greynet can detect scanning, DDoS activities as well as misconfiguration. Moreover, in terms of active monitoring, greynet can identify botnet C&C activities, malware communication, drop locations of stolen information, etc. In a nutshell, greynet can trap various malicious activities and strategies that covers from the first until the last action of a malicious activity.

3.4.3 Greynet: Pros and Cons

Clearly, greynet holds the pros and cons of both darknet and honeypot monitoring systems.

In regard to the advantage of greynet; first, a greynet is probably the most attractive space for adversaries to the fact that it represents a typical organization network having both active and inactive hosts. Hence, the more data is available for analysis. More importantly, greynet can be used to identify various scanning techniques and strategies (Jin et al., 2007). On the other hand, some of the disadvantages behind greynet analysis is the amount and the variety of traces available for analysis. Consequently, analyzing greynet traffic is similar to monitoring a network organization data. The analysis of greynet, in contrary to darknet for instance, is complex to the fact that the traffic is coming from various types of sensors and hence mixing various types of attacks and strategies.

3.5 Honeytokens

Honeytokens were introduce in 2003 by Augusto Paes de Barros. Honeytokens are technologies that go beyond regular honeypots. In fact, honeytokens are honeypots without machines (sensors, computers, etc.). In other word, honeytokens are digital entities. Therefore, honeytokens have all the advantages of traditional honeypots and extend their capabilities beyond physical machines (Spitzner, 2003). In practice, honeytokens can be, but not limited to, the following digital entities: a credit card number, a bogus login or any other information that can be stolen. The concept falls behind the following steps: First, security operators publish or make the aforementioned information accessible to adversaries. Second, assuming that hackers take control over these information and hence, security operators can monitor, track and trace-back hackers' activities.

3.5.1 Honeytokens Deployment

Since honeytokens deployment do not require physical entity, running them is considered simple and fast. In order to elaborate more on the deployment of honeytokens, we provide the following scenario. Imagine cyber security experts are investigating online credit card thefts. Therefore, for monitoring such malicious activities, the experts provide a bogus credit card information online (e.g., on a specific bank database) and wait for malicious activities on this bogus data. Any activities that run on this credit card information is considered a violation to the system's usage policy and hence needs to be investigated. It is noteworthy to note that in general, there is no designed algorithm or configured rules to deploy a honeytoken (Spitzner, 2003).

3.5.2 Honeytokens Data

Honeytokens, similar to any other monitoring system, do not solve all security issues. However, it can help in some security applications such as identifying source of attack and tracing the motive and the behavior of adversaries. Therefore, honeytokens analyzed data contains mainly traces of the attack, namely, handling stolen information, storing stolen information, tracing-back adversaries and their networks, discovering malicious users or users with malicious intent, etc. It is significant to note that honeytokens traps can be in the form of any file or information such as Office documents (PowerPoint, Excel, Word), pdf, databases, SIN, credit card info, bank accounts, signatures, login credentials, etc.

3.5.3 Honeytokens: Pros and Cons

With regard to the advantage of honeytokens, as mentioned before, this technology is considered easy to deploy and extremely effective with low cost. Honeytokens accuracy in detecting malicious users is higher than other trap-based monitoring system to the fact that its digital trap is more attractive and realistic to adversaries since it provide them assets (e.g., financial). For instance, from a law enforcement point of view, tracing back a bogus credit card might have more impact than inferring scanning activities. Further, a major advantage of this technology is the deployment which do not require configuration or/ and setup of hardware devices. Hence, this technology operates dynamically and in a mobile manner. Instead of deploying a sensor on a specific IP address space, honeytokens operate independent of their locations (e.g., web-based). In regard to the disadvantage of this technology, honeytokens cannot trap all network-based information that destined to an IP address space due to the fact that, as mentioned earlier, honeytokens is a digital entity. Therefore, honeytokens fail to trap data regarding scanning activities, worm propagation, etc.

3.6 Comparative Study

In this section, we provide a comparative study of the trap-based monitoring systems, namely, darknet, IP grey space, honeypot, greynet and honeytokens.

3.6.1 Feature Comparison

This section compares the aforementioned monitoring systems based on the following features:

- **Interactivity:** The interactivity is the measure of the interaction level between an adversary and the monitoring system. For example, a darknet, which is inactive and passive monitoring, do not require interaction with adversaries whereas a high-interactive honeypot require a high interactive communication.
- **Complexity:** The complexity is the measure of the difficulties in setting up a monitoring system. In other word, how complex is to deploy a monitoring sensor. For instance, setting up a greynet which can run also honeypot, might be more complex than deploying solely a darknet.
- **Data Collection:** The data collection measure the quantity of data collected from the trap sensor. For instance, obviously, high interactive honeypot which stores bi-directional communication might collect more information than a darknet that saves solely unidirectional data.
- **Security:** The security feature measure the security level of implementing sensor on the monitoring side. For instance, the security of deploying a high interactive honeypot is high as the monitoring sensor might be threatened to become compromised.

Table 1 provides a comparison of network monitoring systems based on several features, namely, type of sensor, interactivity with the adversary, complexity of deployment, data collection or information gathering and the security on the monitoring sensor. First, Darknet and IP gray space share similar

Table 1. Monitoring Systems - Feature Comparison

Monitoring System	Type	Interactivity	Complexity	Data Collection	Security
Darknet	IP-based	N	L	L	S
IP Gray Space	IP-based	N	L	L	S
Low-interactive Honeypot	IP-based	L	L	L	V
Medium-interactive Honeypot	IP-based	M	M	M	V
High-interactive Honeypot	IP-based	H	H	H	V
Greynet	IP-based	N-LMH	LMH	LMH	S-V
Honeytoken	Digital-based	N-L	L	LMH	S

N: Null – L: Low – M: Medium – H: High – S: Safe – V: Vulnerable

Figure 2. Monitoring Systems – Address Space Distribution

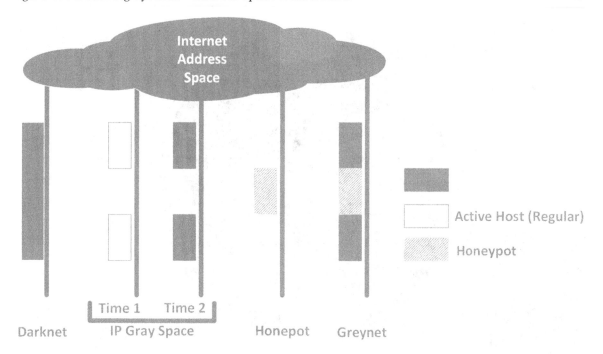

features due to the fact that the latter is darknet but running for a specific period of time. These two safe monitoring systems are running in passive mode (null interactivity) and their deployment and data gathering entities are considered low compared to other monitoring systems. Second, in regard to honeypots, the interactivity, the complexity and the data gathering are mostly proportion to each other. For instance, the more the interaction with the adversary, the more complex is the design and the more data is collected. However, concerning the security aspect, all honeypots which have interactive feature can be vulnerable in terms of security. Third, since greynet consists of darknet and honeypot, it is considered the more comprehensive monitoring system and therefore, it could have all the possibilities in terms of interactivity, complexity, data collection and security. Finally, honeytokens are the only digital-based entity which has null to low interactivity with the adversary depending on the monitored digital entity and low complexity due to the simplicity of running it. Further, this secure and safe monitoring system can have low to high data collection depending on the investigation focus.

Although some trap-based monitoring systems could have hybrid capabilities (e.g., running in both darknet and honeypot), Table 1 provided a high level understanding on typical trap-based sensors and highlighted the thin and gloomy lines that separate among them.

3.6.2 Address Space Distribution

In this section we provide a comparison between IP-based monitoring systems. Therefore, we omit honeytokens monitoring sensors which are digital-based entities. In order to visualize the address space distribution, Figure 2 depicts the address space scenarios of darknet, IP gray space, honeypot and greynet.

First, the darknet IP address space contains only unused addresses running in passive (inactive) mode. Second, the IP gray space (at time 2) is similar to darknet, however, the same address space was already

Figure 3. DAEDALUS-VIZ Overview (Inoue et al., 2012)

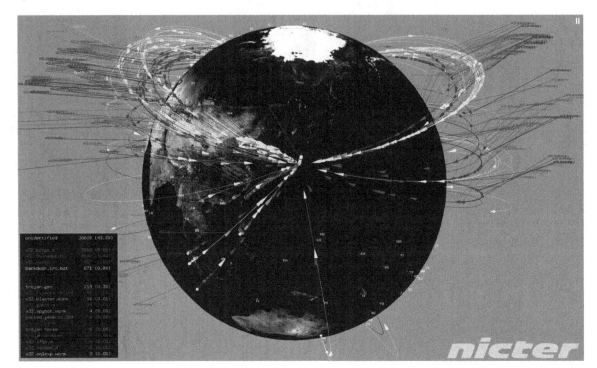

active in a previous period of time (time 1). Third, honeypots can run in any types of network, either solely on a network as shown in Figure 2 or with active hosts or passive host. The latter case represents the final scenario which is the greynet address distribution.

3.7 Case Studies

In this section, we provide two case studies based on the aforementioned monitoring systems. The first is based on a darknet traffic analysis whereas the second focused on honeypots.

3.7.1 Darknet-Based Case Study: DAEDALUS-VIZ

The first case study represents DAEDALUS-VIZ (Inoue, Eto, Suzuki, Suzuki, & Nakao, 2012) which is one of the large-scale cyber security projects (Nicter) that is based on the monitoring and the analysis of one type of trap-based monitoring system, namely, darknet. DAEDALUS-VIZ allows security operators to understand visually and in near real time the worldwide overview of security alerts. Moreover, the project provides high interactive and flexible tools to facilitate the investigation of large-scale cyber threats. An overview of the 3D visualization capability of this project is shown in Figure 3.

DAEDALUS-VIZ visualizes various darknet threat, namely, internal darknet alerts that are based on local scans in addition to external darknet alerts that are based on global scans and backscattered traffic from victims of DDoS (Moore et al., 2006). In addition, the project provides a novel technique to map IPv4 addresses on a sphere and other visualization shapes. Further, to the near real time processing, storing

Figure 4. System Architecture - Inspired by (Li et al., 2011)

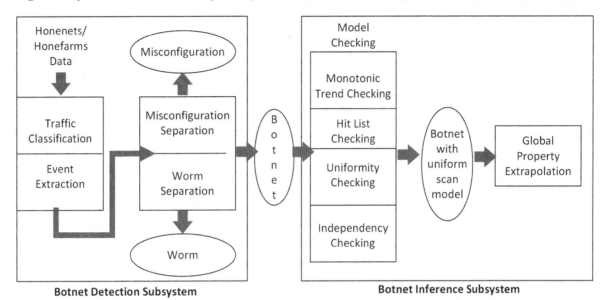

and displaying of information, DEADALUS-VIZ provides an overview system accompanied with drill down capabilities to investigate traces packet per packet. This is all running in an interactive platform which provides flexibility in viewpoint change, zooming capabilities, pausing/resuming services, among others. Most importantly, the system is customizable based on the investigator's need. Hence, security operators can change color, shape, size and position of the platform through a user friendly interface. Further, this visualization tool allows investigators to fine-grained data filtering operations.

3.7.2 Honeypot-Based Case Study: Situational Awareness of Large-Scale Botnet Probing Events

In this case study, we elaborate on a methodology to infer Botnet probing activities through Honeynets (multi honeypots). This case study do not solely infer the malicious activities, but also detect the strategy of the attack, its intention, its uniformity and coordination features. Figure 4 depicts the architecture overview of the botnet probing detection and inference system.

As shown above, the architecture is mainly composed of two main elements, namely the detection and the inference subsystems. In the detection phase, the system takes honeypots information as input, than it classifies traffic before extracting events. The output of the later exercise divide the output into 3 categories, namely, misconfiguration, worm, and botnet. Since this system aims to infer botnet information, the second subsystem takes as input the botnet data for further analysis. The later subsystem is capable, through statistical and probabilistic algorithms, to infer the monotonicity of the botnet, the hit list data, in addition to the uniformity and independency of the strategy (Li, Goyal, Chen, & Paxson, 2011). At the final stage, botnet traces that share similar properties are grouped as one botnet probing event. The output of the approach detected and inferred 203 botnet events that belong to 13 types of probes tackling various services such as HTTP, VNC, NetBIOS, MySQL, Telnet, etc.

4. SECURITY POLICIES AND LEGAL ISSUES

A cybercrime happens when both the action and the will are present. This section provides information on the security policies and legal issues while monitoring the Internet. Therefore, we aim to answer the following questions: Who has the capability to monitor the cyberspace? What are the privacy and security policies behind security analysis and deployment?

Since monitoring sensors (e.g., honeypot) are used to analyze data that is probably based on interactions with users (e.g., adversaries), these monitors might turn to legal responsibilities and several factors might turn them into liability. In this section, we provide an overview on the legal and security aspects of deploying, monitoring and analyzing monitoring data.

In the United States, there are at least three legal concerns to consider while deploying an interactive monitoring system. First, understanding the laws that restrict the owner of the security monitoring systems to monitor user activities. Second, addressing the risk and understanding that the monitoring system might be used by adversaries to harm others. Third, considering the fact that adversaries can argue that the monitoring service was operating undercover and entrapped them. In order to make things work perfectly, the owner of a trap-based monitoring system is recommended to ask a lawyer before implementing an interactive cyber sensor. Further, it is noteworthy to mention that cyber policies and restrictions might change depending on the country where the sensor is being deployed or/and the data is being analyzed.

4.1 Users Monitoring

Running and operating a monitoring system might be a simple exercise. However, having the legal right to monitor network activities of users might be the issue. Many sources might have restrictions on monitoring the cyber space such as privacy and employment policies, terms-of-service agreement, state and provincial laws, etc. Any violation of these laws might lead to civil liability and even criminal sanctions.

It is noteworthy to mention that monitoring cyber activities today takes a big attraction as it produces an exclusive insights for security operators, organizations, law enforcement agencies, governments and even adversaries.

4.1.1 Fourth Amendment

The *Fourth Amendment* limits the authority of government representatives to search or seize for evidence without first obtaining a search warrant from a judge. Since monitoring activities online could constitute a search and seizure, operating a monitoring system under a government agency direction might allow the *Fourth Amendment* of the US Constitution to restrict the monitoring process (Spitzner, 2003). Further, if the *Fourth Amendment* law applies, the evidence obtained from monitoring systems can be suppressed at trial and even individual can face a lawsuit. Only individuals who have a reasonable expectation of privacy can criticize the aforementioned law and complain that the examination was unconstitutional under *Fourth Amendment*. In general, in a lawsuit, hackers do not have a reasonable motive to support their malicious actives. However, a private investigator, who is not under the government direction might analyze monitoring systems data without obeying to the above mentioned amendment.

4.1.2 Wiretap Act

The *Wiretap Act* forbids any individual to intercept or/and sniff network communications unless an exception registered in the act is applied. Even if an adversary do have a reasonable expectation of privacy while trapped in a monitoring system, under the *Wiretap Act*, this does not provide permission of monitoring. It is noteworthy to mention that violating this act can lead to civil liability and even a federal offence. Several exceptions belong to this act such as the *Provider Protection* and the *Consent of a Party* exceptions. Owners of monitoring systems could use these two exceptions to listen to user activities online. However, if the analysis is done under the government's authorities, the owners can utilize the *Computer Trespasser* exception to monitor cyber communication. *Provider Protection* exception allows the owner to monitor data if and only if the purpose of this monitoring activities is to protect the owner's rights or/and property from malicious use of the Internet such as fraud, theft, etc.

Note that, cyber security laws are still not robust due to the fact that this topic is considered new and technology is changing in a rapid manner. For instance, the laws do not include yet honeypot in the *Provider Protection* exception.

Concerning the *Consent of a Party* exception, the owner can monitor the traffic only after providing the consent from the other entity. By doing this act, the other entity agrees to be monitored. In practice, honeypot owners can post/display a consent banner for users who access their monitoring systems. In this case, all users who access this network will be able to see, read and accept the terms on the consent banner. In today's world, this is similar to the case when ISP customers call their company by phone and the voice operator inform the users that this phone call might be recorded for a certain reason. It is noteworthy to mention that consent banner might not work on all network services and must be specific or general depending on the service used (Spitzner, 2003).

4.1.3 Patriot Act

The *Computer Trespasser* is another exception that is part of the US *Patriot Act* that was passed in 2001. This exception allows government to monitor hackers in some cases without securing a warrant. This exception applies to users that are acting as a government agents to monitor adversaries' activities if: i) the network's operator has legally allow the capture; ii) the user who is performing the monitoring service is affiliated to a lawful investigation; and iii) if the person has a convincing reason and believe that the monitored traces will be appropriate to the investigation. This act might be useful when the honeypot is running under the operation of government or law enforcement agencies.

4.2 Harming Others

While communication with hackers, monitoring system might be easily compromised. Therefore, security operators must be careful to reduce the risk of harming others unintentionally. Hackers can control monitoring systems, their bandwidth and network resources to turn them into malicious tools. Some good practices used on the monitoring systems include listening to their output traffic, controlling its parameters such as rates/bandwidth, filtering out suspicious activities and dropping blocking services/domains/IPs when necessary. This exercise require not just proper deployment of sensors, but also maintaining monitoring sensors' activities. Otherwise, monitoring systems can easily and rapidly be transformed to a network entity that belongs to adversaries (e.g., bot). Consequently, this entity can be used for storing malicious files, stolen information, and distributing malicious content such as child pornography and spam emails, etc.

4.3 Entrapment

The supreme court defines entrapment as "the conception and planning of an offense by an officer, and his procurement of its commission by one who would not have perpetrated it except the trickery, persuasion, or fraud of the officers" (Mikell, 1942). Entrapment can be a concern for honeypot owners due to the fact that criminals can use it in an attempt to evade conviction. However, a defendant that was not induced by law enforcement authorities to commit a crime cannot utilize the entrapment to defend the case. It is notable to mention that entrapment policies apply solely in the context of criminal prosecution and hence, it is not applicable to private security monitoring owners.

5. FUTURE RESEARCH DIRECTIONS

For future work, security operators are required to look deeply into, but not limited to, the following areas:

- **IPv6 Security:** IPv6 is going to be the new era of Internet address space due to the fact that IPv4 addresses are about to get congested. Further, hackers are always one step beyond security operators and hence they will focus on new systems to abuse it. IPv6 is one of the most promising targets (Warfield, 2003). For instance, amplified DDoS attacks, which are based on the size of the packets, can be more harmful when using IPv6 (rather than IPv4) since IPv6 packet is larger in size. Moreover, IPv6 packets have built-in packet-level encryption and considered more secure than IPv4 traffic, hence, it might cause more challenges for network operators to investigate malicious behavior within its traffic. As of today, the majority of the current deployment, monitoring and analysis is based on IPv4 traffic. Very few works are done on IPv6 (Baker, Harrop, & Armitage, 2010). Therefore, security operators and researchers are recommended to focus on this area by setting up more IPv6 monitoring sensors to uncover cyber attacks that are embedded in IPv6 traffic.
- **Cloud Security:** Cloud is going to be the first service used on the cyber space. On the cloud, the number of services, users and data is enormous. Therefore, adversaries will consider the cloud as the best place to attack due to the fact that enormous architecture means large impact and easy to obfuscate. Several cloud security issues exist today (Kandukuri, Paturi, & Rakshit, 2009) and very few security measures are deployed. All security operators must think in an enormous scale while installing security services on the cloud. This might require merging several security operators and systems to cope with the cloud security challenge such as a centralized large-scale cyber monitoring service using trap-based monitoring systems as well as firewalls and antivirus tools.

6. CONCLUSION

Internet users are growing intensely in numbers due to the advanced in computer applications today such as social media, cloud services, online shopping, among others. Consequently, information sharing in general and security in particular became a challenge for network operators, Internet service providers, organizations, law enforcement agencies and governments. This provocation is raised due to the lack of big data handling, storing, monitoring and analyses. In order to cope with this challenge, several cyber monitoring systems are used on different IP layers such as networks and applications. In this work, we have discussed that one of the best techniques to monitor the cyber space is to trap adversaries by installing monitoring systems such as darknet, IP gray space, honeypot, greynet and honeytokens. In general, these systems run on unused but routable address space, and hence all traffic destined to them might be suspicious. Darknet and IP gray space operate in passive (inactive) mode whereas honeypot and greynet can operative in active mode. Among all the aforementioned trap-based monitoring systems, only honeytokens is based on a digital entity, whereas the others are focused on IP services. It is noteworthy to mention that some monitoring systems provide hybrid services and can operate in different modes (passive and active) like honeyd (Provos, 2003). Since each type of monitoring system has its own advantages and disadvantages, a good practice is to deploy several services to cover all security aspects. Note that, these systems do not replace other security monitoring and detection services such as intrusion detection systems. In contrary, trap-based monitoring services must run in parallel with IDS and other security services such as firewalls and antivirus tools. Therefore, hybrid monitoring systems are considered to be the best options to choose while deploying a security monitoring system. This chapter discussed various cyber security threats that can be inferred by analyzing traces from the above mentioned monitoring systems such as scanning/probing activities, DDoS attacks, worm propagation, botnet C&C, and malware infections. In general, passive monitoring is decent in inferring scanning/probing and DDoS activities whereas active monitoring, which is interactive with the adversary, is more attractive to botnet and malware activities.

In general, we have seen that deploying passive network monitoring systems is easier than installing and configuring an active monitoring systems. Nevertheless, the easiest trap-based monitoring system to deploy is the honeytoken which is based on providing a bogus digital information such as fake credit card information to an adversary and then monitoring its activities to infer insights on the malicious behavior such as the intention of the attack. However, in general, implementing a trap-based monitoring system is becoming an easy task today as some commercial organizations provide services to install a ready-to-go sensor or even provide the extracted data extracted from the sensor even without deploying it at the client side. Finally, concerning the security policies and legal issues, we have seen that cyber security laws are still in a gray area due to the fact that cyber security is still considered a new topic and therefore several laws are not applicable to specific areas such as trap-based monitoring systems. As a result of the rapid and recent growth in cyber technology, more laws must be updates and new ones must be created.

REFERENCES

Allman, M., Paxson, V., & Terrell, J. (2007, October). A brief history of scanning. In *Proceedings of the 7th ACM SIGCOMM conference on Internet measurement* (pp. 77-82). ACM. doi:10.1145/1298306.1298316

Bailey, M., Cooke, E., Jahanian, F., Myrick, A., & Sinha, S. (2006, March). Practical darknet measurement. In *40th Annual Conference on Information Sciences and Systems*, 2006 (pp. 1496-1501). IEEE.

Baker, F., Harrop, W., & Armitage, G. (2010). IPv4 and IPv6 Greynets.

Bellovin, S. M. (1992, September). There be dragons. In *UNIX Security Symposium III Proceedings* (pp. 1-16).

Bou-Harb, E., Debbabi, M., & Assi, C. (2013). A systematic approach for detecting and clustering distributed cyber scanning. *Computer Networks*, *57*(18), 3826–3839. doi:10.1016/j.comnet.2013.09.008

Dagon, D., Gu, G., Lee, C. P., & Lee, W. (2007, December). A taxonomy of botnet structures. In *Computer Security Applications Conference, 2007. ACSAC 2007. Twenty-Third Annual* (pp. 325-339). IEEE. doi:10.1109/ACSAC.2007.44

Fachkha, C., Bou-Harb, E., Boukhtouta, A., Dinh, S., Iqbal, F., & Debbabi, M. (2012, October). Investigating the dark cyberspace: Profiling, threat-based analysis and correlation. In *Risk and Security of Internet and Systems (CRiSIS), 2012 7th International Conference on* (pp. 1-8). IEEE.

Fachkha, C., Bou-Harb, E., & Debbabi, M. (2014, March). Fingerprinting Internet DNS amplification DDoS activities. In *6th International Conference on New Technologies, Mobility and Security (NTMS)*, (pp. 1-5). IEEE.

Fachkha, C., Bou-Harb, E., & Debbabi, M. (2015). Inferring distributed reflection denial of service attacks from darknet. *Computer Communications*, *62*, 59–71. doi:10.1016/j.comcom.2015.01.016

Freiling, F. C., Holz, T., & Wicherski, G. (2005). *Botnet tracking: Exploring a root-cause methodology to prevent distributed denial-of-service attacks.* (pp. 319–335). Springer Berlin Heidelberg.

Groot, G. J. D., Rekhter, Y., Karrenberg, D., & Lear, E. (1996). Address Allocation for Private Internets.

Harrop, W., & Armitage, G. (2005, November). Defining and evaluating greynets (sparse darknets). In *the IEEE Conference on Local Computer Networks, 2005.* (pp. 344-350). IEEE.

Inoue, D., Eto, M., Suzuki, K., Suzuki, M., & Nakao, K. (2012, October). DAEDALUS-VIZ: novel real-time 3D visualization for darknet monitoring-based alert system. In *Proceedings of the Ninth International Symposium on Visualization for Cyber Security* (pp. 72-79). ACM. doi:10.1145/2379690.2379700

World Internet Users and Population Stats. (2014). *Internet World Stats*. Retrieved from http://www.internetworldstats.com/stats.htm

Jin, Y., Simon, G., Xu, K., Zhang, Z. L., & Kumar, V. (2007, April). Gray's anatomy: Dissecting scanning activities using IP gray space analysis. In *Proceedings of the 2nd USENIX workshop on Tackling computer systems problems with machine learning techniques* (pp. 1-6). USENIX Association.

Jin, Y., Zhang, Z. L., Xu, K., Cao, F., & Sahu, S. (2007, June). Identifying and tracking suspicious activities through IP gray space analysis. In *Proceedings of the 3rd annual ACM workshop on Mining network data* (pp. 7-12). ACM. doi:10.1145/1269880.1269883

Kandukuri, B. R., Paturi, V. R., & Rakshit, A. (2009, September). Cloud security issues. In *IEEE International Conference on Services Computing. SCC'09.* (pp. 517-520). IEEE.

Li, Z., Goyal, A., Chen, Y., & Paxson, V. (2011). Towards situational awareness of large-scale botnet probing events. *IEEE Transactions on Information Forensics and Security, 6*(1), 175–188. doi:10.1109/TIFS.2010.2086445

Lilien, L., Kamal, Z. H., Bhuse, V., & Gupta, A. (2006). Opportunistic networks: the concept and research challenges in privacy and security. *Proc. of the WSPWN*, 134-147.

Mikell, W. E. (1942). The Doctrine of Entrapment in the Federal Courts. *University of Pennsylvania Law Review and American Law Register*, 245-265.

Mirkovic, J., Dietrich, S., Dittrich, D., & Reiher, P. (2004). *Internet Denial of Service: Attack and Defense Mechanisms (Radia Perlman Computer Networking and Security)*. Prentice Hall PTR.

Mokube, I., & Adams, M. (2007, March). Honeypots: concepts, approaches, and challenges. In *Proceedings of the 45th annual southeast regional conference* (pp. 321-326). ACM. doi:10.1145/1233341.1233399

Moore, D. (2003). Network Telescopes: Tracking Denial-of-Service Attacks and Internet Worms Around the Globe. In LISA.

Moore, D., & Shannon, C. (2002, November). Code-Red: a case study on the spread and victims of an Internet worm. In *Proceedings of the 2nd ACM SIGCOMM Workshop on Internet measurement* (pp. 273-284). ACM. doi:10.1145/637201.637244

Moore, D., Shannon, C., Brown, D. J., Voelker, G. M., & Savage, S. (2006). Inferring internet denial-of-service activity. [TOCS]. *ACM Transactions on Computer Systems, 24*(2), 115–139. doi:10.1145/1132026.1132027

Nakashima, E., Miller, G., & Tate, J. (2012). US, Israel developed Flame computer virus to slow Iranian nuclear efforts, officials say. *The Washington Post*.

Pang, R., Yegneswaran, V., Barford, P., Paxson, V., & Peterson, L. (2004, October). Characteristics of internet background radiation. In *Proceedings of the 4th ACM SIGCOMM conference on Internet measurement* (pp. 27-40). ACM. doi:10.1145/1028788.1028794

Provos, N. (2003, February). Honeyd-a virtual honeypot daemon. In *10th DFN-CERT Workshop, Hamburg, Germany* (Vol. 2).

Provos, N. (2004, August). A Virtual Honeypot Framework. In *USENIX Security Symposium* (Vol. 173).

Provos, N., & Holz, T. (2007). *Virtual honeypots: from botnet tracking to intrusion detection*. Pearson Education.

Skoudis, E. (2004). *Malware: Fighting malicious code*. Prentice Hall Professional.

Spitzner, L. (2003). The honeynet project: Trapping the hackers. *IEEE Security and Privacy*, *1*(2), 15–23. doi:10.1109/MSECP.2003.1193207

Spitzner, L. (2003). Honeytokens: The other honeypot.

Stallings, W. (1998). *SNMP, SNMPv2, SNMPv3, and RMON 1 and 2*. Boston, MA: Addison-Wesley Longman Publishing Co., Inc.

Technical Details Behind a 400Gbps NTP Amplification DDoS Attack. (2014CloudFlare. Retrieved from.

Wang, H. J., Guo, C., Simon, D. R., & Zugenmaier, A. (2004, August). Shield: Vulnerability-driven network filters for preventing known vulnerability exploits. [ACM.]. *Computer Communication Review*, *34*(4), 193–204. doi:10.1145/1030194.1015489

Warfield, M. H. (2003). Security implications of IPv6. *Internet Security Systems*, *4*(1), 2–5.

Wustrow, E., Karir, M., Bailey, M., Jahanian, F., & Huston, G. (2010, November). Internet background radiation revisited. In *Proceedings of the 10th ACM SIGCOMM conference on Internet measurement* (pp. 62-74). ACM.

ADDITIONAL READING SECTION

Curran, K., Morrissey, C., Fagan, C., Murphy, C., O'Donnell, B., Fitzpatrick, G., & Condit, S. (2005). Monitoring hacker activity with a Honeynet. *International Journal of Network Management*, *15*(2), 123–134. doi:10.1002/nem.549

Joshi, R. C., & Sardana, A. (Eds.). (2011). *Honeypots: A New Paradigm to Information Security*. CRC Press.

Krawetz, N. (2004). Anti-honeypot technology. *Security & Privacy, IEEE*, *2*(1), 76–79. doi:10.1109/MSECP.2004.1264861

•Pouget, F., & Dacier, M. (2004, May). Honeypot-based forensics. In AusCERT Asia Pacific Information Technology Security Conference.

Pouget, F., Dacier, M., & Pham, V. H. (2005). On the Advantages of Deploying a Large Scale Distributed Honeypot Platform. In *Proceedings of the E-Crime and Computer Evidence Conference*.

Yegneswaran, V., Barford, P., & Paxson, V. (2005). Using honeynets for internet situational awareness. In *Proc. of ACM Hotnets IV*.

KEY TERMS AND DEFINITIONS

Antivirus: An Antivirus is a computer software with an aim to prevent, detect, identify and remove malicious malware and viruses.

ARP: In multiple access networks, the Address Resolution Protocol (ARP) is designed to resolve network layer addresses to link layer addresses.

Backscatter: In a communication protocol, backscatter traffic are packets or traffic that is based on the reply packets (e.g., SYN-ACK, ACK).

CPU: The Central Processing Unit (CPU) is a hardware device inside a computer machine that is responsible on performing basic and logical computer operations.

DDoS: A Distributed DoS (DDoS) is among the most sever cyber attack where adversary bombards the victim with large amount of data/requests in order to exhaust its bandwidth or/and network and host resources.

DNS Amplification: One type of DDoS attack where the attacker try to send amplified replies to the victim in order to exhaust its bandwidth or/and network and host resources.

Firewall: A firewall is a computer hardware or software that has an aim to control the security of the network by applying rule set on the incoming and outgoing traffic.

HTTP: The Hypertext Transfer Protocol (HTTP) is a fundamental data communication process for the World Wide Web (www). It consists of an application protocol for distributing and collaborating hypermedia data systems.

ICMP ECHO: The Internet Control Message Protocol (ICMP) is a core element on the IP layer. This protocol is responsible on the control and error handling of messages among devices such as routers. ICMP messages are many. ECHO message is one type of ICMP.

IRC: Internet Relay Chat (IRC) is a computer program used to transfer text message between two entities.

ISP: An Internet Service Provider is a certified organization for providing Internet services.

Malware: A malware is a piece of code that is malicious.

MySQL: MySQL is one of the most famous open source database with an aim to store, organize and retrieve information.

NetBIOS: A Network Basic Input/output System (NetBIOS) provides communication services related to session layer of the Internet and permitting Local Area Network communications among devices.

P2P: Pear-to-Pear (P2P) is a communication technology where each client can be either client or server.

Root: In Unix Operating Systems, Root is equivalent to a super user with usually full administrative privileges.

SNMP: Simple Network Management (SNMP) protocol is used for managing devises in a network.

Spoof: IP address spoofing is the phenomenon of forging the source IP address for concealing the identity of the sender or impersonating another identity (e.g. victim).

TCP: The Transmission Control Protocol (TCP) is one of the major transport protocol that operates on top of the IP protocol. The aim of this protocol is to transmit data in a reliable manner.

Telnet: Telnet is a network service that provides an interactive text-based communication facilities through a virtual terminal network.

UDP: Similar to the TCP protocol, the User Datagram Protocol (UDP) is another core element on the transport layer. The aim of this protocol is to transmit data in a fast manner.

VM: A Virtual Machine (VM) is a computer program that emulates a real (physical) machine. A virtual machine can be used for several purposes such as (testing, learning, etc.).

VNC: A Virtual Network Computing is a remote desktop sharing protocol used to control another device.

Chapter 5
The Rigorous Security Risk Management Model:
State of the Art

Neila Rjaibi
Department of Computer science, Institut Supérieur de Gestion de Tunis (ISG), Tunisia

Latifa Ben Arfa Rabai
Department of Computer science, Institut Supérieur de Gestion de Tunis (ISG), Tunisia

ABSTRACT

This chapter presents the security concepts terminologies (threat, risk, security risk management, security risk management process, security threat model) and present the state of the art of security risk management models, compare and discuss strengths and weaknesses of such models. Then it presents the Mean Failure Cost (MFC) model for quantifying security threats as a rigorous measure of cyber security, and as a cascade of linear models in order to estimate the system security using the loss of a given stakeholders as a result of security breakdown. Finally it presents an overview of the applicability of the MFC measure to e-systems. In the conclusion, the chapter criticizes the MFC Cyber Security Measure and presents an overview of different perspectives.

INTRODUCTION

Actually the Internet is the main source of all threats and illegal activities. Consequently, E-systems are threatened exponentially, statistics have shown that organizations are currently investing in security resources. It has been shown that through 2005 the total global revenue for security products and service vendors amounted to $21.1 billion. Another source indicated that from 1999 to 2000, the number of organizations spending more than $ 1 million annually on security nearly doubled. So, expenditures have increased from 12% of all organizations revenues in 1999 to 23% in 2000 (Ekelhart et al., 2009). In fact, it is a challenging task for organizations to put the emphasis on security risk management in order to measure and assess security risk and provide a good plan for risk mitigation.

DOI: 10.4018/978-1-4666-8456-0.ch005

They are obliged to put emphasis on security risk management in order to measure and assess security risk and provide a good plan for risk mitigation.

This chapter:

- Presents the security concepts terminologies (threat, risk, security risk management, security risk management process, security threat model)
- Presents the state of the art of security risk management models, compare and discuss strengths and weaknesses of such models
- Presents the MFC model for quantifying security threats as a rigorous measure of cyber security, and as a cascade of linear models in order to estimate the system security using the loss of a given stakeholders as a result of security breakdown.
- Presents an overview of the applicability of the MFC measure to e-systems
- Criticizes the MFC Cyber Security Measure and present an overview of different perspectives.

SECURITY TERMINOLOGIES

The Threat Concept

In the first step it is necessary to define the term 'risk' and 'threat' because there is an important distinction between them. According to Bruce Schneier (2003) a threat is defined as: "a potential way an attacker can attack a system". Commonly known, threats for computers are viruses, network penetrations, theft and unauthorized modification of data, eavesdropping, and non-availability of servers.

A threat is also defined as a category of object, person or other entities that present a danger. Like spam, Trojan horse and fishing (Whitman & Mattord, 2004 ; Stoneburner et al., 2002).

The Risk Concept

A risk is the product of the probability that a particular threat will occur and the expected loss.

According to Bruce Schneier (2003), when we talk about risk, it is the likelihood of the threat and the seriousness of its successful attack. For example a threat is more serious because it is more likely to occur.

Another definition supported the same concept than the product of the financial losses associated with security incidents and the probability that they occur. The risk of security threat as a quantitative measure is a suitable input to decision making (Ryan & Ryan, 2006; Tsiakis & Stephanides, 2005; Mili & Sheldon, 2009; Sommestad et al., 2010). Therefore the purpose of considering risk as a financial measure leads to making decision from business perspective. For example, the return on security investment: ROI measure (Aissa et al., 2010 a; Cavusoglu et al., 2004; Bojanc & Jerman-Blazic, 2008) and the mean failure cost: MFC measure presented in (Mili & Sheldon, 2009; Aissa et al., 2010 a; Aissa et al., 2010 b).

Finally, security is defined as the inverse of risk, because there is a secure system when nothing happens, risk refers to the loss but it is a concept that is difficult to measure (Ryan & Ryan, 2006).

Table 1. The Assessment of threats

Threats	Probability (likelihood)	Damage (cost of failure)	Risk = Probability* Damage
T1	P1	D1	R1= P1*D1
...	...	...	...
Tn	Pn	Dn	R2=Pn*Dn

SECURITY RISK MANAGEMENT DEFINITIONS

Security risk management allows the determination of the worthiest attack and the ignored one, it is one way to focus on the serious attacks to better manage the budget and find the best way to use it. Hence, we need to focus on the risks rather than on the threats. To do so, we need to measure the risk and to quantify it (Scheier, 2003; Ryan & Ryan, 2006). Because sometimes we cannot exclude the risks, our purpose is then to reduce it to a manageable level. Then, security risk management is fundamental in every organization (Cummings et al., 2006). In fact, a threat determines the risk, and for each risk we can determine the countermeasures.

In a quantitative security risk management there are two input variables that need to be fixed, the probability that a threat occurs and the loss suffered from a successful attack (Aissa et al., 2010 a ; Ryan & Ryan, 2006 ; Tsiakis & Stephanides, 2005 ; Sommestad et al., 2010) . Our focus is the risks rather than the threats; it is useful to measure the risk and to quantify it.

In order to assess the risk of the identified threats, we need to prioritize threats by using two factors: damage and likelihood as presented in table 1. First, we need to calculate the risk factor for each threats, second we intend to sort the threat list in decreasing order of risk. Third, we consider the worthiest threat starting at the top of the list, and searching way to better manage it. Therefore, there are four possible ways to manage a risk (Myagmar et al., 2005):

- Accept the risk - The risk is so low and so costly to mitigate that it is worth accepting.
- Transfer the risk - Transfer the risk to somebody else via insurance, warnings etc.
- Remove the risk - Remove the system component or feature associated with the risk if the feature is not worth the risk.

One very important question that may be asked in security management is: why should we quantify security threats? It is clear that by quantifying the two variables, meaningful indication about risk assessment and good business decision makers are provided. Furthermore Mohd Alwi and Fan (2010 a) also suggest that security information management is useful in increasing competition, adequate cash, profitability and commercial image. Results of analysis security threats may also be useful in practical plan to provide us with pertinent information in order to implement a secure environment.

The second question that may be asked: "How security threats are quantified to provide better business decision?" The answer is provided in the next paragraph; hence it is essential to follow the security risk management process.

SECURITY RISK MANAGEMENT PROCESS

Threatened organizations are obliged to emphasize on security risk management in order to measure and assess security risks and provide a good risk mitigation plan. It is a good solution to determine the critical threats, the ignored ones and the most serious attacks in order to better manage them.

Each project needs to have a security risk analysis process to assess security threats and their potential impact in order to anticipate attacks, to weaken their impact and to propose some countermeasures. Therefore, security risk management should uses guidelines (MohdAlwi & Fan, 2010 b; Ekelhart et al., 2009; Stoneburner et al., 2002; Bojanc & Jerman-Blazic, 2008) which can be summarized as follows:

a. Identification of assets: We need to examine security characteristics in compliance with the supported infrastructure application and mention some related security incidents and problems. A survey methodology for expert users is recommended in order to better understand the main threats of the related environment.
b. Estimation of threats and risks calculation: By understanding the main threats and particular situation in the related environment, the framework for information security management can be easily designed.
c. Setting priority and security decision
d. Implementation of controls and counter measures: It covers the future preventive actions and appropriate controls
e. Monitoring of risks and of the effectiveness of counter measures.

Despite the best efforts of security researchers, it is impossible to guarantee 100% security. But we can establish a good security system strikes using the risk management process. In addition, risk management consists of risk assessment and risk reduction (Myagmar et al., 2005).

That is why we need to use security risk management models whether it is quantitative or qualitative because they are fundamental in every organization, in fact, threats determine the risks, and for risks, we envision the countermeasures (Scheier, 2003; Ryan & Ryan, 2006).

THE SECURITY THREAT MODEL

Based on security requirements, the first step in all security management process is to define a security threat model, according to Nickolova and Nickolov (2007). It is necessary and not sufficient to implement a secure system with high quality, to choose strong authentication and encryption techniques. Quantitative solution needed to be implemented to help in computing actual attacks. In general, it is difficult to reach 100% rate of system security, that's why we need to imagine preventive threats in the secure system design phase. We may often ask the following question: Secure against what? And the answer is provided by the threat model. Threat model can help us to anticipate attacks, their impact and countermeasures, that's why we need to model security threat because it will:

•   Characterize the attacker: to identify its goals, motivation and capabilities
•   Identify assets and entry points
•   Identify and classify the threats: make a description of threats in order to prepare to mitigation techniques.

To quantify security threat a quantitative threat model needed to be designed, it is a description of a set of security aspects specific to a system and a set of possible attacks. Also, more than one model can be defined to one computer system when the system is complex. This model is needed to help us to assess threat probability and the risk of attacks. Threat modeling focuses on the idea that any system has assets, for each asset we can identify a set of vulnerabilities that could be protected from internal or external threat. Then we can conclude some countermeasures to mitigate this threat.

Furthermore Mohd Alwi and Fan (2010 a) suggest that the advantage of modeling security threat using the matrix of threats risk can increase the user's awareness when they use the applications and materials and can be a guide for users to protect themselves from threats.

SECURITY RISK MANAGEMENT MODELS

Many security risk management models like Single Loss Expectancy (SLE), the Mean Failure Cost (MFC), The Bayesian Defense Graphs and Architectural Models, The Availability, Integrity, Confidentiality and Authentication (AICA), The improving web application security model (IWAS), CRAMM, NIST SP 800-30, CORAS, OCTAVE, EBIOS, and ISO 27005 and others (Aissa et al., 2012; Aissa et al., 2010a; Nickolova & Nickolov, 2007; MohdAlwi & Fan, 2010 a ; Fenz & Ekelhart, 2009; Sommestad et al., 2009; Karabacak & Sogukpinar, 2005) are introduced to assess the risk and define the best schedule that we need to follow in order to monitor the critical risk in the best time with a low budget. The next section will discuss some well known security risk management models and their related characteristics.

The Mean Failure Cost (MFC): A Cascade of Linear Models

Anis et al. (2010 b, 2012) have presented a recent value based measure of cyber-security, it computes for each stakeholder of the given system his or her loss of operation ($/H). They used the Mean Failure Cost (MFC) metric which is a cascade of linear models to quantify security threat in term of loss that results from system vulnerabilities (Mili & Sheldon, 2007). In addition, Anis et al. (2009) implemented a tool that automatically computes the MFC for a given system, it calculates MFC metrics. The MFC is the estimation of system security using the loss of a given stakeholder as a result of security breakdown.

The Automated Risk and Utility Management (AURUM) Model

The AURUM is a recent risk management approach; it presents a detailed security knowledge domain based on ontological framework structure using a variety of information gathering techniques like questionnaires, interviews, document reviews, and automated scanning tools, the AURUM prototype is useful in supporting decision makers and choosing the appropriate security measures (Fenz & Tjoa, 2008; Fenz & Ekelhart, 2009; Ekelhart et al., 2009).

The Bayesian Defense Graphs and Architectural Model

This model presents a new and recent approach for security risk management based on the creation of trees and graph structures to derive probabilities. The framework uses Bayesian statistics and especially the Extended Influence Diagrams to represent attack graphs and related countermeasures; it forms a compact representation of attack graphs and defense mechanisms (Sommestad et al., 2010 ; Abercrombie et al., 2011). Further refinements are created on developing abstract classes, then, on deriving the dependency model and its assets relationships (Sommestad et al., 2009).

The Single Loss Expectancy (SLE)

The Single Loss Expectancy (SLE) is the measure of the monetary value (euros, dollars, yens, etc.) expected from the occurrence of a risk on an asset. The mathematical formula is (Karabacak & Sogukpinar, 2005):

$$Single\ Loss\ Expectancy\ (SLE) = Asset\ Value\ (AV)\ x\ Exposure\ Factor\ (EF) \tag{1}$$

Where:

- The (EF) is the impact of the risk, or the percentage of asset lost.
- As an example: when the (AV) is reduced by two thirds then the exposure factor value is about .66. When we have a complete loss of the asset, the Exposure Factor is 1.0.

Other Metrics of Security

Quantitative models are provided to measure reliability and safety of a given system. A variety of system reliability measure is discussed in the literature (Mili & Sheldon, 2009; Abercrombie et al., 2009 ; Mili & Sheldon, 2007): the Mean Time to Failure (MTTF), other variations of it are the: mean time to detection of a vulnerability (MTTD), and the mean time to exploitation of vulnerability (MTTE), they are adopted to measure security dependability.

The MTTF has some inconvenience comparing to the MFC system reliability measure:

- Independence of failure cost with respect to sub specificities: The MTTF makes no distinction between requirements
- Independence with respect to stakeholders: It is not dependent on the stakeholder but depends exclusively on the system under observation.
- Independence of failure probability with respect to sub specificities: any failure with respect to any sub specificity is a failure with respect to the whole specificity

COMPARING AND DISCUSSING SECURITY RISK MANAGEMENT MODELS

Regarding the quantitative MFC model applied to an E-commerce application we note that it is independent from the system architecture based on a three matrix and a vector.

The AURUM approach uses Bayesian networks to determine threat probabilities objectively, and based on a consistent structure of security ontology model that provides information on threat dependencies to the risk manager. It also incorporates existing best-practice guidelines and information security standards for threat/vulnerability authentication and control recommendations. Other benefits regarding existing approaches are the computing of threat impacts. In addition, the decision makers can visualize various security scenarios and characteristics using the interactive decision support. Decisions are easily taking in an objective way of cost and danger of the problem (Fenz & Ekelhart, 2009; Ekelhart et al., 2009) . But this approach seems not appropriate in probability and risk number determination, it defines a number for each scale, for example: High (> 50 to 100), Medium (> 10 to 50), Low (1 to 10) regarding the first threat 3x3 risk matrix and following the NIST SP 800-30 guidelines (Ekelhart et al., 2009).These numbers are not precise enough.

The Bayesian networks probabilistic network is advantageous in creating a structured diagram and reducing the complexity of graphs. Second it is useful in presenting attack graphs and defense mechanisms on the same graph, third the framework can be refined iteratively by adding a large amount of information, therefore uncertainty is reduced and a good knowledge about attacks and countermeasures are concluded (Sommestad et al., 2009 ; Sommestad et al., 2010). This is beneficial to managing security within such a complex system.

The Single Loss Expectancy metrics give us the monetary value when the asset is threatened.

Other known approaches such as CRAMM, NIST SP 800-30, CORAS, OCTAVE, EBIOS, and ISO 27005 deal with a variety of features (Ekelhart et al., 2009):

- They cover a set of security guidelines
- The French EBIOS standard provides a full knowledge about threats, vulnerabilities, and countermeasures, but without referring to an expert, it does not consider complex relationships between security concepts-
- The information security standards ISO 27001 is a very abstract implementation for risk mitigation
- They determine the threat probabilities based on subjective evaluation
- They need a domain expert who is very expensive in the whole process.

For the MFC it is a measure of dependability, it varies by stakeholders, threats, requirements and architectural component, it is more than a cyber security metric. It is quantified in economic terms as a monetary value per unit of operational time, and measure the amount of risk that each stakeholder is incurring as a result of security threats and system vulnerabilities. This leads to further good quantitative analysis.

The MTTD and the MTTE present the same shortcomings presented in the discussion of MTTF; they form an abstract measure of the failure rate of the considered system. In front of the proposed limits of the MTTF measure, the MFC is the best solution to measure system security reliability; it considers the variance in failure cost from one sub-specification to another, the variance in failure probability from one sub-specification to another, and the variance in failure cost from one stakeholder to another. The reality that MFC is more meaningful than MTTF is proved by Mili and Sheldon in (Mili & Sheldon, 2007).

The MFC measure of dependability takes into account complex system specifications, and considers variations by stakeholder, specification components, and threats.

In order to adopt good quantified security threat measure, we need to adopt the MFC dependability metric. Another idea is to consider the combination of other abstract metrics: MTTD, MTTE and the MTTF. The reason is when using them individually it does not provide good knowledge to security threats management context. Therefore the best way to assess security is the use of a combination of these methods.

E-systems require a quantitative security threats model based on financial business risk measure which is the measure of cost. It is of our interest to illustrate the MFC in a practical security risk assessment process and to highlight its strengths in the science of cyber security estimation.

THE MFC MODEL AS A MEASURE OF SECURITY RISK MANAGEMENT

Origin of the MFC: The Cyber Security Econometrics System (CSES)

The CSES model presents an infrastructure to estimate system security in terms of the loss that each stakeholder stands as a result of security breakdowns (Abercrombie et al., 2008 ; Sheldon et al., 2009).

- The CSES is adapted to eDomain(s) Econometrics System like e-Commerce, e-Learning, e-Goverenment
- It is a quantitative model that measures the reliability and safety of a system
- It calculates the importance of each requirement as a function of one or more stakeholders' interests in that requirement
- Utilizes the concept of Mean Failure Cost (MFC)
    - It is the loss of a stakeholder due to a requirement or component of the system failing
    - It is independent from the system but varies from a stakeholder to another

Presentation of the MFC Features

A recent value based measure of cyber-security is presented in (Aissa et al., 2012), it computes for each stakeholder of the given system his loss of operation ($/H). They used the Mean failure Cost (MFC) metric which is a cascade of linear models to quantify security threat in term of loss that results from system vulnerabilities.

This quantitative model is a cascade of linear models to quantify security threats in term of loss that results from system vulnerabilities. In addition, Anis et al. (2012) implemented a tool that automatically computes the MFC for a given system, it calculate MFC metrics.

Anis et al. (2010 a) discuss the Boehm's model and present a new quantitative security model throughout mean failure cost. The MFC is the estimation of system security using the metric loss of a given stakeholders as a result of security breakdowns or threat. They define the MFC as:

$$MFC = ST \circ DP \circ IM \circ PT \tag{2}$$

Where ST, DP and IM are three matrixes: the stake matrix, the dependency matrix and the impact matrix. Finally the PT is the vector of probability. More details are given in Table 2.

Furthermore, it is explained in the following table, It seems that Anis et al's model is very similar to the top level stakeholders value dependency matrix from Boehm's model expect some difference in the organization of rows and columns and the new contribution is that entries are real number expressed in $/Hour while in the Boehm's model are in discrete sale (e.g., *)

Table 2. The concept of Mean failure Cost (MFC)

MFC	• Is a vector • Entries = system stakeholders	MFC(H)	Is the mean failure cost of stakeholders= cost ($/H)
ST: Stake matrix	• Is a matrix • Rows= stakeholders • Columns= security requirements	ST(H,R)	• Is the stake that stakeholders H satisfy a requirement R • Is quantified in terms of cost per unit of operation time:$/Hour
DP: Dependency matrix	• Is a matrix • Rows= security requirements • Columns= system components	DP(R,C)	The probability that the system fails to meet requirement R if component C is compromise
IM: Impact matrix	• Is a matrix • Rows= system components Columns= security threat	IM(C,T)	The probability that Component C is compromised if Threat T has materialized
PT: Vector of probability	• Is a vector • Entries: Threat	PT(T)	The probability that threat T materialized for a unit of operation time (one hour of operation)

Threats Probability Estimation

- The Stakes matrix (ST) is filled by stakeholders according to the stakes they have in satisfying individual requirements;
- The Dependency matrix (DP) is filled by the system architect (i.e., cyber security operations and system administrators) according to how each component contributes to meet each requirement;
- The Impact matrix (IM) is filled by analysts according to how each component is affected by each threat.
- The vector of threat emergences probabilities (PV) represents the probability of emergence of the various threats, it is done empirically, by simulating and/or operating the system for some length of time and estimating the number of threats that have emerged during that time. Based on these numbers, we infer the probability of emergence of all the threats during one hour of operation.

The Mean Failure Cost: A Cascade of Linear Model

Aissa et al. (2010 b) introduce the concept of Mean Failure cost as a measure of dependency in general, and a measure of cyber security in particular. To compute the values of the mean failure cost for each stakeholder, we need to fill 3 matrixes and a vector: the stakes matrix ST, the dependency matrix DP, the impact matrix IM and the threat vector PT, we can derive the vector of Mean Failure Costs (one entry per stakeholder) by the MFC formula.

Stakes Matrix (ST)

We consider a system S and we let H1, H2, H3,...Hk, be stakeholders of the system, i.e. parties that have a stake in its operation. We let R1, R2, R3, ... Rn, be security requirements that we wish to impose on the system, and we let $ST_{i,j}$, for $1 \leq i \leq k$ and $1 \leq j \leq n$ be the stake that stakeholder H_i has in meeting security requirement R_j as presented in table 3.

Table 3. The Stakes matrix (ST)

ST		Requirements						
		R_1			R_j			R_n
Stakeholders	H_1							
	H_i							
			Stake that stakeholders H_i has in meeting requirement R_j					
	Hm							

Dependency Matrix (DP)

We consider the architecture of system S, and let $C_1, C_2, C_3, \ldots C_h$, be the components of system S. Whether a particular security requirement is met or not may conceivably depend on which component of the system architecture is operational. If we assume that no more than one component of the architecture may fail at any time, and define the following events:

- $E_i, 1 \leq i \leq h$, is the event: the operation of component C_i is affected due to a security breakdown.
- E_{m+1}: No component is affected.

Given a set of complementary events $E_1, E_2, E_3, \ldots E_h, E_{h+1}$, we know that the probability of an event F can be written in terms of conditional probabilities as:

$$P(F) = \sum_{k=1}^{h+1} P(F \mid E_k) \times P(E_k).$$

We instantiate this formula with F being the event: the system fails with respect to some security requirement. To this effect, we let F_j denote the event that the system fails with respect to requirement R_j and we write (given that the probability of failure with respect to R_j is denoted by PR_j), as presented in table 4:

$$PR_j = \sum_{k=1}^{m+1} P(F_j \mid E_k) \times P(E_k).$$

Impact Matrix (IM)

Matrix IM can be derived by analyzing which threats affect which components, and assessing the likelihood of success of each threat, as presented in table 5.

Table 4. The Dependency matrix (DP)

DP		Components							
		C_1			...C_k...				C_{h+1}
Requirements	R_1								
	... R_i...								
			Prob of failing requirement R_i once component C_k has failed						
	R_n								

Table 5. The Impact matrix (IM)

IM		Threats							
		T_1			...T_q...				T_{p+1}
Components	C_1								
	...C_k...								
			Prob that Component C_k fails once threat T_q has materialized						
	C_{h+1}								

Table 6. The Threat Vector (PT)

PT		Probability
Threats	T_1	
	...T_q....	Prob that threat T_q materializes during unitary period of operation
	T_{p+1}	

Threat Vector (PT)

Components of the architecture may fails to operate properly as a result of security breakdowns brought about by malicious activity. In order to continue the analysis, we must specify the catalog of threats that we are dealing with, in the same way that analysts of a system's reliability define a fault model. To this effect, we catalog the set of security threats that we are facing as presented in table 6, and we let T_1, T_2, T_3, ... T_p, represent the event that a cataloged threat has materialized, and we let T_{p+1} be the event that no threat has materialized. Also, we let PT be the vector of size p+1 such that:

- PTq, for 1≤q≤p, is the probability that threat Tq has materialized during a unitary period of operation (say, 1 hour).
- PTp+1 is the probability that no threat has materialized during a unitary period of operation time.

Summary of MFC Formula

Given the stakes matrix ST, the dependency matrix DP, the impact matrix IM and the threat vector PT, we can derive the vector of mean failure costs (one entry per stakeholder) by the MFC formula.

Where matrix ST is derived collectively by the stakeholders, matrix DP is derived by the systems architect, matrix IM is derived by the security analyst from architectural information, and vector PT is derived by the security analyst from perpetrator models.

Strengths of the MFC Measure

Among the strengths of the MFC, we consider that the threats probability estimation is rigorous because it is determined by all the systems stakeholders (Aissa et al., 2012; Mili & Sheldon, 2009). Then MFC is a structured measure of dependability.

To the best of our knowledge, the MFC measure is a rigorous suitable cyber security measure which presents several benefits. In fact the MFC is advantageous in comparison with other known approaches of security threats estimation and metrics of security, reliability and safety:

- The MFC reflects variance between system stakeholders; one user can attach different stakes regarding the same security requirement (Abercrombie et al., 2011).
- It considers the variance in failure cost from one sub-specification to another, the variance in failure probability from one sub-specification to another and the variance in failure cost from one stakeholder to another (Mili & Sheldon, 2007).
- The MFC measure of dependability takes into account complex system specifications, and considers variations by stakeholder, specification components, and threats in order to adopt a good quantified security threat measure.

The MFC offers the following attributes:

- MFC varies by stakeholders: The Mean Failure Cost is not a characteristic of the system but it rather depends on the system and the stakeholder/ user of the system. The same system may have different MFC values for different stakeholders, reflecting the varying stakes they have in the secure operation of the system.
- MFC varies by stakes: The same stakeholder may have different stakes in meeting different security requirements.
- MFC is cognizant of the system architecture: The Mean Failure Cost is calculated by estimating the probability of failure of each component of the system, and the probability that failure of each component may affect each security requirement.
- MFC is cognizant of the threat configuration: The Mean Failure Cost is calculated by cataloging the list of threats that the system is vulnerable to, the probability that each one of these threats may

materialize within a unitary operation time, and the probability that each threat, if it materializes, will affect each component of the architecture.

- MFC is quantified in economic terms: The mean failure cost is computed as a monetary value per unit of operational time, and measure the amount of risk that each stakeholder is incurring as a result of security threats and system vulnerabilities. As such, it provides adequate support for quantitative decision-making.

Applicability of the MFC Model to E-Systems

First of all, on the theoretical side, Anis et al. (2009, 2010 b, 2012) developed the mathematical infrastructure to estimate the MFC using failure cost and failure probabilities. In the practical side, they applied the proposed MFC to an e-commerce sample application using an implemented tool, they recognize four stakeholders which are:

- The customer
- The merchant
- The technical intermediary
- The financial intermediary

As an application of the MFC, the four stakeholders enter data of the stake matrix with respect to security requirements, they specified a premium on each relevant clause, then the vector of mean failure cost is calculated as explained in table 7. The MFC measure is applied to e-commerce system, it is independent from the system but depends on system users.

To the best of our knowledge, the MFC model can be applied to manage and quantify security threats of all e-System like e-Commerce, e-Learning, and e-Government and others. It is independent from the system but varies from a stakeholder to another (Mili & Sheldon, 2007; Abercrombie et al., 2011).

CRITICISMS, PERSPECTIVES ABOUT THE MFC CYBER SECURITY MEASURE

Given strengths and usefulness of the MFC model as a cyber-security measure, it estimates in quantitative way the security threats of the given system in independent way from its architecture. We intend to focus on the MFC model, on its improvements and expansion to all e-systems security facet and context. A variety of methods, approaches, analytical and empirical techniques needed to be highlighted.

Table 7. Failure cost variability

	Exact failure cost $/h	Wrong failure cost $/h
Customer	40	21.20
Merchant	551	292.03
Technical intermediary	150	79.50
Financial intermediary	270	143.10

We look to focus on the possibility to apply it in a practical application to an e-learning context and to put emphasis on the particularities of e-learning systems which is the complexity of system architecture; it has different stakeholders based on a variety of applications. E-learning environment is a complex system which includes several applications and stakeholders; we propose to test the applicability of the MFC model in this context. Hence we intend to focus on security estimation of e-learning system in the whole phases which are: design, programming and usage.

Threat model can help us to anticipate attacks, their impact and countermeasures. In addition, it is beneficial in presenting necessary attributes to support good decisions, for example in choosing alternative security architectures, courses of actions and pertinent decisions about cost. It is benefic to support the information assurance controls to reduce the dangerous risks with a minimum of cost (Abercrombie et al., 2011). We state here our essential and necessary ideas on the subject step by step:

1. Developing a threat model specific to e-learning context using the MFC model discussed in (Aissa et al., 2012). We have to specify:
   a. The system architecture
   b. The stakeholders
   c. The vulnerabilities categories
   d. The threats within e-learning platforms
2. Quantifying security threat model using MFC measures defined in step 1.
3. Computing measures and deducing results in order to manage security threats in an e-learning system.

We search to propose a quantitative threats assessment model in e-learning that highlight necessary security attributes and measure its risk in a well defined process. By applying the MFC model to e-learning, we have to establish the threat vector, to discuss and to use analytical and empirical models and methods (Fenz & Tjoa, 2008; Cummings et al., 2006) to quantify it, as well as for the three matrixes: the dependency matrix, the impact matrix and the stake matrix as presented in (Aissa et al., 2012).

We refer to this vector as the Threat Configuration Vector or simply as the Threat Vector (PT vector). It contains the probability that a threat Tq materializes during unitary period of operation (Aissa et al., 2010 b; Abercrombie et al., 2011). For each threat, the probability is recognized. The PT vector is filled by security analyst from perpetrator models; it can be derived from known perpetrator behavior and known system vulnerabilities. To each threat category we found the probability of its materialization over a unitary period of operation for example one hour (Aissa et al., 2010 b ; Abercrombie et al., 2011). It can also be filled throughout empirical investigation and survey from security expert (MohdAlwi & Fan, 2010 a). The probabilistic forecast can be also based on expert knowledge, expert opinion and historical evidence.

We need an effective quantitative model to estimate security threats based on specific extension and refinement of the MFC model. Once the theoretical quantitative model is ready for a practical assessment, we can synthesize useful preventive and management security actions. This is beneficial also to manage in a quantitative way security threats and risks within complex system architecture. In consequence, this will be beneficial in managing and planning security budget to minimize the most danger risk with the best strategy and the lowest cost.

Among the shortcomings of the application of the MFC model to a complex system:

- The MFC measure provides excellent knowledge about the loss that each stakeholder stands as a result of security breakdowns (Abercrombie et al., 2008; Abercrombie et al., 2009; Sheldon et al., 2009) but it is not able to consider all the complex relationships between relevant information security concepts and its cost when the system in consideration is complex. In consequence, threat probability determination is subjective.

- Security risk analysis study of a complex system is a challenge work, it requires a very big knowledge and it depends on a variety of work collection. In consequence, it is of our need to design and establish a quantitative structured model to support security analysis within complex environment. Results will be better and decisions will be consistent in a limited response time.

- The MFC does not consider the concept of dependency; it seems that the CSES addresses independent events (Abercrombie et al., 2011). In consequence, the concept of dependency needs to be considered as a first fact, we consider the dependency between components, threat occurrence. Therefore, this leads to consider dependency between threat probabilities occurrences. We discuss probabilities dependency between matrices and probabilities dependency between two entities of the same matrix.

With a complex system, the MFC model can underline the estimation of events and consider the complex relationships between security concepts based on analytical researches on the structure of security specifications such requirements, threats, as well as empirical researches in order to facilitate the calculation, the evaluation and the interpretation of the MFC.

The MFC needs to be refined to:

- Extend the MFC formula in order to calculate the critical security requirements for a given system in general. And then offering a complete diagnosis of the system such as the critical requirement presentation, the critical components and the critical threats.

- Optimize the measure of a standard architectural system by defining a complete and detailed taxonomy of security requirements for computer system in order to spread the ST, DP matrix of the MFC measure and to refine it. Therefore the calculation of the MFC for an e-system application in view to get a more precise evaluation and more efficient decisions.

A variety of methods, approaches, analytical and empirical techniques needed to be considered to incorporate the concept of the quantification of attribute, therefore measuring in a structured way security risk regarding the complexity of a given system. This contribution forms intensive improvements in the context of security risk management for all e-systems in general in the theoretical, empirical and practical plan.

CONCLUSION

This chapter illustrates the rigorous cybersecurity measure which is the Mean failure Cost model to quantify security threats of e-systems, its strength reside on the quantification in economic terms as a monetary value per unit of operational time, and measure the amount of risk that each stakeholder is incurring as a result of security threats and system vulnerabilities. It is independent from the system and its architecture but depends on system users. It can be applied to manage and quantify security threats of all e-System like e-Commerce, e-Learning, and e-Government and others context like cloud computing architecture. It takes into account complex system specifications, and considers variations by stakeholder, specification components, security requirements and threats in order to adopt a good quantified security threat measure.

We envision broadening the application of the MFC model to analysis the security attributes of E-learning systems. Practical future works focus of the definition of the system stakeholders and the related security requirements then the refinement of the catalog of threats and the decomposition of the architectural components.

Next works reside on the collection of the needed empirical information:

- The Stake that stakeholders Hi has in meeting requirement Rj
- The Probability of failing requirement Ri. once component Ck has failed
- The Probability that Component Ck fails once threat Tq has materialized
- The Probability that threat Tq materializes during unitary period of operation

The MFC measures help us to better estimate the matrices, then to explore more opportunities for security related decision-making.

REFERENCES

Abercrombie, R. K., Ferragut, E. M., Sheldon, F. T., & Grimaila, M. R. (2011, April). Addressing the Need for Independence in the CSE Model. In Computational Intelligence in Cyber Security (CICS), 2011 IEEE Symposium on (pp. 68-75). IEEE. doi:10.1109/CICYBS.2011.5949395

Abercrombie, R. K., Sheldon, F. T., & Mili, A. (2008, December). Synopsis of evaluating security controls based on key performance indicators and stakeholder mission value. In High Assurance Systems Engineering Symposium, 2008. HASE 2008. 11th IEEE (pp. 479-482). IEEE. doi:10.1109/HASE.2008.61

Abercrombie, R. K., Sheldon, F. T., & Mili, A. (2009, March). Managing complex IT security processes with value based measures. In Computational Intelligence in Cyber Security, 2009. CICS'09. IEEE Symposium on (pp. 69-75). IEEE. doi:10.1109/CICYBS.2009.4925092

Aissa, A. B., Abercrombie, R. K., Sheldon, F. T., & Mili, A. (2010). Quantifying security threats and their potential impacts: A case study. *Innovations in Systems and Software Engineering*, 6(4), 269–281. doi:10.1007/s11334-010-0123-2

Aissa, A. B., Abercrombie, R. K., Sheldon, F. T., & Mili, A. (2012). Defining and computing a value based cyber-security measure. Information Systems and e-Business Management, 10(4), 433-453.

Aissa, A. B. A., Mili, A., Abercrombie, R. K., & Sheldon, F. T. (2010). Modeling stakeholder/value dependency through mean failure cost. In Proceedings of *6th Annual Cyber Security and Information Intelligence Research Workshop (CSIIRW-2010)*. ACM International Conference.

Alwi, N. H. M., & Fan, I. S.MohdAlwi. (2010). Threats analysis for e-learning. *International Journal Technology Enhanced Learning*, 2(4), 358–371. doi:10.1504/IJTEL.2010.035738

Ben Aissa, A., Abercrombie, R. K., Sheldon, F. T., & Mili, A. (2009, April). Quantifying security threats and their impact. In *Proceedings of the 5th Annual Workshop on Cyber Security and Information Intelligence Research: Cyber Security and Information Intelligence Challenges and Strategies*, (pp. 26). ACM.

Bojanc, R., & Jerman-Blazic, B. (2008). An economic modelling approach to information security risk management. *International Journal of Information Management*, 28(5), 413–422. doi:10.1016/j.ijinfomgt.2008.02.002

Cavusoglu, H., Mishra, B., & Raghunathan, S. (2004). A model for evaluating it security investments. *Communications of the ACM*, 47(7), 87–92. doi:10.1145/1005817.1005828

Cummings, M. C., McGarvey, D. C., & Vinch, P. M. (2006), *Homeland Security Risk Assessment Volume II. Methods, Techniques, and Tools*. Retrieved from http://www.homelandsecurity.org/hsireports/Risk%20Assessment%20Volume%202%20 Methods%20Techniques%20and%20Tools.pdf

Ekelhart, A., Fenz, S., & Neubauer, T. (2009). AURUM: A framework for information security risk management. In *Proceedings of the 42nd Hawaii International Conference on System Sciences*.

Fenz, S., & Ekelhart, A. (2009, March). Formalizing information security knowledge. In *Proceedings of the 4th international Symposium on information, Computer, and Communications Security*, (pp. 183-194). ACM. doi:10.1145/1533057.1533084

Fenz, S., & Tjoa, A. M. (2008). Ontology-and Bayesian-based Threat Probability Determination. In *Proceedings of the Junior Scientist Conference 2008*, (pp. 69-70).

Karabacak, B., & Sogukpinar, I. (2005). ISRAM: Information security risk analysis method. *Computers & Security*, 24(2), 147–159. doi:10.1016/j.cose.2004.07.004

Mili, A., & Sheldon, F. (2007, November). Measuring reliability as a mean failure cost. In *High Assurance Systems Engineering Symposium, 2007. HASE'07. 10th IEEE*, (pp. 403-404). IEEE. doi:10.1109/HASE.2007.42

Mili, A., & Sheldon, F. T. (2009). Challenging the mean time to failure: Measuring dependability as a mean failure cost. In *Proceedings of 42nd Hawaii International Conference on System Sciences (HICSS-42)*, Waikoloa, HI. (pp. 10).

MohdAlwi, N. H., & Fan, I. S. (2010). e-Learning and information security management. *International Journal of Digit Society (IJDS)*, 1(2), 148-156.

Myagmar, S., Lee, A. J., & Yurcik, W. (2005, August). Threat modeling as a basis for security requirements. In *Symposium on Requirements Engineering for Information Security (SREIS)*.

Nickolova, M., & Nickolov, E. (2007). Threat model for user security in e-learning systems. *International Journal Information Technologies and Knowledge*, 1(1), 341–347.

Ryan, J. J. C. H., & Ryan, D. J. (2006). Expected benefits of information security investments. *Computers & Security*, 25(8), 579–588. doi:10.1016/j.cose.2006.08.001

Scheier, B. (2003). *Beyond fear: Thinking sensibly about security in an uncertain world*. New York, NY: Springer-Verlag New York, Inc.

Sheldon, F. T., Abercrombie, R. K., & Mili, A. (2009, January). Methodology for evaluating security controls based on key performance indicators and stakeholder mission. In *System Sciences, 2009. HICSS'09 42nd Hawaii International Conference*, (pp. 1-10). IEEE.

Sommestad, T., Ekstedt, M., & Johnson, P. (2009, January). Cyber security risks assessment with bayesian defense graphs and architectural models. In *System Sciences, 2009. HICSS'09. 42nd Hawaii International Conference*, (pp. 1-10). IEEE.

Sommestad, T., Ekstedt, M., & Johnson, P. (2010). A probabilistic relational model for security risk analysis. *Computers & Security, 29*(6), 659–679. doi:10.1016/j.cose.2010.02.002

Stoneburner, G., Goguen, A., & Feringa, A. (2002). Risk management guide for information technology systems. Nist special publication, 800(30), 800-30.

Tsiakis, T., & Stephanides, G. (2005). The economic approach of information security. *Computers & Security, 24*(2), 105–108. doi:10.1016/j.cose.2005.02.001

Whitman, M. E., & Mattord, H. J. (2004). *Principles of information security*. Boston, MA: Publisher Course Technology Press.

KEY TERMS AND DEFINITIONS

A Threat: Is a category of object, person or other entities that present a danger. Like spam, Trojan horse and fishing.

A Risk: Is the product of the probability that a particular threat will occur and the expected loss.

Security Risk Management: Is the determination of the worthiest attack and the ignored one, it is the one way to focus on the serious attacks to better manage the budget and find the best way to use it.

Security Risk Analysis Process: Is used to assess security threats and their potential impact in order to anticipate attacks, to weaken their impact and to propose some countermeasures.

The Mean Failure Cost: Is a recent value based measure of cyber-security, it computes for each stakeholder of the given system his or her loss of operation ($/H). it is a cascade of linear models to quantify security threat in term of loss that results from system vulnerabilities.

The Stakes Matrix (ST): Is filled by stakeholders according to the stakes they have in satisfying individual requirements.

The Dependency Matrix (DP): Is filled by the system architect (i.e., cyber security operations and system administrators) according to how each component contributes to meet each requirement.

The Impact Matrix (IM): Is filled by analysts according to how each component is affected by each threat.

The Threat Vector: Is emergences probabilities (PV) represents the probability of emergence of the various threats. It is done empirically, by simulating and/or operating the system for some length of time and estimating the number of threats that have emerged during that time.

Chapter 6
Cybersecurity Requires a Clear Systems Engineering Approach as a Basis for Its Cyberstrategy

Dr. Raymond J. Curts
George Mason University, USA

Dr. Douglas E. Campbell
Syneca Research Group, USA

ABSTRACT

Systems engineering is the branch of engineering concerned with the development of large and complex systems, where a system is understood to be an assembly or combination of interrelated elements or parts working together toward a common objective. Past experience has shown that formal systems engineering methodologies have not always been successfully applied to large and complex cybersecurity systems. These complex systems have become commonplace when applying cyberstrategies in cybersecurity operations. The ability to build, operate and maintain such systems is crucial to the effectiveness of cybersecurity operations. Most importantly, a cyberstrategy program must surround these systems on a global scale across multiple inter-related platforms. In this chapter, the authors demonstrate why a systems engineering approach is best suited for large and complex information systems used in cybersecurity, as well as the overall cyberstrategies that must also reside over these systems.

INTRODUCTION

Without robust systems engineering methodologies, the realization of complex information systems involving numerous interacting components would be prohibitively expensive, prone to failure and involve timescales unacceptable in today's cybersecurity industry. By following appropriate, best practice methodologies, highly integrated and complex cybersecurity information systems can be built to interact securely on a global scale. The purpose of this chapter is to build an understanding of systems engineering processes as they apply to a large and complex information system within a cybersecurity environment. By the end of this chapter, the reader should have an appreciation for the environment within which

DOI: 10.4018/978-1-4666-8456-0.ch006

systems engineering occurs; understand the management skills needed to facilitate the development of complex information systems and the cyberstrategies needed in such an environment; and have a clear appreciation of systems engineering as applied to cybersecurity information operations.

It is the intention of the authors to present this chapter along the usual systems engineering lines including some discussion of the basic concepts of system engineering, cybersecurity, interoperability, life cycle support, cyberstrategy operational considerations, and automated tools that can assist with various processes along the way.

BASIC CONCEPTS OF SYSTEMS ENGINEERING, CYBERSECURITY, AND INTEROPERABILITY

Systems Engineering. Systems Engineering is defined as an interdisciplinary process that ensures that the customer's needs are satisfied throughout a system's *iterative* life cycle (*see* Figure 1). When the system under consideration is something manufactured, like a computer, then its system life cycle usually has seven phases: (1) requirements development, (2) concept development, (3) full-scale engineering design and development, (4) manufacturing and deployment, (5) system integration and test, (6) operation, maintenance and modification, and (7) retirement, disposal or replacement. The system life cycle is different for different industries, products and customers (Chapman, Bahill and Wymore, 1992; Wymore, 1993; Kerzner, 1995; Shishko, 1995). However, even when a system life cycle is defined within the manufacturing process, the authors still question why requirements development comes before concept development (Figure 1). Concept development is the high-level process of determining and understanding customer needs. Without understanding what the customer wants in the first place, it becomes very difficult to discover system requirements. With apologies to Chapman, Bahill, Wymore, Kerzner, Shishko and other developers of the systems engineering process, there still remains a good argument as to why concept development should come first. Some authors refer to phase 2 as prelimi-

Figure 1. The Iterative Systems Engineering Process from A. T. Bahill and B. Gissing, Re-evaluating systems engineering concepts using systems thinking, IEEE Transaction on Systems, Man and Cybernetics, Part C: Applications and Reviews, 28 (4), 516-527, 1998.

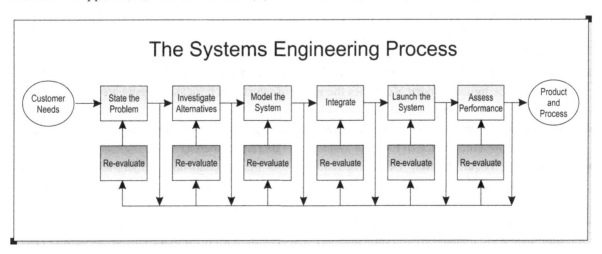

nary design rather than concept development. Perhaps this terminology is a better description of what actually happens at this stage of system development, while the task of 'concept' development is more closely aligned with phase 1.

The systems engineering process includes, but is not limited to: understanding customer needs, discovering system requirements, defining performance and cost measures, prescribing tests, validating requirements, conducting design reviews, exploring alternative concepts, sensitivity analyses, functional decomposition, system modeling, system design, designing and managing interfaces, system integration, total system test, configuration management, risk management, reliability analysis, total quality management, project management, and documentation. Very briefly, each of these processes are explained as follows:

- **Understanding customer needs.** The customer may or may not be fully aware of the details of what they need nor what, in the way of technology, is available. Non-technical customers are also not proficient at expressing their basic needs, opting instead to specify a solution as opposed to a real requirement such as, "We need Norton Anti-Virus" as opposed to "We need a way to deal with intrusive malware." In any case, talking to the customer, understanding the problem to be solved and gleaning the customer's underlying needs is by far the most important first step in systems engineering. This, in turn, defines the overall mission essential needs statement and a product-free "concept of operations." Once completed, "needs" become "requirements."

- **Discovering system requirements.** There are two types of specified system requirements: mandatory (using terms such as *shall* and *will*) and preferred (using terms such as *should* or *want*). Mandatory requirements insure that the system satisfies the customer's operational needs. These mandatory requirements typically rest on legal issues, such as not violating federal or international laws, or budgetary requirements. Mandatory requirements are not subject to trade-offs. There are also unspecified requirements, such as the laws of physics, not addressed in this chapter.

- **Optimizing design.** After understanding the mandatory requirements, the preferred requirements are evaluated to determine the most optimum design. The preferred requirements should use scoring functions to evaluate the figures of merit (Chapman, Bahill and Wymore, 1992) and should be evaluated with a multi-criteria decision aiding technique (Szidarovszky, Gershon and Duckstein, 1986) because none of the feasible alternatives is likely to optimize all the criteria and, thus, there will be trade-offs between these requirements. The words optimize, maximize and minimize should not be used in stating requirements (Grady, 1993). Quality Function Deployment (QFD) and similar Multi-Attribute Utility (MAU) based analyses can help identify system requirements (Bahill and Chapman, 1993; Bicknell and Bicknell, 1994).

- **Defining performance and cost measures.** A technical performance measurement, often called a performance figure of merit, describes the result of a test. Such measurements are made throughout the evolution of the system.

- **Prescribing tests.** Early in the system life cycle the upcoming tests should be described in detail so as to prove compliance of the final system with its requirements.

- **Validating requirements.** Validating requirements means ensuring that the requirements are consistent and that a real-world solution can be built and tested to prove that it satisfies the requirements.

- **Conducting design reviews.** After the system model has been simulated and validated the requirements are reanalyzed and reformulated. This is called a Preliminary Design Review (PDR).

- **Exploring alternative concepts.** Alternative designs should be proposed. Multi-criteria decision aiding techniques should be used to reveal the *best* alternatives based on the requirements, performance and cost figures of merit. For the design of any complex system, alternative designs can highlight and potentially reduce project risk.

- **Sensitivity analyses.** Sensitivity analyses can be used to point out the requirements and parameters that have the biggest effects on cost, schedule and performance. They are used to help allocate resources (Karnavas, Sanchez and Bahill, 1993).

- **What-If analysis.** Closely akin to sensitivity analysis, what-if analyses allow designers to try specific trade-off options by changing parametric values to determine the overall impact upon the resultant system. Many respected engineers consider sensitivity and what-if analyses to be one and the same thing, and the terms are often used interchangeably. Although these may, in fact, represent two sides of the same coin, the authors find both concepts distinct, unique and useful.

- **Functional decomposition.** Systems engineers do functional decomposition on new systems (1) to map functions to physical components, thereby ensuring that each function has an acknowledged owner, (2) to map functions to system requirements, and (3) to ensure that all necessary tasks are listed and that no unnecessary tasks are requested. This list becomes the basis for the work breakdown structure. Recently object-oriented analysis has been replacing function decomposition for re-engineering existing systems (Jacobson, Ericsson and Jacobson, 1995). Although a newer and, in some cases, more robust concept, object-oriented techniques are still in their infancy, relatively speaking, and are not suitable for every situation. The fact remains that the mapping of functional requirements and physical components must be done. The best approach depends upon a number of factors, not the least of which is the experience and hence, the 'comfort level' of the practitioners.

- **System modeling.** Many types of system models can be used, such as physical devices, equations, block diagrams, flow diagrams, object models, and computer simulations. Models are developed for alternative concepts to evaluate their relative merits.

- **System design.** It is called System Design for new systems and Systems Analysis for existing systems. The overall system must be broken down into subsystems, and subsystems are then decomposed into assemblies or components, etc. Once in its simplest form, systems engineering can then look at life cycle issues of reusability, purchasing Commercial-Off-The-Shelf (COTS) parts, etc.

- **Designing and managing interfaces.** Interfaces between subsystems, and interfaces between the main system and the external world must be designed. Subsystems should be defined to optimize the amount of information to be exchanged between the subsystems.

- **System integration.** System integration is bringing subsystems together to produce the desired result and ensure that the subsystems will interact to satisfy the customer's needs. This is where courses, manuals and training are needed (Grady, 1994).

- **Total system test.** The system that is finally built must be tested to see if it is acceptable to the customer and how well it satisfies the preferred requirements.

- **Configuration management.** Configuration management ensures that any changes in requirements, design or implementation are controlled, carefully identified, and accurately recorded.

- **Risk management.** There is always the risk of project failure (due to cost overruns, schedule overruns or failure to meet performance specifications) and risk of harm to people. Project risk can be reduced by supervising quality and timely delivery of purchased items (Kerzner, 1995).

- **Reliability analysis.** Major failure modes must be analyzed for probability of occurrence and severity of occurrence (Kapur and Lamberson, 1977; O'Connor, 1991).
- **Total quality management.** Everyone must continually look for ways to improve the quality of the system. Major tools used in this process include basic concurrent engineering, Multi-Attribute Utility Theory (MAUT), Quality Function Deployment (QFD) and Taguchi's quality engineering techniques among others (Bicknell and Bicknell, 1994).
- **Project management.** Project management is the planning, organizing, directing, and controlling resources to meet specific goals and objectives within time and cost constraints and at the desired performance level (Kerzner, 1995).
- **Documentation.** All of these Systems Engineering activities must be documented in a common repository, often called the Engineering Notebook. Results of trade-off analyses should be included. The reasons for making critical decisions should be stated (Chapman, Bahill and Wymore, 1992; Wymore, 1993). In today's age of automation, this concept can and should be taken one step further. The concept of Engineering Notebooks and written reports are important and required by many customers. Still, we should be able to capture much of the engineering data, trade-offs and other rationale in some form of data structure using off-the-shelf tools. In this way, the things that we learn along the way can be made more available for search, retrieval and analysis. Figure 2 shows how such a database can be utilized to capture the entire lifecycle of a project including the Enterprise Architecture (EA), Configuration Management (CM), and Test & Evaluation Master Plans (TEMP) as well as a complete Requirements Traceability Matrix (RTM).

Cybersecurity. The world of cybersecurity increasingly relies upon critical digital electronic information capabilities to store, process and move essential data in planning, directing, coordinating and

Figure 2. The aggregated lifecycles of system architecture, development, deployment, design, test, configuration management (CM), Certification & Accreditation (C&A), requirements traceability, etc.

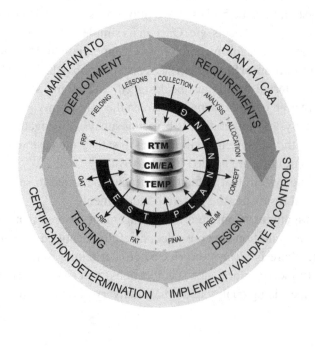

executing cyber operations. Powerful and sophisticated threats can exploit security weaknesses in many of these systems. Weaknesses that can be exploited become vulnerabilities that can jeopardize the most sensitive components of information capabilities. However, we can employ deep, layered defenses to reduce vulnerabilities and deter, defeat and recover from a wide range of threats. From a cyberstrategy perspective, the capabilities that we must defend can be viewed broadly in terms of four major elements: local computing environments, their boundaries, networks that link them together and their supporting infrastructure (Woodward, 2000).

Within this chapter, the term "Cybersecurity" is used to cover a simple but widely-applicable security model called the "CIA triad"; standing for **C**onfidentiality, **I**ntegrity and **A**vailability. This principle is applicable across the whole subject of cybersecurity, from access to a user's internet history to security of encrypted data across the internet. If any one of the three can be breached it can have serious consequences for the parties concerned.

- **Confidentiality.** Confidentiality is the ability to hide information from those people unauthorized to view it. It is perhaps the most obvious aspect of the CIA triad when it comes to security; but correspondingly, it is also the one which is attacked most often. Encryption methods is an example of an attempt to ensure confidentiality of data transferred from one computer to another.
- **Integrity.** The ability to ensure that data is an accurate and unchanged representation of the original information. One type of security attack is to intercept some important data and make changes to it before sending it on to the intended receiver.
- **Availability.** It is important to ensure that the information concerned is readily accessible to the authorized viewer at all times. Some types of security attack attempt to deny access to the appropriate user, either for the sake of inconveniencing them, or because there is some secondary effect. For example, by breaking the website for a particular search engine, a rival's website may become more popular.

So then the term "cybersecurity" applies to the collection, storage, transmission and use of information in the cyber domain. The strategy encompassing cybersecurity is to protect users, business units, and enterprises from the negative effects of corruption of information or denial of services. For example, if the financial data in a payroll database is valid in the sense that it could be correct, but is not in fact correct, there may be no negative impact on the information system, but the enterprise may suffer when people get the wrong amount of money in their paychecks. Similarly, if an order for an engine part in a supply and logistics system is lost in the sub-system that dictates which pallets get loaded onto which aircraft, the information system continues to operate, but the supply service is denied to the person requiring the parts. Naturally, if the information systems processing, storing, or communicating information become corrupt or unavailable, that may also affect the enterprise as a whole, but simply protecting the systems without protecting the information, processing, and communication is not adequate (Management Analytics, 1995).

As the world's information systems are being tied together, the points of entry and exposures increase, and thus risks increase. The technological advancement toward higher bandwidth communications and advanced switching systems has reduced the number of communications lines and further centralized the switching functions. Survey data indicates that the increased risk from these changes is not widely recognized (Loch, 1992). Efforts made by the U.S. Defense Information Systems Agency (DISA) to promulgate standards for the Defense Information Infrastructure (DII) and the Global Information Grid

(GiG) are just two examples that have made a positive impact on cybersecurity and resultant cyberstrategies that are now extending beyond the U.S. Department of Defense (DoD) and impacting all segments of the national economy.

Interoperability. (Note: This Interoperability section comes from the authors' paper "Architecture: The Road to Interoperability" presented at the 1999 Command & Control Research & Technology Symposium at the Naval War College in Newport, RI). The ability to generate and move information has increased many thousands of times over the past 30 years. The services have all become much more reliant on information technology. Unfortunately, the current capability to generate information far exceeds our ability to control and use it effectively. To ensure information interoperability, system developers must comply with international and domestic data and interface standards. Understandable descriptions of databases and the data that they store are the keys to data interoperability (ITSG, 1998). The U.S. Department of the Navy's Information Technology Standards Guidance (ITSG) along with the Technical Architecture for Information Management (TAFIM), attempted to add structure to the process. The acronym C^4ISR stands for Command, Control, Computers, Communications (C^4), Intelligence, Surveillance, and Reconnaissance (ISR). The C^4ISR Architecture Framework Version 2.02, also commonly referred to as the DoD Architecture Framework (DoDAF), provides comprehensive architectural interoperability guidance for all related U.S. Department of Defense (DoD) domains, in order to ensure interoperable and cost-effective military systems. It has emerged in recent years as a successor to the TAFIM.

In addition there is a requirement to develop data metrics to assess and support system data interoperability. Studies done by the U.S. Center for Naval Analysis (CNA) and the C^4ISR Core Architecture Data Model (CADM) provide a foundation for addressing this information architecture.

Where did we begin? In a paper presented at the 1997 DoD Database Colloquium, James Mathwich made the case that the seamless flow of information is one of the most ambitious visions of information warfare. "And yet within the Department of Defense, database integration and information interoperability efforts are more often characterized as false-starts rather than successes. … Commercial data warehouse programs, which are highly bounded database integration efforts, are doing no better with no more than a 50 percent success rate. … Managing information in an interoperable community will fail unless it is automated to the greatest degree possible. Automation of information management cannot be done on a community-wide basis unless there exists a community-wide policy with sufficient detail so that it can be predictably executed in an automated tool. Integrated databases bring new information interoperability challenges. The definition and management of the linkage between information and mission has in the past been lacking. Establishing this linkage will provide critical context and metrics for managing database integration and building effective interoperable systems." (Mathwick, 1997).

From a briefing given to the U.S. Department of the Navy (DoN) Chief Information Officer (CIO) two years later, it was still obvious that we continue to be concerned with interoperability issues. "Data efforts are uncoordinated and there is no process in being to fix the problem. Many [cybersecurity] systems are incapable of sharing and exchanging data, an interoperability problem that could result in the possible 'loss of life, equipment or supplies'. To correct the problem requires both an information architecture and a repository of systems' databases." (Michaels, 1999).

The Joint Interoperability Test Command (JITC) performs the joint interoperability test and certification mission as prescribed in the U.S. Joint Chiefs of Staff instruction CJCSI 6212.01A (JITC, 1998). From JITC we have this definition of interoperability:

- Interoperability – "The ability of systems, units, or forces to provide services to and accept services from other systems, units, or forces, and to use the services so exchanged to enable them to operate effectively together."

In review, information systems and the cybersecurity measures that they embody must be interoperable. They must co-exist in the same environment and not conflict with each other. They cannot impose unacceptable computing, communications or organizational burdens or obstacles that hamper accomplishment of vital operations. They should work together in such functions as sharing data and providing cues, indications or triggers to perform actions (Woodward, 2000).

CYBERSTRATEGIES IN CYBERSECURITY OPERATIONAL CONSIDERATIONS

The purpose of this section is to acknowledge that the development and implementation of a cyberstrategy methodology can be the most demonstrable indicator of support toward an aggressive, proactive approach to secure information and critical information infrastructures. By incorporating "best practices" from defense, industry and global government initiatives, the cyberstrategy methodology becomes a complete solution within a cybersecurity environment. A comprehensive cyberstrategy should accommodate a full range of information systems security needs – assessment, protection (implementation), validation, training, monitoring and management. The authors believe that a full life cycle, defense-in-depth approach that is supported by the best cybersecurity technologies and strategies available is the proper approach to protecting critical information and infrastructures.

The fundamental principle of the cyberstrategy methodology requires that security measures must be implemented with the intent of providing multiple layers of long-term, continuous protection. The logic is simple: even if a cybersecurity's infrastructure is secure today, it may not be tomorrow. New risks and vulnerabilities are introduced at an alarming rate and new technologies are being developed and implemented just as fast. New hardware and software platforms are constantly being installed; new features, functions, and capabilities are being created, etc. More ominously, the skill, sophistication, and motivation of system hackers seem to be increasing proportionally. The critical challenge, then, is to keep IT configurations current and to do it on a continuing basis.

The cyberstrategy should be a framework best represented by a series of five basic operational phases that protect critical cybersecurity assets. The protection is accomplished by establishing a defensive perimeter around them. Each phase is a precursor to or continuation of every other phase in the cyberstrategy life cycle, forming a secure barrier that offers uninterrupted protection as systems grow and evolve.

At the core of this protective perimeter is the security architecture, surrounded closely by security policies and procedures, physical security and any other available security measures that make up a robust security posture. Therein lies the critical data that the cybersecurity staff becomes responsible for protecting.

In 1998 the U.S. General Accounting Office (GAO) reviewed whether DoD organizations were complying with interoperability testing and certification requirements for Command, Control, Communications, Computers, And Intelligence (C^4I) systems; and what actions, if any, were needed to improve the current certification process (U.S. General Accounting Office, 1998). The GAO review was not promising. Of the 15 fundamental weaknesses noted by the GAO, the Command & Control area is the most fitting for this chapter:

COMMAND & CONTROL: *DoD does not have an effective process for certifying existing, newly developed, and modified C⁴I systems for interoperability; many C⁴I systems have not been certified for interoperability and, in fact, DoD does not know how many require certification; and improvements to the certification process are needed to provide DoD better assurance that C⁴I systems critical to effective joint operations are tested and certified for interoperability.*

Perhaps a Cyberstrategy Life Cycle Methodology would be the foundation for such an effective process.

The Cyberstrategy Life Cycle Methodology. With special thanks to Terry DiVittorio, CISSP Senior Cybersecurity Engineer/Consultant, EDS Cybersecurity Services, the authors propose a simple 5-phase life cycle approach to Cybersecurity: assess, protect, validate, train and monitor/manage.

Phase 1: Assess. Assessing an organization's current security posture is generally the first step to resolving the myriad complex cybersecurity issues facing it today. The question, put bluntly, is not whether information system resources and critical assets will be compromised but when. Far too many organizations have little notion of the risks their information infrastructures face, the value of the information systems themselves, or the value of their intellectual capital and sensitive data. Most organizations confront these issues only when sifting through the debris left behind following a disastrous breach in what was supposed to be a secure system, or following the misappropriation of critical assets.

Cybersecurity assessment establishes the baseline that is the current state of cybersecurity within an organization. Using this baseline as a starting point, the cybersecurity staff can help its organization develop strategic and tactical security objectives that evolve along with the organization. The assessment process evaluates the security of an organization (both physical and logical), identifies assets to be protected, identifies security vulnerabilities, and then recommends protective options for eliminating or mitigating security risks.

The complex cybersecurity issues in open networks (e.g., the Internet) and Wide Area Networks (WANs), as well as on closed networks, is a reality in today's IT environment. Under such conditions, the cybersecurity staff becomes responsible for meeting the cybersecurity needs, protecting intellectual property, safeguarding financial transactions, and having reliable and secure activity.

The optimal life cycle strategy begins with an assessment from multiple perspectives, ranging from physical security, to the configuration of the firewalls, to the reliability of personnel. Cybersecurity remains cohesive throughout the life cycle. It takes a system perspective to ensure that any new partial solutions remain compatible with the remainder of the system. Clients, servers, databases, infrastructure protocols and links, router and firewall configurations, policies, and procedures all have their individual issues, as well as an impact on the overall level of trust placed on cybersecurity.

Assessing the risks inherent in each must be done in the context of the cybersecurity policy and objectives. Topics typically covered in an assessment include:

- Physical network architecture
- Onsite review of operations and physical security
- Network description (functions, topology and components)
- Network services and protocols
- Audit trials logging, alarms, and intrusion detection
- Firewall, clients, servers, routers, bridges
- Internal and external connections
- Information security standards, procedures, and policies

- Procedures, responsibilities, tasks, and authorizations
- Management network infrastructure
- Management access
- Management functions (e.g., change, problem, security)

Phase 2: Protect. Every organization must clearly demonstrate their efforts to protect their information and the underlying information infrastructure from a breakdown in accountability, privacy, confidentiality, availability, and data integrity.

Preventing unauthorized access to information assets, protecting against intentional or accidental damage – especially as the use of information technology grows among non-technical users – creating systems that are easy to use, and maintaining a protective shield around those systems requires a sure, methodical approach that addresses forward-thinking strategies as well as current goals. Cybersecurity protection provides enhanced levels of total system security by implementing advanced security technologies using field-proven secure system engineering methodologies. Public Key Infrastructure (PKI) technologies identify and authenticate users over the Internet, intranets, or extranets. Privacy and data integrity are achieved using encryption technologies and hashing algorithms. Digital signatures (now as binding in court as inked ones) provide the basis for non-repudiation. Access control allows only trusted users to view confidential data. Smart Cards, tokens, and biometrics facilitate the positive identification of users so they can be quickly and automatically routed to the information they require.

The principle task accomplished during this phase of the cyberstrategy life cycle is the implementation of solid architectures, plans, and policies for integrating robust security practices enterprise-wide that ensure maximum levels of security and productivity.

Phase 3: Validate. The third phase in securing an organization's information systems and infrastructure is to validate that the security mechanisms put in place during the protection phase do indeed adequately address security policy and address the risks and vulnerabilities identified during the assessment phase. How? By comparing the results of the protection phase against (1) the original requirements, (2) additional exposures, (3) vulnerabilities identified in the assessment phase, and any intervening changes in requirements and/or the IT environment.

Validation should always be done following the implementation of any new protective measure, whether the measure is as simple as the installation of a new firewall or as complicated as developing and testing a command security policy. Indeed, continual re-verification of an organization's cybersecurity posture is one of the requirements for re-accreditation if the systems need government security level certifications.

Cybersecurity validation consists of a set of standardized capabilities and processes that help determine the suitability of a system for a given operational environment. These capabilities help reduce fraud, mission failures, and embarrassing information and data leaks while increasing overall information system assurance. The defined processes provide standardization for the acquisition, operation, and sustainability of IT systems that collect, store, transmit, or process information.

It is essential for organizations to look at information system validations as a basic necessity – a tool for ensuring confidence in the data from which decisions are made. Cybersecurity validation provides organizations with a high degree of certainty that the IT systems will operate within an acceptable risk environment. As appropriate, the strategy for information systems infrastructure is to periodically re-test to determine how well products, applications, policies, and procedures are functioning in accordance with a given standard – defined from government-wide to organizational levels – and reassessed to determine the impact of any new threats.

These validations target existing technologies, as well as emerging ones. System, plan, and procedure reviews are conducted to verify that all components are operating within established parameters and that contingencies are addressed and newly implemented technologies are appropriately configured.

Phase 4: Train. Cybersecurity training, the fourth phase in this cyberstrategy life cycle model, ensures that organizational support personnel as well as users are appropriately trained and skilled in all cybersecurity service areas. In short, it confirms that support personnel have acquired the precise technical expertise necessary for an organization's protective security measures to achieve optimum results and that users understand the need to comply with these protective measures. The training phase also provides more generalized security awareness training for staff and management to help them understand the importance of maintaining a rigorous defensive perimeter. Industry-recognized certifications are offered through a variety of cybersecurity programs. The following are just a few of the more well-known:

- **Certified Information Systems Security Professional (CISSP).** This certification is from the International Information Systems Security Certification Consortium, or ISC^2 (www.isc2.org) and is arguably the most well recognized and prestigious in the industry.
- **Certified Protection Professional (CPP).** The American Society for Industrial Security (www.asisonline.org) administers the Certified Protection Professional program.
- **Certified Information Systems Auditor (CISA).** With more than 23,000 members in over 100 countries, the Information Systems Audit and Control Association (www.isaca.org) is a recognized global leader in IT governance, control and assurance.
- **Business Continuity Professional Certifications.** DRI International's (DRII) world-renowned professional certification program acknowledges an individual's effort to achieve a professional level of competence in the industry. The program includes:
  ◦ **Certified Business Continuity Professional (CBCP).**
  ◦ **Associate Business Continuity Planner (ABCP).**
  ◦ **Master Business Continuity Professional (MBCP).**

In addition to the organizations listed above, many accredited colleges and universities – not to mention the U.S. government - have developed certification and/or degree bearing programs in the fields of Cybersecurity and Information Security.

Phase 5: Monitor/Manage. The fifth and final phase in Cyberstrategy addresses the need for constant, active vigilance at the defensive perimeter, including security policies, practices, procedures, and processes, as well as disaster recovery and business continuity plans.

The broad adoption of the new communications media, new ways of doing business, and the Internet presents organizations with some thorny challenges. Virtually every organization in the world has become heavily influenced by the possibilities of worldwide distribution and dissemination of their information. Organizations that process high-volume / highly-sensitive requirements and also rely on an Internet / Cloud presence are faced with the very real possibility of lost or compromised information if they cannot ensure the availability, performance, privacy, confidentiality, and integrity of their new globally visible Web-based infrastructures and applications.

Cybersecurity monitoring and management services facilitates continued, secure electronic utilization over the Internet, intranets, extranets, and virtual private networks. It provides a layered, defense-in-depth strategy to adequately secure, monitor, protect, and manage an organization's critical information environment, including intrusion detection and response. The capabilities within this service assist in controlling the major security threats faced by today's digital enterprises, providing proactive as well as reactive network operations center services 24 hours a day, 365 days per year.

Cyberstrategy Summary. Cycling just once through the five-step cyberstrategy life-cycle model is simply not enough. Change is happening at a rapid rate – in any organization, in technology, in the economy. And with each new change comes a new set of cybersecurity challenges that must be assessed, protected against, validated, trained for, and monitored. The cyberstrategy life cycle approach must be rigorous, repeatable, and measurable. The cybersecurity staff must be able to get the continual assurance they need that their applications, systems, and critical data are secure when accessed or deployed anytime, anywhere.

The cybersecurity staff may also be responsible for building security into IT solutions based on a cyberstrategy life cycle methodology that integrates cybersecurity requirements into each phase of the systems development life cycle. Integrating cybersecurity into the development and maintenance of secure applications is more than just another good cybersecurity strategy. It becomes an imperative. Integrated security mechanisms result in a higher level of cost-effective cybersecurity. One must realize that the right amount of security must be integrated into an organization's applications from the outset. This further reduces costs typically associated with "grafting" cybersecurity features onto existing systems after the fact.

Unlike many niche solutions, a rigorous, repeatable, and measurable process such as a cyberstrategy life-cycle methodology would be standardized and far-reaching, embracing a wide variety of security products, systems, and mechanisms. A comprehensive life cycle cyberstrategy solution must be based on proven processes.

While the opportunities and rewards are great, potential security hazards lurk at every juncture, every interface, and every portal. Establishing and maintaining effective policies that address the security, integrity, availability, confidentiality, and privacy of critical information system assets is crucial to the survival of any organization.

Specifically, organizations must put into operation and institutionalize a set of security measures (hardware, software, firmware and data), along with their controlling policies, practices, and procedures. These must address the full range of exposures, vulnerabilities, threats, and risks created by the new model. To that end, a truly robust set of security services, implemented in accordance with a cyberstrategy life cycle methodology, is the surest way to mitigate risk now and in the future.

An effective cyberstrategy methodology will provide the full range of security services required to protect the organization on an ongoing basis including:

- Security assessments to assess the organization's current security posture and recommend the appropriate security policies, processes, and procedures.
- Development and implementation of protective measures, including security policies, plans, and architectures that address the identified exposures.
- Validation of the organization's information systems infrastructure, following the implementation of security measures.
- Personnel training to ensure the continued security of the organization's information systems.
- Procedures to continuously monitor the security status of systems and to manage and administer the organization's security policies, processes, procedures, and security technologies.

The Cyberstrategy life cycle methodology delivers the skills, tools, and resources needed to keep data secure and to protect physical, financial and intellectual capital from assault and compromise. End-to-end, the cyberstrategy methodology helps organizations gain control over user access, simplify security management and administration processes, improve accountability and data integrity, ensure privacy and confidentiality, and guard against costly security breaches . . . across platforms, over the Internet, and around the world.

AUTOMATED TOOLS

Anyone operating a cybersecurity program will learn to recognize the value and limitations of automated cybersecurity tools. There is an entire range of tools that can assist in managing a cybersecurity program, including: attribute tools; information handling tools such as database management systems and data visualization tools; architecture tools; interoperability tools; risk, threat and vulnerability assessment tools; requirements tools; network security auditing and anti-virus tools; policy and process tools; graphical interface tools; simulation and modeling tools; and even the tools that attackers use to attempt to access and compromise automated information. This section, with special thanks to Stephen Quinn at the U.S. National Institute of Standards and Technology, will briefly mention a few so that the reader can get an idea of the types of tools that are available.

- **Information Handling Tools** include database management systems like MS Access® and Oracle®, including Open Source systems like PostgreSQL or data visualization tools such as Visualize® by jQuery. An example of how this might be useful was presented in Figure 2.
- **Architecture Tools** range from simple databases to sophisticated analysis models. An example would be Info-Tech's Security Architecture Roadmap Tool. With the emphasis on cloud computing as a cybersecurity strategy, one should look at the cloud computing security patterns provided by the Open Security Architecture organization at www.opensecurityarchitecture.org.
- **Interoperability Tools** come in lots of flavors. Some simply catalog functionality; some, like Levels of Information System Interoperability (LISI)® by Mitre Corporation provide a subjective assessment of interoperability issues; and some actually assist the Security Assessment & Authorization (SA&A), formerly called the Certification and Accreditation (C&A) process and recently revised under the U.S. National Institute of Standards and Technology (NIST) Risk Management Framework (RMF) discussed in NIST Special Publication (SP) 800-37 (NIST SP 800-37, 2010). The Secure Interoperability Testing Database currently under development by the Joint Interoperability Test Command (JITC) is a good example of the SA&A process.
- **Risk, Threat and Vulnerability Assessment Tools,** like interoperability tools are ubiquitous. Some are designed specifically for physical security modeling, some for the "Cyber" or information venue, and some are more generic. Examples include RiskWatch® by RiskWatch, Inc., and the Common Criteria Toolbox®, originally developed by Sparta under the sponsorship of the National Information Assurance Partnership (NIAP) and the international Common Criteria community. Various Protection Profiles have been recently enabled for the Toolbox.
- **Requirements Tools** range from simple database implementations like the Defense Information Systems Agency's (DISA) Requirements Traceability Matrix (RTM), the database shown in Figure

2, the Common Criteria Toolbox® mentioned above, and Computer Aided Systems Engineering (CASE) tools such as Secure Tropos, or ST-Tool, created by the University of Trento, Italy.

- **Internal Vulnerability Scanning/Auditing Tools** would include things like the Computer Oracle and Password System (COPS)® package from Purdue University, and Cisco's Net Ranger®.

- **Password Enhancing Tools/Authentication and System Security Tools** are often built into operating systems and application packages but there are also add-on programs that provide additional services and enhanced security such as OPIE® (One Time Passwords in Everything) developed at the US Naval Research Laboratory (NRL).

- **Password Breaking Tools** abound on the Internet making them readily available to anyone with an interest; e.g., Wfuzz, RainbowCrack, Brutus, etc. Brutus was first made publicly available in October 1998. Many downloads, no doubt, were by those who wanted to break the passwords on your system!

- **Access Control Tools** would include tools like Kerberos®, the network authentication protocol from the Massachusetts Institute of Technology (MIT).

- **Surveillance/Activity Monitoring Tools** like SpyTech's SpyAgent Professional, KeyStroke Spy and NetVizor.

- **Mail Security Tools** help ensure the privacy and confidentiality of email and other documents. One of the most popular examples is Pretty Good Privacy (PGP) ® from Symantec Corporation.

- **Anti-Virus Tools** form a large segment of the industry today. Many examples are available such as Check-Up®, Dr. Solomon's Anti-Virus Toolkit®, F-PROT®, and VIRUSCAN® but probably the most well-known are McAfee VirusScan® and Norton Anti-Virus®.

- **Intrusion Detection Tools/Network Monitoring Tools** would include ASAX® (Advanced Security audit trail Analysis on unix), Cisco's NetRanger® and Tripwire's Enterprise®.

- **Policy/Process Tools** help develop, enforce and measure the effectiveness of organizational policies, processes and procedures. Many are text based question and answer tools designed to help assess the state of the environment and capture that information in some form of database. The Requirements Traceability Matrix (RTM), and the Common Criteria Toolbox® are good examples.

- **Modeling and Simulation** tools tend to be very domain dependent, specifically developed to focus on a particular problem, situation or environment. However, some generic shells do exist to help develop these domain specific models. Commercial modeling tools like Microsoft's Visio® and IBM's Rational Rose® fit this category.

- **A quick summary of other tools and utilities that may be useful include:**
  - **Logging Utilities** such as traceroute. The traceroute command is available on a number of modern operating systems. On Apple Mac OS, it is available by opening 'Network Utilities' then selecting the 'Traceroute' tab. On other Unix systems, such as FreeBSD or Linux, it is available as a 'traceroute(8)' command. On Microsoft Windows, it is named 'tracert'.
  - **System Status Reporting Tools** like the Identification Protocol (ident) in the Unix OS and discussed at length at http://tools.ietf.org/html/rfc1413;
  - **Packet Filtering Tools** such as the IP packet filter for SunOS;
  - **Firewall Tools** such as Socket Secure (socks) discussed at length at http://tools.ietf.org/html/rfc1928;
  - **Real-time Attack Response Tools** such as a dummy "su" program, and example of which can be found at http://www.softpanorama.org/Security/IDS/honeypots.shtml;
  - **Encryption Tools** like IBM's Data Encryption Standard (DES)® Package;

- ○ **Host Configuration Tools** that includes its Message Op Code, discussed at length at http://tools.ietf.org/html/rfc1541;
- ○ **Cryptographic Checksum Tools** such as Snefru.® RHash, an open source command-line tool, can calculate and verify Snefru-128 and Snefru-256 and can be downloaded from http://rhash.anz.ru/; and
- ○ **Other miscellaneous tools** such as PC-Sentry® (a collection of programs and utilities to provide security and accountability on PC's and PC networks from www.sentrypc.com) and SATAN® (System Administrator Tool for Analyzing Networks), a freeware network security analyzer that scans systems connected to the network noting the existence of known and often exploited vulnerabilities. It can be downloaded at http://www.porcupine.org/satan/.

SUMMARY AND CONCLUSION

As stated in the Introduction, the purpose of this chapter was to build an understanding of the systems engineering process as it applies to large and complex information systems covered by cybersecurity requirements. Hence, we focused on cyberstrategy life cycle management within the systems engineering methodology. Systems Engineering models, practices and methodologies are not new but, until recently, they have been applied mostly to large-scale hardware or specific software application development. But these same methods applied to any large-scale system and their application within the world of cybersecurity could yield enormous benefits.

If we have been true to our purpose, the reader should now have an appreciation of the environment within which systems engineering occurs; understand the management skills needed to facilitate the development of complex information systems and the cyberstrategies needed in such an environment; and have a clear appreciation of systems engineering as applied to cybersecurity operations. Consideration of Systems Engineering concepts and their application to cybersecurity architectures, interoperability and cyberstrategies is an area deserving greater emphasis and more in-depth study.

REFERENCES

Bahill, A. T., & Chapman, W. L. (1993). A tutorial on quality function deployment. *Engineering Management Journal, 5*(3), 24–35. doi:10.1080/10429247.1993.11414742

Bicknell, K. D., & Bicknell, B. A. (1994). *The Road Map to Repeatable Success: Using QFD to Implement Changes*. Boca Raton, FL: CRC Press.

Chapman, W. L., Bahill, A. T., & Wymore, W. (1992). *Engineering Modeling and Design*. Boca Raton, FL: CRC Press.

Curts, R., & Campbell, D. (1999). Architecture: The Road to Interoperability. Paper presented at the *Command & Control Research & Technology Symposium*. Newport, RI.

Joint Military Operations: Weaknesses in DoD's Process for Certifying C4I Systems' Interoperability (1998). *General Accounting Office* (Letter Report, 03/13/98, GAO/NSIAD-98-73).

Grady, J. O. (1993). *System Requirements Analysis*. New York, NY: McGraw Hill, Inc.

Grady, J. O. (1994). *System Integration.* Boca Raton, FL: CRC Press.

Grady, J. O. (1995). *System Engineering Planning and Enterprise Identity.* Boca Raton, FL: CRC Press.

Guide for Applying the Risk Management Framework to Federal Information Systems. (2010, February). *National Institute of standards and technology NIST SP 800-37.*

Information Technology Standards. (1998). *Information Technology Standards Guidance – Information Management. Final Draft Version 1.0.* Washington, DC: Department of the Navy.

Jacobson, I., Ericsson, M., & Jacobson, A. (1995). *The Object Advantage: Business Process Reengineering with Object Technology.* New York, NY: Addison-Wesley.

Joint Interoperability Test Command. (1998, October 21). *C⁴I Interoperability–JITC Certification Process.* http://jitc.fhu.disa.mil/

Kapur, K. C., & Lamberson, L. R. (1977). *Reliability in Engineering Design.* New York, NY: John Wiley & Sons.

Karnavas, W. J., Sanchez, P., & Bahill, A. T. (1993). Sensitivity analyses of continuous and discrete systems in the time and frequency domains. *IEEE Transportation Systems, Man and Cybernetics Conference (SMC).* paper SMC-23, (pp. 488-501). doi:10.1109/21.229461

Kerzner, H. (1995). *Project Management: A Systems Approach to Planning, Scheduling, and Controlling.* New York, NY: Van Nostrand Reinhold.

Loch, K. D., Carr, H. H., & Warkentin, M. E. (1992, June). Threats to Information Systems: Today's Reality, Yesterday's Understanding. *Management Information Systems Quarterly, 16*(2), 173–186. doi:10.2307/249574

Management Analytics (15 December 1993). *Planning Considerations for Defensive Information Warfare – Cybersecurity.* Fort George G. Meade, Columbia, MD: Prepared for Defense Information Systems Agency (DISA) Joint Interoperability and Engineering Organization (JIEO) Center for Information Systems Security (CISS).

Mathwick, J. E. (1997). *Database Integration, Practical Lessons-Learned.* San Diego, CA: DoD Database Colloquium.

Michaels, R. (1999, February 18). *Department of the Navy Data Interoperability,* Briefing to Mr. Dan Porter, DoN CIO. Arlington, VA: GRC International.

Shishko, R. (1995). NASA Systems Engineering Handbook, Special Publication (SP) SP-6105.

Szidarovszky, F., Gershon, M., & Duckstein, L. (1993). *Techniques for Multi-objective Decision Making in Systems.* Boca Raton, FL: CRC Press.

Woodward, J. L., Jr., LGEN, USAF, Director for Command, Control, Communications and Computer Systems (February 2000). *Cybersecurity through Defense-in-Depth.* Washington, DC: The Joint Staff, Pentagon.

Wymore, W. (1993). *Model-Based Systems Engineering.* Boca Raton: CRC Press.APPENDIX

APPENDIX

Table 1. Acronyms

Acronym	Definition
ABCP	Associate Business Continuity Planner
ASAX	Advanced Security Audit trail Analysis on unix
ATO	Authority / Authorization To Operate
BASIC	Beginner's All-Purpose Symbolic Instruction Code
C&A	Certification And Accreditation
C⁴I	Command Control Communications Computers And Intelligence
C⁴ISR	Command Control Communications Computers Intelligence Surveillance And Reconnaissance
CA	California
CADM	Core Architecture Data Model
CASE	Computer Aided Software Engineering
CBCP	Certified Business Continuity Professional
CDR	Critical Design Review
CEO	Chief Executive Officer
CIO	Chief Information Officer Command Intelligence Officer
CISA	Certified Information Systems Auditor
CISS	Center for Information Systems Security
CISSP	Certified Information Security Systems Professional
CJCSI	Chairman Of The Joint Chiefs Of Staff Instruction
CM	Configuration Management
CNA	Center for Naval Analysis
COPS	Communications Operational Planning System
COTS	Commercial Off The Shelf
CPP	Certified Protection Professional
CRC	Cyclic Redundancy Check
DAVE	Data Analysis and Visualization Environment
DC	District of Columbia
DES	Data Encryption Standard
DII	Defense Information Infrastructure
DISA	Defense Information Systems Agency
DoD	Department of Defense
DoDAF	DoD Architecture Framework
DoN	Department of the Navy
DRI	Disaster Recovery Institute
DRII	DRI International
EA	Enterprise Architecture

continued on following page

Table 1. continued

Acronym	Definition
F-PROT	FRISK Software International – Protect
FRP	Full Rate Production
GAO	General Accounting Office
GiG	Global Information Grid
IBM	International Business Machines
IEEE	Institute Of Electrical And Electronics Engineers
IP	Internet Protocol
ISC2	International Information Systems Security Certification Consortium
IT	Information Technology
ITSG	Information Technology Standards Guidance
JIEO	Joint Interoperability Engineering Organization
JITC	Joint Interoperability Test Command
JTA	Joint Technical Architecture
LGEN	Lieutenant General
LISI	Levels of Information System Interoperability
LRIP	Limited Rate Initial Production
MAU	Multi Attribute Utility
MAUT	Multi Attribute Utility Theory
MBCP	Master Business Continuity Professional
MIS	Management Information System (OSHA)
MIT	Massachusetts Institute Of Technology
MS	Microsoft
NASA	National Aeronautics and Space Administration
NIAP	National Information Assurance Partnership
NIST	National Institute of Standards and Technology
NRL	Naval Research Laboratory
OPIE	One Time Passwords in Everything
PC	Personal Computer
PDR	Preliminary Design Review
PGP	Pretty Good Privacy
PKI	Public Key Infrastructure
QFD	Quality Function Deployment
RI	Rhode Island
RTM	Requirements Traceability Matrix
SA&A	Security Assessment & Authorization
SATAN	System Administrator Tool for Analyzing Networks
SMC-23	Systems, Man, and Cybernetic
SP-6105	Special Publication
SPAWAR	Space And Naval Warfare Systems Command

continued on following page

Table 1. continued

Acronym	Definition
SunOs	Sun Operating System
TAFIM	Technical Architecture Framework For Information Management
TAGS	Theater Air-Ground System
TEMP	Test And Evaluation Master Plan
US	United States
USA	United States Of America
USAF	United States Air Force
VA	Vulnerability Assessment
WANs	Wide Area Network

Chapter 7
Towards Protecting Critical Infrastructures

Filipe Caldeira
University of Coimbra and Polytechnic Institute of Viseu, Portugal

Tiago Cruz
University of Coimbra, Portugal

Paulo Simões
University of Coimbra, Portugal

Edmundo Monteiro
University of Coimbra, Portugal

ABSTRACT

Critical Infrastructures (CIs) such as power distribution are referred to as "Critical" as, in case of failure, the impact on society and economy can be enormous. CIs are exposed to a growing number of threats. ICT security plays a major role in CI protection and risk prevention for single and interconnected CIs were cascading effects might occur. This chapter addresses CI Protection discussing MICIE Project main results, along with the mechanisms that manage the degree of confidence assigned to risk alerts allowing improving the resilience of CIs when faced with inaccurate/inconsistent alerts. The CockpitCI project is also presented, aiming to improve the resilience and dependability of CIs through automatic detection of cyber-threats and the sharing of real-time information about attacks among CIs. CockpitCI addresses one MICIE's shortcoming by adding SCADA-oriented security detection capabilities, providing input for risk prediction models and assessment of the operational status of the Industrial Control Systems.

INTRODUCTION

Critical Infrastructures provide services that support our society and economy. Telecommunications infrastructures allow interactions among people and businesses within local or remote locations. Transport and air traffic infrastructures allow citizens to travel for tourism or business activities and also support the global commerce flow. One vital CI, which supports the majority of CIs is the electricity infrastructure

DOI: 10.4018/978-1-4666-8456-0.ch007

that enables a variety of services and applications that we take for granted. Can we take it for granted? Unfortunately, we are able to mention several examples that highlight how much actual society depend on services provided by CIs. Natural disasters as, for example, hurricane Katrina (2005), the earthquake and tsunami that affected Fukushima nuclear reactor in Japan (2011) made perceptible that services provided by CIs can cause chaos and difficulties for citizens and the economy, when unavailable. Those scenarios reveal that CIs are one of the most important technical or industrial systems that have a strong impact on peoples' lives and the operation of economy worldwide. Those types of infrastructures provide services that are vital as they provide services that are usually basic inputs to other simple or complex systems. This dependency on services provided by CIs can, in case of an improper operation of the CI, lead to the disruption of other dependent services. Recent efforts to improve security and protection in CIs are predominantly focusing on each CI individually, in order to achieve more secure CIs with increased robustness, security and resilience. An important aspect relates to the interdependency existent among CIs. This interdependency can lead, in an extreme situation, to a global failure in an undefined number of CIs, started by a single trivial incident in one CI. This scenario is known by cascading effect.

Governments from various countries around the world are already aware of the importance of their Critical Infrastructures not only for the well-being of their Citizens but also for the survivability of their nations in terms of economy and defence. More recently, the awareness about the increasing interdependency among CIs steered to the definition of legislation or encouraging policies aiming to improve the information sharing among Critical Infrastructure owners. Examples on legislation addressing this subjects can be found in several countries or regions such as the European Union (European Commission, 2008), the United States of America (Obama, 2013) and Australia (TISN, 2011).

More recently, on the 13th of February 2013, the President of the United States of America, Barack Obama, issued the Executive Order 13636 "Improving Critical Infrastructure Cybersecurity" (Obama, 2013) on which it is proposed that the Policy of the United States Government should help improve the cyber threat information sharing among private sector entities that control CIs, so that those entities can improve the weapons available in the fight against cyber threats.

The European Commission is also committed to enhancing security on Critical Infrastructures. The Directorate-General of the European Commission in charge of the policy area known as "Home Affairs" states that *"Reducing the vulnerabilities of critical infrastructure is one of the major objectives of the EU. An adequate level of protection must be ensured and the detrimental effects of disruptions on the society and citizens must be limited as far as possible."* (European Commission, 2012).

An important element of the European Program for the Protection of Critical Infrastructure (EPCIP) program is a Directive on European Critical Infrastructures as it establishes a procedure for identifying and designating European Critical Infrastructures (ECI) and a common approach to improve the protection of such infrastructures. Understanding the importance of the role that the exchange of information about threats and vulnerabilities plays in protecting CIs, an information network has been created for that role - Critical Infrastructure Warning Information Network (CIWIN) (European Commission, 2008). CIWIN has two main objectives: the establishment of an electronic forum for the purpose of exchanging information on the protection of CIs; and the development of a rapid alert system for the delivery of early warnings for Member States to inform the Commission regarding risks and threats.

The efforts made in the Critical Infrastructure Protection in ICT area in- creased, especially after "Stuxnet" attack. "Stuxnet" is a computer worm and, as reported in 2010, it was the first malware specifically targeting control systems as the ones used in many existing Critical Infrastructures. In a similar way as viruses and worms, "Stuxnet" exploited some vulnerabilities that were unknown at the time of the attack in order to replicate and spread itself among the exploitable equipment. However, the main goal of this worm was to attack the industrial control systems, by introducing changes (not visible to the sys- tem operator) in the Programmable Logic Controllers (PLCs), modifying their normal behaviour, to make them work as the attacker intended (Falliere et al., 2011).

Considering the above, it is clear that CIs are one of the most ICT dependent areas of contemporary societies where we should ensure the highest security levels.

In line with the actual efforts to improve CIP, the MICIE FP7 project (MICIE Consortium, 2008) aimed at the development of an alerting system that identifies, in real time, the risk level induced on a given CI caused by undesired events or malicious attacks happening in the reference CI or in dependent CIs. The MICIE project was able to gather risk information from CIs and also to integrate risk informa- tion received from dependent CIs. As an improvement to the project, we proposed to use a Policy Based Management System (PBMS), allowing the system Operator to manage the system in a simple way, us- ing policies. Those policies, apart from the common conditions used in access control systems are also able to use risk information in order to improve decision taking. From this point it become clear that, in addition to the risk exchange information from dependent CIs and integration of this information in the risk evaluation, it should also be possible to infer on the exchanged information in order to minimise the use of incorrect information.

As it was not foreseen by the MICIE system, to infer on the exchanged information, this gap was identified and a framework for Trust and Reputation Management has been proposed. Since the results of the application of the framework on the MICIE project were promising, an independent architecture has been defined and validated by using also different CI risk models and risk evaluation tools. This architecture contributes to the improvement of CIs security, by addressing problems that result from a scenario were it is intended to evaluate risk levels from CIs and share those risks among multiple (inter) dependent CIs in order to help them in improving their own risk evaluation. The main contributions discussed can be summarised as the following: (1) A Policy Management Architecture able to manage the MICIE system; (2) The conception and development of a Trust and Reputation framework able to infer trust information from the exchanged information in the MICIE system; (3) Integrate the trust model approach in CI risk models.

In order to improve the results obtained by the MICIE project, a follow- up project named CockpitCI is under development (CockpitCI Consortium, 2011). The CockpitCI project aims on one hand to improve and update the online risk assessment framework deployed within the MICIE project and, on the other hand, to introduce ICT detection capabilities in order to get a wider perspective in terms of security, to identify in near real time the CI functionalities impacted by cyber-attacks and to assess the impact on CI delivered services. CockpitCI aims to classify the existent risk level and implement containment measures of the possible consequences of cyber-attacks together with the moving some intelligence to field equipment, allowing it to perform local decisions in order to self-identify and self-react to abnormal situations induced by cyber attacks.

The rest of this chapter is organised as follows: In the next Section, related work associated with Critical Infrastructure security and protection are discussed. The MICIE project and the solutions to incorporate CIs interdependencies in the online risk assessment framework are described in Section *"The MICIE project"*. The subsequent Section describes the employed approach to evaluate Trust and Reputation indicators on the exchanged risk information. Simple validation scenarios are also presented.

Section "*The CockpitCI project*" describes the CockpitCI project including an overview on SCADA security issues and the detailed description of the CockpitCI architecture. In the last Section, this work is concluded and an outlook on future work is given.

PROTECTING CRITICAL INFRASTRUCTURES

An overview of some major research problems associated with Critical Infrastructure security and protection are described in this section, including problems that may arise from the existent CI (inter) dependencies and how these problems are being currently addressed by the research community. This section also presents a brief review of some of the most representative research work done in Critical Infrastructure modelling, simulation techniques and risk assessment. Open issues and challenges associated with them will also be covered. Selected European Projects that deal with CI protection are also presented.

Critical Infrastructures

As already defined, CIs provide vital services for the normal functioning of a community or a country. As the academics become more aware of the impact that a disruption in those services can have, Critical Infrastructure Protection has become an important research topic in the last years.

Among the sectors of activity that encompasses Critical Infrastructures, the electricity and telecommunications CIs are the sectors that are getting more attention from researchers. Nowadays, the power grids are vital to the society causing major losses when they are not available.

As many Critical Infrastructures, Power Grids are usually managed by Industrial Control Systems (ICSs) that include Supervisory Control and Data Acquisition (SCADA) systems, Distributed Control System (DCS), PLC, among other systems typically used in industrial contexts such as utilities (electricity distribution and production, water supply, etc.). An ICS allows, for instance, the CI Operator to remotely control some equipment and perform control tasks. In such a system as SCADA, the data accuracy and is timely reception (real-time) allow the CI Operator to have more reliable information thus allowing a more efficient and safer operation. SCADA systems are frequently used to control dispersed assets using centralised data acquisition and supervisory control. In order to achieve their goals, these systems now rely, for instance, on proper communication availability, in the quality of the information gathered and also on the quality and reliability of the ICT systems that support those activities.

The evolution of the Industrial Control Systems used in CIs is occurring by passing from proprietary and closed architectures to open standard based solutions. As usual while dealing with security, it is important to balance Confidentiality, Integrity and Availability. In this case, ICS systems are becoming more available within the CI and even among partner CIs. While improving availability it is important to focus also on maintaining ICS data confidential and reliable. Currently, ICSs are considered a critical and strategic asset that produces information about all the CI. The failure or just the existence of false or inadequate information in the ICSs has a huge potential for catastrophic consequences within the CI.

It is commonly agreed that a damage or loss of critical services in CI may cause adverse effects on several others. This risk is gradually increasing as some of the infrastructures control systems are making part of a larger interconnected network. It needs to be emphasised that actual infrastructure sectors do not exist isolated but interact among each other as represented in *Figure 1*.

Figure 1. Critical Infrastructure interdependency example (Rinaldi et al., 2001)

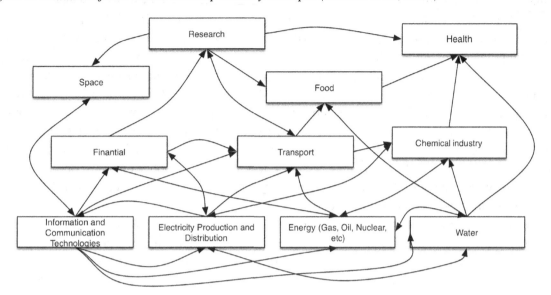

Critical Infrastructure (Inter)Dependency

It is possible to find multiple publications related to the identification of the various kinds of dependencies that may occur among CIs. One major study in the area of Critical Infrastructure (inter)dependency has been carried by Rinaldi et al.. In this work (Rinaldi et al., 2001) a Critical Infrastructure is defined as an agent in a Complex Adaptive System (CAS) due to the complex and continuously changing set of interacting components. Rinaldi et al. intends to clarify and discuss the existing dependencies or interdependencies among CIs, in particular, it provides an excellent overview on the dimensions in which (inter) dependencies can occur. According to Rinaldi et al. each CI can be either dependent or interdependent to other CI determined by whether it is a supporting or supported CI. According to Rinaldi et al., the current state of operation of an infrastructure has a direct impact on the state of operation of interdependent infrastructure. The states of operation can range from normal to stressed/disrupted and repair/restoration (Rinaldi et al., 2001). In this chapter, the cyber interdependency type is addressed with the objective of minimising the effects that this type of dependency can have on the state change of an infrastructure.

A key characteristic of interdependencies is the failure that can occur in an infrastructure and how it may spread to other interdependent infrastructures. As CIs become more interconnected, a failure in a node of this complex network of interdependent infrastructures, can results in disastrous failures including some that are not yet foreseen. These types of failures result from the propagation of some small failure through other interdependent systems. This propagation effect is known as the cascading effect and has been the subject of multiple research works (Rinaldi, 2004).

The research that has been carried out for studying the structure and behaviour of Critical Infrastructures is frequently divided in two main distinct but interrelated groups. The first is involved with the study and analysis of the infrastructures while the second focuses on the understanding of the CIs dynamic behaviour.

Actual research in these areas aims to describe the current status of an infrastructure by identifying and developing new techniques and tools. This is an important aspect, as the cascading effect can be minimised if one knows the actual or predicted state of an infrastructure on which one depends. In order to gather detailed information from CIs, researchers exploit multiple CI vulnerability, risks and threats, aiming to reveal the potential points of failure and to describe the expected consequences of each failure.

Several publications address the problem of how to identify the various kinds of dependencies that can occur among CIs. Rinaldi et al. specifies an overview on the multiple dimensions in which (inter) dependencies can occur (Rinaldi et al., 2001). Rinaldi (Rinaldi, 2004), discusses and analyses different modelling techniques applied to CI (inter)dependencies. Another important publication, among others, that proposes CI models based on various different modelling techniques was presented by Sokolowski et al.. This publication (Sokolowski et al., 2008) describes a conceptual modelling method for CIs that aims to create an abstract and simplified view of a CI. It is important to notice that most of the published work dealing with CI models and CI risk models is very heterogeneous with respect to their purpose and the extent to which they might be implemented.

A significant work is also been carried out by Panzieri et al. (Panzieri et al., 2005), in which the Complex Adaptive System approach is used in order to allow CI modelling. In particular, this approach is focused on analysing performance degradation and fault propagation that can occur after one or more failures, not including recovery or repair procedures that may take place after one failure (Panzieri et al., 2005).

De Porcellinis et al. described the Mixed Holistic Reductionist (MHR) approach as a methodology able to model Critical Infrastructures including the existent interdependencies, considering the predefined level of Quality-of-Service that should be provided to customers or other dependent CIs (De Porcellinis et al., 2009). A reductionist approach aims to model systems into small parts while the holistic method looks globally at systems including the existing interactions. One interesting aspect of the MHR approach is, as stated (De Porcellinis et al., 2009), that holistic blocks are able to represent the holistic perspective of the infrastructures, and are able to interact with other existing holistic blocks in order to inform of their status (De Porcellinis et al., 2009). For example (Simões et al., 2009), the failure block allows modelling social events (e.g. strike, panic) that are difficult to model on a more focused abstract level. Holistic blocks have the possibility to impact the operative conditions of a service, based on feedback received from reductionist elements (Simões et al., 2009).

Also, major work, able to use CI models to infer risk information in CIs, was also proposed by some authors. For instance, Haslum and Arnes describe the use of continuous-time hidden Markov models for real-time risk calculation and estimation (Haslum and Arnes, 2006). Baiardi et al. presents a risk management strategy based on a hyper-graph model in order to detect complex attacks while also supporting risk mitigation (Baiardi et al., 2009).

The recently described CI security model, presented by Schaberreiter et al. is, as stated by the author, based on a different approach that differs greatly from the models previously published (Schaberreiter et al., 2011a). By applying the CI Security Model, Schaberreiter et al. aims to simplify the infrastructure complexity in the model through the use of security properties in order to create an abstraction layer over the physical implementation of the services. Aubert et al. suggests that this abstraction can be applied to a wider range of systems (e.g. energy, telecommunication, air traffic) as they share the same security objectives. Another major benefit of this model is that the information exchanged among CIs is specifically related to the security belonging to shared services, thus keeping confidential information inside each CI. As providers usually hesitate to share the information that would enhance the security of their CIs, it is assumed that the abstraction to a small set of common parameters will encourage service providers to share them with (inter)dependent providers (Aubert et al., 2010).

Critical Infrastructure Protection Projects

The European Union is significantly committed in improving the security level of European CIs. In order to address those objectives, in the past years the European Commission, in the scope of community research and development strategies, promoted research projects related to CI Protection. This section briefly describes three of those projects while in the rest of the Chapter, the projects MICIE and CockpitCI are described in detail.

IRRIIS (Integrated Risk Reduction of Information-based Infrastructure Systems)

The IRRIIS project aimed to enhance the dependability of large complex Critical Infrastructures. This was achieved by developing and applying appropriate modelling and simulation techniques and by developing proper middleware based communication technologies (MIT) among CIs (Klein et al., 2009).

Two application scenarios have been defined for the project, representing, respectively, one electrical power infrastructure and one telecommunication infrastructure that support the first. For each of those scenarios the authors analyse the way CIs are connected to the exterior by the use of networks such as Internet (IRRIIS, 2008). One main challenge addressed by Integrated Risk Reduction of Information-based Infrastructure Systems (IRRIIS) is the different type and comportment of different Critical Infrastructures. IRRIIS approach to this was to build information models able to model physical aspects, as well as information and control aspects of CIs. Simultaneously, the project addressed the variety of existing CIs. Including the dependencies that may exist to other CIs while trying to maintain the model able to be generally used by multiple CI types.

Project IRRIIS has developed a set of applications called Middleware Improved Technology (MIT) allowing the communication among different heterogeneous CIs that usually have incompatible applications. MIT's main objective is to permit a simple, fast and reliable information exchange among CIs, thus reducing response time to incidents that may occur within the CIs, by maintaining network managers well informed about the CI state (IRRIIS, 2008). According to Klein et al., the IRRIIS information model provides an important framework for CI interdependencies simulation, risk estimation and decision support within CIs.

CRUTIAL (CRitical UTility InfrastructurAL Resilience)

CRitical UTility InfrastructurAL Resilience (CRUTIAL) project (CRUTIAL, 2008) aimed to improve the resilience of Critical Infrastructures in order to avoid or minimise problems that may occur due to the large and complex CI ICT systems and also to the increasing number of interconnections among CIs (CRUTIAL, 2008). According to Verissimo et al., the CRUTIAL project provides an architecture including multiple tools and algorithms aimed at improving resilience on global critical information infrastructures, taking into account computer-borne attacks and faults (Verissimo et al., 2008b). Although the CRUTIAL architecture is focused on the computer systems that support an electrical utility infrastructure, Verissimo et al. describes it as a useful reference for all types of Critical Infrastructures. In actual fact, the CRUTIAL architecture is used as a reference to various studies and in particular to multiple European projects.

The existing interdependencies among CIs are analysed and the need of an architecture that considers the global view on those interconnected infrastructures is identified by the CRUTIAL approach, which provides a global view on the interconnected infrastructures. It is also discussed that conventional security mechanisms cannot be directly applied to CI protection (Verissimo et al., 2008b,a; Bessani et al., 2007).

CRUTIAL architecture is established with an intrusion tolerant design in mind on which the resilience of infrastructures is achieved by deploying a trust- worthy operation supported by secure and trusted hardware. Despite the possible existence of faults and intrusions, the non-stop CI operation is enabled by the developed methodologies (proactive-resilience). The components behaviour is monitored over time in order to detect deviations (components that have a behaviour different from the expected). This information is analysed by a state diagnosis component (that guesses the internal state of a component based on the deviation detection) in order to reason whether some individual components may or may not affect the rest of the system. This detection is particularly useful to lower the risk of spreading cascading events (Verissimo et al., 2008b).

The main purpose of the CRUTIAL project was to enable the collection of improved knowledge about Critical Infrastructures, permitting the development of more resilient infrastructures. The validated results obtained within the CRUTIAL project are considered a major contribution to the development of the state of the art in CI protection (CRUTIAL, 2008; Verissimo et al., 2008b; Dondossola et al., 2008; Verissimo et al., 2008a; Bessani et al., 2007). The CRUTIAL developed methodologies and tools are highly focused on ICT and the Electricity Power Systems thus the applicability in different areas becomes more difficult. As the main goal of CRUTIAL is to develop more resilient infrastructures, it does not consider the existence of alerting systems or risk information exchange among CIs.

INSPIRE (INcreasing Security and Protection through Infras- tructure REsilience)

As described by D'Antonio et al., the INSPIRE project aimed to enhance the European potential in the field of security by ensuring the protection of Critical Infrastructures through the identification of their vulnerabilities and the development of innovative techniques for securing networked process control systems (D'Antonio et al., 2009).

The core idea of the INSPIRE project is to protect Critical Infrastructures by appropriately configuring, managing, and securing the communication net- work which interconnects the distributed control systems. A working prototype has been implemented as a final demonstrator of selected scenarios.

The main research objectives addressed by the INSPIRE project were: the design and implementation of traffic engineering algorithms to provide SCADA traffic with quantitative guarantees, thus increasing SCADA resilience to at- tacks or malfunctions; the use of peer-to-peer overlay routing mechanisms for improving the resilience of SCADA systems; the design of an architectural framework for SCADA systems monitoring, diagnosis and reconfiguration and also the development of diagnosis and recovery techniques for SCADA systems (INSPIRE, 2010).

THE MICIE PROJECT

As mentioned in previous sections, it is now agreed that CIs are one of the areas where it is vital to ensure highest security levels. In this context, the European Commission, within the EPCIP, plans the implementation of the Critical Infrastructure Warning Information Network (CIWIN) able to provide a platform for the exchange of rapid alerts among CIs in order to help European Member States and CI Operators to share information on common threats and vulnerabilities. This platform aims to allow

Figure 2. MICIE system overview

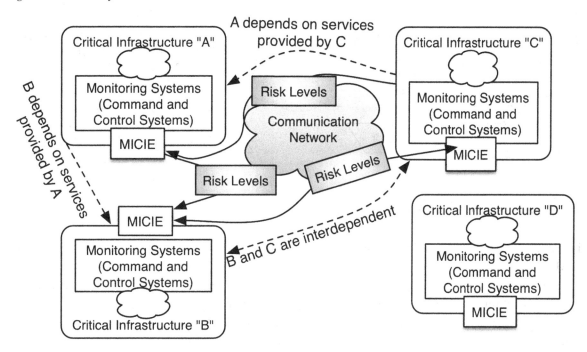

CI Operators to have a real time view on the risk level associated with their services and with services provided by interconnected CIs. Sharing this information allow to increase the accuracy of the CI risk models, by introducing risk information related to external failures (Simões et al., 2010).

In order to improve CIs' service levels and resiliency, a robust, resilient and inter-dependencies-aware alerting system was designed and implemented. This was the main goal of MICIE (Tool for systemic risk analysis and secure mediation of data exchanged across linked CI information infrastructures) FP7-ICT project, aiming the design and implementation of a real-time risk level dissemination and alerting system (MICIE Consortium, 2008).

Figure 2. represents a top-level view of the MICIE system. In this Figure, four CIs operating the system are represented. It is notable the existence of CIs that depend on services provided by partner CI and also CIs that are interdependent. For instance, CI A depends on services provided by CI C and provides services to CI B. CI B depends on services provided by CI A and CI B. CI C only depends on services provided by CI B. One independent CI (CI D) is also represented, highlighting the fact that MICIE can also be used in an independent manner. In this case, only local risk prediction is evaluated and used without information being exchanged.

In the MICIE system, a distributed on-line Prediction Tool (PT) is constantly evaluating the risk level indicators. The PT is updated by incorporating received information gathered from the field of each CI. The MICIE alerting system includes a communication infrastructure, the Secure Mediation Gate-way (SMGW), which provides secure communication channels across the MICIE system. The SMGW retrieves, from each CI, all the information needed to evaluate a real-time risk prediction. Additionally, the system implements information sharing mechanisms according to a highly available and secure framework (*Figure 3*) (Capodieci et al., 2010). The MICIE consortium tested the system in a portion of the electrical and telecommunication infrastructures of Israel, both managed by the Israel Electric Corporation.

Figure 3. MICIE overall system architecture

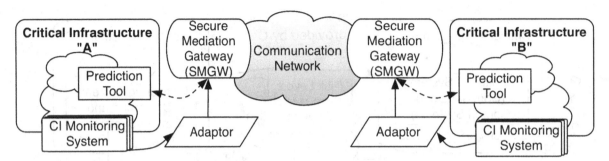

MICIE Overall System Architecture

Since multiple CIs are disposed to cooperate in order to improve the provided Quality-of-Service (QoS), the MICIE system allows CIs to predict and exchange risk information across trusted or untrusted networks. The information exchange is critical as it supports the risk analysis and predictions gathered from each CI, thus it must be kept within the system in a secure manner.

Figure 3. represents the MICIE's system overall architecture with the main following entities (Caldeira et al., 2010a; Castrucci et al., 2012):

- Critical Infrastructure: the infrastructure from which the MICIE system predicts the risk. Multiple CIs might participate in the MICIE system even if they are heterogeneous and even if they are situated in remote locations.
- Prediction Tool (PT): the entity responsible for undertaking risk prediction within CIs. Each CI has at least one local Prediction Tool. However, in order to achieve all the project benefits, it requires, in addition to local information, information related to remote (inter)dependent CIs.
- CI Monitoring System: the local framework able to perform monitoring activities within an infrastructure. This system is able to detect failures, degradation of QoS, among others. As it is assumed that the participant CIs are or can be heterogeneous, each CI can have its own specific monitoring system. Due to the fact that monitoring systems are closely related to the CI physical components, it is assumed that this component is a legacy system completely decoupled from the MICIE system.
- Adaptor: the entity employed for interconnecting each CI's particular monitoring system with the MICIE system. It is able to connect to the CI's monitoring system collecting information from it and providing the necessary translation to a common data representation format. It also performs operations such as filtering, aggregation and translation of information with the main goal to provide the MICIE system with all the information needed to accomplish risk prediction.
- Secure Mediation Gateway (SMGW): the entity that provides to the PT, the information needed for risk prediction. It is able to gather and com- pile local information retrieved by the adaptor(s) and to receive remote information from peer SMGWs. It has also the role of providing the necessary information to remote peer SMGWs in order to assist them with performing their functionalities with proper knowledge. Since the information treated by the SMGW is sensitive, it fulfils a number of security requirements including also the secure communication with remote peer SMGWs.

In order to design and implement the complete MICIE system a reference scenario has been defined, with the stakeholder accordance, and modelled including the discovered (inter)dependencies. Three new functional modules were fully designed and implemented, namely the Adaptor, the SMGW and the PT.

MICIE - Critical Infrastructure Modelling

One of the problems that the MICIE project had to overcome was Critical Infrastructures modelling. Despite the existence of several proposals for CI modelling this was a heavy task. The difficulty was mainly due to the usual complexity and size that such an infrastructure entails. In order to build a representative and realistic model for the MICIE project, a reference scenario has been defined within the project consortium supported by the expertise of the stakeholder, the Israel Electric Corporation. The use of a reference scenario was a fundamental decision thus narrowing down what should be in the model, and providing a concrete context of operation, focused on CI (inter)dependencies.

The reference scenario encompasses the ICT systems and two distinct CIs (energy and telecommunications). It has been established from one set of the Israel Electric Company infrastructures, systems and their interconnections. The main components of the reference scenario are (Simões et al., 2010; Ciancamerla et al., 2010b, 2009):

- a section of an electricity distribution network, including a Medium Volt- age (MV) power grid at 22 KV and a High Voltage (HV) power grid at 160 KV;
- a supervisory control and data acquisition (SCADA) system that remotely monitors and controls the power distribution grid and Remote Terminal Units for remote operations;
- a section of the Israel Electric Corporation (IEC) telecommunications network with fiber optics and radio links used mainly to control the electricity distribution network;
- the interconnection of SCADA with the portion of IEC telecommunications transmission network;
- the ICT infrastructure.

A top-level view of the reference scenario is represented in *Figure 4*. On the left side of the Figure, some examples of possible adverse events, that can eventually occur and cause some impact in the normal operation of the services provided by the CIs, are represented. The represented adverse events can be triggered due to multiple causes, namely, natural causes, malicious attacks or simply due the malfunction of some equipment. A simple event can affect just one of the represented CIs or services, for instance the electrical CI or the telecommunications CI, and, as both of the represented CIs are interdependent, the effect triggered by such a small event may propagate and reach the customers of the medium voltage grid causing, for instance, the interruption of power supply.

MICIE models were evaluated and tested based on multiple heterogeneous models (stochastic versus deterministic, agent based, dynamic simulation, etc.) with the main objective of evaluating a short-term estimate for the Quality- of-Service supplied by the different Critical Infrastructures. The models were created based on the underlying interconnected networks that collaborate for service delivery and, as represented in *Figure 4*, according to multiple possible adverse events (for example, attacks to critical elements, sequences of characteristic failures and congestions or failure in communication networks).

One major aspect that has been addressed is the impact that the potential degradation of the QoS on the SCADA system might have on the quality of the power supply provided by the power grid Operator to power grid customers. Capodieci et al. describes that the MICIE project was able to identify

Figure 4. High level view of the reference scenario (adapted from Ciancamerla et al. (2010a))

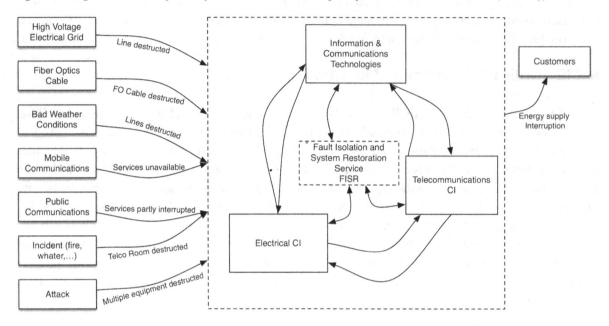

the inter- connected networks that support the Fault Isolation and System Restoration Service (FISR) service, namely, the SCADA system, the telecommunication network and the power distribution grid. This identification was made in terms of topologies, functionalities, performances, rerouting and failure behaviours and interconnections at physical, geographical and logical layers (Capodieci et al., 2010). Different techniques and tools are used to represent the reference scenario. Bertoni et al. describes in detail the application of such techniques and tools within the MICIE project (Bertoni et al., 2010).

Online Risk Prediction Tool

According to Capodieci et al., the MICIE Project applied a realistic approach based in a decentralised scenario able to synchronise with external scenarios. In that approach, each control centre should include a global model representing all existent systems. Each infrastructure has a tool that receives information originated from inside the infrastructure. As the different tools must be inter- connected in order to achieve a global prediction, it is important to maintain them synchronised. An example of how to achieve model synchronisation has been presented by Gasparri et al. for the case of linear distributed interdependency estimators with complete information sharing (Gasparri et al., 2009).

On the proposed framework for the MICIE project, all of the existent pre- diction tools have the same overall model. The Mixed Holistic Reductionist approach has been adopted along with the CISIA (De Porcellinis et al., 2008) simulation framework. CISIA allows to manage multiple heterogeneous models into a single framework, with the desired level of granularity (Capodieci et al., 2010).

More information regarding the results achieved in this area is available from the MICIE work package 3000 – Risk prediction system design documentation and from several publications describing in detail this subject (Panzieri et al., 2010; Simões et al., 2010; Gasparri et al., 2009; De Porcellinis et al., 2009; Oliva et al., 2010; Ciancamerla et al., 2010a).

MICIE Secure Mediation Gateway

The identification and modelling of interdependencies, together with CI state prediction can help to limit the effects of a failure in a CI and even to prevent cascading effects, in case the CI Operator has the opportunity to be informed of the status of the existing interdependencies. In this scenario the Operator can undertake specific actions in order to prevent the failure of the CI if failures occur in interdependent CIs. To reach this goal, it was fundamental to develop a communication system interconnecting different CIs. In the MICIE project, the SMGW is the key element of the existent communication infrastructure that is composed by a set of SMGWs (one for each CI in the system).

The MICIE SMGW architecture, represented in *Figure 5*, is able to interact with four main entities through the following interfaces (Castrucci et al., 2010; Caldeira et al., 2010a; Castrucci et al., 2012):

- to the local CI monitoring system through the SMGW-Adaptor Standard interface;
- to the local Prediction Tool through the SMGW-PT interface;
- to other remote SMGWs through the SMGW-SMGW interface;
- to the system administrator through the SMGW control interface.

Within the MICIE system, the main tasks performed by the SMGW are briefly described as: (i) collecting information about the local CI (i.e. the CI where the SMGW is located); (ii) retrieving information about the other inter- dependent CIs in the system; (iii) sending information about the local CI to remote CIs; (iv) providing all the collected information to the Prediction Tool. In order to implement the main SMGW functionalities proposed in the architecture, five independent entities were developed, namely, the Data/Metadata Database, the Information Discovery Framework, the Communication Engine, the SMGW Manager and the Auditing Engine (Castrucci et al., 2010; Caldeira et al., 2010a; Castrucci et al., 2012).

Figure 5. MICIE SMGW architecture (Castrucci et al., 2012)

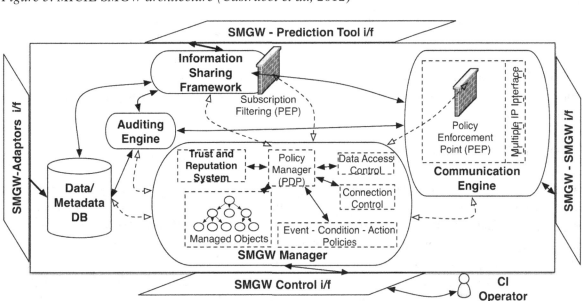

SMGW Management

Information exchanged among SMGWs is extremely sensitive, as it is related to the Critical Infrastructures, their status, and their services. It is clear that non-authorised third parties should not be able to acquire the information ex- changed among CIs. In this context, the problem of how to manage the system has been addressed. Management strategies were developed that address security aspects while permitting an easy definition of security rules by the system administrators.

The MICIE project integrates a Policy Based Management Architecture, allowing an easy and flexible manner to manage all security and operation aspects related to the SMGW (Caldeira et al., 2010c,a,d; Castrucci et al., 2012) The employed management approach offers the CI Operator a management tool where it is possible to define, in a high level manner, the intended behaviour of the system. In this tool the concepts of Policy Decision Point - the SMGW Manager - and Policy Enforcement Point - the entities that must enforce policies are applied for instance, in the Communication Engine and the Subscription Filter. In *Figure 5* the proposed Policy Decision Point (PDP) and the existing Policy Enforcement Point (PEP) are represented. In particular, the one intended to enforce policies related to data subscription and the other enforcing policies related to the remote connections in the Communication Engine. It is also possible to deploy PEP acting outside the SMGW, able to manage, for instance, communication aspects that are not visible within the SMGW. The SMGW Manager includes the PDP, all defined policies, the Managed Objects and also a Trust and Reputation System.

The SMGW Manager handles issues regarding authorisation, authentication and accounting, super-vising existent interaction with peer SMGWs and also the internal operation of the SMGW. It is also responsible for the management of testing, alarming, intrusion prevention, detection functions and the Trust and Reputation System (Caldeira et al., 2010a). The SMGW Manager within the SMGW architecture is represented in *Figure 5*.

The proposed management approach offers the CI Operator a tool on which it is possible to define, in a high level manner, the expected system's behaviour. The CI Operator can define policies addressing the relations between local SMGW and foreign SMGWs, including defining how each particular CI can connect and data access policies. The SMGW manager GUI allow to browse existent information and define actions that remote SMGWs can perform. All data access controls are implemented with a high level of granularity thus maintaining simplicity (Castrucci et al., 2010; Caldeira et al., 2010c).

Policies are represented using a policy specification language and stored in a policy repository. The SMGW Manager interacts with other entities on the SMGW through a dedicated Application Programming Interface (API). The SMGW Manager is based on the PONDER2 Toolkit (Twidle et al., 2009; Ponder, 2010).

Trust and Reputation System for the MICIE System

Considering the sensitive nature of the information exchanged within the MI- CIE system, special attention has been given to the security requirements. In contribution to the security requirements, we proposed the evaluation and usage of Trust and Reputation indicators in the SMGW Manager, allowing also these indicators to become available to the Prediction Tool (Castrucci et al., 2012, 2010; Lev et al., 2011). The main goals of these indicators are: to improve the accuracy of the existent information; to help the SMGW Manager to protect each CI from receiving and using inconsistent information; to gather Trust and Reputation information regarding the behaviour of each involved CI (Caldeira et al., 2010b). The proposed Trust and Reputation framework is described in the following Section.

A FRAMEWORK FOR TRUST AND REPUTATION MANAGEMENT IN CIS

Current research in CI Protection is mostly focused on understanding and modelling (inter)dependencies among CIs and the use of these models in allowing the development of risk prediction tools that receive inputs from several sources, such as, monitoring and control equipment, Operator information and risk in- formation provided by (inter)dependent CIs (Bertoni et al., 2010). Although the existing risk evaluation methodologies are able to merge risk information arriving from multiple sources, the lack of mechanisms allowing to observe and reason about the confidence one can have in the information collected from these sources, was identified. It is also relevant to understand the behaviour of the involved sources and to infer trust information regarding that behaviour. In short, it is intended to answer, at least, one main question that remains open - "How can information used for risk calculation be evaluated for correctness?".

Although the presented Trust and Reputation framework was initially focused on the MICIE project, it can be considered a general framework and thus can be applicable within different models and scenarios (Caldeira et al., 2011, 2013; Schaberreiter et al., 2011b).

Trust and Reputation Model

It is assumed that systems exchanging CI risk information enforce strong security mechanisms, usually focused on the communication and not on the ex- changed data itself. In this context, it may be possible for a CI to offer inaccurate information thus affecting the dependent CIs. These scenarios are possible due to malicious intentions or due to the existence of faulty components in the CI monitoring frameworks. In such a environment, we propose to introduce mechanisms able to allow reasoning on the exchanged information quality and also about the context on which the information is being exchanged.

The proposed framework intends to evaluate the information received from a dependency, considering the previous observations made on that dependency and also to understand the behaviour of the participant CIs. This evaluation is achieved by building a trust relationship between CIs or CI services through a Trust and Reputation System by using gathered trust level indicators to eval- uate the correctness of the received CI information (Caldeira et al., 2010b). One of the faced problems is that each CI can have different information being compared and evaluated. Building a Trust and Reputation System considering numerous dependencies on multiple contexts, can be a fairly complex task to which this framework makes a significant contribution, as it allows a methodical and simple approach to the process. From the Trust and Reputation System (TRS) point of view, it is not relevant for its usage if dependency or interdependency among services refers to relations among different CIs and/or to relations among services existent inside one CI.

The need for a TRS, employed in each CI, able to maintain real-time trust information concerning (inter)dependent CIs and CI services, was identified. This system is able to monitor information exchanged among CIs or among CI services and also to monitor their behaviour in order to gather a trust level for each CI service and to infer CI reputation (Caldeira et al., 2010d,b,c; Bertoni et al., 2010; Castrucci et al., 2012).

The proposed Trust and Reputation Model focuses in two main areas (*Figure 6*). First, to a trust indicator about the information received from (inter)dependent CIs (risk alerts), evaluated in the following ways: for each service, evaluating each service provided by a remote CI, reflecting the trust on the risk alerts received from each dependent service (Risk Alerts Trust); for each CI, evaluating an indicator representing the reputation of that particular CI. Second, the Trust and Reputation System understands

Figure 6. Trust and reputation model

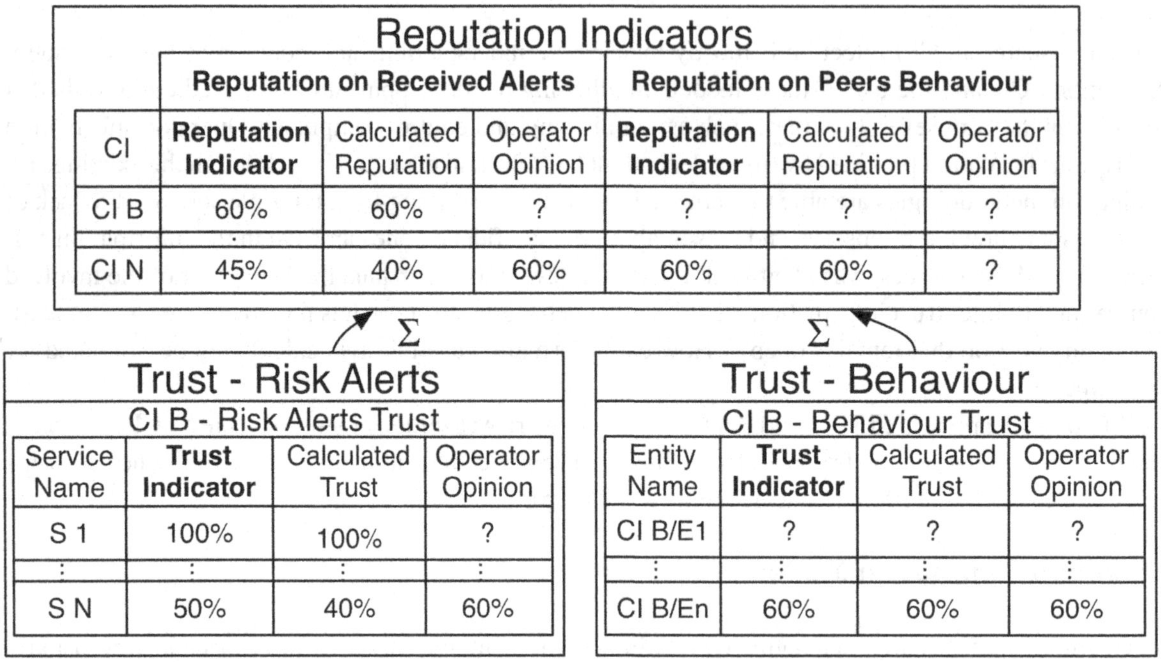

Reputation Indicators						
	Reputation on Received Alerts			Reputation on Peers Behaviour		
CI	**Reputation Indicator**	Calculated Reputation	Operator Opinion	**Reputation Indicator**	Calculated Reputation	Operator Opinion
CI B	60%	60%	?	?	?	?
·	·	·		·	·	·
CI N	45%	40%	60%	60%	60%	?

Σ   Σ

Trust - Risk Alerts			
CI B - Risk Alerts Trust			
Service Name	**Trust Indicator**	Calculated Trust	Operator Opinion
S 1	100%	100%	?
⋮	⋮	⋮	⋮
S N	50%	40%	60%

Trust - Behaviour			
CI B - Behaviour Trust			
Entity Name	**Trust Indicator**	Calculated Trust	Operator Opinion
CI B/E1	?	?	?
⋮	⋮	⋮	⋮
CI B/En	60%	60%	60%

the (inter)dependent CIs' behaviour, for instance, in terms of ICT security (Behaviour Trust). This evaluation is built from multiple entities, each one representing one particular aspect of the CI/Service. The aggregation of the behaviour evaluation, from multiple entities belonging to the same CI/Service represents the Reputation of that CI/Service.

The presented Trust and Reputation Model relies on three main information sources: Historical data provided by the (inter)dependent CI services, the information regarding the behaviour of a CI/Service and also the CI Operator trust on each CI/Service (Caldeira et al., 2010b,d,c). The historical data is analysed in order to compare, for each service, the service risk alerts received, against the actual QoS level of each service. To achieve this analysis, it is mandatory to have available, at each moment, the QoS level measurement for each service based on which it is planned to evaluate trust. The analysis of (inter)dependent CI/Service behaviour is supported by the knowledge gathered from the security entities existent in the CI and on the knowledge gathered by analysing the existing deviations from normal behaviour that may exist, for instance, among CIs, services or CI components. A human factor is also included in the model, allowing to reflect the perception of the CI Operator of each (inter)dependent CI/Service on the evaluated trust indicators. This factor is included, as the CI Operator should have significant knowledge about the CIs.

Trust and Reputation System

In the TRS, the information required to evaluate the proposed indicators is gathered from the system using two types of Agents: (1) The Risk Alerts Trust Agents, that continuously observe the QoS of each service and collect the risk alerts received from peer CIs or CI services. From this real-time information, these Agents are able to detect and evaluate an accuracy value for each risk alert event (a risk alert event is a situation in which the received risk is different from normal, the monitored service QoS decreased or both); (2) The Behaviour Trust Agents, receive and normalise all behaviour events. A behaviour event can be any kind of abnormal situation observed by the existent security entities. Each agent sends the discovered events to the TRS Discovery Tool, aiming to compute in real-time all the Trust and Reputation indicators. The computed indicators are provided to external entities, for example, in the MICIE system, both CI SMGW Manager and the CI Prediction Tool are able to make use of these indicators. A graphical interface provides the CI Operator with an overall view of Trust and Reputation indicators while allowing the CI Operator to also update his opinion.

Risk Alerts Trust Agents

The Risk Alerts Trust Agent receives from the CI Monitoring System, the service QoS measurements. It also collects the risk alert information as received from the dependent services. The received risk alert is then compared with the service measured QoS. To allow comparing them, a simple normalisation pro- cess is required. For this normalisation it is necessary to have a good definition for the obtained values in order to be able to compare and interpret them. For example, it is possible to have a received risk alert of 1 meaning no risk and 5 meaning high risk. For the measured service QoS, value 5 could mean that the service has the lowest admitted QoS. A value of 1 could mean that the service QoS is within the optimum values.

For each event $A(Event_n)$ detected by the Agent, the accuracy is defined as the average of all comparisons made during the event (value T), between the observed service level (Sl_t) and the received risk level (Rl_t), as defined in Equation 1. A sample rate, regarding the time factor, needs to be used, which can be different on each service depending on the information available on the system. A smaller sample rate yields more realistic observations.

$$A(Event_n) = \frac{\sum_{t=1}^{T} f(Sl_t, Rl_t)}{T}, \text{ where } f(Sl_t, Rl_t) = |Sl_t - Rl_t|^k, k \in \mathbb{R}^+ \tag{1}$$

The value k was introduced with the intent to penalise the larger differences or the small differences and should be assigned considering the degree of importance of each service. For instance, during an event, if the measured QoS of a service is always above the defined threshold (normal situation), it will make more sense to penalise more the risk alerts as $Rl_t = 100\%$ than the ones that refer a $Rl_t = 5\%$. By defining a value $k < 1$, it means that the TRS is willing to trust, even in the cases where large differences $|Sl_t - Rl_t|$ are observed. Applying a value $k > 1$ the biggest differences will suffer a higher penalisation. In this approach, the duration of an event is not considered as the agent is only focusing on the accuracy of each received risk alert.

The satisfaction degree for each event is expressed by $A(Event_n)$ which results in a value within the $[0..1]$ range. It is possible to interpret this value and for example, to say that one particular alert was very satisfactory (1.0), satisfactory (0.6), unsatisfactory (0.2), or very unsatisfactory (0). Each $A(Event_n)$ value is sent by the agent to the TRS Discovery Tool in order to be incorporated within the CI/Service Trust and Reputation indicators.

Behaviour Trust Agents

The security issues that may arise from a system with multiple collaborating CIs were particularly focused on throughout author's research. Considering the MICIE project, it is possible to denote the existence of several security entities. For instance, the MICIE SMGW through the SMGW Manager is aware of possible security faults thus able to provide the collection and analysis of data related to security aspects. The possibility to use this information was identified, in order to better understand the behaviour of the partnership, and also to infer a more complete indicator aiming to improve the trust indicator related to the received risk alerts.

The Behaviour Trust Agent's main goal is to gather all types of information that might characterise the behaviour of a CI/Service. In this case, the TRS is focused on receiving behaviour events (a type of abnormal event that is occurring in the system and is able to help characterise a service or a CI). Each behaviour event sent to the TRS, is composed of its origin and the respective trust level. Each Behaviour Trust Agent includes at least one Behaviour Security Model that contains a representation of how the normal behaviour of the system should be and also, a set of identified abnormal behaviours. Furthermore, it contains quantitative information, defined by an expert. This information defines how much one should trust a CI or a service, in case of the presence of a particular, previously identified, abnormal behaviour. For example, if its supposed one must receive a new risk alert within every five minutes and this is not happening, the expert can, for instance, state that this fact indicates a decrease of 10% in the trust of behaviour of that alert. If no alert is received within one hour, the decrease can be greater.

TRS Discovery Tool

Regarding the confidence on the received risk alerts, the TRS is able to evaluate two main indicators: (1) The Risk Alerts Trust indicator represents the confidence one has in the received risks related to one particular dependent service. (2) An indicator is evaluated in order to describe the confidence one may have on the risk alerts received from one particular CI (Risk Alerts Reputation), incorporating the trust, related to all the services provided by each particular CI. Both indicators are able to incorporate the CI Operator's opinion.

As detailed in (Caldeira et al., 2010b), the trust we have in the service risk of service X is represented by $T_{(X)}$ and is calculated by the average of the accuracy of each past event for that particular service (Equation 2). The concept of ageing is used, applying a discount factor D, to give more weight onto recent events. The ageing factor should always depend on the context. $T'_{(X)}$ can be computed for the *Nth* event as:

$$T'_{(X)=} \frac{\left(D*\left(N-1\right)*T_{(X)}\right)+A(Event_N)}{D*\left(N-1\right)+1} \tag{2}$$

D belongs to the $[0..1]$ interval and a small value of D will raise the importance of the last events while a value of D near 1 will provide less ageing for the oldest events. A human factor reflecting the CI operator opinion and contribution to the trust calculation is also considered in trust evaluation (Equation 3).

$$T(final)_{(X,t)} = \alpha\left(T_{(X)}\right) + (1-\alpha)\left(TO_{(X)}\right), (0 < \alpha < 1) \tag{3}$$

The factor α is assigned by the CI Operator depending on the confidence he or she has in $TO_{(X)}$. $T(final)_{(X,t)}$ represents the confidence in the service risk taking into account also the CI operator perspective. In order to understand how the risk alert trust indicators evolve over time, and to define a relation among them, a time value is associated with each $T(final)$.

Concerning the behaviour, we expect to receive alerts only when misbehaviour is detected, leading to a situation where almost only negative events are received and used in the evaluation. This situation would generate low behaviour trust over time. In order to evaluate a precise indicator, the factor time and the concept of inactivity were introduced. Time is divided into a set of time slots. Inactivity in one slot means that the entity behaviour indicators will have the maximum value for that period. If information is received during one slot, the value for that slot becomes the average of all values received during that slot (Caldeira et al., 2010b). For the time slot s, the trust in entity $E\left(T'_{(E,s)}\right)$ is calculated using Equation 4, where D is the ageing factor, $T_{(E)}$ is the indicator evaluated for the slot $(s-1)$ and $Event_{(Slot\ s)}$ is the event value of the slot s.

$$T'_{(E,s)} = \frac{\left(D*(s-1)*T_{(E)}\right) + Event_{(Slot\ s)}}{D*(s-1)+1} \tag{4}$$

Using Equation 5 the operator trust is included. The θ factor is assigned by the CI operator representing the confidence in the subjective trust $\left(TO_{(E,B)}\right)$ that he or she has on the behaviour of CI B concerning entity E.

$$T(final)_{(E)} = \theta\left(TO_{(E)}\right) + (1-\theta)\left(T_{(E)}\right)\quad,\quad (0 < \theta < 1) \tag{5}$$

As stated, the TRS trust model also evaluates one indicator encompassing all monitored entities. Using a weight factor for each entity, the service behaviour reputation can be computed. This indicator, $TBehaviour'_{(X,t)}$, represents the reputation of the behaviour of service X at time t (Caldeira et al., 2010b). In this work the behaviour reputation for a service is generally referred to as behaviour trust and includes the behaviour trust of all managed service entities. Using a similar calculation as used in Equation 5, the Operator trust on the behaviour indicators can also be included (Caldeira et al., 2010b).

Application Scenarios and Validation Example

The proposed framework has already been validated using simulation and also using data from a real CI. A small example from that validation is described. Detailed validation work can be found found in (Caldeira et al., 2010a), (Caldeira et al., 2010b), (Caldeira et al., 2010d), (Caldeira et al., 2010c), (Caldeira et al., 2011), (Caldeira et al., 2013), (Schaberreiter et al., 2011b).

Table 1. Simulation Scenario (% of events for each range of event accuracy values)

Scenarios	Event % of occurrence									
	[0-10]	]10-20]	]20-30]	]30-40]	]40-50]	]50-60]	]60-70]	]70-80]	]80-90]	]90-100]
S1	0	0	0	0	0	0	5	5	10	80
S2	0	0	0	0	10	10	10	10	20	40
S3	40	20	10	10	10	10	0	0	0	0
S4	80	10	5	5	0	0	0	0	0	0

The scenarios described in Table 1, represent the following: (S1) The system behaves as expected with small errors (event accuracy is always above 60% and mainly higher than 90%); (S2) System is not accurate but can still be trustworthy (event accuracy is always above 40%); (S3) Received alerts are inaccurate between 40% and 60% of the cases; (S4) The System is not trustworthy.

For this example, the Risk Alert and Behaviour events were generated using random numbers, according to each defined scenario. The following TRS parameters are used: penalisation factor $k = 2$; ageing factor $D = 0.3$. A threshold of 10%, meaning that events with accuracy above 90% are rated as 100%. The simulation was performed using R (R Development Core Team, 2009).

Figure 7 (A) represents an attack or faulty component situation with a scenario change on every 100 events. The better scenario (S1) abruptly changes to the worst (S4) after 100 events. This change is rapidly incorporated into the trust indicator. Following 100 events from scenario S4, the trust indicator clearly indicates that one should not trust on the received alerts for this service. After 200 events, the received risk alerts become reliable again. Due to the ageing factor, the trust indicator rapidly incorporates new scenarios. From the 300th to the 400th event, the scenario changes to S3, decreasing the trust indicator. This simulation also illustrates that the trust indicator rapidly reacts on changes. It his also clear that even with an abrupt change on the scenarios, the indicator changes gradually due to the ageing factor.

Figure 7 (B) represents a simulation planned to validate that the TRS is still accurate when receiving a small number of events. In this case, the received alerts are not reliable between the 20th and the 30th event, leading to a very low trust value that gradually grows after the 30th event (S2). If the CI Operator

Figure 7. Trust on received risk alerts

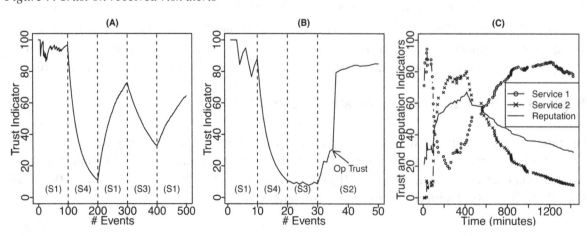

Figure 8. Trust on peer behaviour

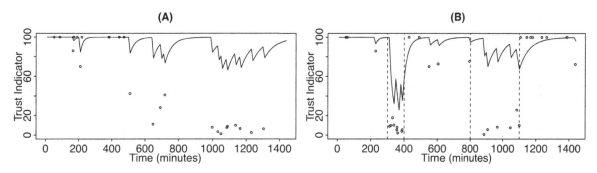

is aware that the situation causing this scenario was already solved, he can update the trust indicator with his opinion about the service, assigning a value of trust of 90% with a contribution of 0.8 to the indicator. Although the indicator continues to incorporate changes from the events, the value will increase. It is important that the Operator know the consequence of that action.

Figure 7 (C) represents the reputation indicator for one CI from which two separated services are received. Each service has an average of 5 events / 60 minutes from a combination of scenarios one to four. The operator assigned a weight of 0.3 to service 1 and 0.7 to service 2. A value of D = 1 (simple average) was used to calculate the Reputation indicator. In this simulation, when the service more important (due to the weight assigned by the Operator) is becoming unreliable, the CI reputation is decaying even when the other service is trusty.

In order to simulate security events (behaviour), the arrival time of each event is generated from random numbers, with an average of x events/minute. The values for each event are generated based on the scenarios defined in Table 1. *Figure 8* represents the results of two different simulations with common parameters: time slot=10, D = 0.05 and simulation period=1140 minutes. The dots on *Figure 8*(A) and *Figure 8*(B) represent the received events.

The first simulation (*Figure 8*(A)) has a rate of 1 event/60 minutes from scenarios (S1), (S3) and (S4). With few events, the trust indicator does not drop below 60% due to influence of the slots where the system has normal behaviour. This simulation demonstrates the importance of the value defined for the time slot. In this case, a larger time slot would lead to a lower behaviour trust indicator. The simulation of a situation with two possible attacks or misbehaviour is presented in *Figure 8*(B). During the first 300 minutes, events from (S1) are triggered at a rate of 1/60 minutes. During a period of 100 minutes, the scenario changes to (S4) with an event rate of 5/60 minutes. The behaviour trust indicator rapidly decays below 50% indicating a problem. Next, the behaviour is simulated using (S2) with a lower event rate leading the indicator to raise. Between the 800th and 1100th minutes, the scenario changes to (S4) with a event rate of 1/60 minutes. It is observable that even with only a few events, the CI Operator can infer that the peer behaviour is not normal. With this indicator, the Operator or an automated system can react. The last simulated minutes represent the scenario S1 at a rate of 1/60 minutes. On this scenario and with a lower event rate, the trust indicator clearly indicates the resolution of the past situation.

As stated, results obtained from multiple validation scenarios are found in references cited at the beginning of this section. In particular, we would like to highlight the validation of the TRS by using data collected on the Grid'5000 project (Caldeira et al., 2013). The Grid'5000 project (Grid5000, 2013) supports an academic computing grid with clusters distributed at numerous locations. This validation scenario (Caldeira et al., 2013) focuses on evaluating a dependency between the computing grid and the telecommunication infrastructure used to interconnect each site of the infrastructure. The trust is evaluated based on a dataset of measurements gathered by the available monitoring tools.

THE COCKPITCI PROJECT

In order to improve the results obtained by MICIE, a follow-up project named CockpitCI was started in 2011. CockpitCI departs from the MICIE approach, by adding cyber-awareness capabilities to CIs, particularly focused on SCADA-based ICS. In this way, CockpitCI addresses one of the fundamental shortcomings of MICIE by adding SCADA-oriented security detection capabilities, which are used to provide input to risk prediction models and ongoing assessment of the operational status of the ICS.

In fact, as they were originally restricted to isolated environments, SCADA systems were considered relatively safe from external intrusion. However, as architectures evolved, these systems started to assimilate technologies from the Information and Communication Technologies (ICT) world, such as TCP/IP and Ethernet networking, encouraging the interconnection of the ICS with organizational ICT network infrastructures, and even with the exterior (e.g., for remote management). This trend, together with the increasing adoption of open, documented protocols, exposed serious weaknesses in SCADA architectures and brought a wave of security problems that weren't even remotely conceivable when such systems were first designed, prompting a significant increase in the number of externally initiated attacks on ICS systems, especially when compared with internal attacks (Kang et al., 2011).

Therefore, ICS constitute a critical and strategic asset that is being increasingly targeted by malicious attacks with potentially catastrophic consequences. The CockpitCI FP7 European project (CockpitCI Consortium, 2011) project is a natural successor of MICIE, combining the strengths of the latter with ICS-oriented cyber-awareness capabilities, particularly focused on SCADA systems. CockpitCI is focused on improving the resilience and dependability of CIs, providing automatic detection of cyber-threats and the sharing of real-time information about attacks among CI operators.

The idea behind the CockpitCI project is to allow the community of CI owners to exchange real-time information about attacks (and tentative attacks). In this scope, each CI incorporates its own real-time Distributed Monitoring System and Perimeter Intrusion Detection System (PIDS). These systems are able to aggregate the filtered and analyzed information of potential cyberattacks against systems used to support the operation of CIs and to identify the potential unsecured area of the CIs.

The PIDS provides the cyber-awareness capabilities of CockpitCI, also constituting its core contribution regarding MICIE. The PIDS performs many of the tasks traditionally associated with a Distributed Intrusion Detection System, with support for diversified and closely integrated detection and analysis techniques and tools. Each PIDS is to be deployed in the targeted area of a CI, in order to detect coordinated cyber-attacks and in order to deploy prevention strategies of isolation. Through coordinated PIDS operations, it is possible to put in place a specific perimeter to detect potential coordinated cyber-attacks on CIs for each type of detected attacks or for mixed cyber-attacks. The CockpitCI PIDS is based on a state-of-the-art distributed intrusion detection architecture encompassing a set of detection agents that feed real-time and soft real-time automated correlation and anomaly detection mechanisms, and are orchestrated together by a management platform.

SCADA ICS security

The development of the CockpitCI PIDS architecture was preceded by a requirements analysis phase, with the purpose of understanding the specific characteristics and differences between ICS (with particular relevance to SCADA systems) and conventional ICT infrastructures, from a security standpoint. This study revealed several significant differences between ICT and ICS domains that are deeply rooted in their own particular characteristics, down to the fundamental priorities that define which are the most important operational and functional properties of the system.

SCADA Technology

SCADA is a common designation for several technologies, protocols and platforms used in ICS for control and automation of production lines, power plants (nuclear, thermoelectric, wind farms), management of distribution grids (electricity, gas, oil, water) and many other applications. *Figure 9* illustrates a SCADA system for controlling the water level of a tank, including components such as:

Figure 9. Architecture of a simple SCADA system (adapted from (Bailey and Wright, 2003))

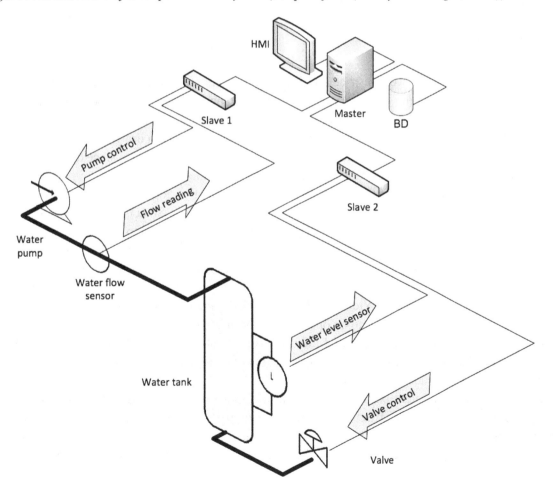

- **Master Stations** (deployed on the process network) supervise processes, controlling and monitoring Slaves and often providing support for HMI (Human-Machine Interface) consoles. They are also frequently connected to other applications, such as databases, to log process data.
- **Slave devices** (PLCs and RTUs – deployed on the control network) are embedded systems connected to one or more Master Stations, and also to sensors and actuators, being responsible for most of the monitoring and control activities. RTUs have limited control capabilities, connecting to sensors that monitor the controlled process and sending data to master stations, while PLCs are more sophisticated, supporting several programming languages and complex control scenarios. Due to their superior capability/cost ratio, PLCs frequently replace RTUs.
- **Field devices** (deployed on the field network) constitute the physical interface with the process, providing information about it (sensors) and enabling the execution of actions affecting its behavior (actuators).

These components are interconnected among them using technologies, such as RS-485 (EIA, 1983), CAN (ISO, 2003), EtherCAT (IEC, 2005), Profinet (PI Organization, 1999) or Industrial Ethernet, among others, accordingly with the needs of the ICS infrastructure scope. The control flow between the Master Station and the PLC/RTU allows exchanging process-related data or execute actions by modifying process control parameters mapped on device registers. This process involves SCADA specific protocols, such as Modbus (Modbus Organization, 2012), IEC 60870-5-104 (IEC 104) (IEC, 2006) or DNP3 (IEEE, 2010), among others.

SCADA Security Issues

In the past SCADA systems were restricted to isolated environments, relatively safe from external intrusion. These original systems were very simple by nature, mainly because there were no formal data processing or memory mechanisms involved, being little more than reactive systems interconnecting sensors and visual indicators. However, that simplicity was also their main drawback, being unfeasible for usage anything other than small-scale and physically limited scenarios. Also, since data logging was impossible, error or failure-debugging capabilities were very limited.

With time, SCADA systems evolved to their present situation, by adopting data processing and networking technologies, the latter replacing legacy telemetry system interconnects. While original systems were isolated and self-contained by nature, they progressively started to open to the exterior world, making use of data communication networks for its own internal purposes and to share information with the outside world or even other systems. These connections might exist for various reasons: with the general purpose corporate Local Area Network (LAN), to exchange information with performance auditing or stock management applications; a Wide Area Network (WAN) connection to connect to other facilities (for instance, two power stations) or to an operations control center, separated miles away. Such WAN connections might be ensured using leased lines, dial-up or, more recently, the Internet itself (Ten et al., 2008), (Davis et al., 2006). Additionally, it is frequent for original device manufactures to provide remote assistance using such mechanisms.

Also, proprietary equipment and protocols were also the norm on older ICS/SCADA systems, limiting interoperability between devices from different manufacturers (and sometimes, even between different models of the same manufacturer). This created a situation of vendor lock-in that forced the customer to remain attached to a specific device family form a particular manufacturer due to the cost of migration.

Presently, equipment and protocols have been standardized, with the adoption of COTS (*Commercial Off-The-Shelf*) equipment whenever possible – for instance for LAN communication (Igure et al., 2006).

As a consequence of the introduction of data processing capabilities to SCADA systems, together with the evolution of embedded systems, operating systems also became part of the SCADA ICS ecosystem that evolved with time. From proprietary systems, the situation evolved up to the point where Windows or Unix-derivatives (Creery et al., 2005) are being used, together with real-time operating systems such as VXWorks or Real-Time Linux (Davis et al., 2006). This evolution brought significant benefits to SCADA systems, in terms of functionality, rationality and cost. However, it is also closely related with some of the most important security issues that currently affect those systems, which over time became increasingly exposed to more open environments where they started to show their limits. The progressive move to more open scenarios, together with the use of Information and Communication Technologies (ICT) and the increasing adoption of open, documented protocols, exposed serious security weaknesses.

Moreover, the growing trend towards the interconnection of the ICS network with organizational ICT network infrastructures, and even with outside networks (for instance, for connection with internal company systems or for remote management by external contractors) created a new wave of security problems and incidents. In fact, there is a growing trend in the number of externally initiated attacks on ICS systems, when compared with internal attacks (Kang et al., 2011). As a result, the old practice of security by obscurity has become unfeasible. Still, the problem of security in SCADA systems has been more or less ignored for several years, and even now serious issues persist.

In fact, when it comes to their fundamental governing principles, ICS and ICT infrastructures have an inverted set of priorities, a situation that is one of the main causes of SCADA infrastructure security problems. This is partly due to the fact that, as the ICS paradigm evolved, it was not accompanied by an equal progression in terms of the industry mind set. As a result, and due to its critical nature, ICS operation and design practices frequently privilege availability and reliability over confidentiality and data integrity—a perspective that is quite the opposite from the ICT philosophy, which privileges confidentiality and security, followed by communications integrity, and, finally, by availability (ISA, 2007). This contrast explains why it is common to find a lack of agreement between the control systems teams and the security IT staff within the same organization. This difference of priorities, illustrated in *Figure 10*, has a real impact when it comes to choosing and implementing security mechanisms. Furthermore, it imposes a significant burden when importing security mechanisms from the ICT world to the ICS domain.

Figure 10. ICT vs. ICS priorities (adapted from (ISA,2007))

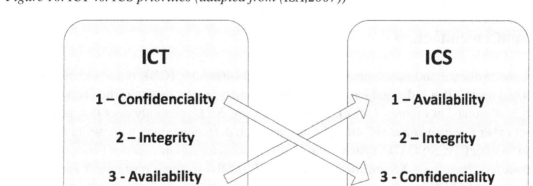

The differences between the ICT and ICS contexts also mean that there is no 'one size fits all' solution when it comes to choose and to implement security mechanisms. Despite this conceptual difference, importing solutions from the ICT world is often a necessity, which might lead to undesirable side-effects. This situation, together with inadequate systems lifecycle management procedures (Krutz, 2006), increases the probability of a successful attack. While such procedures are trivial matters which are part of the regular maintenance routine in the ICT world, they must be dealt with in an entirely different way when it comes to ICS, mainly for three reasons: 1) some components have to work on a continuous basis without interruptions, up to the point of working years without being reinitialized – frequently due to the impediment/high cost of stopping production (Zhu et al., 2011); 2) any software release must be carefully tested by equipment manufacturers before being released (as an example, a SCADA system customer may be unable to install an update on an operating system unless the manufacturer certifies their software for the update); and 3) due to end-of-life support for specific devices or software frameworks.

Product lifecycle is another matter that separates ICT from ICS systems, with the former having substantially shorter lifecycles, when compared with the latter. In ICS it is frequent for mature systems to be kept in operation, sometimes far beyond their projected lifetime - the 'if it ain't broke, don't fix it' philosophy. This limits the possibility of implementing some security mechanisms due to the limited capabilities of existing equipment (Igure et al., 2006).

Moreover, SCADA communication protocols, which are responsible for the interaction between field devices, such as PLC (Programmable Logic Controllers) or RTU (Remote Terminal Units) components and the stations that control and monitor them, pose security concerns. One of such examples is the Modbus protocol (Modbus Organization, 2012), originally developed by Modicon in 1979 and currently part of the Schneider Electric Group. Modbus is one of the most popular protocols for SCADA applications, thanks to its simplicity and ease of use. However, Modbus suffers from security problems: the lack of encryption or any other protection measures exposes it to different vulnerabilities (Triangle MicroWorks, 2002). If we take into consideration that it is not uncommon to find situations where the ICT and ICS networking contexts are blended within the corporate network, it becomes clear to what degree some ICS are vulnerable. Despite this vulnerability, protocols such as Modbus have a large lifespan and are still being massively deployed and used.

Simply put, when it comes to ICS, technology and platform maturity are valued as an implicit recognition of value and reliability, and even the disclosure of security issues related to them seems to have no effect in discouraging their usage or prompting the adoption of security measures to protect them. This has become the root cause of many ICS security issues that have ultimately been exploited with a variable degree of success in recent times, such as the Stuxnet Trojan (Falliere et al., 2011).

The CockpitCI architecture

To improve the resilience and dependability of Critical Infrastructures (CIs), the CockpitCI project proposes an architecture that is divided into several modules/components; the interaction between these components is illustrated in *Figure 11* (CockpitCI Consortium, 2011). Not only does this architecture aim to detect cyber threats using novel strategies for intrusion detection, along with devices specially conceived to monitor CI ICS/SCADA systems, but it also accounts for communication between multiple interdependent CIs, by using a Secure Mediation Network (SMN) to share operational and security information, much like MICIE.

Figure 11. The CockpitCI General Architecture (CockpitCI Consortium, 2013)

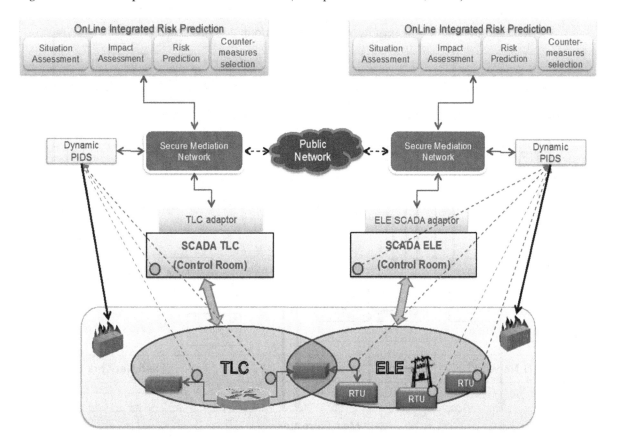

Among the multiple components that make up the CockpitCI architecture, the Dynamic PIDS provides the core cyber-analysis and detection capabilities, by being responsible for continuously assessing and protecting the electronic security perimeter of each CI. The automatic analysis and detection mechanisms for each PIDS are fed by several field adaptors and detection agents deployed within each CI, which constitute its 'eyes', and providing the basic information from which the ongoing security status of the CI is determined. Also, the PIDS encompasses semi-autonomous reaction capabilities, as it is able to deploy and to activate countermeasures, in line with predefined security reaction policies.

For each CI, an Online Integrated Risk Predictor module (IRP – much like MICIE, despite being enhanced to incorporate cyber-awareness capabilities) works as a decision support system for management teams, by feeding operational indicators (such as process-level data, gathered using the SCADA TLC and ELE adaptors shown on *Figure 11*) and cyber-security information (generated by the PIDS) into a set of modelling tools, to assess and to predict propagation and threat levels for potential cyber attacks on the CI. In this scope, SCADA adaptors translate SCADA data from various components into a common data format, which makes it possible to use devices from different vendors and legacy SCADA HW/SW (Hardware/Software) while sharing data with the detection layer and the IRP.

The Secure Meditation Network (SMN) provides the means for exchanging security information between CIs, also enabling the use of risk prediction and other analysis mechanisms to assess threats on a global scale. Moreover, it accounts for CI interdependencies (as exemplified by *Figure 11*, which

Figure 12. The CockpitCI Cyber Detection and Analysis Layer (red flows=management, green=eventing)

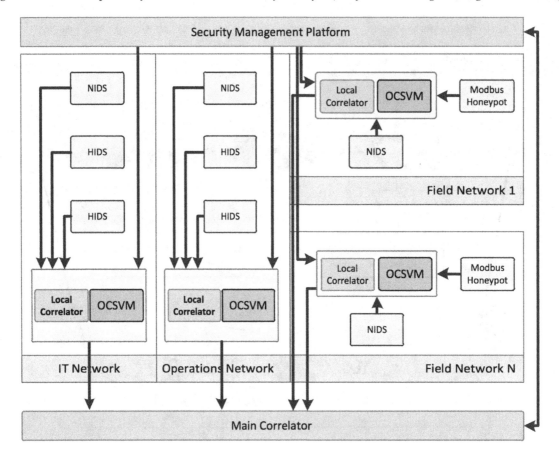

represents two kinds of CIs that are frequently dependent on each other: Telecommunications and Electric Power Distribution).

Among these components, the CockpitCI PIDS cyber analysis and detection architecture constitutes the main subject of this section, which is focused on the presentation and analysis of the basic components of the PIDS, by explaining how they work together to continuously monitor and to analyze the ICS/SCADA system components of a given ICS in order to perform threat detection. Also, the event correlation and anomaly detection mechanisms that constitute the cyber security analysis capabilities of the PIDS will be addressed, together with the description of the agents and probes that feed each with information about ICS/SCADA system's state and its data flows.

Cyber Detection Approach

The CockpitCI PIDS incorporates several advanced real-time detection and analysis mechanisms, integrated to constitute a cyber analysis and detection layer for the CI, as shown in *Figure 12*. It is structured along the three different zones of the CI, each one with its own internal security perimeter: the Field Network, SCADA Process/Operations Network, and the IT (Information Technology) Network. For each zone, the PIDS has the ability to deploy agents and security policies customized to the specific needs and characteristics of each network scope.

This scope separation corresponds to an three-level ICS system infrastructure: the **IT Network**, comprising corporate devices (workstations, servers) and services (such as e-mail, accounting and stock or asset management); the **operations network**, where the supervisory components, such as master stations or Human-Machine Interface (HMI) devices, and historic process databases are - corresponding to Level 2 of ISA-95 (ISA, 2000); and the **field networks** (where basic control and process devices, such PLCs and RTUs are deployed, controlling and monitoring a critical process – corresponding to Level 1 of the ISA-95 recommendations). These two scopes roughly correspond to the process control network levels on ISA-95 – it should be mentioned that there is not a distinction between the automation and device networks in *Figure 12*, for the sake of simplicity (due to the evolving capabilities of PLC devices, the distinction between PLCs and RTUs is somehow vanishing, something that also contributes to somehow fuse the automation and device networks in a single network scope).

This architecture was designed to deal with several attack scenarios, from known threats to rogue events, such as: man-in-the-middle attacks, device impersonation, non-authorized tampering, worms, Trojans, denial-of-service attacks, or flooding, among others. For this purpose, the PIDS is designed in such a way that it integrates different detection strategies, distributed along different levels, namely:

- Detection agents and field adaptors, including agents, adaptors and extensions for existing system components, as well as specialized network probes and honeypots (Spitzner, 2002) to be added to the network, which are able to capture behaviour or traffic patterns (as performed by NIDS– Network IDS components) as well as host (using tools such as HIDS/Host IDS, or antivirus software) and field device monitoring.
- A distributed multi-zone, multi-level correlation structure that processes the information provided by the security sensors, complemented by machine-learning capabilities, in the form of One-Class Support Vector Machine (OCSVM) (Ma and Perkins, 2003) anomaly detection module, based on adaptive machine learning.
- Aggressive usage of topology and system-specific detection mechanisms, based on the fact that the role and behaviour of each system component in an ICS are expected to be more consistent over time than other types of networks; analysis components are fed with knowledge provided by a number of system specific sources, such as topology databases, policy databases, and trust-based mechanisms, as well as strategically placed honeypots.

The operation of the PIDS components is orchestrated through a Security Management Platform (SMP), which is responsible for managing all the involved components of the solution (see *Figure 12*). It includes the mechanisms for managing the security and components of the infrastructure. The SMP is responsible for the maintenance and management of monitoring probes such as IDS and the analysis components, also including monitoring of in-place security and vulnerabilities within the network as well as with the maintenance of the latter. Therefore, the SMP has a dual role, dealing with both security audit and maintenance mechanisms.

The SMP performs the configuration of detection agents on the field, providing the means to define their detection thresholds and other relevant parameters. This detection threshold depends on both the risk level of the overall infrastructure (the level of detection shall be higher if the probability of an attacks is higher) and specific detection needs (for example, in case of abnormal event detection, the SMP shall be able to verify all similar components in the CIs to check their security level).

Due to the demanding availability requisites and little tolerance to delays, the detection architecture is to be implemented using a network that is separate from the SCADA system network (eventually it can use the same physical network, using VLAN (Virtual Local Area Network) or other types of overlay techniques for traffic separation), in order to guarantee that it does not interfere with the normal operation of the control network.

The PIDS Analysis Layer

The analysis components of the PIDS provide a way to extract information from the data collected by the agent layer or directly from network traces. These components are arranged in a two-level architecture with local instances fine-tuned for each network scope.

Local and Global Correlators

Local correlators perform the first step of correlation, by filtering and reducing the number and noise of the alarms generated by the detection layer while, at the same time, providing a mechanism for security event generation that is able to filter, process, and relate events within a network segment. For instance, this provides the means to implement event reduction capabilities, aggregating alarms generated by two or more detection agents or multiple events from the same source.

Local correlators receive the events from local detection agents (for example HIDS) on their network scope and process them accordingly with a set of rules, and forward significant results to a global correlation engine. This approach provides context separation and, at the same time, allows for better efficiency and scalability for real-time event processing. After local correlation, events are sent to the global correlators and from there to the SMN, by using the Intrusion Detection Message Exchange format (Debar et al., 2007). IDMEF defines an experimental standard for exchanging intrusion detection related events. As a standard, it provides a uniform and vendor-independent mechanism to provide communication between different agents such as NIDS or honeypots.

As illustrated by *Figure 12*, local correlators receive events from the different agents such as NIDS, HIDS, and honeypots, among others. These agents are distinct, according to network zone, in which the local correlator is positioned. Despite the range of different agents, the local correlator should use the same interface for all of them, as messages are received through an Event Bus (further discussed in next sections). This interface will allow subscribing to the events published by the agents. Local correlators also have an agent adaptor interface that allows for management, via the SMP.

Regarding the event interfaces for the main correlator there are several different types: one to receive events from the local correlators and another one to send events to the SMP, both using an Event Bus. As local correlators have already previously processed received events, the main correlator can focus on Multi-Step, Attack Focus Recognition correlation as well as Alert Prioritization. A management adaptor provides the interface for the SMP to configure the correlator (see *Figure 13*).

The correlators are implemented using the Esper (Bernhardt and Vasseur, 2007) Complex Event Processing (CEP) tool. This was due to the fact that Esper is a multi-platform, flexible and mature tool, in development since 2006. Also, performance tests have shown Esper to exhibit a good balance between memory usage, CPU usage, and execution time when processing hundreds of thousands of events. The Java-based version of Esper is available as a set of Java packages that can be integrated into a full solution using their Java API. Esper uses an SQL-like approach for rule description, designated by Event

Figure 13. Overview of the Correlator Architecture.

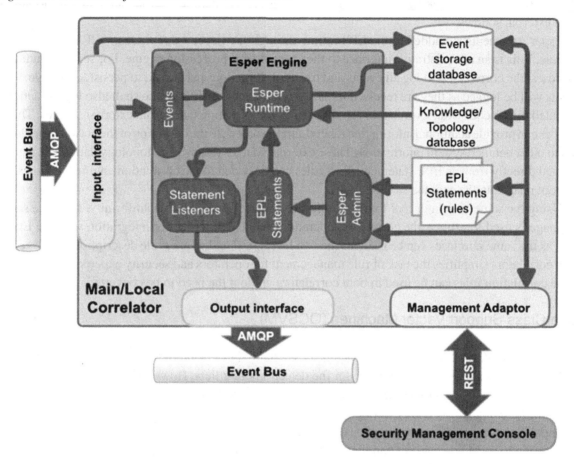

Processing Language (EPL), providing pattern-matching mechanisms via state machines. Esper loads the EPL query set and performs matching within the incoming stream of events, implicitly incorporating a time-based correlation logic that accounts for ordering and sequencing, within a time-window.

Esper can natively accept events represented in XML, among other formats, which is useful, as IDMEF, used by the PIDS, is an XML-based format. If a XML schema document (XSD file) is provided, Esper can read the schema and properly present event type metadata and validate statements that use the event type and its properties. To access the elements of the event the correlator uses XPath expressions. If a schema for the XML is provided, the XPath expression needed to reference the attribute can be inferred automatically. Otherwise, expressions can be manually configured.

An overview of the architecture of a PIDS correlator based on Esper, is pictured in *Figure 13*. The events received from the input adaptor are sent to the Esper Runtime (EPRuntime); this provides the interface to the event stream processing runtime services. The statements are registered in the EPRuntime and represent the event stream queries and/or event pattern. Each statement can have one or more Statement listeners bound to them. When the condition of a query is verified, Esper can trigger the listener(s) bound to the rule, can insert the result of the statement into another stream (that already exists or is created at that time), or can do both. If a rule generates a new event that need to be sent by the correlator to the Event Bus, the listener will interface with the output adaptor to send it. Output events are generated by rules making use of input events, cached events, the internal state, and information from external sources.

Esper statements are added to the EPRuntime through the Esper Administrator (EPAdministrator) module. This is an administrative interface to the event stream-processing engine. For security auditing purposes, the correlator will log all events and traces of the actions performed to persistent storage. The events will be logged as they are received in the correlator and the EPRuntime shall also log the actions executed by the correlator. Correlation can make use of information taken from external sources. These sources can provide additional information related, among others, to the definition of the network topology and to other detailed system information. These external sources (knowledge/topology databases) can be queried directly from an EPL statement. New rules can be added to the correlation engine dynamically, without restarting the engine.

Using the same correlator tool for the two levels of correlation provides uniformity, since the same language is used to express the correlation operations, which allows easier integration with the Event Bus, as the same interfaces can be used for the two levels. Using the same rule description language for both correlators simplifies the task of rule management for operators and security experts. Additionally, some correlation rules can be used in both correlators without the need to be converted.

One-Class Support Vector Machines (OCSVM)

OCSVMs (One-Class Support Vector Machine) are a natural extension of the support vector algorithm to the case of unlabelled data, especially for the detection of outliers. However, unlike SVM or any another classification algorithm, OCSVM does not need any labelled data for training or any information about the kind of anomaly it is expecting for the detection process. OCSVM principles have shown great potential in the area of anomaly detection (Ma and Perkins 2003; Li et al., 2003; Schölkopf et al., 2001). Moreover, OCSVM is capable of handling multiple attributed data (Hsu et al., 2003; Wang et al., 2004), which is well suited for SCADA systems.

The advantages of the OCVSM component are manifold: since OCSVM does not require any signatures of data to build the detection model, it is well suited for anomaly-based intrusion detection in the SCADA environment. Since the detection mechanism does not require any prior information of the expected attack types, OCSVM is capable of detection both known and unknown (novel) attacks, besides being robust to noise in training sets. Also, algorithm behaviour can be controlled and fine-tuned by the user to regulate the percentage of anomalies expected (thresholds, as defined via SMP, via the OCSVM management adaptor).

OCSVM operation consists of two steps: training and testing. During the training stage, OCSVM builds a model from training on normal data (that is, obtained from a system operating under normal conditions, without any attack in progress) and then classifies the new data as either normal or attack, based on its geometrical deviation from the training data in the testing stage. Since the OCSVM detection approach is still effective when samples include noise, the training data set can include some noise samples (that is data which does not correspond to the normal behaviour). An OCSVM component is deployed in IT, Operation, and Field network zone(s), therefore requiring different training sets.

Once the training phase is complete, the OCSVM module is capable of detecting possible intrusions (abnormal behaviour) to the SCADA system, based on real-time capture of network traffic traces. The detection module will classify each event as a normal event or a possible intrusion. This information will then be encoded in an IDMEF message and sent to the main correlator, who will use an adaptor for the Event Bus, in order to react to the detected intrusions.

Detection Agents

The detection agents are the lowest level of the detection layer. Their purpose is to gather information from the system. As the format of information provided depends on the type of detection agents used (type of probe), adaptors allow the acquisition of data from the system in a recognised format. Detection agents and adaptors are essential to feed the local correlators of the detection layer with input data regarding suspicious activity. The PIDS encompasses several kinds of probes and detection agents. The most relevant of these are next described:

- **Network IDS:** the perimeter for each network scope is monitored using NIDS components for each one: IT Network NIDS, Operations Network NIDS, and Field Network NIDS. These have interfaces to report the security events to the zone correlator within their network scope. In the PIDS, Snort (Snort IDS) is used for this purpose, but other NIDS could be used.
- **Host IDS:** the Host IDS is deployed in the hosts/servers of the system. It is capable of reporting anomalous behaviour in the machine where it is deployed. In the CockpitCI PIDS, OSSEC is used for this purpose, but other HIDS could be used.
- **Honeypots:** acting as decoys and being capable of detecting attackers probing the network, honeypots provide another source of data for correlation. There are three types of honeypots in the detection layer: IT Network, Operations Network, and Field Network honeypots (Simões et al., 2013).
- **Exec Checker (linux hosts):** capable of detecting malicious network frames by sniffing the traffic, the Exec Checker (in active or passive mode) captures the different parts of an executable in the network traffic to recreate the file and to send it to an analysis tool.
- **Shadow Security Unit (originally named "Shadow RTU"):** the Shadow Security Unit is a low-cost device deployed in parallel with a PLC or Remote Terminal Unit (RTU), being capable of transparently intercepting its communications control channels and physical process I/O lines to continuously assess its security and operational status. The proposed device does not require significant change to the existing control network, being able to work in standalone or integrated within an ICS protection framework.
- **Output Traffic Controls (linux hosts):** capable of detecting Remote Access Trojans, this specific tool regularly scans system components to check if a remote access toolbox has been installed on components to facilitate external attacks.
- **Vulnerability Checker (windows hosts):** this tool provides a regular control of system vulnerability to check if the monitored systems are vulnerable or not according to an updated database. This tool can be customized for IT or SCADA host profiles.
- **Configuration Checker (linux/windows hosts):** this tool provides a regular control of system configurations to check for unauthorized modification.
- **Behaviour checker (linux/windows hosts):** capable of detecting attacks/threats by analyzing low-level hardware/software behaviour, this specific family of detection agents retrieves hardware/software information, such as temperature and CPU (Central Processing Unit) activity, in order to avoid accidental or malicious outage.

Security events generated by detection agents are encoded using the IDMEF format. All detection agents have a separate channel (another interface or secure channel) for management purposes, which enables the security staff to adjust the configurations with the scenario requirements via the SMP. The detection agents send their messages by means of an Event Bus described in the following section, which also details the management interfaces for the agent adaptors. These interfaces (eventing and management) were designed to ease integration of several types of detection capabilities (such as antivirus) by providing wrapper components for event generation and the management API.

Innovative Threat Detection Agents: The SCADA Honeypot and the Shadow Security Unit

One of the innovations of the CockpitCI is the SCADA honeypot, designed to operate in the process control network of a SCADA/ICS system, coexisting with the existing array of PLCs, RTUs and sensors/actuators that populate the network, binding to the network's unused IP addresses. Its fundamental operating principle is based on the assumption that, by faithfully emulating the behaviour and service footprint of a commercial PLC, the network honeypot is able to faithfully persuade an attacker that it is a worthwhile target, acting as a decoy which actively reports any suspicious activity, by reporting events to the distributed IDS of the ICS, where they will be processed and correlated.

The proposed honeypot is designed to behave and operate as a PLC. Under normal conditions, the honeypot waits for a connection attempt from someone probing the network or accessing it with the intent of impersonating a master station. In practice, any attempt at contacting the honeypot device may potentially generate a security event since, by definition, any activity in the honeypot is illegal and unauthorized (with the possible exception of management operations).

The proposed architecture is generic and compatible with the majority of SCADA protocols. However, Modbus was selected as the preferential protocol to be supported in the proof-of-concept prototype we developed, due to *three factors: standardization, popularity and because it is based in an open specification, whose documentation is easily obtainable.* For this reason, from now on we will specifically mention Modbus components, even though those components could be easily switched to add support for other SCADA protocols.

The architecture for the proposed honeypot for monitoring automation/field networks is presented in *Figure 14*. This is a hybrid Modbus honeypot architecture, in the sense that it runs both simulated and complete implementations of services commonly available on PLC devices. More details about it can be found in (Simoes et al., 2013).

Also, during the development of the CockpitCI cyber-security detection framework, authors were faced with the problem of effectively protecting PLCs and RTUs. While playing an important role in the ICS context, such devices often lack adequate security mechanisms, having been successfully targeted in the past by a wide array of attacks, such as flooding, buffer overflow exploits or man-in-the-middle, just to mention a few. To address this problem, several authors have proposed the use of techniques such as bump-in-the wire VPNs, tight access control list mechanisms or introducing mutual authentication – countermeasures whose deployment is not feasible in all scenarios, for reasons such as latency overhead, reliability or the need for introducing profound changes on well-established protocols and architectures.

This situation has led to the research of an alternative for PLC/RTU security, capable of providing continuous device monitoring with minimal disruption: the Shadow Security Unit (SSU), depicted on *Figure 15*.

Figure 14. SCADA Honeypot Architecture.

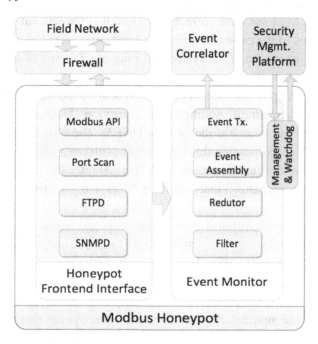

Figure 15. Shadow Security Unit deployment (dashed lines connect optional components)

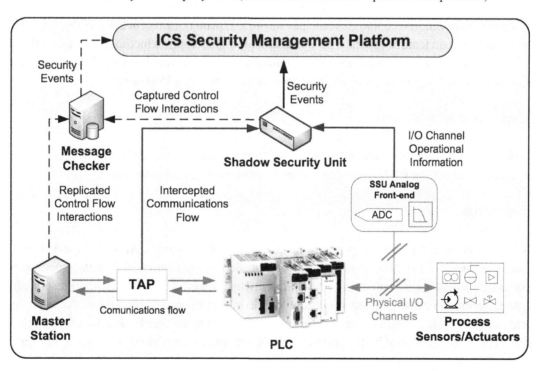

The SSU is a device that is attached in parallel to RTU/PLCs, intercepting the command flow and physical process interfaces to assess their correct operation. It is transparent to the production system, requiring minimum changes to the existing architecture and, since it is out of the critical control path it cannot interfere with the operation of the system, also minimizing any other potential impact on the monitored device from an eventual malfunction.

The SCADA protocols that provide data and control synchronization between devices and supervisory/master stations range from simple, polling-based, operation (Modbus, IEC-104) to more sophisticated models, based on eventing (as it is the case for DNP3). The SSU is able to capture and decode this protocol information flow, correlating this information with the status of the physical I/O modules that interface with sensors and actuators on the field. This enables the possibility of implementing a redundant security-checking mechanism that follows a "black box" approach regarding the analysis of the monitored device.

The SSU has several security capabilities, namely: intercepted command stream processing, continuous network flow monitoring, message integrity/trust checks and abnormal behaviour detection. Apart from these benefits, the SSU can also provide information on the operational and health status of the device. Once the information is collected, the SSU may feed it to an SIEM or it may perform first-stage correlation itself and generate security events to the Security Control Room or SIEM, reporting anomalies that are taking place at the moment. A heartbeat mechanism ensures that the Security Management Platform of the SCADA operator is able to check the status and reachability of the SSU. The heartbeat, management, message checking and eventing mechanisms are provided on a separate network for offband operations, connected to a network interface of the SSU that is physically separated from the one used for security monitoring purposes.

The SSU is a neutral concept that can be ported to other protocols (for example, Profinet/(I)RT or DNP3) and communication technologies (such as RS-485, Profinet or Ethernet/IP). However, it must be emphasized that certain features, such as the communication interception methods depend on the nature of the physical medium and communications technology being used (for instance, Ethernet-based, star and industrial ring topologies require different approaches than RS-485 buses).

Interfaces and Integration

This section describes the transport mechanisms and interfaces for event data flowing between the several existing components of the PIDS, and also addresses their management interfaces.

The Event Bus

The Event Bus is the component responsible for managing the communication of the events between the different elements of the PIDS, whose architecture is detailed in *Figure 16*. Events generated by the different agents within each zone are sent to an Event Bus broker. The broker is then responsible for routing these events to a queue, from which the local correlator can consume them. After processing and correlating the events, each local correlator sends the events to another broker, which feeds the main correlator. The events produced by the main correlator are sent to the main broker that routes them to a queue, and, from there, they can be sent to the SMP.

The Event Bus uses a Message Oriented Middleware (MOM) (Banavar et al., 1999) to provide efficient event communication among the (sometimes, heterogeneous) components that comprise the

Figure 16. Event Bus Architecture

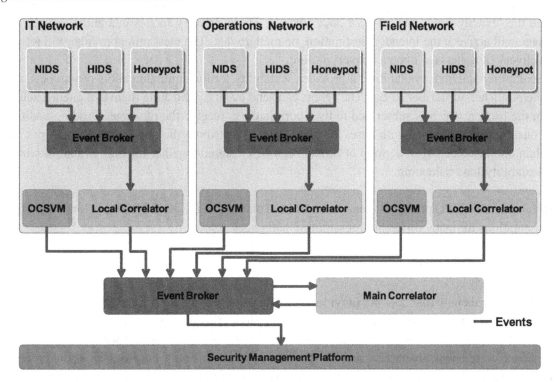

PIDS. Several MOM implementations depend on a Message Queue (MQ) system to allow asynchronous message delivery, by providing a temporary storage, on memory or on a disk, for the messages. Messaging applications communicate with each other through a messaging system, acting either as a message producer (sender) or consumer (receiver). Producers and consumers are loosely coupled, being connected through virtual channels called publish-and-subscribe (one-to-many) channels or point-to-point (one-to-one) channels.

For the integration of eventing interfaces, the CockpitCI PIDS adopted an Event Bus based on the Advanced Message Queuing Protocol (AMQP) (OASIS, 2011), a wire-level, open standard application layer protocol for MOM that defines a neutral (IDMEF-compatible) encoding scheme of byte sequences to pass over the network. An AMQP messaging system consists of three main components: publisher(s) (which assemble messages and send them to a message queue); consumer(s) (which receive messages from a message queue); and broker(s)/server(s) (responsible for receiving messages from publishers and or routing them to the right consumers).

The AMQP-based MOM brings a set of important features to the PIDS architecture, namely:

- Security: it supports authenticated and/or encrypted transport, using Transport Layer Security (TLS) or Simple Authentication and Security Layer (SASL) to protect events from tampering and/or eavesdropping.
- Message reliability: it can guarantee message ordering using a queuing broker, which ensures that messages are delivered to the receiver in the same order in which the sender sent them, with support for disconnection. Messages may be held in a queue for deferred delivery.

- Resiliency: message delivery semantics provide a range of delivery options, with special emphasis on the 'exactly-once' and 'at-least-once' modes. These delivery modes guarantee that the message will arrive at the intended destination, no matter what. The messaging provider will retry the delivery of a message upon a delivery failure.
- Scalability and high availability: it provides scalability for the communication system because of the publisher-subscriber model. The agents can send events, publishing them to a queue/exchange in the broker, which is subscribed to by a correlator, to receive the messages. Adding additional consumers can be done with ease, for failover or to distribute the correlation load across more than one instance. Also, a group of brokers can be clustered together for high availability and/or scalability/load-balancing.

Moreover, the AMPQ protocol is vendor-neutral and platform-agnostic. There are several open source implementations for many different programming languages.

Management Interfaces

For each managed entity that does not provide a suitable management interface, a management adaptor/coupling architecture provides a uniform API and Data Model for each component that does not expose its own native management interface (*Figure 17*). This adaptor is able to interact with the specific interfaces of each component, abstracting and mapping data model attributes. For instance, if the properties or configurations of a certain device are provided via a text configuration file, the management adaptor layer must be able to parse its contents and provide them to the other components of the adaptor through a standardized interface, with the original device configuration properties being mapped into a standardized data model structure by means of an abstraction class.

The Management Adaptor also embeds an API/Data Model module that is responsible for maintaining the data model (state and semantics) properties and also to provide the web service API interface to manipulate them. Accordingly with the mapping rules from the Abstraction Class, attributes exposed by the API layer might have several properties, defining and describing their access mode (read, write), or data types. The API makes use of REST (REpresentative State Transfer) (Fielding, 2000) web services, with security being provided with the help of HTTPS with other authentication mechanisms such as client certificates or signed requests.

The data model structure for management adaptors is standardized, being inspired on hierarchical models usually found on management protocols such as SNMP (Case, 2002), being arranged as a tree, with a root node from which all data model structure is expanded. Also, similarly to SNMP traps or CWMP asynchronous events, the generic model supports the inclusion of eventing properties that enable a specific attribute to generate notification events, for instance, to report when there is a change in the state or value of an attribute.

CONCLUSION

The problematic of Critical Infrastructure Security and Protection is still the subject of an on-going effort in the research community. The evaluation of the proposals presented in this chapter has shown

Figure 17. Security management platform component adaptor (CockpitCI 2014)

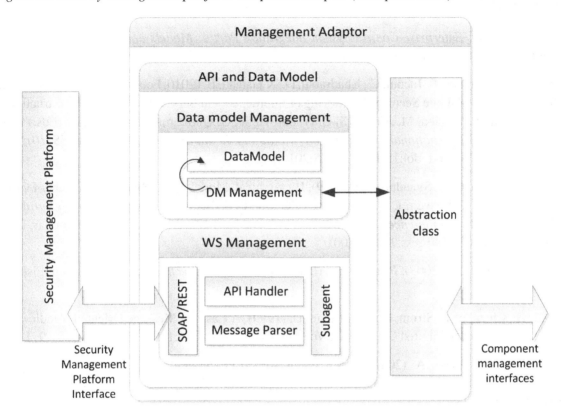

interesting results on improving the accuracy of risk prediction and the manageability and security of a system able to exchange risk information among CIs.

In this context, two recent European projects have been discussed. In this scope, a Policy-Based Management Architecture was presented in order to improve the management of the MICIE Secure Mediation Gateway, responsible for implementing the risk exchange mechanisms. The Trust and Reputation framework able to infer trust information on exchanged information and also on the behaviour of the subjacent system was discussed highlighting the ability to help the CI Operator to reason about the exchanged information and also to dynamically include the risk assessment in the defined management policies.

Also, this chapter presented the architecture of the CockpitCI distributed Intrusion Detection System, designed to address the special cyber-security needs of CIs, such as ICS/SCADA systems. Its approach is based on a distributed approach that attempts to bring the most effective detection mechanisms and tools together with correlation and anomaly detection analysis techniques, in order to create a solution that starts with the state-of-the-art in CI security as its baseline. A strong point of this architecture lies in its capability for assimilation of a diverse range of detection tools in a coherent framework with homogeneous coordination and orchestration. Using distributed two-level correlation capabilities the PIDS is able to get a micro and macro-perspective on the ongoing status of the monitored CI, while being capable of dealing with unknown threats, thanks to the incorporation of machine-learning anomaly detection features. Future work will address improved integration with the SMN, while expanding on functionality and diversity of detection components.

REFERENCES

ANSI/ISA-95.00.01, Enterprise-Control System Integration Part 1: Models and Terminology. (2000). International Society of Automation.

Aubert, J., Schaberreiter, T., Incoul, C., Khadraoui, D., & Gateau, B. (2010, February 15-18). Risk-Based Methodology for Real-Time Security Monitoring of Interdependent Services in Critical Infrastructures. In M. Takizawa, A. M. Tjoa, M. Aleksy, S. Ghernouti-Hélie, G. Quirchmayr, & E. Weippl (Eds.) *Proceedings of the Fifth International Conference on Availability, Reliability, and Security (ARES '10),* (pp. 262–267). Krakow, Poland. doi:10.1109/ARES.2010.102

Baiardi, F., Telmon, C., & Sgandurra, D. (2009). Hierarchical, Model-based Risk Management of Critical Infrastructures. In T. Aven, J. E. Vinnem, & C. G. Soares (Eds.) *Proceedings of the 18th European Safety and Reliability Conference (ESREL 2007)* (Vol. 94, pp. 1403–1415). Stavanger, Norway. June 25–27, 2007. doi:10.1016/j.ress.2009.02.001

Bailey, D., & Wright, E. (2003). *Practical SCADA for Industry (IDC Technology).* Amsterdam: Elsevier Press.

Banavar, G., Chandra, T., Strom, R., & Sturman, D. (1999). A Case for Message Oriented Middleware. Em P. Jayanti (Ed.), Distributed Computing, Vol. 1693, (pp. 1–17). doi:10.1007/3-540-48169-9_1

Bernhardt, T., & Vasseur, A. (2007). Esper: Event Stream Processing and Correlation. *O'Reilly On Java.* Retrieved from http://www.onjava.com/pub/a/onjava/2007/03/07/esper-event-stream-processing-and-correlation.html

Bertoni, A., Ciancamerla, E., di Prospero, F., Lefevre, D., Minichino, M., Lev, L., et al. (2010). Interdependency modelling framework, indicators and models – Final Report. Ciancamerla, E. & Minichino, M., (Eds.) MICIE Project Deliverable D2.2.3. European Commission FP7.

Bessani, A., Sousa, P., Correia, M., & Neves, N. (2007). *Intrusion-tolerant protection for critical infrastructures* (Technical Report). University of Lisbon. Retrieved from http://www.di.fc.ul.pt/~nuno/PAPERS/TR-07-8.pdf

Caldeira, F., Castrucci, M., Aubigny, M., Aubert, J., Macone, D., & Monteiro, E., … Suraci, V. (2010a). Secure Mediation Gateway Architecture Enabling the Communication Among Critical Infrastructures. In P. Cunningham & M. Cunningham (Eds.), *Proceedings of the Future Network and MobileSummit 2010 Conference (2010, June 16-18).* Florence, Italy.

Caldeira, F., Monteiro, E., & Simões, P. (2010b). Trust and Reputation for Information Exchange in Critical Infrastructures. In C. Xenakis, & S. Wolthusen (Eds.), *Proceedings of the 5th International Workshop on Critical Information Infrastructures Security (CRITIS 2010), (2010, September 23-24),* Vol. 6712, pp. 140–152). Athens, Greece. doi:10.1007/978-3-642-21694-7_12

Caldeira, F., Monteiro, E., & Simões, P. (2010c). Trust and Reputation Management for Critical Infrastructure Protection. In S. Tenreiro de Magalhães, H. Jahankhani, & A. G. Hessami (Eds.), *Proceedings of the 6th International Conference on Global Security, Safety, and Sustainability (ICGS3 2010), (2010, September 1-3),* Vol. 92, (pp. 39–47). Braga, Portugal. doi:10.1007/978-3-642-15717-2_5

Caldeira, F., Monteiro, E., & Simões, P. (2010d). Trust and reputation management for critical infrastructure protection. In H. Jahankhani & S. Tenreiro de Magalhães (Eds.), Special Issue on Global Security, Safety and Sustainability, Vol. 3(3), (pp. 187–203).

Caldeira, F., Schaberreiter, T., Monteiro, E., Aubert, J., Simões, P., & Khadraoui, D. (2011). Trust based interdependency weighting for on-line risk monitoring in interdependent critical infrastructures. In F. Cuppens, S. Foley, B. Groza, & M. Minea (Eds.), *Proceedings of the Sixth International Conference on Risks and Security of Internet and Systems (CRiSIS), (2011, September 26-28),* (pp. 1–7). Timisoara, Romania. doi:10.1109/CRiSIS.2011.6061545

Caldeira, F., Schaberreiter, T., Varrette, S., Monteiro, E., Simões, P., Bouvry, P., & Khadraoui, D. (2013). Trust based interdependency weighting for on-line risk monitoring in interdependent critical infrastructures. In K. M. Khan (Ed.), International Journal of Secure Software Engineering (IJSSE) (Vol. 4(4)). IGI Global. doi:10.4018/ijsse.2013100103

Capodieci, P., Diblasi, S., Ciancamerla, E., Minichino, M., Foglietta, C., & Lefevre, D., … Aubigny, M. (2010). Improving Resilience of Interdependent Critical Infrastructures via an On-Line Alerting System. In A. Rizzo (Ed.), *Proceedings of the first International Conference COMPENG, Complexity in Engineering, (2010, February 22-24),* (pp. 88–90). Rome, Italy. doi:10.1109/COMPENG.2010.28

Case, J., Mundy, R., Partain, D., & Stewart, B. (2002). *Introduction and Applicability Statements for Internet-Standard Management Framework* (No. RFC3410). RFC Editor. Retrieved from https://www.rfc-editor.org/info/rfc3410

Castrucci, M., Macone, D., Suraci, V., Inzerilli, T., Neri, A., Panzieri, S., Foglietta, C., Oliva, G., Aubert, J., Incoul, C., Caldeira, F., Aubigny, M., Harpes, C., & Kloda (2010). Secure Mediation Gateway Architecture – Final Version. In Castrucci, M., (Ed.). *MICIE Project Deliverable D4.2.2. European Commission FP7.*

Castrucci, M., Neri, A., Caldeira, F., Aubert, J., Khadraoui, D., & Aubigny, M. … Capodieci, P. (2012). Design and implementation of a mediation system enabling secure communication among Critical Infrastructures. In S. Shenoi (Ed.), International Journal of Critical Infrastructure Protection Vol. 5(2), (pp. 86–97).

Ciancamerla, E., di Blasi, S., Fioriti, V., Foglietta, C., Minichino, M., Lefevre, D., ... (2009). Interdependency modelling framework, interdependency indicators and models – First Interim Report. Ciancamerla, E. & Minichino, M., (Eds.). MICIE Project Deliverable D2.2.1. European Commission FP7.

Ciancamerla, E., Foglietta, C., Lefevre, D., Minichino, M., Lev, L., & Shneck, Y. (2010a). Discrete Event Simulation of QoS of a SCADA System Interconnecting a Power Grid and a Telco Network. In J. Berleur, M. Hercheui, & L. Hilty (Eds.), What Kind of Information Society? Governance, Virtuality, Surveillance, Sustainability, Resilience. Proceedings of the *9th IFIP TC 9 International Conference, HCC9 2010 and 1st IFIP TC 11 International Conference, CIP 2010.* Vol. 328, (pp. 350–362). Brisbane, Australia

Ciancamerla, E., Minichino, M., Lev, L., Simões, P., Panzieri, S., Oliva, G., ... (2010b). CI Reference Scenario and service oriented approach (Final Report). Ciancamerla, E. & Minichino, M., (Eds.). MICIE Project Deliverable D2.1.2. European Commission FP7.

CockpitCI FP7-SEC-2011-1 Project 285647. (2011). Cockpit, C. I., & the Consortium. Retrieved from http://CockpitCI.eu

Creery, A., & Byres, E. J. (2005). Industrial cybersecurity for power system and SCADA networks. *Petroleum and Chemical Industry Conference, 2005. Industry Applications Society 52nd Annual, (September 2005),* (pp. 303–309). Denver, USA. doi:10.1109/PCICON.2005.1524567

CRitical Utility InfrastructurAL resilience. (2008). CRUTIAL. Retrieved from http://crutial.rse-web.it/

Davis, C. M., Tate, J. E., Okhravi, H., Grier, C., Overbye, T. J., & Nicol, D. (2006). SCADA Cyber Security Testbed Development. *Power Symposium, 2006. NAPS 2006. 38th North American (2006, September 17-19),* 483–488. Carbondale, IL, USA. doi:10.1109/NAPS.2006.359615

De Porcellinis, S., Panzieri, S., & Setola, R. (2009). Modelling critical infrastructure via a mixed holistic reductionistic approach. In C. Chaudet, G. L. Grand, & V. Rosat (Eds.), Special Issue on Critical Infrastructures as Complex Systems, 5(1/2), 86–99. doi:10.1504/IJCIS.2009.022851

De Porcellinis, S., Panzieri, S., Setola, R., & Ulivi, G. (2008). Simulation of heterogeneous and interdependent critical infrastructures. In S. Bologna (Ed.), Special Issue on Complex Network and Infrastructure Protection Vol. 4(1/2), (pp. 110–128). Inderscience Publishers. doi:10.1504/IJCIS.2008.016095

Debar, H., Curry, D., & Feinstein, B. (2007). *The Intrusion Detection Message Exchange Format (ID-MEF)* (No. RFC4765). RFC Editor. Retrieved from https://www.rfc-editor.org/info/rfc4765

Dondossola, G., Garrone, F., Szanto, J., & Gennaro, F. (2008). A laboratory testbed for the evaluation of cyber attacks to interacting ICT infrastructures of power grid operators. In E. de Jaeger (Ed.), *Proceedings of the CIRED Seminar: SmartGrids for Distribution, (2008, June 23-24),* (pp. 1–4). Frankfurt, Germany. doi:10.1049/ic:20080459

Electrical Characteristics of Generators and Receivers for Use in Balanced Multipoint Systems. (1983). *EIA Standard* [Electronic Industries Association]. *RS-485,* 1983.

European Commission. (2012). *European Commission - Home Affairs.* Retrieved from http://ec.europa.eu/home-affairs/policies/terrorism/terrorism_infrastructure_en.htm

Falliere, N., Murchu, L. O., & Chien, E. (2011). W32.Stuxnet Dossier [Technical report]. *Symantec - Security Response.* Retrieved from http://www.symantec. com/connect/blogs/w32stuxnet-dossier

Fielding, R. (2000). *Architectural styles and the design of network-based software architectures.* (Ph.D. Dissertation). University of California, Irvine.

Gasparri, A., Oliva, G., & Panzieri, S. (2009). On the distributed synchronization of on-line IIM Interdependency Models. In D.-T. Pham & A. Colombo (Eds.), *Proceedings of the 7th IEEE International Conference on Industrial Informatics (INDIN 2009)* (pp. 795–800). Cardiff, Wales, United Kingdom, 24–26 June 2009: IEEE Computer Society. doi:10.1109/INDIN.2009.5195904

Haslum, K., & Arnes, A. (2006). Multisensor Real-time Risk Assessment using Continuous-time Hidden Markov Models. In Y. Cheung, Y. Wang, & H. Liu (Eds.), *Proceedings of the 2006 International Conference on Computational Intelligence and Security, (2006 November 3-6),* (Vol. 2, pp. 1536–1540). Guangzhou, China. doi:10.1109/ICCIAS.2006.295318

Hsu, C., Chang, C., & Lin, C. (2003). *A practical guide to support vector classification.* Retrieved from https://www.cs.sfu.ca/people/Faculty/teaching/726/spring11/svmguide.pdf

IEC. (2005). *P-IEC/PAS 62407 ed1.0, Real-time Ethernet control automation technology (EtherCAT)*. International Electrotechnical Comission.

IEEE Standard for Electric Power Systems Communications. (2010). IEEE Power & Energy Society.

Igure, V. M., Laughter, S. A., & Williams, R. D. (2006, October). Security issues in SCADA networks. *Computers & Security, 25*(7), 498–506. doi:10.1016/j.cose.2006.03.001

Infrastructure REsilience. The INSPIRE Project. In R. Setola, & S. Geretshuber (Eds.), *Proceedings of the 3th International Workshop on Critical Information Infrastructures Security (CRITIS 2008), (2008, October 13-15)* Vol. 5508, (pp. 109–118). Rome, Italy.

INSPIRE Project Web Site. (2010). *INSPIRE*. Retrieved from http://www. inspire-strep.eu

IRRIIS Project Web Site. (2008). *IRRIIS*. Retrieve from http://www.irriis.org

ISA-99.00.01 - Security for Industrial Automation and Control Systems - Part 1. (2007). *International Society of Automation Standard*. Retrieved from http://isa99.isa.org/Documents/Drafts/ISA-62443-1-1-PUB-A4.pdf

ISO 11898-1:2003, Road vehicles -- Controller area network (CAN) -- Part 1. (2003). *International Standards Organization*.

Kang, D. J., Lee, J. J., Kim, B. H., & Hur, D. (2011). Proposal strategies of key management for data encryption in SCADA network of electric power systems. *International Journal of Electrical Power & Energy Systems, 33*(9), 1521–1526.

Klein, R., Rome, E., Beyel, C., Linnemann, R., Reinhardt, W., & Usov, A. (2009). Information Modelling and Simulation in Large Interdependent Critical Infrastructures in IRRIIS. In R. Setola, & S. Geretshuber (Eds.), *Proceedings of the Third International Workshop on Critical Information Infrastructures Security (CRITIS), (2008, October 13-15)*, Vol. 5508, (pp. 36–47). Rome, Italy. doi:10.1007/978-3-642-03552-4_4

Krutz, R. L. (2006). *Securing SCADA systems*. Indianapolis, USA: Wiley Publishing.

Kun-Lun Li. Hou-Kuan Huang, Shen-Feng Tian, & Wei Xu. (2003). Improving one-class SVM for anomaly detection. *Machine Learning and Cybernetics, 2003 International Conference, Vol. 5*, (pp. 3077–3081).

Lev, L., Tanenbaum, D., Ohana, R., Holzer, R., Hunovich, T., Adar, A., et al. Jager, Pascoli, Aubigny, M., & Harpes, C. (2011). Validation Activities. Lev, L. & Baruch, Y., (Eds.). MICIE Project Deliverable D6.3. European Commission FP7.

Ma, J., & Perkins, S. (2003). Time-series novelty detection using one-class support vector machines. *Neural Networks, 2003. Proceedings of the International Joint Conference on, Vol. 3*, (pp. 1741–1745).

MICIE - Tool for systemic risk analysis and secure mediation of data exchanged across linked CI information infrastructures. (2008). *MICIE Consortium*.

Modbus Application Protocol Specification V1.1b3. (2012). MICIE Consortium Retrieved from http://www.modbus.org/docs/Modbus_Application_Proftocol_V1_1b3.pdf

Advanced Message Queuing Protocol (AMQP), version 1.0. (2012). OASIS. Retrieved from https://www.oasis-open.org/committees/tc_home.php?wg_abbrev=amqp

Obama, B. (2013). Executive Order 13636 - Improving Critical Infrastructure Cybersecurity. *USA Federal Register*, (2013-03915):11737–11744.

Oliva, G., Panzieri, S., & Setola, R. (2010). Agent-based input–output interdependency model. In S. Shenoi (Ed.), International Journal of Critical Infrastructures, 3(2), 76–82.

Panzieri, S., Oliva, G., Foglietta, C., Minichino, M., Ciancamerla, E., Macone, D., et al. (2010). Common Ontology and Risk Prediction Algorithms – Final Version. In S. Panzieri (Ed.), MICIE Project, European Commission FP7.

Panzieri, S., Setola, R., & Ulivi, G. (2005). An approach to model complex interdependent infrastructures. In P. Zítek (Ed.), *Proceedings of the 16th IFAC World Congress, (2005, July 4-8),* (pp. 67–67). Prague, Czech Republic.

Ponder (2010). *Ponder2 project*. Retrieved from http://ponder2.net/

PROFIBUS & PROFINET International. (1999). Retrieved from www.profibus.com

Proposal for a council decision on a Critical Infrastructure Warning Information Network (CIWIN). (2008). *Communication from European Commission*, COM (2008) 676.

R: A Language and Environment for Statistical Computing. (2009). Vienna, Austria: R Foundation for Statistical Computing.

Rinaldi, S. M. (2004). Modeling and simulating critical infrastructures and their interdependencies. In R. H. Sprague (Ed.), *Proceedings of the 37th Hawaii International Conference on System Science (HICSS–37), (2004, January 5-8),* Vol. 2, (pp. 20054a). Big Island, Hawaii, USA. doi:10.1109/HICSS.2004.1265180

Rinaldi, S. M., Peerenboom, J. P., & Kelly, T. K. (2001). Identifying, Understanding, and Analyzing Critical Infrastructure Interdependencies. In R. D. Braatz (Ed.), IEEE Control Systems Magazine, 21(6), 11–25.

Schaberreiter, T., Aubert, J., & Khadraoui, D. (2011a). Critical infrastructure security modelling and RESCI-MONITOR: A risk based critical infrastructure model. In P. Cunningham (Ed.), *Proceedings of the 2011 IST-Africa Conference, (2011, May 11-13),* (pp. 1–8). Gaborone, Botswana.

Schaberreiter, T., Caldeira, F., Aubert, J., Monteiro, E., Khadraoui, D., & Simões, P. (2011b). Assurance and trust indicators to evaluate accuracy of on-line risk in critical infrastructures. In S. Bologna, & S. Wolthusen (Eds.), *Proceedings of the 6th International Workshop on Critical Information Infrastructures Security (CRITIS), (2011, September 8-9).* Lucerne, Switzerland.

Schölkopf, B., Platt, J. C., Shawe-Taylor, J. C., Smola, A. J., & Williamson, R. C. (2001). Estimating the Support of a High-Dimensional Distribution. *Neural Computation Journal, 13*(7), 1443–1471. doi:10.1162/089976601750264965 PMID:11440593

Simões, P., Capodieci, P., Minicino, M., Panzieri, S., Castrucci, M., & Lev, L. (2010). An Alerting System for Interdependent Critical Infrastructures. In J. Demergis (Ed.), *Proceedings of the 9th European Conference on Information Warfare and Security (ECIW), (2010, July 1-2),* (pp. 275–283). Thessaloniki, Greece.

Simões, P., Cruz, T., Gomes, J., & Monteiro, E. (2013). On the use of Honeypots for detecting cyber attacks on Industrial Control Networks, *Proceedings of 12th European Conference on Information Warfare and Security*, eds. R Kuusisto & E Kurkinen, (pp 264–270). ACPI International.

Simões, P., Curado, M., Panzieri, S., Oliva, G., Minichino, M., Ciancamerla, E., et al. (2009). Common Ontology and Risk Prediction Algorithms – Preliminary Version. Panzieri, S., (Ed.). MICIE Project Deliverable D3.2.1. European Commission FP7.

Sokolowski, J., Turnitsa, C., & Diallo, S. (2008). A Conceptual Modeling Method for Critical Infrastructure Modeling. In T. F. Znati, & H. D. Karatza (Eds.), *Proceedings of the 41st Annual Simulation Symposium (ANSS), (2008, April 14-16),* (pp. 203–211). Ottawa, Canada. doi:10.1109/ANSS-41.2008.31

Spitzner, L. (2002). *Honeypots: Tracking hackers*. Addison-Wesley Professional.

Telecontrol equipment and systems - Part 5-104: Transmission protocols. (2006). International Electrotechnical Commission.

Ten Chee-Wooi, Chen-Ching Liu, & Manimaran, G. (2008). Vulnerability Assessment of Cybersecurity for SCADA Systems. *Power Systems, IEEE Transactions on, 23*(4), 1836–1846.

The grid 5000 project web site. (2013). *Grid5000*. Retrieved from http://www. grid5000.fr

Trusted Information Sharing Network (TISN) for Critical Infrastructure Resilience. (2011). *TISN*. Retrieved from http://www.tisn.gov.au

DNP3 Overview. (2002). *Triangle MicroWorks*. Retrieved from http://trianglemicroworks.com/docs/default-source/referenced-documents/DNP3_Overview.pdf

Twidle, K., Dulay, N., Lupu, E., & Sloman, M. (2009). Ponder2: A Policy System for Autonomous Pervasive Environments. In R. Calinescu, F. Liberal, M. Marin, L. Herrero, C. Turro, & M. Popescu (Eds.), *Proceedings of the Fifth International Conference on Autonomic and Autonomous Systems (ICAS), (2009, April 20-25),* (pp. 330–335). Valencia, Spain. doi:10.1109/ICAS.2009.42

Verissimo, P., Neves, N., & Correia, M. (2008). The CRUTIAL reference critical information infrastructure architecture: a blueprint. In A. Gheorghe (Ed.), International Journal of System of Systems Engineering, 1/2, 78–95. doi:10.1504/IJSSE.2008.018132

Verissimo, P., Neves, N., Correia, M., Deswarte, Y., Kalam, A., Bondavalli, A., & Daidone, A. (2008b). The CRUTIAL Architecture for Critical Information Infrastructures. In R. Lemos, F. Giandomenico, C. Gacek, H. Muccini, & M. Vieira (Eds.), *Architecting Dependable Systems V,* 5135, 1–27). Springer Berlin Heidelberg. doi:10.1007/978-3-540-85571-2_1

Wang, Y., Wong, J., & Miner, A. (2004). Anomaly intrusion detection using one class SVM. *Information Assurance Workshop, 2004. Proceedings from the Fifth Annual IEEE SMC*, 358–364. doi:10.1109/IAW.2004.1437839

Zhu, B., Joseph, A., & Sastry, S. (2011). A Taxonomy of Cyber Attacks on SCADA Systems. In *Proceedings of the 2011 International Conference on Internet of Things and 4th International Conference on Cyber, Physical and Social Computing,* (pp. 380–388). doi:10.1109/iThings/CPSCom.2011.34

Chapter 8

Cyber–Attacks, Retaliation and Risk:
Legal and Technical Implications for Nation–States and Private Entities

Cameron S. D. Brown
Australian National University, Australia

ABSTRACT

This chapter examines legal and technical issues that arise when considering strategic retaliatory countermeasures to cyber-attacks. Implications connected with endorsing techniques of active defense for nation-states are viewed alongside challenges faced by private entities. Proactive avenues for tackling cyber-security threats are evaluated and shortcomings within the international system of governance are analyzed. Retributive justice as a legal and philosophical concept is viewed through the lens of customary international law pertaining to use of force and self-defense. Difficulties in adapting rules governing kinetic warfare to instances of cyber-conflict are elucidated. The danger of executing counterstrikes for private entities is explained with reference to cross-border dilemmas, conflict of laws, and risks stemming from civil, criminal, and also administrative liability. Protocols for safeguarding anonymity are observed and the problem of attribution is illustrated. Costs and benefits associated with adopting methods of active defense are presented and solutions to avoid accountability failure are recommended.

INTRODUCTION

For nation-states and private sector entities alike the interconnectivity and transnational reach of the Internet has facilitated a significant shift in economic wealth and power. The potential for cyber-attacks to target governments and corporations is a by-product of the anonymous and decentralized nature of the Internet (Lin, 2010). Computer hacking is a phenomenon that challenges existing notions of warfare, espionage, competitive intelligence (Kovacich, Jones & Luzwick, 2002), and also of crime (Yasin, 1998). The capacity of nation-states and private entities to protect themselves from cyber-attacks is constantly in flux as new attack methods are developed and reactive defenses are devised. Ultimately, strategic

DOI: 10.4018/978-1-4666-8456-0.ch008

advantage lies with the aggressor and the defensive posture adopted by those under siege typically leads to initial loss or damage before vulnerabilities are patched and armored ("Microsoft Security," 2015). Between 2013 and 2015 the average cost of a data breach is estimated to have increased by 23% (Ponemon Institute, 2015).

Cyber-security may be seen to function within an adversary-based paradigm where defensive security innovators and consumers are pitted against persistent rogue attackers and highly organized operatives. In this cat-and-mouse struggle, defense cannot afford a single mistake, whilst those in offence have the advantage of time and need only achieve success on one occasion. In the digital domain, even minor breaches can be critical as data is syphoned out of governmental agencies and departments of defense, and intellectual property is pilfered from corporate networks. The vulnerability of nation-states and their critical infrastructure to Distributed Denial of Service Attacks (DDoS) also raises issues concerning to use of force, self-defense, and rules of engagement. Cyber-threats have become diversified and often comprise multi-stage attacks that use an assortment of attack tools that target a wide spectrum of technologies. The adversarial nature of this digital skirmish is multidimensional and the whole concept of retaliation is laden with risk, posing unique legal and technical problems.

The continuum of potential methods for seeking cyber-retribution is variously labelled 'hacking back', 'striking back', 'active defense', 'offensive retaliation', 'countermeasures', 'counteroffensives', 'counterattacks', 'counterstrikes' or 'forcible cyber-defense', amongst others. This chapter examines the legality and technical feasibility of conducting counteroffensives for both nation-states and private entities. The implications of retaliation for the public and private sphere are analyzed from a legal and operational standpoint. Uncertainties and risks are evaluated across a range of contexts, including the potential for reprisals to escalate conflict and intensify crisis situations.

BACKGROUND

In the wake of recent reports of persistent cyber-exploitation globally, coupled with disclosures concerning unabashed national cyber-surveillance programs (Gorman & Valentino-Devries, 2013), the issue of cyber-defense and retaliation is very topical (Limnell, 2014; Sorcher, 2015; Yadron, 2015). Following the lead of corporate giants like Google (Nakashima, 2013; Richmond, 2010) it seems nation-states and the private sector may resort to the use of forcible cyber-defense following instances of cyber-harm and transnational transgressions via the Internet (Kesan & Hayes, 2012; Messerschmidt, 2013). In 2010, Google announced that a group purportedly identified as the 'Elderwood Gang' (also known as the 'Beijing Group') infiltrated the Company's network, and breached at least thirty other corporations based in the United States (Cha & Nakashima, 2014; Clayton, 2012). The attackers utilized malware known as Hydraq, also referred to as Aurora, in combination with a zero-day exploit (O'Gorman & McDonald, 2012). Nicknamed "Operation Aurora", the cyber-attack was allegedly traced to servers located at two Chinese educational institutions (Kurtz, 2010; "Protecting your critical assets," 2010). Once identified, it is reported that Google launched a counteroffensive targeting the perceived attack source (Sanger & Markoff, 2010).

Unlike passive defense mechanisms, which endeavor to identify or prevent cyber-attacks before harm occurs, active defense aims to proactively retaliate by striking-back against intruders using counter-intelligence, deception, disruption, and destructive means (Kesan & Majuca, 2010). Hacking back encompasses everything from intrusive collection of intelligence to convict culprits, through to launch-

Table 1. Common modes of retaliation to cyber-attacks

Mode	Form
Measures that impede individual attacks	Seeks to identify an attack and block or delay the source. Detection can be facilitated via signature-based security controls, and countermeasures may include use of Dynamic Packet Filtering on a Firewall (i.e., Shunning) and sending Transmission Control Protocol Reset packets (TCP RST) to disable a connection with an adversary. Intrusion Prevention Systems (IPS) can automate this process.
Measures that deceive and camouflage	Seeks to confuse or hide from an adversary. Based on disinformation campaigns and use of counterintelligence. Measures can encompass deceptive responses to ping requests, as well as more complex technical masquerading or physical posturing that impersonates another system or organization.
Measures that target a specific attack tool	Seeks to interfere with tools used by an adversary during an attack, which typically fall within distinct categories. There is little variation in the functionality of each tool, even in instances where an adversary uses customized exploits (e.g., Port Scanners, Packet Sniffers, etc.), thereby presenting a target for retaliation. As such, it is possible to manipulate the presentation of the data that a particular tool is pursuing.
Measures that attack the adversary's host or network	Seeks to forcefully debilitate the capacity of the adversary and/or deter further malicious activity (e.g., Sinkholing). In most circumstances an attacker's chief concerns relate to identifying and circumventing Intrusion Detection Systems (IDS), IPS, Honey Pots, and Tarpits. In the absence of attribution issues, the possibility of targeted reprisals poses a potential challenge to the security and resilience of an adversary's system.

ing counteroffensives designed to deflect malicious activity or deceive an adversary (Menn, 2012) (see *Table 1*). Retaliatory measures might also include scanning and exploiting network vulnerabilities on a target system, as well as disruptive elements that circumvent security, poison data, incapacitate, or deny service (Holz & Raynal, 2013; Karnow, 2005; Kopstein, 2014). Irrespective of the range of potential countermeasures, private actors must be cognizant that use of forcible cyber-defense is strictly prohibited under the laws of most western democratic states where striking back is construed as an offense, rather than as an act of self-defense.

Companies such as FireEye, CrowdStrike, Endgame, CloudFare, Shape Security, Caspida, Fidelis, Palantir, RSA, Palo Alto Networks, Lancope, and Prolexic, amongst others, claim to have developed technology that can profile behavior and defend against persistent cyber-attacks. Yet, the market for proactive services has not emerged recently. In 2004 the security firm Symbiot offered various counteroffensive models, including: exploiting vulnerabilities on attacking systems; accessing, disabling or destroying assets used in the commission of an attack; and offering disproportionate retaliatory counterstrikes to discourage further attacks (Kotadia, 2004; West, 2013). For the private sector, a counteroffensive that impinges upon a third party system is akin to self-help rather than self-defense. For nation-states, the status of intrusive cyber-activity is far less clear.

LEGAL AND TECHNICAL IMPLICATIONS

Promoting a Strategy of Self-Help

Interest on the part of nation-states and private corporations in perusing methods of active defense is being driven by perceived inequities at local and international levels (Bradsher, 2014; Fallon, 2012; Nakashima, 2012; Sanger, 2013). In the private domain, hacking back may circumvent some of the challenges associated with seeking justice via traditional avenues, such as "lengthy prosecutions, thorny jurisdictional matters, technologically unsophisticated juries, and slow courts" (Katyal, 2005, p. 60). The capacity of law enforcement to respond to targeted cyber-attacks is mostly limited in terms of expertise and resources (Karnow, 2005), and trans-jurisdictional matters are hampered by bureaucratic entanglements (Lemos, 2001). Many cyber-attacks are technically sophisticated and well-conceived ("APT30," 2015a), requiring both forensic expertise and deductive reasoning to unravel complex *modus operandi* and substantiate elements of an offence (Bromby, 2006; Endgame, 2015). Despite the pervasiveness of digital information many police and legally trained personnel in criminal justice systems globally are still hesitant to collect and present electronic sources of evidence (Zavrsnik, 2010). Lack of leading edge tools and shrinking defense budgets for procuring resources are ongoing problems (Mislan, 2010).

Nevertheless, defenders can gain insight into the motivations and identities of attackers using open source intelligence, social networks, digital and network forensics, and by following blacklists. The issue then becomes one of precision. Digesting the vast quantity of information and developing actionable intelligence in order to identify trends and accurately profile a specific adversary is complicated for even well-resourced operations. Intelligence must be interpreted objectively, communicated succinctly and placed into the hands of people who can react to the threat in a short amount of time, lest it lose value (Carter & Carter, 2009; Ratcliffe, 2008). Common threat actors and incentives which impel cyber-attacks are outlined in *Table 2*, although like the virtual geography of cyberspace, such categories are increasingly indistinguishable (Finklea & Theohary, 2013; Henry, 2012; Stokes & Weedon, 2015). "State and non-state threats often also blend together; patriotic entities often act as cyber surrogates for states; and non-state entities can provide cover for state-based operators" (US Department of Defense, 2015, p. 9).

A prevailing tendency towards underreporting cyber-attacks has arisen due to: a lack of public confidence in the capacity of police to investigate cyber-attacks (Collier & Spaul, 1992); the belief that law enforcement agencies are inflexible and intrusive (Davies, 1999; Walden, 2005; Wolf, 2000); a deeper reluctance to report due to shame or embarrassment (United Nations Office on Drugs and Crime, 2013); and the perception that many incidents may simply be too insignificant to warrant police attention (Herrera-Flanigan & Ghosh, 2010). Some victims fear that prosecutors will not take on their case, or if they do, will publicize the incident widely to raise the profile of the prosecutor or department concerned, without due regard to the impact of such exposure for the victim (Goodno, 2007; Shafritz, 2001). Private corporations have exhibited great concern that disclosure of cyber-security breaches may: magnify damage created by a cyber-attack; prompt stock prices to plummet (Campbell, Gordon, Loeb & Zhou, 2003); undermine commercial reputation and branding (Cashell, Jackson, Jickling, & Webel, 2004); and telegraph vulnerabilities to competitors in the marketplace (Menn, 2011). Ultimately, many corporations are leaning towards counteroffensives because "there currently is no better method to enforce cyberspace violations" (Epstein, 2005, p. 26; Messerschmidt, 2013), and swift proactive measures may deter future cyber-attacks.

Although many developed countries have the capacity to retaliate against individual cyber-attacks originating outside their borders (Baker, 2010), the sheer magnitude of the problem has become a global epidemic that governments are ill-equipped to resolve ("Public must be warned," 2013; Nakashima, 2012). The rise of non-state actors during the past two decades has challenged the legitimacy of warfare and complicated the process of attributing accountability for cross-border incursions (Bobbitt, 2008). Non-state operatives are obtaining access to sophisticated technology and acquiring the skillsets essential to use that technology (Australian Institute of Criminology, 2006). A range of highly specialized

Table 2. Cyber-threat actors and attack incentives

Actors	Incentives
Cybercriminals	• Making money through fraud or from the sale of valuable information. • Realizing gains on the stock market by obtaining information prior to announcement of official transactions. • Extorting money from private entities by holding data to ransom or interfering with online transactions of a commercial nature. • Indulging in depravity by disseminating abusive material and satisfying predatory urges.
Industrial competitors	• Stealing intellectual property and trade secrets. • Gaining advantage in the marketplace by acquiring commercially sensitive data, such as key negotiating positions. • Furthering privatization strategies by discrediting counterparties to a transaction.
Foreign intelligence agencies	• Obtaining sensitive research and development information from leading manufacturers, governments, and defense contractors. • Toppling hostile regimes. • Sabotaging the technical developments of enemy states.
State sponsored operatives	• Advancing homeland security through ubiquitous surveillance. • Collaborating with likeminded nation-states to solve shared problems. • Monitoring political speech online and silencing dissidents. • Sabotaging international deals to safeguard and enhance domestic commercial interests, or to give local industries an economic advantage.
Hackers	• Interfering with computer systems as an intellectual challenge or to earn respect among peers. • Penetration testing to identify vulnerabilities. • Reverse engineering systems to gain knowledge.
Non-state actors	• Disrupting government services and impeding capacity of industry to function. • Exploiting information security weaknesses to raise awareness, exact revenge, or expose wrongdoing. • Attacking critical infrastructure for political or ideological reasons. • Circulating graphic material to traumatize adversaries and defacing digital resources to further a political agenda.
Employees and common users	• Accidental or deliberate system misuse by users who have legitimate user access, or escalated privileges. • Punishing an employer for perceived grievances. • Monitoring or stalking a significant other. • Strategically planting malicious insiders within a department or organization to gain access to information.

technical freelancers and resolute service providers are also available for hire in the global marketplace (Shelley, 2004).

A nation-state, non-state group, or individual actor can purchase destructive malware and other capabilities on the black market. State and non-state actors also pay experts to search for vulnerabilities and develop exploits. This practice has created a dangerous and uncontrolled market that serves multiple actors within the international system, often for competing purposes (US Department of Defense, 2015, p. 10).

In view of this evolving threat landscape it is expected that use of active defense measures will increase. Therefore, the question is not whether hacking back will occur, but rather how the international community can manage unilateral and multilateral cyber-conflict, and how states themselves intend to control retaliation by legal and natural persons within their borders.

If not the state, who will protect the property of normal citizens and safeguard the commercial interests of private sector entities from transborder cyber-threats (Office of the National Counterintelligence Executive, 2011)? In 1998 the US Government responded in kind to DDoS attacks launched by hacktivists against the Pentagon. In doing so, the US demonstrated that the military already had capacity for active neutralization of threats against public sector entities (Kesan & Hayes, 2012). However, the substance of this issue relates to the willingness of nation-states to engage in retaliation and the availability of strong evidence to support that course of action. It is difficult to justify acting in self-defense when an offender can muster plausible deniability for an infringement, or there is manifest uncertainty about the territorial origin of an attack. Many nation-states are now investing "significantly in cyber as it provides them with a viable, plausibly deniable capability" (US Department of Defense, 2015, p. 9).

At the global level it is the principle of reciprocity in international law which is relied upon to justify retaliation for cyber-incursions (Ferzan, 2008). In essence, this approach mirrors the "eye for an eye" philosophy (Simons, 2008, p. 51), and is based on a decentralized system where compliance is enforced by other nation-states, rather than by an overarching authority. *Lex talionis* derives from Roman law and is a term referring to rules governing acts of revenge or retaliation (Fellmeth & Horwitz, 2011). This law prescribes retributive justice for a crime, such that punitive measures should match in magnitude and form the transgression of the malefactor. Similar examples may be found in the Code of Hammurabi (c.1700 BC), and the Torah (Exodus 21:23–25), which establish moral grounds on permissible revenge (i.e., take no more in retaliation than an eye for an eye, etc.) (Honderich, 2005). It also establishes the norm in a society bound by the rule of law that the punishment for a crime should be proportional to the crime itself.

If indeed cyber-attacks can be characterized as 'use of force', Article 51 of the UN Charter recognizes an "inherent right of…self-defense" following an "armed attack" (*Charter of the United Nations*, 1945). Moreover, when a nation-state fails to exercise due diligence in preventing its territory from being used to cause significant harm to another it is in violation of international law (Kesan & Majuca, 2010). This is also enshrined in Article 2(4) of the UN Charter which provides for a nation-state to be free from the threat of use of force (D'Aspremont, 2011). In instances where a nation-state is unable or unwilling to address an ongoing international threat within its borders, the right of self-defense may also extend to use of force against non-state actors (Deeks, 2012). The military intervention in Mali by France in 2013 is a case in point (Erforth & Deffner, 2013).

Legal Quagmire

Given the decentralized nature of the international system, traditional countermeasures taken by one nation-state as a reprisal to perceived wrongful conduct by another, are widely regarded as a lawful method of redress (Hathaway & Shapiro, 2011). Yet, forcible cyber-defense is practically unregulated by international law and there are no specific provisions for addressing cyber-conflict (Schmitt, 2012). This is partly due to the difficulty in adapting traditional rules of international law to advances in technology. Conflict has become multi-layered and non-linear with engagements occurring "simultaneously at multiple levels and multiple locations, and in virtual spaces" (O'Hagan, 2013, p. 563). Cyber-attacks "not only stretch across a global battle space, but now exceed the normal confines of time, place and meaning" (Der Derian, 2013, p. 575). Most principles of international law are physical in nature and the Internet does not translate well within this paradigm (Wu, 2006). For instance the right of self-defense enshrined in the UN Charter is limited to cases of "armed attack".

The bodies of law that apply to warfare are derived from customary international law (e.g., *Geneva Convention*, 1949, & *Additional Protocols*, 1977; *Hague Convention*, 1907). *Jus ad bellum* is the legal framework governing a decision to resort to the use of force and theoretically informs decision makers about whether an incident justifies an armed response under Article 51 of the UN Charter (i.e., self-defense). *Jus in bello* comprises the actual laws governing the conduct of hostilities (Lewis, 2013a). Article 38 of the *Statute of the International Court of Justice* (1945) provides sources for both of these legal frameworks which may include: international conventions; internationally recognized rules; international custom; general legal principles acknowledged by civilized nations; and established judicial precedent and published works by highly qualified experts worldwide, which may function as a subsidiary source for the determination of rules of law.

The self-defense justification is premised upon several conditions, irrespective of the judicial system: "the reality of the attack, the immediate response whose purpose is to thwart the attack (i.e. excluding revenge) and the proportionality principle" (Bénichou & Lefranc, 2005, p. 25). However, determining the circumstances where a cyber-attack meets these conditions is uncertain at best. To trigger the right of self-defense, a nation-state would need to demonstrate that a cyber-incident amounted to an armed attack which threatened its sovereignty or political independence. Currently, authoritative information available within the public domain concerning actual instances of cyber-conflict, and known cases establishing precedent for determinations about cyber-incidents, both fail to meet this threshold. Experts also agree that espionage (i.e., intelligence gathering), criminal activity (i.e., cyber-theft), and cyber-operations that cause intermittent impairment of non-critical services, are not regarded as an armed attack (Schmitt, 2013). Time will ultimately tell if the intensity of conflict ignited in the Ukraine in 2014 meets the threshold of forcible cyber-warfare (Gonzales & Harting, 2014; Leyden, 2014; Tucker, 2014). The US has assured that any decision to conduct cross-border cyber operations will be "made with the utmost care and deliberation and under strict policy and operational oversight, and in accordance with the law of armed conflict" (US Department of Defense, 2015, p. 6).

According to Rule 11 of *The Tallinn Manual on the International Law Applicable to Cyber Warfare* (the Manual), "A cyber operation constitutes a use of force when its scale and effects are comparable to non-cyber operations rising to the level of a use of force" (Schmitt, 2013, p. 45). The comparison here is necessarily vague as international jurisprudence offers very little in terms of practical guidance. Rule 13 provides that, "A State that is subject to a cyber operation that rises to the level of an armed attack may exercise its inherent right of self-defence. Whether a cyber operation constitutes an armed attack depends on its scale and effects" (Schmitt, 2013, p. 56). Unfortunately the specificities for evaluating the magnitude and repercussions stemming from an act of cyber-conflict, and determining the point where a forcible cyber operation meets the threshold of an armed attack, are unclear. In the absence of criteria, a cumulative approach to differentiating the spectrum of grave uses of force is presented in the Manual. Accordingly, where a series of related cyber operations originating from one or more sources acting in concert individually falls beneath the threshold of an armed attack then the pattern of incidents may be aggregated to qualify as a composite armed attack to trigger the right of self-defense (Schmitt, 2013, para. 8, p. 56). However this 'accumulation of events' model muddies the distinction between Article 51 and Article 2(4) of the UN Charter and has been rejected by the judiciary and various legal commentators (Gazzini, 2006; Lubell, 2010). Judge Simma's Separate Opinion in *Islamic Republic of Iran v. United States of America* (2003, para. 14) stipulates that "there is in the international law on the use of force no "qualitative jump" from iterative activities remaining below the threshold of Article 51". A strict interpretation of the UN Charter also signifies that "states can only deploy force when responding to an "armed attack" or when they are authorized to act by formal resolution of the UN Security Council" (Rabkin & Rabkin, 2012, p. 3).

Like kinetic conflict, the commitment to engage in retaliation, either legitimately or illegitimately, is also a decision complicated by matters of diplomacy and capacity. In fact, if not in law, acts of war are in the eye of the beholder. Nation-states have gone to war over practically nothing. By contrast some nation-states have suffered substantial violations of sovereignty and other insults, but have turned the other cheek. International norms governing the use of force have lost some of their potency and the authoritative interpretation by International Court of Justice (ICJ) of Article 51 cannot necessarily be relied upon to give staunch guidance to policy-makers globally (Glennon, 2002). For example, in *Nicaragua v. United States of America* (1986, paras. 210, 249) the ICJ reasoned that a nation-state which is subjected to a use of force which falls below the threshold of an armed attack may take proportional countermeasures, however the use of force in retaliation is not specified. The court is more precise in its consideration of interventions initiated by third-states: "a use of force of a lesser degree of gravity [than an armed attack] cannot...produce any entitlement to take collective counter-measures involving the use of force." Contrastingly, Judge Simma's Separate Opinion in *Islamic Republic of Iran v. United States of America* (2003, paras. 210, 249) specifies: "hostile military action not reaching the threshold of an "armed attack" within the meaning of Article 51 of the United Nations Charter may be countered by proportionate and immediate defensive measures equally of a military character". These cases demonstrate that there is significant international jurisprudential uncertainty about quantifying the gravity of an attack, and the legal status of forcible countermeasures. Consequently, any determination by the ICJ regarding cyber-countermeasures is likely to be heavily contested.

Although pockets of the international community contend that existing international law can regulate cyber-attacks by implicating the law of armed conflict (Hathaway et al., 2012; Koh, 2012; Kostadinov, 2014a; Kostadinov, 2014b; Schmitt, 1999), this legal framework is wholly inadequate for addressing cyber-attacks that do not amount to an armed conflict or use of force, but are significantly harmful or disruptive nonetheless. In such circumstances, nation-states may ultimately resort to 'retorsions,' 'reprisals,' or 'proportionate countermeasures' equally of a military nature. This notion of 'equivalence' is gaining momentum in the US, such that when a cyber-attack "produces the death, damage, destruction or high-level disruption that a traditional military attack would cause, then it would be a candidate for a "use of force" consideration, which could merit retaliation" (Gorman & Barnes, 2011; Marks, 2015). Yet, due to lack of international regulation in this area, questions of legitimacy quickly become very murky as nation-states choose to engage in lawful unfriendly countermeasures taken in response to hostile acts (i.e., retorsions) (Zemanek, 1987; Zoller, 1984), or alternatively adopt illegal countermeasures "for the purpose of obtaining justice for an international delinquency by taking the law into its own hands" (i.e., reprisals) (Bedernan, 2002, p. 252). In the context of modern cyber-warfare, the sanctions imposed on Russia for incursions against Ukraine may be construed as retorsions (CrowdStrike, 2015; Lookingglass, 2015), and the 'Stuxnet worm' attack on Iran's nuclear centrifuge enrichment program a form of reprisal (Foltz, 2012). In 2015 the US emphasized its "right to use all necessary means, including economic, trade and diplomatic tools, as appropriate in order to defend our nation and our partners, our friends, our allies" (US Department of State, 2015). The sanctions imposed against North Korea are a case in point, exemplifying the use of retorsions in response to "DPRK's provocative, destabilizing and repressive actions, including the cyberattack on Sony Pictures" (US Department of State, 2015).

The US has made clear its intent to employ countermeasures in retaliation to transnational cyber-attacks ("Administration strategy on mitigating," 2013; US Department of Defense, 2015). Similarly, the North Atlantic Treaty Organization (NATO) plans to invoke the collective defense provisions of Article V of its charter (*The North Atlantic Treaty*, 1949) for a severe cyber-attack against any member of the alliance (Leyden, 2014; Sanger, 2014). Interestingly, whilst NATO has not specified when a cyber-attack would trigger an aggregated response, the use of military force in retaliation is potentially within scope (Croft, 2014). China has also indicated its intention to defend cyberspace and take all necessary measures to protect its territorial integrity and national sovereignty (Information Office of the State Council of the People's Republic of China, 2011). Other major powers have largely remained silent on the issue of retaliation, although evidence points toward a torrent of cyber-reprisals occurring beneath the surface of international diplomacy (Suciu, 2014). In a practical sense, the contentious issue here is not the extent to which retaliatory measures are constrained by international law, but rather the manner in which the international community intends to govern the form and use of those measures (Goldsmith, 2013). Even in the unlikely event that a nation-state is able to gather compelling evidence that engenders support by the international community for its use of forcible cyber-defense, there still exists a legal minefield domestically with potential international ramifications.

At the local level in the US and elsewhere, there is considerable debate about enacting legislation that would allow private entities to retaliate against cyber-incidents (US-China Economic and Security Review Commission, 2013; Commission on the Theft of American Intellectual Property, 2013; Baker, 2013; Fisher, 2013; Hutchinson, 2013; Kallberg, 2013; Messmer, 2011; Sanger, 2013; Vijayan; 2013a). Article 12 of the *Council of Europe Convention on Cybercrime* (2001) (the Budapest Convention) specifies corporate liability (i.e., criminal, civil or administrative) for a criminal offence established in accordance with the Convention, which encompasses proposed acts of private retaliation by legal persons (i.e., offences against the confidentiality, integrity and availability of computer data and systems, in addition to computer-related offences) (Brustein, 2013). Put simply, nation-states are afforded use of force privileges to safeguard their sovereignty. For good reasons, private sector entities and natural persons are not (Lewis, 2013b).

There is "widespread criminalization" of hacking behavior among nation-states, and measures of active defense that stretch beyond localized network perimeters and into foreign jurisdictions are likely to transgress the laws of both the originating and target countries (UNODC, 2013, pp. 77-116; Westby, 2012). Ultimately, unauthorized access by private entities or natural persons is just that, unauthorized, irrespective of motive or who is initiating the activity. *Prima facie*, various international legislative frameworks make it illegal to attack or disable computers, including networked devices (Karnow, 2005). These laws apply equally to acts of retaliation (US Department of Justice, 2012; Webb, 2012). If detected, acts of transborder retaliation by private entities could spark an international incident, particularly for countries that have poor diplomatic relations or are not signatory to the Budapest Convention.

In a networked world the territoriality of criminal law does not always coincide with territorial sovereignty (Cassese, 2003), and an act may be initiated in one jurisdiction and the effect or harm felt in another. In the case of data driven hostilities, "a jurisdictional distinction between the initiation and termination of an act becomes the norm", unlike kinetic hostilities where "the initiatory and terminatory elements are generally concurrent" (Walden, 2003, p. 295). Positive and negative conflict of laws may arise, depending on the cyber-attack point of origin (i.e., *locus delicti*), which can present a raft of jurisdictional complexities (Brenner & Koops, 2004). Beyond criminal liability, misdirected countermeasures can harm third-parties and lead to protracted litigation ending in tortious liability (Wilson, 2006, p. 10). Any nation-state that sanctions 'self-help' by private entities would at least need to develop rules, laws or best practices to ensure private actors are responding precisely and proportionately. The lawfulness and proportionality of conducting any act of retaliation must be considered in light of all technical limitations that may impede accurately identifying a target.

Technical Uncertainty

During the Internet's infancy it was possible to rely on an Internet Protocol (IP) address to locate and identify the source of a transmission or the location of a host. IP addresses did not change - they were temporarily unique. Network nodes did not have the same IP address - they were spatially unique. Nowadays, widespread use of Point-to-Point Protocol (PPP), Serial Line Internet Protocol (SLIP), Dynamic Host Configuration Protocol (DHCP), and Classless Inter-Domain Routing (CIDR) has convoluted the process of locating and identifying hosts. This is complicated further by the widespread use of Firewalls, Proxy Socket Servers, Port Forwarding, IP Masquerading, and other network address translators which reroute traffic as it moves between internal and external networks. Consequently, disparate hosts may appear to have identical IP addresses, and disparate IP addresses may actually originate from the same host (Chambers, Dolske, & Iyer, n.d.). Therefore, an IP address is no longer a reliable source for authenticating a unique host on the Internet and there is little comfort that a datagram has originated from where its source field claims it does. Such technical challenges to network security have been highlighted for decades, particularly problems related to 'identification' and 'authentication' (i.e., user identity verification and validity of data transmissions), and 'nonrepudiation' (i.e., preventing deniability of data transmissions) (Shane, 1996).

Nevertheless, geolocation technologies (e.g., geofusion, geotags, exchangeable image file format, credit card transactions, cell tower triangulation, geospatial tools which match phone signals and voice prints, etc.) can help deduce the location of individuals with some accuracy ("Geolocation," 2004; Boyle, 2007; Reidenberg, 1996; Wu, 1999). IP address mapping and media access control (MAC) mapping is widely used by nation-states to regulate Internet usage by users located within its territory (Goldsmith, 1998a; Goldsmith, 1998b). For well-resourced nation-states the possibility of accurately attributing Internet activity to an end user can be magnified by employing 'active intelligence' gathering techniques (e.g., Echelon, Carnivore/DCS1000, DCSNet, Prism, SORM, Skynet 5, Central Monitoring System, Tempora, X-Keyscore, The Golden Shield Project, MonsterMind, and possible implementations of the D-Wave Two quantum computer) (Barrie and Taverna, 2006; Clarke and Knake, 2010; Gallagher, 2013; Jones, 2013; Keefe, 2006; Lupsha, 1996; Mankotia, 2013; Tracy, 2000; Trope, 2014; Shubber, 2013; Spencer 2007; Zetter, 2014). In particular, quantum computing has the potential to substantially increase processing power, thereby reducing the time taken to break encryption algorithms (Poeter, 2012; Simonite, 2014; Thompson, 2014; Wadhwa, 2015). Even when faced with very secure ciphers, encrypted data transmissions may be profiled using statistical clustering techniques that can infer contents of encrypted payloads by modelling packet sizes, timing and direction (Wright, Monrose, & Masson, 2006; Yu, Schwier, Craven, Brooks, & Griffin, 2013).

Unfortunately, sensitive technologies formerly retained exclusively by nation-states are increasingly finding their "way into the hands of disaffected individuals and disruptive groups" and the capacity to inflict harm has "spread to a growing number of illicit actors" (Gridneff, 2012; Odierno 2013). This trend is driven in part by a tendency on the part of international surveillance companies based in technologically advanced countries to unscrupulously peddle their wares globally. Moreover, the complexity of cyber-attacks is increasing exponentially and the seemingly sophisticated exploits of yesteryear are now packaged in automated suites of downloadable tools that are simple to deploy and demand very little by way of technical aptitude from the user (e.g., Bozok, Poison Ivy, PlugX, Sakula, Gh0st, HiKit, etc.) ("Buying remote administration," 2014; CrowdStrike, 2015; "Poison ivy: Assessing damage," 2014; Moran & Haq, 2013).

Law enforcement faces the greatest challenges associated with attribution in cyberspace due to the high standards of proof required to prosecute serious offences, trans-jurisdictional issues, and inadmissibility of some sources of intelligence (e.g., uncorroborated information from anonymous sources). Intelligence analysis is a fundamental step in the process of evidence gathering, yet the admissibility of intelligence material in court must be treated on a case-by-case basis. Accordingly, due consideration should be given to the reliability of the intelligence and whether it constitutes information upon which to base proof. This is less of a problem for the military where the fog of uncertainty that plagues commanders and policymakers during times of war is no different in instances of cyber-conflict (Lewis, 2013a). Similarly, the covert nature of espionage demands that decisions be made with unreliable or incomplete information. Intelligence here is evaluated "in a kind of twilight, which, like fog or moonlight, often tends to make things seem grotesque and larger than they really are" (Clausewitz, 1976, p. 140).

By its very nature attribution is probabilistic, employing trace and link analysis of artefacts left by suspects, or in the absence of 'breadcrumbs', implementing an imperfect analysis of competing hypotheses to narrow the scope of potential adversaries. Evaluating information in this manner is vulnerable to cognitive bias and appraisals may suffer from the dilemma of certainty versus probability. For example, police investigations usually commence by targeting one or two suspects and gradually expand toward other core or peripheral participants. Oftentimes the prime suspect who is regarded by investigators as the main perpetrator within an inquiry is usually the individual who was central, or the starting point, for the investigation. Like iatrogenic complications arising from diagnostic choices made by physicians, this form of investigative bias must also be considered a potential confounding variable associated with attribution in cyberspace.

For nation-states and private entities 'effective retaliation' depends on 'precise attribution' and attribution in cyberspace can be an immense source of bewilderment (see *Table 3*). There exists a variety of techniques that can be employed to enhance anonymity and disguise the perpetrator behind a cyber-attack. Seasoned attackers move laterally between countries with 'friendly' jurisdictions and strategically traverse proxy servers to conceal their identity (Baker, 2010). Like international law, it is the decentralized nature of the Internet that often confounds efforts to redress grievances (Knake, 2010). Evidence only gains weight when both the attacking device and the operator in control of the device can be identified conclusively (Clarke & Knake, 2010). Unfortunately, the Transmission Control Protocol/Internet Protocol (TCP/IP) industry-standard suite does not provide a mechanism for authentication of individual packets of data, and physically placing an offender behind a keyboard is difficult without use of concealed camera or other forensic evidence pointing to a particular user (National Research Council, 2009). This inherent lack of veracity has encouraged the development of techniques and tools to exploit vulnerabilities associated with TCP/IP (e.g., IP spoofing, connection hijacking, SYN flooding, etc.). Many of the solutions that have been developed to overcome these flaws have not been widely adopted (e.g., Kerberos, Simple Key-Management for Internet Protocol, TCP Wrappers, etc.), and implementations of IPv6 have actually opened the way to more targeted attacks due to a much larger address space than IPv4 (i.e., 128bit versus 32bit), which also makes IP address blacklisting potentially ineffective.

Anonymization encompasses the use of techniques to conceal the identity of a user whilst navigating the Internet or sending electronic communications (Morris, 2004). Encryption involves the application of mathematical algorithms to encode 'data in transit' and 'data at rest' which has the effect of obscuring the content of both transmissions and stored information, thereby enhancing confidentially. Cyber-attackers exploit proxy services and encryption technologies when establishing connections to networks (Carr, 2013; White, 2013; O'Brien, 2011). Proxy servers handle queries to and from the Internet on

Table 3. The problem of attribution arising in various contexts of cyber-exploitation

Threat landscape	Attribution issues
Cyber conflict	Depending on the magnitude of an attack, identifying an adversary based on the relatively small proportion of nation-states with advanced assets capable of waging full spectrum cyber-warfare may be possible. Yet, the market for engaging intermediaries to deliver cyber-attacks, coupled with the potential for acquiring access to advanced technologies from allied nation-states, cannot be disregarded.
Targeted breach	Attribution is impeded by lack of effective cooperation at local and international levels, due in part to competition, suspicion and broader politics. Insider threats and vulnerabilities created by third-party vendors are difficult to contain. Nation-states and private entities are also reluctant to report significant events.
Organized cybercrime	Avenues for pursuing offenders between jurisdictions is impeded by delays in processing requests for mutual legal assistance (MLA), lack of consensus regarding international conventions related to cybercrime, and resource inadequacies among many law enforcement departments and agencies. Crime scenes now extend across the globe and forensic services are challenged by the tyranny of distance and barriers to access.
Espionage	Opportunities to identify adversaries are impeded by the widespread use of deception, anonymization, and the sheer pervasiveness of the problem globally. The rise of non-state actors and state sponsored operatives also magnifies possibilities for repudiation.
Pests and sociopaths	It is technically feasible to attribute malicious activity to less sophisticated offenders online, however more robust international frameworks are needed to promote and accelerate transborder collaborative initiatives in support of investigations and legal processes.

behalf of clients and can differ in terms of levels of functionality and sophistication (e.g., access control, caching, security, etc.). They also enable varying degrees of anonymity for clients, whether to mask, impersonate, or conceal network traffic (Spence-Diehl, 2003). Hex-encoding techniques are also used by cyber-attackers to deceive signature-based security controls on IDS and IPS that lack capacity to convert hex-encoded Uniform Resource Locator (URL) requests (Prosise & Sha, 2013). Similarly, adversaries use 'dead drop' resolvers and encoded IP addresses embedded within legitimate websites, as opposed to revealing malicious IP waypoints in plain text, to delay detection and thwart discovery during binary analysis ("Hiding in plain sight," 2015).

Onion routing facilitates anonymous data transmission across computer networks by encrypting the information and transmitting the data through a series of random network nodes before data reaches its intended destination (Dingledine, Mathewson, & Syverson, 2004). Technical variations on the principle of onion routing include: 'Freenet', 'Invisible IRC Project', 'Crowds', 'Tazan', 'Invisible Internet Project (I2P)', and the popular 'The Onion Ring Router (TOR)'. The degree of difficulty in tracing the origin of a suspect transmission is magnified when proxy servers reroute traffic through network nodes located in disparate jurisdictions (Li, Erdin, Güneş, Bebis, & Shipley, 2011). Cyber-attackers also target public and private networks to funnel data transmission through their IP addresses, thereby acting as a stepping-stone to disguise the origin of malicious online activity. Attributing an act to an individual user or organization can also be complicated where the recorded entity for a particular domain name or IP address is not be the entity in control of that domain. Domains can be registered with holding companies that function as intermediaries for the domain user, and blocks of IP addresses can be leased and subleased. Wireless access points are also used by cyber-attackers to maintain anonymity and mobility (Herrera-Flanigan & Ghosh, 2010). Dedicated network protocols such as Secure/Multipurpose Internet Mail Extensions (S/MIME), Direct Internet Message Encapsulation (DIME), Secure Sockets Layer (SSL), Internet Protocol Security (IPsec), Secure Shell (SSH), Address Resolution Protocol (ARP), SOCKet Secure (SOCKS),

Remote Management and Control Protocol (RMCP), and Virtual Private Network (VPN) tunneling can be used to launch cyber-attacks and conceal or obscure traffic (Distributed Management Task Force, 2003; Harris, 2013; Nicks, 2014; Vijayan, 2014). Ultimately, cyber-attacks are "transnational, anonymous, and deceptive with their source often difficult to identify" ("China defense ministry refutes," 2013).

However, let us assume for a moment that, despite the aforementioned challenges presented by anonymization, encryption, and methods of deception, a retaliator is capable of precise attribution when launching a counteroffensive that will, for instance, lead to the recovery of information to substantiate claims of industrial espionage. In this scenario any prudent commercial lawyer will tell you that the key question relates not to whether a breach occurred, but rather, to whom liability for the breach may be attributed? Indeed, one need only look at the reported counterstrike performed by Google in 2010 to demonstrate that even the best resourced organizations with the brightest technical minds can be defeated by the problem of attribution, despite a preponderance of circumstantial evidence (Sanger & Markoff, 2010). In essence, Google succeeded in recovering stolen goods but failed to attribute direct responsibility or state sponsorship for the theft.

Similarly, problems of attribution are evident in the cyber-attacks launched upon Estonia in 2007, and South Korea in 2009. The Estonian authorities were convinced that the Russian government perpetrated the cyber-attack. They admonished the Russians publicly and requested military assistance from NATO. Yet, some follow-up investigations contend that Russia was not the protagonist, with attack sources reportedly traced to Brazil and Vietnam (Gable, 2010). In the case of cyber-attacks against South Korea, the government was certain that the source of attack was unequivocally North Korea. However, in was subsequently conceded that the cyber-attacks may have originated from at least six countries, including the United Kingdom and the United States (Reich, Weinstein, Wild & Cabanlong, 2010; Williams, 2009). Evidently, targeting an adversary in cyberspace can be like shooting billiard balls with a length of rope. The firm finger of authority that confidently points at the perceived source of an attack may in fact be based on little more than the source field in an IP packet. It cannot be disregarded that the problem of attribution serves as a potentially significant technical and legal pitfall (Mudrinich, 2012).

Attribution complexities in cyberspace and risks associated with misattribution are best illustrated using examples. *Figure 1* is consistent with a scenario where an instigator of a cyber-attack engages with another network node directly from his or her device. Here tracing is possible for the Retaliator (i.e., the victim) and would lead to the accurate identification of the attack source (i.e., the Agitator) and precise attribution. For the Retaliator, risk of collateral damage and liability is minimized, provided the response is proportionate. Nevertheless, this situation is quite rare. In the case of more sophisticated cyber-attacks a perpetrator will avoid being identified.

Figure 1. Attribution success due to conspicuousness of the attack source

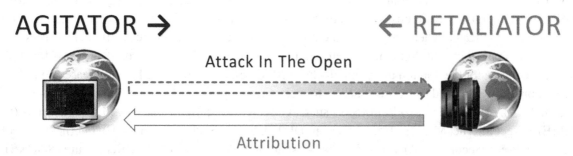

Figure 2. Attribution failure due to system compromise of an intermediary which obfuscates the attack source

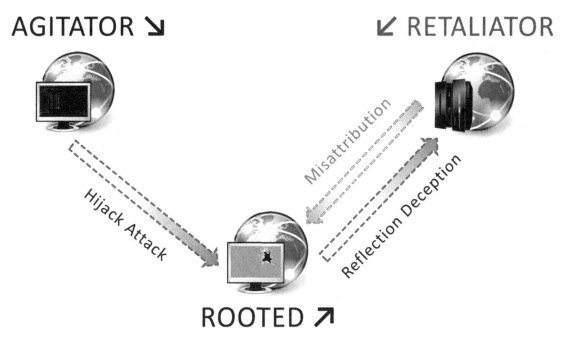

Figure 2 is characteristic of a scenario where an Agitator launches an attack via a compromised intermediary (i.e., Rooted) to create a diversion. Here tracing by the Retaliator would misattribute the attack source to Rooted and any counteroffensive launched by the Retaliator against Rooted would be misdirected. In failing to accurately target the Agitator, the Retaliator risks being subjected to civil, criminal or administrative legal action where Rooted is a corporate entity. In circumstances where Rooted is another nation-state, the Retaliator risks debilitating reprisals, retorsions, and countermeasures, particularly if an aggregated response is deemed appropriate (i.e. NATO).

Figure 3 is evidently the most dangerous scenario for nation-states and is specifically crafted to ignite animosity. In spoofing its identity to resemble that of Beta and then attacking Alpha, the Agitator is provoking antagonism that could lead to an escalation of conflict between Alpha and Beta (Bénichou and Lefranc, 2005). Interestingly, the Agitator has only to send one 'lighting packet' to effect the deception and provoke hostility. If the Agitator is a serious trouble maker, the identity of Beta would also lend credibility to a politically motivated attack against Alpha that would inevitably undermine fragile relations between the two nation-states. In failing to correctly identify the Agitator, both Alpha and Beta expose themselves to possible diplomatic scandal and scathing rebuke from the international community. Given existing political hypersensitivities, the grave potential for retorsions, reprisal, and countermeasures, including kinetic use of force, need not be emphasized. This is the modus operandi behind DNS Reflection and DNS Amplification attacks that exploit botnets or networks of compromised webservers to magnify the impact on targeted systems. Such attacks require little from an offender in terms of computing resources or programming expertise to overwhelm an adversary and instigate acrimony.

Security analysts are discussing the use of 'poisoned data", "beaconing technology" (including "meta-tagging" and "watermarking") to address the problem of data theft (McGee, Sabett, & Shah, 2013, p. 10; Menn, 2012; Romm, 2013; Vijayan, 2013b). Accordingly, stolen data that has been 'branded' or

Figure 3. Attribution failure due to use of deception which disguises the attack source to masquerade as another adversary

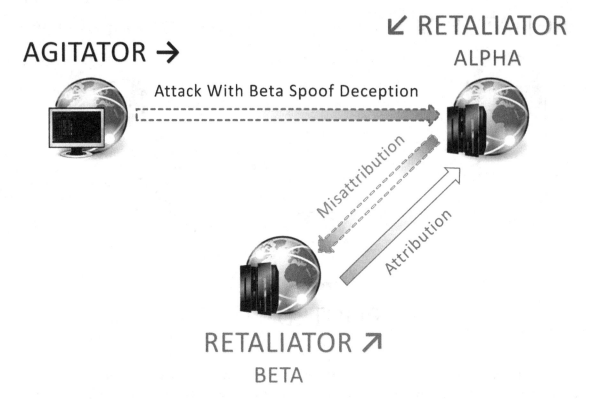

'adulterated' may be able to transmit its location back to the owner, theoretically overcoming uncertainties associated with attribution. Secretly embedded code could also perform similar functions to a Remote Administration Tool (RAT) and create vulnerabilities to facilitate counteroffensives against attackers, including deletion or encryption of exfiltrated data, "photographing the hacker using his own system's camera," or even destruction of the host system when the data is stowed (Commission on the Theft of American Intellectual Property, 2013, p. 81). However, adoption of these proactive measures is not without significant risks.

Firstly, the host system may be owned by an innocent third-party (e.g., compromised Command and Control servers). The use of RATs and beaconing technology also presupposes that the thief has placed the data on a networked device with Internet connectivity which is not impeded by egress filtering. Furthermore, assuming a perceptive adversary detects the beaconing device using behavioral heuristics, or the RAT trigger IDS or is discovered by an endpoint vulnerability scanner, this may prompt the adversary to deliver a bout of debilitating punitive attacks for the impertinence. Nation-states and private entities should be mindful that the technical aptitude of independent talented hackers and elite cyber operatives serving within departments of defense in technologically sophisticated countries (e.g., NSA's Tailored Access Operations, GCHQ's Joint Threat Research Intelligence Group, etc.) are likely to have superior 'arsenals' to most 'middle-power' nations. In operating from the shadows, cybercriminals, state sponsored hackers, and non-state actors are also less amenable to legal process. Moreover, they likely have forged dark support networks spanning the globe and these 'alliances' may be called upon to magnify offensive and defensive activity ("Behind the Syrian conflict's," 2015). It is therefore reasonable to posit that many nation-states and most private entities risk being ill-equipped to deal with the destructive blowback that may flow from direct engagement with an adversary in furtherance of retribution.

Unmitigated counteroffensives also pose a risk to ongoing investigations and retaliatory actions may violate prohibitions against hindering prosecutions or obstructing justice (Alexis, 2013). Any activity on a computer can destroy or alter potential sources of evidence, and persistent network scanning or intrusive cyber-operations may signify danger for a targeted offender and alert them to employ subterfuge, thereby undermining further monitoring activities by authorities. In order to pursue cyber-attack sources, a trace back through transnational networks is often necessary which usually requires the assistance of foreign Internet Service Providers, cross-border investigative support, and engagement of diplomatic resources. Clumsy counterstrikes that miss the mark or derail an official inquiry are unlikely to pave the way toward cohesive global threat intelligence sharing. Ultimately, it is the preservation of robust international relations that is key to tracing and tackling cyber-attacks, deescalating global conflict, and safeguarding the reliability and resilience of telecommunication networks (Wilson, 2006).

SOLUTIONS AND RECOMMENDATIONS

The vast network of international telecommunications systems which facilitate cross-border cyber-attacks demands a common universal framework that is not just regionally centered or organizationally exclusive. Ideally, this should take the form of a binding legal instrument such as a convention under the auspices of the United Nations. Whilst the Budapest Convention has been signed by non-member states, it is nonetheless a product of a regional organization, which is based mostly on the premises and conditions of Council of Europe members. Contrastingly, a United Nations convention would be regarded a joint product of its much more inclusive membership and arguably offer broader appeal to the international community, thereby limiting safe harbor opportunities for perpetrators of cyber-exploitation. A mix of domestic and external policy measures combined with the enactment of common minimum standards and confidence-building security measures is needed. Strengthening cybersecurity requires the collective delineation and enforcement of shared international rules of conduct, standards and norms.

A joint letter containing the International Code of Conduct for Information Security was submitted to the United Nations in 2011 by the permanent representatives of China, Russia, Tajikistan and Uzbekistan (United Nations General Assembly, 2011). The Annex to the letter calls for consensus on a series of guidelines or principles aimed at standardizing the behavior of nation-states in cyberspace so as to "bolster bilateral, regional and international cooperation, promote the important role of the United Nations in formulating international norms, peaceful settlements of international disputes and improvements in international cooperation in the field of information security". The Code also advocates for the establishment of a transparent and democratic international Internet governance mechanism to dissuade use of information and communications technologies to conduct hostile behavior and acts of aggression which "pose threats to international peace and security". The rights and obligations of nation-states to protect their "sovereignty, territorial integrity and political independence" from "threats, interference and sabotage attacks" to critical information and networking infrastructure is emphasized. Most significantly, the Code is offered as an instrument for settling disputes "through peaceful means and to refrain from the threat or use of force".

In 2015 Secretary of State John Kerry affirmed the view espoused by the US during his remarks to an audience in South Korea. He stated that "basic rules of international law apply in cyberspace" and "countries that are hurt by an attack have a right to respond in ways that are appropriate, proportional, and that minimize harm to innocent parties" (US Department of State, 2015). He also promoted five principles to strengthen conflict prevention and stability during times of peace:

First, no country should conduct or knowingly support online activity that intentionally damages or impedes the use of another country's critical infrastructure. Second, no country should seek either to prevent emergency teams from responding to a cybersecurity incident, or allow its own teams to cause harm. Third, no country should conduct or support cyber-enabled theft of intellectual property, trade secrets, or other confidential business information for commercial gain. Fourth, every country should mitigate malicious cyber activity emanating from its soil, and they should do so in a transparent, accountable and cooperative way. And fifth, every country should do what it can to help states that are victimized by a cyberattack (US Department of State, 2015).

Yet, multilateral efforts to regulate cyber-conflict through alliances, legal frameworks, international instruments and norms alone are wholly insufficient to deal with this global problem. Cooperation between law enforcement, security agencies, and private sector entities is essential for broadening awareness concerning emerging attack vectors, foreign mechanisms of criminal justice, and identifying diplomatic channels for helpful dialogues. Responsibility for facilitating such cooperative initiatives should be shared between the United Nations, the European Union, the Organisation for Economic Co-operation and Development, the Council of Europe, NATO, the Group of Eight, the Organization for Security and Co-operation in Europe, the Shanghai Cooperation Organization, the Association of Southeast Asian Nations, the Arab League, the African Union, as well as other international and regional organizations. Independent Internet security research firms, such as Team Cymru, have created crucial platforms for the facilitation of trusted exchanges between multinational key stakeholders in government and the private sector.

The imposition of regulatory obligations upon individuals and organizations to implement passive cyber-security measures would also manifestly reduce vulnerability to data driven attacks. However, any approach that places compliance burdens upon private entities should be aligned with efforts to increase public awareness concerning information security. "We must educate people about basic security. The owners of machines without basic security, patches, or updates are leaving their doors wide open. That campaign should be part of the government's role as well…" (UNODC, 2013, p. 234).

If active defense forms part of a country's cyber-security strategy at the local or international level, several imperative questions must first be answered. What is the level of certainty needed to trigger a cyber-counteroffensive? What are the technical and practical limits of attribution? Where is the line of demarcation that distinguishes between offensive and defensive cyber-activity, including use of intrusive scanning, tracking and testing tools employed by analysts and scientists? How can retaliation provide effective deterrence in an interconnected world? To answer these questions, it is recommended that nation-states conduct a comprehensive legal review to determine what magnitude of cyber-exploitation meets their 'attack' threshold. This distinction is required in order to make clear whether an exploit should be regarded as an attack or an intelligence collection operation, and which counteroffensives may appropriately be taken in self-defense. The review should also determine if prevailing international 'authorities' regard cyber-counterstrikes as a proper form of retaliation. Finally, a legal framework should be structured that applies to discrete forms of cyber-attacks emanating from within and from beyond national borders. In contemplating these recommendations value may be found in revisiting implications associated with adopting active defensive postures to cyber-attacks, as outlined in this chapter. These considerations are presented as a non-exhaustive cost/benefit analysis in *Table 4* and *Table 5*. There is significant overlap here and any assessment would need to be done on a case-by-case basis to factor in circumstantial variables and objective insights.

Table 4. Implications that discourage the adoption of methods of active defense for nation-states and private entities

Risks triggered by vulnerabilities and uncertainties (costs)	
Nation-states	• Collateral damage caused by invasive cyber-activity undermines diplomatic efforts to create international cyber-norms. • Misattributed counterstrikes may prompt aggrieved nation-states to use retorsions as a form of retribution (e.g., sanctions, embargos, etc.). • Repressive, aggressive, or rogue nation-states who treat transborder cyber-intrusions with contempt may be tempted to respond with kinetic reprisals to provocative cyber-activity. • Disrespect for customary international law by one nation-state may be taken as establishing a precedent by others in the international community. • Active intelligence gathering is regarded by some nation-states as an encroachment upon state sovereignty and a serious affront to diplomatic relations. • Public backlash and admonishment from the international community following an ineffectual cyber-operation can erode political support and unhinge economic relations.
Private entities	• The expense of enabling active defensive measures may be hard to justify, particularly given the potential for adverse consequences. • Inadvertent damage to the information systems of innocent third-parties can lead to criminal, civil, and administrative liability. • Negative publicity surrounding use of active defense measures can undermine commercial reputation and branding, thereby reducing market share. • Endorsing methods of self-help for private entities affords excessive scope for invasion of privacy without sufficient levels of oversight. • An international arrest warrant may be issued where countermeasures are deemed to be in violation of established treaties and conventions. • Parties to the Budapest Convention may cooperate in furtherance of an order for extradition following a finding of substantiated trans-boundary cyber-harm.
Collective risks	• Offensive retaliation lacks any semblance of natural justice as retaliators assume the role of judge, jury, and executioner. • Perpetrators of cyber-attacks tend to be more technologically sophisticated than both defenders and victims, and deniability issues permit many offenders to operate with impunity. • Unmitigated counterstrikes may be disproportionate or otherwise excessive. • Endorsing the idea of a full-scale cyber-offensive risks complete accountability failure. • It is significantly easier for a perpetrator to mask or disguise the origin of a cyber-attack than for a defender or victim to accurately attribute the source of an attack. • Any perceived value in using proactive measures to recover exfiltrated data must be weighed against the real possibility that the information has already been exploited and potentially duplicated in multiple locations. • Forcible counteroffensives may incite an adversary and prompt escalation of cyber-conflict. • Use of anonymizing technologies, obfuscation techniques, and multi-stage attacks significantly impedes expeditious attribution. • Active defensive measures may contaminate or destroy crucial evidence which is of interest to an ongoing official investigation. • Offensive retaliation does nothing to combat the cyber-security threat posed by malicious insiders. • The mere existence of strategies that employ counterintelligence and methods of deception significantly extends the margin of error for any analytical inquiry seeking to pursue a cyber-attack source.

Table 5. Implications that encourage the adoption of methods of active defense for nation-states and private entities

Enhancements for security assurance (benefits)	
Nation-states	• Targeted cyber-reprisals may provide direct intelligence support through identification of an adversary's plans, capabilities, and intentions. • The status of customary international law regarding the use of force and the right of self-defense is uncertain in the case of cyber-activity, making unilateral and multilateral cyber-security initiatives that combine active defensive measures more appealing. • Collective defensive postures forged through global alliances may deter malicious cyber-activity by repressive, aggressive, or rogue nation-states.
Private entities	• The expense of enabling active defensive measures and potential for adverse outcomes from initiating forcible counterstrikes may be regarded as insignificant when compared to the palpable value of securing trade secrets and intellectual property. • Corporations are often better positioned to proactively respond to targeted and persistent attacks against commercial infrastructure, compared to reliance on the limited resources and bureaucratic difficulties faced by many national authorities. • Adopting an active defensive posture may circumvent loss of service, theft of information, and data corruption, thus avoiding embarrassing mandatory breach notification provisions in some countries, in addition to averting claims by clients or business partners for breach of contract, breach of privacy, copyright infringement, or professional negligence. • Many governments have shown a manifest lack of interest in leading efforts to enhance cybersecurity for corporations and natural persons, ostensibly shifting responsibility to private entities for the self-management of risks emanating from cyberspace.
Collective benefits	• Expenses associated with incident response, investigation, recovery and remediation can dwarf the immediate financial cost of a security incident, thereby lending support for proactive, rather than reactive, defensive measures. • Attribution can be greatly increased if active methods of intelligence gathering are implemented to monitor the cyber-activity of an adversary. • Avenues of self-help may avoid bureaucratic delays and overcome ineffective judicial remedies. • Successful counteroffensives may impede a perpetrator and mitigate damage from persistent cyber-exploitation. • Effective countermeasures can increase the cost of initiating cyber-operations for an adversary and deter malicious activity.

FUTURE RESEARCH DIRECTIONS

Further research on this topic would benefit from broader consideration of academic literature and press articles published in languages other than English. Comprehensive insights may also be gained through assembling primary materials from a range key stakeholders entrusted with fortifying cyber defenses and implementing information security processes for the private sector, governmental agencies, and international organizations. A comprehensive approach towards gathering first-hand perspectives would also facilitate greater awareness of differing viewpoints concerning the viability of acts of retaliation to cyber-attacks and availability of active defense methods. After all "society's power structure and the vested interests of powerful societal actors have an enormous impact on the way crimes in general and cybercrimes in particular are defined, conceptualized, theorized, measured, responded to and policed" (Kasherti, 2013. p. 28).

CONCLUSION

The use of active defensive measures as a means of retaliation against cyber-attacks is a risky affair for both nation-states and private entities. Certainly there are benefits associated with methods of 'self-help,' but any prudent commander or managing director would realize that the myriad of legal and technical issues discussed in this chapter demands careful attention before executing any strategic cyber-counter-offensive. Failure to balance risk of action vis-à-vis inaction in cyberspace is the digital equivalent to having a complex and interconnected world inhabited by a primitive culture preoccupied with 'mortis' rather than 'rigor'. As the desire for cyber-reciprocity gathers momentum, Gandhi's truism of "an eye for an eye and soon the whole world will be blind" seems particularly fitting. In 1963 Martin Luther King told a story about discourteous drivers who do not follow the etiquette of dimming their lights when passing others on the highway at night. His message conveys the importance exercising sense and tolerance when we encounter those who forget their manners. The need for restraint rings equally true on the information superhighway:

There will be meandering points. There will be curves and difficult moments, and we will be tempted to retaliate with the same kind of force that the opposition will use. But I'm going to say to you, 'Wait a minute...'

REFERENCES

Acquiring high tech crime tools. (2006). *High Tech Crime Brief, 13*. Retrieved from http://www.aic.gov.au/documents/A/B/C/%7bABCFCBC4-541A-4ED8-822E-3A0C3B082644%7dhtcb013.pdf

Alexis, A. (2013, April 9). Debate brewing over whether companies should strike back at their cyber attackers. *Bloomberg*. Retrieved from http://www.bna.com/debate-brewing-whether-n17179873246/

APT30 and the mechanics of a long-running cyber espionage operation. (2015, April 15). *FireEye Threat Intelligence Special Report*. Retrieved from https://www2.fireeye.com/rs/fireye/images/rpt-apt30.pdf

Baker, S. (2012, September 19). Rethinking cybersecurity, retribution, and the role of the private sectors. *Steptoe*. Retrieved from http://www.steptoecyberblog.com/2012/09/19/rethinking-cybersecurity-retribution-and-the-role-of-the-private-sector/?

Baker, S. (2013, November 26). Hackback backers' comeback? *The Volokh Conspiracy*. Retrieved from http://www.volokh.com/2013/11/26/hackback-backers-comeback/

Barrie, D., & Taverna, M. A. (2006). Spy game. *Aviation Week & Space Technology, 165*(23), 74.

Bederman, D. J. (2002). Counterintuiting countermeasures. *The American Journal of International Law, 96*(4), 817–832. doi:10.2307/3070680

Behind the Syrian conflict's digital front lines. (2015, February 1). *FireEye Threat Intelligence Special Report*. Retrieved from https://www.fireeye.com/content/dam/fireeye-www/global/en/current-threats/pdfs/rpt-behind-the-syria-conflict.pdf

Bénichou, D., & Lefranc, S. (2005). Introduction to network self-defense: Technical and judicial issues. *Journal of Computer Virology, 1*(1-2), 24–31. doi:10.1007/s11416-005-0006-5

Bobbitt, P. (2009). *Terror and consent: The wars for the twenty-first century*. New York: Alfred A Knopf.

Boyle, J. (2007). Foucault in cyberspace: Surveillance, sovereignty, and hardwired censors. *University of Cincinnati Law Review, 66*(1), 178–183.

Bradsher, K. (2014, May 20). Retaliatory attacks, online. *The New York Times*. Retrieved from http://www.nytimes.com/2014/05/21/business/international/firms-in-united-states-see-risk-in-challenges-to-beijing.html

Brenner, S. W., & Koops, B. (2004). Approaches to cybercrime jurisdiction. *The Journal of High Technology Law, 4*(1), 1–46.

Bromby, M. (2006). Security against crime: Technologies for detecting and preventing crime. *International Review of Law Computers & Technology, 20*(1-2), 1–5. doi:10.1080/13600860600818235

Brustein, J. (2013, June 3). Letting companies hack the hackers: What could go wrong? *Businessweek*. Retrieved from http://www.businessweek.com/articles/2013-06-03/letting-companies-hack-the-hackers-what-could-go-wrong

Buying remote administration tools. (2014, May 19). *Schwarze Sonne*. Retrieved from http://ss-rat.blogspot.de/2014/05/buying-remote-adminstration-tools.html

Campbell, K., Gordon, L. A., Loeb, M. P., & Zhou, L. (2003). The economic cost of publicly announced security breaches: Empirical evidence from the stock market. *Journal of Computer Security, 11*, 431–438.

Carr, M. (2013). Internet freedom, human rights and power. *Australian Journal of International Affairs, 67*(5), 621–637. doi:10.1080/10357718.2013.817525

Carter, J. G., & Carter, D. L. (2009). Intelligence-led policing: Conceptual and functional considerations for public policy. *Criminal Justice Policy Review, 20*(3), 310–325. doi:10.1177/0887403408327381

Case concerning Military and Paramilitary Activities in and against Nicaragua (*Nicaragua v. United States of America*), Judgment of 27 June 1986, [1986] ICJ Rep. 14.

Case concerning Oil Platforms (*Islamic Republic of Iran v. United States of America*), Judgment of 6 November 2003, (2003) ICJ Rep. 161.

Cashell, B., Jackson, W. D., Jickling, M., & Webel, B. (2004). The economic impact of cyber-attacks. *Congressional Research Service*. Retrieved from http://www.fas.org/sgp/crs/misc/RL32331.pdf

Cassese, A. (2003). Is the bell tolling for universality? A plea for a sensible notion of universal jurisdiction. *Journal of International Criminal Justice, 1*(3), 589–595. doi:10.1093/jicj/1.3.589

Cha, A. E., & Nakashima, E. (2014, January 14). Google China cyberattack part of vast espionage campaign, experts say. *The Washington Post*. Retrieved from http://www.washingtonpost.com/wp-dyn/content/article/2010/01/13/AR2010011300359.html

Chambers, C., Dolske, J., & Iyer, J. (n.d.). TCP/IP security. *Linux Security*. Retrieved from http://www.linuxsecurity.com/resource_files/documentation/tcpip-security.html

Charter of the United Nations (1945).

China defense ministry refutes cyber attack allegations. (2013, February 2). *Xinhua*. Retrieved from http://news.xinhuanet.com/english/china/2013-02/20/c_132180777.htm

Clarke, R. A., & Knake, R. K. (2010). *Cyber war: The next threat to national security and what to do about it*. New York: Ecco.

Clausewitz, C. (1976). *On war* (M. Howard & P. Paret, Trans. & Eds.). New Jersey: Princeton University Press.

Clayton, M. (2012, September 9). Stealing US business secrets: Experts ID two huge cyber 'gangs' in China. *Christian Science Monitor*. Retrieved from http://www.csmonitor.com/USA/2012/0914/Stealing-US-business-secrets-Experts-ID-two-huge-cyber-gangs-in-China

Collier, P. A., & Spaul, B. J. (1992). Problems in policing computer crime. *Policing and Society*, 2(4), 310. doi:10.1080/10439463.1992.9964650

The IP Commission Report. (2013). *Commission on the Theft of American Intellectual Property*. Retrieved from http://ipcommission.org/report/IP_Commission_Report_052213.pdf

Convention for the Amelioration of the Condition of the Wounded and Sick in Armed Forces in the Field (1949) (Geneva Convention No. I).

Convention for the Amelioration of the Condition of the Wounded, Sick, and Shipwrecked Members of Armed Forces at Sea (1949) (Geneva Convention No. II).

Convention Relative to the Protection of Civilian Persons in Time of War (1949) (Geneva Convention No. IV).

Council of Europe Convention on Cybercrime (2001), and *Additional Protocols* (2003).

Croft, A. (2014, September 5). NATO agrees cyber attack could trigger military response. *Reuters*. Retrieved from http://www.reuters.com/article/2014/09/05/us-nato-cybersecurity-idUSKBN0H013P20140905

CrowdStrike. (2015, February 9). 2014 Global Threat Intel Report. *CrowdStrike Threat Intel*. Retrieved from http://go.crowdstrike.com/rs/crowdstrike/images/GlobalThreatIntelReport.pdf

D'Aspremont, J. (Ed.). (2011). *Participants in the international legal system: Theoretical perspectives*. London: Routledge.

Davies, M. (1999, December 2). Failing to deliver on cyber crime. *Birmingham Post*, 2.

Deeks, A. S. (2012). "Unwilling or unable": Toward a normative framework for extraterritorial self-defense. *Virginia Journal of International Law*, 52, 491–495.

Der Derian, J. (2013). From war 2.0 to quantum war: The superpositionality of global violence. *Australian Journal of International Affairs*, 67(5), 570–585. doi:10.1080/10357718.2013.822465

Dingledine, R., Mathewson, N., & Syverson, P. (2004, August 13). Tor: The second-generation onion router. Paper presented at the *Usenet Security Symposium*, San Diego. Retrieved from https://www.usenix.org/legacy/events/sec04/tech/full_papers/dingledine/dingledine_html/index.html

Alert standard format specification. (2003, April 23). *Distributed Management Task Force*. Retrieved from http://www.dmtf.org/sites/default/files/standards/documents/DSP0136.pdf

Epstein, R. A. (2005). The theory and practice of self-help. *Journal of Law Economics & Policy*, *1*, 1–32.

Erforth, B., & Deffner, G. (2013, March 18). Old wine in new bottles? Justifying France's military intervention in Mali. *Think Africa Press*. Retrieved from http://thinkafricapress.com/mali/old-wine-new-bottles-justifying-france-military-intervention

Administration strategy on mitigating the theft of U.S. trade secrets. (2013). *Executive Office of the President of the United States*. Retrieved from http://www.whitehouse.gov/sites/default/files/omb/IPEC/admin_strategy_on_mitigating_the_theft_of_u.s._trade_secrets.pdf

Fallon, W. J. (2012, August 27). Winning cyber battles without fighting. *Time*. Retrieved from http://nation.time.com/2012/08/27/winning-cyber-battles-without-fighting/

Fellmeth, A. X., Horwitz, M., & Oxford University Press (2009). *Guide to latin in international law*. New York: Oxford University Press.

Ferzan, K. K. (2008). Self-defense and the state. *Ohio State Journal of Criminal Law*, *5*(2), 449–478.

Finklea, K. M., & Theohary, C. A. (2013, January 9). Cybercrime: Conceptual issues for Congress and U.S. law enforcement. *Congressional Research Service*, 5-11. Retrieved from http://fas.org/sgp/crs/misc/R42547.pdf

Fisher, M. (2013, May 23). Should the U.S. allow companies to 'hack back' against foreign cyber spies? *The Washington Post*. Retrieved from http://www.washingtonpost.com/blogs/worldviews/wp/2013/05/23/should-the-u-s-allow-companies-to-hack-back-against-foreign-cyber-spies/

Foltz, A. C. (2012). Stuxnet, Schmitt analysis, and the cyber "use-of-force" debate. *Joint Force Quarterly*, *67*, 40–48.

Gable, K. A. (2010). Cyber-apocalypse now: Securing the internet against cyberterrorism and using universal jurisdiction as a deterrent. *Vanderbilt Journal of Transnational Law*, *43*(1), 57.

Gallagher, S. (2013, August 1). NSA's internet taps can find systems to hack, track VPNs and word docs - X-Keyscore gives NSA the ability to find and exploit vulnerable systems. *Ars Technica*. Retrieved from http://arstechnica.com/tech-policy/2013/08/nsas-internet-taps-can-find-systems-to-hack-track-vpns-and-word-docs/

Gazzini, T. (2006). *The changing rules on the use of force in international law*. Manchester: Manchester University Press.

Geneva Convention Relative to the Treatment of Prisoners of War (1949) (Geneva Convention No. III).

Geolocation: Don't fence web in. (2004, July 12). *Wired*. Retrieved from http://archive.wired.com/techbiz/it/news/2004/07/64178?currentPage=all

Glennon, M. (2002). The fog of law: Self-defense, inherence, and incoherence in Article 51 of the United Nations Charter. *Harvard Journal of Law & Public Policy*, *25*(2), 539–558.

Goldsmith, J. (2013, February 2). The USG strategy to confront Chinese cyber exploitation, and the Chinese perspective. *Lawfare*. Retrieved from http://www.lawfareblog.com/2013/02/the-usg-strategy-to-confront-chinese-cyber-exploitation-and-the-chinese-perspective/

Goldsmith, J. L. (1998a). Against cyberanarchy. *The University of Chicago Law Review. University of Chicago. Law School*, 65(4), 1199–1250. doi:10.2307/1600262

Goldsmith, J. L. (1998b). The internet and the abiding significance of territorial sovereignty. *Indiana Journal of Global Legal Studies*, 5(2), 475–491.

Gonzales, D., & Harting, S. (2014, April 29). Exposing Russia's covert actions. *The Rand Blog*. Retrieved from http://www.rand.org/blog/2014/04/exposing-russias-covert-actions.html

Goodno, N. H. (2007). Cyberstalking, a new crime: Evaluating the effectiveness of current state and federal laws. *Missouri Law Review*, 72(1), 125.

Gorman, S., & Barnes, J. E. (2011, May 31). Cyber combat: Act of war. *The Wall Street Journal*. Retrieved from http://online.wsj.com/news/articles/SB10001424052702304563104576355623135782718

Gorman, S., & Valentino-DeVries, J. (2013). New details show broader NSA surveillance reach; programs cover 75% of nation's traffic, can snare emails. *Wall Street Journal*. Retrieved http://online.wsj.com/news/articles/SB10001424127887324108204579022874091732470

Greenwald, G., & MacAskill, E. (2013, June 7). Obama orders US to draw up overseas target list for cyber-attacks. *The Guardian*. Retrieved, from http://www.guardian.co.uk/world/2013/jun/07/obama-china-targets-cyber-overseas

Gridneff, I. (2012, December 31). Organised crime gets smart with technology. *Sydney Morning Herald*. Retrieved from http://www.smh.com.au/it-pro/government-it/organised-crime-gets-smart-with-technology-20121230-2c1iy.html

Hague Convention Respecting the Laws and Customs of War on Land (1907).

Harris, S. (2013). All. In *One CISSP Exam Guide* (6th ed.). New York: McGraw-Hill.

Hathaway, O. A., Crootof, R., Levitz, P., Nix, H., Nowlan, A., Perdue, W., & Spiegel, J. (2012). The law of cyber-attack. *California Law Review*, 100(4), 817–885.

Hathaway, O. A., & Shapiro, S. J. (2011). Outcasting: Enforcement in domestic and international law. *The Yale Law Journal*, 121(2), 252–349.

Henry, S. (2012, March 27). FBI's top cyber official discusses threat. *The Federal Bureau of Investigation*. Retrieved April 16, 2014, from http://www.fbi.gov/news/videos/fbis-top-cyber-official-discusses-threat

Herrera-Flanigan, J. R., & Ghosh, S. (2010). Criminal regulations. In S. Ghosh & E. Turrini (Eds.), *Cybercrimes: A multidisciplinary analysis* (pp. 265–306).

Hiding in plain sight: Fireeye and Microsoft expose obfuscation tactic. (2015, May 14). *FireEye Threat Intelligence Report*. Retrieved from https://www2.fireeye.com/rs/fireye/images/APT17_Report.pdf

Holz, T., & Raynal, F. (n. d.). Malicious malware: attacking the attackers, part 1. *Symantec Connect Community*. Retrieved from www.symantec.com/connect/articles/malicious-malware-attacking-attackers-part-1

Honderich, T. (2005). *The oxford companion to philosophy*. New York: Oxford University Press.

Hutchinson, J. (2013, May 28). Companies should 'hack back' at cyber attackers: Security experts. *Financial Review*. Retrieved from http://www.afr.com/p/technology/companies_should_hack_back_at_cyber_KeoJyUX9HEEtjh9hYAnpgK

Information Office of the State Council of the People's Republic of China. (2011, March 31). China's national defense in 2010. *Xinhua*. Retrieved from http://news.xinhuanet.com/english2010/china/2011-03/31/c_13806851_5.htm

Jones, N. (2013, May 17). Google and NASA snap up quantum computer D-Wave Two. *Scientific American*. Retrieved from http://www.scientificamerican.com/article/google-nasa-snap-up-quantum-computer-dwave-two/

Kallberg, J. (2013, July 28). Private cyber retaliation undermines federal authority. *DefenseNews*. Retrieved from http://www.defensenews.com/article/20130728/DEFREG02/307280007/Private-Cyber-Retaliation-Undermines-Federal-Authority

Karnow, C. E. A. (2005). Launch on warning: Aggressive defense of computer systems. *Journal of Internet Law*, *7*(1), 87–102.

Katyal, N. (2005). Community self-help. *Journal of Law Economics and Policy*, *1*, 33–67.

Keefe, P. R. (2006). *Chatter: Uncovering the Echelon surveillance network and the secret world of global eavesdropping*. New York: Random House.

Kesan, J. P., & Hayes, C. M. (2012). Mitigative counterstriking: Self-defense and deterrence in cyberspace. *Harvard Journal of Law & Technology*, *25*(2), 474–520.

Kesan, J. P., & Majuca, R. (2009). Optimal hackback. *Chicago-Kent Law Review*, *84*(3), 831–835.

Knake, R. K. (2010, July 15). Untangling attribution: Moving to accountability in cyberspace. Statement made before the *Subcommittee on Technology and Innovation, Committee on Science and Technology*, U.S. House of Representatives. Retrieved from http://science.house.gov/sites/republicans.science.house.gov/files/documents/hearings/071510_Knake.pdf

Koh, H. (2012, September 18). International law in cyberspace. Statement made at the meeting of *USCYBERCOM Inter-Agency Legal Conference*, Ft. Meade, MD. Retrieved from http://www.state.gov/s/l/releases/remarks/197924.htm

Kopstein, J. (2013, May 5). Hacking back: Cops and corporations want cybersecurity to go on the offensive. *The Verge*. Retrieved from http://www.theverge.com/2013/5/9/4315228/hacking-back-cops-and-corporations-want-offensive-cybersecurity

Kostadinov, D. (2014a, April 10). Jus in cyber bello: How the law of armed conflict regulates cyber attacks part I. *Infosec Institute*. Retrieved armed conflict regulates cyber attacks part II. *Infosec Institute*. Retrieved from http://resources.infosecinstitute.com/jus-cyber-bello-law-armed-conflict-regulates-cyber-attacks-part-ii/

Kotadia, M. (2004, March 10). Symbiot launches DDoS counter-strike tool. *ZDNet*. Retrieved from http://www.zdnet.com/symbiot-launches-ddos-counter-strike-tool-3039148215/

Kovacich, G. L., Jones, A., & Luzwick, P. G. (2002). Global information warfare: How businesses, governments, and others achieve objectives and attain competitive advantages - Chapter 1, part 2. Information Systems Security, 11(5), 15-23.

Kshetri, N. (2013). Cybercrimes in the Former Soviet Union and Central and Eastern Europe: Current status and key drivers. *Crime, Law, and Social Change, 60*(1), 39–65. doi:10.1007/s10611-013-9431-4

Kurtz, G. (2010, January 14). Operation "Aurora" hit Google, others. *McAfee Blog Central*. Retrieved from http://blogs.mcafee.com/archive/operation-aurora-hit-google-others

Lemos, R. (2001, May 1). Lawyers slam FBI 'hack'. *ZDNet News*. Retrieved from http://www.zdnet.com/lawyers-slam-fbi-hack-2021200883/

Lewis, J. A. (2013a). Conflict and negotiation in cyberspace. *Center for Strategic and International Studies*. Retrieved from http://csis.org/files/publication/130208_Lewis_ConflictCyberspace_Web.pdf

Lewis, J. A. (2013b, May 22). Private retaliation in cyberspace. *Center for Strategic and International Studies*. Retrieved from http://csis.org/publication/private-retaliation-cyberspace

Leyden, J. (2014, September 3). NATO nations 'will respond to a cyber attack on one as though it were on all'. *The Register*. Retrieved from http://www.theregister.co.uk/2014/09/03/nato_article_v_mutual_defence_principle_applies_to_cyberspace/

Leyden, J. (2014, March 4). Cyber battle apparently under way in Russia-Ukraine conflict. *The Register*. Retrieved from http://www.theregister.co.uk/2014/03/04/ukraine_cyber_conflict/

Li, B., Erdin, E., Güneş, M. H., Bebis, G., & Shipley, T. (2011). An analysis of anonymizer technology usage. In J. Domingo-Pascual, Y. Shavitt, & S. Uhlig (Eds.), *Traffic Monitoring and Analysis* (pp. 108–121). Berlin: Springer Berlin Heidelberg. doi:10.1007/978-3-642-20305-3_10

Limnell, J. (2014, August 7). Active defense: Fighting fire with fire leads to a dangerous future. *McAfee Labs*. Retrieved from https://blogs.mcafee.com/executive-perspectives/fighting-fire-fire-will-lead-us-dangerous-future

Lin, H. S. (2010). Offensive cyber operations and the use of force. *Journal of National Security Law & Policy, 4*(1), 63–86.

Lookingglass (2015, April 28). Operation Armageddon: Cyber espionage as a strategic component of Russian modern warfare. *Lookingglass Cyber Threat Intelligence Group*. Report CTIG-20150428-01. Retrieved from https://lgscout.com/operation-armageddon-cyber-espionage-as-a-strategic-component-of-russian-modern-warfare/

Lubell, N. (2010). *Extraterritorial use of force against non-state actors*. Oxford: Oxford University Press. doi:10.1093/acprof:oso/9780199584840.001.0001

Lupsha, P. A. (1996). Transnational organized crime versus the nation-state. *Transnational Organized Crime, 2*(1), 21–48.

Mankotia, A. S. (2013, July 5). Telecom operators will have to help set up government's central monitoring system. *The Economic Times*. Retrieved from http://articles.economictimes.indiatimes.com/2013-07-05/news/40392187_1_telecom-operators-service-provider-uasl

Marks, J. (2015, May 5). U.S. makes new push for global rules in cyberspace. *Politico*. Retrieved from http://www.politico.com/story/2015/05/us-makes-new-push-for-global-rules-in-cyberspace-117632.html#ixzz3afDwS24l

McGee, S., Sabett, R. V., & Shah, A. (2013). Adequate attribution: A framework for developing a national policy for private sector use of active defense. *Journal of Business & Technology Law, 8*(1). http://digitalcommons.law.umaryland.edu/cgi/viewcontent.cgi? article=1187&context=jbtl Retrieved January 12, 2014

Menn, J. (2012, June 18). Hacked companies fight back with controversial steps. *Reuters*. Retrieved from http://www.reuters.com/article/2012/06/18/us-media-tech-summit-cyber-strikeback-idUS-BRE85G07S20120618

Menn, J. (2013, October 10). SEC issues guidelines on hacking. *The Financial Times*. Retrieved from http://www.ft.com/cms/s/0/32e2adae-f5fc-11e0-bcc2-00144feab49a.html#axzz2hR7NpRFX

Messerschmidt, J. E. (2013). Hackback: Permitting retaliatory hacking by non-state actors as proportionate countermeasures to transboundary cyberharm. *Columbia Journal of Transnational Law, 52*(1), 275–324.

Messmer, E. (2011, January 21). Is retaliation the answer to cyber attacks? *Networkworld*. Retrieved from http://www.networkworld.com/article/2199010/malware-cybercrime/is-retaliation-the-answer-to-cyber-attacks-.html

Microsoft Security Intelligence Report, Volume 18. (2015). *Microsoft Corporation*. Retrieved from https://www.microsoft.com/en-us/download/details.aspx?id=46928

Mislan, R. P. (2010, June 30). Cellphone crime solvers. *IEEE Spectrum*, 1–3. Retrieved from http://spectrum.ieee.org/computing/software/cellphone-crime-solvers

Moran, N., & Haq, T. (2013, October, 31). Know your enemy: Tracking a rapidly evolving APT actor. *FireEye Blog*. Retrieved from http://www.fireeye.com/blog/technical/2013/10/know-your-enemy-tracking-a-rapidly-evolving-apt-actor.html

Morris, S. (2004). *The future of netcrime now: Part 1 – threats and challenges*. Home Office Online Report 62/04. Retrieved from http://www.globalinitiative.net/download/cybercrime/europe-russia/Home%20Office%20-%20The%20future%20of%20netcrime%20now%20-%20Part%201%20%E2%80%93%20threats%20and%20challenges.pdf

Mudrinich, E. M. (2012). Cyber 3.0: The Department of Defense strategy for operating in cyberspace and the attribution problem. *The Air Force Law Review, 68*, 167.

Nakashima, E. (2010, January 16). U.S. plans to issue official protest to China over attack on Google. *Washington Post*. Retrieved from http://articles.washingtonpost.com/2010-01-16/news/36816400_1_chinese-search-engine-internet-freedom-chinese-government

Nakashima, E. (2012, September 17). Cybersecurity should be more active, official says. *The Washington Post*. Retrieved from http://www.washingtonpost.com/world/national-security/cybersecurity-should-be-more-active-official-says/2012/09/16/dd4bc122-fc6d-11e1-b153-218509a954e1_story.html

Nakashima, E. (2012, August 10). Pentagon proposes more robust role for its cyber-specialists. *The Washington Post*. Retrieved from http://www.washingtonpost.com/world/national-security/pentagon-proposes-more-robust-role-for-its-cyber-specialists/2012/08/09/1e3478ca-db15-11e1-9745-d9ae6098d493_story.html

National Research Council. (2009). *Technology, policy law and ethics regarding U.S. acquisition and use of cyber attack capabilities*. Washington: The National Academies Press. Retrieved from http://www.lawfareblog.com/wp-content/uploads/2013/01/NRC-Report.pdf

Nicks, D. (2014, August 9). Hackers unveil their plan to change email forever. *Time*. Retrieved from http://time.com/3096341/email-encryption-hackers/

O'Brien, N. (2011, February 6). Bikies' blackberrys beat law. *The Sydney Morning Herald*. Retreived from http://www.smh.com.au/digital-life/mobiles/bikies-blackberrys-beat-law-20110206-1ahmo.html

O'Gorman, G., & McDonald, G. (2012). The Elderwood Project. *Symantec Security Response*. Retrieved from https://www.symantec.com/content/en/us/enterprise/media/security_response/whitepapers/the-elderwood-project.pdf

O'Hagan, J. (2013). War 2.0: An analytical framework. *Australian Journal of International Affairs*, *67*(5), 555–569. doi:10.1080/10357718.2013.823374

Odierno, R. (2013, February 4). The force of tomorrow. *Foreign Policy*. Retrieved from http://www.foreignpolicy.com/articules/2013/02/04/the_force_of_tomorrow

Office of the National Counterintelligence Executive. (2011). *Foreign spies stealing US economic secrets in cyberspace, report to Congress on foreign economic collection and industrial espionage 2009-2011*. Retrieved from http://www.ncix.gov/publications/reports/fecie_all/Foreign_Economic_Collection_2011.pdf

Poeter, D. (2012, February 28). IBM says it's 'on the cusp' of building a quantum computer. *PC Mag*. Retrieved from http://www.pcmag.com/article2/0,2817,2400930,00.asp

Poison ivy: Assessing damage and extracting intelligence. (2014, August 30). *FireEye Special Report*. Retrieved from https://www.fireeye.com/resources/pdfs/fireeye-poison-ivy-report.pdf

Ponemon Institute. (2015, May 23). 2015 cost of data breach study: Global analysis. *Ponemon Institute Research Report*. Retrieved from http://public.dhe.ibm.com/common/ssi/ecm/se/en/sew03053wwen/SEW03053WWEN.PDF

Prosise, C., & Sha, S. U. (2013, January 2013). Hackers' tricks to avoid detection. *Windows Security*. Retrieved from http://www.windowsecurity.com/whitepapers/misc/Hackers_Tricks_to_Avoid_Detection_.html

Protecting your critical assets - Lessons learned from "Operation Aurora" [White paper]. (2010). *McAfee Labs and McAfee Foundstone Professional Services*. Retrieved from http://www.wired.com/images_blogs/threatlevel/2010/03/operationaurora_wp_0310_fnl.pdf

Protocol Additional to the Geneva Conventions (1949), and relating to the *Protection of Victims of International Armed Conflicts* (1977) (Protocol I).

Protocol Additional to the Geneva Conventions (1949), and relating to the *Protection of Victims of Non-International Armed Conflicts* (1977) (Protocol II).

Public must be warned about cyber threat 'like AIDS campaign in the 80s'. (2013, January 9). *The Telegraph*. Retrieved from http://www.telegraph.co.uk/news/uknews/defence/9789743/Public-must-be-warned-about-cyber-threat-like-AIDS-campaign-in-the-80s.html

Rabkin, J. A., & Rabkin, A. (2012). To confront cyber threats, we must rethink the law of armed conflict. *Koret-Taube Task Force on National Security and Law, Hoover Institution, Stanford University*. Retrieved http://media.hoover.org/sites/default/files/documents/EmergingThreats_Rabkin.pdf

Ratcliffe, J. H. (2008). *Intelligence-led policing*. Cullompton: Willan Publishing.

Reich, P. C., Weinstein, S., Wild, C., & Cabanlong, A. S. (2010). Cyber warfare: A review of theories, law, policies, actual incidents - and the dilemma of anonymity. *European Journal of Law and Technology*, *1*(2), 1–58.

Reidenberg, J. R. (1996). Governing networks and rule-making in cyberspace. *Emory Law Journal*, *45*(3), 911.

Richmond, R. (2013, March 3). Flawed security exposes vital software to hackers. *New York Times*. Retrieved October 10, 2013, from http://bits.blogs.nytimes.com/2010/03/05/flawed-security-exposes-vital-software-to-hackers/?_php=true&_type=blogs&_r=0

Romm, T. (2013, March 12). Cyberattacks: The complexities of attacking back. *Politico*. Retrieved March 12, 2013, from http://www.politico.com/story/2013/03/cyberattacks-the-complexities-of-attacking-back-88702.html?hp=r14

Sanger, D. E. (2013, May 21). As Chinese leader's visit nears, U.S. is urged to allow counterattacks on hackers. *The New York Times*. Retrieved from http://www.nytimes.com/2013/05/22/world/asia/as-chinese-leaders-visit-nears-us-urged-to-allow-retaliation-for-cyberattacks.html?emc=tnt&tntemail0=y&_r=2&p%E2%80%A6&

Sanger, D. E. (2014, August 31). NATO set to ratify pledge on joint defense in case of major cyberattack. *The New York Times*. Retrieved from http://www.nytimes.com/2014/09/01/world/europe/nato-set-to-ratify-pledge-on-joint-defense-in-case-of-major-cyberattack.html?_r=1

Sanger, D. E., & Markoff, J. (2010, January 14). After Google's stand on China, U.S. treads lightly. *New York Times*. Retrieved from http://www.nytimes.com/2010/01/15/world/asia/15diplo.html?_r=0

Schmitt, M. (2012). Classification of cyber conflict. *Journal of Conflict and Security Law*, *17*(2), 245–260. doi:10.1093/jcsl/krs018

Schmitt, M. N. (1999). Computer network attack and the use of force in international law: Thoughts on a normative framework. *Columbia Journal of Transnational Law*, *37*(3), 885.

Schmitt, M. N. (Ed.). (2013). *The Tallinn Manual on the international law applicable to cyber warfare*. New York: Cambridge University Press. doi:10.1017/CBO9781139169288

Shafritz, R. (2001). A survey of cyberstalking legislation. *UWLA Law Review*, *32*, 323.

Shane, J. (1996). Information superhighway: An overview of technology challenges U.S. general accounting office. *Journal of Government Information*, *23*(1), 78–80. doi:10.1016/S1352-0237(96)90313-5

Shelley, L. (2004, September 27). Organized crime, cybercrime and terrorism. *Computer Crime Research Center*. Retrieved from http://www.crimeresearch.org/articles/Terrorism_Cybercrime/

Shubber, K. (2013, June 24). A simple guide to GCHQ's internet surveillance program Tempora. *Wired*. Retrieved from http://www.wired.co.uk/news/archive/2013-06/24/gchq-tempora-101

Simonite, T. (2014, June 10). Digital summit: Microsoft's quantum search for the "next transistor". *MIT Technology Review*. Retrieved from http://www.technologyreview.com/news/528256/digital-summit-microsofts-quantum-search-for-the-next-transistor/

Simons, K. W. (2008). Self-defense: Reasonable beliefs or reasonable self-control? *New Criminal Law Review: An International and Interdisciplinary Journal*, *11*(1), 51–90.

Sorcher, S. (2015, April 1). Influencers: Companies should not be allowed to hack back. *The Christian Science Monitor*. Retrieved from http://www.csmonitor.com/World/Passcode/Passcode-Influencers/2015/0401/Influencers-Companies-should-not-be-allowed-to-hack-back

Spence-Diehl, E. (2003). Stalking and technology: The double-edged sword. *Journal of Technology in Human Services*, *22*(1), 5–18. doi:10.1300/J017v22n01_02

Spencer, R. (2007, August 16). China launches 'big brother' surveillance program. *Vancouver Sun*, A11.

Statute of the International Court of Justice (1945).

Stokes, J., & Weedon, J. (2015, May 14). Security in an era of coercive attacks. *FireEye Blogs*. Retrieved from https://www.fireeye.com/blog/executive-perspective/2015/05/security_in_an_erao.html

Suciu, P. (2014, December 21). Why cyber warfare is so attractive to small nations. *Fortune*. Retrieved from http://fortune.com/2014/12/21/why-cyber-warfare-is-so-attractive-to-small-nations/

The North Atlantic Treaty (1949).

Thompson, C. (2014, May 20). The revolutionary quantum computer that may not be quantum at all. *Wired*. Retrieved from http://www.wired.com/2014/05/quantum-computing/

Tracy, J. (2000, January 13). Police get window of access to e-mail. *The Moscow Times*. Retrieved from http://www.themoscowtimes.com/sitemap/free/2000/1/article/police-get-window-of-access-to-e-mail/268089.html

Trope, K. L. (2014). US government eavesdropping on electronic communications: Where are we going? *Scitech Lawyer, 10*(2), 4–9.

Tucker, P. (2014, April 29). Why Ukraine has already lost the cyberwar, too. *Defence One*. Retrieved May 2, 2014, from http://www.defenseone.com/technology/2014/04/why-ukraine-has-already-lost-cyberwar-too/83350/

Turn the map around to prevent damage and loss from cyber attack. (2015, April 16). *Endgame* [White Paper]. Retrieved from http://pages.endgame.com/WC2015-04EnterpriseWhitepaper_WCYYYYM-MDDWebContent.html

United Nations General Assembly. (2011, September 14). Letter dated 12 September 2011 from the Permanent Representatives of China, the Russian Federation, Tajikistan and Uzbekistan to the United Nations addressed to the Secretary-General. Retrieved from https://ccdcoe.org/sites/default/files/documents/UN-110912-CodeOfConduct_0.pdf

United Nations Office on Drugs and Crime. (2013). *The comprehensive study on cybercrime*. Retrieved from http://www.unodc.org/documents/organized-crime/cybercrime/CYBERCRIME_STUDY_210213.pdf

US Department of Defense. (2015, April 17). *The DoD cyber strategy*. Retrieved from http://www.defense.gov/home/features/2015/0415_cyber-strategy/Final_2015_DoD_CYBER_STRATEGY_for_web.pdf

US Department of Justice Computer Crime and Intellectual Property Section Criminal Division. (2012). *Prosecuting computer crimes*. Retrieved from http://www.justice.gov/criminal/cybercrime/docs/ccmanual.pdf

US Department of State. (2015, May 18). An open and secure Internet: We must have both. Remarks made by John Kerry Secretary of State at *Korea University*, Seoul, South Korea. Retrieved from http://origin.www.uscc.gov/sites/default/files/annual_reports/Complete%202013%20Annual%20Report.PDF

Vijayan, J. (2013a, April 6). U.S. urged to let companies 'hack-back' at IP cyber thieves. *Computerworld*. Retrieved from http://www.computerworld.com/s/article/9239503/U.S._urged_to_let_companies_hack_back_at_IP_cyber_thieves

Vijayan, J. (2013b, May 29). Private retaliation in cyberspace a 'remarkably bad idea'. *Computerworld*. Retrieved from http://www.computerworld.com/s/article/9239606/Private_retaliation_in_cyberspace_a_remarkably_bad_idea_

Vijayan, J. (2014, July 2). Hackers hit more businesses through remote access accounts. *IT News*. Retrieved July 3, 2014, from http://itnews.com/security/80848/hackers-hit-more-businesses-through-remote-access-accounts?page=0,0

Wadhwa, V. (2015, May 11). Quantum computing is about to overturn cybersecurity's balance of power. *The Washington Post*. Retrieved from http://www.washingtonpost.com/blogs/innovations/wp/2015/05/11/quantum-computing-is-about-to-overturn-cybersecuritys-balance-of-power/

Walden, I. (2003). Computer crime. In C. Reed & J. Angel (Eds.), *Computer Law*. London: Oxford University Press.

Walden, I. (2005). Crime and security in cyberspace. *Cambridge Review of International Affairs*, *18*(1), 51–68. doi:10.1080/09557570500059563

Webb, J. P. (2012, June 26). The illegality of striking back against hackers. *Cybercrime Review*. Retrieved from http://www.cybercrimereview.com/2012/06/illegality-of-striking-back-against.html

West, Z. (2012). Young fella, if you're looking for trouble I'll accommodate you: Deputizing private companies for the use of hackback. *Syracuse Law Review*, *63*(1), 119–146.

Westby, J. (2012, November 29). Caution: Active response to cyber attacks has high risk. *Forbes*. Retrieved from http://www.forbes.com/sites/jodywestby/2012/11/29/caution-active-response-to-cyber-attacks-has-high-risk/

White, J. (2013). The anti-surveillance state: New products that are challenging law enforcement. *The Journal of the Australian Institute of Professional Intelligence Officers*, *21*(2), 17–36.

Williams, M. (2009, July 14). U.K. not North Korea, source of DDoS attacks, research says. *Computer World*. Retrieved http://www.computerworld.com/s/article/9135492/U.K._not_North_Korea_source_of_DDOS_attacks_researcher_says

Wilson, C. (2006, September 14). *Information operations and cyberwar: Capabilities and related policy issues*. CRS Report for Congress, RL31787. Retrieved from http://fas.org/irp/crs/RL31787.pdf

Wolf, J. B. (2000). War games meets the internet: Chasing 21st century cybercriminals with old laws and little money. *American Journal of Criminal Law*, *28*(1), 95–117.

Wright, C., Monrose, F., & Masson, G. (2006). On inferring application protocol behaviors in encrypted network traffic. *Journal of Machine Learning Research*, *7*, 2745–2769.

Wu, T. (1999). Application-centered internet analysis. *Virginia Law Review*, *85*(6), 1163–1204. doi:10.2307/1073968

Wu, T. (2006). The world trade law of censorship and internet filtering. *Chicago Journal of International Law*, *7*(1), 263–287.

Yadron, D. (2015, January 8). Snowden: Don't hack back. *The Wall Street Journal*. Retrieved January 10, 2015, from http://blogs.wsj.com/digits/2015/01/08/snowden-dont-hack-back/

Yasin, R. (1998). Think twice before becoming a hacker attacker. *InternetWeek*, *745*, 30.

Yu, L., Schwier, J. M., Craven, R. M., Brooks, R. R., & Griffin, C. (2013, July). Inferring statistically significant hidden markov models. *IEEE Transactions on Knowledge and Data Engineering*, *25*(7), 1548–1558. doi:10.1109/TKDE.2012.93

Zavrsnik, A. (2010). Towards an overregulated cyberspace. *Masaryk University Journal of Law & Technology*, *4*(2), 185–188.

Zemanek, K. (1987). Responsibility of states: General principles. In Encyclopaedia of Public International Law (Vol. 10, pp. 362-372).

Zetter, K. (2014, July 3). The NSA is targeting users of privacy services, leaked code shows. *Wired*. Retrieved July 3, 2014, from http://www.wired.com/2014/07/nsa-targets-users-of-privacy-services/

Zoller, E. (1984). *Peacetime unilateral remedies: An analysis of countermeasures. Dobbs Ferry*. Transnational Publishers.

ADDITIONAL READING

American Bar Association. (2013). *The ABA cybersecurity handbook: A resource for attorneys, law firms and business professionals*. Retrieved June 1, 2015, from http://shop.americanbar.org/eBus/Store/ProductDetails.aspx?productId=213569

American Bar Association. (2015, March). A call to cyber norms. *Discussions at the Harvard-MIT–University of Toronto Cyber Norms Workshops, 2011 and 2012*. Retrieved from https://www.americanbar.org/content/dam/aba/uncategorized/GAO/2015apr14_acalltocybernorms.authcheckdam.pdf

American Bar Association Standing Committee on Law and National Security. (2013, October). *A playbook for cyber events*. Retrieved December 17, 2014, from http://shop.americanbar.org/eBus/Default.aspx?TabID=251&productId=217469

Atkinson, J. S., Adetoye, O., Rio, M., Mitchell, J. E., & Matich, G. (2013). Your wifi is leaking: Inferring user behaviour, encryption irrelevant. Paper presented at the *IEEE Wireless Communications and Networking Conference*, 1097-1102. doi:10.1109/WCNC.2013.6554717

Awan, I., & Blakemore, B. (2012). *Policing cyber hate, cyber threats and cyber terrorism*. Farnham: Ashgate Publishing Company.

Barker, J., Hannay, P., & Szewczyk, P. (2011). Using traffic analysis to identify the second generation onion router. Paper presented at the ninth *IEEE/IFIP International Conference on Embedded and Ubiquitous Computing*, 72-78. doi:10.1109/EUC.2011.76

Barnes, D. (2014, January 14). Technology: Cyber security - Under attack. *The Banker*. Retrieved March 14, 2013, from http://search.proquest.com/docview/1475500782?accountid=8330

Barnidge, R. P. J. (2013). *The liberal way of war: Legal perspectives*. Farnham: Ashgate Publishing Company.

Bertino, E., & Takahashi, K. (2011). *Identity management: Concepts, technologies, and systems*. Norwood: Artech House Inc.

Bowyer, K. (2001). *Ethics and computing: Living responsibly in a computerized world*. New York: IEEE Press.

Brenner, S. W. (2007). "At light speed": Attribution and response to cybercrime/terrorism/warfare. *The Journal of Criminal Law & Criminology*, 97(2), 379–475.

Carr, J. (2012). *Inside Cyber Warfare* (2nd ed.). Sebastopol: O'Reilly Media Inc.

Chabrow, E. (2015, January 6). The case against hackback experts calculate the risks of cyberretaliation. *Bank Info Security*. Retrieved from http://www.bankinfosecurity.com/case-against-hack-back-a-7759

Choucri, N. (2012). *Cyberpolitics in international relations: Context, connectivity, and content*. Cambridge: MIT Press.

Condron, S. M. (2007). Getting it right: Protecting American critical infrastructure in cyberspace. *Harvard Journal of Law & Technology, 20*(2), 403–422.

Costigan, S. S., & Perry, J. (2012). *Cyberspaces and global affairs*. Farnham: Ashgate Publishing Company.

Coyne, C. J. (2005). The economics of computer hacking. *Journal of Law. Economic Policy, 1*(2), 511–532.

Denning, P. J., & Denning, D. E. (2010). *The profession of IT: Discussing cyber attack*. New York: Association for Computing Machinery.

Dinstein, Y. (2010). *The conduct of hostilities under the law of international armed conflict*. New York: Cambridge University Press. doi:10.1017/CBO9780511845246

Dittrich, D. (2014, January 11). *Articles/Papers/Audio Related to the Active Response Continuum*. Retrieved from http://staff.washington.edu/dittrich/activedefense.html

Eijkman, Q. (2013). Digital security governance and accountability in Europe: Ethical dilemmas in terrorism risk management. *Journal of Politics and Law, 6*(4), 35. doi:10.5539/jpl.v6n4p35

Epstein, R. A. (2005). Intel v. Hamidi: The role of self-help in cyberspace. *Journal of Law. Economic Policy, 1*(1), 147–170.

Giles, K. (2012). Russia's public stance on cyberspace issues. Paper presented at the 4th *International Conference on Cyber Conflict*, 1-13.

Gross, M. J. (2011, April). Stuxnet worm: A declaration of cyber-war. *Vanity Fair*. Retrieved November 11, 2013, from http://www.vanityfair.com/culture/features/2011/04/stuxnet-201104

Hall, W. M., & Citrenbaum, G. (2010). *Intelligence analysis: How to think in complex environments*. Santa Barbara: Praeger Security International.

Hanover Research. (2015, February). The emergence of cybersecurity law. *Indiana University Bloomington Maurer School of Law*. Retrieved from http://info.law.indiana.edu/faculty-publications/The-Emergence-of-Cybersecurity-Law.pdf

Jarrett, S. M. (2011). Offensive cyber warfare. United States Naval Institute, 137(12), 77-79.

Kelsey, J. T. G. (2008). Hacking into international humanitarian law: The principles of distinction and neutrality in the age of cyber warfare. *Michigan Law Review, 106*(7), 1427–1451.

Kerr, I., Steeves, V. M., & Lucock, C. (2009). *Lessons from the identity trail: Anonymity, privacy, and identity in a networked society*. New York: Oxford University Press.

Kesan, J. P., & Hayes, C. M. (2010). Thinking through active defense in cyberspace. Paper presented at the proceedings of the *Workshop on Deterring Cyberattacks: Informing Strategies and Developing Options*, National Research Council, Washington: National Academies. Retrieved from http://papers.ssrn.com/sol3/Delivery.cfm/SSRN_ID1707527_code291422.pdf?abstractid=1691207&mirid=1

King, R. (2015, March 9). The security download: Anticipating cyberattacks with machine learning. *The Wall Street Journal*. Retrieved from http://blogs.wsj.com/cio/2015/03/09/the-security-download-anticipating-cyberattacks-with-machine-learning/

Knake, R. K. (2011). *Internet governance in an age of cyber insecurity*. Council on Foreign Relations. Retrieved June 17, 2014, from http://www.cfr.org/content/publications/attachments/Cybersecurity_CSR56.pdf

Koch, R., Stelte, B., & Golling, M. (2012). Attack trends in present computer networks. Paper presented at the 4th *International Conference on Cyber Conflict (CYCON)*, 1-12.

Libicki, M. C. (2009). *Cyberdeterrence and cyberwar*. Santa Monica: Rand Corporation. Retrieved June 26, 2014, from http://www.rand.org/content/dam/rand/pubs/monographs/2009/RAND_MG877.pdf

Lindsay, J. R. (2015, May). Exaggerating the Chinese cyber threat. *Belfer Center for Science and International Affairs, Policy Brief*. Reviewed from http://belfercenter.ksg.harvard.edu/files/linsday-china-cyber-pb-final.pdf

Lobel, H. (2012). Cyber war inc.: The law of war implications of the private sector's role in cyber conflict. *Texas International Law Journal*, *47*(3), 617–639.

McGee, S., Sabett, R. V., & Shah, A. (2013). Adequate attribution: A framework for developing a national policy for private sector use of active defense. *Journal of Business & Technology Law*, *8*(1), 1–47.

Mejia, E. F. (2014). Act and actor attribution in cyberspace: A proposed analytic framework. *Strategic Studies Quarterly*, *8*(1), 114–132.

Mitcham, C. (2005). *Encyclopedia of science, technology, and ethics*. Detroit: Macmillan Reference USA.

Nicholson, A., Watson, T., Norris, P., Duffy, A., & Isbell, R. (2012). A taxonomy of technical attribution techniques for cyber attacks. Paper presented at the *European Conference on Information Warfare and Security*, 188-197.

Owens, W. A. (2008). *Technology, policy, law, and ethics regarding U.S. acquisition and use of cyberattack capabilities*. Washington: National Academies Press.

Perrigo, S., & Whitman, J. (2010). *Geneva conventions under assault*. London: Pluto Press.

Pool, P. (2013). War of the cyber world: The law of cyber warfare. *International Lawyer*, *47*(2), 299–323.

Rabkin, J., & Rabkin, A. (2013). Navigating conflicts in cyberspace: Legal lessons from the history of war at sea. *Chicago Journal of International Law*, *14*(1), 197–258.

Reveron, D. S. (2012). *Cyber challenges and national security: Threats, opportunities, and power in a virtual world*. Washington: Georgetown University Press.

Roberts, L. (2008). Jurisdictional and definitional concerns with computer-mediated interpersonal crimes: An analysis on cyber stalking. *International Journal of Cyber Criminology*, *2*(1), 271.

Sales, N. A. (2013). Regulating cyber-security. *Northwestern University Law Review*, *107*(4), 1503–1568.

Schmitt, M. N. (2002, June). Wired warfare: Computer network attack and jus in bello. *RICR Juin IRRC*, *84*(846), 365–399.

Schmitt, M. N. (2007). Asymmetrical warfare and international humanitarian law. In *International Humanitarian Law Facing New Challenges* (pp. 11–48). Berlin: Springer Berlin Heidelberg. doi:10.1007/978-3-540-49090-6_2

Schroeder, S. (2012). *The lure: The true story of how the department of justice brought down two of the world's most dangerous cyber criminals*. Boston: Course Technology / Cengage Learning.

Shahani, A. (2015, April 28). Report: To aid combat, Russia wages cyberwar against Ukraine. *NPR*. Retrieved May 3, 2015, from http://www.npr.org/sections/alltechconsidered/2015/04/28/402678116/report-to-aid-combat-russia-wages-cyberwar-against-ukraine

Simons, K. W. (2008). Self-defense: Reasonable beliefs or reasonable self-control? *New Criminal Law Review: An International and Interdisciplinary Journal, 11*(1), 51–90.

Sklerov, M. J. (2009). Solving the dilemma of state responses to cyberattacks: A justification for the use of active defenses against states who neglect their duty to prevent. *Military Law Review, 201*, 1.

Smith, B. P. (2005). Hacking, poaching, and counterattacking: Digital counterstrikes and the contours of self-help. *Journal of Law. Economic Policy, 1*(1), 171–196.

Swaine, M. D. (2013). Chinese views on cybersecurity in foreign relations. *China Leadership Monitor, 42*. Retrieved June 2, 2015, from http://carnegieendowment.org/email/South_Asia/img/CLM42MSnew.pdf

Tavani, H. T., & Himma, K. E. (2007). *Handbook of information and computer ethics*. New York: John Wiley & Sons.

Teplinsky, M. J. (2013). Fiddling on the roof: Recent developments in cybersecurity. *American University Business Law Review, 2*(2), 225–322.

Tsagourias, N. (2012). Chapter 2: The Tallinn Manual on the international law applicable to cyber warfare: A commentary on chapter II--the use of force. Yearbook of International Humanitarian Law, 15, 19.

Walters, G. J. (2001). *Human rights in an information age: A philosophical analysis*. Toronto: University of Toronto Press.

Watts, S. (2012). The notion of combatancy in cyber warfare. Paper presented at the 4th *International Conference on Cyber Conflict (CYCON)*, 1-15. doi:10.2139/ssrn.2484823

Wilmshurst, E. (2012). *International law and the classification of conflicts*. Oxford: Oxford University Press. doi:10.1093/law/9780199657759.001.0001

Wilson, C. (2007, March 20). Information operations, electronic warfare, and cyberwar: Capabilities and related policy issues. CRS Report for Congress, RL31787. Retrieved from https://www.fas.org/sgp/crs/natsec/RL31787.pdf

Wyler, N. R. (Ed.). (2005). *Aggressive network self-defense*. Burlington: Syngress Publishing.

Zhang, L. (2012, June). A Chinese perspective on cyber war. *International Review of the Red Cross, 94*(886), 801–807. doi:10.1017/S1816383112000823

KEY TERMS AND DEFINITIONS

Adversary: An individual, group, organization, government, or other threat source that executes harmful activities, or has the intent to engage in a course of conduct that is detrimental to another.

Attribution: The analytical process by which sources of intelligence are weighed and explained to determine the identity or location of an adversary, or an adversary's intermediary.

Authentication: The process of verifying the identity or other attributes of an entity (user, process, or device) via a secure information system using cryptographic methods.

Cybersecurity Threat: Any exploit that may cause unauthorized access to, interference with, or damage to the integrity, confidentiality, or availability of an information system, or lead to the exfiltration of data stored on or transmitted through an information system.

Exploit: Code That leverages vulnerabilities in operating systems, web browsers, applications, or software components to access data on an information system or install malware.

Incident: An event or occurrence that results in an adverse consequence, or poses a threat to, the integrity of an information system, including the violation of security policies, security procedures, or acceptable use policies.

Malware: Abbreviation for malicious software which performs unwanted actions on an information system, such as stealing personally identifiable information, locking a system until the user pays a ransom, or using the system to send spam.

Modus Operandi: A Latin term which denotes a pattern of behavior or method of operating that is repeatedly employed by a criminal in the furtherance of committing crime.

Natural Person: An actual human being, rather than a private corporation that is usually treated at law as a legal person or having a legal personality.

Open Source Intelligence: Information of potential value as intelligence that exists in the public domain.

Payload: Intended actions performed by a sample of malware including, but are not limited to, displaying messages, downloading files, logging keystrokes, and changing system settings.

Plausible Deniability: Typically a legal concept referring to the lack of evidence required to prove an allegation, or otherwise related to the capacity of an entity to deny official accountability due to lack of awareness or other cause for repudiation.

Prime Suspect: The individual whom law enforcement investigators believe most probably committed a particular crime.

Private Entity: A broadly defined term which may include a corporation, company, partnership, firm, association, society, or other legal person, as distinct at law from a natural person.

Proxy Server: A service that acts as an intermediary to funnel and separate requests made from a user's Internet gateway to an outside network, or another online resource, which may provide security, anonymity, administrative control, and caching functionality.

Reconnaissance: A phase of an attack where an attacker identifies new information systems, or generates maps of targeted networks or nodes, or probes for specific, exploitable vulnerabilities.

Rooted: Gaining superuser permission or administrative-level access to an information system through the use of exploits.

Signature: An idiosyncratic or distinctive pattern of activity that can be detected on an information system, or profiled against previously identified attacks against information systems, including network traffic attributed to specific attack tools or exploits.

Spoofing: Using electronic means of deception, beguilement, trickery, deceit, bluff, mystification and subterfuge by an unauthorized entity to assume the digital identity of another in order to gain access or interfere with an information system.

Targeted Attack: An attack vector using malware which is customized for a specific group of companies or individuals to facilitate initial access before operations are executed to steal data or disrupt targeted information systems.

Risk: Is the product of correlating the magnitude of a threat with the level of vulnerability which establishes the likelihood of a successful attack against exploitable weaknesses in an information system. Likelihood here is determined by understanding the ease of exploitation and any conditions favorable to exploitation.

Section 3
National Issues, Strategies and Policies

Chapter 9
Developing Confidence Building Measures (CBMs) in Cyberspace between Pakistan and India

Tughral Yamin
National University of Sciences and Technology, Pakistan

ABSTRACT

Cyberspace is at once an area of immense cooperation and a no-holds barred arena for competition. Difficulties in creating a stable environment in cyberspace stem from differing national perceptions regarding the freedom of the Internet, application of international law and problems associated with attribution. Information space has no borders and no recognized rules of engagement or internationally accepted regulatory mechanisms. State parties, freelancers, criminals and terrorists all consider cyber operations beyond the pale of international jurisdiction. Some agreements have emerged concerning cybercrime but cyber warfare remains outside binding legal obligations. In the absence of a consensus on treaty obligations, it is a good idea to begin by constructing credible confidence building measures (CBMs) in information space between rival states. The prospects of an unintentional war as a consequence of a cyber-attack can spell disaster for South Asia. This paper discusses a range of CBMs that can be created between India and Pakistan in cyber space to control malicious cyber behavior and avert an inadvertent war. It advocates cyber cooperation instead of cyber warfare.

THE CONCEPT OF INFORMATION WARFARE (IW)

The success of any management system depends on making quick decisions based on the complete and accurate data shared in real timeing. Means of communication have evolved through the ages from such primitive methods like the word of mouth, drumbeats, smoke signals, bugles, messengers, carrier pigeons, and semaphore to the more sophisticated ones such as the modern computer networks.

Information space is the place, where information resides. In the Internet lexicon terms like cyberspace and information space are used interchangeably. For most people cyberspace signifies the world of computer networks. The *Bing Dictionary* describes **cyberspace** as the "imagined place where electronic

DOI: 10.4018/978-1-4666-8456-0.ch009

data goes," or the "the notional realm in which electronic information exists or is exchanged." Others have defined cyberspace as:

The environment formed by physical and non-physical components, characterized by the use of computers and electro-magnetic spectrum, to store, modify, and exchange data using computer networks (Schmitt 2013).

and

A domain characterized by the use of electronics and the electromagnetic spectrum to store, modify, and exchange data via networked systems and associated physical infrastructures (Publication 2006).

Internet provides the digital oxygen to the contemporary information system. The worldwide web (WWW) has converted the planet into a virtual global village. The international financial system; air, land and maritime transport structures are all digitally connected and controlled by computer networks. Like the commercial sector most of the defense organizations are also fully or partially networked. Digital connectivity has not only speeded up the decision making processes, it has also rendered these systems vulnerable to cyber-attacks. An elaborate system of encryption ranging from simple codes and cyphers to exotic algorithms has been developed to keep the content of the messages secret. However, information vulnerability has become an issue with governments, corporate sector and business houses.

As nations upgrade their net-centric capabilities, they constantly fret about imminent cyber-attacks of 9/11 proportions (Jr 2013). Resultantly they are investing a lot of time, money and effort into developing cyber defenses to protect critical infrastructure like the national command and control (C^2) systems. At the same time technologically advanced countries are enhancing their offensive capabilities to launch cyber-attacks against hostile computer networks. An all pervasive cyber surveillance campaign is in the works. The prospects have become so frightening that countries like Iran, China, Saudi Arabia and Russia are actually working on creating their own Internets (Segal 2013).

Internet is the glue of modern information management system. It holds together governments, defense organizations and financial services. The airlines, maritime industry, railways, the road traffic system are controlled by computer networks. The waterways, logistics services, emergency services, energy management systems, electrical grids and industrial units are operated by SCADA (Supervisory Control & Data Acquisition) type of industrial control system (ICS) (Brodsky 2013). All these are lucrative cyber-targets. Cyber-attacks directed against individual PCs or large networks take place singly or as a large well-coordinated operation. Their cumulative effects can range from minor to major disruptions including interrupted routines to complete breakdown of systems. The aftermath can range from mildly chaotic to absolutely devastating. An element of fear can cause unintended panic and mayhem.

Cyberspace or Cyberia (Rushkof 2002), instead of becoming an area of cooperation has turned out to be the fifth dimension of war fighting (Hardy 2012). The devastating effects of cyber-attacks have significantly altered the landscape of modern warfare (Kuehl). American scholars claim that the first instance of cyber attacks were detected in 1986 (Healy 2013). Ever since then digitally advanced nations are involved in a bitterly intense competition to dominate cyberspace through the unbridled use of Information Warfare (IW) weapons. Information Operations (IO) now form the essential part of all military planning and training. A 2011 survey commissioned by the UN Institute for Disarmament Research (UNIDIR) found that 33 states, including China, Russia and the US, have included cyber warfare in their military planning and organization. At least 12 countries including India have either established or are in the process of establishing military cyber warfare organizations (Timlin 2011).

In order to understand the cyber language some of the more commonly used terms are defined as under. **Cyber-warfare** with both its offensive and defensive facets has been variously defined as:

[A]ctions by a nation-state to penetrate another nation's computers or networks for the purposes of causing damage or disruption (Knake 2010).

[D]eliberate attempt to disable or destroy another country's computer networks (Gjelten 2012).

[D]efending information and computer networks, deterring information attacks, as well as denying an adversary's ability to do the same. It can include offensive information operations mounted against an adversary, or even dominating information on the battlefield (Hildreth 2001).

Cyber-attacks are "deliberate actions to alter, disrupt, deceive, degrade, or destroy computer systems or networks or the information and/or programs resident in or transiting these systems or networks" (William A. Owens 2009). **Cyber exploitation** and **cyber espionage** are long term cyber offensive actions to obtain "information resident on or transiting through an adversary's computer systems or networks," without disturbing "the normal functioning of a computer system or network," and without arousing suspicion (William A. Owens 2009). **Cyber threats** include "external threat actors, insider threats, supply chain vulnerabilities," and threats to the defense establishment (Defense). **IO** is described as the: "Integrated employment, during military operations, of information-related capabilities in concert with other lines of operation to influence, disrupt, corrupt, or usurp the decision-making of adversaries and potential adversaries while protecting our own." It is meant "to influence, disrupt, corrupt, or usurp adversarial human and automated decision making while protecting [one's] own" (Publication 2012). The five forms of IO are electronic warfare (EW), computer network operations (CNO), including computer network attacks (CNA), psychological operations (psy-ops), military deception (MilDec) and operational security (Opsec). Computer network warfare is defined as the employment of complete range of CNO to deny the adversaries the use of its computers, information systems, and networks, while ensuring the effective use of own computers, information systems, and networks. These operations include not only CNA but also Computer Network Exploration (CNE), and Computer Network Defense (CND) (Carr 2010). A combination of these five alongwith related supporting capabilities are used to influence, disrupt, corrupt or usurp adversarial human and automated decision making processes, while protecting one's own (Publication 2012).

As cyber-attacks become increasingly commonplace, new concepts of **cybersecurity** are emerging. This defensive mechanism is described as:

The collection of tools, policies, security concepts, security safeguards, guidelines, risk management approaches, actions, training, best practices, assurance and technologies that can be used to protect the cyber environment and organization and user's assets (X.1205 2011).

One way to ensure cyber-security is by instituting effective local and international laws to check illicit cyber activity. Countries with economies heavily dependent on e-commerce have devised laws to deal with cybercrimes. Federal and state governments in the US have improved cybersecurity through regulations and collaborative efforts with the private-sector. These cyber regulations are governed by the Comprehensive National Cyber Security Initiative (CNCSI) (Security). The purpose of these regulations is to protect companies, organizations and the government from malicious software or malware (Technet n.d), such as viruses, worms, Trojan horses, spam emails, scareware, phishing, spear phishing, denial of service (DOS) or distributed denial of service (DDoS) attacks, unauthorized access (stealing intellectual property or confidential information) and control system attacks (Intenational 2011). An innocuous Universal Serial Bus (USB) thumb drive can introduce a deadly virus into a computer system (Jevans 2013). Similarly Peer-to-Peer (P2P) applications, such as those used to share music files, can also introduce security risks that put information or personal computers (PC) in jeopardy (US-CERT 2013). Numerous measures are available to prevent cyber-attacks. These include <u>firewalls</u>, <u>anti-virus software</u>, intrusion detection and prevention systems, <u>encryption</u> and login passwords (Napolitano).

As an Internet superpower (Eurotopics 2013), US vigorously pursues its commercial, political, as well as military interests in cyberspace. Its actions are driven by worries that its hold on Internet leadership should not loosen up (Segal 2013). The US State Department has created an office of the Coordinator for Cyber Issues to give policy guidelines on cyber affairs. Its mission is to "promote an open, interoperable, secure, and reliable information and communications infrastructure that supports international trade and commerce, strengthens international security, and fosters free expression and innovation" (State 2011). The technical side of the cyber security is handled by the Department of Homeland Security (DHS) and the Department of Defense (DOD). **Office of Cybersecurity and Communications (CS&C)** within the National Protection and Programs Directorate is responsible for the security and reliability of the national cyber and communications infrastructure. It works to prevent and minimize disruptions to critical information infrastructure in order to protect the public, the economy, and government services. The US National Cybersecurity and Communications Integration Center (NCCIC) serves as a 24/7 cyber monitoring, incident response, and management center and as a national point of cyber and communications incident integration.The US Congress recently "passed legislation to encourage businesses to share cyber-threat information with the National Cybersecurity and Communications Integration Center (NCCIC) and with each other" (Hoover 2015).

The US cyber planners have two kinds of cyber threats in mind. Firstly, those aimed against critical infrastructure such as electricity and water supply, transportation and communication networks, and financial services. According to official US sources a 17-fold increase in intrusions into vital infrastructure has been experienced. The ICS running the chemical, electrical, water and transport sectors in the US have all been probed by hackers (CERT n.d). The second area of concern is the large-scale theft/destruction of valuable official and business secrets by state-sponsored hackers and criminals. Widespread hacking activity in the private sector e.g. in August 2012, hackers attacked the networks of Saudi Aramco, destroying data on some 30,000 of the company's computers (Segal 2012). In July 2013, federal prosecutors in New York indicted a group of Russian and Ukrainian hackers for stealing and selling 160 million credit card numbers from more than a dozen companies, causing hundreds of millions of dollars in losses. This has been described as the largest hacking and data breach case in the US (Sengupta 2013). The volume of global online crime is estimated to be between US $110 to 500 billion (Segal 2013). In 2014 significant data breaches in the customer accounts of big businesses like Target, Home Depot and JP Morgan have been reported.

While governments are anxious about rampant theft and crime in cyberspace, they are not averse to buying tantalizing cyber ware from open market for exactly the same purpose. Coding flaws in software like Microsoft Windows known as 'zero days' are being freely sold to the highest bidder by clandestine companies. Big buyers include the American NSA, Iranian Revolutionary Guards and agencies from South Africa to South Korea. Israel, Britain, Russia, India and Brazil are known to be some of the biggest spenders in the field. North Korea, some Middle Eastern intelligence services and countries in the Asian Pacific, including Malaysia and Singapore, are buying too (Sanger 2013). These open market resources add to a country's potential to launch effective cyber-attacks e.g. in June 2013, South Korea blamed the North for attacking 69 websites, including the presidential office and media companies. (*Dawn*, July 16, 2013).

The cyber warfare revolution was triggered by the spectacular display of cutting edge technology by the US military during the first Gulf War. Soon thereafter, US DoD raised cyber and IW units (Sang-Hun 2013). In 1998, the Pentagon created a Joint Task Force Computer Network Defense (JTFCND) (Healy 2013). The task force was subsequently upgraded to a cyber-command (CYBERCOM). This Command became fully operational on October 31, 2010 and now controls all cyberspace operations, cyber resources and military cyber defenses (Command n.d). It is mandated to protect the national security systems from infiltration and disruption. Despite budget cuts (Whitehouse.gov). the US intends to maintain its cyber dominance and intends to quadruple the size of the CYBERCOM by hiring 4,000 information technology (IT) specialists over the next four years. This will happen at an additional cost of US $23 billion (Bumiller 2013). The NSA collects and analyzes huge troves of foreign communications and foreign signals intelligence to monitor and thwart worldwide threats (Nakashima 2013). The NSA also wants more money to deploy a Star Wars kind of cyber defense (Sanger 2013). The scale of NSA global surveillance outreach has sent shock waves around the world, (Rodriguez 2013) alarming both allies (*Washington Post* July 5, 2013), and competitors (Franchi 2013).

The Chinese People's Liberation Army (PLA) seriously studied the emerging trends of cyber warfare and developed indigenous concepts to suit its military strategy (Thomas 2004; Thomas 2007). Sweeping reforms were carried out to establish a fully networked architecture capable of coordinating military operations on land, in air, at sea, in space and across the entire electromagnetic spectrum. Their overarching cyber policy has been guided by the doctrine of fighting "Local War under Informationized Conditions" (Krekel 2009). Informatization requires the armed forces to be more "dynamic, flexible, effective, creative and forward looking" (Thomas 2009). This policy provides the operational framework to the highly trained PLA units engaging in offensive IOs (Paganini 2013). The acquired cyber skills are being sharpened by conducting cyber drills (*Want China Times*, July 4, 2013). China's cyber army is estimated to have more than 100,000 people working for it, with an annual budget of over US$2.71 million (Goldman 2013). The 4th Department of PLA is responsible for Electronic Countermeasures (ECM), while CND and intelligence gathering responsibilities likely belong to the 3rd Department (Signals Intelligence) (Krekel 2009). Reportedly the 2nd Bureau, commonly known as Unit 61398, poses an Advanced Persistent Threat1 (APT1) to US computer networks (Mcwhorter 2013). Western media claims that the Chinese cyber-attacks have expanded beyond the government targets to energy sector corporations (Perlroth 2013), universities (Pérez-Peña 2013), and influential newspapers like the *New York Times* (Perlroth 2013).

In order to cool cyber tempers, the US and China are now talking about the subject in high-level talks (Deutschewelle 2013). Due to differing perceptions, progress is slow but there are indications that they may cooperate on subjects like fighting cybercrime (*Beijing International*) (Government 2013). They could begin by jointly tackling common threats like 'spam' or unsolicited bulk electronic messages sent indiscriminately (Stojanovski 2013). In a summit meeting held in June 2013 the Chinese and the US Presidents agreed that they "needed to develop better military-to-military relations and improve cyber security cooperation" (Service 2013). Cyber security was again on the top of the agenda, when top Chinese and American cabinet level officials met during the annual Strategic and Economic Dialogue in July 2013 in Washington DC. The meeting began on an unfavorable note as accusations were traded about intellectual property theft and large scale digital surveillance. This was in stark contrast to the serious and meaningful meeting held between Chinese and the US cyber experts, two days ahead of the Strategic Dialogue. Many regard this meeting as real progress (Sanger 2013).

While the US and China vie for cyber dominance, the Russians are not far behind. To offset the pervasive US digital surveillance, the Russians want tighter controls over the Internet (Kramer 2013). They are also busy improving the cyber capabilities. In February this year, the Russian Defense Minister Sergei Shoigu instructed the General Staff to complete proposals to set up an army cyber command by the end of 2013 (Lvov 2013). However, since the US and Russia have a long standing tradition of concluding bilateral nuclear arms limitation and reduction treaties dating back to the Cold War, they appear less hesitant in matters concerning cyber cooperation. After their meeting on the sidelines of the G8 summit in Ireland on June 15, 2013, the presidents of Russia and the US announced landmark steps to improve cyber-security, including establishing a communications link to exchange information about computer incidents of national security concern. In a joint statement they pledged to create information sharing mechanisms like secure communication channels between national Computer Emergency Response Teams (CERTs). In order to promptly exchange information related to Information and Communications Technologies (ICT) with the aim of reducing tension, the two presidents agreed to authorize the use of the existing direct communications link between their Nuclear Risk Reduction Centers (NRRCs) to resolve cyber tensions (Defense 2012), and to establish a direct communication link between high-level cyber officials. Furthermore, a bilateral working group was constituted for consultations on cyber-security related issues. This cyber group was tasked to "assess emerging threats, elaborate, propose and coordinate concrete joint measures to address such threats as well as strengthen confidence" (Novosti 2013). Despite this promising beginning the cyber relations between the two countries are currently stalled on account of the asylum that the Russians have granted to the American cyber defector (*New York Times* August 7, 2015).

Cyber-attacks can pose a major decision making dilemma for the victim, in case of a complete breakdown in communication. The US stance to handle such a situation is quite clear. The *International Strategy for Cyber Space* (2011), unambiguously states that the USG reserves the right to "respond to hostile acts in cyberspace," as it "would to any other threat" (House 2011). The Pentagon's Defense Science Board (DSB) believes that China and Russia can develop capabilities to launch an existential cyber-attack:

capable of **causing sufficient wide scale damage for the government potentially to lose control of the country**, *including loss or damage to significant portions of military and critical infrastructure: power generation, communications, fuel and transportation, emergency services, financial services, etc (Ingersoll 2013).*

Senior US security managers feel that a 'cyber Pearl Harbor' is a distinct possibility (Shanker 2012). A 2011 Pentagon report to the Congress, describes a hostile cyber-attack as one directed against the economy, government or military, requiring a response using electronic or conventional military options (Alexander 2011). The officials do not rule out the threat of use of nuclear weapons to deter cyber-attacks (Andreasen 2013). Under the US Constitution, it is the prerogative of the president, as commander in chief of the armed forces, to decide if a cyber-attack is considered sufficiently serious to be declared a hostile act, and thus an act of war. However, it is a moot point as to what kind of cyber-attack could prompt a response and what might be its form and intensity? The Pentagon has recently updated the rules of military engagement for cyber warfare for the first time in seven years, and developed emergency procedures to guide rapid responses to attacks having serious national security or economic consequences (Richardson 2013; Shanker 2013).

The US President Policy Directive (PDP) 20 of October 2012 addresses issues like responses to a cyber-attack (*The Guardian*, June 7, 2013). It explains that the use of cyber weapons would need presidential approval, in case of significant damage like "loss of life, serious levels of retaliation, damage to property, adverse foreign policy consequences or economic impact on the country."As per PDP 20 the Defensive Cyber Effects Operations (DCEO) and the Offensive Cyber Effects Operations (OCEO) are intended to advance US national objectives globally "with little or no warning to the adversary or target and with potential effects ranging from subtle to severely damaging" (*Washington Post,* June 17, 2013). The US policymakers remain alert to the possibility of hostile cyber-attacks. The Fact Sheet issued by the White House regarding the Nuclear Weapon Employment Strategy has codified "an alternative approach to hedging against technical or geopolitical risk, which will lead to more effective management of the nuclear weapons stockpile" (House 2013). Technical risk, in other words, may be construed as a cyber-attack.

The urge to react strongly against a cyber-attack is not new. In early 1998, during a buildup of forces to mount a three day bombing campaign in the Middle East, the US DOD discovered that intruders had broken into numerous secure computers and had obtained 'root access,' allowing them to potentially steal and alter information or damage their networks. The Iraqi government was suspected of sponsoring this subversive activity. When the case was presented to President Clinton both cyber and kinetic countermeasures were considered. An armed response was finally ruled out after it was discovered that a couple of American teenagers and their Israeli mentor were responsible for the mischief (Perrow 2007; Healy 2013).

How would countries, with less developed cyber policies, react to cyber-attacks is largely unknown. What for instance would they do in case their C2 systems are knocked out? How long would they take to respond? Would they take it as a signal to automatically launch their nuclear tipped missiles? How would the launch orders be passed? Would combatant commanders be allowed to launch nuclear weapons as per their own discretion? How would the unsuspecting population be informed about the impending nuclear holocaust? Would the emergency services be ready to handle the situation? What would be the alternate lines of communication to speak with the adversary to get out of a potentially no-win situation? It is reasonable to assume that fallback options would be limited and unpredictable owing to the fog of war. If irrational or erratic cyber behavior goes unregulated, military and non-military cyber-attacks may become an uncontrollable phenomenon in times to come. The confusion in information space is likely to be exacerbated because of the activities of the non-state actors. Not only is there a need to develop reliable measures to protect the national C^2 systems but also to develop a code of conduct among nations to reduce cyber risks. A robust national and international regulatory mechanism can be bolstered through mutually agreed CBMs. This would reduce ambiguity, eradicate doubt and suspicion and improve international cooperation. Such arrangements should increase stability in inter-state relations in military as well as civilian areas, reduce the possibility of cyber conflict and create mechanisms to prevent situations of tension (Lewis 2011).

Information Space CBMs in South Asia

Traditionally South Asia has been a potential conflict zone. The root of disharmony lies in the hasty partition of the South Asian subcontinent in 1947 (Wolpert 2006). Intractable issues like the Kashmir dispute bedevil the relations of the two countries. Since 1998, South Asia has become a veritable nuclear battlefield. Over the years, both India and Pakistan have entered into treaties, agreements and understandings to defuse tensions and prevent wars. One early model of successful negotiations to resolve the issue of the division of water resources was the Indus Basin Treaty of 1960 (Kux 2006; Abbasi 2012). The fragile stability in the region is maintained through an extensive CBM regime. CBMs are a step below formal treaty agreements. These are important means to reduce the risk of conventional and nuclear wars (Hilali 2005). India-Pakistan CBMs have been developed both in military and non-military spheres(Zulfqar 2013). In order to improve the existing mechanism a structured dialogue process was initiated after the meeting of Prime Ministers Nawaz Sharif and I.K. Gujral on the sidelines of the 9th summit of South Asian Association for Regional Cooperation (SAARC) held in Male, the capital of Maldives in 1997. Since then this process has survived a number of crises and continues to sputter along. It broadly covers eight areas (Padder 2012), namely Peace and Security including CBMs, Jammu and Kashmir, Siachen, Wullar Barrage Project/Tulbul Navigation Project, Sir Creek, Terrorism and Drug Trafficking, Economic and Commercial, Cooperation and Promotion of Friendly Exchanges in various fields (Ghosh 2009). The leaders, officials and experts of the two countries regularly meet to improve and add to the existing basket of CBMs (Center n.d). The 7th round of expert-level talks on nuclear CBMs was held in New Delhi in December 2012 (*Zee News* December, 28 2012). Unfortunately cyber security CBMs have never been on the menu of Pakistan-India dialogue.

More worrisome is the fact that the world is getting increasingly suspicious of cyber threats emerging from South Asia. In a statement the US Foreign Affairs Sub-committee on Asia and the Pacific warned that Asia was fast becoming "the cyber security battleground." It was suggested that cyber chain needed to be strengthened by engaging allies, notably India to counter "threats emanating from Pakistan" (Chabot 2013). While, Indians noted with satisfaction the strong pitch the congressman made about the India-US cyber security partnership (Mehdudia 2013), the Pakistanis consider the statement that their country is being considered the weakest link with trepidation. They also fear being isolated in the cyber domain. Cyber mistrust exists in South Asia and will likely aggravate if international cyber battle lines are drawn in the region.

South Asia took most readily to Internet revolution by adopting a wide array of commercially available ICT for managing businesses and private affairs but unfortunately did not do enough to improve the regional cybersecurity environment. Most of its public and private concerns are now digitally linked to the international system and the militaries are in the process of establishing networked C^2 systems. The Indian armed forces have invested heavily in developing net-centric capabilities since the 1980s (India 2013), and are now lobbying for a separate cyber-command (Now 2012). Pakistan tested its fully automated Strategic Command & Control Support System (SCCSS) in November 2012 (ISPR 2012), and its nuclear safety regime caters to cyber threats (*The News* July 10, 2013). The potential of cyber warfare remains because a growing community of cyber warriors in India and Pakistan are actively engaged in defacing government websites (Yusha 2010), in a spirit of patriotic 'hacktivism' without formal sanction (Rouse n.d). Needless to say, this kind of unregulated behavior can cause unnecessary tensions in an already fragile relationship.

Even before the dawn of the digital age both India and Pakistan were aware of the pitfalls of unrestrained information space activity. The need to curb hostile propaganda was recorded in the first government level negotiations between the two states. Article C (8) of the Liaquat-Nehru Agreement of 1950 made it incumbent upon the two governments to

Not permit propaganda in either country directed against the territorial integrity of the other or purporting to incite war between them and shall take prompt and effective action against any individual or organization guilty of such propaganda (Agreement 1950).

As part of the Tashkent (1965) and Simla (1972) Agreements both countries "agreed to 'discourage' and 'prevent' any hostile propaganda directed against each other and 'encourage' the dissemination of such information as would promote the bilateral friendly relations" (ed 2001). Since no monitoring or enforcement mechanisms were enforced, hostile propaganda never ceased. In fact it has increased disproportionately during times of tension, making the situation more combustible.(Sarwar 2013).

There are a number of examples to substantiate this theory. For instance in the first 12 hours after Mumbai attacks on November 26, 2008, "the volume of information and misinformation" grew exponentially – "much of it drawn from social media messages" (Kreppon 2012). Two days later, the two countries almost went to war, when the Pakistani President received a telephone call purportedly from India's External Affairs Minister warning him that his country was about to launch a military response (Times 2008). Pakistan took immediate defensive measures. The air force was placed on high alert and all important countries of the world were informed about these developments (Kreppon 2012). A very flustered US Secretary of State immediately placed a call on her Indian counterpart, whose delayed response caused panic at her end (Rice 2011). She then undertook a visit to South Asia to advise India to exercise restraint (Rice 2011). According to American diplomats in New Delhi one senior official of the Indian Ministry of External Affairs (MEA) had confirmed to them that the call had indeed been made. There were subsequent denials and the entire affair was dismissed as a prank (Nelson 2011).

Another incident that raised tensions between India and Pakistan was the outbreak of ethnic violence in the North Eastern Indian state of Assam in July and August of 2012. Clashes between the indigenous Bodo tribes and Muslim migrants from Bangladesh resulted in killing, violence and internal displacement. Troops were called in to maintain law and order. A rumor soon making the rounds that Bodos living elsewhere in India would be killed after the Muslim holy month of Ramzan, coinciding August 20. This hate campaign was fuelled by sending bulk SMS and MMS over the cell phones and through indiscriminate use of social media platforms like the Facebook. As the rumor mill spun out of control the Bodos fled *en masse* for their native homes, choking the local transport system (Rebello 2012). The Indian government reacted by ordering the telecom services to limit the use of SMS to five per person and the transmission of data beyond 20 KB was banned for 15 days (*The Times of India*, August 18 2012). The Indian businesses rely heavily on cell phone advertisements and suffered massive losses. On the international front India quickly accused Pakistan for sponsoring the unrest (Edward 2012). The Government of Pakistan (GOP) asked India to come up with credible proof (*BBC News*, August 20, 2012). The matter rested there and after the customary period of mutual indignation it was business as usual.

Almost a month later violence broke out in Pakistan over a sacrilegious movie clip uploaded on YouTube. 20 people died and public and private property worth millions of rupees was damaged. Police had a hard time restraining the crowds from storming the US embassy. The repercussions were so severe that President Obama and Secretary Clinton had to make public announcements that the USG had nothing to do with the blasphemous movie (*Al Jazeera*, September 22, 2012). The Pakistani government banned YouTube. The ban continues to-date (Siddique 2013). It has yet to be determined if the movie was uploaded on purpose to provoke religious sentiments and to incite anti US feelings.

Not only countries like India or Pakistan, experience turbulence, when unsubstantiated rumors maliciously or inadvertently go viral. This phenomenon is experienced in other countries as well. On April

23, 2013, a message on the Associated Press Twitter account claimed that two explosions had shaken the White House. Within seven minutes, the Dow Jones Industrial Average dropped by 150 points destroying billions of dollars in value. The tweet was quickly exposed as bogus, the result of hacking by a group identifying itself as the Syrian Electronic Army (SEA). The Dow recovered immediately but the lesson was clear – A single tweet can cause major economic disruption (Rasmussen 2013). This was not the last of the shenanigans of the SEA. On August 15, 2013, the *Washington Post* reported that it had been hacked by none other than the dreaded SEA(Peterson 2013).

These incidents reminds one of the nationwide panic caused in the US after the radio broadcast of H.G. Wells famous fantasy *The War of the Worlds* in 1938 (*New York Times*, October 31, 1998). The power of the social media to perpetuate the rumors is unlimited. If the content is malicious the rumor mill can cause mayhem. A scare can be created about a nuclear attack causing panic in the public or false reports generated to undermine launch notification or nuclear accident agreements can trigger unexpected responses at the decision making levels. Therefore, there is an urgent need to develop an agreed framework for building confidence and trust in information space. A cyber-hotline could be a good way of mitigating disasters created by the malicious spread of dubious information. The US and the Russian Federation are actively considering upgrading their NRRC communication link (State n.d), for cooperating on matters related to cyber security (Nakashima 2012). Similar options are on the table to reduce Sino-US cyber tensions (Segal 2011). The suggestion that Pakistan and India establish their own NRRC has been suggested in the past (Khan 2003).

Thesis and Research Proposal

This study looks at the problem of unchecked cyber activity both from the international as well as the regional perspective. It posits that unregulated behavior in cyberspace can lead to inadvertent wars. Since, consensus is lacking on how, much freedom or control should be exercised in an agreed international information order; it theorizes that cyber-differences can be narrowed to create a stable cyber environment can be created by instituting an information space CBM regime. Based on the experiences of developing CBMs in South Asia, this paper proposes a range of bilateral trust building measures in information space to avert a war triggered by unscrupulous cyber-behavior.

The following questions formed the basis of the research:

Q.1 What is 'acceptable' behavior in information-space?
Q.2 What are the international, regional, non-governmental, private and public initiatives to bring about order in the cyberspace?
Q.3 Is there a model for CBMs in information space?
Q.4 What could be a set of mutually acceptable information-space CBMs between India and Pakistan?
Q.5 What is the way forward?

Literature Review

This research covered diverse areas ranging from cyber security to international law and CBMs. So I had to consult multiple sources of information and subject experts. Some of these books and papers are listed below:

National Cyber Security Policies and Threat Assessments. A number of US cyber policy documents are available online e.g. the National Security Presidential Directive (NSPD) 54/Homeland Security Presidential Directive 23, Cybersecurity Policy (January 2008) and the 2006 Joint Staff National Military Strategy for Cyberspace Operations (NMS-CO) (Publication 2006), the Comprehensive National Cybersecurity Initiative (CNCI) of 2008 and 2010 (House (n.d)), the Cyberspace Policy Review (May 2009) (Whitehouse n.d), the Presidential Policy Directive (PPD) 20 on US Cyber Operations Policy (EPIC n.d), and the International Strategy for Cyber Space (2011). According to the US National Security Council (NSC) key documents guiding their policies on cyber security are the Draft National Strategy for Trusted Identities in Cyberspace, the CNCI, the Cyberspace Policy Reviews and supporting documents, the National Initiative for Cybersecurity Education and the Cybersecurtiy R&D (Whitehouse n.d).

Timothy Thomas's book *Cyber Silhouettes* is used as a standard textbook on IOs in US military colleges and provides interesting insights into how cyber threats are assessed (Thomas 2005). Thomas has also written extensively about the evolution and formulation of Chinese strategic cyber thought. His books have been published by the Foreign Military Studies Office (FMSO) Fort Leavenworth (Thomas 2009). Some thought-provoking information about the future of cyber war is available in Defense Advance Research Projects Agency (DARPA)'s Foundational CyberWarfare Plan-X: The Roadmap for Future Cyber War (Dieterle 2012).

The concepts of cyber war have been elaborated in papers written by experts like Amir Lupovici (Lupovici 2011), and Shmuel Even and David Siman-Tov (Siman-Tov 2012). *Cyber Attacks* by Edward Amoroso provides guidelines in protecting national infrastructures from cyber-attacks (Amoroso 2011). Similar solutions are given in Charles Perrow's book *The Next Catastrophe* (Perrow 2007).

Papers read out at the UNIDIR conference held in Geneva in November 2012 give the national point of views on cyber security and stability of countries like Germany (Wolter 2012), Canada (Hurwitz 2012), India (Gill 2012), and Russia (Fedosov 2012). Indian point of view is also available at the IDSA website (Arvind Gupta 2012). The aforementioned paper indicates that Indian policymakers are in favor of cyber CBMs. A range of cyber CBMs are given in papers authored by Mathias Mielmonka of the German MoD (Miellmonka 2012), John B. Sheldon of Canada Centre for Global Security Studies, University of Toronto (Sheldon 2012), Dave Clemente of Chatham House (Clemente 2012), and Kwon Haeryong, the Ambassador of Republic of Korea to the Conference on Disarmament Permanent Mission (Haeryong 2012).

International Law and Cyber Norms. The applicability of international law is comprehensively covered in the *Tallinn Manual on the International Law Applicable to Cyber Warfar* (Schmitt 2013), and US Department of State's legal advisor Harold Koh's speech on "International Law in Cyber Space" (Koh 2012). A critical analysis of the two documents by Michael N. Schmitt makes for an interesting reading (Schmitt 2012). The need to revise federal laws to provide cyber security has been covered in some detail by Eric A. Fischer (Fischer 2012).

Ambassador Ahmed Kamal, a Pakistani diplomat has produced two monographs regarding developing international cyber norms and laws. The first one, which he co-authored with Eduardo Gelbstein, is titled *Information Insecurity: A Survival Guide to the Uncharted Territories of Cyber-threats and Cybersecurity* (Kamal 2002). A sequel to this book is *The Law of Cyber-Space: An Invitation to the Table of Negotiations* (Kamal 2007). Other works that provide important pointers in this respect are "The Law of Cyber-Attack" (Oona A. Hathaway 2012), "Cyberwarfare and International Law" (Melser 2011), "Cyberattacks and the Use of Force: Back to the Future of Article 2(4)" (Waxman 2011), "The legal application of the prohibition of the threat or use of force in cyberspace: A starting point?"(Arimatsu

2012). A good idea of how the various bodies within the UN are shaping international cyber norms can be obtained from an article that Tim Maurer wrote for the Belfer Center in 2011 (Maurer 2011).

CBMs in South Asia. A number of papers and books have been written on CBMs in South Asia. South Asian scholars have written substantially on this topic e.g. Moonis Ahmer (Ahmer 1997), Feroz Hasan Khan (Khan 2010), Naeem Salik (Salik 1998), Zafar Nawaz Jaspal (Jaspal 2004), Maleeha Lodhi (Lodhi 2012), Kanti Bajpai and Dipanker Banerjee (Bajpai 1999). Another paper that provides useful inputs has been written by Toby Dalton of the Stimson Center (Dalton 2013). So far there has been no work on developing info based CBMs between India and Pakistan.

Organization of the Paper

This paper is organized into four parts. The first section discusses international initiatives to create cyber norms and behavior. The second section takes stock of the existing domestic and international cyber laws and treaties. The third portion studies existing models of CBMs in information space and the final portion suggests a menu of info-based CBMs that can be developed between India and Pakistan. The last section recommends a way forward.

PART I: INTERNATIONAL INITIATIVES TO CREATE CYBER NORMS AND BEHAVIOR

Human society is governed by a host of rules and regulations. Informally these are traditional customs and norms based on social, moral and ethical codes. At spiritual and official levels there are canons, commandments, decrees, dogmas, doctrines, laws, regulations, rules and tenets formally enshrined in religious scriptures, penal codes and state constitutions. At the interstate level activities are regulated and governed by a comprehensive set of international laws and conventions. Irrespective of the fact that at times countries tend to violate these edicts and even get away with it, standardized conventional norms and behavior lie at the heart of international relations. In order to make all transactions legitimate and acceptable, a host of international laws and conventions have been created. This urge to regulate all human activity extends into the realm ICT.

Arguably the modern information age began with the advent of the electrical telegraph in 1837 (Standage 2007). The first electronic language was the Morse code – a simple method of dots and dashes, to relay instant information. The first trans-Atlantic telegraphic message was conveyed in 1858 (New York 1879). The transatlantic telegraph cables have since been replaced by transatlantic telecommunications cables. Telegraph was followed by more novel and secure methods to carry sound as well as image in real time through line, wireless and satellites. The development in technology was complemented by laws to control and regulate these new media of transmitting information. Whereas stringent censorship rules were invoked by governments during times of war and internal strife to protect or isolate their citizens from hostile propaganda, clear cut laws were also developed at the national and international levels to regulate the use of telegraphy and telephony, radio, print and electronic media. Unregulated use of these media, it was feared, could spell chaos and anarchy. Although the Internet has allowed boundless to access and transmit information, no international law has so far been created to regulate cyber activity. Paradoxically, notwithstanding the inherent dangers of cyber terrorism, the digitally advanced countries feel that unfettered access to Internet is good for commerce and therefore, it should be left as it is.

Legality of Cyber-Attacks

An unprotected information space is an open invitation for not only criminals and ideologues but also for nation states to launch cyber-attacks on the sly, without any a formal declaration of war. There has been a debate within the legal community, whether IW operations are covered by the classic definition of Law of War aka Law of Armed Conflict or the International Humanitarian Law (IHL) (Ellis 2001). Unfortunately "the existing legal norms do not offer a clear and comprehensive framework within which states can shape policy responses to the threat of hostile cyber operations" (Schmitt 2010). The argument revolves around a number of issues like what justifies the use of force, how to determine the attribution of the attack and what should be the proportionality of response? Since all cyber-attacks are not state sponsored and are in certain instances the handiwork of sundry freelancers and loose cannons, criminals and terrorists, hence it is legally not possible to pin the blame on a state party. Not at least in the short term. The law of war specifies that the initial attack must be attributed before a counterattack is permitted (Kostadinov 2013). Article 2(4) of the UN Charter explicitly states that "All Members shall refrain in their international relations from the threat or use of force against the territorial integrity or political independence of any state, or in any other manner inconsistent with the Purposes of the United Nations." This, however, does not deny them the right of self-defense under the provisions of *jus in bello* (the international law governing the resort to force by States) and *jus ad bellum* (international law regulating the conduct of armed conflict) (Aldrich 1996; Yurcik 1997; ICRC 2004; Shackelford 2009; Willson 2009), under the principles of proportionality, distinction, and neutrality (Melzer 2011). This begs the question, whether cyber warfare fulfills these conditions? One school of thought believes that cyberspace remains outside the jurisdiction of International Law, while the other is convinced that this is not the case. One strong proponent of the opposing school of thought is Harold Koh, the legal expert of the US State Department. Koh has built an impressive case of justifying that cyber-attacks and cyber counter attacks are governed by international law by answering a set of ten frequently asked questions (Koh 2012). The International Group of Experts hired to draft the *Tallinn Manual* for NATO's Cooperative Cyber Defense Center of Excellence also concur with Koh's version that force can be used in cyberspace under the internationally accepted principles of *jus ad bellum* and *jus ad bello* (Schmidt 2013).

Opinion is also divided about the lethality of cyber weapons (Casey-Maslen 2010; Fulghum 2010). Lethal literally means an activity causing death. High profile cyber-attacks have incapacitated government servers in Georgia, halted banking operations in Estonia and interrupted and delayed Iranian nuclear program (Lindsay 2013), without killing anyone. Therefore, anonymous cyber-attackers do not fit the conventional description of a combatant or someone guilty of war crimes. Deaths in combat can be justified and crimes against humanity like genocide can be persecuted under the Rome statute by the International Criminal Court (ICC) (Court 2002). In the absence of death and destruction and lack of proof with regards attribution, a physical response is difficult to justify. The situation may change if there are casualties as a direct or indirect consequence of a cyber-attack. One can argue that a lethal assault supported by computer technology can be construed as an act of war. So far, this line of thinking has not been pursued against deadly predator strikes in Pakistan using a computer network in Nevada (Oona A. Hathaway 2012).

The use of remotely controlled surveillance planes has been justified as legitimate intelligence gathering exercise and the airspace violations, where these occurred, have been conveniently regretted as inadvertent. A case in point is the US drone that was brought down by the Iranians. On 4th December 2011 Iran announced that it had forced a Lockheed Martin RQ-170 Sentinel unmanned aerial vehicle

(UAV) to land on its territory. The initial American reaction was that the drone had crashed on a recon accident (Starr 2011). The Iranians were able to show the UAV intact. They claimed to have jammed both satellite and land control signals to the UAV, and followed it up by a spoofing attack. The false GPS data fed to the UAV led it into believing that it was landing at its homebase in Afghanistan (Peterson 2011). Since there were no human casualties involved in the accident, the reaction on both sides remained muted. However, things can get serious, if the country being spied upon retaliates against the infringement of its sovereign airspace with disproportionate physical means.

Cyber-attacks are generally aimed against computer systems. It is, however, impossible to separate cybercrime from state sponsored cyber-attacks. Both are overlapping activities because states, criminals and non-state actors all use the same toolkit. Cybercrime broadly refers to illegal activities on computer networks directed against individuals, organizations and governments. It can cause huge losses to common citizens and businesses and can cripple governments and nations. This poses serious challenges to domestic and international law enforcement agencies. The existing laws are not strong enough to seriously curb criminal activity in cyberspace. The threat is enormous and requires unified international legislation and enforcement mechanisms. General countermeasures have been adopted by some governments and organizations to prevent criminal activity in cyber space. This includes legislation and technical measures to track down online crimes, Internet content control, using public or private proxy and computer forensics, encryption and plausible deniability etc. The problem is that each country follows its own set of rules and regulations for dealing with cybercrimes. These laws need to be harmonized into an international regime and relevant provisions and clauses are incorporated into domestic legal codes (Prasad 2012).

Although governments are actively focusing on fighting and preventing cyber criminals from damaging infrastructure, the very nature of cyberspace poses a number of challenges i.e. cyberspace has no political borders and the methods of the cyber-criminal community are continuously evolving, making it more challenging and difficult for governments and companies to keep pace with them. Some 82 countries have signed and/or ratified one of the binding cybercrime instruments. Some countries are members of more than one such instrument. The Council of Europe (CE) Cybercrime Convention (CEC) has the largest number of signatures or ratifications/accessions i.e. 48 countries, including five non-member states. Other instruments have smaller geographic scope e.g. the League of Arab States Convention (18 countries or territories), the Commonwealth of Independent States (CIS) Agreement (10 countries), and the SCO Agreement (6 countries). If signed or ratified by all member states of the African Union (AU), the Draft AU Convention could have up to 54 countries or territories (UNODC 2013). The list of major international and regional instruments on cyber security is given towards the end of this paper.

INTERNATIONAL INITIATIVES

Legal difficulties like affixing culpability and differentiating between cybercrime and cyber-attacks notwithstanding, a number of international and regional instruments have been formulated to promote cyber security and prevent counter cybercrime. These include binding and non-binding instruments. A table listing these instruments on cyber security is given towards the end of this study. Five groups active in creating cyber norms are the CE and the European Union (EU), the CIS and the SCO, inter-governmental African organizations, the League of Arab States, and the UN (UNODC 2013). These initiatives are no doubt motivated by international obligations from not interfering "in any form or for any reason whatsoever in the internal and external affairs of other States" (Justice 1949; UN 1965; UN

1981; Justice 1986). However, the cooperation in cyber security is proceeding at a slow pace. Some of the international initiatives in developing cyber norms are listed below:

The UN

Under Article 11 of its Charter, the UN General Assembly (UNGA) has the mandate to consider general principles of cooperation in the maintenance of international peace and security, including the principles governing disarmament and the regulation of armaments, and makes recommendations to the member states or to the UN Security Council (UNSC). Discussions and decisions at the UNGA on disarmament and international security issues have led to significant developments. The Disarmament and International Security Committee aka the First Committee and the UN Disarmament Commission (UNDC) are two subsidiary bodies dedicated to disarmament issues. Two more bodies namely the UN Institute for Disarmament Research (UNIDIR) and the Advisory Board on Disarmament Matters also deal with disarmament issues. Additionally, the UNGA receives inputs from a number of reporting mechanisms and Groups of Government Experts (GGEs) (UNGA n.d). The 1st Committee explicitly deals with disarmament, global challenges and threats to peace that affect the international community and seeks solutions to the challenges in the international security regime (Nations n.d).

UNGA Resolutions on Cyber Security. The Assembly is only empowered to make non-binding recommendations on international issues within its competence. It has nonetheless, initiated a number of political, economic, humanitarian, social and legal action, affecting the lives of millions of people throughout the world (Nations n.d). With reference to international security, the UNGA has passed a number of resolutions on cyber security. There is no evidence to suggest that the subject has been raised within the UNSC – the highest body within the global organization. The Russian Federation first introduced a draft resolution on information security in the First Committee in 1998 (UNODA n.d). This resolution was based on the agenda item "Developments in Telecommunications and Information in the context of International Security" and was adopted without a vote as UNGA Resolution 53/70 (June 30-July 2, 1999) (UN 1999; Westby 2004). Since then there have been three annual reports on the subject (2010, 2011 and 2012) incorporating the views of the member states have been published. Two related resolutions were passed by the Second Committee (UNGA n.d), on the "Creation of a Global Culture of Cyber-Security and the Protection of Critical Informational Infrastructures" (UNGA 2003), and "Creation of a Global Culture of Cyber-Security and Taking Stock of National Efforts to Protect Critical Information Infrastructures" (UNGA 2010). The 2nd Committee essentially deals with global economic and financial issues.

In August 1999, the UNIDIR organized an international meeting of experts in Geneva to consider the security implications of emerging IT (Nations 2012). Its conclusions were included in UNGA Resolution 57/53, which called upon member states to further consider and discuss information security issues and provide relevant inputs (UNGA 2002). The resolution also called for a new study of international informational security issues, but there was little action on it (UNGA 2002). Similar exhortations in subsequent UNGA sessions failed to produce any meaningful progress (UNGA 2002; UNGA 2003; UNGA 2004; UNGA 2005; UNGA 2006; UNGA 2008; UNGA 2010).

The UN Group of Governmental Experts (GGEs) on Information Security. In 2004, the UNGA first formed a 15 member GGE to examine existing and potential threats from the cyber-sphere and suggest possible cooperative measures to address them. This Group could not come to an agreement on matters like the impact of developments in ICT on national security and military affairs issues and the question whether the discussion should address issues of information content or focus only on information infrastructures. There was particular disagreement regarding the claim that trans-border information content should be controlled as a matter of national security. Other areas of disagreement arose on proposals for capacity-building and technology transfer to developing countries (UNODA 2013; UN n.d).

In July 2010, the second GGE, which included cyber security specialists from major cyber-powers like the US, China, and Russia, submitted a set of recommendations for "building the international framework for security and stability that these new technologies require" (UN 2010). In the foreword to the 2010 GGE Report, the UN Secretary General (UNSG) highlighted the need for further dialogue on the issue of information security and the need to develop 'common perspectives.' The Report itself stressed on the need for dialogue to discuss norms pertaining to state use of ICT, to reduce collective risk and protect critical national and international infrastructure; confidence-building, stability and risk reduction measures to address the implications of state use of ICT, including exchanges of national views on the use of ICT in conflict; information exchanges on national legislation and national information and communications technologies security strategies and technologies, policies and best practices; identification of measures to support capacity-building in less developed countries; and finding possibilities to elaborate common terms and definitions relevant to UNGA Resolution 64/25 (UNODA n.d). The Report had also recommended the need to find possibilities to elaborate common terms and definitions (UNODA 2013). These recommendations represent progress in overcoming a long impasse between the US and Russia on cyber security issues and could become the basis of a multilateral treaooty under the auspices of the UN, which Russia has been advocating (Markoff 2010).

The inputs of the member states were included in the UNGA resolution 66/24, which called for the formation of a new GGE in 2012. The new GGE was asked to continue studying existing and potential threats in the sphere of information security and possible cooperative measures to address them, taking into account the assessments and recommendations contained in the last report. This GGE was tasked to report to the 68th session of the UNGA scheduled in September 2013 (UNGA 2011). The third GGE has met thrice so far – once in 2012 and twice in 2013. Members include Argentina, Australia (Chair), Belarus, Canada, China, Egypt, Estonia, France, Germany, India, Indonesia, Japan, Russia, UK and USA (UNODA n.d). Apparently countries like Germany and India are favorably inclined towards information space CBMs (Ministry of Foreign Affairs 2011; Gupta 2012). Pakistan has clearcut policy position on this subject. Speaking before the 68th session of the UN General Assembly the Pakistani representative declared that "the hostile use of cyber technologies can indeed be characterized as weapons of mass destruction and disruption" and called for their use to be regulated sooner than later (Meyer 2013).

The GGE meeting held in June 2013 agreed that CBMs, such as "high-level communication and timely information sharing, can enhance trust and assurance among states and help reduce the risk of conflict by increasing predictability and reducing misperception." The Group agreed on the "vital importance of capacity-building to enhance global cooperation in securing cyberspace" and the requirement of an open and accessible cyberspace. It was thought that a combination of all these efforts would support a more secure cyberspace. Most importantly the Group affirmed that "international law, especially the UN Charter, applies in cyberspace" (Psaki 2013).

International Code of Conduct on Information Security. On September 12, 2011 China, Russia, Tajikistan and Uzbekistan proposed an international code of conduct on information security to the UNSG. The document discussed security challenges posed to the international community in cyberspace and recommended responsibilities of states in protecting information and cyber-networks, calling upon states to respect domestic laws and sovereignty. It also called for a multilateral approach within the framework of the UN to establish international norms and settle disputes concerning cyberspace. The proposal was discussed within the First Committee but drew sharp criticism from the US officials, who saw it as an exercise in undermining their efforts to keep the Internet free from external interference (Farnsworth n.d). The proposal favored states voluntarily pledging not to use ICTs including networks "to carry out hostile activities or acts of aggression, pose threats to international peace and security or proliferate information weapons or related technologies" (University n.d).

The issue was brought directly in front of the UNGA, on September 21, 2011 by the President of Kazakhstan Nursultan Nazarbayev, who stressed the need for an information and cyber-security pact to deter frequent attacks by hackers against governments, businesses and other institutions. He underlined the need for "an international legal framework of the global information space" based on the nine elements of a global culture of cybersecurity, which the Assembly had adopted in 2002 (Centre 2011).

UN Bodies on Cyber Security. The issue of developing cyber security norms at the UN broadly falls into two areas i.e. cyber warfare and cybercrime. The first one concerns the political-military stream and the other one the economic stream. The organizational platforms dealing with the political-military issues are the International Telecommunication Union (ITU), UNIDIR and Counter-Terrorism Implementation Task Force (CTITF) Working Group. The organizations tackling cybercrimes are the UN Office on Drug and Crime (UNODC) and the UN Interregional Crime and Justice Research Institute (UNICRI) (Maurer 2011). UNIDIR not only organizes conferences and participates in others; it also produces documents on disarmament (Vignard 2011).

UN ICT Task Force (TF) and the Global Alliance for ICT & Development (GAID). The UN ICT TF was set up in November 2001 to build broad-based partnerships, find the means to spread the benefits of the digital revolution in information and communication technologies and avert the prospect of a two-tiered World Information Society. The TF included multiple stake holders from the public and private sectors, civil society and the scientific community, and leaders of the developing and transition economies as well as the most technologically advanced economies. The UN ICT TF organized the World Summit on Information Society (WSIS) in 2005 but these two are separate processes. While, the WSIS could issue documents in the name of the global community, the ICT TF acted as a catalyst inside and outside the UN for ideas and partnerships for the Information Society It lacked the democratic legitimacy of WSIS. The mandate of the ICT TF ended in December 2005. The GAID can be considered, to some extent, as a successor to the UN ICT TF, but its composition is different. While the TF was composed of a limited number of persons selected by the UNSG, the GAID is an informal and open platform for all stakeholders interested in the Information Society (Union n.d).

ICT4Peace Project. This project was launched in 2004 after the publication of a book by the UN ICT TF on the practice and theory of ICT in the conflict cycle and peace building and the approval of paragraph 36 of the Tunis Commitment of the WSIS in 2005. ICT4Peace is primarily concerned with improving crisis information management by the international community through better use of ICT. It also advocates the use of ICTs in helping countries in conflict zones to achieve the UN Millennium Development Goals (MDG). Since 2006 the ICT4Peace project is serving as the hub for research, advocacy and networking on the use of ICT to prevent, respond to and recover from conflict (Education (n.d)). Besides NGOs such as the ICT4Peace and researchers like the Estonian IT specialist Eneken Tikk, have also provided rules of conduct in cyber space (Tikk 2011).

ITU. This Geneva based organization is a member of the UN Development Group (UNDG). It was originally founded as the International Telegraph Union and is now a specialized UN agency on ICT issues (ITU n.d). It is active in areas such as broadband Internet, latest-generation wireless technologies, aeronautical and maritime navigation, radio astronomy, satellite-based meteorology, convergence in fixed-mobile phone, Internet access, data, voice, TV broadcasting and next-generation networks. It coordinates the shared global use of the radio spectrum, promotes international cooperation in assigning satellite orbits, works to improve telecom infrastructure in the developing world, and assists in the development and coordination of worldwide technical standards. It has 193 Member States and around 700 Sector Members and Associates (Group n.d).

As a result of the Tunis WSIS of 2005, the ITU became the lead agency in coordinating international efforts as the sole facilitator of Action Line C5 i.e. "Building Confidence and Security in the use of ICTs" (ITU n.d). This was followed up by a UNGA resolution formalizing its role (UNGA 2006). In order to fulfill its mission the ITU has prepared an elaborate Global Cybersecurity Agenda (GCA) (Touré 2011). It has also revised and updated a 24 year old global telecommunications treaty. The new treaty was signed at an international conference in Dubai in December 2012. This treaty facilitates interconnection and interoperability of an efficient IT system and endorses information access to people with disability, assistance to developing countries in telecom development policies, and emphasize the right to freedom of expression over the ICT systems. It also aims to cut down e-waste, makes mobile roaming charges transparent to people, consistent number of users across the globe for the access of emergency services. Some issues, however, remain unresolved such as: network security, principles associated with unbiased sharing or access to other countries network, language barriers in the context of freedom of expression as outlined in the treaty. The US, UK, Australia and a few other major countries have rejected the treaty because of objections against centralizing the global governance model of regulations on Internet access and the available online content (Nagaraj 2013). This is symbolic of sharp differences of opinion on Internet governance between the developed countries and the developing world. Countries like Russia and China want more national oversights, while those in the former category want the Internet to be a free domain governed by voluntary standards set by the industry. It is widely believed that the Internet is already controlled to a degree by the US alone, and thus it draws the major advantages from its use. Other governments like China and Russia would like to have a greater control over online content and users, which they sometime see as threats to their national policies. They are also concerned about legitimate problems with access like spam and other issues. The terms of the new treaty gives the ITU an explicit role in regulating online content, specifically, spam and cybersecurity. This also extends the treaty's regulatory umbrella to Internet Service Providers (ISP). The ITU will meet again in 2014, when it may consider amending its constitution to formally assert jurisdiction over the technical side of the Web (*Los Angeles Times*, December 16, 2012). ITU has a number of cooperative agreements with other groups like Association of South East Asian Nations (ASEAN) and the Caribbean Community (CARICOM). The ITU has a joint project with the CARICOM and the Caribbean Telecommunications Union (CTU) known as Harmonization of ICT Policies, Legislation and Regulatory Policies in the Caribbean. Under the auspices of this project model legislative texts were prepared on Cybercrime/e-Crimes and Electronic Evidence in 2010 (ITU n.d).

Internet Governance Forum (IGF). There is no central authority controlling the Internet. It is a globally distributed network comprising many voluntarily interconnected autonomous networks. It operates without a central governing body with each constituent network setting and enforcing its own policies. Its governance is conducted by a decentralized and international multi-stakeholder network of interconnected autonomous groups drawing from civil society, the private sector, governments, the academic and research communities and national and international organizations. They work cooperatively from their respective roles to create shared policies and standards that maintain the Internet's global interoperability for public good. Internet governance includes the development and application of shared principles, norms, rules, decision-making procedures, and programs that shape the evolution and use of the Internet.

The IGF was established at the Tunis summit of the WSIS as a multi-stakeholder forum for policy dialogue on issues of Internet governance. It brings together all stakeholders in the Internet governance debate, whether they represent governments, the private sector or civil society, including the technical and academic community, on an equal basis and through an open and inclusive process (Forum n.d). The establishment of the IGF was formally announced by the UNSG in July 2006. It has since then been holding its annual sessions regularly. Its mission is to carry out non-binding conversation among stakeholders about the future of Internet governance. The term 'Internet governance' has been broadened beyond narrow technical concerns to include a wider range of Internet-related policy issues. The UN has also constituted a committee to update worldwide rules governing the Internet. The basic issue remains a tussle between the US and the Russian Federation about the extent of governmental controls over online content (Jones 2012). In April 2013 the second-in-command at the US DHS Jane Holl Lute was hired to write the Internet laws for the UN (More 2013).

Internet Corporation for Assigned Names and Numbers (ICANN), Internet Engineering Task Force (IETF) and Society for Worldwide Interbank Financial Tele- Communication (SWIFT)

The interoperability part of the Internet and several key technical and policy aspects of the underlying core infrastructure and the principal namespaces are administered by ICANN, a not for profit organization headquartered in Los Angeles, California. This body oversees the assignment of globally unique identifiers on the Internet, including Domain Names System (DNS), Internet Protocol (IP) addresses, application port numbers in the transport protocols, and many other parameters. This seeks to create a globally unified namespace to ensure the global reach of the Internet. The ICANN is governed by an international board of directors drawn from across the Internet's technical, business, academic, and other non-commercial communities. However, the National Telecommunications and Information Administration, an agency of the US Department of Commerce, continues to have final approval over changes to the DNS root zone. This authority over the root zone file makes ICANN one of a few bodies with global, centralized influence over the otherwise distributed Internet. Proposals are already being mooted to resolve the 15 year controversy over the US government's special relationship to the ICANN (Ross 2014).

The technical underpinning and standardization of the Internet's core protocols (IPv4 and IPv6) is an activity of the Internet Engineering Task Force (IETF), a non-profit organization of loosely affiliated international participants that anyone may associate with by contributing technical expertise (ICANN n.d). Another example of digital monopoly by the advanced countries over the Internet is the Society for Worldwide Interbank Financial Telecommunication (SWIFT) located in La Hulpe, Belgium (Codes n.d). The SWIFT connects the international banking system and all international banking transactions are conducted through it.

The Institute of Electrical and Electronics Engineers (IEEE) and NIST

The IEEE is the world's largest organization for the advancement of technology (IEEE n.d). It develops technical standards through its Standards Association, in conjunction with the US National Institute of Standards and Technology (NIST) (NIST n.d).

International Electrotechnical Commission (IEC) and the International Organization for Standardization (ISO)

The IEC prepares and publishes international standards and provides conformity assessments for government, business, and society for all electrical, electronic and related technologies. World Trade Organization (WTO) agreements permit use of these standards in international trade. Its membership includes national committees from over 70 nations, comprising representatives from each country's public and private sectors ((IEC) n.d). ISO/IEC JTC 1 is the Joint Technical Committee 1 of the ISO and the IEC. Its purpose is to develop, maintain, promote, and facilitate standards in the fields of IT and ICT. It has developed information security standards for all types of organizations, including commercial enterprises, government agencies, and not-for-profit organizations. Tens or hundreds of thousands of organizations worldwide use the standards developed by it (ISO 1987).

The ISO/IEC 27001:2005 or the "Information technology - Security techniques - Code of practice for information security management" is the internationally-accepted standard of good practice for information security (ISO n.d). The landmark ISO/IEC 27032:2012 provides guidance for improving the state of cyber security, in particular with respect to information security, network security, internet security, and critical information infrastructure protection (CIIP). It covers the baseline security practices for stakeholders in the cyberspace and provides a framework to stakeholders to collaborate on resolving cyber security issues.(ISO n.d).

Organization for Advancement of Structured Information Standards (OASIS)

This is another international, non-profit consortium that drives the development of e-business and web services standards through 70 technical committees. It has done much of its work pursuant to UN request that led ultimately to an important, widely implemented standard, ISO 15000((OASIS) n.d).

Organization of Economic Cooperation and Development (OECD)

The OECD has seriously considered cyber threats to international economy. It has constituted an anti-spam task force, which submitted a detailed report, with several background papers on spam problems in developing countries, best practices for Internet Service Providers (ISPs), e-mail marketers etc (OECD 2006). It has also commissioned works on the information economy (OECD n.d), and the future of the Internet economy (OECD 2008). In 2002, the OECD adopted the Guidelines for the Security of Information Systems and Networks. This established a framework of principles that apply to all participants to enhance the security of information systems and networks in order to foster economic prosperity and social development. In 2012, these Guidelines were comprehensively reviewed (OECD n.d). After the adoption of the Guidelines, the OECD monitored their implementation and organized events to share experience and best practices by governments, with the business community and civil society (OECD n.d).

Virtual Global Task Force (VGT)

The VGT combats online sexual exploitation of children. Twelve police organizations are members of the VGT. These include the Australian National Police, National Child Exploitation Coordination Centre (NCECC) – a national program of the Royal Canadian Mounted Police's Canadian Police Centre for Missing and Exploited Children (CPCMEC), European Police (Europol), International Criminal Police Organization (Interpol), Italian postal and telecommunication police service, Dutch National Police, New Zealand Police, Indonesian National Police, Korean National Police Agency Cyber Terror Response Center, Ministry of the Interior for the United Arab Emirates, Child Exploitation and online Protection Centre UK, DHS and US Immigration and Enforcement (Force (n.d)).

Interpol

Under an ambitious plan, the Interpol is setting up a Global Complex for Innovation in Singapore. This state of the art facility is expected to be complete by 2014. It is meant to complement the work of its General Secretariat in Lyon, France, and in Buenos Aires, Argentina and enhance its presence in Asia. It would provide cutting-edge research and development facility for the identification of crimes and criminals, innovative training, operational support and partnerships. The Complex will have Digital Crime Centre and a forensic laboratory to support digital crime investigations. It will provide research facilities to test protocols, tools and services and to analyze trends of cyber-attacks and will develop practical solutions in collaboration with police, research laboratories, academia and the public and private sectors. It will addresses issues such as Internet security governance, capacity building and training, research into training and methodology and the transfer of this research into police activities on the ground. It will provide classrooms, field and online training programs for National Central Bureaus; Anti-corruption training, particularly in sport. It will set quality standards and provide and accreditation. It will also provide operational and investigative support (Interpol n.d).

World Federation of Scientists (WFS), Information Security Permanent Monitoring Panel (PMP)

Founded in 1973, the WFS is a voluntary organization of more than 10,000 scientists from 110 countries. It promotes international collaboration in science and technology between scientists and researchers. One of its principal aims is to mitigate planetary emergencies. The WFS has identified the threats emanating from cyberspace as a major indicator of the fragility of modern, integrated societies and of undoubted relevance to the functioning and security of the world system. As of today, information security is an important priority for the WFS. In this regard, it advocates unified effort by the entire international community to ensure cyber security (Group 2003). The Information Security PMP was established in 2001 to examine emerging threat to the functioning of ICT systems and it has made appropriate recommendations in this regard (Security 2003).

The Erice Declaration on Principles for Cyber Stability and Cyber Peace was drafted by the PMP and was adopted by the Plenary of the WFS on the occasion of the 42nd Session of the International Seminars on Planetary Emergencies in Erice (Sicily) on August 20, 2009. The Declaration has urged a common code for cyber conduct (ITU n.d).

London Conference on Cyber Space

A number of international seminars have been convened on the subject of cyber security. A number of good suggestions have come out of these. One such seminar was held in London in November 2011. Hosted by the UK Foreign Office with support from Chatham House and the International Chamber of Commerce, it brought together internet experts and cyber security practitioners from governments, the private-sector, and NGOs from around the world. Speakers included William Hague, British Foreign Secretary; Joe Biden, US Vice-President; Jimmy Wales, Co-founder Wikipedia; and Carl Bildt, the Swedish Foreign Minister. It discussed issues ranging from potential cyber-attacks on intelligence information and infrastructure to intellectual property rights and copyright infringement, the evolving cyber security vulnerabilities of governments, businesses, and individuals require a comprehensive dialogue on how to create a safe online environment while utilizing the Internet's full potential for economic growth and as a forum for the exchange of information (House (n.d)).

Forum of Incident Response and Security Teams (FIRST) & CERTs

FIRST was formed in 1990 to respond to incidents like the worm attack against the computer systems in 1989. It is now a reputable international confederation coordinating the operations of 276 CERTs across 60 nations. It cooperatively handles computer security incidents and promotes accident prevention programs. Bringing together the educational, government, military and commercial sectors, it provides access to best practices and tools, and to trusted communication with member teams. Among other things it aims to counteract challenges arising from issues like language, time zones and international standards. Such initiatives, while originating from a very specific need, contribute greatly to the internationalization of best practices of cyber security. This is of special relevance for states with less capacity in cyber security. It is imperative that the international security community looks to mechanisms such as these and ensures that the governmental action at the multinational level is harmonized with the services of operators and other stakeholders, such as private businesses relying on cyberspace infrastructure. CERT India (CERT-In) is listed as a member of the FIRST.(FIRST n.d)

CERTs are also known as Computer Security Incident Response Team (CSIRT, pronounced "see-sirt"), CIRC (Computer Incident Response Capability), CIRT (Computer Incident Response Team), IRC (Incident Response Center or Incident Response Capability), IRT (Incident Response Team), SERT (Security Emergency Response Team) and SIRT (Security Incident Response Team). A CSIRT typically receives reports of security breaches, conduct analyses of the reports and responds to the senders. These teams work either as part of an established group or an ad hoc assembly within the parent organization, such as a government, a corporation, a university or a research network. National CSIRTs are units designated to oversee incident handling for an entire country. These gather periodically throughout the year for proactive tasks such as Disaster Recovery (DR) testing, and in the event of a security breach. External CSIRTs provide paid services on either an on-going or as-needed basis (Gibilisco 2012).

REGIONAL INITIATIVES

At the regional level, important initiatives have been undertaken by groups like the Shanghai Cooperation Organization (SCO), the Commonwealth of Independent States (CIS), the European Union (EU), the Council of Europe (CE), the G8 Group of States, Asian Pacific Economic Cooperation (APEC), Organization of American States (OAS), ASEAN, the League of Arab States, the African Union (AU) and Network Operations Groups (NOG). No initiative has been taken in South Asia within the framework of either the South Asian Association for Regional Cooperation (SAARC) or at the bilateral level.

SCO

SCO is a Eurasian security organization, which was founded in Shanghai in 2001. Besides Russia and China, it includes four former Soviet Central Asian Republics as permanent members. India, Pakistan, Mongolia and Iran have observer status and there are two dialogue partners – Belarus and Sri Lanka (SCO n.d). The President of Afghanistan was invited to attend the 2012 summit meetings (Summit 2012). As leaders of the SCO, Russia and China have used this platform to actively pursue their cyber security agenda.

International information security figures prominently on the SCO's agenda. The SCO is seriously concerned about threats arising from the cyber space and the West dominance of the Internet. These concerns were highlighted in the declaration of the heads of states after their meeting in Shanghai in June 2006. It was stated that:

[A] real danger is currently appearing of ICT being used for purposes capable of bringing serious harm to the security of people, society, and the state in the destruction of foundational principles of equality and mutual respect, non-interference in internal affairs of sovereign states, peaceful regulation of conflicts, non-use of force, and observation of human rights. In this regard the threat of ICT being used in criminal, terrorist, and military-political goals incompatible with the maintenance of international security may be realized in both the civil and military realms and may lead to serious political and socio-economic consequences in individual countries, regions, and the world as a whole, and to the destabilization of the public life of states.(FIDH 2006).

The 2008 SCO Agreement in the Field of International Information Security underlined the 'digital gap' between states. It feared that the more developed parties were monopolizing the production of software/hardware, creating dependence on these products from the less developed states whose chances of participating in international IT collaborations were dwindling. SCO member states believe that the current conventions lack adequate codes of conduct in communications between different countries, omitting a broad spectrum of cyber security abuses, which could escalate into cyber-conflict. Russia's SCO National Coordinator, Ambassador Barsky has described the Council of Europe (CE) Convention on Cybercrime as less than satisfactory (Kizekova 2012).

On June 15, 2009 the landmark SCO Agreement on Cooperation in the Field of International Information Security was signed in Yekaterinburg. The Yekaterinburg Declaration stressed the significance of ensuring international information security as one of the key elements of the common system of international security (FMPRC 2009). The Agreement defined cyber war as confrontation between two or more states in the information space aimed at damaging information systems, processes and resources, and undermining political, economic and social systems, mass brainwashing to destabilizing society and state, as well as forcing the state to take decisions in the interest of an opposing party (Moscow 2009). It clearly described cyberwarfare as dissemination of information "harmful to the spiritual, moral and cultural spheres of other states" and considers it a "security threat." The SCO accord identified 'information war,' in part, as an effort by a state to undermine another's "political, economic, and social systems" (SCO 2013; Healey n.d). SCO presents itself as a possible center of gravity in international legal action on cyber-attacks (Oona A. Hathaway 2012). In 2009 another agreement was concluded among the Governments of the SCO member states on Cooperation in the Field of Ensuring International Information Security with the ASEAN (China n.d; Xinghuanet n.d). The US is wary that other countries may use the SCO Accord template to crackdown on domestic dissent (Boland 2011). On September12, 2011 Russia and China used the forum of the SCO to present an international code of conduct for Internet to the UNGA (China 2011).

CIS

The CIS was founded after the breakup of the Soviet Union in 1991. Its member states are the former Soviet Republics of Armenia, Azerbaijan, Belarus, Kazakhstan, Kyrgyzstan, Moldova, Russia, Tajikistan, and Uzbekistan. Turkmenistan and Ukraine are the unofficial members (States n.d). Georgia left the CIS in 2009, after the Georgia-Russia crisis(*Radio Free Liberty* August 18, 2009). Cyber-security is an important issue for the CIS. An Agreement on Establishment of the Regional Commonwealth in the field of Communications (RCC) was signed by CIS members in 1992. The RCC's mission is to carry out cooperation between the member states in the field of telecommunication and postal communication. Ukraine, Georgia and Turkmenistan are also official members of the RCC. RCC participants determine collaboration around information security and trans-border information exchange between member states. In 1998, the Information Security Commission of the Coordination Council of the CIS member states was established within the RCC. The commission is responsible for developing cooperative proposals on information security matters and for harmonizing national legislation systems accordingly (Communications n.d). It has been alleged that the members of the CIS practice strict Internet censorship. There is also active cooperation between Belarusian and Russian special services in cyberspace. In 2000 the CIS concluded agreement among themselves on Cooperation in Combating Offences related to Computer Information (Fyodor Pavlyuchenkoa n.d).

In the last decade, the region witnessed two cyber wars. The first was a campaign by pro-Russian (and allegedly state-sponsored) hackers, which paralyzed the Estonian Internet in May 2007. The second was a similar campaign (also allegedly organized by nationalist pro-government Russian hackers) that occurred at the same time as major combat operations in Georgia (August 2008). The latter campaign targeting Georgian online media and government websites led Georgian authorities to filter access to Russian Internet sites, allegedly as a means of self-defense against Russian cyber propaganda. This resulted in an information vacuum in Tbilisi during the critical days where it was unclear whether Russian troops would stop their advance into Georgia. The CIS informational controls are similar to those adopted by China and Iran like Internet filtering (Initiative n.d).

CE

The 2001CE Convention on Cybercrime (CEC) – aka the Budapest Convention on Cybercrime or just the Budapest Convention – remains to date, the only binding international legal device. It has the widest possible outreach. It is the first international treaty seeking to address computer and Internet crimes by harmonizing national laws, improving investigative techniques and increasing international cooperation. It provides an effective platform to expand the outreach of the municipal procedural law powers for investigating and prosecuting cyber offences. It deals particularly with infringements of copyright, computer-related fraud, child pornography, hate crimes and violations of network security. Its main objective is to pursue a common criminal policy aimed at the protecting the society against cybercrime by adopting appropriate legislation and fostering international cooperation (Ahsan 2008). The Convention has accomplished three key goals i.e. establishment of a specific list of domestic criminal offenses and conduct that are prohibited; it has adopted a set of procedural tools and powers to properly and effectively investigate crimes. Lastly, it has established strong mechanisms for fostering international cooperation (Cybercrime 2001).

Not all 41 member states of the CE have either signed or ratified the Convention. Signatories include non-European countries from Asia, Africa, Oceania, North and South America. 12 countries have signed but not ratified. 39 have signed and ratified (Cybercrimes n.d). The US ratified the Convention in August 2006. India and Pakistan are not members of the Convention. The Convention not only requires that parties adopt legislative and other measures to establish criminal offences under its domestic law but also to criminalize the willful infringement of copyright and related rights when done on a commercial scale and by means of a computer system. In addition, parties are also required to ensure that all the listed offenses are punishable by effective, proportionate and dissuasive sanctions, which include deprivation of liberty.

The CEC sets out mechanisms by which parties are obligated to assist each other in investigating cybercrimes and other crimes involving electronic evidence. It provides them the widest possible base to co-operate with each other for the purposes of investigating, collecting evidence and proceeding against criminal offences related to computer systems and data. This cooperation is, however, contingent on the basis of uniform or reciprocal legislation and domestic laws (Vatis 2010). The CEC, thus far represents the most substantive, and broadly subscribed multilateral agreement on cybercrime in existence today (Europe 2003). In March 2012, the Council adopted an Internet governance strategy (Europe n.d).

EU

In June 2010, the European Police Office (Europol) created the EU Cybercrime Task Force (Europol n.d). The task force comprises an expert group of representatives from Europol, Euro just (the EU judicial cooperation body) and the European Commission (EC). Europol provides the EU members with investigative and analytical support on cybercrime, and facilitates cross-border cooperation and information exchange (Monitor 2011). At the NATO summit of November 2010, the EU, NATO and the US, approved plans for a coordinated approach to tackle cybercrime in member states. Following a feasibility study conducted by Rand Corporation Europe, the EC decided to establish a European Cybercrime Centre (EC3) at Europol. The EC3 was operationalized in January 2013. This Centre is the focal point in the EU's fight against cybercrime, and contributes to faster reactions in the event of online crimes. It supports Member States and the EU institutions in building operational and analytical capacity for investigations and cooperation with international partners (Europol n.d). The Schengen Information System and the Europol Information System, with in-built safeguards to protect privacy and personal data in line with the Charter of Fundamental Rights exchange cross border information. The EU finds these mechanisms quite adequate (Commision 2012). The EU has also established the European Network and Information Security Agency (ENISA) to advance the functioning of the internal market. ENISA serves as the center of excellence for the European Member States and European institutions in network and information security, giving advice and recommendations and acting as a switchboard of information for good practices. It also facilitates contacts between the European institutions, the Member States and private business and industry actors (Report 2011).

EU has produced a number of legislations and policy directives on issues e.g. EU Directive on e-Commerce, EU Decision on Fraud and Counterfeiting, EU Directive on Data Protection, EU Decision on Attacks against Information Systems, EU Directive on Data Retention, EU Directive Proposal on Attacks against Information Systems, and EU Directive on Child Exploitation.

European Telecommunications Standards Institute (ETSI). This is a non-profit, private entity with over 700 members from 62 countries that produces through member-controlled committees globally applicable standards for ICT, including the mobile Internet standards developed by its Third Generation Partnership Project (3GPP) (Institute n.d).

Organization of American States (OAS). The OAS is committed to support member states in fighting cybercrime, through the Inter-American Committee against Terrorism (CICTE) and the Cyber Security Program. It is also cooperating with national and regional entities from the public and private sectors on policy and technical issues, to build and strengthen cyber-security capacity of member states through technical assistance and training, policy roundtables, crisis management exercises, and the exchange of best practices related to ICT (Security n.d). In April 2004 the OAS approved a resolution stating that member states should evaluate the advisability of implementing the principles of the CE's Convention on Cybercrime and should consider the possibility of acceding to that convention. The OAS also adopted a Comprehensive Inter-American Cyber-security Strategy, which aimed at, among other things, adopting cybercrime policies and legislation designed to protect Internet users and prevent/deter criminal misuse of computers and computer networks, while respecting the privacy and individual rights of Internet users.(Oona A. Hathaway 2012).

Organization of Security and Cooperation in Europe (OSCE). The OSCE has produced a draft code of conduct on cyber security (OSCE n.d). In 2011 the 56 participating nations of the OSCE, including the US voted on a resolution to improve cybersecurity cooperation. The proposal called for participants to exchange information about the way they intend to deploy cyber technology during military conflicts. It also requested debates on international legal standards and codes of conduct for operating in cyberspace (OSCEPA n.d). A draft of proposed CBMs floated by the OSCE was circulated among the member states in November 7, 2012 included six proposals concerning national and transnational ICT security. Most of the suggested CBMs are voluntary and therefore difficult to enforce (Carr 2012).

ASEAN

ASEAN member states cooperate and share best practices on ICT and business processes at the forum of Telecommunications and IT Ministers Meeting (TELMIN). It has prepared an ASEAN ICT Masterplan 2015 (AIM2015) and adopted "Connected ASEAN – Enabling Aspirations." The purpose is to reiterate its commitments to promote ICT-driven economic transformation through people engagement and empowerment, innovation, infrastructure development, human capital development and to bridge the Digital Divide. ASEAN is engaging with China, Japan, the Republic of Korea, the EU and the ITU to implement their respective annual ICT work plans and joint activities (ASEAN 2012). The AIM2015 envisions creating a global ICT hub (Heinl 2013). The ASEAN Chiefs of Police (ASEANAPOL) meet regularly to discuss issues like cybercrime laws. They also want to establish a partnership with the Interpol's Global Complex (IGC) in Singapore, to enable it respond effectively against challenges presented by cybercrime.(Law n.d).

ASEAN has created a number of cyber networks with other countries. In 2009, the ASEAN-China Coordination Framework for Network and Information Security Emergency Responses was signed (ed

2010). Japan not only supports the implementation of AIM2015, it also wants to share its experience on the utilization of ICT in disaster management with ASEAN (*Vietnam*, May 1, 2013). In a June this year, in a meeting with senior officials of the ASEAN on Transnational Crime, the US had proposed a Cybercrime Capacity-Building initiative focusing on the requirements and models for national hi-tech crime investigative units and digital forensics programs. On July 1, US Secretary of State John Kerry met with his ASEAN counterparts on the margins of the ASEAN Regional Forum (ARF) meeting and discussed with them issues including cyber security (State 2013). The ARF has also held Cyber Security workshops in collaboration with Australia (Fox n.d).

Asia Pacific Economic Cooperation (APEC). In 2002, the APEC adopted a strategy outlining six areas for co-operation among member economies including legal developments, information sharing and co-operation, security and technical guidelines, public awareness, and training and education. It also recommended that member states adopt legislation and policies criminalizing cybercrime. To supplement the APEC Cybersecurity Strategy, the APEC Telecommunications and Information Working Group (APEC TEL) adopted the Strategy to Ensure a Trusted, Secure and Sustainable Online Environment in 2005.(APEC n.d) The aim of this strategy is to encourage APEC economies to take action for the security of information systems and networks (Wiki n.d).

League of Arab States

The League of Arab States came into being after the Arab-Israel war of 1967 (CFR n.d). It has come a long way since then. Like many other regional groupings, it is concerned about cyber security, especially after the Flame virus attack that hit the Middle East in 2012 (Blount 2012-13). Two legislations have been prepared in this regard i.e. the Model Arab Law on Combating Offences related to IT Systems (2004) and the Arab Convention on Combating IT Offences (2010).

Economic Community of West African States (ECOWAS), African Union (AU) and Common Market for Eastern and Southern Africa (COMESA)

A number of African groups have come up with directives, legal frameworks and model bills concerning cyber security. ECOWAS has produced a number of legislations including Supplementary Act on Electronic Transactions, Supplementary Act on Personal Data Protection and the Directive on Fighting Cybercrime (Akuetteh n.d). In 2011, the AU and the Economic Commission for Africa (ECA) produced a *Draft Convention on the Establishment of a Legal Framework for Cyber Security*. The purpose was to harmonize African cyber legislations on e-commerce organization, personal data protection, cyber security promotion and cybercrime control. Among other things the draft convention sought to establish a common language on matters pertaining to cyber security and encouraging governments to establish National Cyber Security Authorities (NCSAs) and CERTs. In 2011 another African group, the COMESA came up with the Cybersecurity Draft Model Bill (CBC 2011).

Network Operations Groups (NOG)

The NOGs provide regional forums to engineers and operators to meet, network, develop business and technology relationships, discuss job opportunities, share best practices and keep the Internet working. The North American Network Operations Group came into existence in 1994. It now attracts participants from Europe and Asia also. It holds three meetings in a year (Smith 2008).

BILATERAL INTIATIVES

US-Russia Bilateral Cyber Security Initiatives

As mentioned in the introductory section, at a meeting held between the US and the Russian President Presidents in June 2013, new initiatives on cyber security were discussed to extend "traditional transparency and confidence-building measures to reduce the mutual danger we face from cyber threats." These initiatives involve '**Deeper Engagement through Senior-Level Dialogue' and 'ICT CBMs.**' The existing US-Russia Presidential Bilateral Commission has been tasked to establish a working group to assess emerging threats to ICTs and propose joint responses to such threats. The new CBMs are "designed to increase transparency and reduce the possibility that a misunderstood cyber incident could create instability or a crisis in our bilateral relationship." These CBMs seek to strengthen US-Russian relations in cyberspace, expand a shared understanding of cyber threats that appear to originate in each other's territories, and prevent escalation of cybersecurity incidents. The CBMs adopted are as under:

- Links and Information Exchanges between the US and Russian CERTs. This CBM aims to increase information sharing on "technical information about malware or other malicious threats" in order to facilitate "proactive mitigation of threats."
- Exchange of Cyber Security Notifications. This measure will permit communications and "formal inquiries about cybersecurity incidents of national concern." Such information exchanges and inquiries will flow through the existing NRRC, established in 1987 between the US and the former USSR, to facilitate reduction of "misperception and escalation from ICT security incidents."
- Cyber Hotline between the White House and the Kremlin. To provide a secure means to "manage a crisis situation arising from an ICT security incident." The direct cyber hotline will be integrated into the existing Direct Secure Communication System that the two countries maintain.

In June 2013, the US and Russia announced a joint cyber-security agreement, which had taken two years in the making. A joint statement announced the creation of a cyber-hotline and the formation of a bilateral working group. The group will focus on the threat from cyber-attacks to international security, consider emerging threats, and will act to coordinate a collaborative response (Simson 2013). The White House also indicated that to "create predictability and understanding in the political military environment," the two militaries have "shared unclassified ICT strategies and other relevant studies" to understand "one another's perspectives."These steps are important for cybersecurity because the two countries are applying approaches used in arms control contexts e.g. CBMs and hotline communications, to cybersecurity challenges. This strategy dovetails with needs for better "situational awareness" and transparency through increased information exchange and for stronger, more effective cooperation among key countries through functional collaboration at the technical level and political interactions among high-level officials. However, independent experts in the US are wary that these "iCBMs" would be a panacea for all cybersecurity problems. American interest of course that the Internet remains free and open and unfettered by oppressive international laws(Fidler 2013; CSA n.d).

Differing national perceptions have created a lot of ambiguity about what should constitute an acceptable cyber code of conduct. Various ideas have been floated about common management of information space. One proposal gives a technical checklist of ten points to achieve a quasi-global regulatory mechanism short of an international treaty. It argues that cyber CBMs could be a stopgap measure, since many countries "view a treaty as unverifiable, unenforceable and impractical." In order to create robust CBMs it suggests setting up "bodies to share information and best practices, like the Common Assurance Maturity Model (CAMM) and the Cloud Security Alliance (CSA)." It also highlights the need to "improve communication between the various communities, from policy-makers to technological experts to business leaders both at national and international levels." The checklist favors enhancement "in attribution capabilities by investing in new technologies, and establishing rules and standards;" and advises that the adoption of the "Dutch model of a third party cyber-exchange for improved private-public partnership on internet security."[e] In the end it evinces hope that despite practical hurdles in transparency, both for private companies and for governments, ways could be found to establish assurance and trust "through the use of security mechanisms and processes" (stefanomele n.d).

Convention on Cyberspace

Ideally there should be a Convention on Cyberspace. In 2005 Ahmed Kamal, a Pakistani diplomat based in Geneva produced a monograph suggesting laws for the cyber space (Kamal 2005). Experts are of the view that a Convention on Cyber Space can be prepared on lines similar to the UN Convention on the Law of the Sea of 1982. Unfortunately such a Convention has so far not found international acceptability. Apparently cyber space is more choppy and rough than all the oceans of the world combined together. Similar problems have also been experienced in concluding a treaty on preventing arms race in outer space (PAROS). It is difficult to compare the damages caused by aggressive or illicit behavior in information space to a potentially harmful arms race in outer space. The major difference is that while cyber space is nebulous and ill defined, activity in outer space can still be tracked and monitored. It has been suggested that in absence of a cyber-treaty, the law of armed conflict or IHL can be conveniently applied in the cyberspace (ICRC).

Since damage caused by the cyber-attacks in terms of human deaths or destruction to property is not clearly visible, the applicability of these laws is difficult to comprehend (Wegener n.d).

PART III: EXISTING DOMESTIC LAWS AND TREATIES REGULATING ACTIVITY IN THE INFORMATION ENVIRONMENT IN SOUTH ASIA

As mentioned in the Introduction, one important tool to ensure cyber security is an effective legal system to prevent and prosecute illegitimate cyber activity. This area seems to be extremely patchy in South Asia. South Asian states have no game plan to jointly combat cybercrime. In this section I have made an effort to describe the existing rules and regulations in Pakistan and India on the subject of cyber security.

Cybercrime Laws in Pakistan

Due to the mushrooming growth of electronic commerce and massive internet usage, Pakistan has experienced a spurt of cybercrimes but there is no official database for it. Reports posted on the Internet(Records n.d). and the national media indicate a rise in crime such as identity thefts and illicit use of credit cards; (Dalwn, September 13, 2012) and harassment and blackmailing on the social media (*The News*, February 16, 2012). Pakistan currently has no cybercrime laws. The Prevention of Electronic Crimes Ordinance 2009 lapsed without being made into a law (Wasim 2010), and since then no legal regime has been created to replace it. Criminal activity online is presently being dealt with through an amalgamation of certain administrative measures and legal provisions borrowed from different pieces of legislation. Some provisions of Pakistan Penal Code 1860 & Electronic Transactions Ordinance 2002 are used for investigating complaints relating to illegal cyber activity (Hassan 2012), e.g. Sections 483 (counterfeiting a trademark or property mark), 420 (cheating), 468 (forgery) and 471 (using forged document) of Pakistan Penal Code 1860 have been used to press charges in cases of illicit cyber activity (Zafar n.d). These laws are given in Table II (page 99). Cyber complaints are dealt with by the National Response Centre for Cyber Crimes (NR3C) working under the auspices of Federal Investigation Agency (FIA). Among other things it also acts a CERT (FIA n.d).

Cyber Security Bill

Pakistan does not have a national cyber security policy. This indicates a serious capacity deficit at the policy planning levels (Sohail 2013). Official quarters have been jolted out of their complacency by revelations that Pakistan has been extensively spied upon through Internet and online communication systems and that 13.5 billion pieces of its email, phone and fax communications have been intercepted (Record n.d). On June 24, 2013 the Chairman Senate Standing Committee on Defence Senator Mushahid Hussain Sayed announced that a Cyber Security Strategy bill was being prepared. He demanded that since Pakistan ranked second highest in the list of countries being spied upon, sufficient funds should be allocated to execute a Cyber Security Strategy. He also suggested the formation of a Cyber Security task force within the Ministry of IT, to propose counter measures. His proposal was unanimously adopted (MushahidHussain.com n.d).

In a follow up seminar held on July 8, matters related to cyber security and their impact on sectors such as: the national defence, security, intelligence, diplomacy, nuclear and missile program, economy, energy, education, civil aviation as well as industrial and manufacturing units in the private and public sector were discussed. Three fundamental elements were highlighted: A. The ability to defend digital infrastructure must have the ability to resist attacks, cyber penetration and disruption. B. The ability not only to defend against emerging cyber threats from state sponsored as well as other sources and the ability to retaliate regionally, at least. C. The ability to recover quickly from cyber incidents caused by cyber aggression, accidents or natural disasters. The senator informed the audience that there plans to earmark a focal ministry or division to exclusively handle cyber security issues, introduce laws for data protection and extending an invitation to industry experts to join hands with Parliamentarians in this regard. A cyber security Action Plan was announced for:

1. Introducing legislation to preserve, protect and promote Pakistan's cyber security. The drafting for the Cyber Security bill has already been initiated.
2. Establishing Pakistan Computer Emergency Response Team (PKCERT).
3. Establishing a Cyber Security Task Force in collaboration with the MoD, Ministry of IT, Ministry of Interior, Ministry of Foreign Affairs, Ministry of Information, security organizations and security professionals from the private sector to formulate a Cyber Security Strategy for Pakistan.
4. Establishing an Inter Services Cyber Command under the office of the Chairman, Joint Chiefs of Staff Committee to coordinate cyber security and cyber defence for Pakistan's Armed Forces.

5. Initiating talks within the framework of SAARC, among the 8-member states particularly India to establish acceptable norms of cyber behavior so that they do not engage in cyber warfare against each other.

6. Concluding an agreement with India not to engage in cyber warfare patterned on the agreement not to attack nuclear installations.

7. Organizing a special media workshop to promote awareness among the public and educate opinion leaders on the issue of cyber security (*Dawn*, July 12, 2013).

In January 2014, Government of Pakistan announced that it would be setting up a Cyber Authority - a special court to deal with cyber crime and disputes as well as an emergency unit to counter attacks against Pakistan's interests. This decision was part of a larger plan to amend a dozen major laws through a consolidated compendium to be called the Electronic Documents and Prevention of Cybercrimes Act, 2014 (Kiani 2014).

Cyber Law of India

India enacted its IT Act in June 2000. Spread over 32 pages it provides legal recognition for transactions carried out by means of electronic data interchange and other means of electronic communication, commonly referred to as "electronic commerce," which involve the use of alternatives to paper-based methods of communication and storage of information, to facilitate electronic filing of documents with the Government agencies and further to amend the Indian Penal Code, the Indian Evidence Act, 1872, the Bankers' Books Evidence Act, 1891 and the Reserve Bank of India Act, 1934 and for matters connected therewith or incidental thereto. It refers to the UN GA resolution A/RES/51/162, dated the 30th January, 1997 adopting the Model Law on Electronic Commerce adopted by the UN Commission on International Trade Law. Its principal aim is to promote efficient delivery of Government services by means of reliable electronic records (India n.d). The Indian justice system allows cybercrimes to be tried under this Act. These crimes include theft, fraud, forgery, defamation and mischief, all of which are subject to the Indian Penal Code (India n.d).

Cyber Defenses of India

CERT-In was established in 2004 (FIRST n.d). The Crisis Management Plan for Cyber Attacks was issued in 2010 (India 2010). The National Critical Information Infrastructure Protection Centre (NCIIPC) was created to protect energy, transport, banking, telecom, defense, space and other sensitive areas from cyber-attacks, in 2011 (Chander n.d). A government-private sector plan was started in October 2012 to strengthen the country's cyber security capabilities. Indian cyber security planners are presently looking for ways to make up for the deficiency of 500,000 cyber-experts (Mohan 2012). By February 2013, NCIIPC had finalized the national cyber security policy focusing on domestic security solutions reducing dependence on foreign technology (Fitter 2013). The National Cyber Security Policy 2013 (NCSP-2013) was published On July 2, 2013 (Ministry of Communication and Information Technology 2013). After newsbreak that India was among the top five countries targeted by the US global surveillance programs, decision was taken to establish the office of the National Cyber Security Coordinator to coordinate the work of agencies like the National Technical Research Organization (NTRO), the home ministries and the CERT (Bagchi 2013). In May 2013, a full time Cyber Security Coordinator was appointed (*The Indian Express*, May 10 2013).

Foreign Collaboration

India is actively collaborating with countries other than Pakistan in cyber security matters. In July 2011, it signed a Memorandum of Understanding (MOU) with the US to promote closer cooperation and timely exchange of cyber security information between CERT-In and US-CERT (DHS 2011). In October 2012 the Foreign and Defense Secretaries of India and Japan met at the "2+2" in Tokyo to decide among other things an expansion in cyber security collaboration (Softpedia n.d). During his visit to New Delhi in February 2013, the British Prime Minister promised greater collaboration with India in fighting cyber-attacks. A large amount of UK data is on Indian databases. Britain strongly feels that it needs to partner with India in cybercrime and security related matters, to fight cyber criminals and protect itself from states like China. The British are offering the Indians police training exchanges and research into cyber security and a joint task force to share information. Cyber cooperation also includes regular meetings between leaders in cyber security research in academic institutions and industry (Ashwood 2013).

The SEA-ME-WE Internet Cable

Currently the only cyber sharing that India does with Pakistan is the SEA-ME-WE (South East Asia-Middle East- West Asia) submarine Internet cable. This optical fiber cable was laid by an international telecom consortium under an agreement signed on March 27, 2004. It links South East Asia to Europe via the Indian Subcontinent and Middle East with terminal stations in Singapore, Malaysia, Thailand, Bangladesh, India, Sri Lanka, Pakistan, United Arab Emirates, Saudi Arabia, Egypt, Italy, Tunisia, Algeria and France. It is now being upgraded by a group of French and Japanese companies at the cost of US$500 million. The total length of the SEA-ME-WE 4 submarine cable system spans approximately 20,000 kilometers (SEA-ME-WE n.d).

PART IV: INFORMATION CBMs BETWEEN INDIA AND PAKISTAN

CBMs are time honored diplomatic tools to build trust and prevent wars. The peace treaty of Hudaybiyah is the earliest documented CBM in Islamic history. The pact was signed between the Muslim pilgrims from Medina and the tribesmen of Quraiysh on the outskirts of Mecca in 6th Al Hijra (628 CE). Although some of the clauses of the treaty appeared highly unfavorable for the Muslims, the agreement to co-exist peacefully for 10 years, gave them time to establish their state and spread their religion in Arabia (Lings 1991).

In pre-World War I Europe, it was customary to invite observers from different states (friendly and not so friendly) to witness annual military maneuvers as a means to instill confidence and trust among nations. Most contemporary military CBMs include: communication links like hotlines and regional communication centers; mechanisms to ease border tensions; exchange of military data like troop locations, movements and exercises, military budgets, weapon systems (conventional, nuclear, chemical and biological);weapon test notifications; demilitarized or thin-out zones and goodwill visits etc (Center 2012). Non-military CBMs cover political, economic, environmental, social and cultural fields (Europe 2012).

According to Norwegian political scientists Johan Jørgen Holst and Karen Alette Melander "confidence-building involves the communication of credible evidence of the absence of feared threats by reducing uncertainties and by constraining opportunities for exerting pressure through military activities" (Melander 1977). This concept was further refined as "arrangements designed to enhance such assurance of mind and belief in the trust worthiness of states and the fact they create" (Holst 1983). CBMs became part of modern diplomacy at the Helsinki Conference on Security and Cooperation in Europe (CSCE). The Helsinki Final Act 1975 described CBMs as means to eliminate the causes of tensions, to promote confidence and contribute to stability and security and to reduce the danger of armed conflict arising from misunderstanding or miscalculation. CBMs are also referred to as Conflict Avoidance Measures, Trust Building Measures, Conflict Resolution Measures, Confidence and Security Building Measures and Confidence Building and Security Measures, and Tension Reduction Measures.

The concept of CBMs was formalized through UN Resolution 33/91 B of December 16, 1978 (Secretary-General 1982). The UN *Comprehensive Study on CBMs* declares that the main purpose of these measures is to "eliminate the sources of tension by peaceful means and thereby to contribute to the strengthening of peace and security in the world." The study recognized that "Confidence, like security, is a result of many factors, both military and non-military." It further stated that "the final objective of CBMs is to strengthen international peace and security and to contribute to the development of confidence, better understanding and more stable relations between nations, thereby creating and improving the conditions for fruitful international cooperation" (Secretary-General 1982). The primary tools for managing successful CBMs are "communication, constraint, transparency, and verification measures." Together these make the behavior of states more predictable (Centre n.d).

Contemporary CBMs are the legacy of the Cold War and were used extensively to stabilize the East-West relationship (OSCE 1999). The famous hotline between the White House and the Kremlin was established after the 1962 Cuban Missile Crisis "to reduce the danger of an accident, miscalculation or a surprise attack, and especially an incident that might trigger a nuclear war."(Davenport 2012) Initially only teletypewriters were deployed at both terminals. In the 1970s, the hotline was upgraded to a telephonic link (BBC 2003). The NRRC began operations on April 1, 1988 through a digitally linked direct government-to-government communications link (GGCL). It is a round the clock watch center staffed by members of various government agencies. Its expanded role includes the operation of additional international communications links, which allows the US to implement 13 different nuclear, chemical, and conventional arms control treaties and security-building agreements. The NRRC contributes to bilateral and multilateral transparency and mutual understanding through timely and accurate information exchanges (State n.d).

The hotline was followed by the arms control talks between the US and the former USSR. The CBMs negotiations were codified in the Helsinki Final Act of 1975 (OSCE n.d). These new generation measures were classified as Confidence and Security Building measures (CSBMs). The same model was adopted for the Middle East Arms Control and Regional Security (ACRS) working group that was active in the early 1990s (Landau 2012). Typically the CBMs include Transparency, Information Exchange Measures, Observation and Verification Measures, and Constraint Measures (UNODA n.d). In the early 1980s, the UNDC developed a set of guidelines for CBMs, which was presented at a special UNGA session devoted to disarmament. A couple of these guidelines are reproduced below:

1.2.5 A major objective is to reduce or even eliminate the cause of mistrust, fear, misunderstanding and miscalculation with regard to relevant military activities and intentions of other States, factors which may generate the perception of an impaired security and provide justification for the continuation of the global and regional arms buildup.

1.2.6 A centrally important task of confidence-building measures is to reduce the dangers of misunderstanding or miscalculation of military activities, to help prevent military confrontation as well as covert preparations for the commencement of a war, to reduce the risk of surprise attacks and of the outbreak of war by incident; and thereby, finally, to give effect and concrete expression to the solemn pledge of all nations to refrain from the threat or use of force in all its forms and to enhance security and stability (UN 1988).

Military and non-military CBMs have been introduced in a number of global conflict zones in the Middle East, Europe, the Korean peninsula and South Asia.

History of India-Pakistan CBMs

Despite deep rooted mistrust, India and Pakistan have over the years concluded a number of agreements to keep the affairs of the state moving in a mutually beneficial direction. These efforts to seek peaceful solutions to pressing problems make up for a set of practical CBMs. Some of the early agreements between India and Pakistan included matters such as transfer of official assets (1948), prevention of exodus of refugees (1948), protection of right of minorities (1950), maintenance of places of worship (1953 and 1955) and resolution of some unsettled territorial claims (1958, 1959, 1960 and 1963) (Qadeem 1998). A major source of friction has been the supply of water from the upper (India) to the lower riparian (Pakistan). Tensions mounted in 1950 and 1951, when India blocked Pakistan's share of water, resulting in military mobilization. Three successive agreements were made to allow unimpeded water supply to Pakistan till 1957, and from 1959 to 1960. In September 1960, the World Bank brokered Indus Waters Treaty was concluded (Bank 1960).

Pakistan and India formally ended wars through the Karachi Agreement (1949) (Maker n.d), Tashkent agreement (1966) (Peacemakeer n.d), and the Simla Agreement (1972).(GoI 1972). The Rann of Kutch territorial dispute that preceded the 1965 War was resolved through a UN sponsored Boundary Tribunal in 1968.Both states had pre-agreed to accept its recommendations and the border was demarcated accordingly (Ray 1970). Both states also twice accepted UN intervention to monitor the ceasefire along the LOC. The UN Military Observer Group in India and Pakistan (UNMOGIP) still has a presence in the disputed territory of Jammu and Kashmir (Information 1996).

Although India and Pakistan have maintained diplomatic relations even during times of war, both sides realize the importance of direct communication between civil and military officials. In November 1990 it was agreed to establish a hotline between the offices of the two prime ministers (Dixit 2002). There is little evidence to suggest that this channel has been frequently used. During the Kargil war Prime Ministers Nawaz Sharif and Vajpayee spoke on the telephone but this conversation only served to heighten the predicament (Cohn 2011). Indian external affairs secretary J.N. Dixit recalls talking to his Pakistani counterpart Shaharyar M. Khan over the telephone in March 1993 (Dixit 2002). Instead of using the ministry's phone Pakistani foreign minister Sartaj Aziz flew to New Delhi in an abortive attempt to defuse the situation, emerging from the 1999 Kargil crisis (Cohn 2011). In 2004 there were media reports that India and Pakistan had agreed to set up a hotline between their foreign ministries to reduce the threat of accidental nuclear war but since then there has been little to indicate that this channel has been operationalized (Lancaster 2004). A proposed counter terrorism hotline between the interior ministries also remains stalled(Makkar 2011), but media reports indicate that it may still be on the cards (*Hindustan Times*, May 13, 2012). Telephonic conversation has its limitations and diplomats prefer to talk directly to one another or communicate through carefully formal diplomatic communiqués and non-papers. After the infamous call by the Indian foreign minister threatening the President of Pakistan with dire consequences (*Fox News*, December 6), there is a requirement for additional identification filters and protocols.

One of the most dependable communication links India and Pakistan is the DGMO hotline. This direct link was established after the 1971 war and is now routinely used every week (Centre n.d). Flag meetings between Sector Commanders at battalion and brigade level are organized to sort out problems in their areas on case to case basis through prior arrangements (ACCU n.d). As of 2004, there is a system of biannual meetings between the heads of the Indian border security forces and Pakistani Rangers. The Indian Coast Guard (ICG) and the Pakistan Maritime Security Agency (MSA) have a hotline since 2006 (*Hindustan Tim*es, April 28, 2006).

To begin with military CBMs were mainly about maintaining peace along the LOC and reducing the chances of a conventional war. In the 1980s, the South Asian adversaries intensified their efforts to acquire nuclear weapons. During this time India made repeated attempts to launch decapitating air strikes against Pakistani uranium enrichment facilities in Kahuta. The matter came to a head during Exercise Brasstacks in 1986-87, when 400,000 Indian troops began military drills perilously close to the Pakistani border in the Sindh (Menon 2000; P.R. Chari 2007). The aim was to trigger a conventional war and simultaneously strike Kahuta (Khan 2002). The two sides realized that the time had come to craft a new set of CBMs to prevent a nuclear war. After the exercise terminated and the forces pulled back to their peace locations, the political leadership of the two countries concluded the first nuclear CBM titled, the Prohibition of Attack against Nuclear Facilities. This bilateral agreement was signed on December 31, 1988, ratified in 1991 and implemented in January 1992 (Khoja 1998). To make the process more transparent, both parties are required to annually exchange lists of the location of all their nuclear-related facilities. This ritual is being faithfully complied with, despite periods of tension. Since 1991, there has been an agreement to send advance notices of military exercises and maneuvers and prevent airspace violations (Yamin 2012).

India and Pakistan are both signatories to the Chemical Weapon Convention (CWC) ((OPCW) n.d). On August 19, 1992 the two countries also signed a bilateral agreement on chemical weapons (CW) (Studies n.d). After the nuclear tests of 1998, both countries placed a voluntary moratorium on further nuclear testing (UN n.d). In the September 1998 session of the UNGA the prime ministers of India and Pakistan pledged abstinence from further testing (Acronyms 1998). In February 1999, they met in Lahore, Pakistan, and agreed to: a Joint Statement by the Prime Ministers; a Memorandum of Understanding (MOU) by the Foreign Secretaries; and the Lahore Declaration itself. The major concerns identified in Lahore were about nuclear safety and security. In the joint statement by the prime ministers it was recognized that: "the nuclear dimension of the security environment of the two countries added to their responsibility of the avoidance of conflict between the two countries." The MOU aimed at nuclear risk reduction and improving nuclear security and prevent an accidental nuclear exchange. It called for the creation of communication mechanisms similar in some aspects to those required by the Convention on Early Notification of a Nuclear Accident. Specifically, the two sides committed to exchange information on their nuclear doctrines and security concepts; prevent accidental nuclear crises; work on measures to improve control over their nuclear weapons; review existing CBMs and emergency communications (hotlines) arrangements; and strengthen unilateral moratoriums on nuclear testing by making their commitments binding, barring of course extraordinary events jeopardizing supreme national interests (USIP n.d). The Kargil conflict that followed three months later disrupted the Lahore process. There have been no major clashes along the Line of Control (LoC) after 1999. An informal ceasefire was put in place in 2003 (Karl 2013), which barring occasional violations is still holding out (Mahr 2013).

In November 2005 Pakistan and India signed the ballistic missile advance notification agreement (Centre n.d). Under this accord, the country's defense ministries are obligated to provide their counterparts at least 72 hours of notice before conducting a ballistic missile flight test. They are not to allow trajectories of tested missiles to approach or land close either to their accepted borders or the LOC. They are not to allow tested missiles to fly closer than 40 kilometers from these boundaries or land closer than 70 kilometers away. This warning does not extend to cruise missiles (Creegan n.d).

On substantial issues India and Pakistan have not moved from their entrenched positions during the past few years. In the bargain, despite active Track I (formal) and Track II (informal) negotiations, opportunities have been missed to pluck 'low hanging fruits' like Siachen and Sir Creek. Impartial third party studies have also failed to break the proverbial ice on issues like the demilitarization of the Siachen glacier (Rajen 2007). The slow process of the composite dialogue process notwithstanding (Lodhi 2013), optimists keep floating new ideas on CBMs (ACCU n.d). However, no one has yet broached the issue of CBMs in information space.

Although CBMs are not legally binding treaty obligations but this inherent flexibility gives them a chance of success in the long run. There are several phases in the lifecycle of a CBM. In the preparatory phase, the parties concerned prepare grounds for the negotiations by seeking commonality of interests. The negotiation phase is a very delicate one and requires tact and patience from all those involved. Once the differences have been ironed out and broad consensus obtained on substantial issues, the next phase is that of implementation. If CBMs successfully survive this phase, the next one is to improve, strengthen and possibly upgrade these to the status of treaties and formal accords.

The success and failure of CBMs depends on the seriousness of purpose displayed by the stakeholders, the quality of negotiations, and the sincerity with which these are implemented. The chances of a CBM negotiation succeeding depends in the first instance upon the commitment and sincerity of the governments; the charisma of the leadership and the negotiating skills of the interlocutors to steer through road bumps and hurdles. Openness to new ideas and an attitude of give and take is always helpful in nudging things forward. Having subject specialists with specific skill sets on the negotiating teams is always helpful in fine tuning a CBM. The domestic media may help by building a favorable public opinion and by desisting from creating a hype and raising unrealistic expectations. CBMs on delicate issues are best negotiated out of the media glare. The failed Agra summit between India and Pakistan is just one example(NDTV 2001). Finally, the chances of CBMs surviving and standing the test of time, is based on the premise that these are realistic in approach, simple and practical to enforce and easy to monitor and verify. Prolonged periods of non-use can render even the most promising of CBMs ineffective.

South Asia watchers are of the opinion that India and Pakistan have been reactive and not proactive in formulating CBMs (Higgins n.d). This observation may not be germane to South Asia alone. It has happened elsewhere too e.g. the Kremlin-Whitehouse hotline resulted from the 1962 Cuban missile crisis and the Stockholm agreement of 1986 was the result of large scale military exercises that preceded it (Allen 2001). However, the East-West relationship moved on from being reactionary to proactive. The entire range of arms control initiatives both the strategic arms limitation talks (SALT) and the strategic arms reduction talks (START) were forward looking measures aimed to prevent a nuclear arms race. Perhaps there is something to learn from there.

Information CBMs

The first mention of information security CBMs was made at the 2005 WSIS summit held in Tunis. It was agreed here that it was essential to strengthen the "trust framework, including information security and network security, authentication, privacy and consumer protection, is a prerequisite for the development of the Information Society and for building confidence among users of ICTs." In order to do so it was considered appropriate that a global culture of cyber-security should be promoted through "cooperation with all stakeholders and international expert bodies." It was understood that developing a cyber-security culture would require "the protection of data and privacy, while enhancing access and trade." These conflicting requirements would require taking into account "the level of social and economic development of each country and respect the development-oriented aspects of the Information Society." The WSIS resolved to support the activities of the UN "to prevent the potential use of ICTs for purposes that are inconsistent with the objectives of maintaining international stability and security, and may adversely affect the integrity of the infrastructure within States, to the detriment of their security. It is necessary to prevent the use of information resources and technologies for criminal and terrorist purposes, while respecting human rights." It was recognized spam as "a significant and growing problem for users, networks and the Internet as a whole," and therefore it needed to be dealt with at "appropriate national and international levels." Last but not least the WSIS emphasized that "Confidence and security" were "among the main pillars of the Information Society" (Union 2005).

Pre-Requisites for Information CBMs

A necessary precondition for developing cyberspace CBMs is to have good national cybersecurity policies and practices, particularly for the protection of critical infrastructure ((NIST) 2013). Since all countries and most businesses are digitally linked to each other, their mutual interdependence has increased manifold. Axiomatically, therefore, the national cyber practices and policies have regional and international implications. Poor national cybersecurity practices will most likely weaken collective cyber defenses. In this regard it is in the interest of governments, businesses as well as individual users with greater capacity to assist governments, business and users in countries with lesser capacity. Such measures will improve the confidence and trust among nations and will also strengthen global cybersecurity. Shoring up the cyber defenses cannot be done by governments alone and expertise available in the private sector, as well as in the academic circles, civil society and users can be helpful. This mutual collaboration requires:

Capacity Building. As discussed earlier, a lot of guidance is available on cyber capacity building in form of the UN resolutions on the Creation of a Global Culture of Cybersecurity (57/239, 58/199, 64/211), the OECD Guidelines for the Security of Information Systems and Networks, as well as the work of the ITU and other intergovernmental agencies, as well as businesses and non-governmental bodies. The key characteristics of this exercise includes stocktaking of the public key infrastructure (PKI) (Security n.d); investigating threats and vulnerabilities; identifying stakeholders and their responsibilities; raising national awareness; developing public and private cooperation; putting in place national policies and strategies, developing appropriate organizational structures; developing appropriate legal frameworks especially to facilitate law enforcement cooperation across jurisdictions on cybercrime; and perhaps most importantly developing a national incident response and management capacity. In each of these fields international cooperation, linkages and networks are important. Clearly, the plan to develop capacity building mechanisms has to be seen through from basic design questions to the implementation stage (Building n.d).

Raising Awareness. Many governments are blissfully ignorant of emerging cyber threats. The first step, therefore, is to raise awareness among official quarters regarding this sensitive topic. Policymakers need to understand how dependent their countries have become on ICTs and the vulnerabilities this reliance has created. This ignorance void can be covered through dialogue between states at the diplomatic, operational and technical levels, and between the public and private sectors on cyber security issues. This can be supplemented by launching initiatives to raise awareness among businesses and individual users to create good online security practices. This can be done for instance by observing annual Cyber Security Awareness Days. This event can help promote secure online practices. Effective partnerships can be established with the industry to address cybersecurity issues through the development and promotion of good practices guidelines. National Cyber Security Awareness Weeks can also be observed to help users and small businesses to understand cybersecurity risks, and develop effective cyber security practices.

Developing Policies and Structures. Countries without robust cyber security structures are the weak links in the international system. Therefore, it is important to develop sound national cybersecurity policies. The policies would be based on available cyber ideologies and the prevailing cyber philosophy of the country. This will help form cyber crisis management responses. A well-defined strategy would help the government to streamline and coordinate cyber security approaches. Improved coordination within governments on cybersecurity issues is a key ingredient in managing coordinated responses. Improved government coordination on cybersecurity issues would strengthen its capacity to prevent, manage and react to cyber crises. This is also important to harmonize crisis communications measures with other governments. Improved government cyber activity is thus critical in the development of a number of measures between governments.

Establishing Incident Management and Response Systems. A key element of national cybersecurity strategy is the creation of national capacity to manage and respond to incidents. A crisis management plan and cyber exercises to test the plan are critical corollaries, vital for improving the national cyber security potential. The plan would be based on a cyber defence design taking into account the data security standards; the mechanism for Cyber Event Detection; Incident Response; Internal Investigation; Third-party Forensic Investigation; Law Enforcement; Customer Notification; and a Containment and Remediation Plan (Faculty n.d). National incident response capacity is an essential part of the international incident response network. Countries also need to think about their capacity to protect and defend key government networks. The national cyber incident response system requires two bodies i.e. national and organizational CERTs and a Cyber Security Operations Centre for protecting the Government's critical infrastructure.

Holding Cyber Security Incident Response Workshops (Debate 2013). Workshops aimed at developing the national and organizational capacities to respond to cyber emergencies can be useful. The objectives of such workshops could include topics such as the essentials elements of national cyber defenses; information sharing methods in case of an incident; identifying best practice; and prioritizing capacity building activities for those countries with less mature frameworks and mechanisms. A number of practical scenarios can be discussed at such forums based on the level of willingness of the countries.

One challenge could indeed be the information sharing mechanism before an incident occurs, and to improve preparedness and prevention. Such workshops can become important platforms to understand the capabilities and responsibilities of the countries through face to face discussions in an atmosphere of confidence and trust.

Improving Policies. Developing good cybersecurity is an ongoing process. These policies and practices need to be constantly improved and the capabilities of CERTs and Cyber Security Operations Centre should be upgraded to stand up to emerging challenges. In undertaking this work the governments will have find out areas of common interest in the realm of cyber security. In this respect, it would be worthwhile, to encourage the governments to issue Cyberspace White Paper laying down a framework for maximizing opportunities and minimizing the risks of the digital age (*ABC News*, July 29, 2013). The policies outlined in the White Paper should support the development of long-term trust and confidence in the online world and contribute to the development of international norms of behavior in cyberspace.

Crafting Cyber Security Work Plan. Last but not least there is a need to develop national cybersecurity work plans. These work plans should not only provide users a guideline to enforce cyber security measures in government and organizations' offices (DHS n.d), but also seriously consider ways and means for peaceful collaboration with other nations in cyberspace.

Suggested Information CBMs

Keeping in mind the basic building blocks of CBMs i.e. communication, constraint, verification and monitoring, countries genuinely interested in establishing confidence and trust in information space should consider the following:

1. Information Sharing. Sharing information can go a long way in reducing suspicion and mistrust. Non-classified portions of the national cyber security policies; national organizations, programs, or relevant cyber security strategies and standard cyber terminology; emergency response SOPs; and methods of communicating cyber incidents can be conveniently exchanged. A still better way of sharing information can be with regards best practices. This can be done by organizing regional seminars and exchanging visits of experts.

2. Joint Emergency Response Systems. Battling cyber threats jointly can increase the sense of participation in a common cause. A number of countries are already pooling their expertise and resources in regional CERTs and developing joint strategies to respond to ICT emergencies. Emergency drills could be organized to sharpen the skills of first responders.

3. Restraint Agreements. A path breaking form of information space CBM can be an agreement enjoining upon interested parties to refrain from directing malicious cyber activities against critical infrastructure vital to the wellbeing of civilians, such as telecommunications, energy, transportation and financial systems. Experts are of the opinion that adversaries like the "US and China are *both* increasingly vulnerable to each other in strategic domains – nuclear, space, and cyberspace – where great harm can be done" (Saunders n.d). Commonsense therefore demands that countries should exercise mutual restraint in these fields.

4. Means of Recognition and Respect. Cyber bullying has become a common phenomenon in modern societies.(Graeve 2005) Online hate crime is rife (Division n.d). Cyber intimidation and coercion is now considered part of cyber-terrorism (Denning 2007). Such obnoxious behavior can only be controlled by developing an acceptable code of conduct in cyberspace. Unwarranted propaganda

and hacktivism can increase mistrust and sour relations. One way to improve trust and confidence is to enter into agreements to recognize and respect national cyber jurisdictions (Agin 2008).

5. Defining Responsibilities. If governments are held responsible for the cyber misdeeds of companies and organizations located on their sovereign territories, a lot of irresponsible activity can be curtailed. This can in the long run engender trust. It is therefore important to lay down precisely the responsibilities of the governments and their national organizations to behave in cyber-space in accordance with the international and national legislations (GAO n.d).

6. Means of Attribution. One major problem associated with cyber-attacks is that of 'attribution.' It is very difficult to assign responsibility to the perpetrator of a malicious activity either technically or at a human level (Bobert n.d). Yet it is not entirely impossible to investigate cyber-attacks forensically and assign responsibility (Stilts 2013). One way of making attribution easier is by declaring the geographic location of known IP addresses. Exchanging such information on regular basis can become the bedrock of information space CBMs.

India and Pakistan Information Space CBMs

Given their wide experience in negotiating and practicing CBMs India and Pakistan can find areas of building trust in the information space as well. Following are some of the recommended CBMs:

1. Bilateral Agreements. Pakistan and India can choose from a host of bilateral agreements on cyber security, some of which are fairly benign.
    ○   Agreement on Cybercrime Laws. Cybercrime is one area, where both countries can collaborate without agitating the domestic hawks. An agreement to jointly tackle cybercrime can cover broad range of issues like harmonizing laws covering cybercrime like online theft. Social issues like child pornography and human trafficking already find mention in law manuals (Bernadette H. Schell 2006). An international conference was held in Vienna in September-October 1999, where it was agreed to show zero tolerance towards child pornography on the Internet and to criminalize this activity at the worldwide level (Diplomacy 1999). An Optional Protocol to the Convention on the Rights of the Child on the sale of children, child prostitution and child pornography (OP-CRC-CPC) was enacted by the UN in 2000 (UN 2000). The two countries can expand on the existing statutes and develop laws to curb this nefarious activity, involving regional and international rings.
    ○   Agreement on Not to Attack Essential Services. Drawing inspiration from the IHL, Rule 80 of the *Tallinn Manual* recommends that:

In order to avoid the release of dangerous forces and consequent severe losses among the civilian population, particular care must be taken during cyber-attacks against works and installations containing dangerous forces, namely dams, dykes, and nuclear electrical generating stations, as well as installations located in their vicinity.(Schmidt 2013)

This humanitarian tenet has actually been practiced in the South Asian wars fought between 1947 and 1971, where India and Pakistan had both avoided bombing essential services like dams, dykes and electrical works. This spirit can be extended into the cyberspace. The essential services not to be subjected to cyber-attacks could be expanded to include financial institutions, industrial units, water and sewerage systems, nuclear power plants, health and emergency services. The critical C2 systems can in fact be declared as a cyber-attack exclusive zone (Schmidt 2013).

- ○ Agreement on Not to Target National Command Authorities. Cyber-attacks against national/nuclear command authorities (NCAs) can leave individual commanders and weapon handlers with no choice but to make independent decisions with regards conventional as well as nuclear weapons. Such a worst case scenario could have apocalyptic consequences. Fortunately both countries have a CBM, pledging not to attack each other's facilities. Article 1 (i) of this 1988 agreement can be amended by including the cyber dimension through an amendment or an Additional Protocol (Brig Feroz Hassan Khan, personal communication, July 14 2013).

- ○ Agreement to Refrain from Hostile Propaganda. Social media has made the spreading of rumors and fanning hatred much easier than through state controlled media. The governments of Pakistan and India need to seriously study this issue and come up with imaginative ways of curbing uncontrolled activity in this domain. Hostile media effect is a subject of serious study. Case studies indicate that perception management by media can aggravate an already tense situation (Robert P. Vallone 1985). There have been agreements between Pakistan and India in the past to cease hostile propaganda against each other e.g. in the fall of 1974, the foreign secretaries of India and Pakistan had exchanged letters agreeing to a cessation of hostile propaganda through radio broadcasts. This agreement came into force on October 21, 1974 (Lyon 2008). Although this was never followed in letter and spirit, this concept can be extended to the social media, to avoid toxic fallouts from instances like a potentially damaging video clip going viral.

2. Joint Emergency Teams. Both India and Pakistan can become part of joint teams to handle computer emergencies and monitor criminal and terrorist activity in cyberspace. This can be done at the bilateral level or within the framework of regional organizations like the SAARC or SCO. Both countries are members of the SAARC and have observer status in the SCO. Whereas, SAARC has become a moribund organization, a victim of irreconcilable issues between India and Pakistan, SCO is not only very active in security and counter terrorism issues; it is the only regional association which has an agreement on cyber security. Creating a joint CERT within SCO and SAARC is worth exploring.

3. Joint Monitoring &Policing. The two countries can set up a joint cell to monitor illicit activity in cyber space and share vital information. Forming a cyber police force on the pattern of Intepol, Europol and ASEANOPOL can be put on the information space CBM's menu.

4. Training. There is a lot of scope in building trust by sharing common experiences at professional forums. Regional seminars and meets of technical people and cyber security experts can be organized to share best practices and common experiences in dealing with computer emergencies (UNIDIR 2012). Exchanging IT students for fellowships or regular degrees can be another way of reducing mistrust.

5. Information Space Hotline. Hotlines between the national computer emergency response centers will not only enhance reaction times to respond to emergencies but also strengthen the belief in each other's dependability.

These and other meaningful suggestions can be considered in creating a credible cyber security CBM regime between India and Pakistan.

PART V: THE WAY FORWARD

It has been suggested in this paper that before formal laws governing cyber activity are formalized, information space CBMs should be considered. According UN policy guidelines, the ultimate goal of CBMs is to strengthen international peace and security (UNGA 1986). Peace in cyberspace can be greatly facilitated by instituting internationally recognized cyber code of conduct. This will help reduce tensions, enhance transparency and make state behavior predictable (Walker n.d). Imaginative CBMs can precede complex negotiations on treaty agreements and longwinded ratification procedures. CBMs can sometimes even be installed unilaterally. Of course, a well prepared package of CBMs with consensus can set into motion a genuine peace process.

Currently, most activities in cyberspace take place amidst a deep feeling of distrust and high secrecy cyber military applications. Wide disparities of views among states, insufficient research on important regulatory issues and lack of a common vision about the future of cyberspace makes cooperation in this area a complicated issue. Some crucial issues may not lend themselves to a CBM negotiation on broad principles at all. Differences exist on common definitions on cyber warfare, lack of agreement on what constitutes an armed attack or what responses would be justified, and what should be the rules of engagement in cyberspace. It will take a long time before these basic issues are resolved.

At the present juncture there is no movement either on the part of India or Pakistan to broaching the subject of cybersecurity. The issue of collaborating or building cyber CBMs is nowhere on the horizon. Once the governments recognize that there is a need to include this on the negotiation agenda, the process will start and then problems of structure and content will follow. Contributions from outside, including state parties, international and regional organizations, academic community and dedicated NGOs would help shape the proceedings. Local experts can contribute by taking stock of the existing situation and making independent assessment of how new ideas can be incorporated. For the moment this project may sound ambitious but then this may just be the right time to initiate it before things begin to heat up. Clearly, only genuine negotiations based on common interests will help carry forward the process (Churchman 1995). Professional groups can help set the agenda for the negotiation, by pressing for more transparency in the official doctrines and recommending better mechanisms of international cooperation and crisis management. UN urges cooperation among governments on the subject of cyber security and the USG is willing to "build and sustain an environment in which norms of responsible behavior guide states' actions, sustain partnerships, and sustain the law of cyberspace" (House 2011). Well-reflected inputs from published material like the *Tallinn Manual* on the applicability of international law in cyber warfare will prove useful.

Preliminary regional endeavors are already under way, and their dynamics should be used. If a regional approach prevails, some coordinating mechanism should be developed to avoid contrasting or setting contradictory standards. A new forum for cyber security can also be considered outside the existing ones (Wegener 2007). The political implications and acceptance potential of any of these options have to be weighed carefully, and international experts could be invited to provide their inputs.

ROADMAP FOR INDIA PAKISTAN INFORMATION SPACE CBMs

Preliminary Issues

Before earnest negotiations are undertaken, there is a requirement that the two governments start cooperating by building awareness at public and private levels on the necessity and virtues of cyber-security. Simultaneously there is a need to craft robust domestic cyber laws and wholesome cybersecurity policies. The suggested approach for establishing sustainable cyber-contacts should progress through a carefully calibrated process from informal to formal stages. It is reiterated that unnecessary media hype and undue publicity can be fatal for any meaningful dialogue in South Asia and hence should be avoided. The following roadmap is suggested:

Phase I (Informal Contacts and Capacity Building)

1. Contacts between Technical Societies. The first step in initiating cyber-contacts should be between technical societies working on cyber security issues. These societies should be encouraged to form a regional hub to set semi-official cyber ground rules in South Asia. The governments could patronize these societies and offer them guidance by arranging local and international workshops. The IEEE is one international forum with presence both in India and Pakistan. In Pakistan IEEE sections are located in Islamabad, Lahore and Karachi (IEEE n.d). Peshawar subsection also appears in the IEEE map. The Islamabad section has a Computer Society Chapter (IEEE n.d). The IEEE regularly organizes international technical conferences through its computer society (IEEE n.d). A SAARC IEEE could have a meaningful cyber presence in the region.

2. Contacts between Academic Communities/Universities. Another informal forum for exchange on cyber information could be the universities. In this regard it would be useful to organize regional seminars to share best practices and showcase the latest trends in cyber security. Universities can play an important role in building capacities through cross pollination of ideas i.e. through exchange of students and by developing courses that could be useful for cyber security professionals. NUST School of Electrical Engineering & Computer Sciences (SEECS) (SEECS n.d). and FAST National University of Computers and Emerging Sciences (Sciences n.d) are two world class schools of computer sciences in Pakistan with the potential of contributing towards developing a common cyber security culture in South Asia.

3. Capacity Building. Professional organizations can help build national capacities in drafting cyber laws, improving the quality of cyber policing through improved cyber forensics, investigation and prosecution methods. The national parliamentarian training services (Services n.d), bar associations (*The Strait Times*, January 24, 1997), police training academies (National Police Academy n.d), and judicial academies (Pakistan n.d), can provide good forums for cyber capacity building. The telecommunication authorities of both countries also need to be trained to handle emergencies like politically motivated unrest spread through rumor mongering on the social media. So far the telecom agencies in South Asia namely, the Telecommunication Regulatory Authority of India (India n.d), and Pakistan Telecommunication Authority (PTA) (Authority n.d), have both reacted to inflammatory texting or objectionable video clips by shutting down mobile texting services, laying down restrictions on the content of the text (Horn n.d), and banning video sharing and social media sites (*MailOnline*, May 21, 2010).

Phase II (Non Military CBMs)

1. Police Collaboration to Combat Transnational Cybercrime. Collaboration between the police forces can be an ideal way of creating CBMs at the official level. Cybercrime is a trans-border phenomenon. Regional and international police forces are collaborating to fight it and have successfully established joint monitoring and reporting centers. Collaborations among Interpol, Europol and ASEANOPOL can provide useful examples of joint cyber policing in South Asia (Interpol 2013).

2. Legal Collaboration to Frame Cyber Laws. Neither Pakistan nor India is a signatory to the CEC. They can accede to this agreement and also come up with bilateral agreements to harmonize local laws to jointly prosecute transnational cybercrime. The two countries can mutually organize seminars and training sessions to build capacities for lawyers and legislators to frame cyber laws.

3. Joint CERTs. Pakistan and India can combine forces to respond to computer emergencies by forming joint CERTs bilaterally or within the forum of SAARC or the SCO. A joint CERT would be an excellent CBM.

Phase III (Military Cyber CBMs)

1. Define Redlines. Military cyber CBMs can be a hard sell. One way to proceed in this regard could be by setting redlines, which could prompt a response. One way to do so can be by identifying n-go areas, where no cyber operations should be permitted.

2. Decide Upon De-Escalatory Measures. Keeping various scenarios in mind necessary de-escalatory measures could be worked out in advance before a situation gets out of control.

3. Establish Cyber Hotline. A dedicated hotline linking professionals and policy planners would help first responders to react immediately and the political leadership to undertake de-escalatory measures quickly.

Phase IV (Cyber Cooperation through Treaties)

1. Bilateral Treaties on Cybercrime. The next step to CBMs are regular treaties. Bilateral treaties criminalizing cybercrime would help both countries to efficiently combat cybercrime and increase trust in each other.

2. Bilateral Military Treaties. Areas can be selected, where the two countries would find it agreeable to collaborate. Binding agreements not to attack each other's national C2 centers could be a major coup, if it can be brokered.

CONCLUSION

Cyber CBMs have yet to be accepted as a means to establishing trust in conflict zones. Yet this is exactly the area, where the nations need to make progress. This is indeed a complex issue involving integration of high technology with low technology, understanding the implications of international law, seeing cybercrime and cyber military attacks as overlapping activities and building a common perception about Internet governance. Of course these ideas have been synchronized with other issues like national security exceptions, human rights and privacy policies, which need careful study (Abraham D. Sofaer n.d). Since cyberspace is becoming dangerous by the day, there is a dire need to institute international and regional measures to create a healthy respect for national sovereignty in cyberspace.

CBMs between India and Pakistan have a checkered history. Yet in times of crises these have proven extremely useful in preventing wars and facilitating conflict resolution. The first step towards conflict resolution is removal of mistrust and suspicion. Only then, can the dialogue process begin. It is a hard task to popularize the concept of CBMs between the two countries without removing suspicions and misunderstanding among people about the implied objectives and application of such measures.

In order to institutionalize the process of information based CBMs, it is necessary to create basic awareness among governments, organizations and the common man to embrace this concept. Currently, there is little knowledge at policy making circles about the vulnerabilities associated with ICT tools used for governance and management. This awareness can be created with the assistance of international organizations and local NGOs. Workshops, seminars, track II and track III efforts will help.

Multiple factors should be kept in mind, while formulating information space CBMs. First, the process should be kept out of media glare. Second, it should begin informally and should steadily progress upto official levels. Thirdly, a regional approach may help and facilitate India and Pakistan move out of the vicious circle of bilateral animosity. SAARC needs to be resuscitated. It can draw some inspiration from ASEAN by constructively keeping a low-key approach to contentious issues.(Parameswaran 2012). Balance between military and non-military CBMs is essential for creating conditions for peace. Non-military CBMs such as collaboration between the police forces, the legal, technical and academic communities can certainly make things easier for sustaining the dialogue process between antagonistic parties.

It would be foolish to expect miracles from information space CBMs overnight. It had taken a considerable amount of time for CBMs to work out in other areas. However, one cannot help but repeat that the need for India and Pakistan to begin negotiating cybersecurity CBMs is both immediate and vital.

REFERENCES

A Comprehensive Approach to Cyber Security. (n. d.). *OSCE*. Retrieved from http://www.osce.org/event/cyber_sec2011

A New Philosophy and Approach to Incident Response. (n. d.). Retrieved from http://www.poole.ncsu.edu/erm/index.php/articles/entry/Cyber-Crisis-Management

Abbasi, A. H. (2012). *Indus Basin Treaty*. Pildat Report, Pildat.

Abraham, D. Sofaer, D. C., & Whitfield D. (n. d.). Cyber Security and International Agreements. *Proceedings of workshop on Deterring Cyber Attacks: Informing Strategies and Developing Options for US Policy.*

India-Pakistan Military CBMs Project – Phase 1: Final Report. (n. d.). *ACCU*. Retrieved from http://www.acus.org/files/Final%20Project%20report%20-%20Phase%201_Sept%2025.pdf

Additional Protocol to the Convention on Cybercrime ETS 189. (2003). *Council of Europe*. Retrieved from http://conventions.coe.int/Treaty/en/Treaties/Html/189.htm

Agin, W. E. (2008, March 26). Internet Law Liability Report #3: Jurisdictions in Cyberspace. *American Bar Association, Law Cyberspace Law Committee.*

Agreement between India and Pakistan on Pre-Notification of Flight Testing of Ballistic Missiles. (n. d.). *Stimson.org.* Retrieved from http://www.stimson.org/research-pages/agreement-between-india-and-pakistan-on-pre-notification-of-flight-testing-of-ballistic-missiles/

Agreement between Military Representatives of India and Pakistan Regarding the Establishment of a Ceasefire Line in the State of Jammu and Kashmir (Karachi Agreement). (1949, July 27). *United Nations Peacemaker.* Retrieved from http://peacemaker.un.org/indiapakistan-karachiagreement49

Ahmar, M. (Ed.) (2001). The Challenges of Confidence Building in South Asia. New Delhi: Har-Anand Publications.

Ahmer, M. (Ed.). (1997). *Internal and External Dynamics of South Asian Security.* Karachi: Fazleesons.

Ahsan, S. A. (2008). *Current Situation and Issues of Illegal and Harmful Activities in the Field of Information and Communication Technology in Pakistan* [participant papers]. 140th International Training Course.

Akuetteh, T. (n. d.). Creating the Enabling Environment within the ECOWAS Region [Visual Presentation].

Aldrich, R. W. (1996, Fall). The International Legal Implications of Information Warfare. *Airpower Journal.*

Alexander, D. (2011). U.S. reserves right to meet cyber attack with force.

Allen, K. W. (2001). *Confidence Building Measures and the People's Liberation Army. In C. Cao & B. J. Dickson (Eds.) Remaking the Chinese State: Strategies, Society and Security.* (pp. 228-252). London: Routledge.

Amoroso, E. G. (2011). *Cyber Attacks: Protecting National Infrastructure. Burlington MA.* El SevierInc.

Andreasen, S. & Clarke, R. A. (2013, June 14). Cyberwar's threat does not justify a new policy of nuclear deterrence. *The Washington Post.*

Arimatsu, L. (2012). *The legal application of the prohibition of the threat or use of force in cyberspace: A starting point? Proceedings of Cyber Security Conference 2012: The Role of Confidence-Building Measures in Assuring Cyber Stability.* Geneva, Switzerland: UNIDIR.

Arvind Gupta (2012). CBMs in Cyber Space: What should be India's Approach? *Institue for Defence Studies and Analyses.*

ASEAN Cybercrimelaw. (n. d.). *Cybercrimelaw.net.* Retrieved from http://www.cybercrimelaw.net/ASEAN.html

Joint Media Statement of 12th ASEAN Telecommunications and IT Ministers. (2012, November 19). *Association of Southeast Asian Nations.* Retrieved from http://www.asean.org/news/asean-statement-communiques/item/joint-media-statement-of-the-12th-asean-telecommunications-and-it-ministers-meeting-and-its-related-meetings-with-dialogue-partners

Ashwood, W. (2013). David Cameron pledges UK collaboration with India to fight Cyber Attacks. *ComputerWeekly.com.*

APEC Strategy to Ensure Trusted, Secure and Sustainable Online Environment. (n. d.). *Asia-Pacific Economic Cooperation.* Retrieved from http://www.apec.org/Groups/SOM-Steering-Committee-on-Economic-and-Technical-Cooperation/Working-Groups/~/media/Files/Groups/TEL/05_TEL_APEC-Strategy.pdf

At UN, Kazakhstan calls for global cybersecurity treaty to deter hackers. (2011). *UN News Centre.* Retrieved from http://www.un.org/

Bagchi, I. (2013). Government to Roll Out New Cybersecurity Architecture. *The Times of India.*

Bajpai, K. (1999). *Confidence Building Measures in South Asia Regional Centre of Strategic Studies.* Colombo.

Bank, W. (1960). Indus Waters Treaty.

Bernadette, H. S., Martin, M. V., Hung, P. C. K., & Rueda, L. (2006). Cyber child pornography: a review paper of the social and legal issues and remedies – and a proposed technological solution. In Aggression and Violent Behavior, Vol. 12(1), (2007, January/February).

Blount, A. (2012-13). Topic I: Assessing the current state of cybersecurity and its implications for regional defense and economic interest. *Model Arab League.*

Bobert, W. E. (n. d.). A Survey of Challenges in Attribution. Proceedings of workshop *Deterring Cyber Attacks: Informing Strategies and Developing Options for U.S. Policy.* (pp. 43).

Boland, J. (2011, June 20). Ten Years of the Shanghai Cooperation Organization. *21st Century Defense Initiative.*

Brodsky, R. R. J. (Ed.). (2013). *Handbook of SCADA/Control Systems Security.* CRC Press.

Bumiller, E. (2013). Pentagon Expanding Cybersecurity Force to Protect Networks against Attacks. *The New York Times.*

Carr, J. (2010). *Inside Cyber Warfare: Mapping the Cyber Underworld. Sebastopol*, CA: O'Reilly Media Inc.

Carr, J. (2012). OSCE's Cyber Security Confidence Building Measures Revealed by Anonymous. Retrieved from http://jeffreycarr. blogspot.com/2012/11/osces-cyber-security-confidence.htm

Casey-Maslen, S. (2010). Non-kinetic-energy weapons termed 'non-lethal:' A Preliminary Assessment under International Humanitarian Law and International Human Rights Law.

CBC (2011). Report of the 30thMeeting of the Council of Ministers: Harnessing Science and Technology for Development 37.

CET No. 185. (n. d.). *Council of Europe Convention on Cybercrimes.* Retrieved from http://conventions. coe.int/Treaty/Commun/ChercheSig.asp?NT=185&CM=8&DF=&CL=ENG

Chabot, S. (2013) Asia: The Cyber Security Battleground.

Challenges in Cyber Security. (2011). *Risks, Strategies and Confidence Building – Germany* [Conference Report]. Berlin: German Ministry of Foreign Affairs.

Chander, M. (n. d.). *National Critical Information Infrastructure Protection Centre (NCIIPC): Role, Charter & Responsibilities* [Visual Presentation].

Chari, P. R., Cheema, P. I., & Cohen, S. P. (2007). Four Crisis and a Peace Process. Washington, DC: The Brookings Institute. (pp. 39-79).

China, Russia and Other Countries Submit the Document of International Code of Conduct for Information Security to the United Nations.(2011). Ministry of Foreign Affairs of the People's Republic of China. Retrieved from http://www.fmprc.gov.cn/eng/

China, US Agree to Combat Cyber Crime. (2013). *eBeijing, Beijing International.* Retrieved from http://www.ebeijing.gov.cn/

Churchman, D. (1995). *Negotiations: Process, Tactics and Theory. New York*: University Press of America.

Clemente, D. (2012). Building Coherence and Understanding Foundational Work. Proceedings of *Cyber Security Conference 2012*. Geneva, Switzerland.

Cohn, M. K. N. (Ed.). (2011). Crises in South Asia: Trends and Potential Consequences Washington DC: Stimson Center.

Cold War Hotline Recalled. (2003). *British Broadcasting Company.* Retrieved from http://news.bbc.co.uk/2/hi/europe/2971558.stm

Collapse of the Agra Summit: The After-Story. (2001). NDTV.

Commonwealth of Independent States. (n. d.). *OpenNet Initiative.* Retrieved from https://opennet.net/research/regions/cis

Confidence-Building and Nuclear Risk-Reduction Measures in South Asia. (n. d.). *Stimson.org.* Retrieved from http://www.stimson.org/research-pages/confidence-building-measures-in-south-asia-

Confidence Building Measures. (2012). *Stimson.org.* Retrieved from http://www.stimson.org /topics/confidence-building-measures/

Connecting Police for a Safer World. (n. d.). Retrieved from http://www.interpol.int/About-INTERPOL/The-INTERPOL-Global-Complex-for-Innovation

Convention on the Prohibition of the Development, Production, Stockpiling and Use of Chemical Weapons and on their Destruction(OPCW). (n. d). *OPCW.* Retrieved from http://www.opcw.org/chemical-weapons-convention

Council of Europe adopts Internet Governance Strategy. (n. d.). Council of Europe. Retrieved from http://www.coe.int/t/DGHL/cooperation/economiccrime/cybercrime/default_en.asp

Council of Europe *Convention on Cybercrime, Budapest.* (2001). Retrieved from http://conventions.coe.int/Treaty/en/Treaties /Html/189.htm

Creegan, E. (n. d.). India Pakistan sign missile notification pact.

Crisis Management Plan for Cyber Attacks. (2010). Government of India.

CSA Homepage. (n. d.). *Cloud Security Alliance*. Retrieved, from https://cloudsecurityalliance.org/

Cyber Crime. (2011, July). *Issues Monitor*, Vol. 8. Retrieved from https://www.kpmg.com/Global/en/IssuesAndInsights/ArticlesPublications/Documents/cyber-crime.pdf

Cyber-Crime: Pakistan Criminal Records. (n. d.). *Pakistancriminalrecords.com*. from http://pakistan-criminalrecords.com/tag/cyber-crime

Cyber Laws of India. (n. d.). *Government of India*.

Cyber Security. (n. d.). *Oxford Martin School*. Retrieved from http://www.oxfordmartin.ox.ac.uk/institutes/cybersecurity

Cyber Security Planning Guide. (n. d.). Department of Homeland Security. *Dhs.gov*.

Cyber Threat Source Descriptions. (n. d.). *Industrial Control Systems Cyber Emergency Response Team (ICS-CERT)*. Retrieved from http://ics-cert.us-cert.gov/content/cyber-threat-source-descriptions

Cybercrime. (2011, July). Issues Monitor, Vol. 8. KPMG International.

Cybercrimes/e-crimes: Model Policy Guidelines and Legislative Texts. (n. d.). *International Telecommunication Union*. Retrieved from http://www.itu.int/

Cybersecurity. (2013, February 14). *U.S. Government Accountability Office. GAO.gov*.

Dalton, T. (2013). *Beyond Incrementalism: Rethinking Approaches to CBMs and Stability in South Asia*.

Davenport, K. (2012). *Hotline Agreements*.

Declaration for the Future of the Internet Economy. (2008, June 17-18). Proceedings of *Ministerial Meeting on the Future of Internet Economy*. Retrieved from http://www.oecd.org/futureinternet/

Declaration of the Heads of the SCO Member States on International Information Security [Translated]. (2006).

Defense Strategy for Operating in Cyberspace. (n. d.). *US Department of Defense*.

Hakeem, A., Kanwal, G., Vannoni, M., & Rajen, G. (2007, September). Demilitarization of the Siachen Conflict Zone: Concepts for Implementation and Monitoring. Sandia National Laboratories.

Denning, D. E. (2007). *Cyberterrorism: Testimony before the Special Oversight Panel on Terrorism Committee on Armed Services, US House of Representatives. In E.V. Linden (Ed.), Focus on Terrorism*. 9, (pp. 72–75). New York Nova Science Publishers.

Developing a Framework to Improve Critical Infrastructure Cybersecurity. (2013). *National Institute of Standards of Technology*.

Dieterle, D. (2012). *DARPA's Foundational CyberWarfare Plan-X: The Roadmap for Future CyberWar*. Retrieved from http://cyberarms.wordpress.com/2012/12/01/darpas-foundational-cyberwarfare-plan-x-the-roadmap-for-future-cyberwar/

Diplomacy: US, China aligned on North Korea, Climate and Cybercrime. (2013). *Deutschewelle.de*. Retrieved from http://www.dw.de/us-china-aligned-on-n-korea-climate-and-cybercrime/a-16868686

Disarmament and International Security: First Committee. (n. d.). *United Nations*.

Dixit, J. N. (2002). *India-Pakistan in War & Peace*. London: Routledge.

EC3: A Collective EU Response to Cyber-Crime. (n. d.). *Europol*. Retrieved from https://www.europol.europa.eu/ec3

Edward, M. (2012). *India accuses Pakistan of using social media to stir tensions*. ABC News.

Ellis, B. W. (2001). The International Legal Implications and Limitations of Information Warfare: What Are Our Options?.

European Cybercrime Task Force. (n. d.). *Europol*. Retrieved from http://europol.easyred.com/?p=129

European Telecommunications Standards Institute. (n. d.) *ETSI*. Retrieved from http://www.ihs.com/products/industry-standards/organizations/etsi/index.aspx

Farnsworth, T. (n. d.). *China and Russia Submit Cyber Proposal*.

Federal Judicial Academy. (n. d.). *Government of Pakistan*. Retrieved from http://www.fja.gov. pk

Fedosov, S. (2012). *What does a Stable Cyber Environment look like? Cyber Security Conference 2012: The Role of Confidence-Building Measures in Assuring Cyber Stability*. Geneva, Switzerland: UNIDIR.

Fidler, D. P. (2013). Call Me, Maybe: New US-Russia Cybersecurity Initiatives.

FIRST is the global Forum for Incident Response and Security Teams. (n. d.). Retrieved from http://www.first.org/

FIRST Members. (n. d.). Retrievedfrom http://www.first.org/members/teams/cert-in

Fischer, E. A. (2012). *Federal Laws Relating to Cybersecurity: Discussion of Proposed Revisions*. CRS.

Fitter, M. K. P. M. (2013). *Beware of the Bugs. Business Today*.

Agreement between the Governments of the Member States of the SCO on Cooperation in the Field of International Information Security. (2009, June 15). FMPRC. Retrieved from http://www.fmprc.gov.cn/eng/wjdt/2649 /t569701.htm

Fox, H. (n. d.). The Contribution of Capacity Building to Developing Confidence between States in Cyber Space. Proceedings of ARF Seminar on *Confidence Building Measures in Cyber Space*.

Franchi, H. L. (2013). US-China Cybersecurity Talks. *The Christian Science Monitor*. Retrieved from http://www.csmonitor.com/USA/Foreign-Policy/2013/0709/US-China-cybersecurity-talks-Will-Snowden-leaks-thwart-US-goals

Fulghum, D. A. (2010). Cyber Attacks no longer Non-kinetic.

Functions and Powers of the General Assembly. (n. d.). *United Nations*.

Ghosh, S. (2009). Indo-Pak Composite Dialogue - 2008: Revi.

Gibilisco, S. (2012). *Computer Security Incident Response Team*. CSIRT.

Gill, A. (2012). What does a stable cyber environment look like. Proceedings of *Cyber Security Conference 2012*. Geneva, Switzerland.

Gjelten, T. (2012) *Extending the Law of War into Cyberspace*.

Global Surveillance Data: US Places Pakistan on Second Position in NSA Spy List. (n. d.). Retrieved from http://bbcrecord.com/live/ct-menu-item-17/pakistan/10-pakistan/544-global-surveillance-data-us-places-pakistan-on-second-position-in-nsa-spy-list.html

GoI, M. (1972, July 2). *Simla Agreement*.

Goldman, J. (2013). Taiwan Says China's Cyber Army Now Numbers 100, 000.

Gomper, D. C., & Saunders, P. C. (2011). *Mutual Restraint in Cyberspace*. Washington, DC: Institute for National Strategic Studies.

Graeve, J. B. S. (Ed.). (2005). No Room for Bullies: From the Classroom to Cyber Space. Nebraska: Boys Town Press.

Gupta, A. (2012). *CBMs in Cyber Space: What should be India's Approach?*

Haeryong, K. (2012). The ARF perspective on TCBMs. Proceedings of *Cyber Security Conference 2012*. Geneva, Switzerland.

Hardy, C. (2012). Cyber-space now seen as 'fifth dimension of warfare'. Retrieved from http://www.publicserviceeurope. com/article/1485/cyber-space-now-seen-as-fifth-dimension-of-warfare

Hassan, S. R. (2012). *Alarming Rise in Cyber Crimes*. Dawn.

Hathaway, O. A., Crootof, R., Levitz, P., Nix, H., Nowlan, A., Perdue, W. & Spiegel, Julia. (2012). *The Law of Cyber-Attack*. (pp. 54).

Healey, J. (n. d.). The Five Futures of Cyber Conflict and Cooperation. *Georgetown Journal for International Affairs*.

Healy, J. (2013). *The Future of US Cyber Command*.

Healy, R. J. (Ed.). (2013). A Fierce Domain: Conflict in Cyber Space, 1986 to 2012. Washington DC: CCSA Publication.

Heinl, C. H. (2013). Enhancing ASEAN-Wide Cybersecurity: Time For A Hub Of Excellence? *Analysis*.

Helsinki Final Act. (n. d.). *OSCE*. Retrieved from http://www.osce.org/mc/39501

Higgins, H. (n. d.). Applying Confidence-Building Measures in a Regional context.

Hilali, A. Z. (2005). Confidence- and Security-Building Measures for India and Pakistan. *Political*, *30*(2), 31.

Hildreth, S. A. (2001). *Cyberwarfare*. Congressional Research Service.

Holst, J. J. (1983, January/February). Confidence Building Measures: A Conceptual Framework. *Survival, 25*(1), 2–15. doi:10.1080/00396338308442072

Homeland Security top officer to work on UN's new global Internet rules. (2013). *RT.com*. Retrieved from http://rt.com/usa/cyber-lute-un-internet-572/

Hoover, K. (2015). *Cyber threat bill passes, but small biz still faces big problem. The Business Journals*.

Horn, L. (n. d.). Dirty Texting Banned by Pakistan Telecom Authority.

Hurwitz, R. (2012). Cross-domain threat assessment in international security. Proceedings of Cyber Security Conference 2012. Geneva, Switzerland.

ICT4Peace Project. (n. d.). *ICT4Peace.org*. Retrieved from http://ict4peace.org/whoweare/ict4peace-history

ICJ Reports 1949. (1949). *International Court of Justice*.

ICJ Reports 1986.(1986). International Court of Justice.

IEEE Islamabad Section. (n. d.). Retrieved from http://ewh.ieee.org/r10/islamabad/societies.htm

IEEE Karachi Section. (n. d.). Retrieved from http://ewh.ieee.org/r10/karachi/

India and Pakistan Statements to the United Nations General Assembly. (1998). *Acronym.org*. Retrieved from http://www.acronym.org.uk/spsep98.htm

Information Economy. (n. d.). *OECD*. Retrieved from http://www.oecd.org/sti/ieconomy /informationeconomy.htm

Ingersoll, G. (2013). Defense Science Board Warns of Existential Cyber Attack.

Institute of Electrical and Electronic Engineers. (n.d). *IEEE Computer Society*. http://www.ieee.org/index.html

International Conference on Combating Child Pornography on the Internet. (1999, October 1). Vienna.

International Cooperation with ASEANOPOL bolsters Security Landscape. (2013). Interpol. Retrieved from http://www.interpol.int/News-and-media/News-media-releases/2013/PR019

International Electrotechnical Commission. (IEC) (n. d). *IEC*. Retrieved from http://www.iec.ch/index.htm

International Information Security. (2009). Moscow.

International Strategy for Cyberspace: Prosperity Security and Openness in a Networked World. (2011). The White House. *Whitehouse.gov*.

Internet Corporation for Assigned Names and Numbers (ICANN). (n. d.). *ICANN.org*. Retrieved from http://www.icann.org/

Internet Governance Forum (n. d.). *IGF*. Retrieved from http://www.intgovforum.org/cms/

IPSC: PECO Workshop Cybersecurity and Incident Response. (2004). *Timeshighereducation.co.uk*. Retrieved from http://www.timeshighereducation.co.uk/

ISO/IEC 27002:2005 Information Technology – Security Techniques (n. d.). *ISO.org*. Retrieved from http://www.iso27001security.com/html/27002.html

ISO/IEC 27032:2012 Information technology – Security Techniques. (n. d.). Retrieved from http://www.iso.org/iso/catalogue_detail?csnumber=44375

ISO/IEC JTC 1 Information Technology. (1987). *ISO.org*. Retrieved from http://www.iso.org/iso/standards_development/technical_committees/list_of_iso_technical_committees/iso_technical_committee.htm?commid=45020

ITU. (n. d.). *International Telecommunications Union*. Retrieved from http://www.itu.int/en/Pages/default.aspx

Jaspal, Z. N. (2004, May). Nuclear CBMs between India and Pakistan: Utilitarian Approach - How to build Confidence about our Nuclear Intentions. Defence Journal, 7(10).

Jevans, D. (2013). Little thumb drives now a big security threat.

Jingjing, H. (Ed.). (2010, June 8). The Internet in China. *Xinhuanet.com*. http://news.xinhuanet.com/english2010/china/2010-06/08/c_13339232.htm

Jones, S. E. (2012) United Nations set to Define New Worldwide Rules for the Internet: New Rules to Define Internet Use between Countries.

Jr, D. G. (2013). *Cyber Attack is imminent*.

Jus in bello & Jus ad bellum. (n. d.). *The International Red Cross Association*.

Kamal, A. (2002). *Information Insecurity: A Survival Guide to the Uncharted Territories of Cyber-threats and Cyber-security UN ICT Task Force*. New York: UNITAR.

Kamal, A. (2005). *The Law of Cyber-Space an Invitation to the Table of Negotiations*. Geneva: UNITAR.

Kamal, A. (2007). *The Law of Cyber-Space an Invitation to the Table of Negotiations*. New York: UNITAR.

Karl, D. J. (2013). *The Ties that Bind vs. The Line that Divides*. India and Pakistan.

Khan, F. H. (2003). *Nuclear Risk Reduction Centers*.

Khan, F. H. (2002). Pakistan's Nuclear Future. In R. Chambers (Ed.), South Asia in 2020: Future Strategic Balances and Alliances. (pp. 153-190). Strategic Sciences Institute.

Khan, F. H. (2010, Summer). Prospects for Indian and Pakistani Arms Control and Confidence-Building Measures. *Naval War College Review*, *63*(3), 16.

Khartoum Resolution. (n. d.). *Council on Foreign Relations*. Retrieved from http://www.cfr.org/world/khartoum-resolution/p14841

Khoja, K. (1998). A Handbook of CBMs for Regional Security.

Kiani, K. (2014). *Govt to set up cyber authority, court*. Dawn: Dawn.

Kizekova, A. (2012). The Shanghai Cooperation Organisation: Challenges in Cyberspace.

Clarke, R. & Knake, R. (2010). Cyber War: The Next Threat to National Security and what to do about it: New York. HarperCollins Publishers.

Koh, H. H. (2012, December 13). International Law in Cyberspace. *Harvard International Law Journal*.

Kostadinov, D. (2013). The Attribution Problem in Cyber Attacks.

Kramer, A. E. (2013). NSA Leaks Revive Push in Russia to Control Net. *The New York Times*.

Krekel, B. (2009). *Capability of the People's Republic of China to Conduct Cyber Warfare and Computer Network Exploitation*. National Security Archive.

Kreppon, P. N. M. (2012). *The Unfinished Crisis: US Crisis Management after the 2008 Mumbai Attacks Washington DC*. Stimson Center.

Kuehl, D. D. (n. d.). *From Cyberspace to Cyberpower: Defining the Problem*.

Kux, D. (2006). *India-Pakistan Negotiations: Is Past Still Prologue?* Washington, DC: USIP.

Lancaster, J. (2004). India, Pakistan to Set Up Hotline: Talks End With Deal to Maintain Moratorium on Nuclear Testing. *The Washington Post*.

Landau, E. B. (2012). Assessing the Relevance of Nuclear CBMs to a WMD Arms Control Process in the Middle East Today. Proceedings of *2nd EU Non-Proliferation Consortium (November 5-6)*. Brussels.

Lewis, J. A. (2011). Confidence Building Measures and International Agreements in Cyber Security.

Lindsay, J. R. (2013). Stuxnet and the Limits of Cyber Warfare.

Lings, M. (1991). MUHAMMAD (PBUH): His Life based on the Earliest Sources Islamic Texts Society.

Lodhi, M. (2012). *CBMs need a bold approach. Khaleej Times*.

Lodhi, M. (2013). *Pause in the Peace Process. The News*.

Lupovici, A. (2011, December). Cyber Warfare and Deterrence: Trends and Challenges in Research. *Military and Strategic Affairs*, *3*(3), 13.

Lvov, A. (2013). *Russian Army developing Cyberattack Defences*.

Lyon, P. (2008). *Conflict between India and Pakistan: An Encyclopedia*. Santa Barbara: Cal ABC-CLIO Inc.

Mahr, K. (2013). *India-Pakistan Tensions Spike as Two Sides Trade Fire across the Border. Time World*.

Makkar, S. (2011). *Pakistan yet to establish hotline*. India.

Markoff, J. (2010). Step Taken to End Impasse Over Cybersecurity Talks. *The New York Times*.

Maurer, T. (2011). *Cyber Norm Emergence at the United Nations – An Analysis of the Activities at the UN Regarding Cyber-security*.

Mcwhorter, D. (2013). APT1: Exposing one of China's Cyber Espionage Units. *Mandiant.com*.

Mehdudia, S. (2013). Congressional committee calls for strong India-U.S. ties on cyber security. *The Hindu*.

Melander, J. J. H. K. A. (1977, July/August). European security and Confident Building Measures. *Survival*, *19*(4), 147.

Melzer, N. (2011). *Cyberwarfare and International Law*.

Menon, R. (2000). *A Nuclear Strategy for India*. New Delhi: Sage Publications.

Meyer, P. (2013). *Cyber Security Takes the Floor at the UN*.

Miellmonka, M. (2012). Cyber CSBMs. Proceedings of *Cyber Security Conference 2012*, UNIDIR.

Notification on National Cyber Security Policy File No: 2(35)/2011-CERT-In. (2013). (2013). *Ministry of Communication and Information Technology*. Retrieved from http://indiacybersecurity.blogspot.com/

Mohan, I. B. V. (2012). 5 lakh cyber warriors to bolster India's e-defence. *The Times of India*.

Mushahid to table Cyber Security Bill in Parliament. (n. d.). *MushahidHussain.com*. Retrieved from http://www.mushahidhussain.com/news-detail.php?id=MTE0&pageid=media.

Nagaraj, A. (2013, June 21). Global Telecom Treaty 2012 signed in the ITU world conference. *Center for Information and Communication Science (CICS)*. Retrieved from http://cicsworld.centerforics.org/blog/2013/01/3/global-telecom-treaty-2012-signed-in-the-itu-world-conference/

Nakashima, E. (2012). In U.S.-Russia deal, nuclear communication system may be used for cybersecurity. *Washington Post*.

Nakashima, E. (2013). Bush Order Expands Network Monitoring Intelligence Agencies to Track Intrusions. *Washington Post*.

Napolitano, J. (2012, September 19). Homeland Threats and Agency Responses. *Department of Homeland Security*. Retrieved from http://www.dhs.gov/news/2012/09/19/written-testimony-secretary-napolitano-senate-committee-homeland-security-and

National Institute of Standards and Technology (NIST). (n. d.). Retrieved from http://www.nist.gov/index.html

National Military Strategy for Cyberspace Operations (NMS-CO). (2006). *United States Department of Defense*. from http://www.dod.mil/pubs/foi/joint_staff/jointStaff_jointOperations/07-F-2105doc1.pdf

National Police Academy. (n. d.). *Government of Pakistan*. Retrieved from http://www.npa.gov.pk/

Nehru-Liaquat Agreement 1950 (1950). *Governments of India and Pakistan*.

Nelson, D. (2011). *WikiLeaks: hoax phone call brought India and Pakistan to brink of war*. *The Telegraph*.

Network Warfare. (2013). *Armed Forces and NCW*. Government of India.

Novosti, R. (2013). *Cybersecurity high on agenda of Obama-Putin Meeting*.

Now, D. (2012). *India's Forces to Seek Three New Commands from PM*.

NRRC: Confidence Building through Information Exchange. (2012). *US Department of State*. http://www.state.gov/t/avc/rls/199564.htm

Nuclear Weapons Employment Strategy of the United States. (2013). The White House. *Whitehouse.gov*.

Ocean Telegraphy: The Twenty Fifth Anniversary. (1879).

OECD Guidelines for the Security of Information Systems and Networks: (n. d.). Towards a Culture of Security. Retrieved from http://www.oecd.org/internet/ieconomy/ oecdguidelinesforthesecurityofinformationsystemsandnetworkstowardsacultureofsecurity.htm

Online US is still a Superpower. (2013). *Eurotopics.net*. Retrieved from http://www.eurotopics.net/en/home/presseschau/archiv/article/ARTICLE125313-Online-US-is-still-a-superpower

Organization for the Advanced Structured Information Standards (OASIS). (n. d). *OASIS*. Retrieved from https://www.oasis-open.org/

OSCE Guide on Non-Military CBMs. (2012). OSCE Secretariat. Vienna.

Padder, S. (2012). *The Composite Dialogue between India and Pakistan: Structure, Process and Agency* (Vol. 65). Heidelberg Papers in South Asian and Comparative Politics.

Paganini, P. (2013). *China vs US, Cyber Superpowers Compared*. Retrieved from http://resources.infosecinstitute.com/china-vs-us-cyber-superpowers-compared/

Pakistan Telecommunication Authority (PTA). (n. d.). Retrieved from http://www.pta.gov.pk/

Pakistan Tests Medium Range Missile. (2012, November 28). Pakistan Inter Services Public Relations.

Parameswaran, P. (2012). *ASEAN at a Crossroads. The Diplomat*.

Pavlyuchenkoa, F. (2001). *Belarus in the Context of European Cyber Security*.

Pérez-Peña, R. (2013). Universities Face a Rising Barrage of Cyberattacks. *The New York Times*.

Perlroth, N. (2013). Hackers in China Attacked The Times for Last 4 Months. *The New York Times*.

Perlroth, N., & Sanger, D. E. (2013). Cyberattacks against U.S. Corporations are on the Rise. *The New York Times*.

Perlroth, N., & Sanger, D. E. (2013, July 13). Nations Buying as Hackers Sell Flaws in Computer Code. *The New York Times*.

Perrow, C. (2007). *The Next Catastrophe: Reducing our Vulnerabilities to Natural, Industrial, and Terrorist Disaster*. New Jersey: Princeton University Press.

Peterson, A. (2013). The Post just got hacked by the Syrian Electronic Army. *Washington Post*.

Peterson, S. (2011). *Exclusive: Iran hijacked US drone, says Iranian engineer (video). Christian Science Monitor*.

Prasad, K. (2012). Cyber-terrorism: Addressing the Challenges for Establishing an International Legal Framework. Proceedings from 3rd Australian Counter Terrorism Conference. Australia.

Presidental Policy Directive 20. (n. d.). *EPIC.org*. Retrieved from http://epic.org/privacy/cybersecurity/presidential-directives/presidential-policy-directive-20.pdf

Profile of National Response Centre for Cyber Crimes, National Response Centre for Cyber Crime (NR3C). (n. d.). FIA.

Psaki, J. (2013). Statement on Consensus Achieved by the UN Group of Governmental Experts on Cyber Issues. *U.S. Department of State*. Retrieved from http://www.state.gov/r/pa/prs/ps/2013/06/210418.htm

Qadeem, M. (1998). CBMs and Conflict Resolution as Approaches to the South Asian Security: How Relevant and Pragmatic? In M. Ahmer. (Ed.), *Internal and External Dynamics of South Asian Security*. Karachi, Fazleesons. (pp. 79).

Rasmussen, A. F. (2013). NATO's Next War – in Cyberspace. *The Wall Street Journal*.

Ray, J. B. (1970). The Resolution of the Rann of Kutch Boundary Problem. *The Geographic Bulletin*, 6.

Rebello, M. (2012) Assam violence: Where it all began.

Regional Commonwealth in the Field of Communications. (n. d.). Retrieved from http://www.en.rcc.org.ru/index.php/rcc/about-rcc

Report of the OECD Task Force on Spam. (2006). *Organisation for Economic Cooperation and Development*.

Resolution on Overall approach by the OSCE to promote cybersecurity. (n. d.). *OSCEPA*.

Rice, C. (2011). *No Higher Honor: A Memoir of my Years in Washington*. New York: Broadway Paperbacks.

Richardson, M. (2013). *When Cyber Attacks Could Lead to War. The Strait Times*.

Rodriguez, G. (2013). *Read the Guardian's Entire Interview with the Man who Leaked PRISM*. Retrieved from http://www.policymic.com/articles/47355/edward-snowden-interview-transcript-full-text-read-the-guardian-s-entire-interview-with-the-man-who-leaked-prism

Rome Statute. (2002). *International Criminal Court*.

Ross, J. D. (2014) *Plan to End U.S. Control of ICANN*. Submitted to Brazil Meeting on Future of Internet Governance.

Rouse, M. (n. d.). Hacktivism is the act of hacking, or breaking into a computer system, for a politically or socially motivated purpose. *Techtarget.com*. Retrieved from http://searchsecurity.techtarget.com/definition/hacktivism

Rushkof, D. (2002). *Cyberia: Life in the Trenches of Cyberspace. Manchester*: Clinamen Press Ltd.

Salik, N. A. (1998). CBMs –Past, Present and Future. *Pakistan Defense Review*. (pp. 3).

Sang-Hun, C. (2013). South Korea blames North for June Cyber Attacks. *The New York Times*.

Sanger, D. E. (2013). Differences on Cybertheft Complicate China Talks. *The New York Times*.

Sanger, D. E. (2013). N.S.A. Leaks Make Plan for Cyber defense Unlikely. *The New York Times*.

Sarwar, B. (2013) *LOC Tensions: Need Facts not Hype*.

Schmidt, M. N. (Ed.). (2013). *Tallinn Manual on the International Law Applicable on Cyber Operations*. New York: Cambridge University Press.

Schmitt, M. N. (2010). Cyber Operations in International Law: The Use of Force, Collective Security, Self-Defense, and Armed Conflicts," *Proceedings of a Workshop on Deterring Cyber Attacks: Informing Strategies and Developing Options for US Policy, National Research Council of the National Academies*. Washington D.C: 151.

Schmitt, M. N. (2012). International Law in Cyberspace: The Koh Speech and the Tallinn Manual Juxtaposed. *Harvard International Law Journal*, 54.

Schmitt, M. N. (Ed.). (2013). Tallinn Manual on the International Law Applicable to Cyber Warfare New York, Cambridge University Press.

Sciences, N. U. C. E. (n.d). "FAST-NU for Computer and Emerging Sciences." Retrieved August 7, 2013, from http://nu.edu.pk/

SCO. (2013). "SCO – Cooperation on Security." Retrieved February 14, 2013, from http://www.infosco.eu/index.php/aboutsco/activities

SCO. (n.d). "SCO official website." Retrieved September 19, 2012, from http://www.sectsco.org/

SEA-ME-WE. (n.d). "SEA-ME-WE." Retrieved July 10, 2013, from http://www.seamewe4.com/

Secretary-General, D. o. P. a. S. C. A. U. C. f. D. R. o. t. (1982) Comprehensive Study on CBMs.

Secretary-General, D. o. P. a. S. C. A. U. N. C. f. D. R. o. t. (1982) Relationship between Disarmament and International Security.

Security, C. (n.d). "Cyber Security, OAS." Retrieved August 20, 2013, from http://www.oas.org/en/topics/cyber_security.asp

Security, S. (n.d). "PKI (Public Key Infrastructure). " Retrieved July 4, 2013, from http://searchsecurity.techtarget.com /definition/PKI

Security, U. H. "US Homeland Security: Cyber Laws & Regulations." Retrieved July 4, 2013, from http://www.dhs.gov /cybersecurity-laws-regulations

Security, W. F. o. S. P. M. P. P. o. I. (2003) Toward a Universal Order of Cyberspace: Managing Threats from Cybercrime to Cyberwar - Report & Recommendations.

SEECS. N. (n.d). "NUST SEECS." Retrieved August 7, 2013, from http://seecs.nust.edu.pk/

Segal, A. (2011). *US-China Cyber Hotline*. The Diplomat, The Diplomat.

Segal, A. (2012) What to read on Cyber Security.

Segal, A. (2013) Defending an Open, Global, Secure and Resilient Internet. CFR Independent Task Force Report No. 70, 1

Sengupta, N. P. S. (2013). U.S. Says Ring Stole 160 Million Credit Card Numbers. New York Times. New York.

Service, A. F. P. (2013). *Obama, Xi Discuss Military-to-Military Relations*. Cybersecurity.

Services, P. I. o. P. (n.d). "Pakistan Institute of Parliamentary Services ". Retrieved August 7, 2013, from http://www.pips.org. pk

Shackelford, S. J. (2009). "From Nuclear War to Net War: Analogizing Cyber Attacks in International Law." Berkley Journal of International Law: 192.

Shanker, E. B. T. (2012). Panetta Warns of Dire Threat of Cyberattack on U.S. New York Times. New York New York Times.

Shanker, T. (2013). Pentagon is Updating Conflict Rules in Cyberspace. New York Times, New York

Sheldon, J. B. (2012). *Cyber Incident Information Sharing: A First Step towards Confidence Building? Cyber Security Conference 2012: The Role of Confidence-Building Measures in Assuring Cyber Stability*. Geneva, Switzerland: UNIDIR.

Siddique, A. (2013) Pakistan Demands Filters Before Lifting YouTube Ban.

Siman-Tov, S. E. a. D. (2012) Cyber Warfare: Concepts and Strategic Trends.

Simson, E. (2013). The U.S.–Russia Cybersecurity Pact: Just Paper. 2013.

Smith, P. (2008, May). Network Operations Groups [Berlin.]. *Power Point Presentation for RIPE, 56*, 5–9.

Softpedia (n.d). "India Japan to Expand Cyber Security Cooperation." Retrieved August 21, 2013, from http://news.softpedia. com/news/India-and-Japan-to-Expand-Cyber-Security-Cooperation-301524 .shtml

Sohail, H. (2013). *Information Technology Ministry: A Chaos so far*. The News, The News.

South Asia Confidence-Building Measures Timeline. (n. d.). *Stimson.org*. Retrieved from http://www. stimson.org/data-sets /south-asia-confidence-building-measures-cbm-timeline

Standage, T. (2007). *The Victorian Internet: The Remarkable Story of the Telegraph and the Nineteenth Century On-line Pioneers*. New York: Walker & Company.

Starr, B. (2011). *Drone that crashed in Iran was on CIA recon mission*. CNN.

State, T. U. D. o. (n.d). "Agreement between the United States of America and the Union of Soviet Socialist Republics on the Establishment of Nuclear Risk Reduction Centers (and Protocols Thereto)." Retrieved June 15, 2013, from http://www.state.gov/t/isn/5179

State, U. D. o. (2011). "Office of the Coordinator for Cyber Issues." Retrieved June 13, 2013, from http://www.state.gov/s/cyberissues/

State, U. D. o. (2013). "The ASEAN-U.S. Ministerial Meeting: Fact Sheet, Office of the Spokesperson, Washington, DC." Retrieved July 1, 2013, from http://www.state.gov/r/pa /prs/ps/2013/07/211389.htm

State, U. D. o. (n.d). "Welcome to the Nuclear Risk Reduction Center (NRRC): Confidence Building through Information Exchange." Retrieved July 4, 2013, from http://www.state.gov/t/avc/nrrc/

States, C. o. I. (n.d). "Commonwealth of Independent States." Retrieved January 12, 2013, from http://www.cisstat.com/eng/cis.htm

stefanomele (n.d). "Cyber-security. The vexed question of global rules." Retrieved July 4, 2013, from http://www.stefanomele.it/news/dettaglio.asp?id=285

Stilts, S. o. (2013). "Testifying before Senate Judiciary on Attribution and Cybersecurity." Retrieved July 30, 2013.

Stojanovski, D. (2013) Preventing a U.S.-China Cyber War.

Strengthening law enforcement cooperation in the EU: the European Information Exchange Model. (2012). EIXM.

Studies, C. f. N. (n.d) Inventory of International Nonproliferation Organizations and Regimes.

Summit, S. (2012). "Official Website of the Beijing SCO Summit 2012." Retrieved April 25, 2013, from http://www.scosummit 2012.org/english/2012-04/28/c_131558560.htm

Tashkent Declaration. (1966, October 1). *United Nations Peacekeeper.* Retrieved from http://peacemaker.un.org/india-pakistan-tashkent-declaration66

Technet (n.d). "Defining Malware." Retrieved August 14, 2013, from http://technet.microsoft.com/en-us/library /dd632948.aspx

Telecommunication Regulatory Authority of India. (n. d.). Government of India. Retrieved from http://www.trai.gov.in/

The Blue Helmets. (1996). *A Review of the UN Peacekeeping.* UN Department of Public Information.

The Law of Armed Conflict. (n. d.). *The International Red Cross Association.*

The London Conference. (n. d.). London: Chatham House.

The National Military Strategy for Cyberspace Operations (U). (2006). US JS Publication.

The Netherlands Country Report. (2011).

The Promotion of a Culture of Security for Information Systems and Networks in OECD Countries JT00196105. (2005, December 16). Retrieved from http://www.oecd.org/internet/ieconomy/35884541.pdf

The Swift Codes. (n. d.). *Theswiftcodes.com.* Retrieved from http://www.theswiftcodes.com/

The United Nations Disarmament Yearbook. (2012). Vol. 37, Part I (pp. 3–4). New York: United Nations Publications.

Thomas, T. L. (2004). *Cyber Bytes. Fort Leavenworth.* Foreign Military Studies Office.

Thomas, T. L. (2005). *Cyber Silhouettes: Shadows over Information Operations Fort Leavenworth.* Foreign Military Studies.

Thomas, T. L. (2007). *Decoding the Virtual Dragon. Fort Leavenworth.* Foreign Military Studies Office.

Thomas, T. L. (2009). *The Dragon's Quantum Leap: Transforming from a Mechanized to an Informatized Force Ft Leavenworth*. KS: FMSO.

Tikk, E. (2011, June-July). Ten Rules for Cyber Security. *Survival, 53*(3), 119–132. doi:10.1080/0039 6338.2011.571016

Times, E. (2008). "Hoax call pushed Pakistan to brink of war with India." Retrieved October 3, 2012, from http://articles.economictimes.indiatimes.com/2008-12-06/news/28394766_1_india-and-pakistan-mumbai-attacks-mumbai-killings

Timlin, J. A. L. a. K. (2011) Cybersecurity and Cyberwarfare: Preliminary Assessment of National Doctrine and Organization.

Touré, D. H. I. (2011) The Quest for Cyber Peace.

UN (1965). UNGA Resolution 2131 (XX), UN.

UN (1981). UNGA Resolution 36/103. G. Assemble, UN.

UN. (1988). "Special Report of the Disarmament Commission to the UNGA at its 3rd Special Session devoted to Disarmament, UN Document A/S/-15/3 (May 28, 1988)." from http://www.un.org/ga/search/view_doc.asp?symbol=A/S-15/3(SUPP) &Lang=E.

UN. (1999). UNGA Resolutions adopted in the 53rd session. G. Assembly, UN.

UN. (2000). "Optional Protocol to the Convention on the Rights of the Child on the Sale of Children, Child Prostitution and Child Pornography." Retrieved May 1, 2013, from http://treaties.un.org/doc/source/RecentTexts/iv-11c_eng.htm

UN (2010). Report of the Group of Governmental Experts (GGE) on Developments in the Field of Information and Telecommunications in the Context of International Security, UN Document A/65/201 UN.

UN (n.d). "Group of Governmental Experts on Developments in the Field of Information and Telecommunications in the Context of International Security."

UN. (n.d). "International Day against Nuclear Testing." Retrieved July 4, 2013, from http://www.un.org/en/events/againstnucleartestsday/history.shtml

UN Development Group. (n. d.).

UNGA (1986). UNGA Resolution 41/60C, Considerations of Guidelines for Confidence-Building Measures

UNGA (2002). UNGA Resolution 57/53 UNGA.

UNGA. (2002). *UNGA Resolution 63/37*. UNGA.

UNGA (2003). UNGA Resolution 58/32 UNGA.

UNGA. (2003). *UNGA Resolution 58/199, UN Documentation Research Guide. UNGA*. UNGA.

UNGA. (2004). *UNGA Resolution 59/61*. UNGA.

UNGA (2005). UNGA Resolution 60/45 UNGA.

UNGA. (2006). *UNGA Resolution 60/252*. UNGA.

UNGA (2006). UNGA Resolution 61/54 UNGA.

UNGA (2008). UNGA Resolution 62/17 UNGA.

UNGA. (2010). *UNGA Resolution 64/25*. UNGA.

UNGA. (2010). *UNGA Resolution 64/211*. UNGA.

UNGA. (2011). *UNGA 66/24, Developments in the Field of Information and Telecommunications in the Context of International Security*. UNGA.

UNGA (n.d). UNGA: Economic and Financial – The Second Committee. UNGA, UN.

UNGA (n.d). United Nations General Assembly, UN.

UNIDIR. (2012). Cyber Security Conference 2012 (CS12).

Union, I. T. (2005). "World Summit on the Information Society Geneva 2003. " Retrieved June 19, 2013, from http://www.itu.int/wsis/docs/geneva /official/dop.html

Union, I. T. (n.d). "What was the UN ICT Task Force?". Retrieved September 25, 2013, from https://www.itu.int/wsis/basic/faqs_answer.asp?lang=en&faq_id=88

United States and India Sign Cybersecurity Agreement. Department of Homeland Security. (2011). *Dhs. gov*. Retrieved from http://www.dhs.gov/news/2011/07 /19 /united-states-and-india-sign-cybersecurity-agreement

University, B. (n.d) 66th Session of the UN.

UNODA (2013). Fact Sheet: Developments in the Field of Information and Telecommunications in the Context of International Security.

UNODA (n.d). "Confidence Building."

UNODA (n.d). Developments in the Field of Information and Telecommunications in the Context of International Security. UNODA, UNODA.

UNODA (n.d). Developments in the Field of Information and Telecommunications in the Context of International Security, UNDA.

UNODC (2013). Comprehensive Study on Cybercrime, Draft February 2013. New York, UN.

US Army Cyber Command/2nd Army. (n. d.). *Arcyber.army.mil*. Retrieved from http://www.arcyber.army.mil/

US-CERT. (2013). "Security Tip (ST05-007): Risks of File-Sharing Technology." Retrieved February 14, 2013, from http://www.us-cert.gov/ncas/tips/ST05-007

US NSC's Comprehensive National Cybersecurity Initiative. (n. d.). The White House. *Whitehouse. gov*. Retrieved from http://www.whitehouse.gov/cybersecurity/comprehensive-national-cybersecurity-initiative

USIP (n.d) Lahore Declaration, USIP Peace Agreements Digital Collection.

Vallone, R. P., Ross, L., & Lepper, M. R. (1985). The Hostile Media Phenomenon: Biased Perception and Perceptions of Media Bias in Coverage of the Beirut Massacre. In *Journal of Personality and Social Psychology*, *49*(3), 8.

Vatis, M. A. (2010) The Council of Europe Convention on Cybercrime. 207-224

Vienna Document of the Negotiations on Confidence- and Security-Building. Proceedings of the 269th Plenary Meeting the OSCE Forum for Security Co-operation. (1999, November 16). OSCE. Istanbul. Retrieved from http://www.osce.org/fsc/41276

Vignard, K. (2011). Confronting Cyberconflict, UNIDIR Disarmament Forum.

Virtual Global Task Force. (n. d.). Retrievedfrom http://www.virtualglobaltaskforce.com/

Walker, B. B. (n.d) Transparency and Confidence Building Measures in Cyber Space: Towards Norms and Behaviors. 31-40

Wasim, A. (2010). *Placing lapsed ordinance in Senate: Law ministry apologises to committee*. Dawn.

Waxman, M. C. (2011). "Cyberattacks and the Use of Force: Back to the Future of Article 2(4)." The Yale Journal of International Law V ol. 36: 42, 1: 422-459.

Wegener, H. (2007) Harnessing the Perils in Cyberspace: Who is in Charge? 45-52

Wegener, H. (n.d) Regulating Cyber Behaviour: Some Initial Reflections on Codes of Conduct and Confidence-Building Measures.

Westby, J. R. (Ed.). (2004). *International Guide to Cyber Security Chicago*. American Bar Association.

What we investigate. (n. d.). Federal Bureau of Investigation, Albuquerque Division. Retrieved from http://www.fbi.gov/albuquerque/about-us/what-we-investigate

Whitehouse (n.d). "Cyber Security." Retrieved July 10, 2013, from http://www.whitehouse.gov/cyber-security

Whitehouse (n.d). "Cyber Space Policy Review: Assuring a Trusted and Resilient Information and Communications Infrastructure." from http://www.whitehouse.gov/assets/documents/Cyberspace_Policy_Review_final.pdf

Whitehouse.gov. "The Sequester." Retrieved April 25, 2013, from http://www.whitehouse.gov/issues/sequester

Wiki, I. L. (n.d). "APEC Cybersecurity Strategy." Retrieved June 15, 2013, from http://itlaw.wikia.com/wiki/APEC _Cybersecurity_Strategy.

William, A. Owens, K. W. D. a. H. S. L. e. (2009). Technology, Policy Law and Ethics regarding U.S. Acquisition and use of Cyberattack Capabilities. Washington DC, The National Academies.

Willson, D. (2009). "A Global Problem: Cyberspace Threats Demand an International Approach." ISSA Journal August 2009.

Wolpert, S. (2006). *Shameful Flight: The Last Years of the British Empire in India*. USA: Oxford University Press.

Wolter, D. D. (2012). Looking towards the future of cyber security: what does a stable cyber environment look like?" UNIDIR Cyber Security Conference 2012: The Role of Confidence Building Measures in Assuring Cyber Stability. Cyber Security Conference 2012: The Role of Confidence-Building Measures in Assuring Cyber Stability, Geneva, Switzerland, UNIDIR.

World Federation of Scientists Permanent Monitoring Panel on Information Security.(2003).

X.1205, U. I.-T. (2011) Cybersecurity Information Exchange (CYBEX).

Xinghuanet (n.d). The Internet in China,. P. Han.

Yamin, T. (2012). "Nuclear Risk Reduction in South Asia." Journal of Contemporary Studies.

Yekaterinburg Declaration of the Heads of the Member States of the Shanghai Cooperation Organisation. (n. d.). Ministry of Foreign Affairs of the People's Republic of China. Retrieved from http://www.fmprc.gov.cn/eng/

Yurcik, W. (1997). Information Warfare: Legal and Ethical Challenges of the Next Global Battleground," 2nd Annual Ethics and Technology Conference

Yusha, M. (2010). India - Pakistan's Cyber War: CBI Website Still Not Restored. Pakistan Spectator: Candid Blog, Pakistan Spectator: Candid Blog. 2013.

Zafar, K. (n.d). Cyber-crime: Two arrested for forgery, credit card fraud. Express Tribune, Express Tribune.

Zulfqar, S. (2013). Efficacy of Confidence Building Measures (CBMs) in India-Pakistan Relations. *IPRI Journal, XIII*(1), 10.

Chapter 10
Cyber Attacks and Preliminary Steps in Cyber Security in National Protection

Faruk Aydin
Turkish Air Force, Turkey

O. Tolga Pusatli
Cankaya University, Turkey

ABSTRACT

Cyber attacks launched by individuals and/or supported by nation states have increased due to the prevalence of information technologies at critical infrastructure of the states. In this chapter, such attacks and consecutive impacts are visited. In connection with this issue, evolution of cyber threats from annoying malware to serious weapons is studied by examples; hence, precautions against such threats are visited and usage of anti-malware applications as prevalent precautions is assessed within the scope. Selected information security standards and strategies of selected states and precautions for cyber security of Turkey are studied. Our findings underline that educated citizens and companies along with public institutions should cooperate to provide a nationwide cyber security. Consequently, it is defended that governments should play an affective role to protect, educate, and guide governmental and private companies and citizens on the cyber security by promoting the cyber security topic in the successive national development plans.

INTRODUCTION

While the extensive usage of information technologies (IT) in most industries, and hence business, cyber security has gained its importance in the modern world and promises to climb to higher priorities in government agendas in many countries. Nowadays, IT have been ubiquitous at many levels (personal, institutional, systemic) from individual to across the nation and hence global. Thus, cyber security is no longer considered as a subject constrained to personal computer security and/or securing e-mail accounts.

DOI: 10.4018/978-1-4666-8456-0.ch010

With the widening and spreading nature of the topic, literature is fed with studies on cyber security at various levels in many countries. Thus, we acknowledge the increasing importance of cyber security and its position in the development plans of countries. In this chapter, we shall visit pioneer countries and their policies and take Turkey as an example to reveal what to do in order to protect both society and government against cyber attacks.

Quick examples include Tunisian Report (WSIS, 2005) accepted in the World Summit on The Information Society and the current and previous, development plans of Turkey (State Planning Organization, 2006), (Ministry of Development, 2013).

Basically, the Tunisian Report highlights following points;

- Information resources and technologies are being used for crime,
- Terrorism uses information technologies effectively,
- For that reason abuse of IT should be prevented; however, human rights should be considered during monitoring processes.

When we have a glance to Turkey, we easily capture that transformation of Turkey's society to the information society has been stressed in the vision of the 9th development plan covering 2007-2013 years of Turkey. Both the Tunisian report and the development plans, for example, show that the cyber security issue is considered as an important area both in Turkey as well as abroad.

In addition to this motivation, we observe that cyber attacks are not only targeting business for a brutal form of entertainment or for the purposes of theft; such attacks can be parts of extremist actions such as terrorism as well. For instance, Lucent Technologies, which is a multinational technology company, announced that Unity, a pro-Palestinian group, had attacked its web site in November 2000. The purpose of this attack was not to steal any valuable information but because the company did business in Israel as discussed in (Cross & Shinder, 2008).

Cyber crimes are serious threats not only for the world but also for Turkey. According to the 2012 Norton Cyber Crime Report (Norton, 2012) in Turkey more than 10 million people have been aggrieved because of cyber crime in one year. It is stated that the cost of this problem is around 556 million USD. Such a figure highlights the gravity of the topic.

With this quick introduction, we report on our study on cyber threats, common technological precautions and strategies against them as our aim. Within this scope, we try to find out how serious such threats can be for nations, and whether it is too early to speak of serious cyber threats that can put nationwide security in peril, or not. More specifically, we try to seek an answer for "should the state play an affective role in national cyber security? If it has to, what does the state have to do?"

This work takes a larger study conducted and reported in a thesis in Turkey in 2011 and 2012 (Aydin, 2012) and tries to catch subsequent important developments. The findings match with the earlier reported drafts of the current national development plan as in recognizing the cyber security in a higher rank at the time of writing this chapter; thus, the study has already started to prove itself that the topic should be kept as a high priority not only as a sole subject but to be considered by many in both public and private sectors. At the time of writing, the 10th National Development Plan of Turkey (Ministry of Development, 2013) has been published and it is underlined that the necessity of completing regulation on protecting privacy, private data, ensuring security of national information and securing e-commerce still exist. In parallel to this, a sub-department to combat cyber crime has been established under security department in 2011. Additionally, a cyber security board has been set up at the Ministry of Transport, Maritime Affairs and Communications to gain speed in the cyber security.

BACKGROUND

As a direct relation to cyber security, this section surveys vulnerabilities that may cause cyber attacks to cause damage. In this chapter, we adopt the vulnerability definition from (Newman, 2009) as "a characteristic of a computer system or a network that makes it possible for a threat to occur". Basically, vulnerabilities are the holes in the security and functionalities of computer systems through which an abuser can have opportunity to intrude systems. These intrusions can be of different types according to their origins, purpose and severity. Law can and does consider such actions and classifies them as illegal actions based on the country of origin; however, being anonymous and ubiquitous in the digital environment lessens the effectiveness of laws punishing hacking, stealing information and harming computer systems. For this reason, for a country, passing an act of law concerning cyber crime in the government can be just one leg in this fight; another one should be eliminating the vulnerabilities of computer systems by understanding types of attacks.

Cyber Threats

Cyber threat is an attempt of unauthorized access to data, application or system to corrupt integrity, confidentiality, security or availability as defined in (United States Computer Emergency Readiness Team (US-CERT), 2010). Such threats have led to loss of prestige of the victims in addition to obstruction of their services. In the literature, there are attempts to classify these threats; for example, the council of Europe categorizes them based on possible legal responses in (Council of Europe, 2008):

(a) Attacks via the Internet that cause damage not only to essential electronic communication systems and the IT infrastructure but also to other infrastructures, systems, and legal interests, including human life;

(b) Dissemination of illegal content, including threatening public, inciting, advertising, and glorifying terrorism; fundraising for and financing of terrorism; training and recruiting for terrorism; and dissemination of racist and xenophobia material

(c) Other logistical uses of IT systems by terrorists, such as internal communication, information acquisition, and target analysis.

Cyber threats are of various types and the number of occasions increases every day. Naturally, the threats we review in this section are limited; however, we have tried to include important / popular examples to our knowledge. Some cyber threats are well known such as CIH/Chernobyl (1990), Melissa (1999), Code Red (2001), Nimda (2001), Klez (2001), MyDoom aka Norvag worm (2004). Those are among the big virus infections while some examples are to underline that infections are not only to attract attention.

Another classification related to the cyber attacks is based on the attacker. Basically, this covers hackers (white/black), hacktivists, cyber spies, cyber terrorists and insiders.

Popular examples include a group of Chinese hackers who hit U.S. Chamber in Nov 2009-May 2010. The group breached the computer defenses of America's top business-lobbying group and gained access to data stored on its systems. Key informants report that the information stolen includes private data of three million members of the chamber (Gorman, 2011). Another one is reported in June 9, 2011; Citigroup was hacked and 200,000 customer accounts data are exposed as reported in (The Associated Press, 2011). In the same year, just a couple of months before that, on 27 April 2011, Sony announced that PlayStation network has been hacked and 75 million user accounts are stolen (NTVMSNBC, 2011). RedHack is one of the activist group who has hacked 90% of Turkey's police department web site at 29th March 2012 (CNNTurk, 2012). RedHack claimed that it downloaded all the files of Ministry of Internal Affairs by hacking the Ministry of Internal Affairs' sub website on April 20, 2012 (Milliyet, 2012).

When we have a general look at the cyber attacks we see that those are about malware and/or breaking into a system; meanwhile, we observe the literature to address them botnets, denial of Service (DoS) attacks, distributed DoS (DDoS) attacks, DNS root server incidents and malware such as Trojan, worm and viruses targeting boot, application and macro. Rest of this section lists remarkable examples of such attacks.

GhostNet, a malware-based cyber espionage network, has infected computers possess high-value diplomatic, political, economic and military information in 103 countries as of 2009 (Citizen Lab & Group, 2009). An example of DDoS attack targeted Twitter and put the site offline for an extended period on August the 6th, 2009 (Twitter, 2010). According to the 2012 report of TrendMicro anti-malware company (Kruse, Hacquebord, & McArdle, 2010), based on the intelligence gathered during a four-month period of close monitoring, a malware named Tinba focused on Turkey. Tinba is a small data stealing Trojan-banker. It hooks into browsers and steals login data, as well as sniffing network traffic. Cyber criminals specifically target financial institutions inside Turkey with the Tinba virus.

In a study of 900 cases of business (Verizon RISK Team, 2012) "data leakage" over 48% of the breaches is reported to relate to insiders who abused their right to access corporate information. Ciampa (Ciampa, 2008) argues that insider attacks are usually more costly than an attack from the outside. A more recent and popular insider example appeared with the Wikileaks occasion where a U.S. Army private, Bradley E. Manning (Nicks, 2012), downloaded secret files and handed them to Assange's organization which let US government's secrets been exposed to the public.

Examples do not include only exposing private/confidential information but also manipulating ordinary computers without any secret information. In relation to such threat, botnets are one of the considerable threats on the Internet; they are mostly silent. These threats can have various purposes from hosting for illegal purposes (PC Plus, 2010) including phishing, which is directing links to unintended websites on different infected computers, and performing brute force password attacks which are systematically checking all possible keys until the correct key combination is found. Bots are getting popular and as such they spread globally. A botnet can create excessive amount of data network traffic with e-mails and redirection of website links. For example, Conflicker botnet is reported to have 28TB/sec total bandwidth (Chip, 2011). Another example of botnet is TDL4 which was revealed by an antivirus software company, has been reported as using about 5 million computers as zombies, infected machines (Kaspersky, 2011). Such threats are not easy to defeat for example, the administrators ruling the TDL Botnet Network use their own encrypted algorithm and it is almost impossible to solve the system because they update the algorithm, continuously (Mathews, 2011). This feature of TDL indicates that it is not administrated by simple and trivial hackers.

There are many other malware in the history of digital world; however, they are not limited to attacks launched by individuals but also engineered to cause serious attacks against governments. Popular examples include Stuxnet, Duqu, Wiper and Flame. Because national cyber security is within the scope of this article, we shall visit those viruses under a separate subtitle as the following section.

Cyber Weapons

The discussion of international cyber attacks accelerated with four successive attacks, Stuxnet, Duqu, Wiper and Flame (SDWF), to Iran. While the political tension is increasing between Iran and the USA and Israel, it became easier to think that those attacks are planned and are performed by those countries and by using cyber weapons. According to the news on New York Times (Sanger, 2012), Stuxnet has deactivated 1,000 centrifuges of 5,000 in Iran and delayed its nuclear program for 1.5 to 2 years, and this attack was the successor of the cyber attack program started by the Bush government under "Olympic Games" name and accelerated during the Obama government (Sanger, 2012). Some exceptional properties of SDWF include followings:

- Using zero day exploits, previously unknown vulnerability in the (O/S) (Haltaş, 2011),
- Signing itself with legitimate certificates manufactured using stolen keys,
- Having a complex (include Programmable Logic Controllers-PLC) code (Knapp, 2011),
- Manipulating computer equipments to leak sensitive information (Skywiper Analysis Team, 2012),
- Targeting Iran's nuclear program/oil sector

As we have seen structures of some malware affects the countries can use cyber technology to attack each other.

Other examples include the 2007, possibly Russian, cyber attacks against Estonia. This is a series of cyber attacks targeted websites of the prime minister, communication infrastructure, and finance sector. As a temporary solution, Estonia has isolated itself so that no one could get into the country, digitally. This had a consequence that people with bank accounts but outside the country at that time could not access their accounts (House of Lords, 2010). After the attack, NATO's Cooperative Cyber Defense Centre of Excellence was established in Tallinn, Estonia (Gill & Fleck, 2010). This was one of the remarkable and pioneering defense activities that use no physical weapon.

Another attack occurred as a series of Russian assault to Georgia's government agency websites in 2008 as integrated cyber and kinetic attacks by Russia (Tikk et al., 2008). When Russia had declared war on Georgia for the independence of South Ossetia, cyber attacks blocked channels of communication for strategically significant periods of time (Tikk et al., 2008).

Both Estonia and Georgia cases involve nation states and calls for military action.

By their very nature, the cyber attacks target / initiate in software although its damage is not limited to digital environment. Software products, unlike many physical structures, may have / need frequent update due to rapidly changing user needs (Pusatli & Regan, 2012) hence a stronger business connection between the user and the vendor can occur. For example, Symantec (Shearer, 2013) providing protection against Stuxnet, can be seen as "private army" that guards the critical infrastructure of Iran. Such incidents bring on discussions about taking precautions against state targeted cyber attacks. Naturally,

Figure 1. Cyber threats and their targets

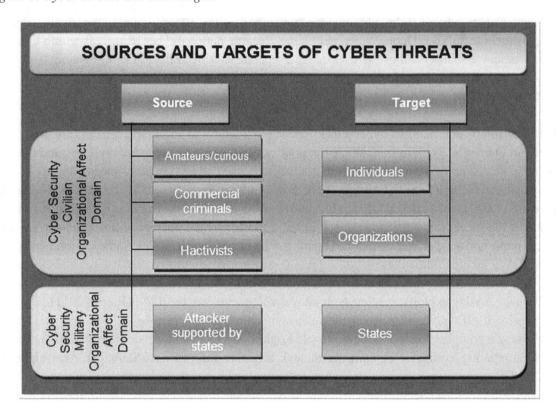

"how can government agencies trust anti-malware companies" and "shall the countries build state owned cyber armies" are among the questions that legislative bodies gather to discuss.

A current example of cyber armies is about to be established by a formal declaration of the state in Turkey as the minister of science, industry and technology announced the training sessions of white hat hackers in 2014 (Cumhuriyet, 2014).

When we look at the nature of cyber threats that are surveyed in this section, we can make a coarse classification of the cyber threats according to their nature and targets (Figure 1).

Findings

Cyber attacks can have severe impacts on the functioning of critical systems both in the public and private sectors. These attacks can be organized rapidly and strike in silence and without warning when compared with physical attacks aimed at similar damage.

Just by looking at the malware based attacks history, we can easily foresee that number of such attacks will increase in the near future. They are less expensive, can cause physical damage without sending any physical material and / or personnel to the target.

Additionally, international cyber threats require common responses of multiple countries coordinated at political, economic, legal and technological level as recommended by the ITU (ITU, 2007) in 2007.

Following is a list of effects of successful cyber attacks, emerged from what we have surveyed in this chapter.

- Provide remote control of systems and collect information to ease further attacks
- Leak sensitive / important / secret information to forge wrong results
- Affect PLC or other type of control systems to damage facilities or cause equipment to slow down or stop production, or remove the control by the systems
- Cause danger to human life because of a malfunctioning system or forged wrong information
- Affect systems to prevent reporting of malicious activities
- Lower the prestige of the institution or country

The literature reviewed informs that there is a variety of threads and anti-malware software products fighting against those threats are both proactive and after the attack activities. However, relying on software vendors to protect a country's critical infrastructure is open to discussion; hence, we examine the necessity of having a national cyber security authority and affiliated defense units such as a separate army force, as discussed next.

CYBER ATTACKS AND STATES

As we have covered major types of attacks and attackers in a previous section, they may be quite harmful for a state owned organization or institution; such an attack may pose more severe damage than to a corporation under the same threat. Especially, a cyber attack to a country's electronic government service and / or critical infrastructure can create a new war place other than land, air or sea which are protected by army forces. An intrusion of an army unit to another country without permission can be a reason to declare war. Fortunately, no nation has declared a cyber war to date; however, many governments have spoken out about cyber attack activities. A recent example is from Iran (BBC News, 2012) where the Hormozgan provincial civil defense chief has announced that they have fend off numerous cyber attacks that target their critical infrastructure including electricity supply facilities in the country. The Iranian officers accuse US and Israel states for such attacks.

Organizations are commonly utilizing anti-malware solutions and they do not have to spend considerable amount of money for such proactive guards, e.g. Kaspersky, McAfee or Norton. Likewise, the governmental agencies are installing such security software. Those software solutions offer safety and backup facilities; however, this may not always cover the total cost of a cyber attack. Furthermore, virus libraries are updated and disinfection methods are developed after such attacks occur, naturally. Hence, anti-malware solutions do not provide total security and recovery. NATO underlines that more combined security schemes are seen as necessities as IT can be used as asymmetric weapons (NATO, 2012) and they can be state initiated attacks.

Consequently, it is known that there are countries developing their cyber weapons capabilities. While NATO took some passive precautions after the 2001 Twin Towers Attack, it mentions Cyber Defence 2.0 (Theiler, 2011) with radical precautions after the 2007 Estonian Cyber Attacks.

Critical Infrastructure

As is well known, infrastructure such as water treatment and distribution, telecommunication, power and energy distribution are vital for countries. Large scale damage to any of them would create considerable impact on the nation, not only in terms of human life but also in the finance sector and to national pride. Cyber attacks can create physical damage; hence, it is necessary to take precautions to protect such infrastructure facilities against digital attacks in peace and wartime. There have been significant declarations and statements created by authorities on this topic; for example, US Space Command boss General William Shelton underlines that it is not easy to even see close future out, given how quickly the cyber-world changes (Ewing, 2012); thus, it is not possible for states to respond against such rapidly changing cyber space.

Today, we depend on control systems more than we used to in the past; hence, to sustain security, maintain economic operations, protect the public health, safety and the environment, countries should keep control systems secure not only against physical damages but also against digital perils. Primary starting point is to determine critical infrastructure.

In the USA, the following sectors are identified as part of critical infrastructure and key asset sectors (Lewis, 2006): agriculture and food, water, public health, emergency services, defense industrial base, energy, transportation, banking and finance, chemicals and hazardous materials, postal and shipping.

Critical infrastructure sectors of the European Union countries are quite similar: energy, nuclear industry, information, communication tech., ICT, water, food, health, financial, transport, chemical industry, space, research facilities (Commission of The European Communities, 2006).

In Turkey, there was no officially published documentation about critical infrastructures till the end of 2012; however, there was a draft documentation prepared about Cyber Security Strategy. This document offers some sectors as critical infrastructure. These are: information, energy, finance, health, food, water, transportation, defense, public security, nuclear-biologic-chemical facilities (Information Security Association, 2012). Cyber Security Institute of The Scientific And Technological Research Council Of Turkey (TÜBITAK) has a center, "Informatics and Information Security Research Center", which runs projects such as information security in critical infrastructure.

Responsibility of the State

The states possess considerable responsibility for making physical security within their borders. However, as we have reviewed cyber attacks previously, digital security should be within the concerns of a nation's defense sector because an attacker may create physical damage by cyber attacks. This damage is not only limited to causing financial waste from changing expensive equipment or shutting down government websites. While we compare cyber weapons to other weapon systems, Cyber Force emerges as a pretty humanist system besides the advantages of cost, effect, and range. However, a cyber weapon more sophisticated than Stuxnet may cause more damage than a missile with a warhead.

The ITU (ITU, 2007) argues that each state has responsibilities other than encouraging research and conferences in cyber security such as creating a cyber security culture in conjunction with the information society. This includes law, finance, industry and social cooperation with other countries' bodies affiliated with the cyber security and coactions of public and private organizations for national strategies.

The same argument implies that responsibilities and the right in ensuring privacy and security in information sharing, reporting and publishing should be defined at the strategic level while best practices in risk management and security are clarified. Those actions are far beyond passing a few acts of law in parliaments. As building an information society is one of the Turkish national targets (State Planning Organization, 2006), it is essential to provide education, information and training in information processing and communication technologies to construct awareness of cyber security hence a cyber code of conduct. As a natural consequence, civil-defense authorities, emergency services, armed forces and security forces would be given not only tactical but also limited operational role against cyber threats to protect, prosecute and recover after an attack.

A discussion can easily start in this point that armies have to have both of defensive and offensive capabilities in the digital world. For that reason, also cyber armies have to have defensive and offensive capabilities and develop these capabilities to get over any possible cyber threat. In 2009, a virtual criminology report prepared by McAfee (McAffe, 2009), informs that countries including China, Russia, USA, Israel and France are not only collecting information about cyber space activities but also developing cyber attack techniques; also North Korea, Iran, Taiwan, Brazil and India are known to have cyber attack programs.

As interpreted from the ITU, it is necessary to structure and develop strategy documents that define priorities and precautions in cyber security. This includes developing a policy for the protection of the information society and the struggle against cybercrime. Following section gives examples from selected countries which put effort in developing national cyber security strategies.

CYBER SECURITY STRATEGIES WITH EXAMPLES

The countries leading international politics need to take strategic precautions which the modern era requires for progressing and not losing their positions. A report of United Kingdom Cabinet Office prepared as "Cyber Security Strategy of United Kingdom" in 2009 (Cabinet Office, 2009) indicates this requirement by the following statements:

...Just as in the 19th century we had to secure the seas for our national safety and prosperity, and in the 20th century we had to secure the air, in the 21st century we also have to secure our advantage in cyber space...

Still from the UK report: "Our vision is for the UK in 2015 to derive huge economic and social value from a vibrant, resilient and secure cyberspace, where our actions, guided by our core values of liberty, fairness, transparency and the rule of law, enhance prosperity, national security and a strong society (Cabinet Office, 2011)

Developed countries started to build up strategies for information security as they have understood the importance of this issue. The EU members are exchanging information and experience through conferences to promote their cyber security strategies even at the time of writing of this article. Examples include 1st International Conference on Cyber Crisis Exercises & Cooperation. This conference is organized for sharing of experiences and enhancing cooperation among the participants.

USA, UK, Germany and France have considerable efforts in structuring national strategies on cyber security. For instance, USA National Strategy Document was issued in 2003 as "The National Strategy to Secure Cyber Space" (The White House, 2003) and another strategic document was prepared in 2008 in which there are directives for protecting military, civilian and governmental computer network and systems and critical infrastructure and strategies to follow in a cyber war; the latest version to our knowledge is published at the government website, White House (The White House, 2010).

Similarly, Cyber Security Strategy of United Kingdom defines the cyber threat as the "very first risk of the 21st century" and in this scope, it determines that international coordination, installing a central cyber security office and defining flaws not only in technology but also in doctrinal, legal and politic regulations are needed (Cabinet Office, 2009), (Cabinet Office, 2011). Germany (Federal Ministry of the Interior, 2011) and France (French Network and Information Security Agency, 2011) also have their own cyber strategies.

A recent example is in Turkey, in which to our knowledge there had been no strategic concept similar to the countries mentioned above till the beginning of 2013. It is better to have a look at the position of anti-malware usage and information security standards in prior to examine plans on strategic cyber security acts.

Anti-Malware and Information Security Standards

A popular defense activity is to adopt anti-malware or anti-virus software; as the name implies those are software that guard computers against malware and remove such threats. With the widespread of the malware, anti-malware programs become essential requisites for any computer that processes sensitive data or accesses the Internet.

There are many vendors providing such kinds of software; hence, institutions should – however, not always do – carefully examine them for maintenance, after sale support and virus list updates before selecting one. Popular anti-malware vendors offer affordable prices for premium services; additionally, most of anti-malware software developers offer free personal usage with limited services.

Standards are also seen as guides to confront cyber threats. There are national and international boards which produce standards in IT for cyber threats such as the ones discussed in this section.

As known, International Electrotechnical Organization (IEC) and International Organization for Standardization (ISO) which are widely recognized organizations, publish standards both in commercial and electro-technical areas, internationally. When we have a glance to the history of the standards focusing information security management systems as a history line (Figure 2), we see that studies on information security were started by the British Standards Institute (BSI) before ISO/IEC, to our knowledge. BSI concentrates on the continuously updated threats, tracking security exploits occurring on hardware or software and how to control human factor.

At the end of the studies, the first part of the BS7799, BS7799-1 was issued in 1995 and second part BS7799-2 was issued in 1999 by BSI. BS7799-1 was accepted in 2000 by ISO as ISO/IEC-17799 after minor modifications and adaptations; consecutively, it has become a globally accepted standard. In 2002, BS7799-2, which is the second part of BS7799, was issued by BSI second time as an English standard after additions and modifications. In 2005, ISO made further changes on ISO/IEC-17799 standard and it was issued again as ISO/IEC-27002:2007 in 2007. The commonly known ISO/IEC:27001 has been published after BS7799-2 of BSI in 2005. ISO/IEC:27001 is a mentor prepared for installing, performing, keeping on and updating information security management system. It was different from the published standards till 2005, because it includes information security checks and information security intrusion management. These additional features are considerably important in taking required precautions to dodge attacks hence, infections and events related to information security.

Although it is argued, for example in (Vural & Sağıroğlu, 2008), that implementing ISO/IEC 27000 standards cannot guarantee organizations' information alone, this standard involves recommendations on information security management.

While the second part of BS-7799 defines how to install information security management system, the first part of BS-7799 provides guidance on how to check information security system. This standard

Figure 2. A Brief Timeline of Selected Standards for Information Security Systems

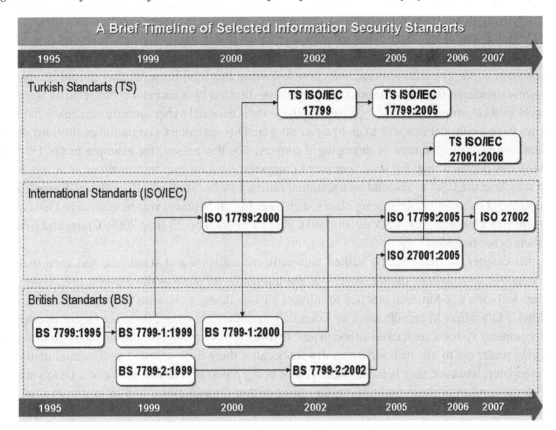

is designed to provide a model for managers and personnel to install and manage effective information security management systems. In this model, plan, implement, check and review steps are defined.

Another British standard related to the information security management systems is prepared as BS7799-3:2005, Information Security Management Systems Risk Management Rules, in December 2005; in 2006 an update is published as BS7799-3:2006.

A more recent and getting popular standard is TS ISO/IEC 15408, the Common Criteria for IT Security Evaluation, in short, Common Criteria (CC). CC includes a basis for evaluating the security specifications of IT software, hardware and systems. With the assessment the product is determined whether to provide the required safety standard or not (Merkow & Breithaupt, 2005). CC certificate is given by a limited number of countries and has 7 evaluation assurance levels (EAL).

It is assessed that a document like a road map for the studies is necessary as the document published by ISA (Information Security Association, 2012), which has been published in 2012.

Results

Although there are discussions in the literature such as (Vural & Sağıroğlu, 2008), adopting information security standards are seen to provide advantages to organizations. Those advantages include guidance on information security management. Still, we should be cautious in saying that cyber security can be guaranteed by adopting standards. We should remember that, systems are only as secure as the people who operate them. Hence, creating awareness in the society should be an overarching national target. For this, leaving this security issue to the IT personnel is no longer a complete solution for the organizations. Organizations should have cyber security documents that dictate principles on digital precautions and what to do in case of an attack. Additionally, users should be trained to adopt such principles. As we have seen so far, organizations are somehow following this line; however, this should be arranged by the government so that organizations' principles are directed by a national cyber security strategy.

Developed countries have already started to shape their national cyber security strategies and many countries have a considerable way to go to cover the gap. Directed attacks on public institutions or vital corporations have the potential of damaging a country. For this reason, for example in the USA, the Pentagon has declared that any state sponsored computer sabotage can be constitute as an act of war which may lead the USA to respond by traditional military force. Similarly, (Gorman & Barnes, 2011) informs us that cyber attacks targeting places such as public institutions will be considered as a reason to declare war. Consequently, USA established Cyber Command on 23 June 2009. China and Iran also have their cyber brigades.

In this chapter, we have briefly visited anti-malware software and standards, and seen that they are not enough to guarantee digital security as the human factor stays as the weakest link. Using anti-malware software is a common practice for almost anyone doing work with a computer; for example, Windows 7 O/S offers Microsoft Security Essentials as default; however, there are lots of examples in which computer systems are hacked although anti-malware software are installed on them. Additionally, users may prefer not to use such security software because there is no private / confidential material in their computer; however, they become under risk of being a part of a Botnet hence of a DDoS attack.

With the support of these findings, we can propose that organizational and mostly individual level security measures are dominant and leaving the cyber security totally to the IT personnel is a poor approach to secure computer systems. One of the vulnerabilities in cyber security is the human factor. For instance, the Botnets are based on the enslaved computers of unconscious users. Obviously, technology should be a part of the solution; however, an integrated approach with the technology, organization and human dimensions would yield more security as individual precautions are not always comprehensive.

When it comes to examining the instance of Turkey, we see that currently, there is no state guidance in securing companies computer systems in Turkey; hence, the organizations are developing their solutions and precautions in isolation. Thus a fully functioning national strategy in cyber security is required.

Even though there are already principal regulations in Turkey, these are far away from meeting the requirements today; further work had to be done on defining sanctions about responsibilities of persons, commercial and public institutions and intrusions in this area so that legal framework can house cyber crimes in a more comprehensive way as stressed in (Aydin, 2012) where cyber security is recommended in the pot of the major targets in the 10th Development Plan. 10th Development Plan's guide of special expertise commissions (Ministry of Development, 2012) has already launched hence time, human and financial resources should be managed carefully and without wasting time.

Parallel information exists in open sources that Turkish Command Forces have precautions individually and Chief of Staff have some directives which arrange the cyber security issues with the Turkish Armed Forces is setting up cyber security structure as in USA, the Cyber Security Command.

FUTURE RESEARCH DIRECTIONS

Precaution against cyber treats is a relatively new topic and there is a considerable room for discussion and proposals for research. One of the primary points is that organizations are not guided by the government in improving digital security; however, putting the government as a stakeholder in this security issue will help improving national cyber strategy. Hence, we support that the state should provide a road map to both public and private sector as well as individuals by:

- Establishing a national warning mechanism managed by the state
- Military precautions
- Designing a non-military structure of cyber defense
- Educating users in cyber security in conjunction with information society
- International coordination and cooperation to promote individual power of the country to a cross border capability in fighting against international threats.

CONCLUSION

Cyber threats are not only annoying malware infects in computer that disrupt files, or send advertising e-mails. This chapter reports that cyber threats target commercial secrets or the secrets of states and are able to paralyze daily life by breaking down the infrastructure of IT on which countries are dependant. Moreover, cyber threats are able to cause physical damages to the critical infrastructures of countries.

Coming back to the research question, "Should the state play an affective role in national cyber security? If it has to, what does the state have to do?" our answer is quite positive. With the example of Turkey which needs to develop a cyber security strategy applicable nationwide; hence, the development agenda needs to include cyber security in, as a separate section. This issue should be given greater importance within short and mid-term targets, performance measures and workshops. Among the activities, authority and responsibilities of the security forces, police and the army, should be discussed in securing the individuals, public and private organizations digital work. To make a body of cyber force possible, there are many regulation works including legal, political, social, financial and public administrational projects. Building such a structure in the armed forces requires extensive preliminary works for the limitations, rights and responsibilities should be defined in a clear-cut manner. Future works should concentrate more on distributing cyber security responsibility among the individuals, private and public sector hence promoting cyber security understanding nationwide.

ACKNOWLEDGMENT

The authors would like to thank Dr. Brian Regan for his efforts in English proofreading and articulation of the text.

REFERENCES

5th Report of Session 2009–10: Protecting Europe against large-scale cyber-attacks, report with evidence (No. HL Paper 68) (2010). *The European Union Committee of the House of Lords.*

Aydin, F. (2012). *Cyber security in the national protection of Turkey.* Ankara: Cankaya University.

Botnets: the new battleground of cybercrime. (2010). *Techradar.* Retrieved from http://www.techradar.com/news/internet/botnets-the-new-battleground-of-cybercrime-719804

Ciampa, M. (2008). *Security+ Guide to Network Security Fundamentals* (3rd Ed.). Cenagae Learning.

Citigroup hacked, customer data exposed. (2011). *CBSNews.* Retrieved from http://www.cbsnews.com/news/citigroup-hacked-customer-data-exposed/

Tracking GhostNet: Investigating a Cyber Espionage Network: The Information Warfare (2009). *Citizen Lab, & Group, T. S.* Monitor.

The European Programme for Critical Infrastructure Protection (EPCIP) (No. MEMO/06/477). (2006). Commission of The European Communities. Brussels.

Cross, M., & Shinder, D. L. (2008). *Scene of the Cybercrime* (2nd Ed.). Burlington: Syngress.

Cyber Security Strategy of the United Kingdom. (2009). *UK Cabinet.*

Cybersecurity guide for developing countries. (2007ITU. Geneva, Switzerland: International Telecommunication Union.

Cyberterrorism - The use of the Internet for terrorist purposes. (2008Council of Europe. Council of Europe Publishing.

Devletin 'hacker'ları geliyor. (2014). *Cumhuriyet.* Retrieved from http://www.Cumhuriyet.com.tr

Ewing, P. (2012). *The cyber war after next.* Retrieved from http://www.dodbuzz.com/2012/03/22/the-cyber-war-after-next/

Cyber Security Strategy for Germany. (2011). *Federal Ministry of the Interior (Germany).*

Information systems defense and security: France's strategy. (2011). *French Network and Information Security Agency.*

Gill, T., & Fleck, D. (2010). *The Handbook of the International Law of Military Operations.* Oxford.

Gorman, S. (2011). China Hackers Hit U.S. Chamber. *The Wall Street Journal.* Retrieved from http://www.wsj.com/articles/SB10001424052970204058404577110541568535300

Gorman, S., & Barnes, J. E. (2011, May 31). Cyber Combat: Act of War; Pentagon Sets Stage for U.S. to Respond to Computer Sabotage With Military Force. *The Wall Street Journal.* Retrieved from http://www.wsj.com/articles/SB10001424052702304563104576355623135782718

Haltaş, F. (2011). DUQU: Yeni Nesil Keşif Uçağı. Retrieved from http://www.bilgiguvenligi.gov.tr/zararli-yazilimlar/duqu- yeni-nesil-kesif-ucagi.html

İçişleri 'bizi seviyor musun' diye 'hack'lendi. (2012). *Milliyet*. Retrieved from http://www.milliyet.com.tr/icisleri-bizi-seviyor-musun-diye-hacklendi/siyaset/siyasetdetay/21.04.2012/1530889/default.htm

National Cyber Security Strategy. (2012). *Information Security Association.*

İnternet'in büyüyen tehlikesi botnet'ler! Mariposa ve Conflicker botnet'leri. (2011). *ChipOnlinetr*. Retrieved from http://www.chip.com.tr

Iran fends off new Stuxnet cyber attack. (2012). *British Broadcasting Company*. Retrieved from http://www.bbc.co.uk/news/world-middle-east-20842113

Kaspersky. (2011). What is the value of your leaked data? Retrieved from http://www.kaspersky.com/about/news/virus/2011/What_is_the_value_of_your_leaked_data_

Knapp, E. D. (2011). *Industrial Network Security: Securing Critical Infrastructure Networks for Smart Grid, SCADA, and Other Industrial Control Systems.* Waltham, MA, USA: Syngress.

Kruse, P., Hacquebord, F., & McArdle, R. (2010). *Threat Report: W32.Tinba (Tinybanker).* The Turkish Incident.

Lewis, T. G. (2006). *Critical Infrastructure Protection in Homeland Security: Defending a Networked Nation.* Hoboken, NJ, USA: Wiley. doi:10.1002/0471789542

Mathews, L. (2011). *TDL4 botnet: smarter, more sophisticated, and not for use in Russia.* Retrieved from http://www.extremetech.com/internet/88770-tdl4-botnet-smarter-more-sophisticated-and-not-for-use-in-russia

McAffe. (2009). *Virtual Criminology Report 2009; Virtually Here: The Age of Cyber Warfare.* McAfee, Inc.

Merkow, M. S., & Breithaupt, J. (2005). *Computer Security Assurance Using the Common Criteria.* Cengage Learning.

Tenth development plan. (2013). Ministry of Development.

NATO and cyber defense. (2012). NATO. Retrieved from http://www.nato.int/cps/en/natolive/topics_78170.htm

Newman, R. C. (2009). *Computer Security: Protecting Digital Resources.* Jones and Barlett Publication.

Nicks, D. (2012). *Private: Bradley Manning, WikiLeaks, and the Biggest Exposure of Official Secrets in American History.* Chicago Review Press.

Norton Cybercrime Report. (2012). *Norton.*

Onuncu Kalkınma Planı (2014-2018). (2012Ministry of Development. Özel İhtisas Komisyonları El Kitabı.

PlayStation: Kullanıcı bilgileri de çalındı! (2011). *NTVMSNBC*. Retrieved from http://www.ntv.com.tr/arsiv/id/25207123

Pusatli, O. T., & Regan, B. (2012). A Model to Assist the Maintenance vs. Replacement Decision in Information Systems. In Z. Belkhamza & S. A. Wafa (Eds.), *Measuring Organizational Information Systems Success: New Technologies and Practices* (pp. 137–157). IGI Global. doi:10.4018/978-1-4666-0170-3.ch008

RedHack'ten emniyete büyük eylem. (2012). *CNNTurk*. Retrieved from http://www.cnnturk.com

Report of the Tunis phase of the World Summit on the Information Society. (2005). WSIS.

Sanger, D. E. (2012). Obama Order Sped Up Wave of Cyberattacks Against Iran. *New York Times*. Retrieved from http://www.nytimes.com/2012/06/01/world/middleeast/obama-ordered-wave-of-cyber-attacks-against-iran.html?pagewanted=all&_r=0

Shearer, J. (2013). *W32.Stuxnet*. Symantec.

sKyWIper: CrySyS Lab. (2012). Budapest University of Technology and Economics Department of Telecommunications.

State Planning Organization. (2006). *Ninth development plan (2007-2013)*.

The UK Cyber Security Strategy Protecting and promoting the UK in a digital world. (2011). *UK Cabinet*.

The National Strategy to Secure Cyberspace. (2003). The White House.

The Comprehensive National Cybersecurity Initiative. (2010). The White House.

Theiler, O. (2011). New threats: the cyber-dimension, Retrieved from http://www.nato.int/docu/review/2011/11-september/Cyber-Threads/EN/index.htm

Tikk, E., Kaska, K., Rünnimeri, K., Kert, M., Talihärm, A.-M., & Vihul, L. (2008). *Cyber Attacks Against Georgia: Legal Lessons Identified*. Tallinn, Estonia: CCDCOE.

Twitter Status. (2010). *Ongoing denial-of-service attack.* Retrieved from http://status.twitter.com/post/157191978/ongoing-denial-of-service-attack

Privacy Impact Assessment for the Initiative Three Exercise. (2010). United States Computer Emergency Readiness Team (US-CERT).

2011 Data Breach Investigations Report. (2012). Verizon RISK Team.

Vural, Y., & Sağıroğlu, Ş. (2008). A Review on Enterprise Information Security and Standards. *Journal of the Faculty of Engineering and Architecture of Gazi University, 23*(2), 507–522.

KEY TERMS AND DEFINITIONS

Cyber Army: A separate force in the armed forces that operates on the digital world; such armies are specialized in recognizing, dodging and organizing cyber attacks.

Cyber Attack: When a cyber threat becomes real i.e. executed, it is considered as a cyber attack.

Cyber Threat: Danger due to prohibited run or obtain control of software, hardware to damage, steal, change, share or expose of electronic information; such threats can involve harming electronic and/or computer systems as well.

Hacktivist: An activist who is trying to raise his voice for his protest and get known by cyber attacks.

National Cyber Strategy: Government initiated strategy that aims to protect the country against cyber attacks.

Vulnerability: A hole in the security and functionalities of computer systems through which an abuser can have opportunity to intrude.

Chapter 11
Conflict in Cyberspace:
The Case of the Middle East

Olivier Danino
French Institute for Strategic analysis (IFAS), France

ABSTRACT

States and non-states actors in the Middle East are totally aware about the strategic importance of cyberspace. They all use it in the conflicts where they are involved in order to improve, for example, their communication, propaganda or intelligence operations. Nevertheless, all these actors have different capabilities in the cyber field. This article sums up how Middle East governments are developing those offensive capabilities and how cyber has changed the way States handle the threat that they are facing. In the other hand, it analyzes how non-states actors are using cyber tools and what kind of targets they are reaching or they want to reach in the near future.

INTRODUCTION

The Middle East is one of the most contentious areas in the world. The issues are strategic, energy-related, religious and political. Territorial disputes are numerous. While the Israeli-Palestinian conflict may dominate the attention, it is not the only one. Iran and the United Arab Emirates, Yemen and Saudi Arabia, Syria and Israel, are examples of territorial disputes still unresolved. One of the major characteristics of the Middle East is the profusion of non-state actors. Some are relatively small. Others are more organized, like Hezbollah in south Lebanon and Hamas in the Palestinian territories. But states and non-state groups have a common point. They use every means at their disposal to defend their interests.

Cyber is especially useful for these objectives. Cyber is a tool for intelligence, sabotage and military operations, but it can also be used for communication and to develop an information and propaganda network. It can be used to launch different types of attacks which are inexpensive and difficult to trace. The actors of the region have different capabilities and different perceptions about the strategic importance of cyber. For some, the cyber domain is a national priority. For others, the focus is mostly to control the Internet and prevent cybercrime.

DOI: 10.4018/978-1-4666-8456-0.ch011

Usually, analysis of cyber issues in the Middle East is devoted to a specific event. The region is rarely studied in its entirety. The consequence is that the data available are scattered and fragmented, which makes synthesis difficult and demands an original approach. This study is therefore based on a variety of information, such as reports available online from university research centers, private and public international organizations, books on cyber, and analyses conducted by computer security firms about viruses detected during the last 5 years. This study is also based on interviews with French and foreign cyber experts, on conferences held in France and abroad, and on a corpus of documents available in French, English and Hebrew.

It must be emphasized that the cyber domain is still maturing. The definition of the word "cyber", and its derivatives, varies according to experts and governments. Russians speak of "information technology" or "information terrorism", where others evoke "cyber" or "cyberterrorism" (Adjemov et al., 2011). Moreover, two countries may use the same term in reference to different realities. The concept of cyberspace fluctuates from one country to another. For the U.S. Department of Defense (2012), cyberspace is "a global domain environment consisting of the interdependent network of information technology infrastructures, including the Internet, telecommunications networks, computer systems, and embedded processors and controllers". In France, the National Agency of Information Systems Security (2011) defines cyberspace as "a communication space consisting of global interconnection equipment automated processing of digital data".

Definition is not an easy matter, but for clarity we have to specify exactly what we understand by cyberspace. As Jean-Loup Samaan (2008) writes, "Security experts recognize three constituent layers of cyberspace: the physical layer, the syntactic stratum, and the semantic stratum. The physical layer consists of infrastructure, cables, routers and switches: it is the most concrete aspect of cyberspace. The syntactic layer links the other two strata formatting information in cyberspace, by giving it standards and protocols such as TCP / IP on which the Internet is based. Finally, the semantic stratum means the raw data transmitted by cyberspace and exploited by humans or machines. This information can range from simple email to the images transmitted by a reconnaissance UAV to its control station on the ground".

An attack against cyberspace may therefore seek one of these three strata. It can be conducted by conventional means such as cyber. The aim of our study is to better understand how the different actors in the Middle East conceive cyberspace. We also examine the possible existence of partnerships between states and between state and non-state groups. In other words, we propose to understand how each actor discusses the cyber domain and the impact of cyber on the balance of forces in the Middle East.

1. CYBER STRATEGIES IN THE MIDDLE EAST

Each country has its own strategy on cyber issues but we can distinguish some common points and then four strategic blocks in the Middle East.

The first block is formed by Turkey alone. Turkey has shifted its global strategy from the goal of joining the European Union to the goal of strengthening certain alliances in the Arab world at the expense of its relationship with Israel. But in the field of cyber, Turkey turns toward organizations outside the Middle East like NATO and the UN. Its first two major participations in cyber exercises and simulation games were with those institutions. A cyber security drill was held in Istanbul on May 15th-16th 2014, in order to strengthen international cooperation and cyber defense. It was jointly organized by the International Telecommunication Union and the International Multilateral Partnership Against Cyber Threats (ITU-

IMPACT), the cyber security arm of the United Nations, along with Turkey's Ministry of Transport, Maritime Affairs and Communications, and the Information and Communication Technologies Authority (ICTA). The second drill was held on May 21st and 22nd 2014. Turkey joined Estonia's cyber exercise, "Locked Shields", which was a simulation of an attack on a fictional nation called "Berylia". Turkey does not just cooperate with NATO, it asked to join the NATO Cooperative Cyber Defense Centre of Excellence in Tallinn.

If the Turkish government is looking for collaboration in order to improve its cyber defense capabilities - Turkey established a cyber defense unit inside the army in 2012 – the authorities are also engaged in a program to reinforce and to develop cyber offensive capabilities. In 2013, Turkey launched a Cyber Warfare Command inside the army to achieve that purpose. Because of the good relations between Turkey and Hamas, Israel is concerned that Turkey may be training Hamas cyber units. Whether or not this is true, we are at the heart of the problem: the possibility for a state to transfer knowledge and technology to a non-state movement.

This is exactly the strategy adopted by Iran and Syria. Regarding the offensive aspect, Iran chooses to promote indirect confrontation with countries it considers hostile. Rather than direct opposition, the Iranian government prefers to spend through interposed opponents. Iran therefore supports movements that are not officially linked with it but act in its interest. Iranian leaders have used the cyber domain to accomplish this for several years now (Géré, 2010). Such a choice allows it to avoid direct involvement and maintain plausible deniability. Thus, when the Saudi authorities accused Iran of being behind the cyber attacks that targeted Aramco, the Saudi Arabian national petroleum and gas company, Iranian officials denied the charge and pointed out that a group called Cutting Sword of Justice had claimed responsibility. This group was unknown before that attack and was never heard from again. For U.S. security services, there is no doubt that Cutting Sword of Justice acted with the support of the Iranian government. Technical experts believe that the computer virus used for this operation could not be designed by a simple group of hackers, but they do not have hard evidence that Iran was behind the attack.

The link with the Iranian government is clearer regarding other groups. This is the case with the Iran Cyber Army (ICA), which consists of IT specialists and professional hackers. The ICA combines several hackers who have been active in the country for years (Nouri, 2010). They are all civilians supported directly by the Revolutionary Guards. The Iranian government also seems to have established a special relationship with a private computer security company, the Ashiyane Security Group, founded in 2002 by Behrooz Kamalian. Ashiyane legally produces and sells computer security software, but the group also claimed responsibility for piracy operations, including against Israeli and U.S. websites. (These were, however, at a relatively low technical level.)

In addition to ICA and Ashiyane, Iranian authorities support a group of hackers called Cyber Hezbollah, composed of hackers who supported the Iranian government during the troubles after the 2009 Presidential election. The aim of Cyber Hezbollah is to mobilize supporters of the Iranian regime and to encourage reflection on the appropriate means of waging Jihad in cyberspace. It holds regular meetings on this topic in Tehran. The conference of 12 July 2012, for example, was devoted to the situation in Syria, with the goal of devising new strategies to help Bashar Al-Assad in cyberspace.

The Meir Amit Intelligence and Terrorism Information Center, an Israeli center established in 2002, describes the action of Cyber Hezbollah: "A memorandum of opinion, released by the organization shortly after it was established, listed its goals and objectives, which include bringing together [Iranian] regime supporters who are active in cyberspace, organizing courses and training for the activists, holding meetings to acquaint the activists with tactics of cyber warfare, and mobilizing the activists for online activities" (Zimmt, 2012). This group of hackers is one of the clearest examples of the strategy adopted by Iran. However, it should not be confused with the Lebanese movement led by Hassan Nasrallah, even if Hezbollah also receives cyber support from its Iranian ally.

To coordinate the strategy of asymmetric warfare in cyberspace, Iran has a cybernetic unit within the Basij Forces Mobilization of Resistance, a branch of the Revolutionary Guards. It is the Council of Cyberspace created in 2010. This council works closely with several groups of hackers and mobilizes cyber specialists within the Revolutionary Guards to recruit new hackers and to help them acquire advanced skills. One of the architects of cyber activities of the Iranian armed forces is Dr. Hassan Abbasi. We note that the election of Hassan Rouhani in June 2013 had no consequences on the Iranian cyber strategy, which remains exactly the same.

Many countries like Saudi Arabia and Qatar regularly accuse Iran of being behind cyber attacks. Israel claims that its information systems are routinely targeted by Iranian infiltration attempts. The United States also blamed Tehran for cyber attacks like the ones on several U.S. banks between September 2012 and January 2013 (ICT, 2013). U.S. authorities believe that these incidents are a response to economic sanctions imposed by the Obama administration on Iran because of the military dimension of its nuclear program.

A few years ago, no expert would have thought to mention Iran among countries with efficient cyber capabilities. Tehran has managed to develop its defensive and offensive capabilities in a very short time. The Iranians have not only learned quickly but they have shown a surprising ability to adapt. Mahdi and Shamoon, two supposed viruses of Iranian origin, illustrate precisely this fact. This rapid progress can be explained by a real motivation to fill the gap and to secure Iranian cyberspace, but also by support from countries with efficient capabilities, like Russia and China. In addition, the Iranian government remains able to mobilize huge sums despite the international economic sanctions in order to support its efforts in the cyber field.

According to Frank J. Cilluffo (2012), Director of the Homeland Security Policy Institute at George Washington University, the Tehran government has mobilized a billion dollars to strengthen its cyber offensive and defensive capabilities. Whatever the exact amount, there is no doubting Tehran's desire to make cyber a priority. For Iran, the cyber domain is an element that must now be integrated into any strategic thinking because it changes the balance of power between states and because it has a direct impact on armed combat. The commander of the anti-aircraft forces of the Revolutionary Guards, General Farzad Esmaili, stated in October 2012 that the next wars that Iran will face have nothing to do with the previous ones (Fars News Agency, 2012).

That is the reason why Iranian authorities are trying to enhance their networks. Iran has begun construction of a "national Internet" parallel "to the global Internet", which will be connected to the population during the year 2013 (Al Jazeera, 2012). The whole area should be covered by 2015-2016. As of mid-2014, only government institutions were connected to that network. We can see here the influence of the China model. Most experts doubt that the creation of a "national Internet" can effectively protect Iran against any sophisticated computer virus, but Tehran believes that the country's security depends on an Internet fully under government control. It is for this reason that in January 2011 the Iranian government created a unit of "cyber police" whose purpose is to monitor the Internet and combat all forms of cyber crime. In November 2011, this "cyber police" integrated hackers to infiltrate sites, email accounts and forums. In addition, in January 2013 Iran established a program to help the authorities monitor social networks. The creation of this software is officially justified by the need to protect against potential malicious software found on these Iranian networks.

That is another key point of the Iranian strategy. The Iranian government wants to support its cyber industry and considerable sums are committed to that purpose. Iran wants to develop and sell its own technology in order to be totally independent from American networks, systems and software. At the end of 2013, Iran launched its own antivirus, called Padvish. Iranian officials claim that Padvish will be ready to be commercialized in 3 years. But the defensive measures adopted by Iran are not limited to this. Since 2010, the Iranian government has rationalized its infrastructure in charge of cyber through the creation of two new bodies: the Cyber Defense Command in November 2010, and the Supreme Council of Cyberspace in March 2012. The Cyber Defense Command is under the authority of the Organization of the Iranian Civil Defense which is in charge of the country's defense and the security of national infrastructure. This initiative is largely due to the discovery of the Stuxnet computer worm in the Iranian nuclear facilities. The Supreme Council of Cyberspace is the central body in the Iranian system. It issues directives to all national organizations in charge of cyber. It is composed of the highest authorities of the country. One of its main tasks is to set up a National Centre of Cyberspace, which will be responsible for developing appropriate responses for all national and international issues related to cyber.

The Gulf States, like Israel, are worried about rapid Iranian progress in the cyber field. It is true that the Arabian Peninsula is far behind Tehran both in defensive and offensive capabilities. They fell behind mainly because in the beginning they gave priority to cybercrime issues. The Stuxnet attack in 2010 and the August 2012 attacks on Aramco in Saudi Arabia and RasGas in Qatar, the second biggest liquefied natural gas producer in the world, were a real wake-up call. This does not mean that they did nothing before that but rather that all cyber initiatives were accelerated after that date.

The uniqueness of the Arabian Peninsula is that the countries have focused mainly on the creation of national Computer Emergency Response Teams (CERTs) instead of national central agencies, like Iran or Israel did, even if those CERTs are usually attached to national organizations related to the government. In Qatar, the CERT, called QCERT, depends on the Supreme Council of Communication and Information Technology, founded in 2004. QCERT works closely with public and private sectors and is responsible for the cyber strategy of the emirate. In Qatar, the private sector is actively involved in the national effort, especially since the attack suffered by RasGas. Qatar Computer Research Institute (QCRI), a national research institute established in 2010 by Qatar Foundation for Education, Science and Community Development, a private non-profit organization, announced in March 2013 that it was setting up an analysis center whose goal is to provide the tools necessary to protect the emirate.

In Saudi Arabia, the CERT is placed under the authority of the Communications and Information Technology Commission (CITC) created in 2001 by King Fahd Ben Abel Aziz Al-Saud. CERT may have broad powers, but all departments of the kingdom are not yet connected to it, thereby limiting its action. In 2011, under the impetus of a resolution adopted by the Ministry of Communications and Information Technology, Saudi Arabia published a text entitled "Developing National Information Security Strategy for the Kingdom of Saudi Arabia". This document sets out the objectives of the Saudi kingdom in cyber matters and has 9 priorities on which Saudi Arabia is particularly engaging its efforts, including human resources, cooperation at the national and international level, and research and innovation. This does not mean that the Saudi authorities had done nothing before about these topics as illustrated by the research center created in 2008 by King Saud University and Al-Elm computer Security Company.

This example of cooperation between the university sector and the industrial sector is not the only one in the Arabian Peninsula. In the United Arab Emirates in 2010, the Khalifa University joined Emiraje Systems to set up a center known as the Cyber Operations Centre of Excellence. The difference with

Saudi Arabia lies in the fact that this project is coordinated with the armed forces and is conducted in collaboration with Cassidian, EADS cyber security branch. The creation of this center of excellence is a perfect example of the UAE dynamism. Indeed, in recent years, the UAE has multiplied initiatives in the cyber field. In 2008, the Telecommunications Regulatory Authority (TRA) put up a CERT whose mission was to coordinate the overall security of the State.

Attacks by Israeli hackers on the website of the stock exchange of Abu Dhabi, and especially the attack against critical infrastructure in Saudi Arabia and Qatar in the summer of 2012, led the UAE to complete this device. The federal government issued a decree at the end of 2012, which stipulates the establishment of the National Electronic Security Authority (NESA) under the direct responsibility of the Supreme Council of National Security. Responsible for the implementation and development of the national policy of the United Arab Emirates on Computer Security, NESA is also responsible for threats and cyber attacks and strengthening the communication network and Emirati information. NESA is guided by a board of directors elected by the Chairman of the Supreme Council of National Security, for a period of three years.

The United Arab Emirates are ahead of many of their neighbors like Bahrain which established its CERT in November 2012. However the Kingdom has several structures, such as the Central Informatics Organization (CIO), which manages the operation of the Internet and its data, and the Directorate for Combatting Corruption and for Electronic and Economic Security, under the responsibility of the Interior Ministry, whose mission is to fight against cybercrime.

Because of the strategy of prioritizing the CERT organism, the first Regional Cyber Security Center (RCSC) was launched in March 2013 into Oman's CERT. This center is the result of cooperation between the Information Technology Authority (ITA) of Oman and the International Multilateral Partnership against Cyber Threat (IMPACT), a branch of the International Telecommunication Union (ITU), the organism in charge of cyber security in the United Nations. The choice of Oman to host RCSC is the result of efforts made by the Sultanate in the cyber domain for several years. ITA was founded on the 31st May 2006 to improve the connectivity of government institutions, economy and citizens of the sultanate. Risk analysis, cyberspace security and protection of the Internet are provided by the CERT of Oman which was established in April 2010.

The objective of RCSC is to assist Arab countries to secure their economic information systems and encourage them to establish national centers in charge of cyber security. RCSC is also responsible for organizing regional simulation exercises to allow its members to respond to major cyber attacks. The first drill took place from the 22nd to the 24th of October 2013 with the participation of Oman, Saudi Arabia, United Arab Emirates, Qatar, Bahrain, Morocco, Libya, Tunisia, Sudan, Mauritania, Egypt, Algeria and Kuwait.

It is worth pointing out that the Organization for Islamic Cooperation (OIC) has had a CERT since June 2005, created to support Cyber cooperation between Muslim countries. But because of tensions between them, this organism is not working well. Indeed, the OIC-CERT participated in February 2012 at the annual simulation exercise organized by its counterpart in Asia Pacific, APCERT, but of the 22 attending countries only Pakistan, Tunisia, and Egypt represented the OIC-CERT which is composed only by 19 countries of the 57 members of the OIC. And if states like Saudi Arabia and the United Arab Emirates are reluctant to participate in exercises with the OIC-CERT, others like Qatar do not even belong to this structure. Turkey is a member of the OIC-CERT, but as we mentioned it seems to prefer to turn toward NATO and the UN rather than the Middle East. Adding to the lack of cooperation, some countries of the OIC-CERT have conflicting relations or controversial partnerships such as Syria, which is a close ally of Iran, and Azerbaijan, which has very close ties with Israel. Some of the 19 members are even suspected of being behind cyber attacks against others. The best example of that is Iran and Saudi Arabia.

This context of tension and suspicion is not ideal to a constructive cooperation and that is the reason why it is not surprising to see the birth of the Regional Cyber Security Center. The creation of RCSC is an important initiative from the perspective of the development of the defensive capabilities of the Gulf States and the overall region. But the main question is whether that center can evolve to form a defense structure against countries like Iran and Syria, and even Israel, or whether it will be a structure dedicated only to some countries with the same strategic interest instead of being for all Arabs states. Iran is excluded from the RCSC (Iran is not an Arab state) but Syria is not. Yet the possibility that Damascus will participate in the activities of the center is unlikely.

The tensions in the region are an obvious obstacle to certain forms of partnership. However, it would not be surprising to see the emergence of unexpected collaborations--between Israel and the countries of the Arabian Peninsula, for example. This link is quite possible given the relationship between the United States and the Gulf States and between the United States and Israel. Moreover, these countries, just like Israel, are worried about the Iranian influence in the region and even if that alliance seems "unnatural" or unlikely, it would not be the first time we see this kind of cooperation in the Middle East, a collaboration motivated only by circumstances and commons interests.

2. THE ISRAELI CYBER STRATEGY

Israel is the last block after the one formed by Turkey, the one composed by Syria and Iran, and the one formed by the Arabian Peninsula. Israel is by far the regional leader in cyber issues (Danino, 2013). It has a real strategy on the matter, a real advance on all the Middle East countries, and the political leaders are totally aware of the importance of cyber. One of the other originalities of Israel is the cyber capabilities of its army. The Israel Defense Forces (IDF) has several specialized cyber units, each with its own skills. The most famous and certainly the largest in number of people is the 8200 unit which is an Israeli Intelligence Corps unit responsible for collecting signal intelligence and code decryption. It has several services under its leadership like the Hatzav unit that collects information in open-source. It also has an elite unit which is regularly projected on the ground. The IDF Cyber Staff, a kind of General Staff whose role is to coordinate and direct the activities of the army in cyberspace, was established in 2009 within the 8200 unit. This structure is composed of soldiers belonging to that unit but also to other units and brigades of the IDF like the Computer Service Directorate (CSD) which is in charge of communications and transmissions within the army. The CSD includes the C4I Corps, an operating brigade (Hayel Ahafala), which deals with operational communications and electronic warfare, and the Telecommunications and Information Technology unit, known in Hebrew as Lotem. This unit is itself divided into several subgroups.

This article cannot go into all the intricacies of the Israeli cyber military organization. What we should remember is that the IDF has several structures ready to deal with cyber issues, its units have different kinds of capabilities, and enhancement is the key to understanding the IDF organization. Indeed, political and military leaders are constantly innovating, creating new structures, new brigades, and new training courses.

In order to coordinate the efforts of Israeli security bodies, the Ministry of Defense established in January 2012 a new central cyber administration. One of its objectives is to support defense industries in developing advanced cyber systems. This is significant. Israel has been aware of the importance of cyber since the 1990's but the priority was given at that time to the security of the military systems at the expense of civilian ones. The Israeli government is now trying to fill the gap accumulated since then by engaging huge sums in the cyber security industries which is really innovating and motivated to propose brand new kinds of solutions. Elbit Systems, for example, announced in June 2012 the creation of a simulator for the training of military and civilian agencies in charge of the defense of Israeli cyberspace. Hybrid Security, for its part, has developed "Telepath", a software capable of detecting suspicious behaviors on the Internet and Intranets. Telepath has been used for more than three years by several national infrastructures in Israel.

If Israel benefits from the presence of numerous cyber industries in its territory, the Israeli government also wants develop its international collaborations. Of course, the United States is the first partner but it is not the only one. In December 2013, Israel and Italy signed a declaration of future cooperation in cyberspace. This is the first document of its kind Israel has signed with a foreign country. The Israeli government also turned to Asia. In May 2014, Japanese Prime Minister Shinzo Abe and Israeli counterpart Benjamin Netanyahu pledged to boost ties between their nations after a meeting in Tokyo, with a particular emphasis on security cooperation and cyber security cooperation. In February 2014, Israel Aerospace Industries (IAI) announced a new Cyber Early Warning Research and Development Center in Singapore. The center will develop prototypes for cyber early warning solutions and market those products both in Singapore and abroad. Initial research at this center will focus on critical and emerging areas: active defense capabilities - aiming to identify cyber attackers in real time; cyber geo-location resolution - aiming to identify the physical location of cyber attackers; advanced anomaly detection capabilities – identifying deviation from routine behavior.

Israel carries out an intense dynamic of cooperation inside and abroad and cross-fertilization in the country. Israel wants to achieve a symbiosis between the education world, the military world and the industrial world. This is why the Israeli Prime minister, Benjamin Netanyahu announced on January, 27th 2014, the creation of an International Cyber Center, called CyberSpark, in Beer-Sheva, in the south of the country. The idea is to get together several cyber military units, like the 8200 unit and Lotem, research and development centers of high-tech companies such as IBM and Deutsche Telekom, university studies specialized in cyber, and public institutions. This huge complex represents an investment estimated by some experts at nearly 9 billion dollars.

As we can see, Israel is extremely proactive in the cyber field. In matters of military strategy it is exactly the same, with the difference that Israel has long adopted a discreet position toward some activities of the IDF in cyberspace. In 2009, the Chief of Staff, General Gabi Ashkenazi said that Israel considers cyberspace as a strategic and operational area but gave no more details. The offensive dimension of Israel's cybernetic strategy has been explicit only since June 2012. Defense Minister, Ehud Barak, was the first politician in authority to break the silence in a speech at an international conference at the University of Tel Aviv. He said that while Israel considers the defensive aspect as the most important and most complex, the IDF has also developed an offensive strategy because the army cannot simply remain in the passive mode of responding to attacks.

This confirmed a note published few days before on the IDF website and entitled "IDF in cyber space: Intelligence gathering and clandestine operations". This very short text discusses the key elements that guide the Israeli army's actions in cyberspace, referring to a document of the IDF Operations Department. In the document we read that "there are many, diverse, operational cyber warfare goals, including thwarting and disrupting enemy projects that attempt to limit operational freedom of both the IDF and the State of Israel, as well as incorporating cyber warfare activity in completing objectives on all fronts and in every kind of conflict. Moreover, it will be used to maintain Israel's quality and advantage over its enemies and prevent their growth and military capabilities, while limiting their operation in this field".

This text is intentionally vague but when we read it, it is difficult not to think of the Israeli raid on the Syrian nuclear reactor in 2007 and various cyber operations against Iran's nuclear program, especially because this note was published just days after the discovery of Flame by Kaspersky Labs, a virus collecting mass information. What is certain is that while Israel takes no responsibility for a series of sophisticated virus attacks all around the Middle East, it does not explicitly deny them either, maintaining an ambiguous position that is similar to its nuclear doctrine. Nevertheless, there is no doubt that Israel is conducting offensive operations in cyberspace and that the country has such capabilities. There is no doubt either that Israel has to face constant attacks or infiltration attempts from states and non-state actors on its networks and on its military and civilian computer systems, just like all Middle East countries. With the current conflicts and tensions in the region, this is not surprising. There is no conflict in the Middle East that is one hundred percent cybernetic, but there are no more conflicts in the region without a cybernetic dimension. Cyber is clearly taken into account by all states and almost all non-states actors, even if they each have different objectives and capabilities.

3. A MULTITUDE OF NON-STATES ACTORS

The Middle East swarms with hackers who act independently of any structured movement. Some may act alone, but they usually belong to a community of hackers who challenge each other and compete to be the most competent and successful. These actors do not always have a well-structured political discourse like other groups such as Telecomix or Anonymous, for example, which are not Middle East movements but operate worldwide. Telecomix and Anonymous are motivated by the will to protect what in their eyes is freedom on the Internet. When they interfered in Middle East affairs for this reason, the tone in their messages moved progressively to a more engaged political discourse. They launched regular cyber operations consisting of denial of service attacks (DoS) or distributed denial of service attacks (DDoS) which are the interruption or the suspension of services of a host connected to the Internet by saturating the target machine with external communications requests. They use also defacement attacks which are attacks that change the visual appearance of a website or even a small detail on a webpage. The more the site is visited, the more the site has a symbolic value, making it more likely to be targeted by DDoS and defacement attacks. Nevertheless, these attacks cause little damage and do not compromise state security even if the cost and the embarrassment are obvious.

Since the popular uprising in Tunisia in late 2010 and early 2011, Anonymous has diversified his forms of engagement by providing logistical support to the people he wants to help. In Tunisia, he did not just participate in piracy operations, he taught opponents of the Ben Ali regime how to share online videos and to hide their identity on the Internet to avoid being identified by the authorities. He distributed books in Arabic but also in French to ease the access to that information for all Tunisians. Anonymous also developed a Greasemonkey script so that opponents do not let themselves be caught by phishing campaigns organized by the Tunisian government. In Egypt, Anonymous and Telecomix worked together to help restore opponents' proxies and sites blocked by the government. They were also particularly active when President Mubarak decided to clip the networks. The actions of Anonymous in Egypt have not stopped after the fall of the Mubarak regime, as illustrated by the numerous threats made against the Muslim Brotherhood and President Morsi.

When this wave of popular protests hit Syria in March 2011, Anonymous launched a large-scale operation to provide technical assistance and regular logistical support to Bashar al-Assad opponents. Made more effective by the experience he gained in Tunisia, Egypt, and Iran in 2009, Anonymous, with the help of other groups of hackers, regularly attacked the interests of the Syrian government. But unlike Egypt or Tunisia, in Syria, the Syrian Electronic Army (SEA) responded against Anonymous. In July 2012, SEA introduced itself into two sites related to the movement and there hacked over 700 accounts belonging to its members. The same month WikiLeaks published with the help of Anonymous million of emails (2,484,899 to be exact) written between August 2006 and March 2012. Those files are known as the Syrian files. These documents show for Anonymous and Wikileaks the double game played by Western companies that have continued to provide the Syrian government with communication equipment and cyber security tools despite the civil war. Anonymous has also targeted Syrian leaders by publishing on the Internet the email addresses and passwords of almost 80 of them. A few days later, it was the turn of President al-Assad himself to be covered by the group who hacked his emails and forwarded them to the Syrian opposition which then released some of them.

Anonymous actions took place in Tunisia, Egypt, Syria, but also in Bahrain and Yemen. Essentially, the movement is engaged in the Middle East wherever it thinks that governments are acting in their own interest rather than in the people's interest. In November 2012, when the Israeli government launched "Pillar of Defense" operation, Anonymous responded immediately by launching an ultimatum accusing Israel of leading an assault against the Palestinian people. In July 2012, the group attacked Dahabshiil, an international money transfer company, based in the United Arab Emirates, which was accused of financing terrorism.

Anonymous and Telecomix have an existence only in cyberspace. They do not fight on the battlefield, just like the International Muslim's Cyber Army or the Muslim Liberation Army which are groups motivated by Islamist ideology. They both target states and groups considered hostile. For them, these actions are the extension of jihad in cyberspace. We can talk then about "cyber jihad" or "e-jihad". The Cyber Hezbollah second conference held in Tehran in September 2011 was on that subject. Entitled "Click of Resistance", this event focused on ways to wage jihad in cyberspace and how to highlight blogs dedicated to the operations of the various jihadist groups. The main speech was given by Dr. Hassan Abbasi, who participates in almost all Cyber Hezbollah conferences.

The Iranians are not the only ones to support cyber jihad. Hamas, for example, considers that this is a new field of resistance against Israel. Religious figures in the Middle East make the same kinds of statements as Tarek Mohammed Al-Suwaidan, a Kuwaiti imam, who called on his twitter account, in January 18, 2012, for a union of Arab hackers to drive "cyber-jihad against the Zionist enemy". For the Israeli Deputy Foreign Minister at that time, Danny Ayalon, any action against Israeli cyberspace was considered a violation of Israel sovereignty, and regarded as an act of terrorism. Israel reserved the right to respond with cybernetic as well as conventional military means. This is also the United States position on that question.

But against whom to retaliate? First, any retaliation means that the victim knows the origin of the attack but in cyberspace it is often difficult to properly identify origin. This is one of the strategic interests of cyber. Second, it is not always easy to know if a group is acting on its own initiative or at the instigation of a state. This is especially true when hackers maintain ambiguity, like the Israel Defense

Forces Team, which uses the official name of the Israeli army, or Ezzedine al-Qassam Cyber Fighters group, which uses the name of the military wing of Hamas. This possible link is even more difficult to establish when a movement becomes known in a single operation, and remains discreet or even disappears completely from the cyber landscape of the Middle East after this one action. This is the case of the Cutting Sword of Justice which claimed responsibility for the attack against Saudi Aramco Hydrocarbon Company in August 2012 but also of Parastoo which probably hacked the International Atomic Energy Agency (IAEA) servers in November 2012.

It is true that the link between certain states and other groups are known, such as between Iran and the Iran Cyber Army and between Syria and the Syrian Electronic Army, but for others it is not always obvious, such as the relationship between Iran and the Islamic Cyber Resistance (ICR). The ICR's first operation on February 25, 2013 was against Bahraini Military systems and United States military personnel located in Bahrain. The Islamic Cyber Resistance also retaliated against the December 4, 2013 assassination of Hezbollah leader, Hassan Laqiss, by leaking documents and sensitive information related to the Saudi Binladin Group, the Saudi Army, and the Israel Defense Forces. What we know for sure is that the ICR has conducted several actions jointly with the Syrian Electronic Army, such as the August 10, 2013 operation against Zain Group, a Kuwait mobile operator.

Usually, operations carried out by these groups of hackers are more "cyber vandalism" than truly dangerous. DDoS attacks and defacement have only minor consequences. There is certainly a financial cost for the affected countries but it does not compromise their security. Operations led by the SEA, the ICR, Anonymous, Telecomix and others, are undoubtedly embarrassing for their victims, and they sometimes complicate the situation on the ground, but in the end they do not really change the balance of power between two enemies. So far, none of these movements has actually managed to infiltrate secure information systems which are the only way to succeed in that objective. In modern society, information systems are a spine where the slightest mistake can cause damage to a greater or lesser extent. The exploitation of the vulnerability of certain SCADA (Supervisory Control and Data Acquisition) systems may actually lead to the paralysis of a country or, in severe cases, the death of several thousand people. This is why Al-Qaeda called in a video released by the U.S. authorities in 2012 to attack the interests of the United States in cyberspace and to target its critical infrastructure, in particular American electric grid systems, identified by Al-Qaeda as one of the major weaknesses of the country. The video compares this vulnerability to aviation vulnerability before the attacks of September 11, 2001, making a parallel between these two types of attack.

It is important to understand that in the Middle East the targets of non-state actors are slowly changing because these groups know that DDoS and defacement attacks have limited consequences. They want to carry out sabotage attacks and to target critical infrastructures. We have an example of this in Israel: in September 2013, a Trojan horse attack targeted the security camera apparatus in the Carmel Tunnels toll road and Israeli experts determined it was not sophisticated enough to be the work of an enemy government. What we know is that a few months before, the Syrian Electronic Army launched an attack on the Haifa water supply systems. The attack failed but was revealed by Israeli experts. These movements are motivated enough to be taken seriously. For the moment they do not have the capabilities but they do have access to improve their skills and they cannot reach this objective without strong state support.

This is exactly how the Lebanese Party of God (Hezbollah) and the Palestinian Islamic Resistance movement (Hamas) have developed their cyber capabilities. Hezbollah has been interested in cyber for several years. As early as 2002, the CIA issued a report stating that the Lebanese movement was preparing attacks against Western countries' information systems. The Secretary General of the Party of God, Hassan Nasrallah, understood the importance of this area and fully integrated cyber by providing Hezbollah with a cybernetic unit in the early years of the twenty-first century. It is difficult to date precisely the creation of this structure but it showed its skills for the first time in November 2004 by sending a drone over Israel. This type of initiative was repeated several times thereafter. In October 2012, Israeli aircraft bombed a drone over the Negev desert that took off from Lebanon three hours earlier and that seemed to be on an intelligence mission. In a speech on television, Hassan Nasrallah confirmed the Israeli accusations against Iran, stating that the aircraft was Iranian-made. He said it had been designed in Iran and assembled by Hezbollah experts in Lebanon. The involvement of Tehran is known and confirmed since the war between Israel and the Lebanese movement during the summer of 2006. During this conflict, the Israeli military were particularly surprised by Hezbollah cybernetic material and technological advance and its capabilities in the cyber field. Iran support to Hezbollah is extensive and not limited to cyber (Levitt, 2013).

Hamas does not possess the same capabilities as Hezbollah even if the movement has also strong ties with Tehran. Nevertheless, the Palestinian movement has adopted the same strategy as its Lebanese ally. During the "Pillar of Defense" operation in November 2012, the Israeli army shelled several drone factories in Gaza, highlighting the cyber capabilities of Hamas and raising the question of its relations with Iran, Syria and Hezbollah in this area. Building drones means that Hamas has the physical infrastructure necessary, such as ground stations, and that its members learned or are learning how to analyze the images transmitted to ground stations. Hamas still has considerable efforts to make in terms of training. For now, the movement has a cybernetic unit whose skills are still fragile. This is why Hamas leaders have launched a recruitment campaign among hackers of the coastal strip. One of the most active groups in the Gaza Strip is the Gaza Hacker Team, which has a website, a Facebook page and has claimed more than 1,726 attacks between January 2011 and January 2013, mainly against Israel, the United States and France. However, Gaza hackers do not have the knowledge. For the Israelis, there is no doubt that Hamas is trained to pilot drones and analyze images by Iranian specialists, just as they trained Hezbollah in Lebanon. The Palestinian movement is in a phase of acquisition of skills and has begun to integrate cyber into the range of its offensive tools. Regarding the defensive aspect, some measures taken by Hamas suggest that strategy is not yet mature but that awareness is underway. On 11 December 2012, the authorities of the Gaza Strip asked the 10 Internet providers present in the coastal territory to stop working with Israeli companies. Referring primarily to economic issues, linked to the competition with Israel, this decision was also motivated by security concerns.

4. DIFFERENT KINDS OF CYBER OPERATIONS IN THE MIDDLE EAST: THE INTELLIGENCE EXAMPLE

Cyber operations have different impacts and different complexities. DDoS attacks and website defacement are the first level of attack. Virus attacks are the second, and sophisticated virus attacks, the third. These are all offensive operations conducted to collect intelligence or to destroy a target. Cyber is used also by state and non-state actors for communication and propaganda. Non-state actors, like Al Qaeda, Hamas or Hezbollah, are mobilizing cyber tools in order to fund their organizations, and to recruit and train their staffs. It is important to keep in mind these other dimensions of cyber activity because they mobilize many people and resources.

Al-Qaeda in the Arabian Peninsula (AQAP) has made "several films in which it had several interviews and portraits of militants, including al-Abtal Wabsaya (Testaments of the hero) and al-Shuhada Muwajahat (Martyrs fighting)". Groups affiliated with Al-Qaeda have "their own websites and their own video production centers" (Canadian Center for Intelligence and Security Studies, 2007). These videos are then posted on the Internet, via platforms like YouTube and Dailymotion and through jihadist forums. Al-Qaeda has its own websites where its members can post videos without any restriction. The movement also publishes texts detailing its ideology, its demands, and its means of action. The target audience is broad. It includes groups that might wish to join the movement, and individuals who might want to act for it. Its online magazine, Inspire, provides instructions on building an explosive device (Jenkins, 2011). Its 12th edition, put online in March 14 2014, even explains how to commit a car bomb attack and lists the possible targets in United-Kingdom, United States and France. Al Qaeda released a second review called Resurgence whose creation was announced on March 4 2014.

Hezbollah and Hamas also have this kind of activity and the two movements have many websites dedicated to their ideology, their armed wing and global information. The Party of God has more than fifty websites divided into information sites, as Moqawama, al-Manar and al-Intiqad, Hezbollah local sites, such as Bint Jbeil, Taybeh, Hula, and sites devoted to associations and social organizations affiliated to Hezbollah like al-Mu'assasat shahid (Information Center on Intelligence and Terrorism, 2006). For all Islamist movements and jihadist groups, cyber can be used in order to gain "hearts and minds". It is a powerful propaganda tool. This is why most of these sites are available in Arabic, English, Spanish, but also French and Hebrew. Communication and propaganda is not our chief subject here. The intelligence aspect of cyber conflict in the Middle East is intriguing and complex.

There are different levels of intelligence operations. The first is open-source intelligence (OSINT) collected by states and non-state actors. Social networks are a good target for this kind of operation. Hezbollah, for example, has created a fake profile on Facebook to get sensitive information about Israel. A charming young woman, named Reut Zukerman, made friends with Israeli soldiers, most of them from an elite unit, and obtained information such as names of soldiers, secret codes, detailed descriptions of bases and training exercises. The Hezbollah members behind that profile spoke perfect Hebrew and they succeeded, step by step, over the course of a year, in maintaining this online illusion. The Taliban did the same thing to ranking American soldiers in Afghanistan in order to collect sensitive information.

Google Earth is also part of OSINT resources. In 2006, the Islamic Army, a Salafist group operating in Iraq, posted on a jihadist website a video explaining how they used Google Earth as part of its rocket attacks against the U.S. army. According to the Foundation of American Scientists (2006), Google's software had been previously mentioned on jihadist forums but it was the first time that a movement actually filmed itself using it. Nevertheless, non-state actors did not wait for this tutorial to prepare their operations on the ground with Google Earth. During the war between Israel and Hezbollah in 2006, the Shiite movement used it to locate Israeli military bases in order to target them. Jihadists in Syria, including the most important of these groups, Jahbat al-Nusra, also known as Nusra Front, are also using Google Earth to identify targets and to organize their attacks (International Crisis Group, 2012).

Of course, OSINT is not used only by non-state actors, but also by the countries of the Middle East. The Israel Police, for example, monitored the Facebook accounts of the social protest movements of 2011 and 2012 and of its leaders, just as the governments of Egypt, Tunisia, Syria, Iran and Bahrain did during the social movements in their countries. In Syria, the authorities went further by creating malwares in order to infiltrate opponents' computer systems. Syrian specialists diverted from its original use a French-made Remote Administration Tool (RAT), called DarkComet, in free access on the net.

The Syrian government also used a Trojan horse, discovered in June 2012 in Syria, called BlackShades. It circulated through a malicious video file which was in fact an install kit program. With BlackShades Syrian security agencies were able to remotely deny access to files, record keystrokes or control webcam on the targeted computer. The United Arab Emirates created a virus of the same type that affected a member of the opposition in January 2013.

If these viruses are used as part of internal frictions, they can also be used as part of foreign tension or opposition, but states remain cautious about doing so, even if they can accuse a country or a non-state actor of an intelligence attack. The Israeli government did not react when the U.S. computer security company FireEye announced in December 2012 that it detected a malware that transferred data from Israel to Kuwait, though Israel did threaten Arab hackers with retaliation for their DDoS attacks. The virus, called BackDoor LV, collected information on the infected machine such as passwords, websites consulted or activity of the webcam. It does not seem to have infected sensitive systems in Israel, and this may explain why Israeli authorities remained silent about it.

More sophisticated viruses have been detected in the Middle East and almost all of them targeting Iranian interests in the region. The connection between them leads experts to conclude that they are part of the same cyber operation and were conceived by the same team or by teams working together or maintaining close ties. The originality of this cyber conflict, which is only one aspect of the greater conflict, is that Iran retaliated and was even inspired by these viruses to make new ones.

5. SOPHISTICATED VIRUSES OPERATIONS IN THE MIDDLE EAST

The sophisticated viruses discovered in the Middle East can be divided into two types: intelligence and sabotage. For the clarity of our remarks, we will say few words about the first category and then about the second.

Flame was accidentally discovered in May 2012 by the Russian computer security company Kaspersky. Flame is by far the most powerful spy tool currently known. With a size of 20 Mb, it is composed of at least 20 modules, each with a specific role. The most surprising one is named Beetlejuice. It is able to identify devices connected via Bluetooth to the infected machine and to copy data from them. While Kaspersky teams were working on Flame they discovered what they at first thought was only one more module. In June/July 2012, they realized it was an independent malware composed of different modules. This Trojan horse called Gauss was probably operational from August to September 2011. It touched banking systems, social networks and e-mail accounts in Lebanon, Israel and the Palestinian Territories. The limited number of Lebanese banks affected by Gauss allows us to guess that it was not a spy virus of criminal nature but a targeted intelligence operation whose aim was to understand the financial activities of Hezbollah and its Iranian ally. On the other hand, MiniFlame, also discovered by Kaspersky, has the profile of a malware used in an intelligence operation with restricted targets. MiniFlame, due to its reduced size and functionality, appears to have been designed to collect specific information while Flame recovered information en masse. It is therefore not surprising that 5000 machines have been infected by Flame while only fifty were infected by MiniFlame. Duqu, for its part, was detected in September 2011. It mainly affected Iran where it flew numerous data on the industrial control systems of the country and the commercial relations of several Iranian organizations. According to some experts, Duqu was developed for the preparation of a massive cyber attack on Iran.

Gauss, discovered in August 2012, has cyber espionage as well as sabotage capacities. It has a module called Godel which can attack SCADA systems. This dual dimension is not unique to Gauss. The malware that attacked the Saudi Aramco hydrocarbon company in August 2012 has these same characteristics. According to the Israeli company Seculert (2012), this computer virus called Shamoon operates in two distinct phases. First, it takes control of a machine directly connected to the Internet and from this unit it contaminates other computers, not necessarily connected to the outside world. Then, in a second step, once Shamoon spreads throughout the system, it is activated by the operator. From there, it retrieves the data of interest and then removes the hard drives of the computers it infected. It is in this way that Shamoon damaged nearly 30,000 workstations -- 75% of Aramco computers, so that it took more than two weeks to restore the entire system.

However, Stuxnet is certainly the most complex sabotage virus known so far. Stuxnet is a computer worm. It evolves independently across networks and has an auto-run module that is activated only when it reaches its target. Stuxnet is the first malicious software designed for a specific and clearly defined industrial control system (ICS) category. It attacks and actually damages a particular model of ICS produced by Siemens, in this case the SIMATIC model, by taking the Step7 software that allows computer use. It benefits at the same time from a vulnerability in Windows that allows it to remain discreetly in the corrupt system (Mueller & Yadegari, 2012). This model of ICS is mainly used by Tehran. Iran is also the country where Stuxnet has done the most damage. The worm destroyed more than 1,000 IR-1 centrifuges in the uranium enrichment plant at Natanz. This represented 11% of centrifuges in use at the site.

Technical analyzes have shown that Stuxnet was composed of many modules, such as module 315 which specifically targets the IR-1 centrifuges, and module 417 which targets a particular model of steam turbine used in the Bushehr central. This means that the creators designed a computer worm for two different types of ICS. This is rare. It takes a programming team with high technical skills and intelligence to fully understand the characteristics of the targets, and the ability to test the worm before inoculation to ensure its functionality. All this requires skills that only few states have. According to the research center of the Congress of the United States, the countries with the knowledge and the motivation for conducting such an attack are "the U.S., Israel, UK, Russia, China and France" (Kerr, Rollins & Theohary, 2010). Whatever the source, Stuxnet, Flame, Gauss and other malwares evidences are more prevalent in the Middle East than anywhere else. This indicates that their use is fully integrated with the tensions in this region and should be linked to the specific issues of the Middle Eastern scene.

The three states most affected at the regional level, Israel, Lebanon and Iran are also the three most affected countries worldwide. However, several elements show that the Islamic Republic is probably the target of these cyber attacks. Why Iran and not Israel or Lebanon? According to David Sanger (2012), President George W. Bush launched a secret cyber operation, called "Olympic Games", in order to attack Iran's nuclear program. David Sanger asserts that this program was carried out by the Americans in partnership with their Israeli ally. The United States and Israel have the knowledge, the financial resources and the capabilities to conduct this kind of operation. They are, however, not alone. Several articles in Forbes also point to Finland and China (Carr, 2011). The articles argue that these two countries are responsible for Stuxnet but not for the other malware that hit Iran. China may have reasons for wanting to sabotage Tehran's nuclear program but its interest in spying on the financial circuits of Hezbollah money remains limited. And we know that Stuxnet and Gauss are related.

Indeed, computer security companies have shown that Stuxnet and Duqu are based on the same programming system. Kaspersky called it the "Tilded Platform". This would seem to establish a connection between the designers of these two malware. On the other hand, Flame, Gauss and MiniFlame, share similarities in their technical design. They are based on the same architectural platform. Because of this, most analysts believe that these two virus families were the work of separate teams that are to some degree affiliated. However, the Kaspersky research teams discovered that one Flame module also exists in Stuxnet. This module, called "resource 207", which allows the propagation of these two viruses via USB port, is similar in both viruses (Kaspersky Labs, 2012). "Resource 207" was discovered in the 2009 version of Stuxnet but not in the 2010 one. "Resource 207" shows that the two projects are linked and that the teams who were working on Stuxnet / Duqu cooperated with the ones working on Flame / Gauss / MiniFlame until 2009. The beginning of this collaboration is difficult to date. Experts think that Stuxnet and Flame were in operation for 5 to 8 years. This means that the two malware were launched between 2005 and 2008. In addition, the oldest MiniFlame protocol known is dated to 2007. If we take into account the time necessary to design these viruses, which is difficult to estimate, we can assume that the decision-making was between 2000 and 2005. This is the moment when two secret nuclear sites were discovered in Iran.

Nevertheless, Tehran's nuclear program is not the only target of these cyber attacks. All Iranian activities have been targeted. Flame showed particular interest in PDF, Microsoft Office and AutoCAD files, suggesting that the industrial sector of the country was the target, including critical infrastructure. However, apart from Israel, Flame mainly affected Iran, Sudan, and to a lesser extent the Palestinian Territories and Lebanon-- all territories accused by the Israeli authorities of hostile activities. Sudan, which was bombed by the Israeli Air Force in October 2012, serves as a logistics base between Iran and the Gaza Strip for weapons traffic (Danino, 2009). The Iranian military support to Palestinian groups arrives in Sudan by sea, then moves to Egypt by land and is then transferred to the various Palestinian movements via the tunnels between the Sinai Peninsula and the Gaza Strip. Is it enough to say that these activities are behind the idea of creating Flame? It is difficult to say, but it is clear that the size of the virus and the many modules that composes it demonstrate that it was designed for a huge variety of targets.

Moreover, Gauss targets Hezbollah's financial activities. The United States and Israel have worked for many years on tracing the financial network of the Shiite movement. Financing for The Party of God depends on Iranian aid but also on illegal activities such as drug trafficking, led by Hezbollah in Latin America and elsewhere in the world (Levitt, 2005). So the United States and Israel seem more likely to be responsible for this malware than Finland and China. Even if none of these states are at the origin of these cyber attacks, it remains that Iran is clearly the target of a vast operation of espionage and sabotage against its nuclear program and against all its activities in the Middle East.

Tehran responded to the attacks in 2012 by combining sophisticated operations with less complex attacks. Parastoo group – parastoo in Farsi means 'swallow' – hacked AIEA servers in November 2012. Two months before, in September, Ezzedine al-Qassam Cyber Fighters group claimed responsibility for "Operation Ababil", as they referred to it in a statement posted on Pastebin. It was a DDoS attack on the websites of several American banks, such as JPMorgan and Bank of America. The group claimed that it was retaliating against the film "Innocence of Muslims," a US filmmaker production. Parastoo and Ezzedine al-Qassam Cyber Fighters group have no clear links with Tehran or the Revolutionary Guards but this does not mean that Iran is not behind these attacks. Despite its vigorous denials, we recall that Iran's cyber strategy is to attack indirectly through groups that seem independent.

Nevertheless, Iran is suspected of being behind two sophisticated attacks. The first was an intelligence attack through a virus called Mahdi, discovered by the Israeli security company Seculert in February 2012. Mahdi collected different kind of information on structures and people linked to the United State in Iran, specifically students, embassies and financial structures. Besides Iran, Mahdi mainly affected

Afghanistan and Israel. It spread in these three countries in a less elaborate way than Duqu, Flame, MiniFlame or Gaus. From a technical point of view, Mahdi is clearly less sophisticated than these four viruses. It spread through malicious e-mails, which included PDF, JPEG and Power Point corrupted files.

The second sophisticated attack, also believed to be Iranian, hit the Saudi hydrocarbon company Aramco and the Qatari gas company RasGas in August 2012. The malware is named Shamoon. Like Mahdi, Shamoon was inoculated by phishing, which is surprising because its effectiveness was enhanced in a more discreet way, by exploiting a vulnerability in Aramco systems. This allows one to assume that the team behind this computer virus did not have the most sophisticated knowledge, though they are far from amateurs. If the technical analysis of Shamoon has not clearly established the responsibility of a state, it is unlikely according to the experts that a simple group of hackers created the virus. Moreover, everything seems to indicate that Shamoon designers were inspired by another virus, called Wiper, the malware that hit the Iranian hydrocarbon installations in April 2012. Indeed, computer security companies found technical similarities between Wiper and Shamoon. However, the designers of Wiper took care to establish a security system erasing the evidences of its passage. As a result, the information available on Wiper is negligible because security companies have very little material on which to base their analysis. Its technical characteristics and its destructive capabilities are much more effective than Shamoon, which remains less sophisticated than other computer viruses that affected the countries of the region.

The link between Shamoon and Wiper raises the issue of "cyber proliferation", the possibility that a virus attack will inspire a state to retaliate by creating an even more destructive virus. In view of the Shamoon case, it is quite possible that Iranian authorities will use the information that it has on these viruses in order to conceive new ones. However, it is clear that a truly efficient virus supposes a conception based on the special characteristics of the target. It is interesting that the second virus of supposed Iranian origin, Mahdi, which is not connected to any particular malware unlike Shamoon, is not a virus used for sabotage, but for purposes of espionage. There is therefore a kind of mimicry from Iran that is inspired by the cyber operation launched against it.

CONCLUSION

Stuxnet is not the first malware created for sabotage purposes. In 1982, the United States designed a Trojan horse on the basis of intelligence collected by French intelligence services. The virus was implemented in a SCADA system purchased by the USSR for Canada and it caused the explosion of a Siberian pipeline being built by the Soviets (Saffire, 2004). It was a sabotage operation probably conceived as an alternative to the use of armed force, exactly like Stuxnet. This episode highlights what we said in the beginning of this article. Cyber can be used alongside old tools, and can be grafted to old practices in order to make them more efficient. States, for example, did not wait to build cyber resources to conduct intelligence operations and sabotage, but it is clear that cyber increased their capabilities in those domains. As we said, there is no conflict anymore in the Middle East without a cyber component but there is no conflict in that region which is totally cybernetic. Operation "Olympic Games" is the perfect example of a vast cyber operation launched in the context of a regional crisis. It must be linked to the region and not be seen as what is sometimes called cyber war. It is the same with cyber attacks between Qatar and Syria or between Syria and Saudi Arabia, which are one aspect of the conflict linked to the Syrian civil war. The cyber operations launched by Hezbollah and Israel against each other in 2006 are also one part of the open war between those enemies at that time. We can multiply the examples in order to show how cyber is present in every conflict of the Middle East. This is an irreversible trend. Cyber will be in all the next conflicts of the region, as demonstrated by the raid led by Israeli warplanes against a Syrian nuclear site near the city of Deir Ez Zor, on the night of 5 to 6 September 2007.

During this operation, Israelis deployed significant cyber means: "eight F-15 fighter-bombers, and electronic warfare aircraft Gulfstream G-550 Nachson [...]. Gulfstream Nachson is equipped to provide electromagnetic shielding bombers and blur detection systems and enemy communications". F-16 fighters have integrated this device "to increase the potential of electronic warfare and anti-radar" (Razoux, 2008). After departure from Israel, the fleets entered Syria through Turkey and blinded the Syrian air defense. According to Pierre Razoux (2008), they then split into two groups. The first one bombed a radar station at the top of Tel el-Abouad and then turned back, while the second continued to the nuclear site and destroyed it. Richard Clarke and Robert Knake (2010), do not mention the bombing of the Syrian radar station. For them, the Israeli air force already had control of Syrian radars screens, ensuring that their aircraft could fly with stealth. Thus, if the Syrian air defense did not see the Israeli planes, it is because nothing at all was displayed on its monitor screens. "When the Israelis attacked Syria, they used light and electric pulses, not to cut like a laser or stun like a taser, but to transmit 1's and 0's to control what the Syrian air defense radars saw. Instead of blowing up air defense radars and giving up the element of surprise before hitting the main targets, in the age of cyber war, the Israelis ensured that the enemy could not even raise its defenses" (Clarke & Knake, 2010).

It is unclear exactly how the Israelis took control of Syrian anti-aircraft defense systems. Richard Clark makes three assumptions including the contamination of the network by a Trojan horse activated during the raid by Israeli warplanes. Whatever the method used, the Israelis succeeded in achieving complete surprise thanks to their cyber skills. If Israel were to attack Iran's nuclear facilities, it is likely that the military authorities would proceed more or less the same way in order to blind the Islamic Republic anti-aircraft defense systems. This may be why the Israelis remain silent on the details of this raid against Syria and in particular on how they took control of the Syrian sky.

The other main point to keep in mind about cyber issues in the Middle East is that non-state actors are totally aware that DDoS attacks or website defacements are limited. They are trying to launch more dangerous cyber attacks and they want in the future to target vital infrastructures. They know that this is where the potential for destruction and destabilization is highest. They have the will. For now they lack the capabilities, despite all the improvements in their attacks in the past few years. In order to launch a sensitive attack, these groups will need help from a state that has the knowledge, the resources and the military infrastructure. Collaboration and transfer of capabilities are essential for non-state actors to reach their goals. This means that states may collaborate with groups that the United-States or Europe considers terrorist organizations. This is one of the main issues of "cyber proliferation" which will need to be resolved in the near future.

REFERENCES

Adjemov, S. A. (2011). *International Information Security: Problems and Decisions.* Moscow, Komov SA.

Iran to launch giant domestic intranet. (2012). Al Jazeera. Retrieved from http://www.aljazeera.com/news/middleeast/2012/09/201292471215311826.html

La stratégie médiatique et de propagande d'Al-Qaïda. (2007). *Canadian Center for Intelligence and Security Studies*. Retrieved from http://www.itac.gc.ca/pblctns/pdf/2007-2-fra.pdf

Carr, J. (2010). Stuxnet's Finnish-Chinese Connection. *Forbes*. Retrieved from http://www.forbes.com/sites/firewall/2010/12/14/stuxnets-finnish-chinese-connection/

Carr, J. (2011). The New York Times fails to deliver Stuxnet's creators. *Forbes*. Retrieved from http://www.forbes.com/sites/jeffreycarr/2011/01/17/the-new-york-times-fails-to-deliver-stuxnets-creators/

Clarke, R. A., & Knake, R. K. (2010). *Cyber War, the next Threat to National Security and what to do about it*. New York: Harper Collins.

Danino, O. (2009). *Le Hamas et l'édification de l'Etat palestinien*. Paris: Karthala.

Danino, O. (2013). La stratégie cybernétique de l'Etat d'Israël. *Sécurité Globale*, *24*(2), 15–24. doi:10.3917/secug.024.0015

Défense et sécurité des systèmes d'information, stratégie de la France. 21. (2011). *Agence nationale de la sécurité des systèmes d'information*. Retrieved from http://www.ssi.gouv.fr/IMG/pdf/2011-02-15_Defense_et_securite_des_systemes_d_information_strategie_de_la_France.pdf

Dictionary of Military and Associated Terms. (2014). *Department of Defense*. (pp. 74-75). Retrieved from http://www.dtic.mil/doctrine/new_pubs/jp1_02.pdf

Iran Boosting Electronic War Capabilities due to Nature of Threats. (2012). *Fars News Agency*. Retrieved from http://english2.farsnews.com/newstext.php?nn=9106243312

Iraqi Insurgency Group utilizes Google Earth for attack planning. (2006). *Foundation of American Scientists*. Retrieved from http://www.fas.org/irp/dni/osc/osc071906.pdf

Gaza Hacker Team operations. (n. d.). Retrieved from http://www.zone-h.org/archive/notifier=Gaza%20Hacker%20Team

Géré, F. (2010). *Iran, état de crise*. Paris: Karthala.

Terrorisme et Internet: le Hezbollah recourt largement à Internet pour diffuser sa haine anti-israélienne, anti-juive et anti-américaine dans le cadre de sa guerre psychologique. (2006). *Centres d'Etudes Spéciales Information Center on Intelligence and Terrorism*. Retrieved from http://www.terrorism-info.org.il/data/pdf/PDF_18674_3.pdf

Jenkins, B. M. (2011). Is Al-Qaeda's Internet Strategy working? *Rand Corporation*. Retrieved from http://www.rand.org/content/dam/rand/pubs/testimonies/2011/RAND_CT371.pdf

Kaspersky Lab. (2012). Resource 207: Kaspersky Lab Research Proves that Stuxnet and Flame Developers are Connected. Retrieved from http://www.kaspersky.com/about/news/virus/2012/Resource_207_Kaspersky_Lab_Research_Proves_that_Stuxnet_and_Flame_Developers_are_Connected

Kerr, P. K., Rollins, J., Catherine, A., & Theohary, C. A. (2010). *The Stuxnet Computer Worm: Harbinger of an Emerging Warfare Capability*. CRS Report for Congress.

Levi, R. (2013). Is Iran behind the attacks on the American banks? *ICT report review*, 12-23. Retrieved from http://www.ict.org.il/Article/60/ICT-Cyber-Desk-Review-Report-2

Levitt, M. (2005). Hezbollah finances, funding the Party of God. *The Washington Institute*. Retrieved from http://www.washingtoninstitute.org/policy-analysis/view/hezbollah-finances-funding-the-party-of-god

Levitt, M. (2013). *Hezbollah: the global footprint of Lebanon's Party of God*. Washington: George Tow University Press.

Developing National Information Security Strategy for the Kingdom of Saudi Arabia. (2013). *Ministry of Communications and Information Technology*. Retrieved from http://www.mcit.gov.sa/Ar/MediaCenter/PubReqDocuments/NISS_Draft_7_EN.pdf

Mueller, P., & Yadegari, B. (n. d.). *The Stuxnet Worm*. Department of Computer Science. University of Arizona. Retrieved from http://www.cs.arizona.edu/~collberg/Teaching/466-566/2012/Resources/presentations/2012/topic9-final/report.pdf

Nouri, K. (2010). Cyber wars in Iran. *Mianeh*. Retrieved from http://mianeh.net/article/cyber-wars-iran

Raff, A. (2012). Shamoon, a two-stage targeted attack. *Seculert*. Retrieved from http://blog.seculert.com/2012/08/shamoon-two-stage-targeted-attack.html

Razoux, P. (2008). Israël frappe la Syrie: Un raid mystérieux. *Politique Etrangere, 1*(1), 9–24. doi:10.3917/pe.081.0009

Saffire, W. (2004). The Farewell Dossier. *The New York Times*. Retrieved from http://www.nytimes.com/2004/02/02/opinion/the-farewell-dossier.html

Samaan, J.-L. (2008). Mythes et réalités des cyberguerres. *Politique Etrangere, 4*(12), 829–841. doi:10.3917/pe.084.0829

Sanger, D. E. (2012). Obama order sped up wave of Cyberattacks on Iran. *New York Times*. Retrieved from http://www.nytimes.com/2012/06/01/world/middleeast/obama-ordered-wave-of-cyberattacks-against-iran.html?pagewanted=all&_r=0

Tentative Jihad: Syria's fundamentalist opposition. (2012). *Middle East Report, 131*(12). *International Crisis Group*. Retrieved from http://www.crisisgroup.org/~/media/Files/Middle%20East%20North%20Africa/Iraq%20Syria%20Lebanon/Syria/131-tentative-jihad-syrias-fundamentalist-opposition.pdf

US House of representatives. (2012). The Iranian Cyber Threat to the United States. *Homeland Security Policy Institute*. Retrieved from http://www2.gwu.edu/~nsarchiv/NSAEBB/NSAEBB424/docs/Cyber-071c.pdf

Zimmt, R. (2012). Spotlight on Iran. *The Meir Amit Intelligence and Terrorism Information Center*. Retrieved from http://www.terrorism-info.org.il/en/article/20370

KEY TERMS AND DEFINITIONS

Denial of Service Attacks (DoS): This is an attack on a network consisting of flooding it with useless traffic.

Defacement Attack: This consists of changing the visual appearance of a website or even a small detail on a webpage.

Distributed Denial of Service Attacks (DDoS): A variation on the denial of service attack. The target machine is saturated with external communications requests, but in a distributed denial of service attack the hacker uses multiple compromised systems in order to reach the goal.

Greasemonkey: A Mozilla Firefox extension that allows users to customize the way a webpage displays or behaves.

Hassan Abbasi: He is the head of the Center for Doctrinal Strategic Studies in the Islamic Revolutionary Guards Corps. He is also special adviser for the Supreme leader Ali Khamenei. Given Iran's cyber strategy, Dr. Hassan Abbasi's participation in Cyber Hezbollah conferences is not a surprise.

Islamic Resistance Movement: Usually known as Hamas, the Islamic Resistance movement was founded in 1987 during the first intifada by the Palestinian branch of the Muslim Brotherhood.

Open-source intelligence (OSINT): This consists of publicly available sources like media, newspapers, public data, or information on the World Wide Web.

Party of God: Usually known as Hezbollah, the Party of God was founded in 1982 during the war between Israel and Lebanon. It is a Shi'a Islamic movement based in Lebanon, particularly in the south of the country.

Phishing: A technique that uses corrupted emails or corrupted attached files in an e-mail in order to scam the user into surrendering private information.

Remote Administration Tool (RAT): A RAT is software that allows a remote operator to take control of a computer from another computer.

SCADA (Supervisory Control and Data Acquisition): SCADA systems organize certain vital infrastructures, particularly in the water, transport, and electrical sectors. SCADA systems belong to industrial control systems.

Trojan Horse: A non-self replicating malware that looks like a benign application but contains a malicious code that allows the attacker to gain unauthorized access to the infected computer.

Chapter 12

Information Warfare in the 2013-2014 Ukraine Crisis

Brett van Niekerk

Transnet SOC Ltd and University of KwaZulu-Natal, South Africa

ABSTRACT

In November 2013 a series of protests in the Ukraine resulted in a change of government, which was followed by a pro-Russian incursion of Crimea in 2014 and an attempted breakaway by Eastern Ukraine. During this crisis information warfare tactics were used extensively, from propaganda and misinformation to cyber-attacks. The chapter discusses these information warfare activities based on reports, social media activity, and secondary data. The time period of interest is up to mid-May 2014, however subsequent major events are considered. An 'ideal' information warfare campaign and possible future repercussions of the conflict are discussed. The information warfare campaigns are discussed in relation to cyber-strategies. The impact of the cyber-strategies of the two nations involved and lessons learned will be discussed.

INTRODUCTION

Information warfare, and in particular cyber-attacks, have been used in Eastern Europe during significant political unrest and conflict. Due to the prevalence of cyber-attacks related to political events in the region, it is unsurprising that there was a strong online component when protests erupted in Ukraine in November 2013, both in support and opposing the pro-Russian government at that time. The incursion by pro-Russian forces into Crimea in February 2014 and subsequent political activity in the region sparked a number of strong online reactions which can be considered as information warfare. For the purposes of this chapter information warfare is considered to comprise of various functional areas, including (Brazzoli, 2007):

- Network warfare, or more commonly known as cyber-warfare, where computer networks are the weapons an targets;

DOI: 10.4018/978-1-4666-8456-0.ch012

- Electronic warfare, which resides in the electro-magnetic spectrum and includes jamming and eavesdropping of signals;
- Psychological operations, which aims at altering the perceptions of the target audience to be favorable to one's objectives.

In addition, the concept of social information warfare is applicable. This can best be illustrated by the Arab Spring events, where online activity played a large part in mobilizing and co-coordinating protestors. The most notable of these events resulted in a change of government in Tunisia and Egypt (van Niekerk & Maharaj, 2013).

The Myriam-Webster Dictionary (2014) provides a short definition for strategy as "a careful plan or method for achieving a particular goal usually over a long period of time" and a more detailed definition: "the science and art of employing the political, economic, psychological, and military forces of a nation or group of nations to afford the maximum support to adopted policies in peace or war". A cyber-strategy would therefore use online activity to leverage the political, economic, psychological and military aspect to achieve the desired goal. From the definitions of information warfare and its functional areas, a cyber-strategy can be considered to be online activities that have an impact on a target's psychological, information, or physical systems. In addition, physical or psychological activities that impact the cyber-based activities can be included in a cyber-strategy. Stonesoft Security (2014) indicates that a cyber-strategy is one which takes advantage of online opportunities whilst mitigating risks from the online environment.

The chapter analyses the information warfare activities surrounding the Ukraine crisis, based on social media activity, reports, and secondary data on DoS attacks. The following sections describe the methodology and theories used in this chapter and provide a background to the region and the crisis. The sections thereafter discuss the influence of social media during the protests, the propaganda and misinformation focusing on the online aspects, the cyber-attacks, and other relevant activities. These sections are followed by a discussion and the conclusion.

METHODOLOGY AND THEORIES

The chapter presents a qualitative analysis of news reports, social media activity, and imagery to determine the flow of events during the crisis, specific incidents and their impact, and the strength and accuracy of reporting. Secondary data is used for cyber-attack data to illustrate the magnitude of the attacks. Two theoretical models underpin the analysis: the IW lifecycle model (shown in Figure 1) and the network warfare attack process. The IW lifecycle model was proposed in van Niekerk and Maharaj (2011) and used to analyze the Arab Spring events in van Niekerk, Pillay and Maharaj (2011). It is a two-layered model, allowing for the overlap of high-level concepts with specific implementations and technologies to conduct the activities. Context is a key factor, and the lifecycle ultimately influences the context, allowing for the closure of the lifecycle or for continuing iterations (van Niekerk and Maharaj, 2011). This model informs the structure of the chapter: the background equates to the initial context of the model. The first iteration can be considered as the protests, which altered the context resulting in a strong pro-Russian resurgence, ultimately leading to the breakaway of Crimea and the attempted breakaway of the Eastern regions of Ukraine. Pro-Russian online rhetoric provided a continuous driver of the context to support their aims.

Figure 1. The IW Lifecycle Model
Source: van Niekerk and Maharaj (2011)

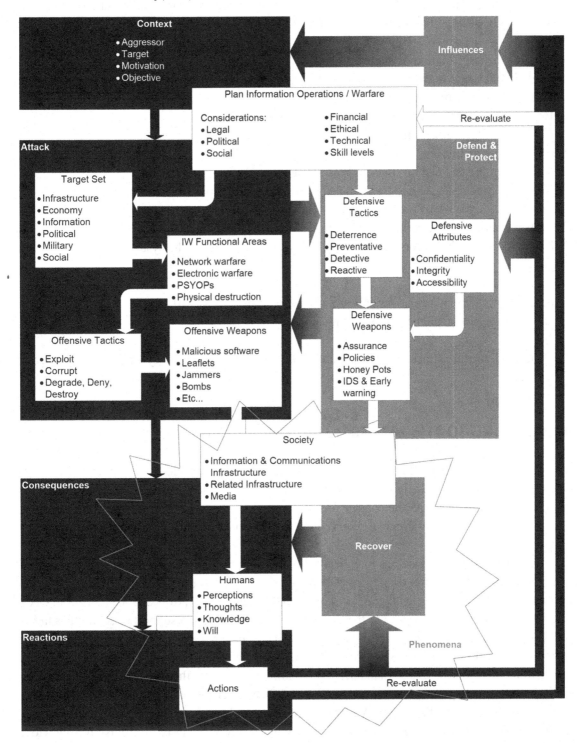

The network warfare attack process described in Jones, Kovacich, and Luzwick (2002) consists of 12 steps taken to compromise a target nation's infrastructure and networks in preparation for conflict extending to cyber-space. The 12 steps are (Jones, Kovacich, and Luzwick, 2002):

1. Identify the target nation or organization
2. Identify interfaces between the global information infrastructure and the target nation's national information infrastructure
3. Research the target nation's systems and networks
4. Gather intelligence information
5. Identify vulnerabilities
6. Covertly probe and test for traps and/or responses
7. Enter the system, locate and transmit sensitive information to safe location
8. Probe for other systems and networks
9. Probe systems and networks for additional information
10. Set logic bombs, trap doors, delete intrusion evidence, and leave the system

11. Search for additional target systems and networks, repeat steps1-10
12. Attack the systems and networks during conflict

This network warfare attack process provides a model against which the cyber-attack campaigns can be analyzed.

BACKGROUND TO THE 2013-2014 UKRAINE CRISIS

This section provides a historical background to the region and an overview of major events during the crisis. The background ultimately sets the context against which the crisis originates, as indicated in the Lifecycle model (Figure 1). As the chapter focuses on the online and information warfare actions during the crisis, the summary of events is required to provide a frame for the political contexts throughout the crisis.

The Eastern European region has long been a hotspot for politically-induced cyber-attacks. In 2007 Estonia was targeted by denial-of-service (DoS) attacks surrounding political dissatisfaction with the relocation of a war memorial (Landler & Markoff, 2007; Nazario, 2007; Rolski, 2007). In 2008, Georgia was targeted by similar attacks prior to the Russian military incursion in support of separatists in South Ossetia (Coleman, 2008; Hart, 2008; Labovitz, 2010). Radio Free Europe/Radio Liberty in Belarus reported DoS attacks on their websites, coinciding with the anniversary of the Estonia attacks (Gandhi, Sharma, Mahoney, Sousan, Zhu & Laplante, 2011). Lithuania was also the victim of alleged pro-Russian hackers in 2008, where a number of websites were defaced over increased political tensions between Lithuania and Russia (Krebs, 2008). A Lithuania news portal was targeted by a DoS attack in 2013 after an article was posted accusing Russians for trying to buy votes in the Eurovision Song Contest (E.L., 2013). Moldova saw one of the first major 'Twitter Revolutions' in 2009 (World Movement for Democracy [WMD], c. 2009).

The Ukrainian and Crimean region has long history of conflict. In 1853 to 1856 the Crimean War was fought between the Russians and the French, British and Ottoman Turks. Ukraine formed part of the USSR, however it broke away in 1991 after an attempted coup in Moscow (British Broadcasting Corporation [BBC], 2014a). In 2004 pro-Russian Victor Yanukovych wins the elections under allegations of vote rigging, and the Orange Revolution begins. Opposition leader Victor Yushchenko won the election re-run. However, Yanukovych won the 2010 elections and Yulia Tymoshenko, his primary opponent, was arrested for abuse of power (BBC, 2014a). Some dissent was shown against an agreement with the European Union. On the 21 November 2013 the Ukrainian cabinet under President Victor Yanukovych sought greater co-operation with Russia over the European Union agreement. This sparks small protests, which began to gain momentum (BBC, 2014a; Temnycky, 2014). The size of the protests varied from 300 000 (al Jazeera, 2014) to over 800 000 (Temnycky, 2014). These protests, with a particular emphasis on the online component, are discussed in the following section. Figure 2 provides a timeline of the protests and related events leading up to the military action in Crimea.

The crisis worsened on the 27 and 28 February when uniformed armed men, without identifying insignia, took control of key buildings and the airport in Simferopol (Crimea) and military airbases. Despite strong international opposition, pro-Russian forces maintained control of Crimea, and a Russian-supported referendum resulted in Crimea electing to break away from Ukraine. This was followed by an attempted breakaway by Eastern Ukraine, resulting in an ongoing internal conflict during which a civilian aircraft was shot down (al Jazeera, 2014; BBC, 2014a). A timeline of activity in Crimea and Eastern Ukraine is presented in Figure 3.

SOCIAL MEDIA DURING THE PROTESTS

The protests, known as EuroMaidan, literally translated as European Square (Bohdanova, 2014), are seen as a continuation of the Orange Revolution. The Orange Revolution did not incorporate social media, however EuroMaidan did, providing observers an opportunity to assess the influence of social media (Satell, 2014). The protests can be considered as social information warfare, in a similar fashion to the Arab Spring events across North Africa and the Middle East (van Niekerk & Maharaj, 2013). The context leading up to the protests is described in the background section above.

Onuch (2014) investigates the importance of social media during the protests: not only did a large proportion learn about the protests through some form of social media or online source (49% Facebook, 35% VKontakte, and 51% from Internet news sites), but they found these online sources more reliable than television reports. However, the study shows television still was the major contributor for potential protestors to learn where the protests are: 48% received information from television, 46% from text messages, 41% from Internet news, and 40% from Facebook (Onuch, 2014). Most protestors joined the protest with company, 32% claiming they came with a group of friends, whereas 18% joined alone (Onuch, 2014). Information dissemination regarding the protests obviously had a strong social component, but also a strong online component. The immediacy of the social media updates provided a more accurate and up-to-date picture of the protest than television did. Facebook in particular seems to have had a strong influence: slogans went viral on Facebook prior to becoming prevalent on the street (Onuch, 2014).

Satell (2014) further illustrates the prevalence of social media in the EuroMaidan protests by comparing them to the Orange Revolution; in 2004 the state controlled the majority of media, but online chat, text

Figure 2. Timeline of events leading up to the military action in Crimea
Sources: al Jazeera (2014), BBC (2014a) and Temnycky (2014)

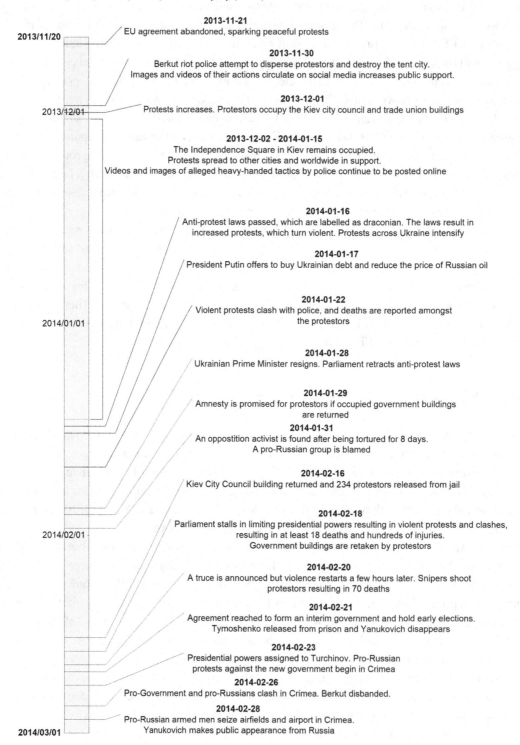

2013-11-21
EU agreement abandoned, sparking peaceful protests

2013/11/20

2013-11-30
Berkut riot police attempt to disperse protestors and destroy the tent city.
Images and videos of their actions circulate on social media increases public support.

2013-12-01
Protests increases. Protestors occupy the Kiev city council and trade union buildings

2013/12/01

2013-12-02 - 2014-01-15
The Independence Square in Kiev remains occupied.
Protests spread to other cities and worldwide in support.
Videos and images of alleged heavy-handed tactics by police continue to be posted online

2014-01-16
Anti-protest laws passed, which are labelled as draconian. The laws result in
increased protests, which turn violent. Protests across Ukraine intensify

2014-01-17
President Putin offers to buy Ukrainian debt and reduce the price of Russian oil

2014-01-22
Violent protests clash with police, and deaths are reported amongst
the protestors

2014/01/01

2014-01-28
Ukrainian Prime Minister resigns. Parliament retracts anti-protest laws

2014-01-29
Amnesty is promised for protestors if occupied government buildings
are returned

2014-01-31
An oppostition activist is found after being tortured for 8 days.
A pro-Russian group is blamed

2014-02-16
Kiev City Council building returned and 234 protestors released from jail

2014-02-18
Parliament stalls in limiting presidential powers resulting in violent protests and clashes,
resulting in at least 18 deaths and hundreds of injuries.
Government buildings are retaken by protestors

2014/02/01

2014-02-20
A truce is announced but violence restarts a few hours later. Snipers shoot
protestors resulting in 70 deaths

2014-02-21
Agreement reached to form an interim government and hold early elections.
Tymoshenko released from prison and Yanukovich disappears

2014-02-23
Presidential powers assigned to Turchinov. Pro-Russian
protests against the new government begin in Crimea

2014-02-26
Pro-Government and pro-Russians clash in Crimea. Berkut disbanded.

2014-02-28
Pro-Russian armed men seize airfields and airport in Crimea.
Yanukovich makes public appearance from Russia

2014/03/01

312

Figure 3. Events in Crimea after pro-Russian Military Intervention
Sources: al Jazeera (2014) and BBC (2014a)

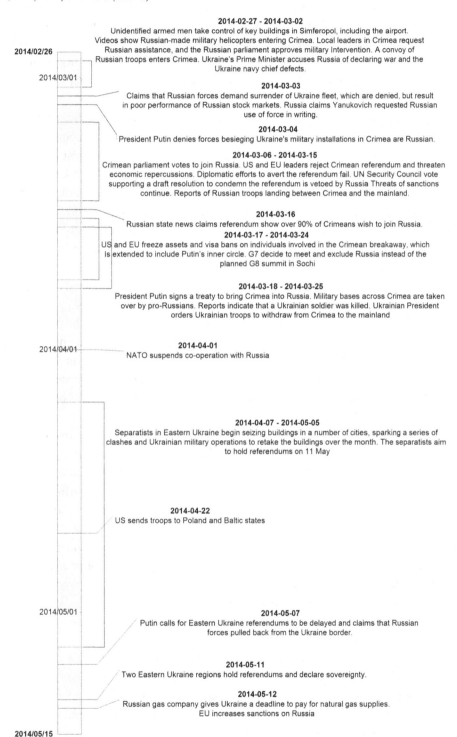

2014-02-27 - 2014-03-02
Unidentified armed men take control of key buildings in Simferopol, including the airport.
Videos show Russian-made military helicopters entering Crimea. Local leaders in Crimea request
Russian assistance, and the Russian parliament approves military Intervention. A convoy of
Russian troops enters Crimea. Ukraine's Prime Minister accuses Russia of declaring war and the
Ukraine navy chief defects.

2014-03-03
Claims that Russian forces demand surrender of Ukraine fleet, which are denied, but result
in poor performance of Russian stock markets. Russia claims Yanukovich requested Russian
use of force in writing.

2014-03-04
President Putin denies forces besieging Ukraine's military installations in Crimea are Russian.

2014-03-06 - 2014-03-15
Crimean parliament votes to join Russia. US and EU leaders reject Crimean referendum and threaten
economic repercussions. Diplomatic efforts to avert the referendum fail. UN Security Council vote
supporting a draft resolution to condemn the referendum is vetoed by Russia Threats of sanctions
continue. Reports of Russian troops landing between Crimea and the mainland.

2014-03-16
Russian state news claims referendum show over 90% of Crimeans wish to join Russia.

2014-03-17 - 2014-03-24
US and EU freeze assets and visa bans on individuals involved in the Crimean breakaway, which
Is extended to include Putin's inner circle. G7 decide to meet and exclude Russia instead of the
planned G8 summit in Sochi

2014-03-18 - 2014-03-25
President Putin signs a treaty to bring Crimea into Russia. Military bases across Crimea are taken
over by pro-Russians. Reports indicate that a Ukrainian soldier was killed. Ukrainian President
orders Ukrainian troops to withdraw from Crimea to the mainland

2014-04-01
NATO suspends co-operation with Russia

2014-04-07 - 2014-05-05
Separatists in Eastern Ukraine begin seizing buildings in a number of cities, sparking a series of
clashes and Ukrainian military operations to retake the buildings over the month. The separatists aim
to hold referendums on 11 May

2014-04-22
US sends troops to Poland and Baltic states

2014-05-07
Putin calls for Eastern Ukraine referendums to be delayed and claims that Russian
forces pulled back from the Ukraine border.

2014-05-11
Two Eastern Ukraine regions hold referendums and declare sovereignty.

2014-05-12
Russian gas company gives Ukraine a deadline to pay for natural gas supplies.
EU increases sanctions on Russia

2014/02/26
2014/03/01
2014/04/01
2014/05/01
2014/05/15

313

messages and the few independent newspaper and television channels provided dissemination points. The difference was that journalists did not have a mass media platform outside of the mainstream media in 2004, whereas during the EuroMaidan protests prominent journalists disseminated information through Facebook and other social media, which is more difficult for influential people to control (Satell, 2014). Even during the EuroMaidan protests, Satell (2014) claims that the state had strong influence over the media, which could account for the study results described above indicating that social media provided more accurate information than traditional broadcast media.

Tucker, Metzger, and Barbera (2014) measured the actual posts on Facebook and Twitter during the protests. Facebook showed peaks from the beginning of the protests to mid-December, then after brief reductions in activity peaked again in late January and late February. The largest peak was during late February, exceeding 250 000 likes per day. The most common form of activity were 'likes' followed by shares (Tucker, Metzger, & Barbera, 2014). Twitter showed similar behavior, with a maximum peak of approximately 2500 tweets per hour. An interesting trend is that on Twitter there was a relatively even distribution across Ukrainian, English, and Russian compared to predominantly Ukrainian languages on Facebook; in particular the amount of English increased dramatically after January 15, indicating that Twitter was being used to target an international audience (Tucker, Metzger, & Barbera, 2014). In addition they showed that the number of Twitter account subscriptions increased drastically during the protests, indicating that the protest initiated an uptake of social media.

Bohdanova's (2014) analysis agrees that Facebook was key in organizing the protests, with Twitter being prominent in informing international audiences about the protests. The main Ukrainian Facebook page made a Ukrainian record by reaching 76 000 likes in the first six days; in addition to this main page, an English and localized Facebook pages were created. They advocated peaceful protest, provided suggestions for dealing with the police, discussed future protests and informed protestors about other urgent issues (Bohdanova, 2014).

A number of social media aggregators were set up in a bid to gather the posts from the relevant social media sites so that the majority of information was available in s single location; these websites include (Bohdanova, 2014): Maidan.in.ua in English, Euromaidan.eu in Ukrainian, Euromaidan.com in Russian, and Euromaidan.tk in all three languages. Some pages were specific to sharing creative ideas such as placard designs, or crowdsourcing funds to provide necessities to protestors; double the requested amount was received by the closing date (Bohdanova, 2014). A number of Facebook pages or groups provided legal support or legal discussions around the protests, such as Euromaidan-SOS (https://www.facebook.com/EvromaidanSOS) and The Revolution's Legal Department (https://www.facebook.com/groups/569879549761649/). In addition to the legal aid, medical volunteers who were providing assistance set up pages such as Maidan.Doctors (https://www.facebook.com/maidanmed) which helped organize the volunteers (Bohdanova, 2014). An example of a webpage to organize volunteers is Galas.org.ua, which uses crowdmapping.

Ukrainian journalists who uncovered documents from the former President Yanukovych's retreat after he fled from Ukraine detailed the recovery of the documents and then posted their contents online through a website named YanukovychLeaks (http://YanukovychLeaks.org) and a Facebook page (https://www.facebook.com/yanukovychleaks/info). These documents are claimed to indicate massive corruption by the government. A number of the journalists tweeted about the discovery, and posted images on Instagram (Lokot, 2014). Whilst this appears reminiscent of the whistleblower website Wikileaks, this website has a key difference: it is not anonymous and the procedure around the source documents appear well documented.

Figure 4. Selected memes relating to the EuroMaidan protests

A number of memes referring to the protests were circulated; Figure 4 illustrates selected memes. Many appear to focus on the violence of the protests, implying heavy-handed tactics by both police and protestors; others show political commentary such as giving opinion on the anti-protest laws. Memes are not necessarily information warfare tactics, but they do help shape opinion and provide an online and global form of 'political cartoon', sometimes with a tongue-in-cheek or sarcastic approach. As the memes are predominantly English, it can be assumed they are targeting an international audience as an alternative means to bring attention to the protests.

The social media landscape surrounding the protests have similar aspects to the Arab Spring events, however there appears to be a far more organized support mechanism to aid the protestors which was managed through social media. In addition to these pages, memes provided a more satirical or tongue-in-cheek look at the protests and eventually there was their own Wikileaks-style website. However, the social media and online component in these protests are undisputable, and clearly illustrate the influence of the new media on political conflict.

Following the lifecycle model in Figure 1, the techniques used were largely psychological in nature; the tools included both online protest and physical protest supported by social networking technology. The traditional and online media aided in the delivery of the social information warfare by furthering the global awareness of the protestor's message. The Ukrainian government at the time responded mostly in the physical domain, and the apparent heavy-handed approach provided the protestors with additional psychological ammunition with which to tarnish the government's image. The internal and global pressure ultimately led to a change in government. The cyber-strategy of the pro-EU protestors proved effective, however there were limited online defensive measures by the pro-Russian government.

The result of the protestor's successful strategy, both online and in the real world, was to alter the context of Ukrainian politics. The pro-Russian government was replaced with an interim pro-EU government. This effectively changed the roles as the pro-Russian population now became the anti-government protestors, and the pro-EU population supported the government. The change in context, with the pro-Russian protests predominantly in Crimea, triggered the next phase, which was the Russian incursion into Crimea.

THE RUSSIAN-UKRAINE CONFLICT

This section focuses primarily on the events after the EuroMaidan protests and the change in Ukrainian government, however some activities did initiate prior to the protests. The context altered significantly due to the government change; the pro-Russian populace went on the offensive after being defenders during the protests.

There are four parts to this section: the cyber-based propaganda, the cyber-attacks, other IW related activities, and a discussion of the significance of the activities and the associated strategies within the context of the conflict.

Propaganda

The changing context of Ukrainian politics, as described in the previous section, prompted pro-Russian media and groups to conduct their own psychological attacks aimed at supporting the ousted government and degrading the image of the new interim government. The tools and techniques remained largely the same in this aspect of the conflict, however there appeared to be an increase in the 'artistic license' used in producing articles and news stories. Whilst the traditional media often led with these stories, they were mirrored in the online environment.

Prior to and during the Russian incursion, a number of releases by various news agencies illustrated that strong propaganda campaigns were being conducted. Many of the claims by pro-Russian sources were refuted online, however a strong pro-Russian influence is seen. This section discusses the propaganda surrounding the pro-Russian incursion into Crimea with a focus on social media.

In the days immediately after the incursion into Crimea, a number of claims were made which were dismissed by the adversary. News of an alleged ultimatum levied against the Ukrainian forces in Crimea by the Russian fleet spread rapidly on the 3 March, however the ultimatum was refuted by the Russian authorities and press (Russia Today, 2014a). An infographic by Nemchenko (2014) and a post by the US Department of State (2014) listed alleged inaccuracies in the Russian media releases, including:

- Many refugee Ukrainians were seeking asylum in Russia in a humanitarian crisis, when there was no evidence of this. Figure 5 shows a Twitter post containing a picture of a largely empty border post between Russia and Ukraine.
- The armed men in Crimea were claimed to be self-defense forces and militia, however they were using Russian equipment not available to civilians, and identified themselves as Russian security forces to journalists.

Figure 5. Example of contradictions to the Russian claims
Source: Eristavi (2014) (https://twitter.com/MaximEristavi)

- Claims of mass attacks against synagogues and orthodox churches, yet the apparent victims report not seeing evidence of such attacks.
- Russian actions are in-line with the 1997 Friendship Treaty between Russia and Ukraine, however the treaty states that Russia needs to respect Ukraine's territorial claims.
- Claims of mass defections of Ukrainian troops to Russia, when only the Ukrainian navy chief defected.
- Misquoting politicians who oppose the intervention.

A claim that 'trolls' tried to attack discredit blog authors, and where this failed tried to redirect the discussion to Russian news sites; some of these posts are claimed to originate from the Kremlin (chornajuravka, 2014). This again implies that the pro-Russians were attempting to dominate the social media environment, and illustrates an example of them attempting to discredit opinions.

By searching Social Mention for "Ukraine" on 2 March, 3 March, and 16 March, the prevalence of the pro-Russian opinion can be seen, as shown in Figure 6. On both the 2 March and 3 March the Russian news network RT was the top user, and on the 2 March Ruptly (part of RT) was also prevalent. The positive sentiment indicates a prevalence of a pro-Russian view, as a negative sentiment would reasonably have been expected due to the strong reaction against the incursion by the international community. As expected, the top keywords were relevant to the situation.

After the EU and US targeted prominent Russian figures with sanctions, Dmitry Rogozin openly mocked President Obama and the sanction on Twitter; a screenshot is shown in Figure 7. A pro-Russian online campaign began leveling joke sanctions against president Obama (Reuters, 2014b). These posts follow the official Russian stance downplaying the impact of the sanctions (Thomson Reuters, 2014). However, earlier reports indicated that the sanctions were having an impact (Kelly & Korsunskaya, 2014).

Figure 6. Social Mention data for search term "Ukraine" on the 2, 3, and 16 March 2014 (left to right)
Source: Social Mention (2014) (http://socialmention.com/)

On the 28 February ousted president Yanukovich made a public broadcast from Russia, claiming to still be president. This resulted in a strong reaction from many Ukrainians, who posted self-portraits of themselves giving his broadcast "the finger" (Dougherty, 2014). This mocking reaction can be seen as an emotional equivalent of showing evidence to disprove claims, as described above.

As with the protests, a number of memes provided political commentary surrounding the Russian incursion into Crimea; selected memes are presented in Figure 8. These memes not only focus directly on the incursion, but the US foreign policy, and imply there is hypocrisy in the attitudes involving US involvement. As with the protests, the memes are not necessarily direct propaganda, but could influence or reinforce opinions, and appear to be aimed at the international community due to the prevalence of English.

Figure 7. Tweets mocking the the imposed sanctions
Source: Rogozin (2014) (https://twitter.com/Rogozin)

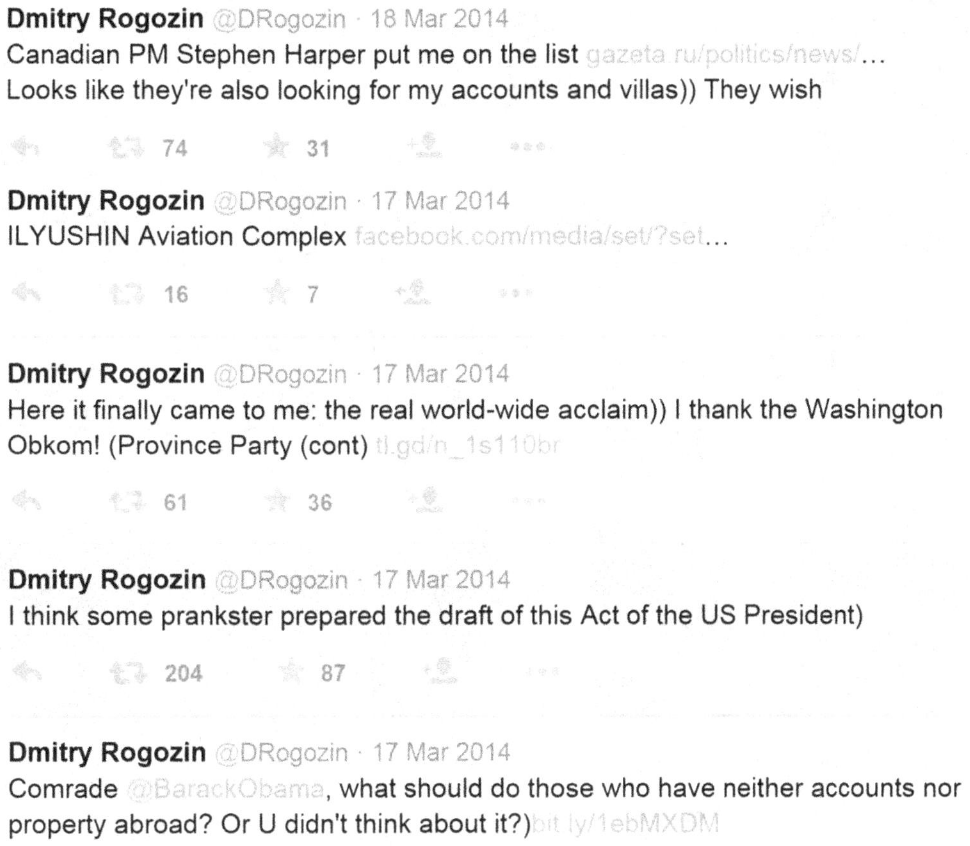

Dmitry Rogozin @DRogozin · 18 Mar 2014
Canadian PM Stephen Harper put me on the list gazeta.ru/politics/news/...
Looks like they're also looking for my accounts and villas)) They wish

74   31

Dmitry Rogozin @DRogozin · 17 Mar 2014
ILYUSHIN Aviation Complex facebook.com/media/set/?set...

16   7

Dmitry Rogozin @DRogozin · 17 Mar 2014
Here it finally came to me: the real world-wide acclaim)) I thank the Washington
Obkom! (Province Party (cont) tl.gd/n_1s110br

61   36

Dmitry Rogozin @DRogozin · 17 Mar 2014
I think some prankster prepared the draft of this Act of the US President)

204   87

Dmitry Rogozin @DRogozin · 17 Mar 2014
Comrade @BarackObama, what should do those who have neither accounts nor
property abroad? Or U didn't think about it?) bit.ly/1ebMXDM

Walker (2014) illustrates the pro-Russian and opposition propaganda, both of which sometimes presented rumors hard truths. The pro-Russian elements presented the protests and pro-EU groups as 'Nazis' and Western interference to destabilize Russia, which evokes strong emotions due to the history from the Second World War; however the pro-EU accused these media channels of telling lies. The Nazi imagery was also apparent in the South Ossetia conflict, where defaced webpages compared Georgian President Saakashvili to Hitler (van Vuuren, Phahlamohlaka, & Brazzoli, 2010). Harding (2014) illustrates "manipulation of the press" through the reporting of the Russian media that Ukrainian naval vessels had defected to Russia, despite no other reports to confirm this. As many of the Ukrainian vessels were captured when the bases were stormed, they obviously had not defected at the time of the Russian reports (Standifer, 2014). On 14 April 2014 reports were made of a Russian fighter aircraft making twelve low-altitude passes of a US warship, USS Donald Cook, in the Black Sea prior to it docking in Romania, apparently related to Russian complaints that the ship had contravened the 1936 Montreux Convention, where ships from non-Black Sea nations had to leave in 21 days (Fishel and Associated Press, 2014; LaGrone, 2014). A week later, Russian media reported the same incident, however claiming the aircraft had a new electronic warfare capability that jammed the ship's Aegis radar system, and that "all the 27 members of the crew filed a letter of resignation" when the ship docked in Romania, and that this was "indirectly confirmed by the Pentagon statement according to which the action demoralized the crew of

Figure 8. Memes regarding the Russian incursion into Crimea

the American ship" (Russia Radio, 2014). These ships typically have over 290 crew (US Navy, 2014), not 27, and no report by the Pentagon indicated the crew was demoralized. The initial reports indicated as the Russian aircraft was unarmed, the ship did not go to battle stations (Fishel and Associated Press, 2014; LaGrone, 2014).

In mid-April 2014, reports surface that Russian propagandists had been "caught red-handed" (Gregory, 2014a) as three Russian channels interviewed the same person, but he played a different role each time: a German spy, a pro-Russian protestor attacked by right-wingers, and as a pediatrician. In addition, claims were made of other suspect reporting claiming protests were diminishing with only a few hundred protestors, whereas estimates indicate nearly a million protestors in the accompanying images have been reported (Bennetts, 2014). A few days later more, whilst Russia was denying involvement, reports surfaced of a YouTube video showing a uniformed man in Eastern Ukraine introducing himself as a Russian lieutenant colonel and a radio interview of a protestor claiming to be Russian (Gregory, 2014b). Photos then surfaced of some of the armed men in Eastern Ukraine and Russian forces, showing the same person in both photos; one appeared to have served in Georgia in 2008, and another appeared to have been in the Crimea earlier in the Ukrainian crisis (BBC, 2014b). These photos were used as further evidence of covert Russian forces in Eastern Ukraine.

Rantapelkonen and Jaitner (2013) discuss the Russian leadership's attempts to dominate mass media, and indicate that in some cases there is inconsistency with how social media is viewed as a political tool. Therefore the strong use of mass media and social media is not unexpected. In 2008 the cyber-attacks against Georgia provided the Russian viewpoint with a monopoly for a number of days (Hart, 2008), however in Ukraine the prevalence of social media has provided the opposition to challenge the Russian media. A Russian professor indicated that television reports create a reality for the viewers, and does not necessarily need to reflect actual events as most television viewers are unlikely to visit the area, and therefore form perceptions based on what they view on the television (Kates & Butorin, 2014). This manipulation of the media then creates a reality that the authorities want their population to perceive, to gain support for the military actions.

The Economist (2014) shows that Ukraine is divided into a pro-Russian East and South, and pro-EU West and North, and it is these divisions which the various rumors and propaganda targeted to polarize the country. The interim government did not counter pro-Russian propaganda, and the Ukrainian prime minister only addressed the ethnic Russian populations into the crisis, which would have allowed the propaganda to seed doubt in that population during this exclusion (*The Economist*, 2014). Walker (2014) indicates that the militia defending the Russian bases in Crimea appeared to have strong nationalist views; indicating a strong polarization, where the Russian-speaking population in Crimea supported the Russian incursion. Just as there are claims of Western meddling, the interim Ukrainian government accuses Russia of sending agents to instigate and influence instability, and it was predicted that Donetsk was vulnerable to Russian influence (*The Economist*, 2014). A few weeks later, in early April, Dontesk did descend into chaos with pro-Russian protestors seizing government buildings (as the Maidan protestors did earlier in the year) and demanding independence (Russia Today, 2014e; *The Guardian*, 2014).

The crisis in Ukraine eventually led to opposition protests in Moscow the day before the referendum in Crimea, the largest since the 2011 Russian elections (Tsvetkova & Bush, 2014). The crisis could therefore potentially influence public opinion in Russia and further destabilize the entire region if the crisis drags on. During President Putin's annual question and answer event, he appeared to reassure the Russian population that Russia has the economic capability to maintain the Crimea, and continued to deny Russian presence in Eastern Ukraine (Kendall, 2014); this further illustrates there are concerns amongst the general Russian population regarding the Russian involvement in the crisis.

In July 2014, after the shooting down of Malaysian flight MH17 over Eastern Ukraine, it was reported that a tool monitoring webpage edits originating from Russian government IP addresses detected an alteration on the Russian-language Wikipedia page discussing Boeing 777 accidents. The edit reportedly change a sentence claiming that the plane had been shot down by terrorists using Russian-made weapons to the plane being shot down by Ukrainian soldiers (Lowensohn, 2014). These postings, made prior to the attribution of fault, further illustrate how the Internet is used in attempts to sway opinion and apportion blame.

Once again there was a mostly one-sided affair in cyber-space, however the roles were reversed along with the context. The superior cyber-strategy regarding propaganda ensured a pro-Russian dominance of rhetoric on social media. This change in context enabled pro-Russian forces to successfully annex the Crimean region. The rapidly shifting antagonism amongst the pro-Russian population also led the Eastern parts of Ukraine into attempts to breakaway, resulting in a civil war which continues at the time of writing. Alongside the cyber-based propaganda, cyber-attacks were being conducted; the following section describes the cyber-attacks related to the crisis and subsequent conflict.

Cyber-Attacks

As with many political incidents in the region, the Ukraine crisis was accompanied by a series of cyber-attacks leading up to and during the crisis, including cyber-espionage campaigns, DoS attacks, and web defacements. The majority of DoS attacks originated from hacktivist groups and appeared with no long-term plan, however there does appear to have been a cyber-campaign targeting Ukraine from prior to the conflict. This Russian cyber-campaign follows along the 12 steps of the network warfare attack process described in the methodology section, and was attributed to Russia.

In early 2014 a report was released regarding a series of related malware, commonly known as Snake or Uroburos, which is a remote access tool that is typically used for accessing information remotely. The majority of the malware samples (32 of 56) submitted originate from Ukraine, with 14 of those occurring in 2014 and eight in 2013. Second was Lithuania, with 11 total reported infections (BAE Systems, 2014). This indicates that Ukraine was targeted by a cyber-espionage campaign. This was not the first time Ukraine has been affected by such activity: in October and November 2012 an espionage campaign (known as Rocra or Red October) targeting government, diplomatic, and corporate organizations was detected and investigated. Whilst this is earlier than the events in Ukraine, it is notable that many of the victims are in the immediate region, the malware appears to originate from a Russian-speaking country, and some of the victim systems in the Ukraine were defense-related (SecureList, 2013). In February 2013 another cyber-espionage campaign known as MiniDuke targeted mostly European nations, and the Adobe PDF documents used to distribute the malware claimed to be documents containing foreign policy and NATO membership plans from Ukraine (Mimoso, 2013). Whilst being a victim of three cyber-espionage campaigns may be a coincidence, being the main target of Snake and the claimed foreign policy documents being instrumental in MiniDuke, which is also one of the pivotal themes of the demonstration, may be more indicative of the following crisis than mere coincidence.

In early November 2013 a series of Ukrainian government websites were defaced, displaying a message purporting to be from NATO's Cooperative Cyber Defense Centre of Excellence (CCD COE); in conjunction a number of fake emails were also distributed under the Centre's name (Kovacs, 2013). However, the complaints of NATO hacking websites and the false emails are reported to come from the same IP address which is associated with botnets (Kovacs, 2013). Estonian military webpages were targeted by DDoS attacks on 1 November, the email campaigns occurred on the 4 November and the NATO CCD COE was targeted by DoS attacks on 7 November in conjunction with website defacements in Estonia (CERT-EE, 2013). These attacks were claimed by Anonymous Ukraine in a campaign they called #OpIndependence, which claimed to have hacked and release emails from the Ukrainian Democratic Alliance for Reform party in February 2014 (Anon, 2014).

Just prior to the pro-Russian incursion into Crimea a series of cyber-attacks occurred, which continued for a week after the incursion. Reports indicate that the attacks disrupted the communications of most of the Ukrainian force in Crimea (Mullish, 2014). A number of Ukrainian websites, some associated with the EuroMaidan protests, were targeted by DoS attacks, and pro-Ukrainians attacked the Kremlin website on the 27 February (Cyber Threat News, 2014). On 28 February Anonymous Ukraine claimed to have defaced over 20 Polish websites warning them about the "Nazis of EuroMaidan" (Revolution News, 2014). On the 3 March the website of Russia Today was defaced with the word 'Nazi' replacing 'Russian' or 'military' (Bitdefender, 2014), and the following day the website of Ruptly, a video news agency owned by Russia Today, was targeted by a DDoS attack which blocked access for 30 minutes (Kovacs, 2014). On the 4 March it was confirmed Ukrainian Parliament mobile phones were suffering from DoS attacks (Vamosi, 2004). This was followed by DDoS attacks against the Ukrainian defense, security and media websites on the 8 March, which appears to have originated from Crimea (Polityuk, 2014; Pultarova, 2014).

Cyber-attacks again became prevalent a few days prior to the Crimean referendum: on 14 March Ukrainian websites experienced attacks, followed by massive DDoS attacks on the Kremlin, Russian Central bank, Foreign Ministry, and media websites. The attacks on Russia were claimed by Anonymous Caucasus, and there were statements that indicated that the attacks were not related to the crisis (Clayton, 2014b; Gallagher, 2014; Reuters, 2014a; Russia Today, 2014d). The website for the Crimean referendum was targeted by a DDoS attack on the evening before the referendum (Russia Today, 2014c). A number of DDoS attacks targeted official websites in both Ukraine and Russia on the day of the referendum (16 March) and continued onto the following day; reports indicate that the 132 attacks against Russia peaked at 124 Gbps whilst those against Ukraine only peaked at 9.8 Gbps (Clayton, 2014c). NATO was again targeted on the 16 March when DDoS attacks took down their websites and affected their unclassified email system. A Ukrainian group calling itself CyberBerkut was behind the attacks protesting against perceived interference in Ukraine; the attacks coincided with the referendum for Crimea to break away from Ukraine (Croft & Apps, 2014; Russia Today, 2014b).

Graphs illustrating the magnitude of the various DDoS attacks are shown in Figure 9. Not all the attacks shown are related to the crisis, particularly in the case of Russia. However, the comparison of the Russian graph prior to 14 March and the graph continuing past that date shows the magnitude of the attacks leveled against the Russian websites. From Figure 9, it can be seen that the attacks against Ukraine appear in groups: leading up to the protest, prior to the incursion, leading up to the referendum, and then during the Eastern Ukraine attempts to break away. The graph illustrating Poland indicates large attacks starting on the 22 April; while this may not necessarily be related to the crisis it did coincide with the announcement of US troops being sent to Poland and the Baltic states.

Observers provide mixed commentary regarding the cyber-attacks during the crisis: Clayton (2014a) initially indicated that whilst attacks are occurring, it was expected that they would be more noticeable. It was proposed that the Ukrainian hackers may be able to retaliate more effectively than Russia's previous adversaries; Gady (2014) also considers the Russian cyber-attacks as being restrained and mentions the quality of the Ukrainian hackers, and indicates that the Ukraine Internet infrastructure may be resilient and attacks could have repercussions on the surrounding nations, including Russia.

Due to the commentary suggesting that the Russian cyber-attacks were restrained, it is worthwhile comparing the DDoS attacks surrounding the crisis with previous attacks in the region and others that occurred closer to the time. During the 2007 Estonian attacks, the largest of the series peaked at 90 Mbps and lasted for ten hours (Nazario, 2007). The largest attack during the 2008 Georgian conflict peaked at 814 Mbps, with the longest lasting 6 hours, and the attack traffic averaging at 211 Mbps (Kerner, 2008; Labovitz, 2010). The 2013 Lithuanian attacks were reported to have peaked at 6 Gbps (E.L., 2013).

Other sizeable DDoS attacks include those against Burma, which peaked at 14 Gbps (Labovitz, 2010), the Cyberbunker/Spamhaus attacks which were recorded at 300 Gbps (Bright, 2013), and Cloudflare reporting attack traffic of 400 Gbps in 2014 (Ashford, 2014).

By comparison, the attacks against Ukraine were similar in magnitude to those previously occurring in the region, where the day with the largest amount of attack traffic reached between 8 and 9 GB, as shown in Figure 9. However, this is relatively small in comparison to other attacks. The DDoS attack against Russia prior to the referendum was far more significant, where 60 GB traffic was recorded, as shown in Figure 9. From this it can be claimed that the attacks against Ukraine were not as strong as the

Figure 9. DDoS attacks over time. a) Ukraine b) Russia before 14 March c) Russia after 14 March d) Poland
Source: Arbor Networks and Google Ideas (2013) Google and the Google logo are registered trademarks of Google Inc., used with permission (http://www.digitalattackmap.com

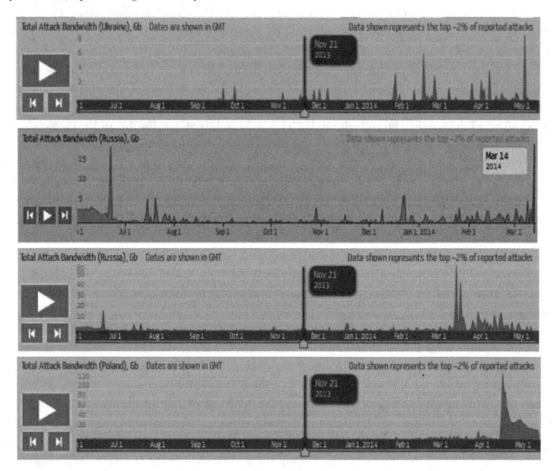

could have been; for the reasons mentioned above or also not to hinder data extraction from potential cyber-espionage campaigns, as Snake would indicate were being conducted. The 120 Gb traffic against Poland was significantly larger than anything seen in the region during the period of the crisis, and indicates the attacker has access to more resources to conduct the attack.

The webpage defacements from the pro-Russian cyber campaign can be seen to follow with the propaganda; the comparison of the opposition to Nazis was common, and was also used in Georgia. Reports of communications outages in Crimea prior to the incursion imply similar tactics to Georgia, where a DDoS attack severely disrupted Georgian communications; the outage in Crimea may have been a similar attempt which aided in the prevalence of the pro-Russian viewpoint online.

One of the initial sets of buildings seized by armed men in Crimea was a number of telecommunications centers, which were taken offline by destroying cables and thus disrupting both landline and Internet services (Finley, 2014; Russon, 2014). At a later stage it was thought these centers were also used in an attempt to monitor the mobile communications of Ukrainian politicians (Russon, 2014). Given the claims of DDoS attacks on the mobile phones, it is possible that they could have originated from these communication centers. The seizure and sabotage of the nodes illustrates physical attacks to disrupt cyber-activity, and like the DDoS attacks in Georgia, could have been an attempt to limited information leaving the region in support of military action.

Gandhi et al. (2011) indicate that the attacks against Estonia and Georgia are attacks triggered by socio-cultural conflict; the same can be said for the cyber-attacks related to the Ukraine crisis, however many can also be considered as politically motivated attacks protesting government actions. Whereas with the previous instances, there were usually two nations primarily involved. During the Ukraine crisis, multiple nations and international organizations (such as NATO) were targeted by cyber-attacks.

Whilst the hacktivist cyber-attacks were sporadic and un-coordinated, and followed major political events, the Russian cyber-strategy appeared to follow the 12 step network attack process. Prior to the conflict, access and intelligence was gained through the use of cyber-espionage campaigns. This probably provided intelligence and could have aided in later attacks, such as the capture and sabotage of key information infrastructure nodes in Crimea and the denial-of-service on the Ukrainian cell phones. The Ukrainian response appeared to have been limited. The hacktivist-originating DoS attacks overshadowed any of the planned attacks in terms of magnitude; particularly the Anonymous Caucasus attacks aimed at Russian government and media websites. However, the Russian campaign was probably the most effective. The strategy of combined physical and cyber-campaigns proved suitable as the Crimea was ultimately annexed with no major cyber-war or physical war.

Other Information Warfare-Related Activities

Other areas that are relevant to information warfare which do not fall into the main areas discussed above will be covered in this section. The areas can be classified as the impact of technology on military operations, electronic warfare, activism, perception, and intelligence.

Videos showing Russian-made military transport and attack helicopters flying over Crimea are posted on YouTube, some of these appear to be taken from mobile devices with cameras (Fındıklı, 2014; GlobalLeaks, 2014; Mighty Mole, 2014; TubeLeaks, 2014). Figure 10 shows a photo of the helicopters posted on the day of the Crimean incursion. On 24 April an unverified footage of what was claimed to be a Russian military helicopter in Eastern Ukraine was posted on YouTube (http://www.youtube.com/watch?v=8xreVTDxg7s). Mobile devices with an integrated cameras and social media connectivity could easily capture military movements and make them globally available minutes later. As indicated in van Niekerk and Maharaj (2012), cameras on mobile devices could be used to identify and monitor surprise attacks. The videos of the helicopters illustrate the legitimacy of this, however there still appeared to be confusion over the exact origin of the helicopters and troops for a few days after the incursion. In a similar manner, a journalist posted photos of Ukrainian forces defecting in Eastern Ukraine, which is shown in Figure 11. Reports that social media identified Russian troops as thus illustrated possible untruths in the official denials of military involvement further illustrates the impact that social media has on documenting surprise attacks and covert operations. Social media also played a role in attributing the downing of MH17 over Eastern Ukraine. Social media reports aided in identifying the location the missile was launched from, and one of the senior separatist figures allegedly bragged about downing a Ukrainian military aircraft on social media, but attempted to remove the post after realizing it was a civilian aircraft (Carroll, 2014; Rushe & Walker, 2014). A series of 'selfies' taken by a Russian soldier with location services enabled on his phone has allowed his movements to be mapped, which adds additional proof that Russian forces were involved in Eastern Ukraine, but they may have also been pres-

Figure 10. Photo of Russian helicoptes posted on Twitter
Source: *Adin of Crimea (2014) (https://twitter.com/RealCrimea)*

 Adin of Crimea @RealCrimea · 28 Feb 2014
photo Mi-24 #Russian helicopter gunships heading to #Sevastopol #Crimea.
Each can carry 8 soldiers

View photo

Figure 11. Photo of defecting Ukrainian units
Source: *Salloum (2014) (https://twitter.com/Ranyah)*

 Raniah Salloum @Ranyah · 16 Apr 2014
One of the six tanks of the Ukranian army that I just saw in #Kramatorsk that
switched sides. Now w Russian flag.

571   85

View photo

ent when the flight was shot down (Li, 2014). These incidents indicate the potential for online sources, and in particular social media, to provide a wealth of open-source intelligence which could impact on conventional military strategy. Deception and surprise attacks may become more difficult without control of the online space. From a defensive point of view, an effective cyber-based intelligence strategy could aid in predicting mass civil disobedience, surprise attacks, and other upcoming physical attacks.

On the 14 March 2014 Russia Today reported that attempts were made to jam Russian television satellites from Western Ukraine, and that Ukraine had blocked Russian television channels (Rehle, 2014). No corroborating reports could be found for this incident, however if it is true it could be an example of using electronic warfare to counter Russian propaganda.

Russian president Vladimir Putin is reported to have an aversion to using a number of communications technologies, and does not own a mobile phone (Shuster, 2014). Rantapelkonen and Jaitner (2013) indicate that whilst Vladimir Putin recognizes the importance of social media, he is not a user. This has resulted in difficulty in intelligence agencies predicting aspects of Russian operations, as there is no technological communications for them to intercept (Shuster, 2014). Calabresi (2014) discusses the possibility of a Russian espionage campaign against the countries surrounding Russia, which include activities such as compromising energy companies and security services, conducting cyber-attacks and stirring nationalist sentiment amongst ethnic Russian minorities in the regions. These activities described by Calabresi appear consistent with the occurrences in Ukraine, and he states that whilst the activity in Ukraine may appear spontaneous or disorganized, it is associated with an underlying plan. These reports illustrate the importance of intelligence in conflict, and how denial of information or deception and possible subversion can give a nation or group a large advantage over their adversaries.

Videos posted to YouTube by the hacker collective Anonymous admitted to them being divided over the Ukraine crisis (OfficialAnonymousTV1, 2014), however their initial activity appeared to support the pro-Russians, or at least took an anti-NATO line, as they targeted the NATO websites and the pro-EU politicians as part of #OpIndependence (Anon, 2014; CERT-EE, 2013). However, prior to the referendum Anonymous Caucasus targeted Russia with a large DDoS attack, protesting against Russian involvement in other countries (Gallagher, 2014). This does indicate a split in the global collective, however the regional incarnations of Anonymous may be internally united. Another form of protest emerged from Ukraine in the form of Femen, where the female protesters use nudity to gain attention; their protests were against the pro-Russian government of Victor Yanukovych (Shevchenko, 2014).

In March 2014 Natalia Poklonskaya was appointed as the new Attorney General for Crimea. After video clips of an interview with her were circulated on social media, a number of Anime representations of her began to appear and went viral (Palmer, 2014). Whilst unexpected, this may prove to aid the Russian propaganda efforts. During the second Gulf War Japanese forces providing support painted Japanese cartoon characters which were popular in the Middle East on their trucks, and attributed this to the trucks not being attacked (Yin & Taylor, 2008). In a similar manner, the Anime indicates an infatuation with Ms. Poklonskaya, and the representations may further add to a softening towards the Russian presence in the Crimea.

Figure 12 illustrates the interest in the keywords 'Ukraine', 'Russia', and 'Crimea' from October 2013 to May 2014, as depicted by a screenshot of Google Trends for Search. As would be expected, the search terms spiked after the incursions into Crimea, however the largest spike was related to Ukraine, as the majority the political crisis revolved around Ukraine rather than purely Russia or the Crimean region. The rapid online increase in interest is significant in that it indicates online propaganda and perception

Figure 12. Screenshot of Google Trends for Ukraine, Crimea, and Russia as Search Terms
Google and the Google logo are registered trademarks of Google Inc., used with permission (http://www.google.com/trends)

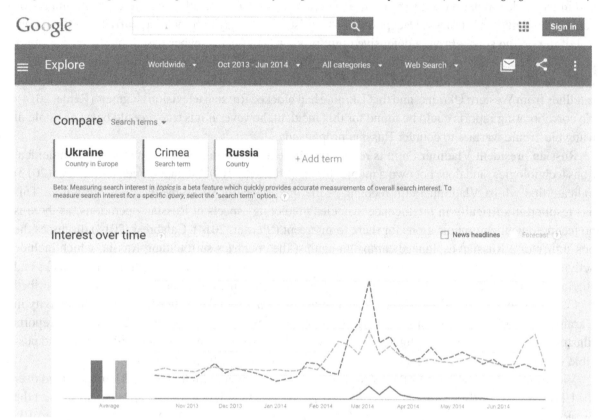

management could reach a large audience, who are actively seeking information, and therefore will have a larger impact.

The events in this section indicate the impact of technology on conventional military and political strategies, and highlight the strength of open-source intelligence from online sources such as social media. Online exposure of physical activism is also noticeable, and cyber-based activity could provide unplanned and unexpected support for reasons not directly related to the conflict; similarly unexpected reasons may introduce antagonism towards one's goals.

SUMMARY DISCUSSION OF IW IN THE UKRAINE CONFLICT

Given the range of cyber-based activities employed by the various actors in the crisis, it is clear that cyber-strategies were involved. Many of the online activities were planned, coordinated, took advantage of online opportunities, and sought to achieve a specific goal. The two main strategies were those of the protestors seeking social and political reform, and the Russian strategy maintain and enhance its influence in the region.

The crisis in Ukraine has provided a platform to study the impacts of cyber-space on conflict. Previous social-media based protests had no recent equivalents with which to compare, however the EuroMaidan protests can be contrasted with the Orange Revolution, and the impact of social media can be seen: ranging from information provision to an entire support structure for the protests.

There have been some differences to previous incidents of this type. Some cyber-attacks began before the protests started, there was a greater variety of attackers and targets, and there appeared to be a split in the Anonymous collective, with one faction targeting NATO and the EU, and another targeting Russia. This indicates that the cyber environment in future regional conflicts are becoming more complex, and will have a far broader scope than the region of the physical conflict.

The information warfare campaign by the pro-Russian elements, whether intentional or not (Calabresi (2014) suggests it was intentional), illustrate a good mix of activities enabling cyber-based propaganda in addition to espionage and cyber-attacks. The potential for an 'ideal' information warfare campaign can be illustrated through the activities that occurred in Ukraine. An initial cyber-espionage campaign to gather relevant information and provide the backdoor access for more damaging cyber-attacks during conflict; this can be considered as 'intelligence preparation of the cyber-battlefield.' Propaganda, both online and through traditional media, can be used to increase support amongst one's own population for possible military action and reduce local resistance on the ground by increasing any ethnic, religious or other social divisions in the area of interest. Opposing narratives can be refuted; all three aspects provide a psychological dominance of the region. When the semi-instigated crisis reaches the point where military intervention is possible, cyber-attacks can be used to disrupt opposition information capabilities and in some cases distract defenders in order to support physical military interventions. Any physical intervention will be accompanied by additional propaganda legitimize the military action. By comparison, an apparent lack of counter-propaganda by Ukrainian authorities did not provide sufficient alternative narrative originating from the region to mitigate fears and animosity generated by Russian narrative. The overarching Russian cyber-strategy, based on Georgia and Ukraine, is to hinder communications and increase the 'fog of war' regarding Russian interventions (Mullish, 2014).

A successful political and physical solution to the crisis may not end the cyber-based conflict, where political statements can continue to be made. A series of DDoS attacks targeted social media in August 2009, with reports that they were aimed at silencing bloggers making political statements related to the Georgian conflict or other cyber-attacks on South Korea (Adhikari, 2009; Menn & Gelles, 2009). As cyber-attacks appeared to have occurred around the anniversary of the Estonia DDoS event, it it possible that there is a trend of recognising the anniversaries of such events with cyber-attacks. Therefore social media and national websites could become targets in the future to mark the anniversary of the Ukrainian crisis.

The crisis already has had a strategic impact in a cyber context: NATO was tasked by the Defense Ministers of member states to improve the cyber-defense policy, which was endorsed in July 2014. A cyber-attack against any NATO member is now considered sufficient for a collective NATO response (Mullish, 2014). Similarly, considerations regarding cyber-attacks were formalized into NATO's first cyber-defense policy as a direct result of the 2007 Estonian DDoS attacks (NATO, 2014).

LESSONS LEARNED FROM THE ROLE OF CYBER-STRATEGY IN THE CONFLICT

From the case of the conflict in Ukraine, it is evident that a cyber-strategy is not limited to cyber-attacks or cyber-warfare scenarios, but also includes the use of cyber-based propaganda and impromptu command

and control platforms. Online platforms have exhibited potential for open-source intelligence gathering in this crisis. In addition, a cyber-strategy is not necessarily associated with a nation, and can be used to great effect by non-state actors.

The protestors had an effective cyber-strategy, even if it was informal, which provided them with a 'force-multiplier' effect, and enhanced the successes enjoyed by the demonstrations. Whilst similar events, in particular Arab Spring, previously indicated that the cyber aspect was a contributor, the Ukrainian case provided further confirmation when compared to the Orange Revolution.

After the change of government, the Russian online activities also indicated that they had a clear and effective cyber-strategy which allowed them information dominance and provided sufficient support when physical action was taken. However, the new Ukraine government did not exhibit and effective cyber-strategy, which further afforded the pro-Russian groups information dominance over the relevant regions, and the Ukrainian government ultimately lost the information-based conflict. This ultimately led to the loss of the Crimean region and a civil-war in Eastern Ukraine. Had the Ukrainian government exhibited an effective cyber-strategy to counter the pro-Russian information activities, they may have successfully prevented, or at least hindered, the Russian physical activities.

Based on the outcomes from the protests and the conflict, cyber-strategy could be said to have profound impact on conflict, particularly when well executed and unopposed. Therefore there is a need to develop and test such strategies in order to be prepared in the event of a conflict with a strong cyber component. Wargaming the strategies to refine them and ensure the multi-faceted components (cyber-espionage, cyber-attack, and cyber-based propaganda) support each other and are coordinated to achieve a single goal will be required.

The responsibilities for implementing the facets of a national and coherent cyber-strategy could be distributed over a number of departments and organizations. As in the case of Ukraine, critical infrastructure was targeted. Critical infrastructure providers, such as telecommunication and information infrastructure service providers, physical transportation infrastructure operators, and utility operators, therefore need to ensure a cyber-security strategy to defend against attacks and can contribute to a cyber-based threat intelligence strategy. The military and intelligence services will contribute to cyber-defense, cyber-espionage, cyber-based intelligence, and cyber-attack strategies. The cyber-based strategic communications need to be led by government communications with support from the media, however all departments and organizations need to play their part to ensure a coherent and coordinated message to promote the 'official line.'

Effective cyber-based intelligence and strategic communications strategies could prove to be instrumental in a cyber-deterrence strategy. Coordinated with a cyber-defense strategy these will be able to mitigate or prevent impact due to cyber-attacks. The case of Ukraine has illustrated the importance of cyber-strategies in a conflict; similar strategies could be employed to prevent conflict, whether physical or online.

As cyber-attacks have proven to disrupt communications, create uncertainty and confusion resulting in hindered decision making, a resilient communications system that can survive the impact of the attacks is required to ensure the relevant leadership and decision makers can effectively lead the targeted nation.

CONCLUSION

The Ukraine crisis began in late 2013 when large-scale protests erupted against the government; this chapter considers the events up until mid-May 2014, which include a change of government, a Russian incursion and cessation of Crimea, and the destabilization and attempted break-away of Eastern Ukraine. The protests provide a clear indication of the role of social media in such events when compared to the Orange Revolution; the support provided to these mass demonstrations by social media is significant, and ranges from providing information about the demonstrations themselves to organizing legal and medical aid to the protestors. The subsequent involvement of Russia illustrated a comprehensive and coordinated use of various information warfare activities, including propaganda aimed at various target populations, cyber-espionage, and cyber-attacks, all of which supported a military incursion. Whilst the Ukrainian protestors used social media to great effect, there was a noticeable lack of counter-propaganda to counter Russian narrative during the crisis. The ramifications of this crisis on the information sphere may be felt long after the immediate physical and information activities have ended. Cyber-attacks may mark the anniversary of various events during the crisis as those who oppose the various political standpoints seek to continue their protest.

From the example of Ukraine, it is evident that a cyber-strategy is not limited to computer network attack and defense, but can include the use of the Internet to support strategic communications, propaganda, and psychological operations. When implemented, these strategies had a noticeable, if not significant, impact on the outcome of the conflict stage. This strategy of cyber-based propaganda is effective in that it provides a continual shift of the overall context to influence behavior and support the end objectives. A coordinated online propaganda, cyber-attack, and cyber-based intelligence strategy will provide any nation or group a significant advantage with information superiority, as the adversary decision-making will be hindered but also be transparent. Therefore a sound cyber-strategy is crucial in future conflicts; both the benefits of a successful cyber-strategy and the repercussions of an ineffective cyber-strategy were highlighted in the Ukraine crisis.

REFERENCES

Adhikari, R. (2009, August 13). Another day, another DDoS blitz for Twitter, *E-Commerce Times*. Retrieved from http://www.ecommercetimes.com/story/67851.html# Adin of Crimea.

al Jazeera. (2014, May 15). *Timeline: Ukraine's political crisis*. Retrieved from http://www.aljazeera.com/news/europe/2014/03/timeline-ukraine-political-crisis-201431143722854652.html

Anon. (2014, February 13). Vitali Klitschko's UDAR party hacked Confidential data leaked. *CyberWarNews*. Retrieved from http://www.cyberwarnews.info/2014/02/13/opindependence-vitali-klitschkos-udar-party-hacked-confidential-data-leaked/

Arbor Networks and Google Ideas. (2013). *Digital Attack Map*. Retrieved from http://www.digitalattackmap.com

Ashford, W. (2014, February 12). NTP-based DDoS attacks a concern, says Cloudflare. *Computer Weekly*. Retrieved from http://www.computerweekly.com/news/2240214216/NTP-based-DDoS-attacks-a-concern-says-Cloudflare

Bennetts, M. (2014, April 15). Inside Russia's gaffe-prone propaganda war. *Vocativ*. Retrieved from http://www.vocativ.com/world/russia/inside-russias-gaffe-prone-propaganda-war/

Bohdanova, T. (2014, December 9). How Internet Tools Turned Ukraine's #Euromaidan Protests Into a Movement. *Global Voices Online*. Retrieved from http://globalvoicesonline.org/2013/12/09/how-internet-tools-turned-euromaidan-protests-into-a-movement/

Brazzoli, M. S. (2007). Future Prospects of Information Warfare and Particularly Psychological Operations. In L. le Roux (Ed.), *South African Army Vision 2020* (pp. 217–232). Pretoria: Institute for Security Studies.

Bright, P. (2013, March 27). Spamhaus DDoS grows to Internet-threatening size. *ARSTechnica*. Retrieved from http://arstechnica.com/security/2013/03/spamhaus-ddos-grows-to-internet-threatening-size/

British Broadcasting Corporation (BBC). (2014a, May 8). *Ukraine crisis timeline*. Retrieved from http://www.bbc.com/news/world-middle-east-26248275

British Broadcasting Corporation (BBC). (2014b, April 22). *Ukraine crisis: What the 'Russian soldier' photos say*. Retrieved from http://www.bbc.com/news/world-europe-27104904

Carroll, L. (2014, July 20). Kerry: Ukrainian separatist 'bragged' on social media about shooting down Malaysia Flight 17. *Politifact*. Retrieved from http://www.politifact.com/truth-o-meter/statements/2014/jul/20/john-kerry/kerry-ukrainian-separatist-bragged-social-media/

CERT-EE. (2013, November 1-7). CERT-EE report: DDoS attacks, e-mail messages with forged sender address and defacements. *Estonian Information System's Authority*. Retrieved from https://www.ria.ee/cert-ee-report-opindependence-november-1-7/

chornajuravka. (2014, March 29). Kremlin's Gremlins: pro-Russian trolls have Kremlin IP addresses. *EuroMaidanPR*. Retrieved from https://euromaidanpr.wordpress.com/2014/03/29/kremlins-gremlins-pro-russian-trolls-have-kremlin-ip-addresses/#more-5957

Clayton, M. (2014a, March 3). Where are the cyberattacks? Russia's curious forbearance in Ukraine. *Christian Science Monitor*. Retrieved from http://www.csmonitor.com/World/Security-Watch/2014/0303/Where-are-the-cyberattacks-Russia-s-curious-forbearance-in-Ukraine.-video

Clayton, M. (2014b, March 14). Major cyber-assaults on Ukraine, then Moscow, on eve of Crimea vote. *Christian Science Monitor*. Retrieved from http://www.csmonitor.com/World/Security-Watch/Cyber-Conflict-Monitor/2014/0314/Major-cyber-assaults-on-Ukraine-then-Moscow-on-eve-of-Crimea-vote-video

Clayton, M. (2014c, March 18). Massive cyberattacks slam official sites in Russia, Ukraine. *Christian Science Monitor*. Retrieved from http://www.csmonitor.com/World/Security-Watch/Cyber-Conflict-Monitor/2014/0318/Massive-cyberattacks-slam-official-sites-in-Russia-Ukraine

Coleman, K. (2008, August 13). Cyberwar 2.0 - Russia vs Georgia. *DefenseTech*. Retrieved from http://defensetech.org/2008/08/13/cyber-war-2-0-russia-v-georgia/

Croft, A., & Apps, P. (2014, March 16). NATO websites hit in cyber attack linked to Crimea tension, *Reuters*. Retrieved from http://www.reuters.com/article/2014/03/16/us-ukraine-nato-idUSBREA2E0T320140316

President Putin's fiction: 10 false claims about Ukraine. (2014, March 5). Department of State. Retrieved from http://www.state.gov/r/pa/prs/ps/2014/03/222988.htm

Dougherty, S. (2014, February 28). On social media, Ukraine gives Yanukovych the finger, *Global Post*. Retrieved from http://www.globalpost.com/dispatch/news/regions/europe/140228/ukraine-social-media-yanukovych-middle-finger

E.L. (2013, June 1). Lithuania under cyber-attack - Greetings to the President [Weblog comment] Retrieved from http://www.economist.com/blogs/easternapproaches/2013/06/lithuania-under-cyber-attack

Eristavi (2014, March 2) Twitter post [Weblog comment]. Retrieved from https://twitter.com/MaximEristavi

Fındıklı, S. (2014). Russian military attack helicopters over the Crimea Ukraine [Video file]. Retrieved from http://www.youtube.com/watch?v=qlW317itFEk

Finley, J. C. (2014, February 28). Telecom services sabotaged in Ukraine's Crimea region, *UPI*. Retrieved from http://www.upi.com/Top_News/World-News/2014/02/28/Telecom-services-sabotaged-in-Ukraines-Crimea-region/7611393621345/

Fishel, J. and Associated Press (2014, April 14) Russian jet passes at close range over US warship in Black Sea, *Fox News*. Retrieved from http://www.foxnews.com/politics/2014/04/14/russian-jet-passes-at-close-range-over-us-warship-in-black-sea/

Gady, F. (2014, March 7). Cyberwar in the Crimea? [Weblog comment]. Retrieved from http://www.usnews.com/opinion/blogs/world-report/2014/03/07/russias-cyberwar-restraint-in-ukraine

Gallagher, S. (2014, March 14). Kremlin gets DDoS'd by Anonymous Caucasus. *ARSTechnica*. Retrieved from http://arstechnica.com/tech-policy/2014/03/kremlin-gets-ddosd-by-anonymous-caucasus/

Gandhi, R., Sharma, A., Mahoney, W., Sousan, W., Zhu, Q., & Laplante, P. (2011). Dimensions of cyber-attacks: Social, political, economic, and cultural. *IEEE Technology and Society Magazine*, (Spring): 28–38.

Russia invading Ukraine [Video file]. (2014). GlobalLeaks. Retrieved from http://www.youtube.com/watch?v=lWvQHpQ12Ws

Gregory, P. R. (2014a, April 12). Russian TV Propagandists Caught Red-Handed: Same Guy, Three Different People (Spy, Bystander, Heroic Surgeon), *Reuters*. Retrieved from http://www.forbes.com/sites/paulroderickgregory/2014/04/12/russian-tv-caught-red-handed-same-guy-same-demonstration-but-three-different-people-spy-bystander-heroic-surgeon/

Gregory, P. R. (2014b, April 14). You Tube shatters Russian lies about troops in Ukraine: Putin denies truth to Obama, *Forbes*. Retrieved from http://www.forbes.com/sites/paulroderickgregory/2014/04/14/you-tube-shatters-russian-lies-about-troops-in-ukraine/

Harding, J. (2014, March 2). Russian manipulation of the press regarding Ukraine [Weblog comment]. Retrieved from http://toinformistoinfluence.com/2014/03/02/russian-manipulation-of-the-press-regarding-ukraine/

Hart, K. (2008, August 14). Longtime battle lines are recast in Russia and Georgia's cyberwar, *The Washington Post*, p. D01.

Jones, A., Kovacich, G. L., & Luzwick, P. G. (2002). *Global Information Warfare*. Boca Raton, FL: Auerbach.

Kates, G., & Butorin, P. (2014, April 16). Russian professor explains media manipulation. *Radio Free Europe Radio Liberty*. Retrieved from http://www.rferl.org/content/unspun-russian-professor-media-manipulation/25351952.html

Kelly, L., & Korsunskaya, D. (2014, March 21). Russia's finance ministry admits sanctions bite. *Yahoo South Africa*. Retrieved from http://za.news.yahoo.com/russias-finance-ministry-admits-sanctions-bite-183735932--business.html

Kendall, B. (2014, Aptil 17) Analysis: Vladimir Putin's veiled threats over Ukraine. *BBC*. Retrieved from http://www.bbc.com/news/world-europe-27063136

Kerner, S. M. (2008, August 15). The Russia Georgia cyberwar [Weblog comment]. Retrieved from http://blog.internetnews.com/skerner/2008/08/the-russia-georgia-cyberwar.html

Kovacs, E. (2013, November 7). Anonymous Ukraine Launches DDOS Attack on NATO's CCDCOE Website. *Softpedia*. Retrieved from http://news.softpedia.com/news/Anonymous-Ukraine-Launches-DDOS-Attack-on-NATO-s-CCDCOE-Website-398063.shtml

Kovacs, E. (2014, March 4). Website of International Video News Agency Ruptly Hit With DDOS Attack. *Softpedia*. Retrieved from http://news.softpedia.com/news/Website-of-International-Video-News-Agency-Ruptly-Hit-With-DDOS-Attack-430390.shtml

Krebs, B. (2008, July 3). Lithuania Weathers Cyber Attack, Braces for Round 2. *The Washington Post*. Retrieved from http://voices.washingtonpost.com/securityfix/2008/07/lithuania_weathers_cyber_attac_1.html

Labovitz, C. (2010). Attack Severs Burma Internet. *Arbour Networks*. Retrieved from http://asert.arbor-networks.com/2010/11/attac-severs-myanmar-internet/

LaGrone, S. (2014, April 14). Russian Fighter Buzzes U.S. Destroyer in Black Sea. *USNI News*. Retrieved from http://news.usni.org/2014/04/14/russian-fighter-buzzes-u-s-destroyer-black-sea

Landler, M., & Markoff, J. (2007, May 29). Digital fears emerge after data siege in Estonia. *The New York Times Online*. Retrieved from http://www.nytimes.com/2007/05/29/technology/29estonia.html?_r=1

Li, D. K. (2014, July 31). Soldier's selfies might prove Russia's direct role in Ukraine. *The New York Post*. Retrieved from http://nypost.com/2014/07/31/soldiers-selfies-might-prove-russias-role-in-ukraine/

Lokot, T. (2014, March 2). Ukrainian journalists take regime's corruption public with YanukovychLeaks. *Global Voices Online*. Retrieved from http://globalvoicesonline.org/2014/03/02/ukrainian-journalists-take-regimes-corruption-public-with-yanukovychleaks/

Lowensohn, J. (2014, July 18). Russia Spotted editing Wikipedia page about downed Malaysia Airlines jet. *The Verge*. Retrieved from http://www.theverge.com/2014/7/18/5917099/russia-spotted-editing-wikipedia-page-of-downed-malaysia-air-jet

Menn, J., & Gelles, D. (2009, August 6). Concerted cyber-attack takes down Twitter. *Financial Times*. Retrieved from www.ft.com/cms/s/.../038b9b54-82a6-11de-ab4a-00144feabdc0.html

Mighty Mole. (2014). Russian helicopters swarm over Ukraine [Video file]. Retrieved from http://www.youtube.com/watch?v=-7OOKecS-WU

Mimoso, M. (2013, February 27). MiniDuke espionage malware hits governments in Europe using Adobe exploits [Weblog comment]. Retrieved from http://threatpost.com/en_us/blogs/miniduke-espionage-malware-hits-governments-europe-using-adobe-exploits-022713

Mullish, J. (2014). NATO and Ukraine Must Ready for Cyber Threats. *Defence IQ*. Retrieved from http://www.cdans.org/media/9255/32455.pdf

Myriam-Webster Dictionary. (2014). *Strategy*. Retrieved from http://www.merriam-webster.com/dictionary/strategy

Cyber Defence. (2014, September 30). NATO. Retrieved from http://www.nato.int/cps/en/natohq/topics_78170.htm

USS Donald Cook – Ship Characteristics. (2014). *U. S. Navy*. Retrieved from http://www.cook.navy.mil/

Nazario, J. (2007, May 17). Estonian DDoS Attacks – A Summary to Date. *Arbor Networks*. Retrieved from http://ddos.arbornetworks.com/2007/05/estonian-ddos-attacks-a-summary-to-date/

Nemchenko, A. (2014, March 11). Top 7 false statements by Russian media about Ukraine. Retrieved from http://visual.ly/top-7-false-statements-russian-media-about-ukraine

OfficialAnonymousTV1. (2014). Anonymous - message from Ukraine 2014 [Video file]. Retrieved from http://www.youtube.com/watch?v=1AWEI9rFYXs

Onuch, O. (2014, January 2). Social networks and social media in Ukrainian "Euromaidan" protests [Weblog comment]. Retrieved from http://www.washingtonpost.com/blogs/monkey-cage/wp/2014/01/02/social-networks-and-social-media-in-ukrainian-euromaidan-protests-2/

Palmer, E. (2014, March 21). Natalia Poklonskaya: Crimean Attorney General becomes surprise Japanese Anime viral hit. *International Business Times*. Retrieved from http://www.ibtimes.co.uk/natalia-poklonskaya-crimean-attorney-general-becomes-surprise-japanese-anime-viral-hit-1441281

Polityuk, P. (2014, March 8). Ukrainian authorities suffer new cyber attacks. *Reuters*. Retrieved from http://www.reuters.com/article/2014/03/08/us-ukraine-cricis-cyberattack-idUSBREA270FU20140308

Pultarova, T. (2014, March 10). Ukraine under cyber attack. *Engineering and Technology Magazine*. Retrieved from http://eandt.theiet.org/news/2014/mar/ukraine-cyber.cfm

Rantapelkonen, J., & Jaitner, M. (2013). Russian state leaders' contradicting narratives on social media. In R. Kuusisto & E. Kurkinen (Eds.), *12th European Conference on Information Warfare and Security*, (pp. 224-230). Reading, UK: Academic Conferences.

Rehle, M. (2014, March 15). Attempt to jam Russian satellites carried out from Western Ukraine. *Russia Today*. Retrieved from http://rt.com/news/ukraine-attacks-television-satellites-990/

Reuters. (2014a, March 15). Kremlin website hit by 'powerful' cyber-attack. *NDTV*. Retrieved from http://gadgets.ndtv.com/internet/news/kremlin-website-hit-by-powerful-cyber-attack-496150

Reuters. (2014b, March 27). No vodka for Obama - Russians impose joke 'sanctions'. *Yahoo South Africa*. Retrieved from https://za.news.yahoo.com/no-vodka-obama-russians-impose-joke-sanctions-090309509. html

Rogozin, D. (2014, March 17) Twitter post [Weblog comment]. Retrieved from https://twitter.com/Rogozin

Rolski, T. (2007, May 17). Estonia: ground zero for World's first cyber war. *ABC News*. Retrieved from http://abcnews.go.com/print?id=3184122

Rushe, D., & Walker, S. (2014, July 20). MH17 crash: Kerry lays out evidence of pro-Russia separatists' responsibility. *The Guardian*. Retrieved from http://www.theguardian.com/world/2014/jul/20/mh17-crash-kerry-evidence-pro-russia-separatists-responsibility

Russia Radio. (2014, April 21). *Russian Su -24 scores off against the American "USS Donald Cook" in Black Sea*. Retrieved from http://indian.ruvr.ru/2014_04_21/Russian-Su-24-scores-off-against-the-American-USS-Donald-Cook-5786/

Russia Today. (2014a, March 3). *Russian Defense Ministry dismisses Ukraine ultimatum reports as 'total nonsense'*. Retrieved from http://rt.com/news/russia-dismiss-ultimatum-ukraine-644/

Russia Today. (2014b, March 16). *Ukrainian CyberBerkut takes down NATO websites*. Retrieved from http://rt.com/news/nato-websites-ddos-ukraine-146/

Russia Today. (2014c, March 16). *Crimean govt: Referendum website downed by cyber-attack from US*. Retrieved from http://rt.com/news/crimea-referendum-attack-website-194/

Russia Today. (2014d, March 14). *Russian media websites hit by 'massive' DDoS attack 'linked to Ukraine'*. Retrieved from http://rt.com/news/russian-media-ddos-ukraine-614/

Russia Today. (2014e, April 7). *Donetsk activists proclaim region's independence from Ukraine*. Retrieved from http://rt.com/news/donetsk-republic-protestukraine-841/

Russia wants a divided Ukraine, and despite the promise of the revolution it may well get one. (2014, March 22). *The Economist*. Retrieved from http://www.economist.com/news/briefing/21599413-russia-wants-divided-ukraine-and-despite-promise-revolution-it-may-well-get

Russon, M. (2014, March 4). Ukraine crisis: cyber war with Russia heating up, *International Business Times*. Retrieved from http://www.ibtimes.co.uk/ukraine-crisis-cyber-war-russia-heating-1438890

Salloum, R. (2014, April 16) Twitter post [Weblog]. Retrieved from https://twitter.com/Ranyah

Satell, G. (2014, January 18). If you doubt that social media has changed the World, take a look at Ukraine. *Forbes*. Retrieved from http://www.forbes.com/sites/gregsatell/2014/01/18/if-you-doubt-that-social-media-has-changed-the-world-take-a-look-at-ukraine/

SecureList. (2013). "Red October" diplomatic cyber attacks investigation. *Kaspersky Lab*. Retrieved from http://www.securelist.com/en/analysis/204792262/Red_October_Diplomatic_Cyber_Attacks_Investigation

Shevchenko, I. (2014). Femen on protests in Kiev: 'Now, it's fight or die.' *Dazed Digital*. Retrieved from http://www.dazeddigital.com/artsandculture/article/18966/1/femen-on-kiev-protests-now-its-fight-or-die

Shuster, S. (2014, March 24). Putin's fear of texting kept U.S. spymasters in the dark. *Time Magazine Online*. Retrieved from http://time.com/35932/ukraine-russia-putin-spies-kgb/

Social Mention. (2014) *Search results*. Retrieved from http://socialmention.com/

Standifer, C. (2014, April 17). Ukraine's last ship, *US Naval Institute*. Retrieved from http://news.usni.org/2014/04/11/ukraines-last-ship

Stonesoft Security. (2014). *Cyberstrategy*. Retrieved from http://www.stonesoft-security.co.uk/solutions/cyber-strategy/

Snake campaign & cyber espionage toolkit. (2014). *B. A. E. Systems*. Retrieved from http://www.bae-systems.com/marketoform/snake_whitepaper.pdf

Temnycky, P. (2014, February 9). Unrest in Ukraine: Summarizing the Euromaidan. *Fordham Political Review*. Retrieved from http://fordhampoliticalreview.org/unrest-in-ukraine-summarizing-the-euromaidan/

Ukraine: pro-Russia activists proclaim independent republic in Donetsk. (2014, April 7). The Guardian. Retrieved from http://www.theguardian.com/world/2014/apr/07/ukraine-officer-shot-dead-russian-soldier-crimea

Thomson Reuters. (2014, March 30). *Ukraine crisis: Russia downplays sanctions ahead of Paris talks*. Retrieved from http://www.cbc.ca/news/world/ukraine-crisis-russia-downplays-sanctions-ahead-of-paris-talks-1.2591839

Tsvetkova, M., & Bush, J. (2014, March 15). Ukraine crisis triggers Russia's biggest anti-Putin protest in two years. *Reuters*. Retrieved from http://www.reuters.com/article/2014/03/15/ukraine-crisis-russia-rallies-idUSL6N0MC0JC20140315

TubeLeaks. (2014). Crimea Crisis - Russian Mi-35 combat helicopters flying over Sevastopol Ukraine [Video file]. Retrieved from http://www.youtube.com/watch?v=PfuCt0ZjzE0

Tucker, J. A., Metzger, M., & Barbera, P. (2014, February 28). *SMaPP Lab Data Report: Ukraine Protests 2013-2014*. Social Media and Political Participation Lab, New York University. Retrieved from http://smapp.nyu.edu/reports/Ukraine_Data_Report.pdf

Twitter Case Study. (WMD). (2009). *World Movement for Democracy* Retrieved from http://www.wmd.org/resources/whats-being-done/information-and-communication-technologies/case-study-twitter

U.S. watching Russia for cyber attack tactics against Ukraine. (2014, March 1). *Flash Critic*. Retrieved from http://flashcritic.com/u-s-watching-russia-cyber-attack-tactics-ukraine/

Vamosi, R. (2014, March 4). DDoS Attacks Silence Ukraine Cell Phones [Weblog comment]. Retrieved from https://mocana.com/blog/2014/03/04/ddos-attacks-hit-ukraine-cell-phones/

van Niekerk, B., & Maharaj, M. (2011). The IW Life Cycle Model, *South African Journal of Information Management,* 13. Available from http://www.sajim.co.za/index.php/SAJIM/article/view/476

van Niekerk, B., & Maharaj, M. (2012). Mobile devices and the military: useful tool or significant threat? In *Proceedings of the 4th Workshop on ICT Uses in Warfare and the Safeguarding of Peace* (IWSP 2012), Pretoria: CSIR and UKZN.

van Niekerk, B., & Maharaj, M. (2013). Social Media and Information Conflict. *International Journal of Communication*, 7, 1162–1184.

van Niekerk, B., Pillay, K., & Maharaj, M. (2011). Analysing the Role of ICTs in the Tunisian and Egyptian Unrest from an Information Warfare Perspective. *International Journal of Communication*, 5, 1406–1416.

van Vuuren, J. J., Phahlamohlaka, J., & Brazzoli, M. S. (2010). The impact of increase in braodband access on South African national security and the average citizen. *Journal of Information Warfare*, 9(3), 9–13.

Walker, S. (2014, March 4). Russian propaganda and Ukrainian rumour fuel anger and hate in Crimea. *The Guardian*. Retrieved from http://www.theguardian.com/world/2014/mar/04/russian-propaganda-ukrainian-rumours-anger-hate-crimea

Web site of Russia Today hacked and defaced over Ukraine conflict. (2014, March 3). *Bitdefender*. Retrieved from http://www.bitdefender.com/security/web-site-of-russia-today-hacked-and-defaced-over-ukraine-conflict.html

Yin, J., & Taylor, P. M. (2008). Information operations from an Asian perspective: A comparative analysis. *Journal of Information Warfare*, 7(1), 1–23.

KEY TERMS AND DEFINITIONS

Cyber-Attack: Attacks conducted in cyber-space primarily aimed at disrupting information services, steal information, or making political statements.

Cyber-Strategy: Co-ordinated operations and activities in cyber-space in order to achieve a strategic objective.

Electronic Warfare: Activities in the electromagnetic spectrum in order to achieve superiority in the spectrum.

Information Operations: Operations conducted in the physical, virtual and cognitive domains to gain information superiority over an adversary.

Information Warfare: Activities in the physical, virtual and cognitive domains during times of conflict to achieve an advantage over an adversary.

Network Warfare: Computer network-based attacks designed to disrupt network services or gain access to information, and defensive measures to mitigate such attacks.

Propaganda: Messages or mass communication, which are not necessarily true, specifically intended to support a political agenda.

Psychological Operations: Messages or activities designed to influence perceptions and ultimately behavior of a target audience.

Strategic Communication: Co-ordinated communications and activities to deliver a coherent message and further a strategic objective.

Section 4
Concluding Remarks and Reflections on the Essence of Cyberwarfare

Chapter 13
The Islamist Cyberpropaganda Threat and Its Counter-Terrorism Policy Implications

Nigel Jones
King's College, UK

Ian Tunnicliffe
Accordance Associates, UK

Paul Baines
Cranfield University, UK

Nicholas O'Shaughnessy
Queen Mary University of London, UK

Russell Craig
Cranfield University, UK

ABSTRACT

This chapter examines Islamist cyberpropaganda case studies live in 2014, namely Al Qaeda, Islamic State, Boko Haram and Al Shabaab. The authors define cyberpropganda as the exploitation of the generative characteristics of online interaction for the production and reproduction of propaganda. The cross-case analysis identifies key messages and themes, how cyberpropaganda is generated and spread, and how it is made attractive to those who may act on it. In the discussion that follows implications for the policy-maker are identified and addressed. These include whether to tackle symptoms or causes of the problems and whether to treat the problems as essentially global or local. The final issue is how the counter-propagandist can make themselves heard.

INTRODUCTION

A layered model of cyberspace is usually represented in defence publications as including the physical space, the physical network of connected equipment, the data and information flowing on the logical network, the electronic personas of people, and the people acting in social groups in the 'real' world and online (United States Army, 2010). This chapter examines an issue that spans all the 'layers' of cyberspace, straddling the organisational boundaries that law enforcement, defence and intelligence organisations (and universities) set themselves in terms of managing expertise, budgets and responsibilities. The study of terrorist and insurgent use of the internet must necessarily work through these layers simply by asking

DOI: 10.4018/978-1-4666-8456-0.ch013

questions such as, who is using which platform to communicate with whom for what effect? This endeavour represents a key challenge for the intelligence community seeking to exploit online interaction to understand the command and control arrangements of a group, their motivations and intentions, gather evidence for prosecution and data for operations support. This context is not without controversy, as highlighted by the arguments between government and private companies arising over statements made by Richard Hannigan, the head of the UK's GCHQ intelligence agency, in November 2014. Hannigan has stated that "... increasingly [internet firms'] services not only host the material of violent extremism or child exploitation, but are the routes for the facilitation of crime and terrorism" (BBC, 2014). This serves to highlight the importance attached to online activities by government agencies.

Conway (2007) argues that terrorist use of the Internet has five key purposes: 1) information provision, 2) recruitment, 3) financing, 4) networking and 5) information gathering. Conway (2007) was right to identify the properties of the internet which differentiate it from traditional media such as volume, speed, two-way communication and global scope. Much of the intended persuasive power implicit in online terrorist activities is driven by propaganda, defined here in its contemporary understanding as "information, especially of a biased or misleading nature, used to promote a political cause or point of view" (Oxford Dictionaries, n.d.). The idea that the internet acts as an echo chamber is considered further in a 2013 RAND study on radicalisation and digital media (Von Behr *et al.*, 2013). It examines individual radicalisation through 15 case studies and argues that these case studies confirm the notion that that the internet "...allows individuals to seek material that they are interested in, and to reject that which does not support their worldview. The Internet can give the illusion of strength of consensus..." (Von Behr *et al.*, 2013:27). The study also discusses the far reach and speedy distribution of extremist material through online active participation (Von Behr *et al.*, 2013:26).

This chapter seeks to examine through a short review and comparison of current Islamist cases studies, what we term *cyberpropaganda*. We define this as the exploitation of the generative characteristics of online interaction for the production and reproduction of propaganda. We do not wish to generalise further on Conway's (2007) work or specifically look at radicalisation as undertaken in the RAND study, but we acknowledge the characteristics of online communications that they outline. Instead this chapter explores the generative characteristics of social communications in cyberpropaganda cases live in 2014. It examines group emergence, specific communication platforms, audiences, messages, themes and possible effects. This is undertaken in the context of understanding the issues and policy implications for trying to counter, when necessary, violent extremist cyberpropaganda.

The four cases chosen in this chapter for examination of this important topic include the cyberpropaganda activities of Al Qaeda, Islamic State, Boko Haram and Al Shabaab. It is of course tempting in choosing these case studies to assume that they are connected as simply local expressions of the same Islamist campaign. A surface reading can focus on shared characteristics such as violent extremist views in an Islamist context and similar social media platforms. Killcullen (2009) has argued that the internet and global communications have served to give the impression of a connected global insurgency emerging from what could be interpreted as essentially local disputes. This raises a question about whether in countering cyberpropaganda similar approaches should be taken to similar dispositions or thematic postures as may be apparent across cases, or whether a highly local or targeted and specific form of counter-measure is required that takes account of critical and, perhaps, not so apparent differences. Each case is examined in turn, before a comparative discussion is presented. The chapter will conclude with recommendations for counter-terrorism (CT) policy.

Case 1: Al Qaeda

Al Qaeda was the first global terrorist organization in history and has been the pioneer of Islamist propaganda. All other modern Islamist groups have drawn their communication stances from its example. As a result, we explain its messaging approach in detail. Its acts have been characterised by first, the extremism of the terror act itself (the propaganda of the deed, see Bolt, 2008), second, the global reach of such acts, and third, the ability to elucidate the message of those acts verbally and visually on a global scale, particularly through the internet. Al Qaeda message appeals focus on sharing a fantasy, that of the global conspiracy against Islam (and the global nature of the internet allows global dissemination of this idea), the iniquity of its enemies, and the notion that they are fighting to save their faith from extinction. Holbrook (2014) terms this a 'grievance narrative'. The terror act, and the cyberspace amplification of that deed (evidenced by the presence of online propaganda), is entirely self-referential. Al Qaeda solicits multiple targets using a range of objectives. Undoubtedly, recruitment is an aim; AQ propaganda seeks to legitimize the excitement and danger of combat as a way of luring bored and unemployed youth (Baines *et al*, 2010) but they also need a source of legitimacy from culturally significant figures. Despite security service successes in a number of countries, Al Qaeda remains fully focused on its murderous mission. An analysis of AQ messaging by IntelCenter revealed a significant increase in the annual production of AQ's propaganda tapes by as-Sahab, its main media production company, from circa 6 in 2002 to 58 by 2006. By the end of 2007, they had produced at least 87 (IntelCenter, 2007) and many more since. The three key figures appearing in as-Sahab propaganda videos between 2002-2007 were Osama bin Laden, Ayman Al Zawahiri and Yahya Al Libi. One particularly noteworthy assessment in the evolution of as-Sahab propaganda was AQ's ability to respond to unpredictable events with audio-visual statements sometimes released within 5-7 days of significant events (usually bombings for which they claimed responsibility).

AQ governance shows recognition that ideas have to be actively sold, so AQ conscripts theatrical devices to present the same messages in different ways. The dramaturgy of AQ messaging explains its surprisingly persuasive power. The suicide bomber narrative, of pious Islamic warrior, melds theatre and ritual. The ritual is well-established in AQ's messaging: the bomber's articulation of his motivations, farewell to friends and family, avowal of the certainty of paradise, the preparation of the vehicle and bomb construction, the hiding of the vehicle, the approach of the enemy convoy and, of course, the explosion. This intermixing of life and death and the emancipation of death as an ideal for the idealistic Muslim is truly an exercise in social creativity. Unfortunately, sufficient numbers of Western citizens appear to believe the myths.

Inviting Fantasies

Much of the AQ product invites viewers to participate in a fantasy. The literature certainly stresses the significance of fantasy in human behaviour. For example, Velleman (2000) cites various categories of behaviour that feature motivation by imagining. Targets are being offered vistas of a truly diabolic enemy fought by truly saintly warriors in the simple binary of good and evil. Target audiences do not have to believe all the particulars of this vision of enmity, or even its principal allegations. What AQ seek is an emotional trigger, an imagistic and rhetorical rationale whose truth or falsehood is not the main point: it does not (necessarily) make the mistake of asking for belief. Le Bon said of the masses that "they turn instinctively, as the insects seek the light, to the rhetoricians who tell them what they want... whoever can supply them with delusions is easily their master; whoever attempts to destroy their illusions is always evicted" (Le Bon, 1908). Fantasies are not beliefs: they are known to be false but believed to be true. Fantasy has been conceived as an internal dialogue that serves some wish-fulfilling function (Poster, 1988). The cyberspace nature of much of the engagement with AQ audio-visual material serves to enhance the opportunities for followers to celebrate their fantasies, individually and in online fora, for it to reach a wider audience.

The Pious Persona

One aspect of superiority, as political Islam's de facto praetorian guard, is a depth of piety manifest in the rejection of all worldly blandishments and siren voices. There is a significant focus on the life of austerity led by the martyrs and the Mujahidin fighters who reject a life of comfort to fight for their cause. They are positioned as supremely moral men. But AQ also aligns the cause of Islam with anti-materialism, since the western adversary represents materialism and all that is evil with such. What is constant throughout these rhetorical essays is the notion of a binary universe for the Al Qaeda world - luxury/austerity: good/ evil: city/country: human/animal: Muslim/infidel: paradise/hell. Such a Manichean perspective is attractive to some because it 'sorts' a complex world, but it may also be facilitated by the hard-wiring of the brain itself. The social anthropologist, Leymore, in line with the structuralism of Levi-Strauss, suggests that the mind is particularly sensitive to contrasts in the human condition (Leymore, 1975).

AQ are the original self-elected and self-appointed defenders of Islam, justified by showing themselves to be the most pure illustrated through martyrdom, with their message amplified in cyberspace. Their videographic material, available online, presents an ideal self, a model to be emulated, but also a challenge since self-detonation is cast as the ultimate test of manhood. Martyrs are not presented as strange men, and the fact of their ostensible normalcy is important to AQ, as is their attractiveness of personality and appearance. Bin Laden fortified these ideas by constantly seeking to give the impression of a scholarly clergyman.

Legitimacy of a Supra-National Movement

AQ seek to demonstrate that their own approach of exacting death in the name of their religion's honour is validated by Islam, that it is *the* exclusive, interpretation of the Qur'an. Hence AQ misuses the language of religion, in a necessarily imprecise way. The mandates of any global religion must have an inherent vagueness because of the millions of different situations in which a particular individual might find themselves. No religion crafts a formula for each conceivable situation. AQ place these general, and generally poetically expressed precepts, alongside the militant text of their own authorship to create an associative emotional connection where none can conceivably be regarded to exist in logic.

AQ re-conceptualises Islam as a nation with its own territoriality. This is an illicit conceptual move: it takes an idea from one realm, politics, and applies it to another, spirituality. If peoples within geographic areas can self-constitute as sovereign nations, so then can a religion. This includes any former Islamic territory such as Spain (Al Andalus). The rhetorical ascription to Islam of the idea of nationhood offers the derivative of a polemic of nationalism, with specific reference to the Umma (the world body of Islamic adherents).

AQ's Key Messages

AQ's propaganda focuses particularly on a message aimed at consolidating a religious anti-Western world-view, espousing a global conspiracy against Islam. The only antidote is to perform Jihad, self-defined as either the conduct of a martyrdom operation, the provision of financial or sympathetic support, or at the very least passive non-engagement with AQ. Its approach has become increasingly sophisticated in terms of production values, its symbolic and its rhetorical argumentation. AQ's material seeks to exploit and capture a mood, not necessarily a dominant one, but one to which some in the Middle East have been obvious target recruits. It is this mood of angry despair- manifest also in secular ways as in the revolutions of the 2011 Arab Spring - which AQ have attempted to direct, although not to present with much success (Holbrook, 2014). Cantril's early (1941) study of deviant social movements like the Nazi party shows how national moods develop. What is clear overall is that despite Bin Laden's death in 2011, the West continues to face a sophisticated ideological battle against AQ propagandists. AQ's ideology is constructed around a perverse and perverted view of Islam. Consequently, there is an urgent need to provide an alternative metaphysical sanctuary for disaffected Muslims (in Pakistan, the Middle East, Europe and the US).

Since its inception in 1988, AQ has spawned or assimilated 7 groups including Egyptian Islamic Jihad in Egypt (2001), Al Qaeda in Iraq (AQI, 2004), Al-Qaeda in the Islamic Maghreb in North Africa (AQIM, 2007), Al-Qaeda in the Arabian Peninsular in Yemen (AQAP, 2009), Al Shabab in Somalia (2011), Jabhat al-Nusra in Syria (JN, 2011), and Al-Qaeda in the Indian Sub-continent (AQIS, 2014). Kimmage (2010) argues that AQ's communications have become less effective because of the changing media environment, growing concern of AQ's murder of Muslims and the failure of AQ to achieve lasting social change. Whilst AQ has survived by spawning various affiliates, these groups are also adversely affecting the coherence of AQ message. Lyons (2013) argues that whilst al-Qaeda's online propaganda is dangerous, relatively few violent incidents in the West have been caused by it (Lyons, 2013). More recently, however, for Western Europe at least, the propaganda threat has come from Islamic State, which appears to have induced 2580 Western Europeans to decamp from their relative luxury to the battle-torn lands of Syria and Iraq (Saltman & Winter, 2014). We turn to Islamic State next.

Case 2: Islamic State

Islamic State (IS) has used the conflict in Syria to seize territory there and in Iraq (Home Office, 2014). In the territories they have seized, IS have targeted minorities for persecution (UN News Centre, 2014), and victory is frequently accompanied by savagery (Rush, 2014). IS threatens Bagdad and seeks to destroy the Iraqi government, in order to remove an existential threat to itself (Lewis, 2014). Their rise has destabilized the entire region as they threaten the interests' of many neighboring countries (Cockburn, 2014), and globally there is a fear of IS terrorism (US DOD, 2014), although some have contested the extent of this threat (Shashank, 2014).

IS's lineage stems from 2002 when it was an insurgent group in Iraq. Over the years it has undergone various brand and allegiance changes. It reached an apogee when it allied with Al Qaeda before being diminished in 2006 by the Iraqi people, who rejected its brutality (BBC, 2014). It is a Sunni organization which has sought to exploit Iraqi Sunnis' dissatisfaction with their government (Connable, 2014), and from 2013 they have used the situation in Syria to battle-harden their troops, create safe havens and seize vast revenues in oil and assets. Since then they have seized more territory and assets, and their leader, al-Baghdadi has declared their territory a revived Islamic state – or Caliphate (Phillips, 2014). IS is and acts as a proto-State.

IS has come forcefully to the attention of Western media. A search of Goggle Trends[1] shows a steep rise in interest at the end of May and the beginning of June 2014; also borne out by an article count by topic on the BBC[2]. During this period, IS had major triumphs in Iraq and declared the Caliphate (BBC, 2014). However, it is not just mainstream media reporting on IS, the organization itself has a prodigious output on the internet. It distributes media through a variety of fronts, such as *Al Furqan Media* (Hashem, 2014) and *Al Hayat Media Center* (Becker, 2014). These appear to direct 'official' IS releases through mediums like Twitter, Facebook and YouTube. However, it also appears to employ regional press offices too (Hashem, 2014). In addition, their fighters tweet pictures and their own experiences. These messages are picked up, echoed and passed on by a fanclub who support IS (Kingsley, 2014). Attempts have been made to stem IS messaging, with Twitter banning their accounts. Despite these efforts, the volume of material on the internet, and the specific nature of programs that censor content, have made it impossible to silence them. IS have tried to evade blocking by retreating to less controlled sites (Lee, 2014), and diversifying their outlets (Shane, 2014). They have even created an app to help the IS fanclub dominate Twitter (Berger, 2014), and practiced spamming techniques where users clicked on a non-IS link to find an unexpected IS video (Ali, 2014).

In addition to offering varied distribution channels, IS varies the use of its media: from tweets and other social media messages to glossy online magazines, short videos, beheading videos and a long documentary (Shane, 2014). They produce in Arabic (with a translation service to English (Hashem, 2014), English[3] and also in languages specific to Pakistan and India (Reuters, 2014). IS media is reasonably well-produced e.g. their documentary, *The Flames of War* has slow-motion, a soundtrack, and intensive post-production. Their snuff-filmesque beheading videos make use of basic editing techniques to retain viewer interest. However, it is likely that this is produced by cheap, consumer level technology, possibly even "one man and a laptop" (Rose, 2014).

The audiences for IS's outpouring are distinct. They target foreign powers such as the US and UK by beheading prisoners from those nations and then releasing videos of the event with comments directed at those countries' leaders. This is either a direct attempt to goad foreign governments into action and, thus, bring legitimacy to the IS cause as they are cast as defending Islam against Western interference (Mardini, 2014) or a failed attempt at psychological operations to sap Western morale and drive Western intervention from the Middle East.

IS appears to be targeting their enemies on the battlefield; their products often feature footage of Iraqi or Syrian soldiers being executed. This has led some commentators to ascribe the mass routing of these soldiers to be, in some part attributed, to IS media (Davidson, 2014). Presently, however, there are no detailed studies of the actual relationship between IS media and their effect, if any, on the battlefield morale of their opponents.

The main target audience is likely to be potential recruits and donors. IS has positioned itself as more fashionable and more successful than other Jihadi groups. It has achieved what others before it have not, namely a proto-State. Its materials make use of modern, and youthful, cultural references, such as online gaming, films and catchphrases (Kingsley, 2014). Despite this, a cursory look at any of IS's materials suggests that they may be appealing to only those who are already primed for such material. IS material may therefore be aimed at already staunch activist supporters in a similar way as party election broadcasts are targeted at party supporters in UK elections. IS material is littered with Islamic references, Arabic words and acts of gross violence – none of which are likely to appeal to the un-initiated. The role of the Internet material is therefore to instil greater commitment to the cause (Gladstone, 2014). It is this last point that may prove to be the Achilles-heel for IS media. Despite their clever distribution methods, modern production techniques and apparent support, their message is one of extremely narrow appeal.

Case 3: Boko Haram

Boko Haram was the target of public outrage generated by its kidnapping of 200-300 schoolgirls on 14 April 2014 from a girls' school in Chibok, Borno State, northern Nigeria. Reports vary on the exact number of those kidnapped, both those who remain in detention and those who have since escaped. This outrage was exacerbated by the release of a Boko Haram video showing the girls in captivity (BBC, 2014c). It drew a global social media response, through the hashtag #BringBackOurGirls, trending through May and early summer 2014. One response from Boko Haram was to issue another video in July 2014, reportedly showing its leader, Abubakar Shekau mocking the campaign (Audu, 2014a). Clearly Boko Haram's actions had driven a highly-charged emotional response from a global audience, and one in which a multi-party engagement was present in digital media.

Whilst there is some disagreement about the exact dates of its formation, Boko Haram and its antecedents can be dated from the early 1990s. It has been known by a number of names in the Nigeria media such as Taliban and Yusufiyya (Loimeier, 2012). The latter is after its founder Muhammad Yusuf (1970-2009). Its official title in Arabic is 'Jama'atu Ahlis Sunna Lidda'awati wal-Jihad' which is translated as 'People Committed to the Propagation of the Prophet's Teachings and Jihad' (Adibe, 2013). Adegbulu argues that the 'ideology and philosophy of the movement can best be understood by explicating the two words – 'Boko' and 'Haram'' (Adegbulu, 2013). Boko, a Hausa word, means 'western' or 'foreign'. Haram is from the Arabic for 'forbidden.' Taken together Boko Haram communicates that everything western, or more specifically 'western education' in the local context, is forbidden. Central to the philosophy is that the state itself is a western construct that should be replaced by an Islamic state governed by Sharia. In the context of northern Nigeria this resonates with Boko Haram's members and supporters in that the western or western-style education of a Nigerian elite and institutions of the Nigerian state have failed to address poverty and disadvantage for young people, particularly young men, creating inequality thereby contributing to the continuing violence (Rakodi, 2012). Oil wealth, for example, is generated in the largely Christian south, driving perceptions of inadequate wealth re-distribution.

The education theme extends to analysis of Boko Haram's membership and religious thinking. Adegbulu (2012) describes Muhammad Yusuf as a 'semi-illiterate,' whilst Gourley (2012) points out its members have traditionally been largely, though not exclusively, poor Qur'anic students working in a manual craft-based labour and madrassa system. Boko Haram should be seen in the broader religious context in Nigeria that is characterized by tensions between the Christian south and Muslim north, as well as intra-Islamic tensions. Dowd (2014) points out that this has included 'anti-innovation' reformists who argue a fundamentalist view of sacred texts rejecting, for example, 'errors and innovations' associated with Sufi forms of Islam. Moreover, as noted by Hansen and Aliyu Musa (2013:287), "Boko Haram's anger and resentment is especially directed at the corrupt and venal Muslim ruling political class in the north whom they view as apostates". Assessment of Boko Haram's anti-western stance has also catalysed discussion of an alternative 'anti-innovation' agenda regarding western technology. It is common to read assessments that Boko Haram rejects modern and western inventions and somehow wishes to take Nigeria back to a period without such technology. This is set against Nigeria's 'mobile telecommunications revolution' (Ulanoff, 2014), a revolution that includes significant growth in mobile phones and internet usage.

Associated with mobile phone penetration is a rise in online activism in Nigeria, amongst not only social rights groups, youths and political activists but even Nigerian politicians (Chiluwa, 2012). One would expect to see in Boko Haram's communications strategy a tension between a principled dismissal of western style digital technology and Nigeria's growth in online activism. There is nothing unequivocal in this regard, with assessments pointing to different viewpoints. Bertram and Ellison (2014) conducted a survey of sub-Saharan African terrorist groups' use of the internet in the months prior to the schoolgirls' kidnap. In it, they found that of the 53 Facebook pages they surveyed, Boko Haram's site had the most 'likes': 6817 likes on 5 August 2013. As of 12 December 2014 it appeared to have 11,885 (Nigerian Terrorism News Arena, n.d.). They note that nairaland.com, a Nigerian generic social platform, had a discussion concerning a new Facebook site purporting to be owned by the Group leader, Shekau, although Bertram and Ellison (2014) contend whether or not it really is his work.

Boko Haram also apparently has a Twitter account, with the strapline, 'To Hate is Human, To Bomb is Divine. We hate western inventions including Twitter: however, we feel the necessity to use it to reach out to our fans'. Whether this account is really Boko Haram's or not, it plays to the narrative of rejection of Western technology, except as necessary for a greater good. Certainly, Facebook, Twitter, other online publishers (including those opposed to Boko Haram) and traditional media, all serve to distribute Boko Haram-attributed statements, images and video. Eveslage (2012) conducted a content analysis of Boko Haram's public statements in 2012 and found that 83% of criticisms and threats were directed towards domestic subjects. These criticisms and threats are targeted at the illegitimacy of Nigeria and its leadership, in particular its President Goodluck Jonathan. Prominent Muslim leaders who criticize Boko Haram are also targeted. Much of the taunting is directed at state institutions, such as Nigeria's military. This includes images of captured weapons and equipment meant to illustrate the capability and enduring power of Boko Haram, relative to the Nigerian armed forces and police. Boko Haram have also been quick to provide footage or images of their successful attacks or aftermath, and to give a rationale for their actions, perhaps with a follow-up threat to the next potential victim. Threats to oil infrastructure (and therefore a corrupt economy) and Nigerian and international media outlets are persistent features of their statements (Audu, 2014b).

One controversial theme is the death of Shekau. When declared in the press or by the Nigerian Government (several times to date) it has been followed-up by videos posted to show he remains alive. Part of this ongoing dialogue includes the apparent mistaken identity of Boko Haram members by Nigerian forces, with photographs distributed online, of suspects killed in attacks (Cocks, 2014). This undermines Government credibility both in terms of the veracity of reporting content and the veracity of information sources. Shekau remains a focus of official statements by Boko Haram and his leadership plays a central role in its video presentation.

From an international dimension, statements often address by name US, UK, Israel and UN leaders both past and present (Allafrica.com, 2014). References to other violent Islamist groups, such as Al Qaeda, show a developing international perspective. For example, the inclusion of images of a black flag replacing its own logo stretched on an armoured vehicle has indicated a larger, more international narrative, perhaps leveraging referent power from other violent groups or suggesting validation of their actions. Use of English is also a persistent feature of the videos. One assessment is that this not only attempts to attract a more international audience ahead of the Nigerian election scheduled for 2015, but also addresses Western-educated and English-speaking Nigerian political leaders and religious leaders

(Soufan Group, 2014). This serves to reinforce the failure of a Western-educated elite and, therefore, the failure of Western culture itself.

The international impact of Boko Haram's actions and media has been highlighted through the attention garnered by the kidnapping of the schoolgirls. Alongside this has been evidence of online discussion amongst the public and in news commentary on the veracity of the propaganda war itself, particularly when multiple deaths are reported of the group's leader, (Premium Times, 2014) when messages from official government sources are treated with suspicion and disbelief (Okino, 2014), or the belief that elements of Nigerian media reporting are compromised by bias[4]. What is clear from the propaganda battle online, and in traditional news reporting, is an unresolved tension between the continued existence of Boko Haram and the claims of success made by the Nigerian establishment in their security efforts to defeat it.

In 2014, Boko Haram's agenda was brought onto the world stage through its kidnapping and forced-conversion to Islam of the Chibok girls. Online platforms have allowed international comment and interaction on Boko Haram's activities. Collins (2014) noted that:

More than any other, the [#Bringbackourgirls] campaign has shown that social media is more than pictures of meals and cocktails – it's a buzzing conversation hub of the important issues of the day. It's populated not just by friends and family; influencers, journalists and politicians are all there too, poised to respond to the problems that matter most to their audience.

Yet, the campaign has faced criticism, with Monnet (2014) arguing that the #Bringbackourgirls campaign has given free publicity to Boko Haram, making it into a world brand for hostage-taking, and has seriously destabilised the Nigerian government. Boko Haram's digital and online propaganda seeks to thrive on North-South, political, economic and religious divisions and perceptions of failure of a Western-style state and governance model. Next we turn to another Jihadist organization, seeking to exploit a weak state, Al Shabaab in Somalia.

Case 4: Al-Shabaab

Since the collapse of the Mohamed Siad Barre government in 1991, Somalia has seen successive waves of civil war and international interventions. The conflict has ravaged the country and, for many years, it has lacked any substantive or coherent central government, allowing a variety of insurgent, tribal and terrorist groups to flourish in the absence of government control. Repeated attempts to establish a national government eventually led to the creation in 2012 of the current, internationally recognised, Federal Government of Somalia. But, in the process, it also led to the creation of Harakat al-Shabaab al-Mujahideen (HSM) more commonly known as al-Shabaab (in Arabic 'The Youth', or 'The Young-sters') - a name which resonates strongly with another criminal group, the Picciotteria ('The Lads'), the forerunners of the Calabrian Mafia ('Ndrangheta) in Italy (Dickie, 2012).

Al-Shabaab has its origins in the emergence of the Islamic Courts Union (ICU) and was originally its youth wing. During the chaos of the 1990s, in the absence of any other law, a number of Sharia law courts were formed to administer justice at the local and district level, with each court having its own militia to help maintain law and order in their area. In 2006, eleven of these courts united to create the ICU and, for a few months, the ICU ruled large areas of Somalia before Ethiopian troops, supporting the then Transitional Federal Government, drove them out of Mogadishu. As a result, the ICU effectively disintegrated and splintered into a number of groups with Al Shabaab subsequently emerging as the most prominent of these. Formally aligned with Al Qaeda since 2012, the group remains opposed to the Federal Government and the African Union Mission in Somalia (AMISOM). It has recently suffered a number of setbacks, including the loss of much of the territory it previously controlled and, on 1st September 2014, the killing of one of its most prominent leaders, Ahmed Abdi Godane. Godane headed a faction within Al Shabaab that advocated closer alignment with al-Qaeda and the 'International Struggle' and it is not immediately known what impact his death might have. Despite this setback, Al Shabaab remains a capable and dangerous organisation estimated to have as many as 5,000 fighters, including several hundred foreign fighters (Harper, 2014).

From the very beginning, Al Shabaab has used the internet and social media (i.e. Twitter), in particular, as an integral part of its operations. In many cases, it has pioneered techniques that are now being used by other extremist Islamic groups e.g. IS. In contrast, the West initially failed to understand the importance of its media efforts. Although Al Shabaab is recognised as a major threat today, the origins of its success lie in its early evolution and online recruitment efforts. Despite its emergence in Somalia in 2007 both the United States and the United Kingdom were slow to respond to it. The United States only designated it as a banned terrorist organisation in February 2008 (US State Department, n.d.), while the British government did not do so until March 2010 (UK Home Office, 2014). By then Al Shabaab was already actively recruiting in the US and in the UK, creating a recruiting network and disseminating videos online. It proved from the outset to be an agile, early adopter of new media for propaganda purposes, using English to appeal mainly to the US and British Somali diaspora. It has also produced a magazine, *Gaidi Mtaani* ("Street Terrorist") in Kiswahili (a dialect used in Kenya and Uganda), to cement its support in neighbouring countries to Somalia (Meleagrou-Hitchens, Maher & Sheehan, 2012).

One of its early American recruits was Omar Shafik Hammami, also known as Abu Mansoor Al-Amriki (the American). Hammami pioneered the use of digital and social media as tools for radicalisation and recruitment, producing slick Westernized recruitment videos for dissemination via YouTube. His YouTube.com *Ghaba Productions* (Ghaba being a variant of the Somali word for poetry) uses the warrior poetry form used by 19th century Somali poet Mohammad Abdullah Hassan and Hammami's poetry-rap videos such as 'Send Me a Cruise' have been widely circulated[5].

Al Shabaab has its own media production group, al Kataib, which employs professional production values to produce jihadist videos. In particular, its creative use of graphics and sophisticated video techniques intended to reach and appeal to a young, mainly diasporic audience, is a key element in the videos. While using YouTube extensively for its videos, the group also became an early adopter of Twitter and posted its first tweet on 7 December 2011 (in Arabic and translated as 'In the name of God the merciful'). Three years later, al-Shabaab's influence on IS seems clear.

The attractiveness of the content produced by al Kataib is not just based on its professional production quality; it is carefully targeted and specifically focuses on youth and their perspective, concentrating what they will find interesting or 'cool'. Some of Al Shabaab's YouTube posts depict an intense combat training regime; others are recorded interviews with American, British and other foreign fighters discussing why they decided to join the group, and seeking to glorify the experience. Another series of videos shows fighters attempting to rap about waging jihad in Somalia. Amidst images of combat, dead bodies, and cheering children, the rap videos also seek to exploit the *gabei* poetry tradition unique to the Somali identity. As a result, the organisation's international recruitment efforts have been very successful. It is estimated that over a period of six years to 2013, approximately 1000 ethnic Somalis and 200–300 non-Somalis were recruited to Al Shabaab from outside Somalia and that over 40 of those were from the United States, recruited mainly from the Minneapolis-St Paul diaspora, while at least 10 were British citizens (Meleagrou-Hitchens, Maher & Sheehan, 2012).

Aside from recruiting and propaganda, the organisation's whole media operation is very professional. Osman (2013), a Channel 4 journalist, describes Al Shabaab as one of the most media savvy:

of all al-Qaeda Islamist groups across the world, Al Shabaab is probably the most accessible. Journalists who cover the east Africa region can reach the al-Shabaab press team through email or phone. Al Shabaab spokesmen give live interviews to local and international media from al-Kataib's offices. Like any communication officers, their press officers use catchy phrases and interesting soundbites to get the attention of the media.

In every case and, regardless of platform, al-Shabaab broadcasts a quasi-professional message stream that seeks to embed and glorify its own critical role as both a key defender and proselytiser of Islam, which is invariably represented as under imminent threat of extinction by Western 'Crusaders'. The posts also seek to magnify the group's role far beyond its actual importance within Somalia and the rest of the world and deliver a relentlessly positive version of Al Shabaab's fighting capability as well as its success in capturing hearts and minds for the Salafist cause.

Al Shabaab has also demonstrated its ability to rapidly respond to events with carefully targeted products to exploit new events and developing situations. Al Shabaab have previously released videos of young Somali's with British accents urging people to join the fight, causing then-head of MI5, Jonathan Evans, to make a statement that it is only a matter of time before Al Shabaab inspires UK terror attacks (Shinn, 2011). Two years later, the organisation's online release of an hour-long film glorifying the slaughter of the British soldier, Lee Rigby, in Woolwich, London in 2013 is one example. Narrated by a man with a British accent, wearing a black mask and a camouflage jacket, the production praises those behind the killing as 'a new and terrifying reality' and incites others to carry out attacks in the UK. Holding an automatic weapon in his hands, the narrator tells viewers to purchase knives: 'do not waste your time trying to reinvent the wheel. If you can't afford to get hold of one of these then certainly a simple knife from your local B&Q will do the job' (Graham, 2013).

Its most recent spectacular attack also demonstrated a new use of social media as an integral part of an operation. During the Westgate Mall attack in Kenya on 21st September 2013, Al Shabaab updated Twitter in near-real time. The account was shut down a total of five times over the four-day siege, only to re-appear almost immediately under a different name, highlighting the difficulty of controlling such social media. In ironic contrast to its own activities online, al Shabaab has responded to the increasing development of the media environment inside Somalia by seeking to restrict the use of the internet. In January 2014, it banned the internet within the areas it controls and, in February 2014, Al Shabaab shut down the mobile internet provider Hormuud Telecom at gunpoint (Mohamed, 2014). It continues to threaten other internet service providers. Perhaps as an organisation that realises the power of social media and its rapid growth on mobile phones in particular, it now fears the potential impact such media might have on the population within its own areas.

In the next section, we discuss the implications of the four cases, in order to determine commonalities and differences in the different terrorist groups' approaches to cyberpropaganda.

Discussion

The purpose of examining four cases is not simply to understand similarities and differences in each of the cases, but to establish a knowledge base upon which policy recommendations might be shaped. This helps us to determine what elements in the cases are of interest by assessing them from the perspective of the policy-maker.

Firstly we assume that cyberpropaganda is perceived by the policy-maker as a problematic phenomenon that either presents a challenge to the policy-maker's interests, or generates fear that it might. This may be a direct challenge in terms of threats to leaders, citizens and property (and sometimes civic values), or an indirect challenge through the recruitment of its citizens to terrorist groups, or choices regarding defence posture and relationships, that would otherwise not be pursued. We recognise that in the propaganda discourse there exist conspiracies regarding complicity with the terrorist group on behalf of officials and suggested ambiguity about who are the 'true' beneficiaries of continued instability and upheaval amongst specific communities and geographies. This often takes the forms of suggesting complicity with intelligence agencies, specifically that the West or others organically created the groups, that governments or their citizens are actually providing arms, training or finance or that powerful businesses benefit despite public assurances. Our position is that such discourse needs to be taken into account by the policy-maker who genuinely views violent extremist propaganda as a problem issue. Secondly, if the first assumption is correct, and that the policy-maker is driven to act against the propaganda (intervene or counter) in some way, what characteristics of cyberpropganda are material to generating options? This is the question we will focus on for the remainder of the chapter. There are many ways in which the characteristics of cyberpropaganda could be divided up, but arguably there are five key questions that emerge from the cases, each with implications for the policy maker. These include:

- What are the key messages and themes?
- How is cyberpropaganda generated and spread?
- What makes it attractive to those who may act on it?
- How local or global is the focus of the propaganda?
- What is the trajectory of the problem issue for the future?

In order to answer these questions, we first summarise the cases against these questions in Table 1 and discuss each in turn next.

What are the Key Messages and Themes?

At a high level, all groups share a similar Islamist ideology, rejecting western notions of statehood and advocating a theocratic model, drawn from a strict interpretation of religious texts. Recruitment and radicalisation is a common issue. However, they play out in different ways. Boko Haram is the least similar in this regard because it does not focus as much on Western recruitment. Where foreign fighters are present, they tend to be drawn from other parts of Africa (Abubakar, 2014). The others have placed emphasis on the international appeal and nature of the struggle. All groups are using fear appeals to goad Western audiences, and pseudo-religious zealotry to appeal to suggestible Muslim converts including white converts. The white convert has particular propaganda value because this inspires greater terror ('we all could be terrorists' is the implication). The relationship with the West is a key aspect of

Table 1. Cross Case Analysis

Analysis Items	Al Qaeda	Islamic State	Boko Haram	Al Shabab
Key messages and themes?	• Recruit and radicalise • Global conspiracy against Islam • The iniquity of its enemies • They are fighting to save their faith from extinction.	• Recruit and radicalise, especially foreign fighters. • Rightful conflict. • A well run Caliphate has been established. • Dissuade enemy from fighting. • Goad foreign nations into attacking IS. • IS's victory in inevitable. • Those who stand against IS will find no mercy and their fate will be grim. • Foreign nations' actions are illegitimate.	• Nigerian elite and institutions of the Nigerian state have failed to address poverty and disadvantage • Illegitimacy of Nigeria and its leadership, in particular its President Goodluck Jonathan • The state itself is a western construct that should be replaced by an Islamic state governed by Sharia • Mocking the west, Nigerian officials, and opposition Muslims. • Threats to Nigerian economic interest and media.	• Recruit and radicalise, including foreign fighters • Islam under threat from the West. • Amplification of its own importance in Somalia and internationally. • Messages of success.
How is cyberpropganda generated and spread?	• Self-referential online propaganda, video of events and statements. • Efficacy established through first hand imagery and timely reporting and response.	• Media distribution media through fronts, such as Al Furqan Media and Al Hayat Media Center. • 'Official' releases on Twitter, Facebook and YouTube; • Regional press offices • Fighters themselves who tweet pictures and their own experiences. • Messages are picked up, echoed and passed on by a 'fanclub' • Glossy online magazines, short videos, beheading videos and a long documentary	• Release of video, often with the leader speaking directly to camera. • First-hand video • Social media such as Facebook and twitter platforms where attribution is unclear. • Supporters generate and redistribute material.	Via: • Al Khataib media production group. • You Tube videos • Twitter • Live interviews and relationship with journalists. • Soundbites and catchy phrases – to suit traditional media. • Live tweeting as incident is in progress.

all groups, where local problems are closely associated with western ills. Messages echo a golden age of Islam with a caliphate spread across the Middle East, North Africa and parts of Southern Europe. Goading and mockery are all consistent features of the propaganda. This is in part to show the weakness of the response against them, and in the case of IS, to deliberately draw a military response. It has been a tactic of many terror groups to try to cause a regime to enact ever-more repressive measures, thereby gaining more support and coherence for the justness of their cause.

How is Cyberpropaganda Generated and Spread?

All groups use 'official' channels to launch much of their 'set piece' videos and media content. Al Shabaab's live tweets have shown the drive to timely material from their actions, as has the use of tweets and individual stories by IS fighters. The difficulty in battling online propaganda by shutting down sources

Table 2. Cross Case Analysis Continued

Analysis Items	Al Qaeda	Islamic State	Boko Haram	Al Shabab
What makes it attractive to those who may act on it?	• Excitement and danger of combat as a way of luring bored/unemployed youth • legitimacy inferred from the appearance of significant spokespersons. • AQ's ability to respond to unpredictable events with audio-visual statements • Dramaturgy, such the suicide bomber narrative, of pious Islamic warrior, melds theatre and ritual, intermixing life and death. • 'Vox populi' method where ordinary Palestinians in the street express their rage - set against other voices - notes of calm authority – the rational centre of an irrational world. • Emancipation of death as an ideal for the Muslim • Opportunities to celebrate fantasy. • Piety. • A binary universe: luxury/austerity: good/evil: Muslim/infidel: paradise/hell – 'sorts' a complex world.	• IS fighters looking happy, mixing with locals – in particular children. • Islamic imagery, music and quotes. • Modern computer games (e.g. *Grand Theft Auto* or *Battlefield series*). • Exciting (slow motion, night time footage). • Graphic violence on the enemy. • The happiness/peacefulness of a death in combat. • Islamic justification for violence and duty to violent struggle (jihad). • Emphasizing the swiftness of victory. • The resources available to IS. • That IS fights with passion and for a good cause but the enemy's is not and so they will lose. • Does not shy from possibility of death, but emphasizes afterlife. • In murdering hostages the blame is entirely placed on foreign nation's leaders. • Varied media targeted at to segmented audiences. They produce in Arabic, with a translation service to English, English and also languages found in Pakistan and India. 'Softer' videos for western eyes, where the execution takes place off camera (compare with execution videos of Syrian soldiers).	• In the context of northern Nigeria this resonates with Boko Haram's members and supporters in that the western or western-style education of a Nigerian elite and institutions of the Nigerian state have failed to address poverty and disadvantage for young people, particularly young men. • Images of captured weapons and equipment meant to illustrate the capability and enduring power of Boko Haram, relative to the Nigerian armed forces and police. • Boko Haram are also quick to provide footage or images of their successful attacks or aftermath, and to give a rationale for their actions, perhaps with a follow-up threat to the next potential victim.	• Use of culturally relevant forms of communciation. • Al Shabaab's YouTube posts depict an intense combat training regime; • There You Tube videos are recorded interviews with American, British and other foreign fighters discussing why they decided to join the group, and seeking to glorify the experience. • Other videos shows fighters attempting to rap about waging jihad in Somalia. Amidst images of combat, dead bodies, and cheering children. • The rap videos also seek to exploit the gabei poetry tradition unique to the Somali identity. • Success is attractive to the Salafist cause. • Responds rapidly to events or tweets live.

has highlighted the 'fan club' effect which generates, retweets and further disseminates uploaded content. Digital media allows supporters to reuse and repackage material so that cyberpropaganda does not only circulate in its original state, but mutates as it spreads through networks of interest and participation. IS has also released a number of propaganda videos in which they have shown the killing by beheading of 5 US and British citizens and a number of Syrian government troops. This snuff-filmesque approach is designed to shock a core group of Islamist fanatics, particularly in the West to support a more hard-core version of Islamist ideology. Given the number of Western foreign fighters in Syria (many of which come from the US, Britain, France, Canada and so on), this propaganda strategy may actually be working. Their reality horror film recruitment video may actually tie into their watchers' deep desire for excitement and the need to be part of something powerful and identify meaning in their lives (see Baines *et al*, 2010). This shock value in turn may influence the degree to which something is shared and spread. There are also examples of the packaging of the material so that it is taken up by traditional media outlets, demonstrating these groups' prowess and mastery of what would now be termed 'spin-doctoring'.

Table 3. Cross Case Analysis Continued

Analysis Items	Al Qaeda	Islamic State	Boko Haram	Al Shabab
How local or global is the focus of the propaganda?	Global in context for explaining grievances and seeking recruitment. Regional in terms of Middle East change and revolution.	Global context for grievance (and possible spill-over to western targets), local focus for battle and territorial gain and control.	Focused largely on Nigeria, with an increasing reference to international Islamist agenda and organisations.	Formally aligned with Al Qaeda. Global recruitment, but a regional dynamics with African troops and neighbours.
What is the trajectory of the problem issue for the future?	A declining AQ influence involved in an intra-Islamist struggle with IS.	Sees itself as taking the lead from Al Qaeda in its attempt to control ground and form a Caliphate.	Continued insurgency in Nigeria with a view to establishing Islamist control, but with increasing possibility of internationalisation in West Africa.	Continued efforts to destabilise the region and exert Islamist control using terror tactics having withdrawn from major urban centres.

What Makes It Attractive to Those Who May Act on It?

It is possible to examine the attractiveness of communications in three ways. First is the degree to which it accords with the audience's worldview. Pious and religious messages will appeal to those exploring religious insight. An anti-western stance will be congruent with a population that is disposed to blaming the West for problems. This reflects the processes at work in the RAND study (Von Behr *et al.*, 2013). At a more social-psychological level is the interplay of poverty, excitement, boredom, escapism and fantasy that suggests a better or more fulfilling life is possible.

Second is the extent to which the media is nested in cultural norms. For example, it may be that young people are attracted to rap, video games and other aspects of youth culture that are transferrable to an Islamist context. They all adapt to their local customs (Al Shabaab with poetry, AQ with Indian-Pakistani enmity content, IS with Syria content) in a parasitic way. It is easy to concentrate on the aberrant nature of the communications: the execution of prisoners, threats of violence and religious extremism. However, there may be elements that reflect norms in the region. In part a greater willingness to show violence in new material or more subtly, in the case of IS's recruitment drive, this could be seen as part of the wider use of ex-patriots in the Middle East, with some GCC countries' populations being over 80% ex-patriot (CIA, 2014) - a figure that may be growing (*Emirates 24/7*, 2013). The ex-patriot populations are a smorgasbord of nationalities (Pretorius, 2013), with many Europeans also living there (Al Qassemi, 2013). From IS's point of view the recruitment drive may be as simple as any 'other' Gulf state wishing to harness the "benefits of foreign labour: foreigners provide a basic workforce as well as specialists to compensate for the limited number of nationals with required skills and attitudes..." (Kapiszewski, 2006). Of course, there are critical differences – it is unlikely that those recruited by IS are there to enjoy the benefits detailed by Kapiszewski (2006) such as better pay, conditions and career advancement. The point being that any analyses, and subsequent counter-propaganda campaign, should be aware of the wider regional norms, and not just concentrate on the aberrant aspects.

Third are the production values. Leaving Boko Haram aside, all cases show considerable effort and innovation in production values. All recognise the requirement to be timely with material during and after events. This gives the propaganda the salience of news.

How Local or Global is the Focus of the Propaganda?

Boko Haram would appear to be the case with the most local focus, though it is increasingly international in its reference to other groups. Of the four cases, Al Qaeda has been the most global, spreading its brand and having an impact across diverse geographical regions. However, it is Al Qaeda that has the weakest tie to geography in terms of its ability to control territory. Indeed it is often framed as Al Qaeda 'in' another country. At the time of 9/11, it was hosted in Afghanistan. Based on the concept of territorial control, the other three cases can be said to have a local focus. Indeed these cases can all trace their roots back to regional tensions and politics. The foreign fighter and anti-western stance has served to disguise the essentially local politics at work. For example, in the case of Boko Haram, the organisation's grievances are situated in a wider political and social discourse that polarises the Nigerian north and south, Christian and Muslim, distribution of wealth and beneficiaries and victims of corrupt practices.

What is the Trajectory of the Problem Issue for the Future?

Despite the regional nature of the problems described above, one can observe a continued internationalisation at work. In part, this is the desire to recruit foreign fighters and, in part, it is the spread of the grievance narrative (Holbrook, 2014) to ethnic and diaspora groups in other countries. In part, it is the nature of the internet-as-echo-chamber that coheres sympathetic views despite the geo-spatial distribution of the individuals who hold them. There is on one hand a desire to develop coherence between the Islamist groups, such that they become affiliates or aligned. On the other, there is the competition currently being played our between IS and Al Qaeda. There is clearly an important distinction between the propaganda conducted by IS and that of Al Qaeda. Some have suggested that the Al Qaeda brand is now dead (Keck, 2014), as a result of the turf war between AQ and Islamic State (Hubbard, 2014), a much more vicious Islamist variant. The leader of Al Qaeda central recommended that the leader of IS, Abu Bakr Al Baghdadi move out of Syria to allow AQ's affiliate there, Al Nusra Front, room for manoeuvre. This was a request that Al Baghdadi flatly turned down. IS has since assassinated a number of AQ figures sent as intermediaries to broker a joint agreement (Ackerman, 2014). The return of foreign fighters is currently exercising the security services of many countries, an example of the blurring of home and abroad through the movement of people and their ideas. There is a dynamic that presents challenges and opportunities for the policy-maker seeking to develop counter strategies. These will be explored next.

Implications: Cyber Counter-Propaganda Policy and Counter-Terrorism

The policy maker is confronted with five key interrelated problems in assessing how to respond to the questions above. First is the pressure of an 'action imperative'[6]. This pressure is characterised by the need to do something; something must be done when the problem is framed as a war, fight or struggle. To do otherwise is to allow an uncontested communication space to be dominated by an adversary or risk being labelled impotent. However, any action feeds the discourse by being interpreted by interested audiences through the lens of their own worldview. Second is whether to tackle symptoms or causes of the problems. In the context of counter-propaganda, this means whether to counter the message or narrative, rather than the problems driving the messaging or narrative. This is certainly harder to separate than it might first appear in the field of communications, as action taken to resolve a dispute also helps address some of the problematic messaging. Again, actions 'speak', or at least are sensed and interpreted.

Third is whether to treat the problems as essentially global or local. For example, to work as though all cases are part of the same problem, or to tackle each as a local manifestation. Fourthly, which audience should be the focus of attention, and how would one define or select it? Fifth, is the problem of how to make oneself heard.

To explore how these interrelated problems can surface in practice, let us consider the case of how to respond to IS propaganda. The output is often described in Western media as 'slick' and well-produced. There is a fear that it is working because one only needs to see the Western recruits appearing in the recruitment videos. Something must be done, because to do otherwise is to fail to stem the recruitment drive, or is tantamount to facilitating returning extremists. Should the focus therefore be on countering the message of recruitment, actions to identify and stop recruits returning or undermine the motives of those who might consider joining up in the first place? Should action be taken to inhibit the technical production and spread of extremist propaganda through the net? This would be with the aim of trying to disrupt the generative characteristics of the internet for production and reproduction of propaganda. Should this be part of the counter-propagandist approach, or someone else's job? Should it be simply left to the 'PR people' to deal with the message part? Clearly it can be taken as read that one would recommend a multi-stranded approach. Perhaps more usefully, one would recommend that all actions and communication be seen in the context of how they are interpreted for the purposes of countering propaganda. In the case of IS's supposedly 'slick' propaganda, it could potentially sap Western will whilst continuing to inspire recruits – the very thing the West does not want the Jihadi messaging to do because it praises the adversary and gives them credit, and causes a kind of paralysis in response, or worse a belief that it can be countered only with force. This, on the face of it, pursues the Jihadists' agendas through counter-productive aggression.

Therefore, let us accept that a multi-stranded approach needs to be pursued and that a number of audiences need to be addressed, and tensions resolved in the communications. One has to assess where energy and resources can best be directed. For example, if we take the echo-chamber idea where a potential recruit looks online for support to their pre-existing sympathies, it is notoriously difficult to change the minds of fans. Consequently, one might be drawn to persuading the friends and families of potential extremists to report their relative or friend to the authorities. This is difficult because it involves the authorities in the first place and potential sanctions against the relative or friend. Alternatively, one might persuade the friend or family member to act as someone who might persuade the potential extremist to not act on their sympathies. In this instance, the cognitive and social barriers may be easier to overcome, but one might not know if the suggested action is occurring. For the policy-maker, it is harder to show a metric of successful intervention.

Having selected an audience, it is important to communicate in a culturally resonant way and by ensuring consistency with the target audience's pre-existing beliefs. IS does this through emotional appeals packaged in ways that are attractive to their target audience, through piety, fun, congruence with grievances, production values and gaming themes. The policy-maker potentially needs to advocate the same but bureaucracies (certainly Western ones) usually avoid religious themes and opt for rationalistic rather than emotional appeals in their communications.

So what does this discussion mean for the four cases as a whole and policy implications? There are clearly home audiences, international audiences and in-theatre audiences that should be addressed; all also require a different treatment. Perhaps the easiest to advocate is a very locally relevant communication approach. Unfortunately for outside agencies, this is perhaps the hardest to implement, given the level of local knowledge, language ability and cultural understanding required. It necessarily drives a partnering approach with local agencies and an overhead in ensuring consistency between in-country messaging and that which feeds back through traditional media, online reporting and diaspora groups. It is tempting to treat the four cases at a global and general level for home and international audiences. Indeed, it is engaging such audiences that makes the policy-maker's strongest case in the eyes of the public that something is being done – when under 'action imperative' pressure. The line between the appearance of activity and effective intervention is hard to publicly discern but is clearly of central importance when trying to make a real difference to the problem situation.

In speaking to the home or international audience, it is unclear whether the collective effect of terrorist strategies is designed to goad the West into indifference or action against them. Western audiences find it hard to shake off the experiences of the decade or more in Afghanistan and Iraq. Indifference over time potentially allows each group to formulate plans to eventually co-ordinate, amass economies of scale and cohere. We see evidence of internationalisation between the cases; this is a frightening scenario. It indicates that all terrorist organizations should be targeted simultaneously, though not necessarily with equal resources, if the West is to be effective in its counter-messaging. To engage actively through force is to risk perpetuating the grievance and emotion, right or wrong, on which these terrorist campaigns feed. Communications therefore require somehow to establish the need for positive action from all audiences (perhaps other than the extremists themselves) whilst allowing space for accepting that direct military and law-enforcement action is sometimes required (when the extremist is not for changing). This will have to have both a rational and emotional base for each audience, perhaps without aiming to have consensus but an acceptance of a price to be paid for a lesser evil. It seems best to err on the side of the limits of what can be achieved than to hope for a fully committed mobilisation when one accepts the rational and emotional trade-offs involved in making the case. For example, it is likely that a family reporting a relative to authorities will do so with a heavy heart and a certain amount of fear.

The 'fan club' phenomenon, driven by authentic support or simply the sharing of controversial and ghoulish content, is technically problematic to stop. A concerted international effort in outlawing such material needs to be pursued, as well as persistent monitoring. The effort involved should not be underestimated, and it is likely that this will be a case of trying to manage rather than solve the problem. Consequently, trying to shape audiences' relationships with such material becomes as important, if not more so. On this issue alone, one might consider a range of audiences, from Internet Service Providers (ISPs) on the one hand to harnessing the power of concerned consumers on the other. One might also try to examine ways in which messaging can interrupt or disrupt the potential extremist at the moment of viewing in an early attempt to deter a move to action.

CONCLUSION AND FURTHER RESEARCH

The rather simple idea that there are home, international and local audiences is seductive, but it is a more complex mix when one takes into account for example, diaspora communities and online communities. We, therefore, recommend a nested counter-propaganda approach, where messages are consistent rather than contradictory in the global communications environment. The diaspora community will be acutely aware of the local drivers of an overseas conflict, but will live amongst people who have a generalised view of a rising Islamist violent extremist movement. The global and the local approach should be joined up. Most importantly, we recommend that each planned action in a multi-stranded approach should be checked through the lens of the counter-propagandist at an early stage – to align actions with words.

The increasingly internationalist claims made by extremist groups serves to legitimise their own ideology and to give an appearance of scale that breeds fear in its audiences. The escalation observed in the increasingly grizzly imagery is worrying. It is hard to assess what the ultimate effect is on audiences. Al Qaeda has allegedly had its own debate on the impact of beheadings with concerns that it was undermining support for the insurgency in Iraq (BBC, 2005). This strategy can backfire when videos are interpreted as showing a loss of humanity first and foremost. On the other hand, the echo-chamber effect, where people who are attracted to graphic violence are motivated to take action, presents a security challenge for those trying to keep the streets of their cities safe from knife-wielding extremists. Moreover, there may be a risk that those who take the most extreme action are seen as being the truest and most committed of actors. This may generate recruits with extreme violence in mind whilst over-shadowing the moderate voice or making it appear weak. The concern of Western counter-terrorism agencies and others studying propaganda/terrorism studies is therefore to ascertain how attractive this new variant of Islamist ideology actually is to their citizens, including Muslim converts, and to what extent it might inspire acts of terrorism. We recommend that further research to establish attractiveness and extent is prioritised by security agencies.

It is important that the voice of the moderate is amplified through emotional appeal and a radical sense of inter-faith and community dialogue and intolerance to violent extremism. Therefore, we recommend that counter-propagandists could advocate an approach that enhances the emotional appeal of messages, rather than simply a cold rationalistic and bureaucratic model. Timeliness and relevance to events and lived experiences is an important feature of tapping emotional appeal. Our case studies show that these are now consistent features of contemporary violent extremist propaganda. We suggest that policy-makers should continue to monitor and develop technical and other means to manage and disrupt the production and reproduction of propaganda through the internet. Further consideration of what the propaganda seeks to achieve, such as the aims of the recruitment drive of IS, should be undertaken to provide a foundation for further study. It appears to have the following objective: to recruit those already primed to their cause. This is suggestive of peer driven interventions in AIDS prevention. There appears to be parallels: a small group of 'primed' individuals who are made aware of interventions through public media and then 'recruited' by volunteers (Broadhead *et al.*, 1998). We recommend a more thorough examination of these parallels and how they could be used to better understand or counter propaganda.

Finally, policy-makers are encouraged to adopt an ambitious multi-stranded approach, but be realistic about the extent to which the audience's world-views can be radically changed. They should develop messages around the lesser of evils in addressing grievances. At the same time, they need to remain confident about their own values and to act in accordance with them. The battle of ideas between Western ideals and those of a minority of Islamist fanatics is taking place in a political marketspace and the sooner we research this important area, the more we can understand this phenomenon and why it's taking place. This, in our view, is a necessary antecedent in dealing with the problem of this dangerous new variant of Islamist terrorist ideology.

Disclaimer

The analysis, opinions and conclusions expressed or implied in this chapter are those of the authors and do not necessarily represent the views of the Joint Services Command and Staff College, the UK Ministry of Defence or any other government agency.

REFERENCES

Ackerman, S. (2014, October 2). Obama maintains Al-Qaida and Isis are 'one and the same' despite evidence of schism. *The Guardian*. Retrieved from http://www.theguardian.com/world/2014/oct/02/isis-al-qaida-obama-administration-argument-same-strikes-break

Abubakar, A. (2014). Boko Haram under scrutiny over foreign fighter claim. Retrieved from http://news.yahoo.com/boko-haram-under-scrutiny-over-foreign-fighters-claim-150350774.html

Adegbulu, F. (2013). Boko Haram: The emergence of a terrorist sect in Nigeria 2009-2013. *African Identities*, *11*(3), 260–273. doi:10.1080/14725843.2013.839118

Adibe, J. (2013). What do we really know about Boko Haram?. Mantzikos, I. (Ed.), *Boko Haram – Anatomy of a Crisis*. Retrieved from http://www.e-ir.info/wp-content/uploads/Boko-Haram-e-IR.pdf

Al Qassemi, S. (2013, November 21). The other special relationship: the UAE and the UK. *The National*. Retrieved from: http://www.thenational.ae/thenationalconversation/news-comment/the-other-special-relationship-the-uae-and-the-uk

Ali, L. (2014, September 22). Islamic State's soft weapon of choice: social media. *LA Times*, Retrieved from http://www.latimes.com/entertainment/la-et-islamic-state-media-20140922-story.html

Vanguard - Nigeria: Boko Haram leader vows to kill elder statesmen, others in new video. (2014). *Allafrica.com*. Retrieved from http://allafrica.com/stories/201402210294.html

Audu, O. (2014a, July 14). *Boko Haram leader, Shekau, mocks #BringBackOurGirls campaign. Premium Times.* Retrieved from https://www.premiumtimesng.com/news/164868-boko-haram-leader-shekau-mocks-bringbackourgirls-campaign.html

Audu, O. (2014b, February 20). Nigeria: Boko Haram Leader, Shekau, Speaks - Vows to attack Nigerian refineries, Buhari, Babangida, others. *Premium Times*. Retrieved from http://allafrica.com/stories/201402210198.html

Baines, P. R., O'Shaughnessy, N. J., Moloney, K., Richards, B., Butler, S., & Gill, M. (2010). The dark side of political marketing: Islamist propaganda, Reversal Theory and British Muslims. *European Journal of Marketing*, *44*(3/4), 478–495. doi:10.1108/03090561011020543

Profile: Abu Musab al-Zarkawi. (2005, November 10). *BBC News*. Retrieved from http://news.bbc.co.uk/1/hi/world/middle_east/3483089.stm

GCHQ's Robert Hannigan says tech firms 'in denial' on extremism. (2014a, November 4). *BBC News*. Retrieved from http://www.bbc.co.uk/news/uk-29891285

What is Islamic State? (2014b, September 26). *BBC News*. Retrieved from http://www.bbc.co.uk/news/world-middle-east-29052144

Nigeria kidnapped girls shown in Boko Haram video. (2014c, May 12). *BBC News*. Retrieved from http://www.bbc.co.uk/news/world-africa-27373287

Becker, O. (2014, July 12). ISIS Has a Really Slick and Sophisticated Media Department. *VICE News*. Retrieved from https://news.vice.com/article/isis-has-a-really-slick-and-sophisticated-media-department

Berger, J. M. (2011). *Jihad Joe: Americans Who Go to War in the Name of Islam*. Washington, DC: Potomac Books.

Berger, J. M. (2014, June 16). How ISIS Games Twitter. *The Atlantic*. Retrieved from http://www.theatlantic.com/international/archive/2014/06/isis-iraq-twitter-social-media-strategy/372856/

Bertram, S., & Ellison, K. (2014). Sub Saharan African terrorist groups' use of the internet. *Journal of Terrorism Research*, *5*, 1. Retrieved from http://ojs.st-andrews.ac.uk/index.php/jtr/article/view/825/704

Bolt, N. (2008). Propaganda of the deed and the Irish Republican brotherhood: From the politics of 'shock and awe' to the 'imagined political community'. *The RUSI Journal*, *153*(1), 48–54. doi:10.1080/03071840801984565

Broadhead, R. S., Heckathorn, D. D., Weakliem, D. L., Anthony, D. L., Madray, H., Mills, R. J., & Hughes, J. (1998). Harnessing peer networks as an instrument for AIDS prevention: Results from a peer-driven intervention. *Public Health Reports (Washington, D.C.)*, *113*(1), 42–57. Retrieved from http://www.ncbi.nlm.nih.gov/pmc/articles/PMC1307726/#reference-sec PMID:9722809

Cantril, H. (1941). *The Psychology of Social Movements*. New York: John Wiley and Sons Inc. doi:10.1037/13593-000

Carter, J. A., Maher, S., & Neumann, P. R. (2014). Greenbirds: Measuring Importance and Influence in Syrian Foreign Fighter Networks. London: ICSR, King's College London; Retrieved from http://www.google.co.uk/url?sa=t&rct=j&q=&esrc=s&source=web&cd=1&ved=0CCQQFjAA&url=http%3A%2F%2Ficsr.info%2Fwp-content%2Fuploads%2F2014%2F04%2FICSR-Report-Greenbirds-Measuring-Importance-and-Infleunce-in-Syrian-Foreign-Fighter-Networks.pdf&ei=_hxBVN3AF4fUat-LgpAG&usg=AFQjCNHRlI4cBTcsCJDeGMw55DKRZ6HhAg&sig2=T4r9hljxs4sW-dCJ_Uf4pA&bvm=bv.77648437,d.bGQ

Chiluwa, I. (2012). Social media networks and the discourse of resistance: A sociolinguistic CDA of Biafra online discourses. *Discourse & Society*, *23*(3), 217–244. doi:10.1177/0957926511433478

The World Factbook. (2014). *CIA*. Retrieved from https://www.cia.gov/library/publications/the-world-factbook/geos/ae.html

Cockburn, P. (2014, October 12). *War against Isis: US strategy in tatters as militants march on - Comment - Voices The Independent*. Retrieved from http://www.independent.co.uk/voices/comment/war-against-isis-us-strategy-in-tatters-as-militants-march-on-9789230.html?origin=internalSearch

Cocks, T. (2014, September 26). Boko Haram 'Leader', killed repeatedly, continue to threaten Nigeria, *Reuters*. Retrieved from http://uk.reuters.com/article/2014/09/26/uk-nigeria-bokoharam-idUKKCN0HL0BL20140926

Collins, M. (2014, May 9). #BringBackOurGirls: the power of a social media campaign. *The Guardian*. Retrieved from http://www.theguardian.com/voluntary-sector-network/2014/may/09/bringbackourgirls-power-of-social-media

Connable, B. (2014). Defeating the Islamic State in Iraq. Cambridge: RAND. Retrieved from http://www.rand.org/pubs/testimonies/CT418.html

Conway, M. (2007). Terrorism and New Media: The Cyber-battlespace. In J.J.F. Forest (Ed), *Countering Terrorism and Insurgency in the 21st Century*. Westport, CT: Praeger Publishers. Retrieved from http://psi.praeger.com/doc.aspx?newindex=1&q=Maura+Conway&imageField.x=7&imageField.y=15&c=&d=/books/gpg/C9036/C9036-3154.xml&i=0

Davidson, J. (2014, August 21). The ISIS Propaganda Machine Is Horrifying and Effective: How Does It Work? *Council for Foreign Relations*, Retrieved from http://blogs.cfr.org/davidson/2014/08/21/the-isis-propaganda-machine-is-horrifying-and-effective-how-does-it-work/?cid=soc-Facebook-in-propaganda_machine-081514

Dickie, J. (2012). *Mafia Brotherhoods: Camorra, Mafia, 'Ndrangheta: The Rise of the Honoured Societies*. London: Sceptre.

Dowd, R. A. (2014). Religious diversity and religious tolerance: Lessons from Nigeria. *The Journal of Conflict Resolution*. doi:10.1177/0022002714550085

UAE, Qatar have highest expat ratio in GCC. (2013, September 11). *Emirates 24/7*. Retrieved from: http://www.emirates247.com/news/emirates/uae-qatar-have-highest-expat-ratio-in-gcc-2013-09-11-1.520659

Evelage, B. S. (2012). Clarifying Boko Haram's transnational intentions, using content analysis of public statements in 2012. *Perspectives on Terrorism*, 7, 5. Retrieved from http://www.terrorismanalysts.com/pt/index.php/pot/article/view/291

Gladstone, B. (2014, June 20). Extremist social media. *On The Media*. Retrieved from: http://www.onthemedia.org/story/extremist-social-media/

Gourley, S. M. (2012). Linkages between Boko Haram and al Qaeda: A potential deadly synergy. *Global Security Studies*, *3*(3), 1–14.

Graham, G. (2013, October 18). British Muslims targeted in Al-Shabaab terror video are offered police protection. *The Telegraph*. Retrieved from http://www.telegraph.co.uk/news/10390026/British-muslims-targeted-in-Al-Shabaab-terror-video-are-offered-police-protection.html

Hansen, W. W., & Musa, U. A. (2013). Fanon, the Wretched and Boko Haram. *Journal of Asian and African Studies*. doi:0021909612467277.

Harper, M. (2014, February 26). Somali's Al Shabab: Striking like mosquitos. *BBC News*. Retrieved from http://www.bbc.co.uk/news/world-africa-26343248

Hashem, A. (2014, August). The Islamic State's social media strategy. *Al-Monitor*. Retrieved from http://www.al-monitor.com/pulse/originals/2014/08/is-clinton-atrocities-social-media-baghdadi-mccain.html

Holbrook, D. (2014). *The Al-Qaeda Doctrine: The Framing and Evolution of the Leadership's Public Discourse*. London: Bloomsbury.

Home Office. (2014). *Proscribed Terrorist Organisations*. London: UK Home Office. Retrieved from https://www.gov.uk/government/publications/proscribed-terror-groups-or-organisations--2#history

Hubbard, B. (2014, January 25). The franchising of Al Qaeda. *The New York Times*. Retrieved from http://www.nytimes.com/2014/01/26/sunday-review/the-franchising-of-al-qaeda.html?_r=0

IntelCenter. (2007, September 9). Al Qaeda Messaging Statistics. *Version 3.3*. Retrieved from: www.intelcenter.com

Kapiszewski, A. (2006). *United Nations Expert Group Meeting On International Migration and Development in The Arab Region. Arab Versus Asian Migrant Workers in The GCC Countries*. United Nations Population Division. Retrieved from: http://www.google.co.uk/url?sa=t&rct=j&q=&esrc=s&source=web&cd=2&cad=rja&uact=8&ved=0CCcQFjAB&url=http%3A%2F%2Fwww.un.org%2Fesa%2Fpopulation%2Fmeetings%2FEGM_Ittmig_Arab%2FP02_Kapiszewski.pdf&ei=cEFcVMHPGcbhaszPgsgL&usg=AFQjCNHnI32FnQn2B2wewOMGhTNMnoOidA&sig2=k4BTDNvZC9pJASWAgqTE5Q

Pretorius, R. (2013, August 17). A bit like attending college: departing expat looks back on his UAE experience. *The National*. Retrieved from: http://www.thenational.ae/thenationalconversation/comment/a-bit-like-attending-college-departing-expat-looks-back-on-his-uae-experience

Keck, Z. (2014, March 17). Al Qaeda's brand is dead. *The National Interest*. Retrieved from: http://nationalinterest.org/commentary/al-qaedas-brand-dead-10059?page=1

Killcullen, D. (2009). *The Accidental Guerrilla: Fighting Small Wars in the Midst of a Big One*. Oxford: Oxford University Press.

Kimmage, D. (2010, May). *Al Qaeda Central and the Internet*. Washington DC: New America Foundation. Retrieved from: http://homelandsecurity.gwu.edu/sites/homelandsecurity.gwu.edu/files/downloads/HSPI_Report_15.pdf, accessed 12th 2014.

Kingsley, P. (2014, June 23). Who is behind Isis's terrifying online propaganda operation? *The Guardian*. Retrieved from: http://www.theguardian.com/world/2014/jun/23/who-behind-isis-propaganda-operation-iraq

Le Bon, G. (1908). *The Sentiments and Morality of Crowds*. London: T Fisher Unwin. doi:10.1037/10878-002

Leymore, V. L. (1975). *The Hidden Myth*. New York: Basic Books.

Lee, D. (2014, August 20). James Foley: Extremists battle with social media. *BBC News*. Retrieved from: http://www.bbc.com/news/technology-28870777

Lewis, J. D. (2014, June 27). *ISIS Battleplan for Bagdhad*. Washington DC: Institute for The Study of War. Retrieved from http://www.understandingwar.org/press-media/staff-bios/jessica-d-lewis

Loimeier, R. (2012). Boko Haram: The development of a militant religious movement in Nigeria. *Africa Spectrum*, *47*(2/3), 137–155.

Lyons, D. K. (2013). Analyzing the effectiveness of Al Qaeda's online influence operations by means of propaganda theory (Master of Science Thesis). El Paso, TX, USA: The University of Texas, El Paso. Retrieved from http://academics.utep.edu/Portals/1892/Theses/Analyzing%20the%20Effectiveness%20of%20Al%20Qaeda%27s%20Online%20Influence%20Operations%20%28Lyons%29.pdf

Mardini, R. (2014, September 12). The Islamic State threat is overstated. *The Washington Post*. Retrieved from http://www.washingtonpost.com/opinions/the-islamic-state-threat-is-overstated/2014/09/12/acbbebb2-33ad-11e4-8f02-03c644b2d7d0_story.html,

Meleagrou-Hitchens, A., Maher, S., & Sheehan, J. (2012). Lights, Camera, Jihad: Al-Shabaab's Western Media Strategy. London: ICSR, King's College London. Retrieved from http://icsr.info/wp-content/uploads/2012/11/ICSR-Lights-Camera-Jihad-Report_Nov2012_ForWeb-2.pdf

Mohamed, H. (2014, January 9). Al Shabab bans internet in Somalia. *Al Jazeera*. Retrieved from http://www.aljazeera.com/news/africa/2014/01/al-shabab-bans-internet-somalia-20141981213614575.html

Monnet, B. (2014, May 21). Bring back our girls campaign giving free publicity to Boko Haram. *The Telegraph*. Retrieved from http://www.telegraph.co.uk/news/worldnews/africaandindianocean/nigeria/10847493/Comment-Bring-back-our-girls-campaign-is-giving-free-publicity-to-Boko-Haram.html

Nigerian Terrorism News Arena. (2014). Facebook.com. Retrieved from: https://wwww.facebook.com/NigerianTerrorismNewsArena

Okino, Z. S. (2014, March 19). Boko Haram: Is the military in false propaganda war? *Premium Times*. Retrieved from https://www.premiumtimesng.com/opinion/157016-boko-haram-is-the-military-in-false-propaganda-war-by-zainab-suleiman-okino.html

Osman, J. (2013, October 25). Al Shabaab: using social media to fight the jihad. *Channel 4*. Retrieved from http://www.channel4.com/news/al-shabaab-jihadist-kenya-westgate-kenya-nairobi-twitter

Propaganda. (n. d.). *Oxford Dictionaries*. Retrieved from http://www.oxforddictionaries.com/definition/english/propaganda

Phillips, A. (2014). The Islamic State's challenge to international order. *Australian Journal of International Affairs*, *68*(5), 495–498. doi:10.1080/10357718.2014.947355

Poster, M. (1988). *Jean Baudrillard: Selected Writings*. Palo Alto, CA: Stanford University Press.

Premium Times. (2014). Controversy trails new video claiming Boko Haram leader, Abubakar Shekau, is alive. Retrieved from: https://www.premiumtimesng.com/news/headlines/168948-controversy-trails-new-video-claiming-boko-haram-leader-abubakar-shekau-is-alive.html

Rakodi, C. (2012). Inter-religious violence and its aftermath: Insights from Indian and Nigerian cities. *Journal of Asian and African Studies*, *48*(5), 557–576. doi:10.1177/0021909612464339

Reuters, T. (2014, September 7). ISIS propaganda material turns up in Pakistan. *CBC News*. Retrieved from: http://www.cbc.ca/news/world/isis-propaganda-material-turns-up-in-pakistan-india-1.2758299

Rosen, A. (2014, August 15). ISIS Is Paying Attention to the experts. *Business Insider*. Retrieved from: http://www.businessinsider.com/isis-is-paying-attention-to-the-experts-2014-8

Rush, J. (2014, October 13). Horror of Kobani: Headless corpses left in the street and victims with their eyes 'cut out', the savagery of Isis laid bare. *The Independent*. Retrieved from http://www.independent.co.uk/news/world/middle-east/horror-of-kobani-headless-corpses-left-in-the-street-and-victims-with-their-eyes-cut-out-the-savagery-of-isis-laid-bare-9791199.html?origin=internalSearch, accessed 15th December 2014.

Saltman, E. M., & Winter, C. (2014). *Islamic State: The Changing Face of Modern Jihadism*. London: Quilliam Foundation.

Shane, S. (2014, August 30). ISIS Displaying a Deft Command of Varied Media. *New York Times*. Retrieved from http://www.nytimes.com/2014/08/31/world/middleeast/isis-displaying-a-deft-command-of-varied-media.html?hp&action=click&pgtype=Homepage&version=LedeSum&module=first-column-region&region=top-news&WT.nav=top-news&_r=2

Shashank, J. (2014, August 22). Islamic State: Biggest threat to United States? *BBC News*. Retrieved from http://www.bbc.co.uk/news/world-middle-east-28896348

Shinn, D. (2011). Al Shabaab's foreign threat to Somalia. *Orbis*, *55*(2), 203–215. doi:10.1016/j.orbis.2011.01.003

Nigeria: Boko Haram surge in capabilities & activity. (2014, April 1). *Soufan Group*. Retrieved from http://soufangroup.com/tsg-intelbrief-nigeria-boko-haram-surge-in-capabilities-activity/

Ulanoff, L. (2014 May 13). Boko Haram won't stop Nigeria's mobile revolution. *Mashable*. Retrieved from http://mashable.com/2014/05/13/nigeria-internet-kidnapped-girls/

'Barbaric' sexual violence perpetrated by Islamic State militants in Iraq. (2014). *UN News Centre*. Retrieved from http://www.un.org/apps/news/story.asp?NewsID=48477

United States Army Cyberspace Operations Concept Capability Plan 2016-2028. (2010). *Tradoc Pamphlet, 525-7-8*, 8. Retrieved from http://fas.org/irp/doddir/army/pam525-7-8.pdf

Department of Defense Press Briefing by Secretary Hagel and General Dempsey in the Pentagon Briefing Room. (2014). Defense.gov Transcript. Retrieved from http://www.defense.gov/transcripts/transcript.aspx?transcriptid=5491

US State Department. (n. d.). *Foreign Terrorist Organisations*. Retrieved from http://www.state.gov/j/ct/rls/other/des/123085.htm

Velleman, J. D. (2000). *The Possibility of Practical Reason*. New York: Clarendon Press.

VICE. (2014, August 15). *The Islamic State (Full Length)*. *VICE News*. Retrieved from https://news.vice.com/video/the-islamic-state-full-length

Von Behr, I., Reding, A., Edwards, C., & Gribbon, L. (2013). *Radicalization in the Digital Era: The Use of the Internet in 15 Cases of Terrorism and Extremism*. Cambridge: RAND.

Winkler, C., & Dauber, C. E. (Eds.). (2014). *Visual Propaganda and E-extremism in the Online Environment*. US Army War College Press & Strategic Studies Institute. Retrieved from http://permanent.access.gpo.gov/gpo51688/pub1213.pdf

ENDNOTES

¹   Search terms used include: 'Iraq ISIS', 'Islamic State of Iraq and Levant', 'IS', 'Deash', 'ISIL'.

²   Using same search terms as in footnote iii above.

³   IS propaganda can be found at: https://archive.org/. Examples include 'documentary 'Flames of War', the *Islamic State Report* (Issues 1-4), the IS newsletter, *Dabiq* (two issues, including 'The Khilafah' and 'The Flood').

⁴   For example, the discussion at http://www.nairaland.com/1871323/boko-harams-latest-propaganda-war accessed 3 October 2014 rehearses themes of evidence, doubt over whether events actually took place or are subject to biased reporting.

⁵   'Send Me a Cruise' debuted online on April 9, 2011. Hummami was eventually killed by Al-Shabaab in 2013 in an internal dispute.

⁶   'Action imperative' is a term most associated with hostage negotiation techniques – 'the pressure that compels police departments to take any action to get things going' (Noesner 1999:9), regardless of whether or not it is the right thing to do.

Chapter 14
Thinking Systemically about Security and Resilience in an Era of Cybered Conflict

Peter Dombrowski
US Naval War College, USA

Chris C. Demchak
US Naval War College,USA

ABSTRACT

The international system now depends on cyberspace, a global 'substrate' of massive, complex, insecurely designed networks providing systemic advantages to masses of predators and adversaries. States today face an unprecedented spectrum of 'cybered conflict' between peace and war with growing existential implications. Their piecemeal searches for defensible jurisdictions are creating a rising Cyber Westphalian world crisscrossed with gateways, holes, national cyber forces, and often partial, uncoordinated, or vague strategies. Over time, the world will have robust, midlevel, and poor cyber powers, with the first tier coercing the others and dominating the rules of exchange. Democratic civil societies are not guaranteed to be robust. For acceptable future societal well-being in a deceptive and opaque cybered world, decision-makers need a systemic approach based on the logic of complex socio-technical-economic systems (STES) to create the systemic resilience and disruption capacities across shareable (across allies/sectors) secure architectures essential to becoming a robust cyber power, which is the focus of this chapter.

INTRODUCTION

Cyber war is not coming (Arquilla and Rondfeldt 1993), but 'cybered conflict' is. For decades we have been warned of the possibility of digital Pearl Harbors (Wilson 2008) where network attacks lead to cascading failures of critical military, public and private systems. Recently, there has been a backlash against the shrillest warnings about cyber war. Contrarians now argue that cyber war not only hasn't occurred but is highly unlikely (Rid 2012). They point to the absence of cyber "battle deaths" to date and

DOI: 10.4018/978-1-4666-8456-0.ch014

the immense difficulty of using cyber weapons for political and military purposes. Botnets and malware can disrupt service and lead to lost data but these are expensive nuisances rather than acts of war. Truly dangerous attacks, targeting, for example, the SCADA systems of military facilities or public utilities while potentially destructive, require exquisite intelligence and dedicated teams of hackers-- capacities beyond the means of most nation-states much less terrorists or common criminals.

Yet worrying about cyber war and arguing about whether it can occur or not misses something important about the contemporary security environment much less the future. Our communications networks and computer are vulnerable. Everyday new reports come of possible Russian attacks on Ukrainian websites; retail stores losing the personal data of customers to criminals, and next generation weapons allegedly developed using stolen engineering specifications. Adversaries of all sorts will seek to influence outcomes by accessing and altering both the systems themselves and the data that resides within. From hot shooting wars to spying by peacetime rivals much of the action now takes place within computer networks. The damage may be financial or reputational but the costs are real. For militaries, boots on the ground and ordinance on targets may be the ultimate determinants of victory, but to deploying soldiers in the field or launching missiles on now requires the secure, accurate, and timely flow of information.

The computer and telecommunications systems that comprise the backbone of modern militaries are both linked to, and part of, cyberspace. Even data encryption, the creation of closed systems and the establishment of air gaps between critical computer systems and outside networks have proved unreliable defensive measures against some advanced persistent threats (Singer and Friedman 2014: 55-60). As such hostile actors can disrupt and perhaps even destroy military systems in crises and wartime using techniques, tactics and procedures similar to those (but not limited to) used against private citizens, commercial firms and civilian government agencies.

If this isn't war, what is it? In this chapter we argue that the globe is enduring a period of cybered conflict in which states (including military organizations, intelligence agencies, and law enforcement), firms, and criminal are using cyberspace as a convenient medium for spying, attacking, and stealing from other entities reliant on computer and communications networks—that is virtually every social organization in the information age.

We conclude that, from the standpoint of nation-states (and social organizations in general), analyses of the security threats posed in and by "cyberspace" should adopt a systemic approach adapted from the logic of complex socio-technological systems (STES) (Trist 1980). Since such systems are "patterns of artifacts, institutions, rules and norms assembled and maintained to perform economic and social activities" (Berkhout, Smith, and Stirling 2003), scholars, policy-makers, and strategists needs to think through how emerging technologies from 3D printing to autonomous private vehicles to adoption of materials like grapheme will change those patterns (Manyika, Chui, et al 2013). Many arguments about how to respond to the security challenges posed by cyberspace taking place today in the government and policy communities are characterized by hype, false or misleading analogies (Betz and Stevens 2013; Goldman and John Arquilla 2014), and, worse, misunderstandings of the technical, engineering and scientific underpinning of critical terms and concepts. Instead, the conversations should be about how computer and communications are being penetrated and data is being lost, corrupted or stolen on a vast scale, and the harm done to victim societies as a whole. The focus of decision-makers must be to design and develop architectures—both technical and institutional—that can survive and prosper in the face of near constant attacks and evolving threats. To complicate matters, emergent technologies, sometimes labeled as disruptive technologies (Christensen 1997), may change the calculus, some reducing scale, proximity, and precision necessary for both bad actors and good to conduct offensive and defense cyber operations at any time (Pierce 2005; Dombrowski and Gholz 2006).

DEFINING CYBERED CONFLICT IN THE CYBER 'SUBSTRATE'

In contrast to common or conventional usage, we believe that cyberspace is not a "domain" but a 'substrate'. The cyber 'substrate' is then underlying layer on which modern, information age society is increasingly built and sustained. Cyberspace as a substrate implies that it intersects with and underlies all other productive dimensions of human society—increasingly economic growth, technological innovation, scientific exploration, commercial vitality and all forms of communications depend upon the networks of networks. It is now a socio-technical-economic system (STES) with unprecedented national and international significance.

Cyberspace also has a topology that is largely (surprisingly to some) territorial (Blum 2012). One reason that cyberspace is in fact not strictly a 'domain' as some suggest is that it is an environment—imagined, created, developed, sustained, and extended by human intentions and actions. One implication of cyberspace's being a completely human built environment is that it can be unbuilt, remodeled, and perhaps in an extreme case even destroyed (say, by electromagnetic pulse), at least temporarily and within spatial limits.

As a global substrate, cyberspace plays a major role in any competition or conflict among states and non-state actors. Its complexity and scale make it both vulnerable to widespread disruptions and yet still relatively resilient as a global phenomenon. The underlying design features of cyberspace and its inherent value to government and commercial actors both contribute to this resilience. Despite widespread accidents and technical breakdowns and various forms of attacks, destroying this substrate is neither acceptable to governments nor desirable to the host adversaries who use cyberspace for their operations. This shared need to at least keep cyberspace functional at basic levels for oneself makes power in, though, or enabled by cyberspace all the more valuable for adversaries or competitors. The substrate is today in effect the technological 'high ground' in any organized struggle, not only for the military and intelligence services but also government, civilian, and commercial sectors as well.

Cybered Conflict. Cyberspace is not then a separate conflict space or host to a particular type of conflict (Dombrowski and Demchak 2014). Cybered conflict occurs along a spectrum that includes conflicts from large to small—total war, small wars, wars of choice, and a host of others. It also hosts hostile actions by disgruntled citizens, criminals (Deibert 2012:265-266), pirates, and, occasionally perhaps, terrorists. In the next twenty years, the tools for attacking and defending in cyberspace will become so ubiquitous that we prefer to use the adjective "cybered," since "cyber" is likely to be taken for granted and abandoned. In the meantime, cyberspace is changing how governments and their militaries and non-state actors fight wars and conflicts. Organizing and operating in joint, interagency, and combined (with friends, partners, and allies) terms for cybered conflicts are not only sensible but strategically and operationally essential for success.

Conflict involving cyber operations will neither stay wholly within networks nor prove over time to be a fad or simply a subset of existing tactical, operational, and technological categories. From either empirical or conceptual perspectives, cybered conflict is neither; it has already proven to be an evolutionary force slowly altering the likely future conditions for interstate competition and potential for kinetic forms of battle. Scholars, analysts, and, most important, operators need to think systematically about how cyber operations-- offensive and defensive if that distinction still makes sense-- affect tactics, operations, and strategies.

THINKING SYSTEMICALLY ABOUT SECURITY IN CYBERSPACE

All societies need in principle to recognize and prepare systemically for the inevitability of "normal" accidents (Perrow 1999) involving their large-scale complex systems (Simon 1962). But the globally open, easy to use cyberspace substrate has added at least two more layers of challenging sources of 'accidents' deliberately imposed by bad actors using the complexity of these systems to harm their users. In the modern deeply cybered world, nations dependent on such critical systems must also guard against "fifth columnists" from within (Farahmand and Spafford 2013; Moore, Cappelili, Andres and Carroll 2008) and enemies seeking to sabotage from without. Further, espionage, whether military and commercial, may not endanger a private firm or a military organization in the short-term, but will likely have long-term consequences. Stolen intellectual property and data related to military planning and weapons system, or the presence of spyware lurking inside critical systems waiting to act until a crisis or the maximum point of advantage may weaken the target organization and potentially lead to catastrophic consequences in extremis.

Achieving institutional resilience is the research focus of scholars in the field of surprise and large-scale complex socio-technical systems. They have developed recommendations for systemic resilience both for individual firms (and other social organizations such as government agencies) and across firms/organizations in networked into critical infrastructures. For the large firm or organizations, individually, three adaptive responses to complexity in general are essential for resilience: (1) assuring redundancy in knowledge at the points of surprise (not mere replication), (2) using slack in time to prepare for "surprises" that are unknowable in advance, and (3) continuously pursuing trial and error learning across the enterprise. Cyber experts might draw upon a related, albeit indirectly, body of scholarship associated with the international national security studies literatures on strategic, military and intelligence surprise (Betts 1983; Knorr and Morgan 1982; Gooch and Perlmutter 2007). Other research by the authors looks more systematically at the intersection of the socio-technical systems literature on surprise and that of security studies scholars; one clear connection is the intersection between defense planning and the need for architectural design to increase the resilience and security of socio-technical systems.

When firms or other organizations are conjoined by telecommunications and computer networks, developing institutional resilience to surprise imposes additional requirements. . Networked firms/organizations need to prepare in advance for disruptions to parts or the whole of the network by (1) developing robust collective sense-making processes, (2) preparing for rapid collective mitigation, all the while investing in innovative forward adaptations. Even were there no globally open cyberspace substrate, the possibility of devastating 'normal accidents' in complex systems still stand and increase with the complexity and criticality of the STESs involved. Recent research by systems engineers argue that resilience in digitized networks stems from the creation of defensive measures that ensure the following: the detection of intrusions/threats that defeat defensive measures, the remediation of harm caused by the intrusion, and, finally, the recovery of the affected system to return it to it "normal," unaffected state (Cetinkaya and Sterbenz 2013). Of course, recovery is not the end of the process if resilience is the ultimate goal: organizations seeking to protect their systems also establish recursive feedback loops to refine the defensive measures that were defeated in the first place to ensure that future attacks are not as successful.

The emergence of cyberspace adds two even more challenging layers of potential systemic threats on top of these two basic layers - the individual enterprise and the network of connected enterprises. First, because the global substrate is, today, relatively open and easily abused, there is third layer formed by a worldwide community of bad actors threatening STESs by reaching across cyberspace. For this layer of surprise to complex systems, the literature is still being written, but scholarship on information systems and complexity theory suggest two basic ways to combat external cyber threats: (1) increasing the difficulty of accessing networked targets (i.e., obstacles to intrusion) or increasing the ability of the targeted networks to resist harm (i.e., transforming the basic technologies with security in the design at the outset). From our perspective, this is not simply a technical challenge best left to engineers and network scientists, but also a social challenge with political and national security dimensions. As nation-states assert their sovereignty and thus authority over cyberspace, they will both need to protect their own networks (civilian and military) and, we believe, play a greater role in defending commercial and other private systems generally. Democratic and capitalist imperatives tend to assure that over time most non-authoritarian, civil society regimes eventually respond to citizen and business pressure to guard personal data and intellectual property while ensuring the functionality of the shared cyber substrate by which all modern systems may effectively and accountably function.

In some respects, currently, the organic evolution of cyberspace itself is undermining the ability of organizations, whether public or private, to increase the difficulty of accessing targeted systems. For example, the rise of the so-called "internet-of-things" (IoT) complicates security efforts to prevent malicious cyber activities. It is an umbrella term covering "various aspects related to the extension of the Internet and the Web into the physical realm, by means of the widespread deployment of spatially distributed devices with embedded identification, sensing and/or actuation capabilities" (Morianda, Scicrib, De Pellegrina, and Chlamtaca 2012). In theory, connecting everything allows bad actors to penetrate even more deeply into target systems. Not only are individuals connected but machines in-creasingly talk automatically and opaquely to other machines while both computer processors and a growing range of sensors are deeply embedded in material things ranging from household appliances to SCADA devices controlling vast enterprises. The proliferation of connectivity, sensors, and analytics are already allow "big data" to reshape social life, commercial transactions and business models, as well as, perhaps, democratic politics as we understand them. But it will also introduce new vulnerabilities, perhaps poorly understood, that bad actors might exploit. Much of today's cyber hygiene regimes target toward on human operators; soon they will need to focus more intensively on designs and architectures that opaquely and deeply link the critical physical, economic, and social equipment of daily life to the global cyber substrate.

The second additional layer of systemic threats imposed by cyberspace is a very special subset of the preceding massive volume of bad actors – the 'wicked' actors. This smaller but individually much more powerful group poses a final type pf potential surprise, the sort of systemic challenges that could, at least in theory, disrupt or destroy important socio-technical economic systems of all sorts. While most bad actors are low or moderately skilled programmers more akin to opportunists than dedicated computer savvy adversaries,, the 'wicked actors' (Demchak 2012) are top 5-15 percent of the bad actors cyber community extraordinarily highly skilled, organized, and able to operate deceptively and opaquely across all four layers. We use wicked actors based on the concept of wicked problems in mathematics. Wicked actors are unlikely to be deterred by most resilience measures, usually able to penetrate more defenses deeply, and their operations are extremely difficult to counter. . Most are well paid employees of states, their proxies, or transnational criminal organizations, not individually income insecure and prone to find the challenge of the penetration a key part of their satisfaction in operating. This group includes the clearly –state-sponsored 'advanced persistent threat' (APTs) because, unlike the mass of criminal bad actors who will abandon tough defenses, wicked actors keep trying to succeed in penetrating networks over time. They will patient wait to find a zero-day flaw or perhaps gathering small bits of intelligence that may, over time, benefit their employers. Wicked actors are able, if not disrupted preemptively, to roam freely across all layers and pose, eventually, the most persistent and potential threats, even when and if the vast numbers of less threatening, nuisance level bad actors are reduced and discouraged over time by systemic resilience. .

It is important to note that the challenges to socio-technical economic systems posed by the global cyber substrate are not just a problem facing nation-states or governments. Systemic resilience and the capacity for forward disruption are not only key for governments in protecting their societies; they are now accepted as critical capabilities for corporations. The recommendations of scholars of STES surprise regarding resilience have been roughly validated by the experiences and conclusions of senior leaders in nongovernment organizations experiencing attacks and intrusions of bad and wicked actors as well. In early 2014 a report by the World Economic Forum and the McKinsey & Company surveyed over 200 major global firms who largely responded that they cannot individually keep up with the assaults on their systems, knowledge, and productive resources. Given the survey responses, the report estimated the cumulative costs to be over three trillion dollars globally. . The report's authors then observed that commercial enterprises were turning to a new model, one we would recognize as a STES model of systemic cyber resilience. In this model, the following seven key requirements were identified: information assets prioritization based on risks, differentiated protection of these assets according to their business critical-ity, the normalization of security concerns as a key factor into all decisions to reduce the scale of threat vectors, continuous testing of incident responses, integration of 'cyber-resistance' into all governance and management processes, socializing frontline members to value and protect information assets, and the deployment of active defenses to proactively uncover attacks as early as possible in their life cycle (Chin, Kaplan and Weinberg 2014). The first six recommendations point to systemic resilience and the last to the need for some capacity to reach forward and preempt some attacks before their initiation or at the earliest point at which they can be discerned.

We therefore conclude that the threats of cyberspace to the embedded critical systems have brought both nations and enterprises to the same challenges of creating a systemic response to significant cyber surprise. To maintain and defend the well-being of large complex socio-technical-economic systems must involve an array of reconceptualizations, tools, and institutional evolutions. For example, the twentieth century notion of a 'rogue community' needs reconceptualization for a cybered world. In the traditional sense, a rogue state was one that wreaked havoc for gain and with impunity before withdrawing behind unassailable walls or water. If a victim city, state, or clan survived and could locate the marauders, they strove to go to war and end the threat. Generally, before the 20th century, most aggrieved victim com-munities resorted to resilient measures, especially using granaries, and cisterns for redundancies, and walls, plus harbor and hill alert systems for warnings in time. Today, in a similar fashion, bad actors en masse impose that uncertainty and lack of foreknowledge experienced historically by the sudden rogue community attacks. Now, the bad actors are able to accomplish globally and minute by minute from distant hidden locations using unknown tools what the 10th century Vikings did only seasonally. The modern marauders succeed with impunity through the exceptionally fast, remote, deceptive, and opaque use of the complexities of cyberspace. Unfortunately, most of history's 'rogue states', including the recent forty years of the internationally controlled world of the Cold War, seem in comparison, exceptionally largely obvious, well identified, and unimpressively geographically bound.

The conceptualizations, tools, and institutions developed especially over the Cold War are not directly helpful with today's bad actor states or communities. For the targeted cybered enterprise or state, the threats can come en masse from any direction at any time. In the Cold War, war was war and peace was peace, and conflicts between states involved easily recognized kinetic weapons, territory, largely known adversaries and distance (generally). The rules of interstate behaviors were developed and enforced by the more kinetically powerful modern civil societies who wrote and promoted the Geneva Convention and the law of armed conflict. In the emerging cybered conflict age, the lack of foreknowledge and clarity is systemically more medieval than postmodern. War is at the end of a spectrum that is not measurable. What appears to be peace can also be a period when the society's systems are being deceptively and opaquely hollowed from the inside by masses of rogue actors. What are in effect the hidden state-disrupting weapons of rogue states look like the tools of innovative economic growth as well.

WHAT CAN BE DONE? DEFINING THE SYSTEMIC NEED FOR RESILIENCE IN A CYBERED WORLD

For most institutions including nation-states, developing cyber disruption defenses and systemic resilience are the keys (Comfort, Boin, and Demchak 2010). With all the attention paid to high profile attacks like Stuxnet, it is sometimes difficult to remember that the most effort—in terms of time, manpower, technology and money— is put into developing defensive systems able to survive well against the vast flood of less well skilled, but no less cumulatively debilitating intrusions. Firewalls, anti-virus programs, cryptographic techniques and the like play important roles in maintaining functionality. Even as this chapter is being written, hardware from submarine cables to data farms is being hardened. The designers of the newest military systems such as the HACMS mini-drone even claim to have created a "hack proof" operating system with software "mathematically" protected against adversaries attempting to seize control of the weapon (Osborne 2014). Regardless of whether those claims are true, the fact that there is a logical commercial demand for hack-proof platforms is evidence of the worries of defense planner, whether in government or in a large enterprise.

Today, both governments and firms are trying to develop the tools, training, tactics, and procedures necessary to protect data, software and hardware against a wide array of known and as yet unseen threats. . . The lack of adequate nationally systemic defenses so far is widespread. When retired General Alexander warned of the "greatest transfer of wealth in human history," he was not referring to a single incident, event or failure. .Rather, he was describing the cumulative impact of hidden penetrations taking place over the course of years into the critical, value-producing data of commercial systems and the nationally sensitive, critical infrastructure and defense government systems. Based on the enormous range of proposals in strategies, technologies, and institutional change being widely distributed today, it is an open question, however, whether the necessary reconceptualizations, new basic technologies, and institutional developments are emerging spontaneously. Without all three, it is not clear that resilience can be built, architectures improved, and material investments made quickly enough to prevent a catastrophic failure, or to mitigate the more likely, proverbial death by a thousand cuts described by Alexander.

In this section, we argue that a systemic approach is necessary to understand how nations need to develop their socio-technical-economic systems (STES) into vibrant, resilient national architectures adapting over time to the globally changing cyberspace substrate. While "hack-proof" single platforms offer some help to those who buy and use them, such in-place defenses of course are not enough. Given the stakes involved and motivations of hackers, it is inevitable that new Zero Day exploits will be employed, new malware will be developed, and internal threats from formerly trusted agents will emerge. The enemy will get through. But when telecommunications and computing systems are inevitably damaged, they must already have evolved systemically to be able to recover quickly. This means building in redundancy and avoiding single points of failure, but it also means having talented, well-trained personnel capable of responding quickly to repair, restore and rebuild.

Rethinking the open, unfettered, near-free structure of the global cyberspace substrate is fundamental to a systemic response to the challenges of the emerging cybered conflict. This reconceptualization is happening across states, their leaders, and the corporate commercial world, but the proposals do not suggest a clear understanding of what has changed over the past 25 years. Today the current and expanding basic technological architecture links strangers with the ability to harm others to the means and the opportunity with little or no personal risk and possibly much to gain. Responses by states need to address the ability of the current cyberspace substrate architecture to intrinsically vastly and systemically diminish three major obstacles to offense: the scale of organising effective attacks, the proximity required to gather critical intelligence, and the costs of precision in targeting and retargeting broadly. Unlike most of human history, today's bad actor, organization, or government may organize like-minded strangers on a large scale, to reach across large geographic distances for information or access, and then to attach a victim's society or well-being at will or under control with varying levels of precision in attack harm, timing, repetition, and skills. With these three advantages, operations are remarkably low cost, low risk, and widely reusable for anyone who has time and internet access, producing a very modern form of democratised predation (Finkle 2010).

Furthermore, if the bad actors ensure two additional attributes- the deception (in tools and techniques) and opaqueness (of their own or community identities and locations), the three systemic advantages are systemically much more useful for states or non-state organisations alike. Both attributes are essential. Deception matters because the tools exploit ignorance of insecurities. Cybered tools are not like tanks which still work even if seen. Once the tool's exploitation method is known, they may not work at all given the corrective responses of the likely targets. Opaqueness is especially important because a revealed aggressor could easily be the victim of equally deceptive and opaque campaigns in return or even attacked pre-emptively by aggrieved targets, proxies, and allies.

These five systemic components then – scale, proximity, precision, deception, and opaqueness are the challenges that nations and enterprises must systemically considering designing their national architectures for a world of cybered conflict. For example, of the three offense advantages, the near elimination of proximity as a problem in particular helps adversaries or their proxies both physically far from victims and also far from suspicion. Unlike the pre-cybered past eras n which conflict was at least generally observable, cybered conflict leaves few 'smoking guns' to provide an easy association with a state level actor who might be forced to accept responsibility by, say, a threat of war. In 2014, Russia moved to simply absorb the Crimea from a sovereign state, the Ukraine. During the first weeks of what was clearly conflict, had the Ukraine been devastated by massive and successfully cyber-attacks, no amount of denial would have kept the world from blaming Russia directly. Instead, cybered events during the first weeks only slowly increase, none devastating, and by the third week or so, there were large attacks but these were not clearly attached to Russia. By then, Russian leaders could argue it was nationalistic teenagers or something, and thus deflect the responsibility from themselves and their nation.

Even relatively active cybered states attempt to maintain both deception and opaqueness in order to avoid losing good tools or access, and risking equally deceptive or opaque retributions by victims or third parties participating just because they can. To date, no active cybered state is willing to forego the advantages of deception and opaqueness by unilaterally publicly announcing campaigns, and incurring the wide range of potential blowback costs. The number of states with national cyber strategies is rising, but few suggest their nation would actively and publicly engage in such operations in retribution. Yet many of the same nations are developing 'active defence', which entails reaching back at cyber aggressors, however vaguely defined. Buried amidst a wide variety of legal prohibitions and surveillance systems across governments and markets, an enormous volume of other bad actors attempt to stay unidentified and unhindered in their use of the scale, proximity, and precision advantages.

What is to be done also involves systemically reconceptualising the power of a nation. It rests more and more on cybered capacities closely tied to a nation's abilities to systemically secure a wide range of vulnerable public and private sectors critically dependent on a highly insecure cyberspace substrate. National security increasingly means national leaders must more explicitly play a key role in ensuring the wider systemic well-being by enabling the cybered security of the critical, internal socio-technical-economic systems (STESs). Responding to the five challenges, the robust cyber power needs to be both resilient to the masses of unskilled 'bad actors' assaulting across societies with botnets and malware, and also able to legally and proportionately disrupt the smaller but highly skilled set of organised hackers, i.e., the 'wicked' actors generally only employed by states or transnational organisations.

For the defender, resilience is important for national power in a cybered world. Since the underground cybercrime black market attackers form the vast majority of these threats, the rise of obstacles, especially national cybered borders, is a logical consequence of national needs to reduce the efficacy of these assaults. The gradual rise of national jurisdictions in a future 'Cyber Westphalia' interstate system is already apparent in trends seen from democratic civil societies to those more autocratic nations which would have been interested in having such virtual borders anyway. These cyber borders are a part of resilience but not all of it. Means of reducing the flood of easy, low cost attacks must be designed into the nation's or enterprise' internal STES architectures as well to reduce the scale, proximity, precision, deception, and opaqueness advantages now freely available to massive volumes of threats from external or internal sources.

In addition to systemic national resilience, and importantly for potential retribution or countermeasures among states, cybered national power for a defender must be designed to have a second component aimed at disrupting the highly skilled proxies or actors of other states, for whom the virtual borders stopping the masses are not effective deterrence. Disruption needs to be proportional and legal, but able to discern and derail these 'wicked' actors who deftly use camouflage, cover, and the tools of the cyberspace substrate. States may take a 'free ride' on their mass of bad actors undertaking 'patriotic hacking'-- this is the term for state tolerance of otherwise illegal hacking as long as the victims are outside the state's geographic borders or those of close allies-- for objectives including economic extractions for market advantage or intelligence for future political, economic, or even military leverage. However, they actively employ the wicked actors for a wide variety of cybered conflict advantages from leverage to economic attrition, or even to wage a 'counter resilience' campaign against other states. The national STES architectures creating robust cyber power will have to develop legal tailored disruptive capacities to reach and change the key elements of the wicked actors' business models and calculations of efficacy and personal risk away for their currently persistent and often successful operations.

A nation's cyber power relative to other states in the future is being built now by the efforts made during this transition era to develop national systemic resilience and forward disruption capacities. It is already difficult to keep up the level of resources needed over the next fifteen to twenty years to anticipate and secure against potentially hundreds of thousands of unidentified bad actors using unknown or unpatched exploits, and to develop the tailored, well skilled, targeted disruption capabilities needed. The open unfettered cyberspace allows for the obscured hollowing out of a nation's economic resources, often over years, and without it seeming to be extensive enough to be dangerous or deliberate enough to require national level responses. Over time, if nothing happens to alter and defend the STES architectures of a victimized state or enterprise the economic resources of either decline, as do the abilities of policy makers or leaders to be able to afford to act systemically in defence of all vulnerable integrated and critical elements or communities. Much more needs to be done.

A TURBULENT FUTURE?

Mastering cybered conflict will be a long and likely painful process. Technologies evolve rapidly; developing defensive and resilient institutions remains a game of catch up. States will try to regulate and govern but will often fail or get things wrong. Gains to be made from cyber exploits—whether stealing intellectual property or disabling military equipment used for in a shooting war or deceiving publics with misinformation transmitted over social media—are simply too great for ambitious generals, corporate buccaneers, and greedy criminals to resist.

Developments in 2013 and 2014, unfortunately, emphasize the high stakes, conflict-ridden nature of the process reaching a modus vivendi over how to govern the global cyber substrate. At a bilateral level, China and the United States are locked in a show-down over cyber-espionage and international property rights that may have long-term implications for the military balance between the two great powers. Great power politics might slow or even stop, at least in the short run,

Even more broadly, the revelations of National Security Agency (NSA) contractor Edward Snowden have greatly complicated multilateral negotiations over the future of internet governance. Few if any governments are comfortable with the news that the NSA systematically spies on them and their citizens, often without the knowledge of their own political leaders or intelligence agencies much less the general publics. Problems are particularly acute within the western alliance. Even before the Snowden transatlantic difference over privacy, data protection and business regulation had made for contentious commercial negotiations between the European Union and the United States; Snowden appeared to confirm the worst fears of some Europeans, not just about the commercial implications of how cyberspace is governed but also how US intelligence agencies exploited advanced technologies (Kerry 2014).

On the other hand, however, we are witnessing ongoing multilateral negotiations within a number of fora that may yet prove productive both in governance terms and, with regard to the concerns of this chapter, cyber security on a global scale. The process of developing secure and resilient socio-technical institutions in the information age will parallel and intertwine with the process of establishing cyber borders and thus states' sovereignty over cyberspace (Demchak an Dombrdowski 2011; Maher 2013). Elsewhere we have argued that establishing a Cyber Westphalian international system "will be nonlinear, dangerous, and lengthy" (Dombrowski and Demchak 2014). During the transition, the technical, institutional, and cultural weaknesses of states will be exploited by amoral or criminal individuals, 'wicked' actors, unethical or ignorant firms, terrorists (Weimann 2005; Dunn-Cavelty 2008) and criminal syndicates as well as states not fully committed to an emerging international rule set. The lack of linear predictability will force most states to seek more predictability in their international interactions, though nothing ensures that search will be peaceful or cooperative.

Nevertheless, in the not-too-distant future, most states will delineate defensible borders in some measure across the formerly ungoverned, even chaotic cyberspace. As this transition era eventually comes to a close, the unfettered web will be complexly crisscrossed with borders, gateways, filters, dark holes between jurisdictions, national cyber security forces, and a plethora of strategies, only some of which will be coordinated. Whether by accident, mutual adjustments, conflicts, or some combination of all three, states will meet the challenge of cyber threats. The relative distributions of national cyber power will be solidifying according to how well each state has developed its own resilience and disruption capacities. The world's states will cluster in groups of robust, midlevel, and poor cyber powers, with the first two more likely to attempt to coerce the third, and the poorer states simply trying to not lose too much in compliance.

They will legislate domestic laws giving themselves the necessary authorities, establish the competent military and law enforcement organizations negotiate international treaties, and perhaps even modify existing international organizations to assert controls to the advantage of states.

However the emergent cyber Westphalian system will be structured is unclear, but conflict will dramatically alter most conceivable future conditions unless new STES national responses alter existing cyberspace substrate's offense advantages in scale, proximity, precision, deception, and opaqueness. The rise of cyber jurisdictions will help if they effectively begin to reinstate the security value of distance in cyberspace and diminish the proximity advantage to the offense. It will be harder to hide in a cyber-bordered state and reach across other bordered states and through encrypted clouds to a target state to acquire the economic and societal intelligence so easily acquired today. In a fully instantiated cyber Westphalian world, it is likely to be harder to stay undetected in exfiltrating huge data streams illegally back through all these gateways or cyber-challenging systems without being detected by someone monitoring big data for anomalies. The vast majority of everyman attackers will not have the expertise to work around these obstacles to get the information or access needed, without incurring personal risk of being identified or the loss of increasingly more expensive tools from the global cybercrime black market. Correctly implemented, the jurisdictional controls will also be more challenging for the highly skilled state sponsored wicked actors, in part because they too must take extra time to work around, though, or deceive those controls. With the reduction of the vast numbers of inferior skilled actors, their actions will be less camouflaged and more likely to be discernible with ever more accurate cybered hunting and monitoring systems.

The potential scale of externally organized attacks will begin to decline, increasingly narrowing to what bad actors are available and willing to operate within one's own cybered borders, where they are more likely to be subjected more directly to the rules of that government in terms of monitoring private communications for criminal controls. Non-nationals, for example, will not be as easily able or persuaded to readily cross monitoring borders to join in organising efforts for cybered campaigns.

With declining hordes of less skilled cyber criminals available for testing new techniques, providing cover, or buying the new tools of criminal coders, the global underground's activities are likely to become more consistently professionalised. Fewer people and less distance for protection means more skill will be needed to take advantage of looser or weaker cybered jurisdictions more reliably and efficiently; more like drug cartels than the cybered street gangs of today. Other than further reducing the numbers of low level actors used for cover, this loss in scale only affects the high skilled state-sponsored actors indirectly. More time and attention of the criminal toolmakers will be diverted from innovative tools to finding ways to undermine the rising variety of national jurisdiction controls just to gain the access and ease that today is virtually free. More of those exploits will be expensive, harder to develop or test, and have to be constructed by the wicked actors themselves, rather than they acquiring and adapting already tested techniques from the criminalized code community.

The advantages of deception (in tools and techniques) and opaqueness (in identity and location) are, in terms of the volumes of possible new tools and new bad actors, also diminished, but not necessarily in terms of possible internal threats. To the extent that rise of national cybered jurisdictions reduce the structural advantage of proximity and scale in cyberspace, low-skill members of the criminal community will try less often to penetrate beyond many borders illegally. They are more likely to turn their focus either on their own nation where they are not prevented by borders from acting or on the poorer cyber power states with ineffective virtual borders. They will, however, attempt even more to be deceptive with tools and techniques and even more opaque personally, so as to extend the value of their increasingly more valuable hacks or botnets and not be arrested. The rise of these borders, therefore, helps the resilience of a nation, but they are not sufficient. The national leaders will need to develop and ensure resilience internally across all the STESs critical to national wellbeing.

Precision remains an advantage in a bordered cybered world. Whether inside a nation or outside, a bad actor, group, or state can still opaquely amass and differentially apply a variety of tools against a wide and diverse array of targets at once, in barrages or in small groups at one's whim. However, staying opaque across defended cyber jurisdictions will be much harder without the cover of millions of low level actors is likely to require more time, as is acting with deceptive, as yet unrecognized new tools over time in complex campaigns. In this regard, the high-skill actors have the same problem as the low-skill actors in attempting deceptive and opaque mass attacks because, for the former, in principle, they are still likely to be attempting mostly to attack outside their nation. The targets can be planned with great precision and skill, but the campaign has to be executed either very slowly at a very low level to maintain deception and opacity, or all at once, thus blowing the reuse of tools but increasing the chances that the one-off nature of the attack will deny any identifying pattern to monitoring systems.

At the end of the day, the national systemic focus on architecture for long-term cyber power and wellbeing means the resilience and disruptive capacities are proportional and embedded capacities in the internal STESs systems and at the edges where cyber jurisdictions meet. This need for systemic responses also implies national efforts to design responses that work well with like-minded other nations able to help dampen the threats collectively while each nation grows along its own path to systemic resilience and disruptive capacities. The advantages of a collective overlay in this systemic approach are the mutuality of protection in transition and permanently embedded in STES architecture designs. For example, in a cybered conflict, one nation may call upon allied nations for help in being resilient to, but also proportionately disrupting attacking state-sponsored, 3rd party opportunistic and criminal actors. While the victim state may not itself be quite robust, with its allies, it can nonetheless go about systemically repulsing or neutralizing attacks. The collective development of such resilience relies on cross alliance redundancies enabling timely knowing and acting, to include common standardized mechanisms for redundancy, slack, and mitigation, technological detection systems harmonised, alert frameworks continuous and efficiently adaptive and validating, and the required responses routinely tested, updated and enforced effectively and communally. One caveat, however, is that, in the current and future cybered world, being resilient also means in some sense being autarchic in key areas for national survival, most of them economic and infrastructural.

Under these admittedly ambitious calls for a more systemic approach, it is wise to keep in view that, over this current transition period and then beyond, the underlying technological designs and economic flows of cyberspace will change again. The architectures being developed over the next 15-20 years will only help a nation avoid being a poor, non-robust cybered state, not guarantee any nation will be the most robust or dominant cyber power. The many lists of emerging 'disruptive' technologies offer windows into what is likely to be available for all cybered actors, from coercers to criminals to opportunists to defenders. In many respects, all nations are developing nations in a deeply cybered world, and many will continue to develop as the Westphalian cybered borders emerge. Nonetheless, it relatively safe to argue that, for most states, the fortuitous combination of being resilient and able to disrupt as desired will not emerge without deliberate effort to reconceptualise and then collectively act upon the basic elements of the systemic challenges of the cyberspace substrate. For most, if not all, good enough will have to be the standard in achieving resilience and disruption capacities essential for a robust cyber power able to meet these five challenges. For some states, robust cyber power not be achievable or, at least, may not be easily or completely achievable. Slowly but surely leading states will take steps, internally and externally, to defend hard fought prerogatives, but even they, over the next ten to fifteen years of transition, have no guarantees of being among the robust cyber powers if, for any number of reasons, they fail to recognize these systemic challenges in time and to act to foster more resilient designs of their own internal their STES architectures appropriately.

REFERENCES

Arquilla, J., & Ronfeldt, D. (1993). Cyberwar is coming! *Comparative Strategy, 12*(2), 141–165. doi:10.1080/01495939308402915

Berkhout, A. Smith and A. Stirling. (2003). Socio-technological regimes and transition contexts. *SPRU Electronic Working Paper no. 106*. Falmer, UK: The Freeman Centre, University of Sussex.

Betts, R. (1983). *Surprise attack: Lessons for defense planning*. Washington: Brookings Institution.

Betz, D., & Stevens, T. (2013). Analogical reasoning and cyber security. *Security Dialogue, 44*(2), 147–164. doi:10.1177/0967010613478323

Blum, A. (2012). *Tubes: A journey to the center of the internet*. New York: Ecco.

Cetinkaya, E., & Sterbenz, J. (2013, March). A taxonomy of network challenges. *Proceedings of the 9th IEEE/IFIP International Conference on the Design of Reliable Communication Networks (DRCN)*. Budapest: IEEE/IFIP.

Chin, D., Kaplan, J., and Weinberg, A. (2014, January) *Risk and responsibility in a hyperconnected world: Implications for enterprises*. McKinsey & Company.

Christensen, C. (1997). *The innovator's dilemma: When new technologies cause great firms to fail*. Cambridge: Harvard Business School Press.

Comfort, L., Boin, A., & Demchak, C. (2010). *Designing resilience: preparing for extreme events*. Pittsburgh: University of Pittsburgh Press.

Deibert, R. (2012). The growing dark side of cyberspace (…and what to do about it). *Penn State Journal of Law & International Affairs, 1*(2), 260–274.

Demchak, C. (2012). Hacking the next war. *The American Interest, 8*(1).

Demchak, C., & Dombrowski, P. (2011). Rise of a 'Cybered Westphalian' age. *Strategic Studies Quarterly*, *5*(1), 32–61.

Dombrowski, P., & Demchak, C. (2014). Cyber war, cybered-conflict and the maritime domain. *Naval War College Review*, *67*(2), 71–96.

Dombrowski, P. and C. Demchak. (2014). Cyber westphalia: asserting state prerogatives in cyberspace. *Georgetown Journal of International Affairs*: 5-13.

Dombrowski, P., & Gholz, E. (2006). *Buying military transformation: technological innovation and the defense industry*. New York: Columbia University Press.

Dunn-Cavelty, M. (2008). Cyber-terror- looming threat or phantom menace? The framing of the US cyber-threat debate. *Journal of Information Technology & Politics*, *4*(1), 19–36. doi:10.1300/J516v04n01_03

Farahmand, F., & Spafford, E. (2013). Understanding insiders: An analysis of risk-taking behavior. *Information Systems Frontiers*, *15*(1), 5–15. doi:10.1007/s10796-010-9265-x

Goldman, E., & Arquilla, J. (Eds.). (2014). *Cyber analogies. Montery*. Naval Post Graduate School.

Gooch, J., & Perlmutter, A. (Eds.). (2007). *Military deception and surprise!* London: Routledge.

Greitzer, F., Moore, A., Cappelli, D., Andrews, D., Carroll, L., & Hull, T. D. (2008, February/March). Combating the insider cyber threat. *IEEE Security and Privacy*, *6*(1), 61–64. doi:10.1109/MSP.2008.8

Kerry, C. (2014, May). *Missed connections: Talking with Europe about data, privacy, and surveillance*. Washington: Center for Technology Innovation at Brookings.

Knorr, K., & Morgan, P. (1982). *Strategic military surprise*. Herndon, VA: Transaction Publishers.

Maher, K. (2013, February 25). The new westphalian web. *Foreign policy magazine online*.

Manyika, J., & Chui, M. et al. (2013). *McKinsey Global Institute Report: Disruptive technologies: Advances that will transform life, business, and the global economy*. McKinsey & Company.

Miorandia, D., Sicarib, S., De Pellegrinia, F., & Chlamtaca, I. (2013, September). Internet of things: Vision, applications and research challenges. *Ad Hoc Networks*, *10*(7), 1497–1516. doi:10.1016/j.adhoc.2012.02.016

Osborn, K. (2014, May 21). "DARPA unveils hack-proof drone. *DefenseTech*

Perrow, C. (1999). *Normal accidents: Living with high-risk technologies*. Princeton: Princeton University Press.

Pierce, T. (2005). *Warfighting and disruptive technologies: disguising innovation*. London: Routledge.

Rid, T. (2012). Cyber war will not take place. *The Journal of Strategic Studies*, *35*(1), 5–32. doi:10.10 80/01402390.2011.608939

Simon, H. (1962). The architecture of complexity. *Proceedings of the American Philosophical Society*, *106*(6), 67–482.

Singer, P., & Friedman, A. (2014). *Cybersecurity and cyberwar: what everyone needs to know*. London: Oxford University Press.

Trist, E. (1980, April). *The evolution of socio-technical systems: A conceptual framework and an action research program*. Centre for the Study of Organizational Innovation, Wharton School, University of Pennsylvania, Philadelphia, PA.

Weimann, G. (2005). Cyberterrorism: The sum of all fears? *Studies in Conflict and Terrorism*, *28*(2), 129–149. doi:10.1080/10576100590905110

Wilson, W. (2008). *Botnets, cybercrime, and cyberterrorism: vulnerabilities and policy issues for congress*. Washington: Congressional Research Service.

KEY TERMS AND DEFINITIONS

Coercion (Cybered): Far beyond and in contrast to traditional notions of coercion requiring a demonstration of threat and a stated demand, cybered coercion elevates the deceptive, opaque, and relatively low-cost manipulation of economic flows and values of 'low politics' by a wide variety of 'everyman' actors to the level of a major national security issues of 'high politics'. First, *'deception in tools'* used is essential because the tools exploit ignorance of insecurities. Once the tool's exploitation method is known, they may not work at all given the corrective responses of the likely targets. Second, *'opaqueness in origins'* is especially important because a revealed aggressor could easily be the victim of equally deceptive and opaque campaigns in return or even attacked preemptively by aggrieved targets, proxies, and alliesbased on deception and opaqueness.

Cyber Power: A measure of a state's ability to influence the international economic and political system by developing 'systemic resilience' to defend against cyber coercion or attacks and having a small but necessary legal forward targeted 'cyber disruption capacities' to respond legally punitively or proactively in self-defense against the small number of sponsored 'wicked actors' or highly skilled aggressors able to defeat the state's cybered defenses.

Cyber Westphalia: A post-industrial international system topologically defined by cybered jurisdictions outlining the limits of state sovereignty in all elements of societal concern in, through, or enabled by cyberspace and acknowledged as such by the actions and reciprocity of other states.

Cybered: Term making the entire socio-technical-economic system part of the discussion; 'cyber' alone is restricted generally to the technical aspects including networks, protocols, coding, data mechanisms, etc. The colloquial use of cyber as an adjective for everything has confused analysis. Furthermore, the term cyber will fall out of fashion in a decade or more because the substrate will be everywhere and the term cyber this or that will be redundant and obvious.

Cybered Conflict: Spectrum between peacetime spying and petty theft and onset of shooting cyber-enabled war as created by Scale-Proximity-Precision offense advantages given to massive amounts of predators able to act against strangers with impunity and immunity due to the highly insecure, near free, ubiquitous, standardized, and complex aspects of the globally linked substrate. 'Cyber war' exists only at the end of the spectrum of cybered conflict where violent organized kinetic ('shooting') cyber-enabled operations are initiated against another state.

Cyberspace 'Substrate': Cyberspace is best viewed as a 'substrate' forming the underlying layer on which modern, information age society is increasingly built and sustained; the combined human-technical assemblies that spread outward and upward into every function of every digitizing society or sector. As a substrate, cyberspace intersects with and underlies all other productive dimensions of human society—increasingly economic growth, technological innovation, scientific exploration, commercial vitality and all forms of communications depend upon the networks of networks.

Offense (Cyber) 3 Systemic Advantages: 'Scale-Proximity-Precision' are the three major systemic advantages made nearly free and always available by the globally unfettered highly complex but insecure cyberspace substrate. '*Scale*' in organizing is historically so expensive that only emperors or superpowers or near neighbors could usually afford to organize a sufficient force to overwhelm defending forces. Cyberspace has made that organizing with people or its equivalent in using botnets nearly free for any predator or adversary. '*Proximity*' historically was needed to know enough about a potential defender in order to plan an attack or even to develop a grievance or jealousy sufficient to justify the costs. Cyberspace has eliminated a cost for proximity because anyone anywhere can spend nearly nothing save time to find out information about intended victims in small groups or en masse. '*Precision*' was a hindrance to conflict historically because only emperors or super powers or possibly close neighbors could afford to design the precisely right array of weapons and organizations to ensure victory over defenses of the victim communities. Emperors could afford to be imprecise and have many of everything; others needed to be precise in order to not lose the battle with the wrong equipment. In cyberspace, not only is every weapon in principle available to every would-be attacking group, the range of victims and tempo can be precisely or imprecisely decided on whim by the aggressors. The three offense advantages in cyberspace were conflict deflators throughout the rest of history.

Resilience (Systemic): Is much more than an ability to return to the status quo at minimal cost. In a deeply cybered world, it is at each level of analysis a continuous state of a complex STES (any lesser socio-technical system) in which urgent, accumulating, systemic debilitating, costly surprises are defused or neutralized by the knowledgeable rapid, accurate preemptions or reactions built into the existing system either through original design (redundancy in knowledge and slack in time), previous events mitigation and then innovation, or by collective pre-surprise discovery trial-and error learning (DTEL) that allowed the right kind of knowledge development, redundancy, substitutability, malleability, and effective decoupling to be systemically continuously tested, innovated, retested, and adopted in advance. 'Systemic Cyber Resilience' involves enterprises, critical infrastructure and industries, and state level functions individually developing redundancy in knowledge, slack in time, and DTEL and collectively developing together processes of sensemaking when surprised urgently and responses in rapid, collective defusion, mitigation, and innovation to make the whole system more immune and adaptive to that or other surprising attacks.

STES: 'Socio-technical-economic systems' - a term developed from the socio-technical systems literature that emerged in the 1970s to explain and prevent surprises across largescale enterprises involving highly complex machine assemblies, organizations, and wide societal concerns for safety, reliability, and resilience to nasty surprises that can immediately or over time devastate the whole system at any level.

Systemic Approach (Cybered): Analysis based on STES analyses beginning with all critical functions of the system, ranging from enterprise, through the coordinating sector or industry, through the society as a whole over time, and to the wider international system as a global STES.

Chapter 15

Cyberinsecurity and Cyberwarfare:
The Case for Social Science and Philosophical Approaches. Reflections from Asia.

Alan Chong
Nanyang Technological University, Singapore

ABSTRACT

This chapter seeks to define the term "cyberinsecurity" as the intersection of human fears and errors with user behaviour in a digital setting. Examining links between psychology and human-computer interaction, the author explores several case studies set against the context of cyber-authoritarianism in Asian countries and argues that any attempts to address or advance studies in cybersecurity and cyberwarfare must be grounded in a solid foundation of current social science theory.

INTRODUCTION

While the study of cyberwarfare has proliferated over the past two decades, scholarship has insufficiently maintained a commensurate intellectual depth. A vast majority of authors have not kept their senses tuned to the ground. (Arquilla & Ronfeldt, 1997; Armistead, 2004) The fundamental fact of cyberspace is that it begins with the social origins of computing. Computers could only be experimented with, and eventually redesigned for office and home, on the basis that they fulfilled human needs. In this regard, the cybernetic idea challenges human capacities to cope with information overload and the readiness to react. Over time, computer usage socializes human behaviour into the pattern that time honoured traditions in many societies prefigure their members' reactions to the capabilities of new technologies. While the use of the human messenger, carried on horseback, elephant or camel, or on his own feet, appeared commonplace across the globe, the embrace of the telegraph, the telephone and the television impacted unevenly. In some societies, early forms of electronic communication displaced Providence

DOI: 10.4018/978-1-4666-8456-0.ch015

and spirituality severely since visions and disembodied voices could now be created by one's fellow humankind and projected in defiance of space and time.

The purpose of such a long exegesis is intended to draw attention to the social grounding of cyberspace, and the consequent need to employ traditional social science and philosophy to examine cyberspatial politics. It is the sole contention of this chapter that research on cyberspace and its implications for national and global security ought to logically begin with the by-product of widespread civilian computer usage – cyberinsecurity. As the renowned industrial sociologist Jacques Ellul had warned, the computer arises from the industrial technique, and it is 'nothing more than means and the ensemble of means.' (Ellul, 1973, p. 19) At this point, the industrial man applies consciousness and judgment into the technical phenomenon: 'the technician takes stock of alternative possibilities. The immediate result is that he seeks to apply the new methods in fields which traditionally had been left to chance, pragmatism, and instinct. The intervention of consciousness causes a rapid and far-flung extension of technique…It is really a question of finding the best means in the absolute sense, on the basis of numerical calculation.' (Ellul, 1973, p. 21) In short, the computer was invented to render calculation and other forms of industrial calibration more accurate, but that very production of precision required also corresponding efforts at 'troubleshooting' possible faults that impeded the attainment of accuracy in any computer. Faults had to be found and isolated in laboratory and actual practice sessions. *Therein lies the beginnings of cyberinsecurity: the computer user's fears are bound up with his search for the perfection of his computing capabilities.* Writing about the initial impact of home computers and 'desktops' in 1983, Otto Friedrich, the then Senior Editor at *Time Magazine*, reflectively queried if the advent of the computer will radically transform the very nature of human thought. His answer was emphatic: 'computers do not think, but they do stimulate many of the processes of the human brain: remembering, comparing, analyzing. And as people rely on the computer to do things that they used to do inside their heads, what happens to their heads?' (Friedrich, 1983, p. 229) In support of this clean distinction, Friedrich goes on to quote Charles Lecht, president of the New York consulting firm Lecht Scientific: '"Computers help teach kids to think. Beyond that, they motivate people to think. There is a great difference between intelligence and manipulative capacity. Computers help us realize that difference."' (Friedrich, 1983, p. 229) This position strays a little from that of Jacques Ellul in suggesting that computers are probably benign instruments in assisting humanity in seeing good from evil, instead of deciding for them.

At the other extreme, there are the proponents of medium theory. These argue that computers are never neutral, and may actually do more than help human discernment. Computers may even prefigure certain options, and construct new horizons for social activity where none had existed before. The writings of Marshall McLuhan exemplify this perspective to a very great degree. For McLuhan, human agency ought to accommodate the likelihood that 'the medium is the message' because the message in any medium 'is the change of scale or pace or pattern that it introduces into human affairs.' (McLuhan, 1974, p. 16) In this regard, McLuhan drew an analogy with the impact of the railway. The latter cannot be described as introducing the idea of movement or transportation into human consciousness, 'but it accelerated and enlarged the scale of previous human functions, creating totally new kinds of cities and new kinds of work and leisure.' (McLuhan, 1974, p. 16) By extrapolation, electric media environments can alter our sensory horizons by speeding up events, encapsulating a remote event in a portable extract, and subvert the association between time and place. This is all abstract until one begins to unpack how the transnational Islamic diaspora exhibits umbrage over cartoons and books depicting the Prophet Mohammed in secular and Christian-majority societies in the western hemisphere. Likewise, tsunami-triggered calamities, ferry disasters and airplane crashes across the globe assume an aspect of global tragedy simply because they are mediated and enlarged via 24/7 satellite and cable television, in tandem with social media, into events that elicit spiritual solidarity from 'safe places' all around the world. The media facilitates, and in some cases, orchestrate in complicity with key human actors, via words and images, an instantaneous community of grief. This community of grief is thereby moved to act to alleviate misery, material distress and so on through acts of monetary donation. In this regard, we realise the foresight contained in McLuhan's warning that computers have revolutionized our political perspectives by extending the human being's nervous systems into mediated experiences in cyberspace:

They[, the electric information environments,] are a form of clothing that can be programmed at will to produce any effect desired. Quite naturally, they take over the evolutionary work that Darwin had seen in the spontaneities of biology....Various people have pointed out that the computer revolution is greater than that of the wheel in its power to reshape human outlook and human organization. Whereas the wheel is an extension of the foot, the computer gives us a world where the hand of man never set foot... As much as the wheel is an extension of the foot, the computer is an extension of our nervous system, which exists by virtue of feedback or circuitry. (McLuhan & Fiore, 1968, pp. 37, 53)

Medium theory, in the way that McLuhan expounded it, can explain why cyberinsecurity is often translated at the office, *and* the government department, into an immediate personal crisis of confidence, as well as an instantaneous disaster for filing systems, procedurally-honed decision-making procedures and the collective prestige of bureaucratic teams. One reads of the qualified success of the Stuxnet attacks on the Iranian nuclear facilities, but one rarely reads openly published accounts of the internal 'shake-ups' in procedures and leaderships that such a cybersecurity lapse triggered. The latter must of course be tremendously painful and damaging to many careers. Likewise, the Chinese penetration into American corporate sanctums must surely have taken a toll on how corporate strategies and professional secrets have to be sustained from that point on. McLuhanite medium theory can also be taken to extremes. The computer might appear to be attributed as the ultimate source of all cyberinsecurity, and this might just lead some misguided organizations to assign the troubleshooting tasks of diminishing cyberinsecurity exclusively to engineers. This is precisely what a nuanced reading of cyberinsecurity should avoid. The human factor and its philosophical and sociological dimensions ought to be considered in every possible relationship to the mechanical and material since one is really assessing how computers and their attendant influence on human insecurities have played out in terms of human 'perceptions' in reacting to those insecurities.

This author has deliberately chosen Asian cases as points of reflection, rather than full case studies, for the evident reason that this region represents a challenging case of being a latecomer to embracing information technology (IT) and a laboratory for 'development as modernization', the socioeconomic and political crucible within which computers and cyber activity is legitimized and facilitated. The United States and Western Europe serve as the incubators of cyberspace as we know it, having hosted the inventors of the prototypes of computers, namely, the cryptographic machines, calculators, the telephone, the television set and their predecessor, the electric telegraph. Therefore, the pre-existing literature, and the research on cyberinsecurity and cyberwarfare suffers a built-in bias: the perspective from the developed world. (Arquilla & Ronfeldt, 1997; Armistead, 2004; Liff, 2012; Landau, 2013) Asia on the other hand, offers a near pristine developmental landscape where IT penetration in society has to contend with pre-electronic norms and approaches to governance. This allows the reader to encounter Asia as a demonstration of the linkages between cyberinsecurity, authoritarianism and democratization. Secondly, it enables the reader to understand why the study of cyberwarfare ought to commence with the uses of cyberspace for dissent. In consonance with the theoretical exposition of cyberinsecurity sketched earlier, one will see that in Asia, cyberinsecurity occurs in tandem with governmental insecurity, all within the context of developing a new nation-state. Finally, Asian approaches to managing cyber vulnerabilities are often couched in terms of cultural understandings of security and warfare, hence the need to study stratagems. Once again, the role of stratagems imitates a recurring feature in Asian politics: the resort to philosophical understandings of what government, public opinion and the national security narrative of the political community ought to be about, and the need to adopt a strong guiding hand, including deception and deviousness in official policy, instead of assuming that democracy is recognized as an immediate and universal good by the populace.

CYBERINSECURITY, AUTHORITARIANISM AND DEMOCRATIZATION

One of the fundamental goals of constructing a modern nation-state is the maintenance of social order. This is perhaps best exemplified by the psychological u-turn made by the former Prime Minister of Malaysia, Dr Mahathir Mohamad, in June 2012. Dr Mahathir had been lauded in the mid-1990s for launching one of the most visionary cyber development projects in Asia: the Multimedia Super Corridor on Malaysian territory which was intended to duplicate California's Silicon Valley and more. At the time, Dr Mahathir guaranteed no censorship of the Internet in Malaysia. His backpedalling on that promise began with the undoing of the Malaysian economy during the Asian financial crisis of 1997-8 and reached a crescendo during his years out of office. In a 2012 interview, following the erosion of his ruling coalition's two-thirds parliamentary majority in the general election a few years earlier, Dr Mahathir blamed the Internet for an 'anything goes' culture where racial bigotry, religious extremism and slander could be practised with impunity: 'When I said there should be no censorship of the Internet, I really did not realise the power of the Internet, the power to undermine moral values, the power to create problems and agitate people.' (Jayasankaran, 2012) Malaysia is widely reported to have instituted a 'Net Patrol' and occasionally hauls authors of overtly political blogs through the courts on the basis of sedition. The current Malaysian premier has proven somewhat more liberal than his predecessors in quashing dissent on the Web but maintains a watchful stance in relation to his ruling coalition's reputational standing amongst the three dominant ethnic groups of Malays, Chinese and Indians. An unofficial rule of thumb that has emerged through practice has been the need to publicly favour the online and mainstream media expressions of vigilance about protecting Malay rights and privileges, including the primacy of Islam as the official religion of the Malays, vis-à-vis the other races. This information policy mirrors the country's unwritten governing 'compact' since gaining independence from Britain in 1957, chiefly that the Malays possess a stronger claim for indigeneity, and hence stronger official protections from political, economic and social encroachments from the other racial communities, and from western influences. In the Malaysian case, cyber policy writ large as information policy, is tasked to police this notion of development as adjusting postcolonial justice towards favouring one ethnic community more than the others, as well as institutionalizing this tilted *status quo* as an unchallengeable psychological reality. (Rodan, 2005, p. ch.2)

Another recent example of the Web revealing lingering inter-ethnic animosities in a developing and democratizing Asian state is Myanmar. The Buddhist-Muslim clashes in Rakhine State have reopened long simmering hatreds between the predominantly Buddhist majority Bamar ethnic group and the

Muslim minority Rohingya. The democratizing orientation of President Thein Sein's government had included the lifting of the censorship of the Internet put in place by the preceding military governments. Unfortunately, the effect of freeing the Internet within Myanmar had not advanced political space for either dialogue or accommodation with minorities. In June 2012, when the Facebook page of the Eleven Media Group, one of the largest private media organizations in the country, reported the discovery of a dead Rohingya in the wake of the most recent violence, one Facebook respondent who identified himself as a Myanmar national from the Bamar majority applauded the discovery for he had been 'waiting for this kind of news for a long time'. (Fuller, 2012) Another reader of the same page commented: 'It's not enough that he is dead.' There were worse postings. Rohingyas had been likened to dogs, thieves, and terrorists. Many urged the government of President Thein Sein to 'make them [the Rohingyas] disappear' and vented anger at the West and the UN for highlighting their plight. According to investigation by the *International Herald Tribune*, the deep seated animosity towards the Rohingyas was rooted in a mixture of religious differences, nationalism, racial bigotry and 'colonial resentment'. (Fuller, 2012) Even pro-democracy icon Daw Aung San Suu Kyi had been evasive in her comments on the plight of the Rohingyas: 'We have to be very clear about what the laws of citizenship are and who are entitled to them.' (Fuller, 2012) A leading moderate Myanmar intellectual has instead described the new climate of Web freedom in his country as follows: 'All these grievances have come out…The voices of reason are on the sidelines for now.' (Fuller, 2012) In this regard, there is a clear continuity with the Malaysian scenario where inter-ethnic relations are cast as vulnerable to cyber-incitement. One can go on to add Indonesia, Singapore, Vietnam, Pakistan and India to the list of Asian states where inter-ethnic and inter-religious tensions require national authorities to artificially sanitize narratives online to ensure offline social peace. In one spectacular move in 2012, India had blocked 245 social media sites and sought the assistance of Google Corporation, Facebook and others to shut down sites containing hate speech and doctored images purportedly fanning outrage and fear amongst Muslim migrants from India's northeastern provinces who were working in major cities such as Chennai, Bangalore and Mumbai. (Bajaj, 2012) It was no small irony that Bangalore and Chennai have been touted as India's equivalent of America's Silicon Valley, and yet vulnerable to cyber panic of the atavistic pre-digital kind.

In the People's Republic of China (PRC), sensitivity towards managing the mentalities of the populace holds sway in the grand scheme of pursuing modernization, but without the consideration of managing a multiethnic balance. In a book edited by Anne-Marie Brady, the Chinese Communist Party's approach to cyber information goes under the moniker of 'thought management' (Brady, 2012); this phrase refers to 'activities to control, guide, adjust, or develop the social or ideological relationships which influence the shaping (change or development) of people's thinking; to make their thinking conform with the dominant ideology; thereby standardizing people's behaviour; in order to put in place a set of objectives.' (Shiwen, Yangtao, & Xinshan, 2001, p. 449; Brady, 2012, pp. 8, fn 1) In August 2013, President Xi Jinping summoned the top cadres of the Chinese Communist Party to a series of closed door briefing sessions where he warned that 'western-inspired notions of media independence and civic participation' were one of seven critical security threats to the ideological integrity of both the Party and people of China and called for a rectification campaign to protect both. (Buckley, 2013) This legitimized ever greater vigilance by the Chinese authorities on the Internet to either remove critical blogs, social media postings, or to sanitize other criticisms online. The key thrust of 'thought control' is to ensure that the development of a modern PRC is organized along the lines of a singular master narrative of a one party state that plans and adjusts modernization to increase the overall material welfare of the Chinese people through controlled interaction with external ideas and technology, while maintaining the territorial and psychological unity of the people. The sources of modernization lie in foreign, primarily western, imports of technology and higher education. Yet these are not to be regarded as undiluted universal positives for the PRC. The Internet exemplifies this double-edged import from the West that is at once enchanting to the hitherto repressed masses and a conduit of possible ideological sapping. One can, of course, treat this according to the social science analogies of framing Chinese development within a so-called Prussian model of authoritarian modernization, or an earnest attempt to find a local filter for the amorphousness of global flows of ideas, consumption and alternative social modes. In this regard, the study of Asian, let alone Chinese, cyberwarfare should best proceed from the comprehension of the sources of Asian national and statist ideological insecurities which have extended into cyber insecurities. In this regard, Asian political elites who have acted conservatively towards embracing the Internet have subconsciously taken the reflections of Jacques Ellul and Marshall McLuhan to heart even if the latter were not publicly credited. For developing nation-states, articulations of contrarian perspectives on cyberspace are tantamount to a national security threat that can undo the collective mass energies required for successful modernization.

THE USES OF CYBERSPACE FOR DISSENT

If there is a strong tendency for many Asian states to adopt authoritarian political communication to assist modernization, it is also because their governments have perceived the intellectual link between the circumventive uses of cyberspace as a medium and its liberal ideational origins. An academic author, Victoria Carty, has for instance made the claim that:

Theories of newly emerging ICTs [Information and Communications Technologies], and particularly those of the Internet, resonate with NSM [New Social Movement] theory and critical theory because both pay attention to the significance of democratic discourse in modern societies and how the recent "technological revolution" is affecting forms of communication and mobilization efforts. Because information has become a crucial resource in postindustrial societies, collective action designed to change the ways in which public discourse is structured is of great significance...Newly emerging ICTs, that in many ways are used and experienced differently from conventional media and information systems, have the potential to redefine social relations, cultural practices, and economic and political orders. (Carty, 2011, p. 16)

Since the 1990s, scholars of transnational civil society and nongovernmental organizations (NGOs) have concurrently hammered at the theme of the Internet, blogs and email as new information devices empowering the underdog in championing causes across multiple borders in spite of governments' disapproval. (Josselin & Wallace, 2001) Margaret Keck and Kathryn Sikkink, followers of the work of Sidney Tarrow on grassroots social movements in the wider branches of social science, have proposed that NGOs operate in network formation with great ease thanks to the Web and email acting as non-technical user friendly media to lower transaction costs and enhance real time coordination in lobbying states on human rights violations, disarmament or environmental causes. (Keck & Sikkink, 1998) One particular strategy they have highlighted is the informational 'boomerang': NGO activists who are silenced by official sanctions and heavy policing in their states of domicile can post calls for action on third party Websites or appeal directly to pre-existing solidarity groups to enact a campaign against their government. (Keck & Sikkink, 1998, pp. 12-14) Moreover, once set in motion, such transnational 'name and shame' campaigns may take on a momentum of their own and damage the targeted state's reputation, as well as trigger other states' sanctions against its activities to a degree far worse than the pain that state inflicted upon the NGO campaigners through incarceration at home. Of course, one might argue that the government in Beijing resisted pressures from the international community for an accounting of human rights abuses far more frequently than others in Asia, but there is little doubt that campaigns of dissent by NGOs were decisive in producing some significant alterations of behaviour by India, Indonesia, Malaysia, Myanmar, Sri Lanka, Thailand, Vietnam and the Philippines. Many of the political boomerang effects of transnational NGO campaigning are of course dependent on wider factors such as the existence of great power support for the campaigners and the beleaguered government, diversified investors' profiles, and the vulnerabilities of export markets, which will determine the degree of pain that might be triggered by sanctions. Nonetheless, the threat of a nongovernmental, civil society orchestrated campaign targeting the local from the global is a constant source of concern for Asian states and societies.

Even where some Asian governments have attempted to buy into the 'knowledge based economy' without wholeheartedly embracing the liberalizing premises of the Web, they must surely be quietly alarmed by Manuel Castells' assertion that in the era of a 'networked' global capitalist economy, 'for the first time in history, the human mind is a direct productive force, not just a discursive element of the production system.' (Castells, 1996, p. 32) Evidently taking a leaf from medium theory, Castells posits that 'computers, communication systems, and genetic decoding and programming are all amplifiers and extensions of the human mind.' Henceforth, 'what we think, and how we think, become expressed in goods, services, material and intellectual output, be it food, shelter, transportation and communications systems, computers, missiles, health, education, or images.' (Castells, 1996, p. 32) Those last two categories of expression can of course be seen via daily updates on Twitter, Facebook and Instagram where NGOs, disgruntled citizens, disenfranchised workers and others with grievances against authority vent their sentiments and assail those public personas they have assigned as objects of their anger. The government of Singapore is frequently in the news headlines covering curbs on freedom of expression on the Web. Not unlike Malaysia and Myanmar, the government of Singapore is actively policing against racial bigotry, and where slander and misrepresentation of political leaders' financial and official reputations are involved. Singapore's offline laws against slander and sedition have been extended by parliamentary vote into governing online speech where it is posted in Singapore and by both foreigners and Singaporeans domiciled in the island state. Likewise, Thailand has been reported to have irregularly blocked up to 50,000 websites between 2008 and 2011 relating to the whole gamut of subjects ranging from pornography, incitements to terrorism, and insults against religion. (Anonymous Compiler, 2010) Moreover, Thailand's lèse-majesté law has been frequently invoked to selectively block YouTube and jail citizens, academics, journalists and politicians for putting up material deemed derogatory to the prestige of the Thai king. (Fuller, 2013) Much in the same vein of protecting political stability and continuity of social peace, Vietnam has not shied away from arresting bloggers who question the Vietnamese Communist Party's leading role in the state. Moreover, so-called 'Internet polemists' have been hired by the government in Hanoi to combat what it calls 'online hostile forces' operating from computers located in basements and cafes. It has been reported that Article 88 of the existing Vietnam Criminal Code treats 'propaganda against the Socialist Republic of Vietnam' as a punishable offence. (Ghosh, 2013) Over the longer term, more Asian governments and 'thought leaders' will have to develop their own philosophy of 'defensive' and 'selective' Internet usage in order to justify their arms length policies towards social media freedoms. This will increasingly mean responding with discourses and logics on the intellectual frequency on which Bernard Kouchner, the French foreign minister and founder of *Medecins Sans Frontieres* (Doctors without Borders), makes the case for treating the disruptiveness of Internet freedoms as coextensive with offline democratization:

...the distortions [of Internet usage] are the exception rather than the rule. The Internet is above all the most fantastic means of breaking down the walls and boundaries that close us off from each other. For the oppressed peoples, who have been deprived of their right to self-expression and the right to choose their own future, the Internet provides power beyond their wildest hopes. In minutes, news and images recorded on a telephone can be disseminated worldwide in cyberspace. It is increasingly difficult to hide a public demonstration, an act of repression or a violation of human rights.

In authoritarian and repressive countries, mobile telephones and the Internet have given rise to public opinion and civil society. They have also given citizens a critical means of expression, despite all the restrictions. (Kouchner, 2010, p. 61)

CYBERWARFARE VIA STRATAGEMS

Bernard Kouchner's warning is also a useful reflection point for how the majority of Asian strategic thought emphasizes the primacy of practising informational strategies as both proxies for physical warfare, as well as supplements for military operations. A fair sampling of the strategic thought of Sun Tzu, Mao Zedong and Vo Nguyen Giap indicate this preference. I choose these three thinkers as samples on the basis that they are probably the most frequently visible in international curricula on 'military studies' and 'security studies' syllabi. Moreover, in one of the most widely read 'textbooks' published in English on military strategy, Peter Paret treats Mao and Giap as simply revolutionary warfare thinkers. (Paret, 1986) Another survey by Robert Bunker categorizes all three as 'unconventional warfare philosophers'. (Bunker, 1999) Why is there an association between these thinkers and revolutionary and unconventional warfare? Sun Tzu's ancient thought, whose intellectual impact casts its shadow over the other two Asian contemporary thinkers, treats war as a moral contest where civilizations are engaged in a trial of values and ingenuity. Superiority through bloodless manoeuvres is the better vindication of prowess than victory attained through the physical clash of arms. Insofar as Sun Tzu speaks directly to cyberwarfare in our time, read as 'information warfare' and 'psychological warfare' in his time, his counsel is to read the opportunity costs of waging war correctly, and never end up with greater losses than those envisioned in the opening gambit. Essentially, cyberwarfare emerges as an art of reading the proverbial 'tea leaves' of achieving national goals using the right policy instruments adapted to circumstances. According to Chong's interpretation of Sun Tzu, the latter does not explicitly address the distinction between peacetime and wartime. (Chong, 2013, pp. 16-17) There is every intimation in Sun Tzu's writings that the two periods exist on a seamless continuum of preparation for the eventuality of combat. To be victorious in the event of war, one's military must be deployed advantageously, akin to the momentum found in nature: torrential water moving boulders, falcons falling upon hapless prey and so forth. (Sun Tzu, 2005, p. 33) Because mental preparations must draw on parallels to the forces of nature, and nature in turn privileges harmony amongst its forces, Sun Tzu denigrates any form of chaos (*luan*), whether in strategic planning, logistics, failure to treat physical terrain as an ally, or the absence of unwavering charismatic inspiration of one's troops. (Sun Tzu, 2005, pp. 77-79) Correspondingly, Sun Tzu extolled the possibilities of sowing *luan* within one's enemy.

Sun Tzu appears to embrace espionage as a lofty form of information warfare in his time. Here it is worth quoting in full: 'The enlightened sovereign and the capable commander conquer the enemy at every move and achieve successes far surpassing those of ordinary people because they possess "fore-knowledge". This "foreknowledge" cannot be obtained from ghosts or spirits, nor from gods, nor by analogy with past events, nor from astrological calculations. It can only come from men who know the enemy situation.' (Sun Tzu, 2005, p. 109) This is from the Art of War's closing Chapter Thirteen, titled 'Using Spies'. Sun Tzu specifies in some detail five types of spy: the native agent, the internal agent, the converted agent, the expendable agent and the surviving agent. The finer details need not concern us; but the various secret roles all involve *the need to penetrate the walls of the enemy's inner sanctums of government and put on a veneer of sincerely empathizing with the enemy*, in order to listen in on their most subtle intentions. There is no right or wrong time for espionage – 'so delicate and so secretive is espionage that there is nowhere you cannot put it to good use.' (Sun Tzu, 2005, p. 109) In employing spies, the overriding goal of gaining "foreknowledge" must always drive action. In this way, asymmetrical information power triumphs.

To slightly different degrees, Mao Zedong established his reputation in asymmetrical warfare during the heat of anti-colonial struggle. In Mao's perspective, the liberation of China from Japanese and western colonialism, along with the latter's surrogate, the Nationalist *Guomindang* government, required an awareness of relative strengths and weaknesses between Mao's ragtag communist guerrillas and their materially better equipped opposition. Mao's answer, elaborated through an abstract multidimensional thesis of exploiting political contradictions, was to strategise victory for the underdog by exploiting moral and symbolic strengths which have no correlation with physical strength or volume of high technology weaponry. The challenge in Maoist informational strategy was to ensure that despite the relative material poverty of the Red Army, the *Guomindang* soldiers would find it morally rewarding to join the righteous cause of fighting for revolution against their former masters. The Red Army would thus gain mass through the conversion of the enemy's ranks:

Apart from the role played by the party, the reason the Red Army can sustain itself without collapse in spite of such a poor standard of material life and incessant engagements, is its practice of democracy. The officers do not beat the men; officers and men receive equal treatment; soldiers enjoy freedom of assembly and speech; cumbersome formalities and ceremonies are done away with; and the account books are open to the inspection of all...They [the captured soldiers] feel that, though in material life they are worse off in the Red Army than in the White [Guomindang] army, spiritually they are liberated. The fact that the same soldier who was not brave in the enemy army yesterday becomes very brave in the Red Army today shows precisely the impact of democracy. The Red Army is like a furnace in which all captured soldiers are melted down and transformed the moment they come over. (Mao, 1968, p. 171)

Under this rubric, psychological operations are treated as both substitute and supplement for the strategies of mass and technological augmentation. Therefore, Mao inherited Sun Tzu's precept of executing one's military campaign with the *Dao* (the Daoist-Confucian Way) of harmonizing the people and their rulers. This likewise extends into propaganda tasks other than fighting. In Mao's words, proper war fighting should transcend 'the purely military viewpoint' and the military 'should also shoulder such important tasks as agitating the masses, organizing them, arming them, and helping them to set up revolutionary political power, and even establishing organizations of the Communist Party.' (Mao, 1968, p. 174) That Mao's undeclared targets are the winning of the populace's 'hearts and minds', and the subversion of the enemy's political command, is obvious in the disproportionate emphasis placed upon informational strategies in his writings. Even when dealing with specific military strategies, his emphasis remains steadfastly fixed upon correctly appraising the terrain and foreknowledge gleaned of the enemy forces. His clarion call is for the flexibility of means to be reconciled with some semblance of centralized command at every level. Mao was set '*against* fixed operational fronts and positional warfare, and *for* fluid operational fronts and mobile warfare; *against* the mere routing of the enemy, and *for* a war of annihilation; *against* the principle of striking with both fists, and *for* the principle of striking with one fist...' (Mao, 1968, p. 182) One can easily extrapolate how the activities of a dedicated national cyber command can efficiently exploit the electronic penetration routes of the World Wide Web to spread propaganda, issue deceptions and filch secrets from across sovereign borders.

The third persona among the three Asian strategists is the Vietnamese, Vo Nguyen Giap. Like Mao, his contemporary, Giap was obsessed with tilting the unlevel Cold War battlefield vis-à-vis a superior military power. In fact, Giap spent time in Mao's camps in southern China in the early 1940s, observing and learning from his communist brethren how to fight successfully as the weaker party. From this experience, Giap helped the Party formulate the overlapping concepts of resistance war, anti-imperialist war, and war for national liberation. These slogans were meant to capture the loyalties of as broad a segment of Vietnamese society as possible for an armed and unified anti-French front. This broad coalition would also discursively alienate collaborators and compel Vietnamese with wavering loyalties to take sides in a 'just war'. (Giap, 1968, pp. 38-40)

Along with consolidating the political front, Giap noted that 'guerrilla war must multiply. To keep itself in life and to develop, guerrilla warfare necessarily has to develop into mobile warfare. This is a general law.' (Giap, 1968, p. 219) Giap subsequently elaborated this guerrilla strategy into a three-stage scenario with: first, the 'stage of contention', second, the 'stage of equilibrium'; and third, the 'stage of counter-offensive'. In the stage of contention, one's forces were both numerically and materially weaker than the enemy's. Small scale attacks on enemy outposts and the killing or capturing of a handful of enemy soldiers counted for important political effects. At every turn, guerrillas were expected to trade ground for safety through retreat into the jungles. With time and steadily growing confidence and supplies, hit-and-run attacks would give way to pitched battles with the enemy. Once the base areas had attained a level of security from large scale harassment by enemy troops, the people's army could then transit from mere guerrilla attacks to concerted regimental and battalion scale campaigns against the enemy.

Giap is therefore relevant to our appreciation of cyberwarfare because he highlights the moral and ideational mobilization of the untapped strength of the physically weak. Psychological and other propaganda manoeuvres to marshal political loyalties in support of one's cause were crucial to constituting the base for subsequent stages. As a communist, Giap interpreted Marx, Lenin and Mao correctly in preparing armed struggle through political engineering. His guerrilla pronouncements suggested that the weaker party in a conflict should always bide its time, staging attacks commensurate with its deployable resources at any given point in time to demonstrate the lively presence of opposition. Incrementally, gains achieved through harassment would build momentum towards full-scale assault. (Rolph, 1972) This is especially relevant to the exploitability of Internet-based information operations – the simple and random acts of hacking displace the enemy's security systems and its state of tranquillity; consequently, when the enemy's information systems prove ever more vulnerable, more decisive denial of service attacks, virus injections and spam waves can be deployed to paralyze him completely.

Between them, Sun Tzu, Mao and Giap make the concerted point to students of cyberwarfare that all war is essentially a game of mental thrust and parry. Information gets into cybernetic loops and can potentially foil decisive leadership and rational calculation without raising any initial alarm. These thinkers lend substance to the age old association of Asian strategy with the idea of 'stratagem', or ploys which are meant to deceive the enemy in order to attain one's political aims. Moreover, stratagems rely on the viability and resilience of pre-existing systems of governance, that is, the nation-state, in order to target an enemy without having the enemy practise the same against one's side. This aspect resonates across the earlier two subsections since Asian governments are diverting their cyber attention to more conventional possibilities of informationalized subversion via the daily use of email, blogs and social media to undermine authoritarian narratives of the domestic social contract as well as venting against the excesses of state power across the globe. Finally, the use of cyberweapons against states and non-state actors appears to have been foreseen by the Asian strategists as a matter that defies distinctions of wartime and peacetime. Instead, the nation-state is treated as a resilient entity that demands good leadership at its helm in order to practice a survival obsession that motivates the sourcing of good intelligence in equal measure with sowing doubt in the minds of foes and third parties. (Chong, 2013, pp. 21-22)

THE POLITICAL CONSEQUENCES OF THE COMPUTER: SOCIAL SCIENCE AND PHILOSOPHY NEEDED TO ANALYSE IT

The abstractions of human-computer interactions are brought into sharp relief when one reflects on the complex and contradictory realities of Asian nation-states' experiences in governing the Internet and its rapidly growing number of users. What is probably evident is that Asians have had difficulties embracing the free flow of information in relation to the maintenance of good government. There are a number of ways to analyze this: government-society relations under the strains of modernization *qua* democratization, prior to the arrival of the Internet; dissent and its resort to the novelty of individual broadcast capabilities afforded by social media; and the roles of media freedoms and their channelling of multicultural, factional politics. And there may be more permutations of these. The scholars of human-computer interactions cited in the early parts of this chapter offer a collective warning to guide inquiry into cyberinsecurity and cyberwarfare: are human agents fully cognizant of the capabilities of computers as simultaneously individuated and massed broadcast channels? McLuhan's words sum this social scientific inquiry up very presciently: 'As much as the wheel is an extension of the foot, the computer is an extension of our nervous system, which exists by virtue of feedback or circuitry.' (McLuhan & Fiore, 1968, p. 53)

Fundamentally, these call for the urgent need to apply social science and philosophy to the study of cyberinsecurity, thence cyberwarfare. Human beings are often assigned rationality and agency but one has to investigate if these operate in spite of the advent of computerization and the Internet. Can human rationality be isolated from the wider patterns of electronic political communication? Or has the ease of electronic communication empowered 'rapid reaction' politics within limited rationality, or worse automated rationality? Philosophy, as a branch of the reflective study of how human beings coexist with one another in governmental relationships, invites the cyber-politics scholar to ponder the normative in relation to cyberspace. At its roots, philosophers have been dubbed by Aristotle as 'those who discourse on nature', which classical political philosophers have taken to mean treating 'nature' as 'the character of a thing, or of a kind of thing, the way in which a thing or a kind of thing looks and acts, and the thing, or the kind of thing, is taken not to have been made by gods or men.' (Strauss & Cropsey, 1987, p. 2) Modern or contemporary political philosophy would go the further step to ask if there are conventions governing nature, that 'nature' by itself is not fully cognizant of. Convention is therefore totally man-made, hence the reason why contemporary political philosophers are obsessed over the distinctions between natural human freedoms and positive human freedoms. (Strauss & Cropsey, 1987, p. 3) These conundrums apply even to electronic social media. Should cyberspace be governed like the newspaper, radio and television before it? What is the definition of the 'collective good' when the Internet openly invites the individuation of media users? Surely, these are tasks that should still be reserved for earnest social scientists and philosophers even in the era of overwhelming cyberspatial extensions of ourselves. A helpful start can thus be commended by the works of firstly, Martin Libicki in speculating about the strategy of the open conquest of cyberspace through open access portals and software subscriptions (Libicki, 2007); or the predictions by Chris Demchak of the need to clarify 'the interconnections of basic large scale human systems security in the emerging age while offering a method of achieving more adept resilience and long-term relative global civility' in a 'cybered conflict age' (Demchak, 2011, p. 290); or Chong's suggestion that cyberwarfare *qua* information warfare following an Asian philosophical model would celebrate the time honoured cunning of a devious strategic mind bent on exploiting government-society relations, social vagaries and attacks on mentalities. (Chong, 2013)

REFERENCES

Anonymous Compiler. (2010, July 31). *2Bangkok.com*. Retrieved from http://2bangkok.com/blocked.shtml

Armistead, L. (2004). *Information Operations: Warfare and the Hard Reality of Soft Power*. Dulles, Virginia, USA: Brassey's Inc.

Arquilla, J., & Ronfeldt, D. (1997). Cyberwar is Coming! In J. Arquilla & D. Ronfeldt (Eds.), *In Athena's Camp: Preparing for Conflict in the Information Age*, (pp. 23–60). Santa Monica, California, USA: RAND.

Bajaj, V. (2012, August 23). India Presses Web Sites over Ethnic Clashes. *International Herald Tribune*, p. 13.

Brady, A.-M. (Ed.). (2012). *China's Thought Management*. Abingdon, UK: Routledge.

Brady, A.-M. (2012). Introduction - Market-Friendly, Scientific, High Tech, and Politics-Lite: China's New Approach to Propaganda. In A.-M. Brady (Ed.), *China's Thought Management* (pp. 1–10). Abingdon, UK: Routledge.

Buckley, C. (2013, August 21). China Memo Reveals Fears of Western Influence. *International Herald Tribune*, (pp. 1, 3).

Bunker, R. J. (1999). Unconventional Warfare Philosophers. *Small Wars & Insurgencies, 10*(3), 136–149. doi:10.1080/09592319908423253

Carty, V. (2011). *Wired and Mobilizing: Social Movements, New Technology, and Electoral Politics*. New York: Routledge.

Castells, M. (1996). The Information Age: Economy, Society and Culture, Vol. I. *The Rise of the Network Society*. Oxford, UK: Blackwell Publishers.

Chong, A. (2013, May 9). Information Warfare? The Case for an Asian Perspective on Information Operations. *Armed Forces and Society*, 1-26. doi:10.1177/0095327X13483444

Demchak, C. (2011). *Wars of Disruption and Resilience: Cybered Conflict, Power and National Security*. Athens, Georgia, USA: University of Georgia Press.

Ellul, J. (1973). *The Technological Society* (J. Wilkinson, Trans.). New York: Alfred A. Knopf.

Friedrich, O. (1983). The Computer Moves In. In F. J. Coppa & R. Harmond (Eds.), *Technology in the Twentieth Century* (pp. 215–231). Dubuque, Iowa, USA: Kendall/Hunt Publishing Company.

Fuller, T. (2012, June 16-17). In Myanmar, Freedom and a Wave of Hate. *International Herald Tribune*, (pp. 1, 3).

Fuller, T. (2013, January 17). In Thailand, a Broader Definition of Insulting Royalty. *International New York Times*. Retrieved from http://www.nytimes.com/2013/01/18/world/asia/in-thailand-a-broader-definition-of-insulting-royalty.html?_r=0

Ghosh, N. (2013, March 12). Vietnam Pushes Back Against Online Critics. *The Straits Times (Singapore)*, p. A9.

Giap, V. N. (1968). *People's War, People's Army. The Vietcong Insurrection Manual for Underdeveloped Countries* (2nd Ed.). New York, USA: Bantam Books.

Giap, V. N. (1968). The Resistance War against French Imperialism. In W. J. Pomeroy (Ed.), *Guerrilla Warfare and Marxism* (pp. 212–216). New York: International Publishers.

Jayasankaran, S. (2012, June 5). Mahathir Calls for Internet Access to be Regulated. *The Business Times (Singapore)*, p. 16.

Josselin, D., & Wallace, W. (2001). Non-State Actors in World Politics: a Framework. In D. Josselin & W. Wallace (Eds.), *Non-State Actors in World Politics*, (pp. 1–20). Basingstoke: Palgrave Macmillan. doi:10.1057/9781403900906

Keck, M. E., & Sikkink, K. (1998). *Activists Beyond Borders: Advocacy Networks in International Politics*. Ithaca, New York, USA: Cornell University Press.

Kouchner, B. (2010). Stand Up to the Enemies of the Internet. *New Perspectives Quarterly*, *27*(3), 61–63. doi:10.1111/j.1540-5842.2010.01188.x

Landau, S. (2013). *Surveillance or Security? The Risks Posed by New Wiretapping Technologies*. Cambridge, Massachusetts, USA: The MIT Press.

Libicki, M. (2007). *Conquest in Cybersapce: National Security and Information Warfare*. Cambridge, UK: Cambridge University Press. doi:10.1017/CBO9780511804250

Liff, A. P. (2012). Cyberwar: A New 'Absolute Weapon'? The Proliferation of Cyberwarfare Capabilities and Interstate War. *The Journal of Strategic Studies*, *35*(3), 401–428. doi:10.1080/01402390.2012.663252

Mao, Z. (1968). Characteristics of China's Revolutionary War. In W. J. Pomeroy (Ed.), *Guerrilla Warfare and Marxism* (pp. 182–185). New York, USA: International Publishers.

Mao, Z. (1968). On the Purely Military Viewpoint. In W. J. Pomeroy (Ed.), *Guerrilla Warfare and Marxism* (pp. 173–176). New York, USA: International Publishers.

Mao, Z. (1968). The Military Problem. In W. J. Pomeroy (Ed.), *Guerrilla Warfare and Marxism* (pp. 168–171). New York, USA: International Publishers.

McLuhan, M. (1974). *Understanding Media: The Extensions of Man* (2nd Ed.). London, UK: Routledge and Kegan Paul Limited/Abacus.

McLuhan, M., & Fiore, Q. (1968). *War and Peace in the Global Village*. New York, USA: Bantam Books.

Paret, P. (Ed.). (1986). *Makers of Modern Strategy: from Machiavelli to the Nuclear Age*. Princeton, New Jersey, USA: Princeton University Press.

Rid, T. (2013). More Attacks, Less Violence. *The Journal of Strategic Studies*, *36*(1), 139–142. doi:10 .1080/01402390.2012.742012

Rodan, G. (2005). *Transparency and Authoritarian Rule in Southeast Asia*. Abingdon, UK: Routledge.

Rolph, H. (1972). Vietnamese Communism and the Protracted War. *Asian Survey*, *12*(9), 783–792. doi:10.2307/2642828

Shiwen, Z., Yangtao, Y., & Xinshan, W. (2001). *Xin shiqi sixiang zhengzhi gongzuo yanjiu lunwen ji*. Wuhan, China: Wuhan Daxue Chubanshe.

Strauss, L., & Cropsey, J. (1987). Introduction. In L. Strauss & J. Cropsey (Eds.), *History of Political Philosophy* (3rd Ed.), (pp. 1–6). Chicago, USA: The University of Chicago Press. doi:10.7208/chicago/9780226924717.001.0001

Sun Tzu. (2005). *Sunzi: the art of war and Sun Bin: the art of war*. (R. Wu, X. Wu, & W. Lin Trans. & Eds.). Beijing, China: Foreign Languages Press.

Compilation of References

Advanced Message Queuing Protocol (AMQP), version 1.0. (2012). OASIS. Retrieved from https://www.oasis-open.org/committees/tc_home.php?wg_abbrev=amqp

Case dropped against hacker accused with breaking into USAF computers. (1997, November 22). *Agence France Presse*.

Commonwealth of Independent States. (n. d.). *OpenNet Initiative*. Retrieved from https://opennet.net/research/regions/cis

Developing National Information Security Strategy for the Kingdom of Saudi Arabia. (2013). *Ministry of Communications and Information Technology*. Retrieved from http://www.mcit.gov.sa/Ar/MediaCenter/PubReqDocuments/NISS_Draft_7_EN.pdf

DNP3 Overview. (2002). *Triangle MicroWorks*. Retrieved from http://trianglemicroworks.com/docs/ default-source/referenced-documents/DNP3_Overview.pdf

Electrical Characteristics of Generators and Receivers for Use in Balanced Multipoint Systems.(1983). *EIA Standard* [Electronic Industries Association]. *RS-485*, 1983.

Framework for Improving Critical Infrastructure Cybersecurity, Version 1.0. (2014, February 12). *National Institute of Standards and Technology*. Retrieved from http://www.nist.gov/cyberframework/upload/cybersecurity-framework-021214.pdf

Graeve, J. B. S. (Ed.). (2005). No Room for Bullies: From the Classroom to Cyber Space. Nebraska: Boys Town Press.

Iraqi Insurgency Group utilizes Google Earth for attack planning. (2006). *Foundation of American Scientists*. Retrieved from http://www.fas.org/irp/dni/osc/osc071906.pdf

ISO/IEC JTC 1 Information Technology. (1987). *ISO.org*. Retrieved from http://www.iso.org/iso/standards_development/technical_committees/list_of_iso_technical_committees/iso_technical_committee.htm?commid=45020

Joint Military Operations: Weaknesses in DoD's Process for Certifying C^{4}I Systems' Interoperability (1998). *General Accounting Office* (Letter Report, 03/13/98, GAO/NSIAD-98-73).

National Cyber Security Strategy. (2012). *Information Security Association*.

Newsmakers with Senator Joe Lieberman. (2012, September 21). *C-Span*. Retrieved from http://www.c-spanvideo.org/program/JoeLiebe

Nigeria kidnapped girls shown in Boko Haram video. (2014c, May 12). *BBC News*. Retrieved from http://www.bbc.co.uk/news/world-africa-27373287

Norton Cybercrime Report. (2012). *Norton*.

Profile of National Response Centre for Cyber Crimes, National Response Centre for Cyber Crime (NR3C). (n. d.). FIA.

Tentative Jihad: Syria's fundamentalist opposition. (2012). *Middle East Report, 131*(12). *International Crisis Group.* Retrieved from http://www.crisisgroup.org/~/media/Files/Middle%20East%20North%20Africa/Iraq%20Syria%20Lebanon/Syria/131-tentative-jihad-syrias-fundamentalist-opposition.pdf

The Comprehensive National Cybersecurity Initiative. (2010). The White House.

The National Strategy to Secure Cyberspace. (2003). The White House.

The United Nations Disarmament Yearbook. (2012). Vol. 37, Part I (pp. 3–4). New York: United Nations Publications.

'Barbaric' sexual violence perpetrated by Islamic State militants in Iraq. (2014). *UN News Centre.* Retrieved from http://www.un.org/apps/news/story.asp?NewsID=48477

2011 Data Breach Investigations Report . (2012). Verizon RISK Team.

5th Report of Session 2009–10: Protecting Europe against large-scale cyber-attacks, report with evidence (No. HL Paper 68) (2010). *The European Union Committee of the House of Lords.*

A Comprehensive Approach to Cyber Security. (n. d.). *OSCE.* Retrieved from http://www.osce.org/event/cyber_sec2011

A New Philosophy and Approach to Incident Response. (n. d.). Retrieved from http://www.poole.ncsu.edu/erm/index.php/articles/entry/Cyber-Crisis-Management

Abbasi, A. H. (2012). *Indus Basin Treaty.* Pildat Report, Pildat.

Abercrombie, R. K., Ferragut, E. M., Sheldon, F. T., & Grimaila, M. R. (2011, April). Addressing the Need for Independence in the CSE Model. In Computational Intelligence in Cyber Security (CICS), 2011 IEEE Symposium on (pp. 68-75). IEEE. doi:10.1109/CICYBS.2011.5949395

Abercrombie, R. K., Sheldon, F. T., & Mili, A. (2008, December). Synopsis of evaluating security controls based on key performance indicators and stakeholder mission value. In High Assurance Systems Engineering Symposium, 2008. HASE 2008. 11th IEEE (pp. 479-482). IEEE. doi:10.1109/HASE.2008.61

Abercrombie, R. K., Sheldon, F. T., & Mili, A. (2009, March). Managing complex IT security processes with value based measures. In Computational Intelligence in Cyber Security, 2009. CICS'09. IEEE Symposium on (pp. 69-75). IEEE. doi:10.1109/CICYBS.2009.4925092

Abraham, D. Sofaer, D. C., & Whitfield D. (n. d.). Cyber Security and International Agreements. *Proceedings of workshop on Deterring Cyber Attacks: Informing Strategies and Developing Options for US Policy.*

Abubakar, A. (2014). Boko Haram under scrutiny over foreign fighter claim. Retrieved from http://news.yahoo.com/boko-haram-under-scrutiny-over-foreign-fighters-claim-150350774.html

Ackerman, S. (2014, October 2). Obama maintains Al-Qaida and Isis are 'one and the same' despite evidence of schism. *The Guardian.* Retrieved from http://www.theguardian.com/world/2014/oct/02/isis-al-qaida-obama-administration-argument-same-strikes-break

Acquiring high tech crime tools. (2006). *High Tech Crime Brief, 13.* Retrieved from http://www.aic.gov.au/documents/A/B/C/%7bABCFCBC4-541A-4ED8-822E-3A0C3B082644%7dhtcb013.pdf

Additional Protocol to the Convention on Cybercrime ETS 189. (2003). *Council of Europe.* Retrieved from http://conventions.coe.int/Treaty/en/Treaties/Html/189.htm

Adegbulu, F. (2013). Boko Haram: The emergence of a terrorist sect in Nigeria 2009-2013. *African Identities, 11*(3), 260–273. doi:10.1080/14725843.2013.839118

Adhikari, R. (2009, August 13). Another day, another DDoS blitz for Twitter, *E-Commerce Times*. Retrieved from http://www.ecommercetimes.com/story/67851.html# Adin of Crimea.

Adibe, J. (2013). What do we really know about Boko Haram?. Mantzikos, I. (Ed.), *Boko Haram – Anatomy of a Crisis*. Retrieved from http://www.e-ir.info/wp-content/uploads/Boko-Haram-e-IR.pdf

Adjemov, S. A. (2011). *International Information Security: Problems and Decisions*. Moscow, Komov SA.

Administration strategy on mitigating the theft of U.S. trade secrets. (2013). *Executive Office of the President of the United States*. Retrieved from http://www.whitehouse.gov/sites/default/files/omb/IPEC/admin_strategy_on_mitigating_the_theft_of_u.s._trade_secrets.pdf

Agin, W. E. (2008, March 26). Internet Law Liability Report #3: Jurisdictions in Cyberspace. *American Bar Association, Law Cyberspace Law Committee.*

Agreement between India and Pakistan on Pre-Notification of Flight Testing of Ballistic Missiles. (n. d.). *Stimson.org*. Retrieved from http://www.stimson.org/research-pages/agreement-between-india-and-pakistan-on-pre-notification-of-flight-testing-of-ballistic-missiles/

Agreement between Military Representatives of India and Pakistan Regarding the Establishment of a Ceasefire Line in the State of Jammu and Kashmir (Karachi Agreement). (1949, July 27). *United Nations Peacemaker*. Retrieved from http://peacemaker.un.org/indiapakistan-karachiagreement49

Agreement between the Governments of the Member States of the SCO on Cooperation in the Field of International Information Security. (2009, June 15). FMPRC. Retrieved from http://www.fmprc.gov.cn/eng/wjdt/2649 /t569701.htm

Ahmar, M. (Ed.) (2001). The Challenges of Confidence Building in South Asia. New Delhi: Har-Anand Publications.

Ahmer, M. (Ed.). (1997). *Internal and External Dynamics of South Asian Security*. Karachi: Fazleesons.

Ahsan, S. A. (2008). *Current Situation and Issues of Illegal and Harmful Activities in the Field of Information and Communication Technology in Pakistan* [participant papers]. 140th International Training Course.

Aissa, A. B. A., Mili, A., Abercrombie, R. K., & Sheldon, F. T. (2010). Modeling stakeholder/value dependency through mean failure cost. In Proceedings of *6th Annual Cyber Security and Information Intelligence Research Workshop (CSI-IRW-2010)*. ACM International Conference.

Aissa, A. B., Abercrombie, R. K., Sheldon, F. T., & Mili, A. (2012). Defining and computing a value based cyber-security measure. Information Systems and e-Business Management, 10(4), 433-453.

Aissa, A. B., Abercrombie, R. K., Sheldon, F. T., & Mili, A. (2010). Quantifying security threats and their potential impacts: A case study. *Innovations in Systems and Software Engineering, 6*(4), 269–281. doi:10.1007/s11334-010-0123-2

Akuetteh, T. (n. d.). Creating the Enabling Environment within the ECOWAS Region [Visual Presentation].

al Jazeera. (2014, May 15). *Timeline: Ukraine's political crisis*. Retrieved from http://www.aljazeera.com/news/europe/2014/03/timeline-ukraine-political-crisis-201431143722854652.html

Al Qassemi, S. (2013, November 21). The other special relationship: the UAE and the UK. *The National*. Retrieved from: http://www.thenational.ae/thenationalconversation/news-comment/the-other-special-relationship-the-uae-and-the-uk

Aldrich, R. W. (1996, Fall). The International Legal Implications of Information Warfare. *Airpower Journal.*

Aldrich, R. J. (2010). *GCHQ*. London: HarperPress.

Alert standard format specification. (2003, April 23). *Distributed Management Task Force*. Retrieved from http://www. dmtf.org/sites/default/files/standards/documents/DSP0136.pdf

Alexander, D. (2011). U.S. reserves right to meet cyber attack with force.

Alexis, A. (2013, April 9). Debate brewing over whether companies should strike back at their cyber attackers. *Bloomberg*. Retrieved from http://www.bna.com/debate-brewing-whether-n17179873246/

Ali, L. (2014, September 22). Islamic State's soft weapon of choice: social media. *LA Times*, Retrieved from http://www. latimes.com/entertainment/la-et-islamic-state-media-20140922-story.html

Allen, K. W. (2001). *Confidence Building Measures and the People's Liberation Army. In C. Cao & B. J. Dickson (Eds.) Remaking the Chinese State: Strategies, Society and Security.* (pp. 228-252). London: Routledge.

Allman, M., Paxson, V., & Terrell, J. (2007, October). A brief history of scanning. In *Proceedings of the 7th ACM SIG-COMM conference on Internet measurement* (pp. 77-82). ACM. doi:10.1145/1298306.1298316

Alperovitch, D. (2011).Towards establishment of cyberspace deterrence strategy. In *Proceedings of the 3rd International Conference on Cyber Conflict (ICCC)*, Tallinn:IEEE.

Alwi, N. H. M., & Fan, I. S.MohdAlwi. (2010). Threats analysis for e-learning. *International Journal Technology Enhanced Learning*, 2(4), 358–371. doi:10.1504/IJTEL.2010.035738

Amoroso, E. G. (2011). *Cyber Attacks: Protecting National Infrastructure. Burlington MA*. El SevierInc.

Andreasen, S. & Clarke, R. A. (2013, June 14). Cyberwar's threat does not justify a new policy of nuclear deterrence. *The Washington Post*.

Anon. (2014, February 13). Vitali Klitschko's UDAR party hacked Confidential data leaked. *CyberWarNews*. Retrieved from http://www.cyberwarnews.info/2014/02/13/opindependence-vitali-klitschkos-udar-party-hacked-confidential-data-leaked/

Anonymous Compiler. (2010, July 31). *2Bangkok.com*. Retrieved from http://2bangkok.com/blocked.shtml

ANSI/ISA-95.00.01, Enterprise-Control System Integration Part 1: Models and Terminology. (2000). International Society of Automation.

APEC Strategy to Ensure Trusted, Secure and Sustainable Online Environment. (n. d.). *Asia-Pacific Economic Cooperation*. Retrieved from http://www.apec.org/Groups/SOM-Steering-Committee-on-Economic-and-Technical-Cooperation/Working-Groups/~/media/Files/Groups/TEL/05_TEL_APECStrategy.pdf

Appelbaum, J., & Poitras, L. (2013). "Als Zielobjekt markiert": Der Enthüller Edward Snowden über die geheime Macht der NSA [Mark as Target: The whistleblower Edward Snowden about the secret power of the NSA]. *Der Spiegel, 28,* 22-24.

APT30 and the mechanics of a long-running cyber espionage operation. (2015, April 15). *FireEye Threat Intelligence Special Report*. Retrieved from https://www2.fireeye.com/rs/fireeye/images/rpt-apt30.pdf

Arbor Networks and Google Ideas. (2013). *Digital Attack Map*. Retrieved from http://www.digitalattackmap.com

Arimatsu, L. (2012). A treaty for governing cyber-weapons: Potential benefits and practical limitations. In *Proceedings of the 4th International Conference on Cyber Conflict (CYCON)*. Tallinn:IEEE.

Arimatsu, L. (2012). *The legal application of the prohibition of the threat or use of force in cyberspace: A starting point? Proceedings of Cyber Security Conference 2012: The Role of Confidence-Building Measures in Assuring Cyber Stability.* Geneva, Switzerland: UNIDIR.

Armistead, L. (2004). *Information Operations: Warfare and the Hard Reality of Soft Power.* Dulles, Virginia, USA: Brassey's Inc.

Arquilla, J., & Ronfeldt, D. (1993). Cyberwar is coming! *Comparative Strategy, 12*(2), 141–165. doi:10.1080/01495939308402915

Arquilla, J., & Ronfeldt, D. (1997). Cyberwar is Coming! In J. Arquilla & D. Ronfeldt (Eds.), *In Athena's Camp: Preparing for Conflict in the Information Age,* (pp. 23–60). Santa Monica, California, USA: RAND.

Arvind Gupta (2012). CBMs in Cyber Space: What should be India's Approach? *Institue for Defence Studies and Analyses.*

ASEAN Cybercrimelaw. (n. d.). *Cybercrimelaw.net.* Retrieved from http://www.cybercrimelaw.net/ASEAN.html

Ashford, W. (2014, February 12). NTP-based DDoS attacks a concern, says Cloudflare. *Computer Weekly.* Retrieved from http://www.computerweekly.com/news/2240214216/NTP-based-DDoS-attacks-a-concern-says-Cloudflare

Ashwood, W. (2013). David Cameron pledges UK collaboration with India to fight Cyber Attacks. *ComputerWeekly.com.*

At UN, Kazakhstan calls for global cybersecurity treaty to deter hackers. (2011). *UN News Centre.* Retrieved from http://www.un.org/

Aubert, J., Schaberreiter, T., Incoul, C., Khadraoui, D., & Gateau, B. (2010, February 15-18). Risk-Based Methodology for Real-Time Security Monitoring of Interdependent Services in Critical Infrastructures. In M. Takizawa, A. M. Tjoa, M. Aleksy, S. Ghernouti-Hélie, G. Quirchmayr, & E. Weippl (Eds.) *Proceedings of the Fifth International Conference on Availability, Reliability, and Security (ARES '10),* (pp. 262–267). Krakow, Poland. doi:10.1109/ARES.2010.102

Audu, O. (2014a, July 14). *Boko Haram leader, Shekau, mocks #BringBackOurGirls campaign. Premium Times.* Retrieved from https://www.premiumtimesng.com/news/164868-boko-haram-leader-shekau-mocks-bringbackourgirls-campaign.html

Audu, O. (2014b, February 20). Nigeria: Boko Haram Leader, Shekau, Speaks - Vows to attack Nigerian refineries, Buhari, Babangida, others. *Premium Times.* Retrieved from http://allafrica.com/stories/201402210198.html

Aydin, F. (2012). *Cyber security in the national protection of Turkey.* Ankara: Cankaya University.

Bagchi, I. (2013). Government to Roll Out New Cybersecurity Architecture. *The Times of India.*

Bahill, A. T., & Chapman, W. L. (1993). A tutorial on quality function deployment. *Engineering Management Journal, 5*(3), 24–35. doi:10.1080/10429247.1993.11414742

Baiardi, F., Telmon, C., & Sgandurra, D. (2009). Hierarchical, Model-based Risk Management of Critical Infrastructures. In T. Aven, J. E. Vinnem, & C. G. Soares (Eds.) *Proceedings of the 18th European Safety and Reliability Conference (ESREL 2007)* (Vol. 94, pp. 1403–1415). Stavanger, Norway. June 25–27, 2007. doi:10.1016/j.ress.2009.02.001

Bailey, D., & Wright, E. (2003). *Practical SCADA for Industry (IDC Technology).* Amsterdam: Elsevier Press.

Bailey, M., Cooke, E., Jahanian, F., Myrick, A., & Sinha, S. (2006, March). Practical darknet measurement. In *40th Annual Conference on Information Sciences and Systems,* 2006 (pp. 1496-1501). IEEE.

Baines, P. R., O'Shaughnessy, N. J., Moloney, K., Richards, B., Butler, S., & Gill, M. (2010). The dark side of political marketing: Islamist propaganda, Reversal Theory and British Muslims. *European Journal of Marketing, 44*(3/4), 478–495. doi:10.1108/03090561011020543

Bajaj, V. (2012, August 23). India Presses Web Sites over Ethnic Clashes. *International Herald Tribune,* p. 13.

Bajpai, K. (1999). *Confidence Building Measures in South Asia Regional Centre of Strategic Studies.* Colombo.

Baker, F., Harrop, W., & Armitage, G. (2010). IPv4 and IPv6 Greynets.

Baker, S. (2012, September 19). Rethinking cybersecurity, retribution, and the role of the private sectors. *Steptoe.* Retrieved from http://www.steptoecyberblog.com/2012/09/19/rethinking-cybersecurity-retribution-and-the-role-of-the-private-sector/?

Baker, S. (2013, November 26). Hackback backers' comeback? *The Volokh Conspiracy.* Retrieved from http://www.volokh.com/2013/11/26/hackback-backers-comeback/

Banavar, G., Chandra, T., Strom, R., & Sturman, D. (1999). A Case for Message Oriented Middleware. Em P. Jayanti (Ed.), Distributed Computing, Vol. 1693, (pp. 1–17). doi:10.1007/3-540-48169-9_1

Bank, W. (1960). Indus Waters Treaty.

Baran, P. (1964). Security, secrecy, and tamper-free considerations. *Distributed Communications*, No. 9.

Barrie, D., & Taverna, M. A. (2006). Spy game. *Aviation Week & Space Technology, 165*(23), 74.

Basu, E. (2013). Hacking Insulin Pumps and Other Medical Devices from Black Hat. *Forbes.com.* Retrieved from www.forbes.com/sites/ericbasu/2013/08/03/hacking-insulin-pumps-and-other-medical-devices-reality-not-fiction

Becker, O. (2014, July 12). ISIS Has a Really Slick and Sophisticated Media Department. *VICE News.* Retrieved from https://news.vice.com/article/isis-has-a-really-slick-and-sophisticated-media-department

Bederman, D. J. (2002). Counterintuiting countermeasures. *The American Journal of International Law, 96*(4), 817–832. doi:10.2307/3070680

Behind the Syrian conflict's digital front lines. (2015, February 1). *FireEye Threat Intelligence Special Report.* Retrieved from https://www.fireeye.com/content/dam/fireeye-www/global/en/current-threats/pdfs/rpt-behind-the-syria-conflict.pdf

Bellovin, S. M. (1992, September). There be dragons. In *UNIX Security Symposium III Proceedings* (pp. 1-16).

Ben Aissa, A., Abercrombie, R. K., Sheldon, F. T., & Mili, A. (2009, April). Quantifying security threats and their impact. In *Proceedings of the 5th Annual Workshop on Cyber Security and Information Intelligence Research: Cyber Security and Information Intelligence Challenges and Strategies*, (pp. 26). ACM.

Bénichou, D., & Lefranc, S. (2005). Introduction to network self-defense: Technical and judicial issues. *Journal of Computer Virology, 1*(1-2), 24–31. doi:10.1007/s11416-005-0006-5

Bennetts, M. (2014, April 15). Inside Russia's gaffe-prone propaganda war. *Vocativ.* Retrieved from http://www.vocativ.com/world/russia/inside-russias-gaffe-prone-propaganda-war/

Bergen, P., Sterman, D., Schneider, E., & Cahall, B. (2014). *Do NSA's Bulk Surveillance Programs Stop Terrorists?* Washington, DC: New America Foundation.

Berger, J. M. (2014, June 16). How ISIS Games Twitter. *The Atlantic.* Retrieved from http://www.theatlantic.com/international/archive/2014/06/isis-iraq-twitter-social-media-strategy/372856/

Berger, J. M. (2011). *Jihad Joe: Americans Who Go to War in the Name of Islam.* Washington, DC: Potomac Books.

Berkhout, A. Smith and A. Stirling. (2003). Socio-technological regimes and transition contexts. *SPRU Electronic Working Paper no. 106.* Falmer, UK: The Freeman Centre, University of Sussex.

Bernadette, H. S., Martin, M. V., Hung, P. C. K., & Rueda, L. (2006). Cyber child pornography: a review paper of the social and legal issues and remedies – and a proposed technological solution. In Aggression and Violent Behavior, Vol. 12(1), (2007, January/February).

Bernhardt, T., & Vasseur, A. (2007). Esper: Event Stream Processing and Correlation. *O'Reilly On Java*. Retrieved from http://www.onjava.com/pub/a/onjava/2007/03/07/esper-event-stream-processing-and-correlation.html

Bertoni, A., Ciancamerla, E., di Prospero, F., Lefevre, D., Minichino, M., Lev, L., et al. (2010). Interdependency modelling framework, indicators and models – Final Report. Ciancamerla, E. & Minichino, M., (Eds.) MICIE Project Deliverable D2.2.3. European Commission FP7.

Bertram, S., & Ellison, K. (2014). Sub Saharan African terrorist groups' use of the internet. *Journal of Terrorism Research*, *5*, 1. Retrieved from http://ojs.st-andrews.ac.uk/index.php/jtr/article/view/825/704

Bessani, A., Sousa, P., Correia, M., & Neves, N. (2007). *Intrusion-tolerant protection for critical infrastructures* (Technical Report). University of Lisbon. Retrieved from http://www.di.fc.ul.pt/~nuno/PAPERS/TR-07-8.pdf

Betts, R. (1983). *Surprise attack: Lessons for defense planning*. Washington: Brookings Institution.

Betz, D., & Stevens, T. (2013). Analogical reasoning and cyber security. *Security Dialogue*, *44*(2), 147–164. doi:10.1177/0967010613478323

Bevan, M. (1997). History. Retrieved from http://www.kujimedia.com/articles/

Bevan, M. (2012, November 9). [Details about information leading to the arrest].

Bicknell, K. D., & Bicknell, B. A. (1994). *The Road Map to Repeatable Success: Using QFD to Implement Changes*. Boca Raton, FL: CRC Press.

Billo, C., & Chang, W. (2004). *Cyber warfare an analysis of the means and motivations of selected nation states*. Retrieved from http://www.ists.dartmouth.edu/docs/cyberwarfare.pdf

Black, I., & Sample, I. (2013, August 29). UK report on chemical attack in Syria adds nothing to informed speculation. *The Guardian*. Retrieved from http://www.theguardian.com/world/2013/aug/29/uk-report-chemical-attack-syria

Blanchard, C. (2014, January 27). Promises to be Another Banner Year for Cybersecurity. *Aerospace & Defense Law, 360.*

Blount, A. (2012-13). Topic I: Assessing the current state of cybersecurity and its implications for regional defense and economic interest. *Model Arab League.*

Blueprint for a Secure Cyber Future . (2011US Department of Homeland Security Washington, DC: US Department of Homeland Security. (pp. 50).

Blum, A. (2012). *Tubes: A journey to the center of the internet*. New York: Ecco.

Bobbitt, P. (2009). *Terror and consent: The wars for the twenty-first century*. New York: Alfred A Knopf.

Bobert, W. E. (n. d.). A Survey of Challenges in Attribution. Proceedings of workshop *Deterring Cyber Attacks: Informing Strategies and Developing Options for U.S. Policy.* (pp. 43).

Bodeau, D., & Graubart, R. (2011, September). Cyber Resiliency Engineering Framework, Version 1.0. *mitre.org*. Retrieved from http://www.mitre.org/sites/default/files/publications/pr-14-4035-cyber-resiliency-engineering-aid-techniques.pdf

Bodeau, D., & Graubart, R. (2013). Cyber Resiliency Assessment: Enabling Architectural Improvement. *mitre.org*. Retrieved from www.mitre.org/sites/default/files/pdf/12_3795.pdf

Boebert, W. E. (2010). A Survey of Challenges in Attribution. In *Proceedings of a Workshop on Deterring Cyberattacks: Informing Strategies and Developing Options for U.S. Policy.*Washington, DC: The National Academies Press.

Bohdanova, T. (2014, December 9). How Internet Tools Turned Ukraine's #Euromaidan Protests Into a Movement. *Global Voices Online*. Retrieved from http://globalvoicesonline.org/2013/12/09/how-internet-tools-turned-euromaidan-protests-into-a-movement/

Bojanc, R., & Jerman-Blazic, B. (2008). An economic modelling approach to information security risk management. *International Journal of Information Management, 28*(5), 413–422. doi:10.1016/j.ijinfomgt.2008.02.002

Boland, J. (2011, June 20). Ten Years of the Shanghai Cooperation Organization. *21st Century Defense Initiative*.

Bolt, N. (2008). Propaganda of the deed and the Irish Republican brotherhood: From the politics of 'shock and awe' to the 'imagined political community'. *The RUSI Journal, 153*(1), 48–54. doi:10.1080/03071840801984565

Botnets: the new battleground of cybercrime. (2010). *Techradar*. Retrieved from http://www.techradar.com/news/internet/botnets-the-new-battleground-of-cybercrime-719804

Bou-Harb, E., Debbabi, M., & Assi, C. (2013). A systematic approach for detecting and clustering distributed cyber scanning. *Computer Networks, 57*(18), 3826–3839. doi:10.1016/j.comnet.2013.09.008

Boyle, J. (2007). Foucault in cyberspace: Surveillance, sovereignty, and hardwired censors. *University of Cincinnati Law Review, 66*(1), 178–183.

Bradsher, K. (2014, May 20). Retaliatory attacks, online. *The New York Times*. Retrieved from http://www.nytimes.com/2014/05/21/business/international/firms-in-united-states-see-risk-in-challenges-to-beijing.html

Brady, A.-M. (2012). Introduction - Market-Friendly, Scientific, High Tech, and Politics-Lite: China's New Approach to Propaganda. In A.-M. Brady (Ed.), *China's Thought Management* (pp. 1–10). Abingdon, UK: Routledge.

Brady, A.-M. (Ed.). (2012). *China's Thought Management*. Abingdon, UK: Routledge.

Brandt, A. (2005, May 5). Stupid hacker tricks, part two: The folly of youth. *InfoWorld Daily News*.

Brazzoli, M. S. (2007). Future Prospects of Information Warfare and Particularly Psychological Operations. In L. le Roux (Ed.), *South African Army Vision 2020* (pp. 217–232). Pretoria: Institute for Security Studies.

Brenner, S. W. (2007). At Light Speed: Attribution and Response to Cybercrime/Terrorism/Warfare. *The Journal of Criminal Law & Criminology, 97*(2), 379–476.

Brenner, S. W., & Koops, B. (2004). Approaches to cybercrime jurisdiction. *The Journal of High Technology Law, 4*(1), 1–46.

Bright, P. (2013, March 27). Spamhaus DDoS grows to Internet-threatening size. *ARSTechnica*. Retrieved from http://arstechnica.com/security/2013/03/spamhaus-ddos-grows-to-internet-threatening-size/

Brink, D. (2010, October 7). *Quantifying Business Value of Application Security: Cost Avoidance, Cost Savings*. Retrieved from http://blogs.aberdeen.com/it-security/quantifying-business-value-of-application-security-cost-avoidance-cost-savings/

British Broadcasting Corporation (BBC). (2014a, May 8). *Ukraine crisis timeline*. Retrieved from http://www.bbc.com/news/world-middle-east-26248275

British Broadcasting Corporation (BBC). (2014b, April 22). *Ukraine crisis: What the 'Russian soldier' photos say*. Retrieved from http://www.bbc.com/news/world-europe-27104904

Broad, W. J., Markoff, J., & Sanger, D. E. (2011, January 15). Israeli Test on Worm Called Crucial in Iran Nuclear Dela. *The New York Times*.

Broadhead, R. S., Heckathorn, D. D., Weakliem, D. L., Anthony, D. L., Madray, H., Mills, R. J., & Hughes, J. (1998). Harnessing peer networks as an instrument for AIDS prevention: Results from a peer-driven intervention. *Public Health Reports (Washington, D.C.), 113*(1), 42–57. Retrieved from http://www.ncbi.nlm.nih.gov/pmc/articles/PMC1307726/#reference-sec PMID:9722809

Brodsky, R. R. J. (Ed.). (2013). *Handbook of SCADA/Control Systems Security.* CRC Press.

Bromby, M. (2006). Security against crime: Technologies for detecting and preventing crime. *International Review of Law Computers & Technology, 20*(1-2), 1–5. doi:10.1080/13600860600818235

Brown, I. (2010). Communications Data Retention in an Evolving Internet. *International Journal of Law and Information Technology, 19*(2), 95–109. doi:10.1093/ijlit/eaq016

Brown, I., & Korff, D. (2009). Terrorism and the Proportionality of Internet Surveillance. *European Journal of Criminology, 6*(2), 119–135. doi:10.1177/1477370808100541

Brustein, J. (2013, June 3). Letting companies hack the hackers: What could go wrong? *Businessweek.* Retrieved from http://www.businessweek.com/articles/2013-06-03/letting-companies-hack-the-hackers-what-could-go-wrong

Buckley, C. (2013, August 21). China Memo Reveals Fears of Western Influence. *International Herald Tribune,* (pp. 1, 3).

Bumiller, E. (2013). Pentagon Expanding Cybersecurity Force to Protect Networks against Attacks. *The New York Times.*

Bunker, R. J. (1999). Unconventional Warfare Philosophers. *Small Wars & Insurgencies, 10*(3), 136–149. doi:10.1080/09592319908423253

Buying remote administration tools. (2014, May 19). *Schwarze Sonne.* Retrieved from http://ss-rat.blogspot.de/2014/05/buying-remote-adminstration-tools.html

Caldeira, F., Castrucci, M., Aubigny, M., Aubert, J., Macone, D., & Monteiro, E., … Suraci, V. (2010a). Secure Mediation Gateway Architecture Enabling the Communication Among Critical Infrastructures. In P. Cunningham & M. Cunningham (Eds.), *Proceedings of the Future Network and MobileSummit 2010 Conference (2010, June 16-18).* Florence, Italy.

Caldeira, F., Monteiro, E., & Simões, P. (2010d). Trust and reputation management for critical infrastructure protection. In H. Jahankhani & S. Tenreiro de Magalhães (Eds.), Special Issue on Global Security, Safety and Sustainability, Vol. 3(3), (pp. 187–203).

Caldeira, F., Schaberreiter, T., Varrette, S., Monteiro, E., Simões, P., Bouvry, P., & Khadraoui, D. (2013). Trust based interdependency weighting for on-line risk monitoring in interdependent critical infrastructures. In K. M. Khan (Ed.), International Journal of Secure Software Engineering (IJSSE) (Vol. 4(4)). IGI Global. doi:10.4018/ijsse.2013100103

Caldeira, F., Monteiro, E., & Simões, P. (2010b). Trust and Reputation for Information Exchange in Critical Infrastructures. In C. Xenakis, & S. Wolthusen (Eds.), *Proceedings of the 5th International Workshop on Critical Information Infrastructures Security (CRITIS 2010), (2010, September 23-24),* Vol. 6712, pp. 140–152). Athens, Greece. doi:10.1007/978-3-642-21694-7_12

Caldeira, F., Monteiro, E., & Simões, P. (2010c). Trust and Reputation Management for Critical Infrastructure Protection. In S. Tenreiro de Magalhães, H. Jahankhani, & A. G. Hessami (Eds.), *Proceedings of the 6th International Conference on Global Security, Safety, and Sustainability (ICGS3 2010), (2010, September 1-3),* Vol. 92, (pp. 39–47). Braga, Portugal. doi:10.1007/978-3-642-15717-2_5

Caldeira, F., Schaberreiter, T., Monteiro, E., Aubert, J., Simões, P., & Khadraoui, D. (2011). Trust based interdependency weighting for on-line risk monitoring in interdependent critical infrastructures. In F. Cuppens, S. Foley, B. Groza, & M. Minea (Eds.), *Proceedings of the Sixth International Conference on Risks and Security of Internet and Systems (CRiSIS), (2011, September 26-28)*, (pp. 1–7). Timisoara, Romania. doi:10.1109/CRiSIS.2011.6061545

Caltagirone, S., Pendergast, A., & Betz, C. (2013). *The Diamond Model of Intrusion Analysis.* Arlington, VA: Threat Connect. (pp. 1–61).

Campbell, K., Gordon, L. A., Loeb, M. P., & Zhou, L. (2003). The economic cost of publicly announced security breaches: Empirical evidence from the stock market. *Journal of Computer Security, 11,* 431–438.

Cantril, H. (1941). *The Psychology of Social Movements.* New York: John Wiley and Sons Inc. doi:10.1037/13593-000

Capodieci, P., Diblasi, S., Ciancamerla, E., Minichino, M., Foglietta, C., & Lefevre, D., … Aubigny, M. (2010). Improving Resilience of Interdependent Critical Infrastructures via an On-Line Alerting System. In A. Rizzo (Ed.), *Proceedings of the first International Conference COMPENG, Complexity in Engineering, (2010, February 22-24)*, (pp. 88–90). Rome, Italy. doi:10.1109/COMPENG.2010.28

Carr, J. (2010). Stuxnet's Finnish-Chinese Connection. *Forbes.* Retrieved from http://www.forbes.com/sites/firewall/2010/12/14/stuxnets-finnish-chinese-connection/

Carr, J. (2011). The New York Times fails to deliver Stuxnet's creators. *Forbes.* Retrieved from http://www.forbes.com/sites/jeffreycarr/2011/01/17/the-new-york-times-fails-to-deliver-stuxnets-creators/

Carr, J. (2012). OSCE's Cyber Security Confidence Building Measures Revealed by Anonymous. Retrieved from http://jeffreycarr. blogspot.com/2012/11/osces-cyber-security-confidence.htm

Carr, J. (2010). *Inside Cyber Warfare: Mapping the Cyber Underworld. Sebastopol,* CA: O'Reilly Media Inc.

Carr, M. (2013). Internet freedom, human rights and power. *Australian Journal of International Affairs, 67*(5), 621–637. doi:10.1080/10357718.2013.817525

Carroll, L. (2014, July 20). Kerry: Ukrainian separatist 'bragged' on social media about shooting down Malaysia Flight 17. *Politifact.* Retrieved from http://www.politifact.com/truth-o-meter/statements/2014/jul/20/john-kerry/kerry-ukrainian-separatist-bragged-social-media/

Carter, J. A., Maher, S., & Neumann, P. R. (2014). Greenbirds: Measuring Importance and Influence in Syrian Foreign Fighter Networks. London: ICSR, King's College London; Retrieved from http://www.google.co.uk/url?sa=t&rct=j&q=&esrc=s&source=web&cd=1&ved=0CCQQFjAA&url=http%3A%2F%2Ficsr.info%2Fwp-content%2Fuploads%2F2014%2F04%2FICSR-Report-Greenbirds-Measuring-Importance-and-Infleunce-in-Syrian-Foreign-Fighter-Networks.pdf&ei=_hxBVN3AF4fUat-LgpAG&usg=AFQjCNHRlI4cBTcsCJDeGMw55DKRZ6HhAg&sig2=T4r9hljxs4sW-dCJ_Uf4pA&bvm=bv.77648437,d.bGQ

Carter, J. G., & Carter, D. L. (2009). Intelligence-led policing: Conceptual and functional considerations for public policy. *Criminal Justice Policy Review, 20*(3), 310–325. doi:10.1177/0887403408327381

Carty, V. (2011). *Wired and Mobilizing: Social Movements, New Technology, and Electoral Politics.* New York: Routledge.

Case concerning Military and Paramilitary Activities in and against Nicaragua (*Nicaragua v. United States of America*), Judgment of 27 June 1986, [1986] ICJ Rep. 14.

Case concerning Oil Platforms (*Islamic Republic of Iran v. United States of America*), Judgment of 6 November 2003, (2003) ICJ Rep. 161.

Case, J., Mundy, R., Partain, D., & Stewart, B. (2002). *Introduction and Applicability Statements for Internet-Standard Management Framework* (No. RFC3410). RFC Editor. Retrieved from https://www.rfc-editor.org/info/rfc3410

Casey-Maslen, S. (2010). Non-kinetic-energy weapons termed 'non-lethal:' A Preliminary Assessment under International Humanitarian Law and International Human Rights Law.

Cashell, B., Jackson, W. D., Jickling, M., & Webel, B. (2004). The economic impact of cyber-attacks. *Congressional Research Service*. Retrieved from http://www.fas.org/sgp/crs/misc/RL32331.pdf

Cassese, A. (2003). Is the bell tolling for universality? A plea for a sensible notion of universal jurisdiction. *Journal of International Criminal Justice, 1*(3), 589–595. doi:10.1093/jicj/1.3.589

Castells, M. (1996). The Information Age: Economy, Society and Culture, Vol. I. *The Rise of the Network Society*. Oxford, UK: Blackwell Publishers.

Castrucci, M., Macone, D., Suraci, V., Inzerilli, T., Neri, A., Panzieri, S., Foglietta, C., Oliva, G., Aubert, J., Incoul, C., Caldeira, F., Aubigny, M., Harpes, C., & Kloda (2010). Secure Mediation Gateway Architecture – Final Version. In Castrucci, M., (Ed.). *MICIE Project Deliverable D4.2.2. European Commission FP7*.

Castrucci, M., Neri, A., Caldeira, F., Aubert, J., Khadraoui, D., & Aubigny, M. … Capodieci, P. (2012). Design and implementation of a mediation system enabling secure communication among Critical Infrastructures. In S. Shenoi (Ed.), International Journal of Critical Infrastructure Protection Vol. 5(2), (pp. 86–97).

Caton, J. (2013). Exploring the prudent limits of automated cyber attack. In *Proceedings of the 5th International Conference on Cyber Conflict (CYCON)*, Tallinn:IEEE.

Cavusoglu, H., Mishra, B., & Raghunathan, S. (2004). A model for evaluating it security investments. *Communications of the ACM, 47*(7), 87–92. doi:10.1145/1005817.1005828

CBC (2011). Report of the 30thMeeting of the Council of Ministers: Harnessing Science and Technology for Development 37.

CERT-EE. (2013, November 1-7). CERT-EE report: DDoS attacks, e-mail messages with forged sender address and defacements. *Estonian Information System's Authority*. Retrieved from https://www.ria.ee/cert-ee-report-opindependence-november-1-7/

Certification of Information Systems Security Principles (n. d.). Retrieved from http://mhprofessional.com/downloads/products/0072254238/0072254238_ch01.pdf

CET No. 185. (n. d.). *Council of Europe Convention on Cybercrimes*. Retrieved from http://conventions.coe.int/Treaty/Commun/ChercheSig.asp?NT=185&CM=8&DF=&CL=ENG

Cetinkaya, E., & Sterbenz, J. (2013, March). A taxonomy of network challenges.*Proceedings of the 9th IEEE/IFIP International Conference on the Design of Reliable Communication Networks (DRCN)*. Budapest: IEEE/IFIP.

Cha, A. E., & Nakashima, E. (2014, January 14). Google China cyberattack part of vast espionage campaign, experts say. *The Washington Post*. Retrieved from http://www.washingtonpost.com/wp-dyn/content/article/2010/01/13/AR2010011300359.html

Chabinsky, S. (2013). *Cyber Warfare*. Paper presented at *the American Center for Democracy*. http://www.youtube.com/watch?v=Uiz2R_f1Lxo

Chabinsky, S., Henry, S., & Painter, C. (2012, May 16). Lessons from Our Cyber Past: The First Cyber Cops. *Atlantic Council*. Retrieved from http://www.atlanticcouncil.org/index.php?option=com_content&view=article&id=9693:lessons-from-our-cyber-past-the-first-cyber-cops&catid=8:events&Itemid=101

Chabot, S. (2013) Asia: The Cyber Security Battleground.

Challenges in Cyber Security. (2011). *Risks, Strategies and Confidence Building – Germany* [Conference Report]. Berlin: German Ministry of Foreign Affairs.

Chambers, C., Dolske, J., & Iyer, J. (n.d.). TCP/IP security. *Linux Security*. Retrieved from http://www.linuxsecurity.com/resource_files/documentation/tcpip-security.html

Chander, M. (n. d.). *National Critical Information Infrastructure Protection Centre (NCIIPC): Role, Charter & Responsibilities* [Visual Presentation].

Chapman, W. L., Bahill, A. T., & Wymore, W. (1992). *Engineering Modeling and Design*. Boca Raton, FL: CRC Press.

Chari, P. R., Cheema, P. I., & Cohen, S. P. (2007). Four Crisis and a Peace Process. Washington, DC: The Brookings Institute. (pp. 39-79).

Charter of the United Nations (1945).

Chiluwa, I. (2012). Social media networks and the discourse of resistance: A sociolinguistic CDA of Biafra online discourses. *Discourse & Society, 23*(3), 217–244. doi:10.1177/0957926511433478

Chin, D., Kaplan, J., and Weinberg, A. (2014, January) *Risk and responsibility in a hyperconnected world: Implications for enterprises*. McKinsey & Company.

China defense ministry refutes cyber attack allegations. (2013, February 2). *Xinhua*. Retrieved from http://news.xinhuanet.com/english/china/2013-02/20/c_132180777.htm

China, Russia and Other Countries Submit the Document of International Code of Conduct for Information Security to the United Nations.(2011). Ministry of Foreign Affairs of the People's Republic of China. Retrieved from http://www.fmprc.gov.cn/eng/

China, US Agree to Combat Cyber Crime. (2013). *eBeijing, Beijing International*. Retrieved from http://www.ebeijing.gov.cn/

China's Views of Sovereignty and Methods of Access Control, (2008).

Chong, A. (2013, May 9). Information Warfare? The Case for an Asian Perspective on Information Operations. *Armed Forces and Society*, 1-26. doi:10.1177/0095327X13483444

chornajuravka. (2014, March 29). Kremlin's Gremlins: pro-Russian trolls have Kremlin IP addresses. *EuroMaidanPR*. Retrieved from https://euromaidanpr.wordpress.com/2014/03/29/kremlins-gremlins-pro-russian-trolls-have-kremlin-ip-addresses/#more-5957

Christensen, C. (1997). *The innovator's dilemma: When new technologies cause great firms to fail*. Cambridge: Harvard Business School Press.

Churchman, D. (1995). *Negotiations: Process, Tactics and Theory. New York*: University Press of America.

Ciampa, M. (2008). *Security+ Guide to Network Security Fundamentals* (3rd Ed.). Cenagae Learning.

Ciancamerla, E., di Blasi, S., Fioriti, V., Foglietta, C., Minichino, M., Lefevre, D., ... (2009). Interdependency modelling framework, interdependency indicators and models – First Interim Report. Ciancamerla, E. & Minichino, M., (Eds.). MICIE Project Deliverable D2.2.1. European Commission FP7.

Ciancamerla, E., Foglietta, C., Lefevre, D., Minichino, M., Lev, L., & Shneck, Y. (2010a). Discrete Event Simulation of QoS of a SCADA System Interconnecting a Power Grid and a Telco Network. In J. Berleur, M. Hercheui, & L. Hilty (Eds.), What Kind of Information Society? Governance, Virtuality, Surveillance, Sustainability, Resilience. Proceedings of the *9th IFIP TC 9 International Conference, HCC9 2010 and 1st IFIP TC 11 International Conference, CIP 2010.* Vol. 328, (pp. 350–362). Brisbane, Australia

Ciancamerla, E., Minichino, M., Lev, L., Simões, P., Panzieri, S., Oliva, G., ... (2010b). CI Reference Scenario and service oriented approach (Final Report). Ciancamerla, E. & Minichino, M., (Eds.). MICIE Project Deliverable D2.1.2. European Commission FP7.

Citigroup hacked, customer data exposed. (2011). *CBSNews.* Retrieved from http://www.cbsnews.com/news/citigroup-hacked-customer-data-exposed/

Clapper, J. R. (2012, February 2). Unclassified Statement for the Record on the Worldwide Threat Assessment of the United States Intelligence Community for the House Permanent Select Committee on Intelligence.

Clarke, R. & Knake, R. (2010). Cyber War: The Next Threat to National Security and what to do about it: New York. HarperCollins Publishers.

Clarke, R. A., & Andreasen, S. (2013, June 15). Cyberwar's threat does not justify a new policy of nuclear deterrence. *The Washington Post.* Retrieved from http://js.washingtonpost.com/opinions/cyberwars-threat-does-not-justify-a-new-policy-of-nuclear-deterrence/2013/06/14/91c01bb6-d50e-11e2-a73e-826d299ff459_story.html

Clarke, R. A., & Knake, R. (2010). *Cyber War: The Next Threat to National Security and What to Do About It.* New York, NY: HarperCollins.

Clarke, R. A., & Knake, R. K. (2010). *Cyber war: The next threat to national security and what to do about it.* New York: Ecco.

Clarke, R. A., Morell, M. J., Stone, G. R., Sunstein, C. R., & Swire, P. (2013). *Liberty and Security in a Changing World: Report and Recommendations of The President's Review Group on Intelligence and Communications Technologies.* Washington, DC: The White House.

Clausewitz, C. (1976). *On war* (M. Howard & P. Paret, Trans. & Eds.). New Jersey: Princeton University Press.

Clayton, M. (2012, September 9). Stealing US business secrets: Experts ID two huge cyber 'gangs' in China. *Christian Science Monitor.* Retrieved from http://www.csmonitor.com/USA/2012/0914/Stealing-US-business-secrets-Experts-ID-two-huge-cyber-gangs-in-China

Clayton, M. (2014a, March 3). Where are the cyberattacks? Russia's curious forbearance in Ukraine. *Christian Science Monitor.* Retrieved from http://www.csmonitor.com/World/Security-Watch/2014/0303/Where-are-the-cyberattacks-Russia-s-curious-forbearance-in-Ukraine.-video

Clayton, M. (2014b, March 14). Major cyber-assaults on Ukraine, then Moscow, on eve of Crimea vote. *Christian Science Monitor.* Retrieved from http://www.csmonitor.com/World/Security-Watch/Cyber-Conflict-Monitor/2014/0314/Major-cyber-assaults-on-Ukraine-then-Moscow-on-eve-of-Crimea-vote-video

Clayton, M. (2014c, March 18). Massive cyberattacks slam official sites in Russia, Ukraine. *Christian Science Monitor*. Retrieved from http://www.csmonitor.com/World/Security-Watch/Cyber-Conflict-Monitor/2014/0318/Massive-cyberattacks-slam-official-sites-in-Russia-Ukraine

Clemente, D. (2012). Building Coherence and Understanding Foundational Work. Proceedings of *Cyber Security Conference 2012*. Geneva, Switzerland.

Cockburn, P. (2014, October 12). *War against Isis: US strategy in tatters as militants march on - Comment - Voices The Independent*. Retrieved from http://www.independent.co.uk/voices/comment/war-against-isis-us-strategy-in-tatters-as-militants-march-on-9789230.html?origin=internalSearch

CockpitCI FP7-SEC-2011-1 Project 285647. (2011). Cockpit, C. I., & the Consortium. Retrieved from http://CockpitCI.eu

Cocks, T. (2014, September 26). Boko Haram 'Leader', killed repeatedly, continue to threaten Nigeria, *Reuters*. Retrieved from http://uk.reuters.com/article/2014/09/26/uk-nigeria-bokoharam-idUKKCN0HL0BL20140926

Cohen, T. (2013, September 5). Obama: It's the world's 'red line' on Syria; Senate panel backs military strike plan. *CNN*. Retrieved from http://edition.cnn.com/2013/09/04/politics/us-syria/

Cohn, M. K. N. (Ed.). (2011). Crises in South Asia: Trends and Potential Consequences Washington DC: Stimson Center.

Cold War Hotline Recalled. (2003). *British Broadcasting Company*. Retrieved from http://news.bbc.co.uk/2/hi/europe/2971558.stm

Coleman, K. (2008, August 13). Cyberwar 2.0 - Russia vs Georgia. *DefenseTech*. Retrieved from http://defensetech.org/2008/08/13/cyber-war-2-0-russia-v-georgia/

Collapse of the Agra Summit: The After-Story. (2001). NDTV.

Collier, P. A., & Spaul, B. J. (1992). Problems in policing computer crime. *Policing and Society*, 2(4), 310. doi:10.1080/10439463.1992.9964650

Collins, M. (2014, May 9). #BringBackOurGirls: the power of a social media campaign. *The Guardian*. Retrieved from http://www.theguardian.com/voluntary-sector-network/2014/may/09/bringbackourgirls-power-of-social-media

Comfort, L., Boin, A., & Demchak, C. (2010). *Designing resilience: preparing for extreme events*. Pittsburgh: University of Pittsburgh Press.

Confidence Building Measures. (2012). *Stimson.org*. Retrieved from http://www.stimson.org/topics/confidence-building-measures/

Confidence-Building and Nuclear Risk-Reduction Measures in South Asia. (n. d.). *Stimson.org*. Retrieved from http://www.stimson.org/research-pages/confidence-building-measures-in-south-asia-

Connable, B. (2014). Defeating the Islamic State in Iraq. Cambridge: RAND. Retrieved from http://www.rand.org/pubs/testimonies/CT418.html

Connecting Police for a Safer World. (n. d.). Retrieved from http://www.interpol.int/About-INTERPOL/The-INTERPOL-Global-Complex-for-Innovation

Convention for the Amelioration of the Condition of the Wounded and Sick in Armed Forces in the Field (1949) (Geneva Convention No. I).

Convention for the Amelioration of the Condition of the Wounded, Sick, and Shipwrecked Members of Armed Forces at Sea (1949) (Geneva Convention No. II).

Convention on the Prohibition of the Development, Production, Stockpiling and Use of Chemical Weapons and on their Destruction(OPCW). (n. d). *OPCW.* Retrieved from http://www.opcw.org/chemical-weapons-convention

Convention Relative to the Protection of Civilian Persons in Time of War (1949) (Geneva Convention No. IV).

Conway, M. (2007). Terrorism and New Media: The Cyber-battlespace. In J.J.F. Forest (Ed), *Countering Terrorism and Insurgency in the 21st Century.* Westport, CT: Praeger Publishers. Retrieved from http://psi.praeger.com/doc.aspx?new index=1&q=Maura+Conway&imageField.x=7&imageField.y=15&c=&d=/books/gpg/C9036/C9036-3154.xml&i=0

Council of Europe adopts Internet Governance Strategy. (n. d.). Council of Europe. Retrieved from http://www.coe.int/t/DGHL/cooperation/economiccrime/cybercrime/default_en.asp

Council of Europe Convention on Cybercrime (2001), and *Additional Protocols* (2003).

Council of Europe *Convention on Cybercrime, Budapest.* (2001). Retrieved from http://conventions.coe.int/Treaty/en/Treaties /Html/189.htm

Creegan, E. (n. d.). India Pakistan sign missile notification pact.

Creery, A., & Byres, E. J. (2005). Industrial cybersecurity for power system and SCADA networks. *Petroleum and Chemical Industry Conference, 2005. Industry Applications Society 52nd Annual, (September 2005),* (pp. 303–309). Denver, USA. doi:10.1109/PCICON.2005.1524567

Crisis Management Plan for Cyber Attacks. (2010). Government of India.

CRitical Utility InfrastructurAL resilience. (2008). CRUTIAL. Retrieved from http://crutial.rse-web.it/

Croft, A. (2014, September 5). NATO agrees cyber attack could trigger military response. *Reuters.* Retrieved from http://www.reuters.com/article/2014/09/05/us-nato-cybersecurity-idUSKBN0H013P20140905

Croft, A., & Apps, P. (2014, March 16). NATO websites hit in cyber attack linked to Crimea tension, *Reuters.* Retrieved from http://www.reuters.com/article/2014/03/16/us-ukraine-nato-idUSBREA2E0T320140316

Cross, M., & Shinder, D. L. (2008). *Scene of the Cybercrime* (2nd Ed.). Burlington: Syngress.

CrowdStrike. (2015, February 9). 2014 Global Threat Intel Report. *CrowdStrike Threat Intel.* Retrieved from http://go.crowdstrike.com/rs/crowdstrike/images/GlobalThreatIntelReport.pdf

CSA Homepage. (n. d.). *Cloud Security Alliance.* Retrieved, from https://cloudsecurityalliance.org/

Cummings, M. C., McGarvey, D. C., & Vinch, P. M. (2006), *Homeland Security Risk Assessment Volume II. Methods, Techniques, and Tools.* Retrieved from http://www.homelandsecurity.org/hsireports/Risk%20Assessment%20Volume%20 2%20 Methods%20Techniques%20and%20Tools.pdf

Curts, R., & Campbell, D. (1999). Architecture: The Road to Interoperability. Paper presented at the *Command & Control Research & Technology Symposium.* Newport, RI.

Cyber Crime. (2011, July). *Issues Monitor,* Vol. 8. Retrieved from https://www.kpmg.com/Global/en/IssuesAndInsights/ArticlesPublications/Documents/cyber-crime.pdf

Cyber Defence. (2014, September 30). NATO. Retrieved from http://www.nato.int/cps/en/natohq/topics_78170.htm

Cyber Laws of India. (n. d.). *Government of India.*

Cyber Security Planning Guide. (n. d.). Department of Homeland Security. *Dhs.gov.*

Cyber Security Strategy for Germany. (2011). *Federal Ministry of the Interior (Germany).*

Cyber Security Strategy of the United Kingdom. (2009). *UK Cabinet.*

Cyber Security. (n. d.). *Oxford Martin School.* Retrieved from http://www.oxfordmartin.ox.ac.uk/institutes/cybersecurity

Cyber Threat Source Descriptions. (n. d.). *Industrial Control Systems Cyber Emergency Response Team (ICS-CERT).* Retrieved from http://ics-cert.us-cert.gov/content/cyber-threat-source-descriptions

Cybercrime. (2011, July). Issues Monitor, Vol. 8. KPMG International.

Cyber-Crime: Pakistan Criminal Records. (n. d.). *Pakistancriminalrecords.com.* from http://pakistancriminalrecords.com/tag/cyber-crime

Cybercrimes/e-crimes: Model Policy Guidelines and Legislative Texts. (n. d.). *International Telecommunication Union.* Retrieved from http://www.itu.int/

Cybersecurity Act of 2012. (2012). U.S. Congress.

Cybersecurity guide for developing countries. (2007ITU. Geneva, Switzerland: International Telecommunication Union.

Cybersecurity Update (2011, October 18). US Department of State. Retrieved from http://fpc.state.gov/175773.htm

Cybersecurity. (2013, February 14). *U.S. Government Accountability Office. GAO.gov.*

Cyberterrorism - The use of the Internet for terrorist purposes. (2008Council of Europe. Council of Europe Publishing.

D'Aspremont, J. (Ed.). (2011). *Participants in the international legal system: Theoretical perspectives.* London: Routledge.

Dagon, D., Gu, G., Lee, C. P., & Lee, W. (2007, December). A taxonomy of botnet structures. In *Computer Security Applications Conference, 2007. ACSAC 2007. Twenty-Third Annual* (pp. 325-339). IEEE. doi:10.1109/ACSAC.2007.44

Dalton, T. (2013). *Beyond Incrementalism: Rethinking Approaches to CBMs and Stability in South Asia.*

Danino, O. (2009). *Le Hamas et l'édification de l'Etat palestinien.* Paris: Karthala.

Danino, O. (2013). La stratégie cybernétique de l'Etat d'Israël. *Sécurité Globale, 24*(2), 15–24. doi:10.3917/secug.024.0015

Davenport, K. (2012). *Hotline Agreements.*

Davidson, J. (2014, August 21). The ISIS Propaganda Machine Is Horrifying and Effective: How Does It Work? *Council for Foreign Relations,* Retrieved from http://blogs.cfr.org/davidson/2014/08/21/the-isis-propaganda-machine-is-horrifying-and-effective-how-does-it-work/?cid=soc-Facebook-in-propaganda_machine-081514

Davies, M. (1999, December 2). Failing to deliver on cyber crime. *Birmingham Post,* 2.

Davis, C. M., Tate, J. E., Okhravi, H., Grier, C., Overbye, T. J., & Nicol, D. (2006). SCADA Cyber Security Testbed Development. *Power Symposium, 2006. NAPS 2006. 38th North American (2006, September 17-19),* 483–488. Carbondale, IL, USA. doi:10.1109/NAPS.2006.359615

De Porcellinis, S., Panzieri, S., & Setola, R. (2009). Modelling critical infrastructure via a mixed holistic reductionistic approach. In C. Chaudet, G. L. Grand, & V. Rosat (Eds.), Special Issue on Critical Infrastructures as Complex Systems, 5(1/2), 86–99. doi:10.1504/IJCIS.2009.022851

De Porcellinis, S., Panzieri, S., Setola, R., & Ulivi, G. (2008). Simulation of heterogeneous and interdependent critical infrastructures. In S. Bologna (Ed.), Special Issue on Complex Network and Infrastructure Protection Vol. 4(1/2), (pp. 110–128). Inderscience Publishers. doi:10.1504/IJCIS.2008.016095

Debar, H., Curry, D., & Feinstein, B. (2007). *The Intrusion Detection Message Exchange Format (IDMEF)* (No. RFC4765). RFC Editor. Retrieved from https://www.rfc-editor.org/info/rfc4765

Declaration for the Future of the Internet Economy. (2008, June 17-18). Proceedings of *Ministerial Meeting on the Future of Internet Economy*. Retrieved from http://www.oecd.org/futureinternet/

Declaration of the Heads of the SCO Member States on International Information Security [Translated]. (2006).

Deeks, A. S. (2012). "Unwilling or unable": Toward a normative framework for extraterritorial self-defense. *Virginia Journal of International Law, 52,* 491–495.

Defence and Cyber Security. (2012).

Défense et sécurité des systèmes d'information, stratégie de la France. 21. (2011). *Agence nationale de la sécurité des systèmes d'information.* Retrieved from http://www.ssi.gouv.fr/IMG/pdf/2011-02-15_Defense_et_securite_des_systemes_d_information_strategie_de_la_France.pdf

Defense Strategy for Operating in Cyberspace. (n. d.). *US Department of Defense.*

Deibert, R. (2012). The growing dark side of cyberspace (...and what to do about it). *Penn State Journal of Law & International Affairs, 1*(2), 260–274.

Demchak, C. (2011). *Wars of Disruption and Resilience: Cybered Conflict, Power and National Security.* Athens, Georgia, USA: University of Georgia Press.

Demchak, C. (2012). Hacking the next war. *The American Interest, 8*(1).

Demchak, C., & Dombrowski, P. (2011). Rise of a 'Cybered Westphalian' age. *Strategic Studies Quarterly, 5*(1), 32–61.

Denning, D. E. (2000). Reflections on cyberweapons controls. *Computer Security Journal, 16*(4), 43–53.

Denning, D. E. (2007). *Cyberterrorism: Testimony before the Special Oversight Panel on Terrorism Committee on Armed Services, US House of Representatives. In E.V. Linden (Ed.), Focus on Terrorism.* 9, (pp. 72–75). New York Nova Science Publishers.

Department of Defense Cyberspace Policy Report: A Report to Congress Pursuant to the National Defense Authorization Act for Fiscal Year 2011 US Department of Defense. (2011). Washington, D.C.: Department of Defense.

Department of Defense Press Briefing by Secretary Hagel and General Dempsey in the Pentagon Briefing Room. (2014). Defense.gov Transcript. Retrieved from http://www.defense.gov/transcripts/transcript.aspx?transcriptid=5491

Department of Defense Strategy for Operating in Cyberspace. (2011, July). *U.S. Department of Defense.*http://www.defense.gov/news/d20110714cyber.pdf

Der Derian, J. (2013). From war 2.0 to quantum war: The superpositionality of global violence. *Australian Journal of International Affairs, 67*(5), 570–585. doi:10.1080/10357718.2013.822465

Developing a Framework to Improve Critical Infrastructure Cybersecurity. (2013). *National Institute of Standards of Technology.*

Dever, J., & Dever, J. (2013). Cyberwarfare: Attribution, Preemption, and National Self Defense. *Journal of Law and Cyber Warfare, 2*(1), 25–66.

Devletin 'hacker'ları geliyor. (2014). *Cumhuriyet.* Retrieved from http://www.Cumhuriyet.com.tr

Dickie, J. (2012). *Mafia Brotherhoods: Camorra, Mafia, 'Ndrangheta: The Rise of the Honoured Societies.* London: Sceptre.

Dictionary of Military and Associated Terms. (2014). *Department of Defense*. (pp. 74-75). Retrieved from http://www. dtic.mil/doctrine/new_pubs/jp1_02.pdf

Dieterle, D. (2012). *DARPA's Foundational CyberWarfare Plan-X: The Roadmap for Future CyberWar*. Retrieved from http://cyberarms.wordpress.com/2012/12/01/darpas-foundational-cyberwarfare-plan-x-the-roadmap-for-future-cyberwar/

DiMeglio, R. P., Condrom, S. M., Bishop, O. B., Musselman, G. S., Lindquist, T. L., & Gillman, A. D. ...Stigall, D.E. (2012). Law of Armed Conflict Deskbook. Johnson, W.J., & Gillman, A.D. (Eds.). US Army: Virginia.

Dingledine, R., Mathewson, N., & Syverson, P. (2004, August 13). Tor: The second-generation onion router. Paper presented at the *Usenet Security Symposium*, San Diego. Retrieved from https://www.usenix.org/legacy/events/sec04/tech/full_papers/dingledine/dingledine_html/index.html

Dipert, R. R. (2010). The Ethics of Cyberwarfare. *Journal of Military Ethics*, *9*(4), 384–410. doi:10.1080/15027570.2010.536404

Diplomacy: US, China aligned on North Korea, Climate and Cybercrime. (2013). *Deutschewelle.de*. Retrieved from http://www.dw.de/us-china-aligned-on-n-korea-climate-and-cybercrime/a-16868686

Disarmament and International Security: First Committee. (n. d.). *United Nations*.

Dixit, J. N. (2002). *India-Pakistan in War & Peace*. London: Routledge.

DOD announces the expansion of Defense Industrial Base (DIB) Voluntary Cyber Security Information Sharing Assurance. (2012, May 11). *U.S. Department of Defense (CS/IA)*. [Press Release]. Retrieved from http://www.defense.gov/releases/release.aspx?releaseid=15266

Dombrowski, P. and C. Demchak. (2014). Cyber westphalia: asserting state prerogatives in cyberspace. *Georgetown Journal of International Affairs*: 5-13.

Dombrowski, P., & Demchak, C. (2014). Cyber war, cybered-conflict and the maritime domain. *Naval War College Review*, *67*(2), 71–96.

Dombrowski, P., & Gholz, E. (2006). *Buying military transformation: technological innovation and the defense industry*. New York: Columbia University Press.

Dondossola, G., Garrone, F., Szanto, J., & Gennaro, F. (2008). A laboratory testbed for the evaluation of cyber attacks to interacting ICT infrastructures of power grid operators. In E. de Jaeger (Ed.), *Proceedings of the CIRED Seminar: SmartGrids for Distribution, (2008, June 23-24)*, (pp. 1–4). Frankfurt, Germany. doi:10.1049/ic:20080459

Dougherty, S. (2014, February 28). On social media, Ukraine gives Yanukovych the finger, *Global Post*. Retrieved from http://www.globalpost.com/dispatch/news/regions/europe/140228/ukraine-social-media-yanukovych-middle-finger

Dourado, E. (2013, October 10). Put trust back in the Internet. *The New York Times*.

Dowd, R. A. (2014). Religious diversity and religious tolerance: Lessons from Nigeria. *The Journal of Conflict Resolution*. doi:10.1177/0022002714550085

Dunn-Cavelty, M. (2008). Cyber-terror- looming threat or phantom menace? The framing of the US cyber-threat debate. *Journal of Information Technology & Politics*, *4*(1), 19–36. doi:10.1300/J516v04n01_03

E.L. (2013, June 1). Lithuania under cyber-attack - Greetings to the President [Weblog comment] Retrieved from http://www.economist.com/blogs/easternapproaches/2013/06/lithuania-under-cyber-attack

Easton, N. (2013, July22). The CEO Who Caught the Chinese Spies Red-Handed. *Fortune*, *168*, 80–88.

Eberle, C. J. (2013). Just War and Cyberwar. *Journal of Military Ethics*, *12*(1), 54–67. doi:10.1080/15027570.2013.782638

EC3: A Collective EU Response to Cyber-Crime. (n. d.). *Europol*. Retrieved from https://www.europol.europa.eu/ec3

Edward, M. (2012). *India accuses Pakistan of using social media to stir tensions*. ABC News.

Ekelhart, A., Fenz, S., & Neubauer, T. (2009). AURUM: A framework for information security risk management. In *Proceedings of the 42nd Hawaii International Conference on System Sciences*.

Ellis, B. W. (2001). The International Legal Implications and Limitations of Information Warfare: What Are Our Options?.

Ellul, J. (1973). *The Technological Society* (J. Wilkinson, Trans.). New York: Alfred A. Knopf.

Epstein, R. A. (2005). The theory and practice of self-help. *Journal of Law Economics & Policy*, *1*, 1–32.

Erforth, B., & Deffner, G. (2013, March 18). Old wine in new bottles? Justifying France's military intervention in Mali. *Think Africa Press*. Retrieved from http://thinkafricapress.com/mali/old-wine-new-bottles-justifying-france-military-intervention

Eristavi (2014, March 2) Twitter post [Weblog comment]. Retrieved from https://twitter.com/MaximEristavi

European Commission. (2012). *European Commission - Home Affairs*. Retrieved from http://ec.europa.eu/home-affairs/policies/terrorism/terrorism_infrastructure_en.htm

European Cybercrime Task Force. (n. d.). *Europol*. Retrieved from http://europol.easyred.com/?p=129

European Telecommunications Standards Institute. (n. d.) *ETSI*. Retrieved from http://www.ihs.com/products/industry-standards/organizations/etsi/index.aspx

Evelage, B. S. (2012). Clarifying Boko Haram's transnational intentions, using content analysis of public statements in 2012. *Perspectives on Terrorism*, *7*, 5. Retrieved from http://www.terrorismanalysts.com/pt/index.php/pot/article/view/291

Ewing, P. (2012). *The cyber war after next*. Retrieved from http://www.dodbuzz.com/2012/03/22/the-cyber-war-after-next/

Fachkha, C., Bou-Harb, E., Boukhtouta, A., Dinh, S., Iqbal, F., & Debbabi, M. (2012, October). Investigating the dark cyberspace: Profiling, threat-based analysis and correlation. In *Risk and Security of Internet and Systems (CRiSIS), 2012 7th International Conference on* (pp. 1-8). IEEE.

Fachkha, C., Bou-Harb, E., & Debbabi, M. (2014, March). Fingerprinting Internet DNS amplification DDoS activities. In *6th International Conference on New Technologies, Mobility and Security (NTMS)*, (pp. 1-5). IEEE.

Fachkha, C., Bou-Harb, E., & Debbabi, M. (2015). Inferring distributed reflection denial of service attacks from darknet. *Computer Communications*, *62*, 59–71. doi:10.1016/j.comcom.2015.01.016

Falliere, N., Murchu, L. O., & Chien, E. (2011). W32.Stuxnet Dossier [Technical report]. *Symantec - Security Response*. Retrieved from http://www.symantec. com/connect/blogs/w32stuxnet-dossier

Fallon, W. J. (2012, August 27). Winning cyber battles without fighting. *Time*. Retrieved from http://nation.time.com/2012/08/27/winning-cyber-battles-without-fighting/

Farahmand, F., & Spafford, E. (2013). Understanding insiders: An analysis of risk-taking behavior. *Information Systems Frontiers*, *15*(1), 5–15. doi:10.1007/s10796-010-9265-x

Farnsworth, T. (n. d.). *China and Russia Submit Cyber Proposal*.

Federal Judicial Academy. (n. d.). *Government of Pakistan*. Retrieved from http://www.fja.gov. pk

Fedosov, S. (2012). *What does a Stable Cyber Environment look like? Cyber Security Conference 2012: The Role of Confidence-Building Measures in Assuring Cyber Stability.* Geneva, Switzerland: UNIDIR.

Fellmeth, A. X., Horwitz, M., & Oxford University Press (2009). *Guide to latin in international law.* New York: Oxford University Press.

Fenz, S., & Ekelhart, A. (2009, March). Formalizing information security knowledge. In *Proceedings of the 4th international Symposium on information, Computer, and Communications Security,* (pp. 183-194). ACM. doi:10.1145/1533057.1533084

Fenz, S., & Tjoa, A. M. (2008). Ontology-and Bayesian-based Threat Probability Determination. In *Proceedings of the Junior Scientist Conference 2008,* (pp. 69-70).

Fernandez Vazquez, D., Pastor Acosta, O., Brown, S., Reid, E., & Spirito, C. (2012). Conceptual framework for cyber defense information sharing within trust relationships. In *Proceedings of the 4h International Conference on Cyber Conflict (CYCON),* Tallinn:IEEE.

Ferzan, K. K. (2008). Self-defense and the state. *Ohio State Journal of Criminal Law, 5*(2), 449–478.

Fidler, D. P. (2013). Call Me, Maybe: New US-Russia Cybersecurity Initiatives.

Fielding, R. (2000). *Architectural styles and the design of network-based software architectures.* (Ph.D. Dissertation). University of California, Irvine.

Fight Cyber Crime infographic. (2013, October). Ponemon Institute. Retrieved from www.hp.com/hpinfo/newsroom/press/2013/309_ponemon.jpg

Fındıklı, S. (2014). Russian military attack helicopters over the Crimea Ukraine [Video file]. Retrieved from http://www.youtube.com/watch?v=qlW317itFEk

Finklea, K. M., & Theohary, C. A. (2013, January 9). Cybercrime: Conceptual issues for Congress and U.S. law enforcement. *Congressional Research Service,* 5-11. Retrieved from http://fas.org/sgp/crs/misc/R42547.pdf

Finley, J. C. (2014, February 28). Telecom services sabotaged in Ukraine's Crimea region, *UPI.* Retrieved from http://www.upi.com/Top_News/World-News/2014/02/28/Telecom-services-sabotaged-in-Ukraines-Crimea-region/7611393621345/

FIRST is the global Forum for Incident Response and Security Teams. (n. d.). Retrieved from http://www.first.org/

FIRST Members. (n. d.). Retrievedfrom http://www.first.org/members/teams/cert-in

Fischer, E. A. (2012). *Federal Laws Relating to Cybersecurity: Discussion of Proposed Revisions.* CRS.

Fishel, J. and Associated Press (2014, April 14) Russian jet passes at close range over US warship in Black Sea, *Fox News.* Retrieved from http://www.foxnews.com/politics/2014/04/14/russian-jet-passes-at-close-range-over-us-warship-in-black-sea/

Fisher, M. (2013, May 23). Should the U.S. allow companies to 'hack back' against foreign cyber spies? *The Washington Post.* Retrieved from http://www.washingtonpost.com/blogs/worldviews/wp/2013/05/23/should-the-u-s-allow-companies-to-hack-back-against-foreign-cyber-spies/

Fitter, M. K. P. M. (2013). *Beware of the Bugs. Business Today.*

Flaherty, A. (2013, February 20). A look at Mandiant, allegations on China hacking. *The Associated Press.*

Foltz, A. C. (2012). Stuxnet, Schmitt analysis, and the cyber "use-of-force" debate. *Joint Force Quarterly, 67,* 40–48.

Fox, H. (n. d.). The Contribution of Capacity Building to Developing Confidence between States in Cyber Space. Proceedings of ARF Seminar on *Confidence Building Measures in Cyber Space*.

Franchi, H. L. (2013). US-China Cybersecurity Talks. *The Christian Science Monitor*. Retrieved from http://www.csmonitor.com/USA/Foreign-Policy/2013/0709/US-China-cybersecurity-talks-Will-Snowden-leaks-thwart-US-goals

Freiling, F. C., Holz, T., & Wicherski, G. (2005). *Botnet tracking: Exploring a root-cause methodology to prevent distributed denial-of-service attacks*. (pp. 319–335). Springer Berlin Heidelberg.

Fresco, A. (1997, March 22). Schoolboy hacker was 'No 1 threat' to US security. *The Times*.

Friedrich, O. (1983). The Computer Moves In. In F. J. Coppa & R. Harmond (Eds.), *Technology in the Twentieth Century* (pp. 215–231). Dubuque, Iowa, USA: Kendall/Hunt Publishing Company.

Friesen, T. L. (2009). Resolving tomorrow's conflicts today: How new developments within the U.N. Security Council can be used to combat cyberwarfare. *Naval Law Review*, *58*, 89–127.

Fulghum, D. A. (2010). Cyber Attacks no longer Non-kinetic.

Fuller, T. (2012, June 16-17). In Myanmar, Freedom and a Wave of Hate. *International Herald Tribune*, (pp. 1, 3).

Fuller, T. (2013, January 17). In Thailand, a Broader Definition of Insulting Royalty. *International New York Times*. Retrieved from http://www.nytimes.com/2013/01/18/world/asia/in-thailand-a-broader-definition-of-insulting-royalty.html?_r=0

Functions and Powers of the General Assembly. (n. d.). *United Nations*.

Gable, K. A. (2010). Cyber-apocalypse now: Securing the internet against cyberterrorism and using universal jurisdiction as a deterrent. *Vanderbilt Journal of Transnational Law*, *43*(1), 57.

Gady, F. (2014, March 7). Cyberwar in the Crimea? [Weblog comment]. Retrieved from http://www.usnews.com/opinion/blogs/world-report/2014/03/07/russias-cyberwar-restraint-in-ukraine

Gady, F.-S. (2010, November 25). The Cyber Fortress Mentality. *Foreign Policy Journal*.

Gallagher, S. (2013, August 1). NSA's internet taps can find systems to hack, track VPNs and word docs - X-Keyscore gives NSA the ability to find and exploit vulnerable systems. *Ars Technica*. Retrieved from http://arstechnica.com/tech-policy/2013/08/nsas-internet-taps-can-find-systems-to-hack-track-vpns-and-word-docs/

Gallagher, S. (2014, March 14). Kremlin gets DDoS'd by Anonymous Caucasus. *ARSTechnica*. Retrieved from http://arstechnica.com/tech-policy/2014/03/kremlin-gets-ddosd-by-anonymous-caucasus/

Gandhi, R., Sharma, A., Mahoney, W., Sousan, W., Zhu, Q., & Laplante, P. (2011). Dimensions of cyber-attacks: Social, political, economic, and cultural. *IEEE Technology and Society Magazine*, (Spring): 28–38.

Gartzke, E. (2013). The myth of cyberwar: Bringing war in cyberspace back down to earth. *International Security*, *38*(2), 41–73. doi:10.1162/ISEC_a_00136

Gary McKinnon v. Government of the USA, No. EWHC 762 (High Court of Justice Queen's Bench Division 2007).

Gasparri, A., Oliva, G., & Panzieri, S. (2009). On the distributed synchronization of on-line IIM Interdependency Models. In D.-T. Pham & A. Colombo (Eds.), *Proceedings of the 7th IEEE International Conference on Industrial Informatics (INDIN 2009)* (pp. 795–800). Cardiff, Wales, United Kingdom, 24–26 June 2009: IEEE Computer Society. doi:10.1109/INDIN.2009.5195904

Gaza Hacker Team operations. (n. d.). Retrieved from http://www.zone-h.org/archive/notifier=Gaza%20Hacker%20Team

Gazzini, T. (2006). *The changing rules on the use of force in international law*. Manchester: Manchester University Press.

GCHQ's Robert Hannigan says tech firms 'in denial' on extremism. (2014a, November 4). *BBC News*. Retrieved from http://www.bbc.co.uk/news/uk-29891285

Gellman, B., & Soltani, A. (2013, October 14). NSA collects millions of e-mail address books globally. *The Washington Post*. Retrieved from http://www.washingtonpost.com/world/national-security/nsa-collects-millions-of-e-mail-address-books-globally/2013/10/14/8e58b5be-34f9-11e3-80c6-7e6dd8d22d8f_story.html

Geneva Convention Relative to the Treatment of Prisoners of War (1949) (Geneva Convention No. III).

Geolocation: Don't fence web in. (2004, July 12). *Wired*. Retrieved from http://archive.wired.com/techbiz/it/news/2004/07/64178?currentPage=all

Géré, F. (2010). *Iran, état de crise*. Paris: Karthala.

Ghosh, N. (2013, March 12). Vietnam Pushes Back Against Online Critics. *The Straits Times (Singapore)*, p. A9.

Ghosh, S. (2009). Indo-Pak Composite Dialogue - 2008: Revi.

Giap, V. N. (1968). *People's War, People's Army. The Vietcong Insurrection Manual for Underdeveloped Countries* (2nd Ed.). New York, USA: Bantam Books.

Giap, V. N. (1968). The Resistance War against French Imperialism. In W. J. Pomeroy (Ed.), *Guerrilla Warfare and Marxism* (pp. 212–216). New York: International Publishers.

Gibilisco, S. (2012). *Computer Security Incident Response Team*. CSIRT.

Giles, K., & Hagestad, W. (2013). Divided by a common language: Cyber definitions in Chinese, Russian and English. In *Proceedings of the 5th International Conference on Cyber Conflict (CYCON)*, Tallinn:IEEE.

Gill, A. (2012). What does a stable cyber environment look like. Proceedings of *Cyber Security Conference 2012*. Geneva, Switzerland.

Gill, T., & Fleck, D. (2010). *The Handbook of the International Law of Military Operations*. Oxford.

Gjelten, T. (2012) *Extending the Law of War into Cyberspace*.

Gladstone, B. (2014, June 20). Extremist social media. *On The Media*. Retrieved from: http://www.onthemedia.org/story/extremist-social-media/

Glaser, E. L. (1967, April 18-20). A brief description of privacy measures in the multics operating system. In Proceedings of the *Spring Joint Computer Conference (AFIPS '67)*. New York, NY, USA. (pp.303-304). doi:10.1145/1465482.1465529

Glaser, E. L., Couleur, J. F., & Oliver, G. A. (1965, November 30-December 1). System design of a computer for time sharing applications. In Proceedings of the Fall Joint Computer Conference (AFIPS '65). ACM, New York, NY, USA. (pp. 197-202). doi:10.1145/1463891.1463913

Glennon, M. (2002). The fog of law: Self-defense, inherence, and incoherence in Article 51 of the United Nations Charter. *Harvard Journal of Law & Public Policy*, 25(2), 539–558.

Global Surveillance Data: US Places Pakistan on Second Position in NSA Spy List. (n. d.). Retrieved from http://bbcrecord.com/live/ct-menu-item-17/pakistan/10-pakistan/544-global-surveillance-data-us-places-pakistan-on-second-position-in-nsa-spy-list.html

GoI, M. (1972, July 2). *Simla Agreement*.

Goldman, J. (2013). Taiwan Says China's Cyber Army Now Numbers 100, 000.

Goldman, E., & Arquilla, J. (Eds.). (2014). *Cyber analogies. Montery*. Naval Post Graduate School.

Goldsmith, J. (2013, February 2). The USG strategy to confront Chinese cyber exploitation, and the Chinese perspective. *Lawfare*. Retrieved from http://www.lawfareblog.com/2013/02/the-usg-strategy-to-confront-chinese-cyber-exploitation-and-the-chinese-perspective/

Goldsmith, J. (2013b, October 10). We Need an Invasive NSA. *New Republic*. Retrieved from http://www.newrepublic.com/article/115002/invasive-nsa-will-protect-us-cyber-attacks?utm_content=bufferc47b9&utm_source=buffer&utm_medium=twitter&utm_campaign=Buffer

Goldsmith, J. (2013a). How Cyber Changes the Laws of War. *European Journal of International Law*, *24*(1), 129–138. doi:10.1093/ejil/cht004

Goldsmith, J. L. (1998a). Against cyberanarchy. *The University of Chicago Law Review. University of Chicago. Law School*, *65*(4), 1199–1250. doi:10.2307/1600262

Goldsmith, J. L. (1998b). The internet and the abiding significance of territorial sovereignty. *Indiana Journal of Global Legal Studies*, *5*(2), 475–491.

Golling, M., & Stelte, B. (2011). Requirements for a future EWS – cyber defence in the internet of the future. In *Proceedings of the 3rd International Conference on Cyber Conflict (ICCC)*, Tallinn:IEEE.

Gomper, D. C., & Saunders, P. C. (2011). *Mutual Restraint in Cyberspace*. Washington, DC: Institute for National Strategic Studies.

Gonzales, D., & Harting, S. (2014, April 29). Exposing Russia's covert actions. *The Rand Blog*. Retrieved from http://www.rand.org/blog/2014/04/exposing-russias-covert-actions.html

Gooch, J., & Perlmutter, A. (Eds.). (2007). *Military deception and surprise!* London: Routledge.

Goodno, N. H. (2007). Cyberstalking, a new crime: Evaluating the effectiveness of current state and federal laws. *Missouri Law Review*, *72*(1), 125.

Gorman, S. (2011). China Hackers Hit U.S. Chamber. *The Wall Street Journal*. Retrieved from http://www.wsj.com/articles/SB10001424052970204058404577110541568535300

Gorman, S. (2013, July 22). Annual U.S. Cybercrime Costs Estimated at $100 Billion. *Wall Street Journal*. Retrieved from http://online.wsj.com/news/articles/SB10001424127887324328904578621880966242990

Gorman, S., & Barnes, J. E. (2011, May 31). Cyber Combat: Act of War; Pentagon Sets Stage for U.S. to Respond to Computer Sabotage With Military Force. *The Wall Street Journal*. Retrieved from http://www.wsj.com/articles/SB10001424052702304563104576355623135782718

Gorman, S., & Valentino-DeVries, J. (2013). New details show broader NSA surveillance reach; programs cover 75% of nation's traffic, can snare emails. *Wall Street Journal*. Retrieved http://online.wsj.com/news/articles/SB10001424127887324108204579022874091732470

Gourley, S. M. (2012). Linkages between Boko Haram and al Qaeda: A potential deadly synergy. *Global Security Studies*, *3*(3), 1–14.

Grady, J. O. (1993). *System Requirements Analysis*. New York, NY: McGraw Hill, Inc.

Grady, J. O. (1994). *System Integration*. Boca Raton, FL: CRC Press.

Grady, J. O. (1995). *System Engineering Planning and Enterprise Identity*. Boca Raton, FL: CRC Press.

Graham, G. (2013, October 18). British Muslims targeted in Al-Shabaab terror video are offered police protection. *The Telegraph*. Retrieved from http://www.telegraph.co.uk/news/10390026/British-muslims-targeted-in-Al-Shabaab-terror-video-are-offered-police-protection.html

Greenwald, G. (2013, July 31). XKeyscore: NSA tool collects nearly everything a user does on the internet. *The Guardian*. Retrieved from http://www.theguardian.com/world/2013/jul/31/nsa-top-secret-program-online-data

Greenwald, G., & MacAskill, E. (2013, June 7). Obama orders US to draw up overseas target list for cyber-attacks. *The Guardian*. Retrieved, from http://www.guardian.co.uk/world/2013/jun/07/obama-china-targets-cyber-overseas

Gregory, P. R. (2014a, April 12). Russian TV Propagandists Caught Red-Handed: Same Guy, Three Different People (Spy, Bystander, Heroic Surgeon), *Reuters*. Retrieved from http://www.forbes.com/sites/paulroderickgregory/2014/04/12/russian-tv-caught-red-handed-same-guy-same-demonstration-but-three-different-people-spy-bystander-heroic-surgeon/

Gregory, P. R. (2014b, April 14). You Tube shatters Russian lies about troops in Ukraine: Putin denies truth to Obama, *Forbes*. Retrieved from http://www.forbes.com/sites/paulroderickgregory/2014/04/14/you-tube-shatters-russian-lies-about-troops-in-ukraine/

Greitzer, F., Moore, A., Cappelli, D., Andrews, D., Carroll, L., & Hull, T. D. (2008, February/March). Combating the insider cyber threat. *IEEE Security and Privacy*, *6*(1), 61–64. doi:10.1109/MSP.2008.8

Gridneff, I. (2012, December 31). Organised crime gets smart with technology. *Sydney Morning Herald*. Retrieved from http://www.smh.com.au/it-pro/government-it/organised-crime-gets-smart-with-technology-20121230-2c1iy.html

Groot, G. J. D., Rekhter, Y., Karrenberg, D., & Lear, E. (1996). Address Allocation for Private Internets.

Guide for Applying the Risk Management Framework to Federal Information Systems. (2010, February). *National Institute of standards and technology NIST SP 800-37*.

Guitton, C. (2013, 11-12 July). *Modelling Attribution*. Paper presented at the *12th European Conference on Information Warfare and Security*, Jyväskylä.

Guitton, C., & Korzak, E. (2013). The Sophistication Criterion for Attribution. *The RUSI Journal, 158*(4).

Guitton, C. (2012). Criminals and Cyber Attacks: The Missing Link Between Attribution and Deterrence. *International Journal of Cyber Criminology*, *6*(2), 1030–1043.

Guitton, C. (2014). (Forthcoming). Attribution of Cyber Attacks and Its Reliance on Judgement Calls. *Security Dialogue*.

Gupta, A. (2012). *CBMs in Cyber Space: What should be India's Approach?*

Haeryong, K. (2012). The ARF perspective on TCBMs. Proceedings of *Cyber Security Conference 2012*. Geneva, Switzerland.

Hague Convention Respecting the Laws and Customs of War on Land (1907).

Hakeem, A., Kanwal, G., Vannoni, M., & Rajen, G. (2007, September). Demilitarization of the Siachen Conflict Zone: Concepts for Implementation and Monitoring. Sandia National Laboratories.

Halliday, J. (2010, September 24). Stuxnet worm is the work of a national government agency. *The Guardian*.

Haltaş, F. (2011). DUQU: Yeni Nesil Keşif Uçağı. Retrieved from http://www.bilgiguvenligi.gov.tr/zararli-yazilimlar/duqu- yeni-nesil-kesif-ucagi.html

Hansen, W. W., & Musa, U. A. (2013). Fanon, the Wretched and Boko Haram. *Journal of Asian and African Studies*. doi:0021909612467277.

Harding, J. (2014, March 2). Russian manipulation of the press regarding Ukraine [Weblog comment]. Retrieved from http://toinformistoinfluence.com/2014/03/02/russian-manipulation-of-the-press-regarding-ukraine/

Hardy, C. (2012). Cyber-space now seen as 'fifth dimension of warfare'. Retrieved from http://www.publicserviceeurope.com/article/1485/cyber-space-now-seen-as-fifth-dimension-of-warfare

Hare, F. (2012). The significance of attribution to cyberspace coercion: A political perspective. In *Proceedings of the 4h International Conference on Cyber Conflict (CYCON)*, Tallinn:IEEE.

Harper, M. (2014, February 26). Somali's Al Shabab: Striking like mosquitos. *BBC News*. Retrieved from http://www.bbc.co.uk/news/world-africa-26343248

Harris, S. (2013). All. In *One CISSP Exam Guide* (6th ed.). New York: McGraw-Hill.

Harrop, W., & Armitage, G. (2005, November). Defining and evaluating greynets (sparse darknets). In *the IEEE Conference on Local Computer Networks, 2005.* (pp. 344-350). IEEE.

Hart, K. (2008, August 14). Longtime battle lines are recast in Russia and Georgia's cyberwar, *The Washington Post*, p. D01.

Hashem, A. (2014, August). The Islamic State's social media strategy. *Al-Monitor*. Retrieved from http://www.al-monitor.com/pulse/originals/2014/08/is-clinton-atrocities-social-media-baghdadi-mccain.html

Haslum, K., & Arnes, A. (2006). Multisensor Real-time Risk Assessment using Continuous-time Hidden Markov Models. In Y. Cheung, Y. Wang, & H. Liu (Eds.), *Proceedings of the 2006 International Conference on Computational Intelligence and Security, (2006 November 3-6)*, (Vol. 2, pp. 1536–1540). Guangzhou, China. doi:10.1109/ICCIAS.2006.295318

Hassan, S. R. (2012). *Alarming Rise in Cyber Crimes*. Dawn.

Hathaway, O. A., Crootof, R., Levitz, P., Nix, H., Nowlan, A., Perdue, W. & Spiegel, Julia. (2012). *The Law of Cyber-Attack*. (pp. 54).

Hathaway, O. A., Crootof, R., Levitz, P., Nix, H., Nowlan, A., Perdue, W., & Spiegel, J. (2012). The law of cyber-attack. *California Law Review, 100*(4), 817–885.

Hathaway, O. A., & Shapiro, S. J. (2011). Outcasting: Enforcement in domestic and international law. *The Yale Law Journal, 121*(2), 252–349.

Healey, J. (n. d.). The Five Futures of Cyber Conflict and Cooperation. *Georgetown Journal for International Affairs*.

Healy, J. (2013). *The Future of US Cyber Command*.

Healy, R. J. (Ed.). (2013). A Fierce Domain: Conflict in Cyber Space, 1986 to 2012. Washington DC: CCSA Publication.

Heinl, C. H. (2013). Enhancing ASEAN-Wide Cybersecurity: Time For A Hub Of Excellence? *Analysis*.

Helsinki Final Act. (n. d.). *OSCE*. Retrieved from http://www.osce.org/mc/39501

Henry, S. (2012, March 27). FBI's top cyber official discusses threat. *The Federal Bureau of Investigation*. Retrieved April 16, 2014, from http://www.fbi.gov/news/videos/fbis-top-cyber-official-discusses-threat

Herrera-Flanigan, J. R., & Ghosh, S. (2010). Criminal regulations. In S. Ghosh & E. Turrini (Eds.), *Cybercrimes: A multidisciplinary analysis* (pp. 265–306).

Heuer, R. J. (1999). *Psychology of Intelligence Analysis*. Washington, D.C.: Centre for the Study of Intelligence.

Heywood, A. (2004). *Political theory: an introduction*. New York: Palgrave Mcmillan.

Hider, J. (2012, May 29). Iran attacked by Israeli computer virus. *The Times*.

Hiding in plain sight: Fireeye and Microsoft expose obfuscation tactic. (2015, May 14). *FireEye Threat Intelligence Report*. Retrieved from https://www2.fireeye.com/rs/fireye/images/APT17_Report.pdf

Higgins, H. (n. d.). Applying Confidence-Building Measures in a Regional context.

Hilali, A. Z. (2005). Confidence- and Security-Building Measures for India and Pakistan. *Political, 30*(2), 31.

Hildreth, S. A. (2001). *Cyberwarfare*. Congressional Research Service.

Holbrook, D. (2014). *The Al-Qaeda Doctrine: The Framing and Evolution of the Leadership's Public Discourse*. London: Bloomsbury.

Holst, J. J. (1983, January/February). Confidence Building Measures: A Conceptual Framework. *Survival, 25*(1), 2–15. doi:10.1080/00396338308442072

Holz, T., & Raynal, F. (n. d.). Malicious malware: attacking the attackers, part 1. *Symantec Connect Community*. Retrieved from www.symantec.com/connect/articles/malicious-malware-attacking-attackers-part-1

Home Office. (2014). *Proscribed Terrorist Organisations*. London: UK Home Office. Retrieved from https://www.gov.uk/government/publications/proscribed-terror-groups-or-organisations--2#history

Homeland Security top officer to work on UN's new global Internet rules. (2013). *RT.com*. Retrieved from http://rt.com/usa/cyber-lute-un-internet-572/

Honderich, T. (2005). *The oxford companion to philosophy*. New York: Oxford University Press.

Hoover, K. (2015). *Cyber threat bill passes, but small biz still faces big problem. The Business Journals*.

Horn, L. (n. d.). Dirty Texting Banned by Pakistan Telecom Authority.

Hsu, C., Chang, C., & Lin, C. (2003). *A practical guide to support vector classification*. Retrieved from https://www.cs.sfu.ca/people/Faculty/teaching/726/spring11/svmguide.pdf

Hubbard, B. (2014, January 25). The franchising of Al Qaeda. *The New York Times*. Retrieved from http://www.nytimes.com/2014/01/26/sunday-review/the-franchising-of-al-qaeda.html?_r=0

Hunker, J., Gates, C., & Bishop, M. (2011). *Attribution Requirements for Next Generation Internets*. Paper presented at the *International Conference on Technologies for Homeland Security*, Waltham.

Hurwitz, R. (2012). Cross-domain threat assessment in international security. Proceedings of Cyber Security Conference 2012. Geneva, Switzerland.

Hutchinson, J. (2013, May 28). Companies should 'hack back' at cyber attackers: Security experts. *Financial Review*. Retrieved from http://www.afr.com/p/technology/companies_should_hack_back_at_cyber_KeoJyUX9HEEtjh9hYAnpgK

İçişleri 'bizi seviyor musun' diye 'hack'lendi. (2012). *Milliyet*. Retrieved from http://www.milliyet.com.tr/icisleri-bizi-seviyor-musun-diye-hacklendi/siyaset/siyasetdetay/21.04.2012/1530889/default.htm

ICJ Reports 1949. (1949). *International Court of Justice*.

ICJ Reports 1986.(1986). International Court of Justice.

ICT4Peace Project. (n. d.). *ICT4Peace.org*. Retrieved from http://ict4peace.org/whoweare/ict4peace-history

IEC. (2005). *P-IEC/PAS 62407 ed1.0, Real-time Ethernet control automation technology (EtherCAT)*. International Electrotechnical Comission.

IEEE Islamabad Section. (n. d.). Retrieved from http://ewh.ieee.org/r10/islamabad/societies.htm

IEEE Karachi Section. (n. d.). Retrieved from http://ewh.ieee.org/r10/karachi/

IEEE Standard for Electric Power Systems Communications. (2010). IEEE Power & Energy Society.

If you see something, say something. (2014). *Department of Homeland Security*. Retrieved from http://www.dhs.gov/see-something-say-something

Igure, V. M., Laughter, S. A., & Williams, R. D. (2006, October). Security issues in SCADA networks. *Computers & Security*, 25(7), 498–506. doi:10.1016/j.cose.2006.03.001

Improving Critical Infrastructure Cybersecurity. (2013The White House.

India and Pakistan Statements to the United Nations General Assembly. (1998). *Acronym.org*. Retrieved from http://www.acronym.org.uk/spsep98.htm

India-Pakistan Military CBMs Project – Phase 1: Final Report. (n. d.). *ACCU*. Retrieved from http://www.acus.org/files/Final%20Project%20report%20-%20Phase%201_Sept%2025.pdf

Information Economy. (n. d.). *OECD*. Retrieved from http://www.oecd.org/sti/ieconomy /informationeconomy.htm

Information Office of the State Council of the People's Republic of China. (2011, March 31). China's national defense in 2010. *Xinhua*. Retrieved from http://news.xinhuanet.com/english2010/china/2011-03/31/c_13806851_5.htm

Information systems defense and security: France's strategy. (2011). *French Network and Information Security Agency*.

Information Technology Standards. (1998). *Information Technology Standards Guidance – Information Management. Final Draft Version 1.0*. Washington, DC: Department of the Navy.

Infrastructure REsilience. The INSPIRE Project. In R. Setola, & S. Geretshuber (Eds.), *Proceedings of the 3th International Workshop on Critical Information Infrastructures Security (CRITIS 2008), (2008, October 13-15)*Vol. 5508, (pp. 109–118). Rome, Italy.

Ingersoll, G. (2013). Defense Science Board Warns of Existential Cyber Attack.

Inoue, D., Eto, M., Suzuki, K., Suzuki, M., & Nakao, K. (2012, October). DAEDALUS-VIZ: novel real-time 3D visualization for darknet monitoring-based alert system. In *Proceedings of the Ninth International Symposium on Visualization for Cyber Security* (pp. 72-79). ACM. doi:10.1145/2379690.2379700

INSPIRE Project Web Site. (2010). *INSPIRE*. Retrieved from http://www. inspire-strep.eu

Institute of Electrical and Electronic Engineers. (n.d). *IEEE Computer Society*. http://www.ieee.org/index.html

IntelCenter. (2007, September 9). Al Qaeda Messaging Statistics. *Version 3.3*. Retrieved from: www.intelcenter.com

International Committee of the Red Cross. (1977). *Protocol Additional to the Geneva Conventions of 12 August 1949, and relating to the Protection of Victims of International Armed Conflicts (Protocol I)*.

International Committee of the Red Cross. (1996, May 3). *Protocol on Prohibitions or Restrictions on the Use of Mines, Booby-Traps and Other Devices*.

International Conference on Combating Child Pornography on the Internet. (1999, October 1). Vienna.

International Cooperation with ASEANOPOL bolsters Security Landscape. (2013). Interpol. Retrieved from http://www.interpol.int/News-and-media/News-media-releases/2013/PR019

International Electrotechnical Commission. (IEC) (n. d). *IEC*. Retrieved from http://www.iec.ch /index.htm

International Group of Experts. (2013). *Tallinn Manual on the International Law Applicable to Cyber Warfare*. Cambridge: Cambridge University Press.

International Information Security. (2009). Moscow.

International Strategy for Cyberspace: Prosperity Security and Openness in a Networked World. (2011). The White House. *Whitehouse.gov*.

Internet Corporation for Assigned Names and Numbers (ICANN). (n. d.). *ICANN.org*. Retrieved from http://www.icann.org/

Internet Governance Forum (n. d.). *IGF*. Retrieved from http://www.intgovforum.org/cms/

İnternet'in büyüyen tehlikesi botnet'ler! Mariposa ve Conflicker botnet'leri. (2011). *ChipOnlinetr*. Retrieved from http://www.chip.com.tr

IPSC: PECO Workshop Cybersecurity and Incident Response. (2004). *Timeshighereducation.co.uk*. Retrieved from http://www.timeshighereducation.co.uk/

Iran Boosting Electronic War Capabilities due to Nature of Threats. (2012). *Fars News Agency*. Retrieved from http://english2.farsnews.com/newstext.php?nn=9106243312

Iran fends off new Stuxnet cyber attack. (2012). *British Broadcasting Company*. Retrieved from http://www.bbc.co.uk/news/world-middle-east-20842113

Iran to launch giant domestic intranet. (2012). Al Jazeera. Retrieved from http://www.aljazeera.com/news/middleeast/2012/09/201292471215311826.html

IRRIIS Project Web Site. (2008). *IRRIIS*. Retrieve from http://www.irriis.org

ISA-99.00.01 - Security for Industrial Automation and Control Systems - Part 1. (2007). *International Society of Automation Standard*. Retrieved from http://isa99.isa.org/Documents/Drafts/ISA-62443-1-1-PUB-A4.pdf

ISO 11898-1:2003, Road vehicles -- Controller area network (CAN) -- Part 1. (2003). *International Standards Organization*.

ISO/IEC 27002:2005 Information Technology – Security Techniques (n. d.). *ISO.org*. Retrieved from http://www.iso27001security.com/html/27002.html

ISO/IEC 27032:2012 Information technology – Security Techniques. (n. d.). Retrieved from http://www.iso.org/iso/catalogue_detail?csnumber=44375

ITU. (n. d.). *International Telecommunications Union*. Retrieved from http://www.itu.int/en/Pages/default.aspx

Jabbour, K. & Muccio, S. (2011, Summer). The Science of Mission Assurance. *Journal of Strategic Security*, IV(2), pp. 61-74.

Jackson, W. (2012, April 19). Former FBI cyber cop: Hunt the hacker, not the hack, *Government Computer News*.

Jacobson, I., Ericsson, M., & Jacobson, A. (1995). *The Object Advantage: Business Process Reengineering with Object Technology*. New York, NY: Addison-Wesley.

Jaspal, Z. N. (2004, May). Nuclear CBMs between India and Pakistan: Utilitarian Approach - How to build Confidence about our Nuclear Intentions. Defence Journal, 7(10).

Jayasankaran, S. (2012, June 5). Mahathir Calls for Internet Access to be Regulated. *The Business Times (Singapore)*, p. 16.

Jenkins, B. M. (2011). Is Al-Qaeda's Internet Strategy working? *Rand Corporation*. Retrieved from http://www.rand.org/content/dam/rand/pubs/testimonies/2011/RAND_CT371.pdf

Jevans, D. (2013). Little thumb drives now a big security threat.

Jinghao, Y., & Wuning, D. (2013, February 21). Regular cyber attacks from US: China. *Global Times*. Retrieved from http://www.globaltimes.cn/content/763142.shtml

Jingjing, H. (Ed.). (2010, June 8). The Internet in China. *Xinhuanet.com.* http://news.xinhuanet.com/english2010/china/2010-06/08/c_13339232.htm

Jin, Y., Simon, G., Xu, K., Zhang, Z. L., & Kumar, V. (2007, April). Gray's anatomy: Dissecting scanning activities using IP gray space analysis. In *Proceedings of the 2nd USENIX workshop on Tackling computer systems problems with machine learning techniques* (pp. 1-6). USENIX Association.

Jin, Y., Zhang, Z. L., Xu, K., Cao, F., & Sahu, S. (2007, June). Identifying and tracking suspicious activities through IP gray space analysis. In *Proceedings of the 3rd annual ACM workshop on Mining network data* (pp. 7-12). ACM. doi:10.1145/1269880.1269883

Joint Intelligence Organisation. (2013). *JIC assessment of 27 August on Reported Chemical Weapons use in Damascus London*. Cabinet Office.

Joint Interoperability Test Command. (1998, October 21). *C⁴I Interoperability–JITC Certification Process*. http://jitc.fhu.disa.mil/

Joint Media Statement of 12ᵗʰ ASEAN Telecommunications and IT Ministers. (2012, November 19). *Association of Southeast Asian Nations*. Retrieved from http://www.asean.org/news/asean-statement-communiques/item/joint-media-statement-of-the-12th-asean-telecommunications-and-it-ministers-meeting-and-its-related-meetings-with-dialogue-partners

Joint Publication JP 3-12 Cyberspace Operations Final Coordination. (2012, April 10).

Jones, N. (2013, May 17). Google and NASA snap up quantum computer D-Wave Two. *Scientific American*. Retrieved from http://www.scientificamerican.com/article/google-nasa-snap-up-quantum-computer-dwave-two/

Jones, S. E. (2012) United Nations set to Define New Worldwide Rules for the Internet: New Rules to Define Internet Use between Countries.

Jones, A., Kovacich, G. L., & Luzwick, P. G. (2002). *Global Information Warfare*. Boca Raton, FL: Auerbach.

Josselin, D., & Wallace, W. (2001). Non-State Actors in World Politics: a Framework. In D. Josselin & W. Wallace (Eds.), *Non-State Actors in World Politics,* (pp. 1–20). Basingstoke: Palgrave Macmillan. doi:10.1057/9781403900906

Jr, D. G. (2013). *Cyber Attack is imminent.*

Jus in bello & Jus ad bellum. (n. d.). *The International Red Cross Association.*

Kallberg, J. (2013, July 28). Private cyber retaliation undermines federal authority. *DefenseNews*. Retrieved from http://www.defensenews.com/article/20130728/DEFREG02/307280007/Private-Cyber-Retaliation-Undermines-Federal-Authority

Kamal, A. (2002). *Information Insecurity: A Survival Guide to the Uncharted Territories of Cyber-threats and Cyber-security UN ICT Task Force*. New York: UNITAR.

Kamal, A. (2005). *The Law of Cyber-Space an Invitation to the Table of Negotiations*. Geneva: UNITAR.

Kamluk, V. (2011, November 30). The Mystery of Duqu: Part Six (The Command and Control servers), *SecureList*. Retrieved from http://www.securelist.com/en/blog/625/The_Mystery_of_Duqu_Part_Six_The_Command_and_Control_servers

Kandukuri, B. R., Paturi, V. R., & Rakshit, A. (2009, September). Cloud security issues. In *IEEE International Conference on Services Computing. SCC'09*. (pp. 517-520). IEEE.

Kang, D. J., Lee, J. J., Kim, B. H., & Hur, D. (2011). Proposal strategies of key management for data encryption in SCADA network of electric power systems. *International Journal of Electrical Power & Energy Systems*, *33*(9), 1521–1526.

Kapiszewski, A. (2006). *United Nations Expert Group Meeting On International Migration and Development in The Arab Region. Arab Versus Asian Migrant Workers in The GCC Countries*. United Nations Population Division. Retrieved from: http://www.google.co.uk/url?sa=t&rct=j&q=&esrc=s&source=web&cd=2&cad=rja&uact=8&ved=0CCcQFjAB&url=http%3A%2F%2Fwww.un.org%2Fesa%2Fpopulation%2Fmeetings%2FEGM_Ittmig_Arab%2FP02_Kapiszewski.pdf&ei=cEFcVMHPGcbhaszPgsgL&usg=AFQjCNHnI32FnQn2B2wewOMGhTNMnoOidA&sig2=k4BTDNvZC9pJASWAgqTE5Q

Kaplan, D. (2012). *Offensive line: Fighting back against hackers. SC Magazine*.

Kapur, K. C., & Lamberson, L. R. (1977). *Reliability in Engineering Design*. New York, NY: John Wiley & Sons.

Karabacak, B., & Sogukpinar, I. (2005). ISRAM: Information security risk analysis method. *Computers & Security*, *24*(2), 147–159. doi:10.1016/j.cose.2004.07.004

Karl, D. J. (2013). *The Ties that Bind vs. The Line that Divides*. India and Pakistan.

Karnavas, W. J., Sanchez, P., & Bahill, A. T. (1993). Sensitivity analyses of continuous and discrete systems in the time and frequency domains. *IEEE Transportation Systems,Man and Cybernetics Conference (SMC)*. paper SMC-23, (pp. 488-501). doi:10.1109/21.229461

Karnow, C. E. A. (2005). Launch on warning: Aggressive defense of computer systems. *Journal of Internet Law*, *7*(1), 87–102.

Kaspersky Lab. (2012). Resource 207: Kaspersky Lab Research Proves that Stuxnet and Flame Developers are Connected. Retrieved from http://www.kaspersky.com/about/news/virus/2012/Resource_207_Kaspersky_Lab_Research_Proves_that_Stuxnet_and_Flame_Developers_are_Connected

Kaspersky. (2011). What is the value of your leaked data? Retrieved from http://www.kaspersky.com/about/news/virus/2011/What_is_the_value_of_your_leaked_data_

Kates, G., & Butorin, P. (2014, April 16). Russian professor explains media manipulation. *Radio Free Europe Radio Liberty*. Retrieved from http://www.rferl.org/content/unspun-russian-professor-media-manipulation/25351952.html

Katyal, N. (2005). Community self-help. *Journal of Law Economics and Policy*, *1*, 33–67.

Keck, Z. (2014, March 17). Al Qaeda's brand is dead. *The National Interest*. Retrieved from: http://nationalinterest.org/commentary/al-qaedas-brand-dead-10059?page=1

Keck, M. E., & Sikkink, K. (1998). *Activists Beyond Borders: Advocacy Networks in International Politics*. Ithaca, New York, USA: Cornell University Press.

Keefe, P. R. (2006). *Chatter: Uncovering the Echelon surveillance network and the secret world of global eavesdropping*. New York: Random House.

Kelly, L., & Korsunskaya, D. (2014, March 21). Russia's finance ministry admits sanctions bite. *Yahoo South Africa*. Retrieved from http://za.news.yahoo.com/russias-finance-ministry-admits-sanctions-bite-183735932--business.html

Kendall, B. (2014, Aptil 17) Analysis: Vladimir Putin's veiled threats over Ukraine. *BBC*. Retrieved from http://www.bbc.com/news/world-europe-27063136

Kerner, S. M. (2008, August 15). The Russia Georgia cyberwar [Weblog comment]. Retrieved from http://blog.internet-news.com/skerner/2008/08/the-russia-georgia-cyberwar.html

Kerr, P. K., Rollins, J., Catherine, A., & Theohary, C. A. (2010). *The Stuxnet Computer Worm: Harbinger of an Emerging Warfare Capability*. CRS Report for Congress.

Kerry, C. (2014, May). *Missed connections: Talking with Europe about data, privacy, and surveillance*. Washington: Center for Technology Innovation at Brookings.

Kerzner, H. (1995). *Project Management: A Systems Approach to Planning, Scheduling, and Controlling*. New York, NY: Van Nostrand Reinhold.

Kesan, J. P., & Hayes, C. M. (2012). Mitigative counterstriking: Self-defense and deterrence in cyberspace. *Harvard Journal of Law & Technology*, 25(2), 474–520.

Kesan, J. P., & Majuca, R. (2009). Optimal hackback. *Chicago-Kent Law Review*, 84(3), 831–835.

Khan, F. H. (2002). Pakistan's Nuclear Future. In R. Chambers (Ed.), South Asia in 2020: Future Strategic Balances and Alliances. (pp. 153-190). Strategic Sciences Institute.

Khan, F. H. (2003). *Nuclear Risk Reduction Centers*.

Khan, F. H. (2010, Summer). Prospects for Indian and Pakistani Arms Control and Confidence-Building Measures. *Naval War College Review*, 63(3), 16.

Khartoum Resolution. (n. d.). *Council on Foreign Relations*. Retrieved from http://www.cfr.org/world/khartoum-resolution/p14841

Khoja, K. (1998). A Handbook of CBMs for Regional Security.

Kiani, K. (2014). *Govt to set up cyber authority, court*. Dawn: Dawn.

Killcullen, D. (2009). *The Accidental Guerrilla: Fighting Small Wars in the Midst of a Big One*. Oxford: Oxford University Press.

Kimmage, D. (2010, May). *Al Qaeda Central and the Internet*. Washington DC: New America Foundation. Retrieved from: http://homelandsecurity.gwu.edu/sites/homelandsecurity.gwu.edu/files/downloads/HSPI_Report_15.pdf, accessed 12ᵗʰ 2014.

King, S. (2011, November 8). Office of Secretary of Defense Research and Engineering's Cyber S&T Priority Steering Council Research Roadmap. Proceedings of *National Defense Industrial Association Disruptive Technologies Conference*. 8 November 2011.

Kingsley, P. (2014, June 23). Who is behind Isis's terrifying online propaganda operation? *The Guardian*. Retrieved from: http://www.theguardian.com/world/2014/jun/23/who-behind-isis-propaganda-operation-iraq

Kizekova, A. (2012). The Shanghai Cooperation Organisation: Challenges in Cyberspace.

Klein, R., Rome, E., Beyel, C., Linnemann, R., Reinhardt, W., & Usov, A. (2009). Information Modelling and Simulation in Large Interdependent Critical Infrastructures in IRRIIS. In R. Setola, & S. Geretshuber (Eds.), *Proceedings of the Third International Workshop on Critical Information Infrastructures Security (CRITIS), (2008, October 13-15),* Vol. 5508, (pp. 36–47). Rome, Italy. doi:10.1007/978-3-642-03552-4_4

Knake, R. K. (2010, July 15). Untangling attribution: Moving to accountability in cyberspace. Statement made before the *Subcommittee on Technology and Innovation, Committee on Science and Technology*, U.S. House of Representatives. Retrieved from http://science.house.gov/sites/republicans.science.house.gov/files/documents/hearings/071510_Knake.pdf

Knapp, E. D. (2011). *Industrial Network Security: Securing Critical Infrastructure Networks for Smart Grid, SCADA, and Other Industrial Control Systems*. Waltham, MA, USA: Syngress.

Knorr, K., & Morgan, P. (1982). *Strategic military surprise*. Herndon, VA: Transaction Publishers.

Koh, H. (2012, September 18). International law in cyberspace. Statement made at the meeting of *USCYBERCOM Inter-Agency Legal Conference*, Ft. Meade, MD. Retrieved from http://www.state.gov/s/l/releases/remarks/197924.htm

Koh, H. H. (2012). *International Law in Cyberspace*. Paper presented at the *USCYBERCOM Inter-Agency Legal Conference*, Fort Meade, Maryland.

Koh, H. H. (2012, December 13). International Law in Cyberspace. *Harvard International Law Journal*.

Kopstein, J. (2013, May 5). Hacking back: Cops and corporations want cybersecurity to go on the offensive. *The Verge*. Retrieved from http://www.theverge.com/2013/5/9/4315228/hacking-back-cops-and-corporations-want-offensive-cybersecurity

Koskenniemi, M. (1990). The Politics of International Law. *Journal of International Law, 1*, 5–32.

Kostadinov, D. (2013). The Attribution Problem in Cyber Attacks.

Kostadinov, D. (2014a, April 10). Jus in cyber bello: How the law of armed conflict regulates cyber attacks part I. *Infosec Institute*. Retrieved armed conflict regulates cyber attacks part II. *Infosec Institute*. Retrieved from http://resources.infosecinstitute.com/jus-cyber-bello-law-armed-conflict-regulates-cyber-attacks-part-ii/

Kotadia, M. (2004, March 10). Symbiot launches DDoS counter-strike tool. *ZDNet*. Retrieved from http://www.zdnet.com/symbiot-launches-ddos-counter-strike-tool-3039148215/

Kouchner, B. (2010). Stand Up to the Enemies of the Internet. *New Perspectives Quarterly, 27*(3), 61–63. doi:10.1111/j.1540-5842.2010.01188.x

Kovacich, G. L., Jones, A., & Luzwick, P. G. (2002). Global information warfare: How businesses, governments, and others achieve objectives and attain competitive advantages - Chapter 1, part 2. Information Systems Security, 11(5), 15-23.

Kovacs, E. (2013, November 7). Anonymous Ukraine Launches DDOS Attack on NATO's CCDCOE Website. *Softpedia*. Retrieved from http://news.softpedia.com/news/Anonymous-Ukraine-Launches-DDOS-Attack-on-NATO-s-CCDCOE-Website-398063.shtml

Kovacs, E. (2014, March 4). Website of International Video News Agency Ruptly Hit With DDOS Attack. *Softpedia*. Retrieved from http://news.softpedia.com/news/Website-of-International-Video-News-Agency-Ruptly-Hit-With-DDOS-Attack-430390.shtml

Kramer, A. E. (2013). NSA Leaks Revive Push in Russia to Control Net. *The New York Times*.

Krebs, B. (2008, July 3). Lithuania Weathers Cyber Attack, Braces for Round 2. *The Washington Post*. Retrieved from http://voices.washingtonpost.com/securityfix/2008/07/lithuania_weathers_cyber_attac_1.html

Krekel, B. (2009). *Capability of the People's Republic of China to Conduct Cyber Warfare and Computer Network Exploitation*. National Security Archive.

Kreppon, P. N. M. (2012). *The Unfinished Crisis: US Crisis Management after the 2008 Mumbai Attacks Washington DC*. Stimson Center.

Kruse, P., Hacquebord, F., & McArdle, R. (2010). *Threat Report: W32.Tinba (Tinybanker)*. The Turkish Incident.

Krutz, R. L. (2006). *Securing SCADA systems*. Indianapolis, USA: Wiley Publishing.

Kshetri, N. (2013). Cybercrimes in the Former Soviet Union and Central and Eastern Europe: Current status and key drivers. *Crime, Law, and Social Change, 60*(1), 39–65. doi:10.1007/s10611-013-9431-4

Kuehl, D. D. (n. d.). *From Cyberspace to Cyberpower: Defining the Problem*.

Kun-Lun Li. Hou-Kuan Huang, Shen-Feng Tian, & Wei Xu. (2003). Improving one-class SVM for anomaly detection. *Machine Learning and Cybernetics, 2003 International Conference, Vol. 5*, (pp. 3077–3081).

Kurtz, G. (2010, January 14). Operation "Aurora" hit Google, others. *McAfee Blog Central*. Retrieved from http://blogs.mcafee.com/archive/operation-aurora-hit-google-others

Kux, D. (2006). *India-Pakistan Negotiations: Is Past Still Prologue?* Washington, DC: USIP.

La stratégie médiatique et de propagande d'Al-Qaïda. (2007). *Canadian Center for Intelligence and Security Studies*. Retrieved from http://www.itac.gc.ca/pblctns/pdf/2007-2-fra.pdf

Labovitz, C. (2010). Attack Severs Burma Internet. *Arbour Networks*. Retrieved from http://asert.arbornetworks.com/2010/11/attac-severs-myanmar-internet/

LaGrone, S. (2014, April 14). Russian Fighter Buzzes U.S. Destroyer in Black Sea. *USNI News*. Retrieved from http://news.usni.org/2014/04/14/russian-fighter-buzzes-u-s-destroyer-black-sea

Lancaster, J. (2004). India, Pakistan to Set Up Hotline: Talks End With Deal to Maintain Moratorium on Nuclear Testing. *The Washington Post*.

Landau, E. B. (2012). Assessing the Relevance of Nuclear CBMs to a WMD Arms Control Process in the Middle East Today. Proceedings of *2nd EU Non-Proliferation Consortium (November 5-6)*. Brussels.

Landau, S. (2013). *Surveillance or Security? The Risks Posed by New Wiretapping Technologies*. Cambridge, Massachusetts, USA: The MIT Press.

Landler, M., & Markoff, J. (2007, May 29). Digital fears emerge after data siege in Estonia. *The New York Times Online*. Retrieved from http://www.nytimes.com/2007/05/29/technology/29estonia.html?_r=1

Laprise, J. (2006). Cyber-warfare seen through a mariner's spyglass. *Technology and Society Magazine, IEEE, 25*(3), 26–33. doi:10.1109/MTAS.2006.1700019

Le Bon, G. (1908). *The Sentiments and Morality of Crowds*. London: T Fisher Unwin. doi:10.1037/10878-002

Lee, D. (2014, August 20). James Foley: Extremists battle with social media. *BBC News*. Retrieved from: http://www.bbc.com/news/technology-28870777

Lemos, R. (2001, May 1). Lawyers slam FBI 'hack'. *ZDNet News*. Retrieved from http://www.zdnet.com/lawyers-slam-fbi-hack-2021200883/

Lev, L., Tanenbaum, D., Ohana, R., Holzer, R., Hunovich, T., Adar, A., et al. Jager, Pascoli, Aubigny, M., & Harpes, C. (2011). Validation Activities. Lev, L. & Baruch, Y., (Eds.). MICIE Project Deliverable D6.3. European Commission FP7.

Levi, R. (2013). Is Iran behind the attacks on the American banks? *ICT report review*, 12-23. Retrieved from http://www.ict.org.il/Article/60/ICT-Cyber-Desk-Review-Report-2

Levin, A., & Goodrick, P. (2013). From cybercrime to cyberwar? The international policy shift and its implications for Canada. *Canadian Foreign Policy Journal, 19*(2), 127–143. doi:10.1080/11926422.2013.805150

Levitt, M. (2005). Hezbollah finances, funding the Party of God. *The Washington Institute*. Retrieved from http://www.washingtoninstitute.org/policy-analysis/view/hezbollah-finances-funding-the-party-of-god

Levitt, M. (2013). *Hezbollah: the global footprint of Lebanon's Party of God*. Washington: George Tow University Press.

Lewis, J. A. (2011). Confidence Building Measures and International Agreements in Cyber Security.

Lewis, J. A. (2013a). Conflict and negotiation in cyberspace. *Center for Strategic and International Studies*. Retrieved from http://csis.org/files/publication/130208_Lewis_ConflictCyberspace_Web.pdf

Lewis, J. A. (2013b, May 22). Private retaliation in cyberspace. *Center for Strategic and International Studies*. Retrieved from http://csis.org/publication/private-retaliation-cyberspace

Lewis, J. D. (2014, June 27). *ISIS Battleplan for Bagdhad*. Washington DC: Institute for The Study of War. Retrieved from http://www.understandingwar.org/press-media/staff-bios/jessica-d-lewis

Lewis, P., & Williams, H. (2013, September 19). Syria under Scrutiny: Chemical Weapons Inspections, *Expert Comment*. Retrieved from http://www.chathamhouse.org/media/comment/view/194267

Lewis, T. G. (2006). *Critical Infrastructure Protection in Homeland Security: Defending a Networked Nation*. Hoboken, NJ, USA: Wiley. doi:10.1002/0471789542

Leyden, J. (2014, March 4). Cyber battle apparently under way in Russia-Ukraine conflict. *The Register*. Retrieved from http://www.theregister.co.uk/2014/03/04/ukraine_cyber_conflict/

Leyden, J. (2014, September 3). NATO nations 'will respond to a cyber attack on one as though it were on all'. *The Register*. Retrieved from http://www.theregister.co.uk/2014/09/03/nato_article_v_mutual_defence_principle_applies_to_cyberspace/

Leymore, V. L. (1975). *The Hidden Myth*. New York: Basic Books.

Li, D. K. (2014, July 31). Soldier's selfies might prove Russia's direct role in Ukraine. *The New York Post*. Retrieved from http://nypost.com/2014/07/31/soldiers-selfies-might-prove-russias-role-in-ukraine/

Li, B., Erdin, E., Güneş, M. H., Bebis, G., & Shipley, T. (2011). An analysis of anonymizer technology usage. In J. Domingo-Pascual, Y. Shavitt, & S. Uhlig (Eds.), *Traffic Monitoring and Analysis* (pp. 108–121). Berlin: Springer Berlin Heidelberg. doi:10.1007/978-3-642-20305-3_10

Libicki, M.C. (2012). Cyberspace is not a warfighting domain. *I/S: A Journal of Law and Policy for the Information Society, 8*(2), 325–340.

Libicki, M. (2007). *Conquest in Cybersapce: National Security and Information Warfare*. Cambridge, UK: Cambridge University Press. doi:10.1017/CBO9780511804250

Libicki, M. C. (2009). *Cyberdeterrence and Cyberwar*. Santa Monica, CA: RAND Corporation.

Lichtblau, E. (2013, July 6). In Secret, Court Vastly Broadens Powers of N.S.A. *The New York Times*. Retrieved from http://www.nytimes.com/2013/07/07/us/in-secret-court-vastly-broadens-powers-of-nsa.html?_r=0

Lichtblau, E., & Schmidt, M. S. (2013, August 3). Other Agencies Clamor for Data N.S.A. Compiles, *The New York Times*. Retrieved from http://www.nytimes.com/2013/08/04/us/other-agencies-clamor-for-data-nsa-compiles.html?pagewanted=all

Liff, A. P. (2012). Cyberwar: A New 'Absolute Weapon'? The Proliferation of Cyberwarfare Capabilities and Interstate War. *The Journal of Strategic Studies*, *35*(3), 401–428. doi:10.1080/01402390.2012.663252

Liles, S., Rogers, M., Dietz, J., & Larson, D. (2012). Applying traditional military principles to cyber warfare. In *Proceedings of the 4h International Conference on Cyber Conflict (CYCON)*, Tallinn:IEEE.

Lilien, L., Kamal, Z. H., Bhuse, V., & Gupta, A. (2006). Opportunistic networks: the concept and research challenges in privacy and security.*Proc. of the WSPWN*, 134-147.

Limnell, J. (2014, August 7). Active defense: Fighting fire with fire leads to a dangerous future. *McAfee Labs*. Retrieved from https://blogs.mcafee.com/executive-perspectives/fighting-fire-fire-will-lead-us-dangerous-future

Lindsay, J. R. (2013). Stuxnet and the Limits of Cyber Warfare.

Lings, M. (1991). MUHAMMAD (PBUH): His Life based on the Earliest Sources Islamic Texts Society.

Lin, H. S. (2010). Offensive cyber operations and the use of force. *Journal of National Security Law & Policy*, *4*(1), 63–86.

Lin, P., Allhoff, F., & Rowe, N. C. (2012). War 2.0: Cyberweapons and ethics. *Communications of the ACM*, *55*(3), 24–26. doi:10.1145/2093548.2093558

Li, Z., Goyal, A., Chen, Y., & Paxson, V. (2011). Towards situational awareness of large-scale botnet probing events. *IEEE Transactions on Information Forensics and Security*, *6*(1), 175–188. doi:10.1109/TIFS.2010.2086445

Loch, K. D., Carr, H. H., & Warkentin, M. E. (1992, June). Threats to Information Systems: Today's Reality, Yesterday's Understanding. *Management Information Systems Quarterly*, *16*(2), 173–186. doi:10.2307/249574

Lodhi, M. (2012). *CBMs need a bold approach.Khaleej Times*.

Lodhi, M. (2013). *Pause in the Peace Process. The News*.

Loimeier, R. (2012). Boko Haram: The development of a militant religious movement in Nigeria. *Africa Spectrum*, *47*(2/3), 137–155.

Lokot, T. (2014, March 2). Ukrainian journalists take regime's corruption public with YanukovychLeaks. *Global Voices Online*. Retrieved from http://globalvoicesonline.org/2014/03/02/ukrainian-journalists-take-regimes-corruption-public-with-yanukovychleaks/

Lookingglass (2015, April 28). Operation Armageddon: Cyber espionage as a strategic component of Russian modern warfare. *Lookingglass Cyber Threat Intelligence Group*. Report CTIG-20150428-01. Retrieved from https://lgscout.com/operation-armageddon-cyber-espionage-as-a-strategic-component-of-russian-modern-warfare/

Lowensohn, J. (2014, July 18). Russia Spotted editing Wikipedia page about downed Malaysia Airlines jet. *The Verge*. Retrieved from http://www.theverge.com/2014/7/18/5917099/russia-spotted-editing-wikipedia-page-of-downed-malaysia-air-jet

Lubell, N. (2010). *Extraterritorial use of force against non-state actors*. Oxford: Oxford University Press. doi:10.1093/acprof:oso/9780199584840.001.0001

Lukasik, S. (2011, September). Protecting Users of the Cyber Commons. *Communications of the ACM, 54*(9), 54–61. doi:10.1145/1995376.1995393

Lupovici, A. (2011, December). Cyber Warfare and Deterrence: Trends and Challenges in Research. *Military and Strategic Affairs, 3*(3), 13.

Lupsha, P. A. (1996). Transnational organized crime versus the nation-state. *Transnational Organized Crime, 2*(1), 21–48.

Lvov, A. (2013). *Russian Army developing Cyberattack Defences.*

Lynn, W. J. (2010, September/October). Defending a New Domain. *The Pentagon's Cyberstrategy.*

Lynn, W. J. (2011, September). One Year Later. *The Pentagon's Cyberstrategy.*

Lyon, P. (2008). *Conflict between India and Pakistan: An Encyclopedia.* Santa Barbara: Cal ABC-CLIO Inc.

Lyons, D. K. (2013). Analyzing the effectiveness of Al Qaeda's online influence operations by means of propaganda theory (Master of Science Thesis). El Paso, TX, USA: The University of Texas, El Paso. Retrieved from http://academics. utep.edu/Portals/1892/Theses/Analyzing%20the%20Effectiveness%20of%20Al%20Qaeda%27s%20Online%20Influence%20Operations%20%28Lyons%29.pdf

MacAskill, E., Borger, J., Hopkins, N., Davies, N., & Ball, J. (2013, June 21). GCHQ taps fibre-optic cables for secret access to world's communications. *The Guardian.* Retrieved from http://www.guardian.co.uk/uk/2013/jun/21/gchq-cables-secret-world-communications-nsa

Maher, K. (2013, February 25). The new westphalian web. *Foreign policy magazine online.*

Mahr, K. (2013). *India-Pakistan Tensions Spike as Two Sides Trade Fire across the Border. Time World.*

Ma, J., & Perkins, S. (2003). Time-series novelty detection using one-class support vector machines. *Neural Networks, 2003.Proceedings of the International Joint Conference on, Vol. 3,* (pp. 1741–1745).

Makkar, S. (2011). *Pakistan yet to establish hotline.* India.

Management Analytics (15 December 1993). *Planning Considerations for Defensive Information Warfare – Cybersecurity.* Fort George G. Meade, Columbia, MD: Prepared for Defense Information Systems Agency (DISA) Joint Interoperability and Engineering Organization (JIEO) Center for Information Systems Security (CISS).

Mandiant Hires Travis Reese as Vice President of Federal Services. (2006, April 25). *Business Wire.*

Mankotia, A. S. (2013, July 5). Telecom operators will have to help set up government's central monitoring system. *The Economic Times.* Retrieved from http://articles.economictimes.indiatimes.com/2013-07-05/news/40392187_1_telecom-operators-service-provider-uasl

Manyika, J., & Chui, M. et al. (2013). *McKinsey Global Institute Report: Disruptive technologies: Advances that will transform life, business, and the global economy.* McKinsey & Company.

Mao, Z. (1968). Characteristics of China's Revolutionary War. In W. J. Pomeroy (Ed.), *Guerrilla Warfare and Marxism* (pp. 182–185). New York, USA: International Publishers.

Mao, Z. (1968). On the Purely Military Viewpoint. In W. J. Pomeroy (Ed.), *Guerrilla Warfare and Marxism* (pp. 173–176). New York, USA: International Publishers.

Mao, Z. (1968). The Military Problem. In W. J. Pomeroy (Ed.), *Guerrilla Warfare and Marxism* (pp. 168–171). New York, USA: International Publishers.

Mardini, R. (2014, September 12). The Islamic State threat is overstated. *The Washington Post*. Retrieved from http://www.washingtonpost.com/opinions/the-islamic-state-threat-is-overstated/2014/09/12/acbbebb2-33ad-11e4-8f02-03c644b2d7d0_story.html,

Markoff, J. (2010). Step Taken to End Impasse Over Cybersecurity Talks. *The New York Times*.

Marks, J. (2015, May 5). U.S. makes new push for global rules in cyberspace. *Politico*. Retrieved from http://www.politico.com/story/2015/05/us-makes-new-push-for-global-rules-in-cyberspace-117632.html#ixzz3afDwS24l

Masters, J. (2011, May 24). Here's How The U.S. Plans To Plug The Holes In Its Cybersecurity Policy. *The Business Insider*.

Mathews, L. (2011). *TDL4 botnet: smarter, more sophisticated, and not for use in Russia*. Retrieved from http://www.extremetech.com/internet/88770-tdl4-botnet-smarter-more-sophisticated-and-not-for-use-in-russia

Mathwick, J. E. (1997). *Database Integration, Practical Lessons-Learned*. San Diego, CA: DoD Database Colloquium.

Maurer, T. (2011). *Cyber Norm Emergence at the United Nations – An Analysis of the Activities at the UN Regarding Cyber-security*.

Maybury, M. (2012, December 13). Air Force Cyber Vision 2025. United States Air Force Cyberspace S&T Vision 2012-2025. *USAF Office of the Chief Scientist*. Retrieved from http://www.defenseinnovationmarketplace.mil/resources/cyber/cybervision2025.pdf

Maybury, M. (2013, August 1). Global Horizons. *Armed Forces Journal*. Retrieved from http://www.armedforcesjournal.com/global-horizons/

McAffe. (2009). *Virtual Criminology Report 2009; Virtually Here: The Age of Cyber Warfare*. McAfee, Inc.

McConnell, M. (2010, February 28). Mike McConnell on how to win the cyber-war we're losing. *The Washington Post*. Retrieved from http://www.washingtonpost.com/wp-dyn/content/article/2010/02/25/AR2010022502493.html

McGee, S., Sabett, R. V., & Shah, A. (2013). Adequate attribution: A framework for developing a national policy for private sector use of active defense. *Journal of Business & Technology Law*, 8(1). http://digitalcommons.law.umaryland.edu/cgi/viewcontent.cgi? article=1187&context=jbtl Retrieved January 12, 2014

McLuhan, M. (1974). *Understanding Media: The Extensions of Man* (2nd Ed.). London, UK: Routledge and Kegan Paul Limited/Abacus.

McLuhan, M., & Fiore, Q. (1968). *War and Peace in the Global Village*. New York, USA: Bantam Books.

Mcwhorter, D. (2013). APT1: Exposing one of China's Cyber Espionage Units. *Mandiant.com*.

Mehdudia, S. (2013). Congressional committee calls for strong India-U.S. ties on cyber security. *The Hindu*.

Melander, J. J. H. K. A. (1977, July/August). European security and Confident Building Measures. *Survival*, 19(4), 147.

Meleagrou-Hitchens, A., Maher, S., & Sheehan, J. (2012). Lights, Camera, Jihad: Al-Shabaab's Western Media Strategy. London: ICSR, King's College London. Retrieved from http://icsr.info/wp-content/uploads/2012/11/ICSR-Lights-Camera-Jihad-Report_Nov2012_ForWeb-2.pdf

Melzer, N. (2011). *Cyberwarfare and International Law*.

Menn, J. (2012, June 18). Hacked companies fight back with controversial steps. *Reuters*. Retrieved from http://www.reuters.com/article/2012/06/18/us-media-tech-summit-cyber-strikeback-idUSBRE85G07S20120618

Menn, J. (2013, October 10). SEC issues guidelines on hacking. *The Financial Times*. Retrieved from http://www.ft.com/cms/s/0/32e2adae-f5fc-11e0-bcc2-00144feab49a.html#axzz2hR7NpRFX

Menn, J., & Gelles, D. (2009, August 6). Concerted cyber-attack takes down Twitter. *Financial Times*. Retrieved from www.ft.com/cms/s/.../038b9b54-82a6-11de-ab4a-00144feabdc0.html

Menon, R. (2000). *A Nuclear Strategy for India*. New Delhi: Sage Publications.

Merkow, M. S., & Breithaupt, J. (2005). *Computer Security Assurance Using the Common Criteria*. Cengage Learning.

Messerschmidt, J. E. (2013). Hackback: Permitting retaliatory hacking by non-state actors as proportionate countermeasures to transboundary cyberharm. *Columbia Journal of Transnational Law*, *52*(1), 275–324.

Messmer, E. (2011, January 21). Is retaliation the answer to cyber attacks? *Networkworld*. Retrieved from http://www.networkworld.com/article/2199010/malware-cybercrime/is-retaliation-the-answer-to-cyber-attacks-.html

Meyer, P. (2013). *Cyber Security Takes the Floor at the UN*.

Michaels, R. (1999, February 18). *Department of the Navy Data Interoperability*, Briefing to Mr. Dan Porter, DoN CIO. Arlington, VA: GRC International.

MICIE - Tool for systemic risk analysis and secure mediation of data exchanged across linked CI information infrastructures. (2008). *MICIE Consortium*.

Microsoft Security Intelligence Report, Volume 18. (2015). *Microsoft Corporation*. Retrieved from https://www.microsoft.com/en-us/download/details.aspx?id=46928

Miellmonka, M. (2012). Cyber CSBMs. Proceedings of *Cyber Security Conference 2012*, UNIDIR.

Mighty Mole. (2014). Russian helicopters swarm over Ukraine [Video file]. Retrieved from http://www.youtube.com/watch?v=-7OOKecS-WU

Mikell, W. E. (1942). The Doctrine of Entrapment in the Federal Courts. *University of Pennsylvania Law Review and American Law Register*, 245-265.

Mili, A., & Sheldon, F. (2007, November). Measuring reliability as a mean failure cost. In *High Assurance Systems Engineering Symposium, 2007. HASE'07. 10th IEEE,* (pp. 403-404). IEEE. doi:10.1109/HASE.2007.42

Mili, A., & Sheldon, F. T. (2009). Challenging the mean time to failure: Measuring dependability as a mean failure cost. In *Proceedings of 42nd Hawaii International Conference on System Sciences (HICSS-42)*, Waikoloa, HI. (pp. 10).

Mimoso, M. (2013, February 27). MiniDuke espionage malware hits governments in Europe using Adobe exploits [Weblog comment]. Retrieved from http://threatpost.com/en_us/blogs/miniduke-espionage-malware-hits-governments-europe-using-adobe-exploits-022713

Miorandia, D., Sicarib, S., De Pellegrinia, F., & Chlamtaca, I. (2013, September). Internet of things: Vision, applications and research challenges. *Ad Hoc Networks*, *10*(7), 1497–1516. doi:10.1016/j.adhoc.2012.02.016

Mirkovic, J., Dietrich, S., Dittrich, D., & Reiher, P. (2004). *Internet Denial of Service: Attack and Defense Mechanisms (Radia Perlman Computer Networking and Security)*. Prentice Hall PTR.

Mislan, R. P. (2010, June30). Cellphone crime solvers. *IEEE Spectrum*, 1–3. Retrieved from http://spectrum.ieee.org/computing/software/cellphone-crime-solvers

Modbus Application Protocol Specification V1.1b3. (2012). MICIE Consortium Retrieved from http://www.modbus.org/docs/Modbus_Application_Proftocol_V1_1b3.pdf

Mohamed, H. (2014, January 9). Al Shabab bans internet in Somalia. *Al Jazeera*. Retrieved from http://www.aljazeera.com/news/africa/2014/01/al-shabab-bans-internet-somalia-20141981213614575.html

Mohan, I. B. V. (2012). 5 lakh cyber warriors to bolster India's e-defence. *The Times of India*.

MohdAlwi, N. H., & Fan, I. S. (2010). e-Learning and information security management. *International Journal of Digit Society (IJDS)*, 1(2), 148-156.

Mokube, I., & Adams, M. (2007, March). Honeypots: concepts, approaches, and challenges. In *Proceedings of the 45th annual southeast regional conference* (pp. 321-326). ACM. doi:10.1145/1233341.1233399

Monnet, B. (2014, May 21). Bring back our girls campaign giving free publicity to Boko Haram. *The Telegraph*. Retrieved from http://www.telegraph.co.uk/news/worldnews/africaandindianocean/nigeria/10847493/Comment-Bring-back-our-girls-campaign-is-giving-free-publicity-to-Boko-Haram.html

Moore, D. (2003). Network Telescopes: Tracking Denial-of-Service Attacks and Internet Worms Around the Globe. In LISA.

Moore, D., & Shannon, C. (2002, November). Code-Red: a case study on the spread and victims of an Internet worm. In *Proceedings of the 2nd ACM SIGCOMM Workshop on Internet measurement* (pp. 273-284). ACM. doi:10.1145/637201.637244

Moore, D., Shannon, C., Brown, D. J., Voelker, G. M., & Savage, S. (2006). Inferring internet denial-of-service activity. [TOCS]. *ACM Transactions on Computer Systems*, 24(2), 115–139. doi:10.1145/1132026.1132027

Moran, N. (2012). A Cyber Early Warning Model. In J. Carr (Ed.), Inside Cyber Warfare (179-189). O'Reilly Media Inc.: Sebastopol, CA.

Moran, N., & Haq, T. (2013, October, 31). Know your enemy: Tracking a rapidly evolving APT actor. *FireEye Blog*. Retrieved from http://www.fireeye.com/blog/technical/2013/10/know-your-enemy-tracking-a-rapidly-evolving-apt-actor.html

Morris, S. (2004). *The future of netcrime now: Part 1 – threats and challenges*. Home Office Online Report 62/04. Retrieved from http://www.globalinitiative.net/download/cybercrime/europe-russia/Home%20Office%20-%20The%20future%20of%20netcrime%20now%20-%20Part%201%20%E2%80%93%20threats%20and%20challenges.pdf

Mudrinich, E. M. (2012). Cyber 3.0: The Department of Defense strategy for operating in cyberspace and the attribution problem. *The Air Force Law Review, 68*, 167.

Mueller, P., & Yadegari, B. (n. d.). *The Stuxnet Worm*. Department of Computer Science. University of Arizona. Retrieved from http://www.cs.arizona.edu/~collberg/Teaching/466-566/2012/Resources/presentations/2012/topic9-final/report.pdf

Mullish, J. (2014). NATO and Ukraine Must Ready for Cyber Threats. *Defence IQ*. Retrieved from http://www.cdans.org/media/9255/32455.pdf

Mushahid to table Cyber Security Bill in Parliament. (n. d.). *MushahidHussain.com*. Retrieved from http://www.mushahidhussain.com/news-detail.php?id=MTE0&pageid=media.

Myagmar, S., Lee, A. J., & Yurcik, W. (2005, August). Threat modeling as a basis for security requirements. In *Symposium on Requirements Engineering for Information Security (SREIS)*.

Mydans, S. (2000, May 11). Student Sought In Virus Case In Philippines. *The New York Times*. Retrieved from http://www.nytimes.com/2000/05/11/business/student-sought-in-virus-case-in-philippines.html?ref=oneldeguzman

Myriam-Webster Dictionary. (2014). *Strategy*. Retrieved from http://www.merriam-webster.com/dictionary/strategy

Nagaraj, A. (2013, June 21). Global Telecom Treaty 2012 signed in the ITU world conference. *Center for Information and Communication Science (CICS)*. Retrieved from http://cicsworld.centerforics.org/blog/2013/01/3/global-telecom-treaty-2012-signed-in-the-itu-world-conference/

Nakashima, E. (2010, January 16). U.S. plans to issue official protest to China over attack on Google. *Washington Post*. Retrieved from http://articles.washingtonpost.com/2010-01-16/news/36816400_1_chinese-search-engine-internet-freedom-chinese-government

Nakashima, E. (2012). In U.S.-Russia deal, nuclear communication system may be used for cybersecurity. *Washington Post*.

Nakashima, E. (2012, August 10). Pentagon proposes more robust role for its cyber-specialists. *The Washington Post*. Retrieved from http://www.washingtonpost.com/world/national-security/pentagon-proposes-more-robust-role-for-its-cyber-specialists/2012/08/09/1e3478ca-db15-11e1-9745-d9ae6098d493_story.html

Nakashima, E. (2012, September 17). Cybersecurity should be more active, official says. *The Washington Post*. Retrieved from http://www.washingtonpost.com/world/national-security/cybersecurity-should-be-more-active-official-says/2012/09/16/dd4bc122-fc6d-11e1-b153-218509a954e1_story.html

Nakashima, E. (2013). Bush Order Expands Network Monitoring Intelligence Agencies to Track Intrusions. *Washington Post*.

Nakashima, E. (2013a, February 11). Cyber-spying said to target U.S. business. *The Washington Post*.

Nakashima, E. (2013b, February 11). U.S. said to be target of massive cyber-espionage campaign. *The Washington Post*. Retrieved from http://www.washingtonpost.com/world/national-security/us-said-to-be-target-of-massive-cyber-espionage-campaign/2013/02/10/7b4687d8-6fc1-11e2-aa58-243de81040ba_story.html?hpid=z1

Nakashima, E. (2014, January 12). NSA phone record collection does little to prevent terrorist attacks, group says. *The Washington Post*. Retrieved from http://www.washingtonpost.com/world/national-security/nsa-phone-record-collection-does-little-to-prevent-terrorist-attacks-group-says/2014/01/12/8aa860aa-77dd-11e3-8963-b4b654bcc9b2_story.html

Nakashima, E., & Soltani, A. (2013, December 18). Panel urges new curbs on surveillance by U.S. *The Washington Post*. Retrieved from http://www.washingtonpost.com/world/national-security/nsa-shouldnt-keep-phone-database-review-board-recommends/2013/12/18/f44fe7c0-67fd-11e3-a0b9-249bbb34602c_story.html

Nakashima, E., Miller, G., & Tate, J. (2012). US, Israel developed Flame computer virus to slow Iranian nuclear efforts, officials say. *The Washington Post*.

Napolitano, J. (2012, September 19). Homeland Threats and Agency Responses. *Department of Homeland Security*. Retrieved from http://www.dhs.gov/news/2012/09/19/written-testimony-secretary-napolitano-senate-committee-homeland-security-and

National Institute of Standards and Technology (NIST). (n. d.). Retrieved from http://www.nist.gov/index.html

National Military Strategy for Cyberspace Operations (NMS-CO). (2006). *United States Department of Defense*. from http://www.dod.mil/pubs/foi/joint_staff/jointStaff_jointOperations/07-F-2105doc1.pdf

National Police Academy. (n. d.). *Government of Pakistan*. Retrieved from http://www.npa.gov.pk/

National Research Council. (2009). *Technology, policy law and ethics regarding U.S. acquisition and use of cyber attack capabilities*. Washington: The National Academies Press. Retrieved from http://www.lawfareblog.com/wp-content/uploads/2013/01/NRC-Report.pdf

NATO and cyber defense. (2012). NATO. Retrieved from http://www.nato.int/cps/en/natolive/topics_78170.htm

Nazario, J. (2007, May 17). Estonian DDoS Attacks – A Summary to Date. *Arbor Networks*. Retrieved from http://ddos.arbornetworks.com/2007/05/estonian-ddos-attacks-a-summary-to-date/

Needham, R. (1972). Protection systems and protection implementations. In FJCC, AFIPS Conf. Proc., Vol. 41, pt. 1, pp. 571-578.

Nehru-Liaquat Agreement 1950 (1950). *Governments of India and Pakistan.*

Nelson, D. (2011). *WikiLeaks: hoax phone call brought India and Pakistan to brink of war. The Telegraph.*

Nemchenko, A. (2014, March 11). Top 7 false statements by Russian media about Ukraine. Retrieved from http://visual.ly/top-7-false-statements-russian-media-about-ukraine

Network Warfare. (2013). *Armed Forces and NCW.* Government of India.

Newman, R. C. (2009). *Computer Security: Protecting Digital Resources.* Jones and Barlett Publication.

Nguyen, V. (2013). Attribution of Spear Phishing Attacks: A Literature Survey (C. a. E. W. Division, Trans.). Edinburgh, South Australia: Australian Government.

Nicholson, A., Janicke, H., & Watson, T. (2013). *An Initial Investigation into Attribution in SCADA Systems.* Paper presented at *the International Symposium for ICS & SCADA Cyber Security Research*, Leicester.

Nicholson, A., Janicke, H., & Watson, T. (2013). An initial investigation into attribution in SCADA systems. In *Proceedings of the 1st International Symposium for ICS & SCADA Cyber Security Research.*Leicester, UK: BCS.

Nickolova, M., & Nickolov, E. (2007). Threat model for user security in e-learning systems. *International Journal Information Technologies and Knowledge, 1*(1), 341–347.

Nicks, D. (2014, August 9). Hackers unveil their plan to change email forever. *Time*. Retrieved from http://time.com/3096341/email-encryption-hackers/

Nicks, D. (2012). *Private: Bradley Manning, WikiLeaks, and the Biggest Exposure of Official Secrets in American History.* Chicago Review Press.

Nigeria: Boko Haram surge in capabilities & activity. (2014, April 1). *Soufan Group*. Retrieved from http://soufangroup.com/tsg-intelbrief-nigeria-boko-haram-surge-in-capabilities-activity/

Nigerian Terrorism News Arena. (2014). Facebook.com. Retrieved from: https://wwww.facebook.com/NigerianTerrorismNewsArena

Notification on National Cyber Security Policy File No: 2(35)/2011-CERT-In. (2013). (2013). *Ministry of Communication and Information Technology.* Retrieved from http://indiacybersecurity.blogspot.com/

Nouri, K. (2010). Cyber wars in Iran. *Mianeh*. Retrieved from http://mianeh.net/article/cyber-wars-iran

Novosti, R. (2013). *Cybersecurity high on agenda of Obama-Putin Meeting.*

Now, D. (2012). *India's Forces to Seek Three New Commands from PM.*

NRRC: Confidence Building through Information Exchange. (2012). *US Department of State.* http://www.state.gov/t/avc/rls/199564.htm

Nuclear Weapons Employment Strategy of the United States. (2013). The White House. *Whitehouse.gov.*

O'Brien, N. (2011, February 6). Bikies' blackberrys beat law. *The Sydney Morning Herald*. Retreived from http://www. smh.com.au/digital-life/mobiles/bikies-blackberrys-beat-law-20110206-1ahmo.html

O'Connell, M. E. (2012). Cyber security without cyber war. *Journal of Conflict and Security Law*, *17*(2), 187–209. doi:10.1093/jcsl/krs017

O'Gorman, G., & McDonald, G. (2012). The Elderwood Project. *Symantec Security Response*. Retrieved from https:// www.symantec.com/content/en/us/enterprise/media/security_response/whitepapers/the-elderwood-project.pdf

O'Hagan, J. (2013). War 2.0: An analytical framework. *Australian Journal of International Affairs*, *67*(5), 555–569. doi:10.1080/10357718.2013.823374

Obama, B. (2013). Executive Order 13636 - Improving Critical Infrastructure Cybersecurity. *USA Federal Register*, (2013-03915):11737–11744.

Obama, B. (2013, February 12). Remarks by the President in the State of the Union Address. *The White House*. Retrieved from http://www.whitehouse.gov/the-press-office/2013/02/12/remarks-president-state-union-address

Obama, B. (2014, January 17). Remarks by the President on Review of Signals Intelligence. *The White House*. Retrieved from http://www.whitehouse.gov/the-press-office/2014/01/17/remarks-president-review-signals-intelligence

Ocean Telegraphy: The Twenty Fifth Anniversary. (1879).

Odierno, R. (2013, February 4). The force of tomorrow. *Foreign Policy*. Retrieved from http://www.foreignpolicy.com/ articules/2013/02/04/the_force_of_tomorrow

OECD Guidelines for the Security of Information Systems and Networks: (n. d.). Towards a Culture of Security. Retrieved from http://www.oecd.org/internet/ieconomy/ oecdguidelinesforthesecurityofinformationsystemsandnetworkstowardsa-cultureofsecurity.htm

Office of the National Counterintelligence Executive. (2011). *Foreign spies stealing US economic secrets in cyberspace, report to Congress on foreign economic collection and industrial espionage 2009-2011*. Retrieved from http://www.ncix. gov/publications/reports/fecie_all/Foreign_Economic_Collection_2011.pdf

OfficialAnonymousTV1. (2014). Anonymous - message from Ukraine 2014 [Video file]. Retrieved from http://www. youtube.com/watch?v=1AWEI9rFYXs

Okino, Z. S. (2014, March 19). Boko Haram: Is the military in false propaganda war? *Premium Times*. Retrieved from https://www.premiumtimesng.com/opinion/157016-boko-haram-is-the-military-in-false-propaganda-war-by-zainab-suleiman-okino.html

Oliva, G., Panzieri, S., & Setola, R. (2010). Agent-based input–output interdependency model. In S. Shenoi (Ed.), International Journal of Critical Infrastructures, 3(2), 76–82.

Online US is still a Superpower. (2013). *Eurotopics.net*. Retrieved from http://www.eurotopics.net/en/home/presseschau/ archiv/article/ARTICLE125313-Online-US-is-still-a-superpower

Onuch, O. (2014, January 2). Social networks and social media in Ukrainian "Euromaidan" protests [Weblog comment]. Retrieved from http://www.washingtonpost.com/blogs/monkey-cage/wp/2014/01/02/social-networks-and-social-media-in-ukrainian-euromaidan-protests-2/

Onuncu Kalkınma Planı (2014-2018). (2012Ministry of Development. Özel İhtisas Komisyonları El Kitabı.

Organisation for the Prohibition of Chemical Weapons. (2014). *Chemical Weapons Convention: Genesis and Historical Development*. Retrieved May 14, 2015, from http://www.opcw.org/chemical-weapons-convention/genesis-and-historical-development

Organization for the Advanced Structured Information Standards (OASIS). (n. d). *OASIS*. Retrieved from https://www.oasis-open.org/

Osborn, K. (2014, May 21). "DARPA unveils hack-proof drone. *DefenseTech*

Osborne, C. (2013, February 1). US government debates action over alleged Chinese cyberattacks. *ZDNet*. Retrieved from http://www.zdnet.com/us-government-debates-action-over-alleged-chinese-cyberattacks-7000010679/

OSCE Guide on Non-Military CBMs. (2012). OSCE Secretariat. Vienna.

Osman, J. (2013, October 25). Al Shabaab: using social media to fight the jihad. *Channel 4*. Retrieved from http://www.channel4.com/news/al-shabaab-jihadist-kenya-westgate-kenya-nairobi-twitter

Padder, S. (2012). *The Composite Dialogue between India and Pakistan: Structure, Process and Agency* (Vol. 65). Heidelberg Papers in South Asian and Comparative Politics.

Paganini, P. (2013). *China vs US, Cyber Superpowers Compared*. Retrieved from http://resources.infosecinstitute.com/china-vs-us-cyber-superpowers-compared/

Pakistan Telecommunication Authority (PTA). (n. d.). Retrieved from http://www.pta.gov.pk/

Pakistan Tests Medium Range Missile. (2012, November 28). Pakistan Inter Services Public Relations.

Palmer, E. (2014, March 21). Natalia Poklonskaya: Crimean Attorney General becomes surprise Japanese Anime viral hit. *International Business Times*. Retrieved from http://www.ibtimes.co.uk/natalia-poklonskaya-crimean-attorney-general-becomes-surprise-japanese-anime-viral-hit-1441281

Pang, R., Yegneswaran, V., Barford, P., Paxson, V., & Peterson, L. (2004, October). Characteristics of internet background radiation. In *Proceedings of the 4th ACM SIGCOMM conference on Internet measurement* (pp. 27-40). ACM. doi:10.1145/1028788.1028794

Panzieri, S., Oliva, G., Foglietta, C., Minichino, M., Ciancamerla, E., Macone, D., et al. (2010). Common Ontology and Risk Prediction Algorithms – Final Version. In S. Panzieri (Ed.), MICIE Project, European Commission FP7.

Panzieri, S., Setola, R., & Ulivi, G. (2005). An approach to model complex interdependent infrastructures. In P. Zítek (Ed.), *Proceedings of the 16th IFAC World Congress, (2005, July 4-8),* (pp. 67–67). Prague, Czech Republic.

Parameswaran, P. (2012). *ASEAN at a Crossroads.The Diplomat*.

Paret, P. (Ed.). (1986). *Makers of Modern Strategy: from Machiavelli to the Nuclear Age*. Princeton, New Jersey, USA: Princeton University Press.

Parker, T., Devost, M. G., Sach, M. H., Shaw, E., & Stroz, E. (2004). *Cyber Adversary Characterisation*. Rockland: Syngress Publishing.

Parks, R., & Duggan, D. (2011). Principles of cyberwarfare. *Security Privacy, IEEE, 9*(5), 30–35. doi:10.1109/MSP.2011.138

Parrish, K. (2013, February 6). Panetta warns cyber threat growing quickly. *American Forces Press Service*. Retrieved from http://www.defense.gov/news/newsarticle.aspx?id=119214

Pavlyuchenkoa, F. (2001). *Belarus in the Context of European Cyber Security*.

Pérez-Peña, R. (2013). Universities Face a Rising Barrage of Cyberattacks. *The New York Times*.

Perlroth, N. (2012, May 30). Researchers Find Clues in Malware, *The New York Times*. Retrieved from http://www.nytimes.com/2012/05/31/technology/researchers-link-flame-virus-to-stuxnet-and-duqu.html?_r=1&ref=world

Perlroth, N. (2013). Hackers in China Attacked The Times for Last 4 Months. *The New York Times*.

Perlroth, N. (2013a, December 19). Target Struck in the Cat-and-Mouse Game of Credit Theft. *The New York Times*. Retrieved from http://www.nytimes.com/2013/12/20/technology/target-stolen-shopper-data.html?src=me&ref=general&_r=0

Perlroth, N. (2013b, December 27). Target's Nightmare Goes On: Encrypted PIN Data Stolen, *The New York Times*. Retrieved from http://bits.blogs.nytimes.com/2013/12/27/targets-nightmare-goes-on-encrypted-pin-data-stolen/?ref=technology

Perlroth, N., & Sanger, D. E. (2013). Cyberattacks against U.S. Corporations are on the Rise. *The New York Times*.

Perlroth, N., & Sanger, D. E. (2013, July 13). Nations Buying as Hackers Sell Flaws in Computer Code. *The New York Times*.

Perlroth, N., Sanger, D. E., & Schmidt, M. S. (2013, March 3). As Hacking Against U.S. Rises, Experts Try to Pin Down Motive. *The New York Times*. Retrieved from http://www.nytimes.com/2013/03/04/us/us-weighs-risks-and-motives-of-hacking-by-china-or-iran.html?_r=0

Perrow, C. (1999). *Normal accidents: Living with high-risk technologies*. Princeton: Princeton University Press.

Perrow, C. (2007). *The Next Catastrophe: Reducing our Vulnerabilities to Natural, Industrial, and Terrorist Disaster*. New Jersey: Princeton University Press.

Peterson, A. (2013). The Post just got hacked by the Syrian Electronic Army. *Washington Post*.

Peterson, S. (2011). *Exclusive: Iran hijacked US drone, says Iranian engineer (video). Christian Science Monitor*.

Phillips, A. (2014). The Islamic State's challenge to international order. *Australian Journal of International Affairs*, *68*(5), 495–498. doi:10.1080/10357718.2014.947355

Pierce, T. (2005). *Warfighting and disruptive technologies: disguising innovation*. London: Routledge.

PlayStation: Kullanıcı bilgileri de çalındı! (2011). *NTVMSNBC*. Retrieved from http://www.ntv.com.tr/arsiv/id/25207123

Poeter, D. (2012, February 28). IBM says it's 'on the cusp' of building a quantum computer. *PC Mag*. Retrieved from http://www.pcmag.com/article2/0,2817,2400930,00.asp

Poison ivy: Assessing damage and extracting intelligence. (2014, August 30). *FireEye Special Report*. Retrieved from https://www.fireeye.com/resources/pdfs/fireeye-poison-ivy-report.pdf

Poitras, L., Rosenbach, M., & Stark, H. (2013, September 16). Follow the Money': NSA Monitors Financial World. *Der Spiegel*. Retrieved from http://www.spiegel.de/international/world/how-the-nsa-spies-on-international-bank-transactions-a-922430.html

Polityuk, P. (2014, March 8). Ukrainian authorities suffer new cyber attacks. *Reuters*. Retrieved from http://www.reuters.com/article/2014/03/08/us-ukraine-cricis-cyberattack-idUSBREA270FU20140308

Ponder (2010). *Ponder2 project*. Retrieved from http://ponder2.net/

Ponemon Institute. (2015, May 23). 2015 cost of data breach study: Global analysis. *Ponemon Institute Research Report*. Retrieved from http://public.dhe.ibm.com/common/ssi/ecm/se/en/sew03053wwen/SEW03053WWEN.PDF

Poster, M. (1988). *Jean Baudrillard: Selected Writings.* Palo Alto, CA: Stanford University Press.

Power, R. (2000, October 30). Joy Riders: Mischief That Leads to Mayhem. *informIT.* Retrieved from http://www.informit.com/articles/article.aspx?p=19603&seqNum=3

Prasad, K. (2012). Cyber-terrorism: Addressing the Challenges for Establishing an International Legal Framework. Proceedings from 3rd Australian Counter Terrorism Conference. Australia.

Premium Times. (2014). Controversy trails new video claiming Boko Haram leader, Abubakar Shekau, is alive. Retrieved from: https://www.premiumtimesng.com/news/headlines/168948-controversy-trails-new-video-claiming-boko-haram-leader-abubakar-shekau-is-alive.html

Prescott, J. M. (2013). *Autonomous Decision-Making Processes and the Responsible Cyber Commander.* Paper presented at the *5th International Conference on Cyber Conflict,* Tallinn. doi:10.2139/ssrn.2283767

President Putin's fiction: 10 false claims about Ukraine. (2014, March 5). Department of State. Retrieved from http://www.state.gov/r/pa/prs/ps/2014/03/222988.htm

Presidental Policy Directive 20. (n. d.). *EPIC.org.* Retrieved from http://epic.org/privacy/cybersecurity/presidential-directives/presidential-policy-directive-20.pdf

Pretorius, R. (2013, August 17). A bit like attending college: departing expat looks back on his UAE experience. *The National.* Retrieved from: http://www.thenational.ae/thenationalconversation/comment/a-bit-like-attending-college-departing-expat-looks-back-on-his-uae-experience

Privacy Impact Assessment for the Initiative Three Exercise . (2010). United States Computer Emergency Readiness Team (US-CERT).

PROFIBUS & PROFINET International. (1999). Retrieved from www.profibus.com

Profile: Abu Musab al-Zarkawi. (2005, November 10). *BBC News.* Retrieved from http://news.bbc.co.uk/1/hi/world/middle_east/3483089.stm

Propaganda. (n. d.). *Oxford Dictionaries.* Retrieved from http://www.oxforddictionaries.com/definition/english/propaganda

Proposal for a council decision on a Critical Infrastructure Warning Information Network (CIWIN). (2008). *Communication from European Commission,* COM (2008) 676.

Prosise, C., & Sha, S. U. (2013, January 2013). Hackers' tricks to avoid detection. *Windows Security.* Retrieved from http://www.windowsecurity.com/whitepapers/misc/Hackers_Tricks_to_Avoid_Detection_.html

Protecting your critical assets - Lessons learned from "Operation Aurora" [White paper]. (2010). *McAfee Labs and McAfee Foundstone Professional Services.* Retrieved from http://www.wired.com/images_blogs/threatlevel/2010/03/operationaurora_wp_0310_fnl.pdf

Protocol Additional to the Geneva Conventions (1949), and relating to the *Protection of Victims of International Armed Conflicts* (1977) (Protocol I).

Protocol Additional to the Geneva Conventions (1949), and relating to the *Protection of Victims of Non-International Armed Conflicts* (1977) (Protocol II).

Provos, N. (2003, February). Honeyd-a virtual honeypot daemon. In *10th DFN-CERT Workshop, Hamburg, Germany* (Vol. 2).

Provos, N. (2004, August). A Virtual Honeypot Framework. In *USENIX Security Symposium* (Vol. 173).

Provos, N., & Holz, T. (2007). *Virtual honeypots: from botnet tracking to intrusion detection.* Pearson Education.

Psaki, J. (2013). Statement on Consensus Achieved by the UN Group of Governmental Experts on Cyber Issues. *U.S. Department of State.* Retrieved from http://www.state.gov/r/pa/prs/ps/2013/06/210418.htm

Public must be warned about cyber threat 'like AIDS campaign in the 80s'. (2013, January 9). *The Telegraph.* Retrieved from http://www.telegraph.co.uk/news/uknews/defence/9789743/Public-must-be-warned-about-cyber-threat-like-AIDS-campaign-in-the-80s.html

Pultarova, T. (2014, March 10). Ukraine under cyber attack. *Engineering and Technology Magazine.* Retrieved from http://eandt.theiet.org/news/2014/mar/ukraine-cyber.cfm

Pusatli, O. T., & Regan, B. (2012). A Model to Assist the Maintenance vs. Replacement Decision in Information Systems. In Z. Belkhamza & S. A. Wafa (Eds.), *Measuring Organizational Information Systems Success: New Technologies and Practices* (pp. 137–157). IGI Global. doi:10.4018/978-1-4666-0170-3.ch008

Qadeem, M. (1998). CBMs and Conflict Resolution as Approaches to the South Asian Security: How Relevant and Pragmatic? In M. Ahmer. (Ed.), *Internal and External Dynamics of South Asian Security.* Karachi, Fazleesons. (pp. 79).

R: A Language and Environment for Statistical Computing. (2009). Vienna, Austria: R Foundation for Statistical Computing.

Rabkin, J. A., & Rabkin, A. (2012). To confront cyber threats, we must rethink the law of armed conflict. *Koret-Taube Task Force on National Security and Law, Hoover Institution, Stanford University.* Retrieved http://media.hoover.org/sites/default/files/documents/EmergingThreats_Rabkin.pdf

Raff, A. (2012). Shamoon, a two-stage targeted attack. *Seculert.* Retrieved from http://blog.seculert.com/2012/08/shamoon-two-stage-targeted-attack.html

Rakodi, C. (2012). Inter-religious violence and its aftermath: Insights from Indian and Nigerian cities. *Journal of Asian and African Studies, 48*(5), 557–576. doi:10.1177/0021909612464339

Rantapelkonen, J., & Jaitner, M. (2013). Russian state leaders' contradicting narratives on social media. In R. Kuusisto & E. Kurkinen (Eds.), *12th European Conference on Information Warfare and Security,* (pp. 224-230). Reading, UK: Academic Conferences.

Rashid, F. Y. (2012, November 21). Eugene Kaspersky: Definition Of 'Cyberwar' In Flux, Threat Of Cyber Weapons Underestimated. *SecurityWeek.* Retrieved from http://www.securityweek.com/eugene-kaspersky-definition-cyberwar-flux-threat-cyber-weapons-underestimated

Rasmussen, A. F. (2013). NATO's Next War – in Cyberspace. *The Wall Street Journal.*

Ratcliffe, J. H. (2008). *Intelligence-led policing.* Cullompton: Willan Publishing.

Rauscher, K. F., & Korotkov, A. (2011). *Working towards rules for governing cyber conflict.* New York: The East-West Institute.

Ray, J. B. (1970). The Resolution of the Rann of Kutch Boundary Problem. *The Geographic Bulletin,* 6.

Razoux, P. (2008). Israël frappe la Syrie: Un raid mystérieux. *Politique Etrangere, 1*(1), 9–24. doi:10.3917/pe.081.0009

Rebello, M. (2012) Assam violence: Where it all began.

RedHack'ten emniyete büyük eylem. (2012). *CNNTurk.* Retrieved from http://www.cnnturk.com

Regional Commonwealth in the Field of Communications. (n. d.). Retrieved from http://www.en.rcc.org.ru/index.php/rcc/about-rcc

Rehle, M. (2014, March 15). Attempt to jam Russian satellites carried out from Western Ukraine. *Russia Today*. Retrieved from http://rt.com/news/ukraine-attacks-television-satellites-990/

Reich, P. C., Weinstein, S., Wild, C., & Cabanlong, A. S. (2010). Cyber warfare: A review of theories, law, policies, actual incidents - and the dilemma of anonymity. *European Journal of Law and Technology*, *1*(2), 1–58.

Reidenberg, J. R. (1996). Governing networks and rule-making in cyberspace. *Emory Law Journal*, *45*(3), 911.

Report of the Defense Science Board Task Force on High Performance Microchip Supply. (2005, February). *DTIC* Report ADA435563. Retrieved from http://www.dtic.mil/docs/citations/ADA435563

Report of the OECD Task Force on Spam. (2006). *Organisation for Economic Cooperation and Development.*

Report of the Tunis phase of the World Summit on the Information Society. (2005). WSIS.

Resolution on Overall approach by the OSCE to promote cybersecurity. (n. d.). *OSCEPA.*

Reuters, T. (2014, September 7). ISIS propaganda material turns up in Pakistan. *CBC News*. Retrieved from: http://www.cbc.ca/news/world/isis-propaganda-material-turns-up-in-pakistan-india-1.2758299

Reuters. (2013, September 16). Belgium investigates suspected cyber spying by foreign state. *Reuters*. Retrieved from http://www.reuters.com/article/2013/09/16/us-usa-security-belgium-idUSBRE98F0A320130916)

Reuters. (2014a, March 15). Kremlin website hit by 'powerful' cyber-attack. *NDTV*. Retrieved from http://gadgets.ndtv.com/internet/news/kremlin-website-hit-by-powerful-cyber-attack-496150

Reuters. (2014b, March 27). No vodka for Obama - Russians impose joke 'sanctions'. *Yahoo South Africa*. Retrieved from https://za.news.yahoo.com/no-vodka-obama-russians-impose-joke-sanctions-090309509.html

Rice, C. (2011). *No Higher Honor: A Memoir of my Years in Washington*. New York: Broadway Paperbacks.

Richard, M., & Sain, J. J. (2012, October 14). Security Intelligence: Attacking the Cyber Kill Chain. *SansDfir*. Retrieved from http://digital-forensics.sans.org/blog/2009/10/14/security-intelligence-attacking-the-kill-chain

Richardson, M. (2013). *When Cyber Attacks Could Lead to War. The Strait Times.*

Richmond, R. (2013, March 3). Flawed security exposes vital software to hackers. *New York Times*. Retrieved October 10, 2013, from http://bits.blogs.nytimes.com/2010/03/05/flawed-security-exposes-vital-software-to-hackers/?_php=true&_type=blogs&_r=0

Rid, T. (2012). Cyber war will not take place. *The Journal of Strategic Studies*, *35*(1), 5–32. doi:10.1080/01402390.2011.608939

Rid, T. (2013). More Attacks, Less Violence. *The Journal of Strategic Studies*, *36*(1), 139–142. doi:10.1080/01402390.2012.742012

Rinaldi, S. M., Peerenboom, J. P., & Kelly, T. K. (2001). Identifying, Understanding, and Analyzing Critical Infrastructure Interdependencies. In R. D. Braatz (Ed.), IEEE Control Systems Magazine, 21(6), 11–25.

Rinaldi, S. M. (2004). Modeling and simulating critical infrastructures and their interdependencies. In R. H. Sprague (Ed.), *Proceedings of the 37th Hawaii International Conference on System Science (HICSS–37), (2004, January 5-8),* Vol. 2, (pp. 20054a). Big Island, Hawaii, USA. doi:10.1109/HICSS.2004.1265180

Risen, J., & Poitras, L. (2013a, September 28). N.S.A. Gathers Data on Social Connections of U.S. Citizens. *The New York Times*. Retrieved from http://www.nytimes.com/2013/09/29/us/nsa-examines-social-networks-of-us-citizens.html?hp&_r=0

Risen, J., & Poitras, L. (2013b, November 22). N.S.A. Report Outlined Goals for More Power. *The New York Times*. Retrieved from http://www.nytimes.com/2013/11/23/us/politics/nsa-report-outlined-goals-for-more-power.html?ref=international-home&_r=0

Robertson, J. (2013, July 23). Medical device hackers find government ally to pressure industry. *Bloomberg.com*. Retrieved from http://www.bloomberg.com/news/articles/2013-07-22/medical-device-hackers-find-government-ally-to-pressure-industry

Rodan, G. (2005). *Transparency and Authoritarian Rule in Southeast Asia*. Abingdon, UK: Routledge.

Rodriguez, G. (2013). *Read the Guardian's Entire Interview with the Man who Leaked PRISM*. Retrieved from http://www.policymic.com/articles/47355/edward-snowden-interview-transcript-full-text-read-the-guardian-s-entire-interview-with-the-man-who-leaked-prism

Rogers, M. (2014). *Rebooting Trust? Freedom vs. Security in Cyberspace*. Paper presented at the *Munich Security Conference*, Munich.

Rogozin, D. (2014, March 17) Twitter post [Weblog comment]. Retrieved from https://twitter.com/Rogozin

Rolph, H. (1972). Vietnamese Communism and the Protracted War. *Asian Survey*, *12*(9), 783–792. doi:10.2307/2642828

Rolski, T. (2007, May 17). Estonia: ground zero for World's first cyber war. *ABC News*. Retrieved from http://abcnews.go.com/print?id=3184122

Rome Statute. (2002). *International Criminal Court*.

Romm, T. (2013, March 12). Cyberattacks: The complexities of attacking back. *Politico*. Retrieved March 12, 2013, from http://www.politico.com/story/2013/03/cyberattacks-the-complexities-of-attacking-back-88702.html?hp=r14

Rosen, A. (2014, August 15). ISIS Is Paying Attention to the experts. *Business Insider*. Retrieved from: http://www.businessinsider.com/isis-is-paying-attention-to-the-experts-2014-8

Ross, J. D. (2014) *Plan to End U.S. Control of ICANN*. Submitted to Brazil Meeting on Future of Internet Governance.

Rouse, M. (n. d.). Hacktivism is the act of hacking, or breaking into a computer system, for a politically or socially motivated purpose. *Techtarget.com*. Retrieved from http://searchsecurity.techtarget.com/definition/hacktivism

Rowe, N. (2010). The ethics of cyberweapons in warfare. *International Journal of Cyber Ethics*, *1*(1), 20–31.

RT. (2012, 16 October). Global cyber war: New Flame-linked malware detected, *RT*. Retrieved from http://rt.com/news/mini-flame-malware-kaspersky-519/

Rubin, H., Fraser, L., & Smith, M. (1995). US and International Law Aspects of the Internet: Fitting Square Pegs Into Round Holes. *International Journal of Law and Information Technology*, *3*(2), 117–143. doi:10.1093/ijlit/3.2.117

Rush, J. (2014, October 13). Horror of Kobani: Headless corpses left in the street and victims with their eyes 'cut out', the savagery of Isis laid bare. *The Independent*. Retrieved from http://www.independent.co.uk/news/world/middle-east/horror-of-kobani-headless-corpses-left-in-the-street-and-victims-with-their-eyes-cut-out-the-savagery-of-isis-laid-bare-9791199.html?origin=internalSearch, accessed 15th December 2014.

Rushe, D., & Walker, S. (2014, July 20). MH17 crash: Kerry lays out evidence of pro-Russia separatists' responsibility. *The Guardian*. Retrieved from http://www.theguardian.com/world/2014/jul/20/mh17-crash-kerry-evidence-pro-russia-separatists-responsibility

Rushkof, D. (2002). *Cyberia: Life in the Trenches of Cyberspace. Manchester*: Clinamen Press Ltd.

Russia invading Ukraine [Video file]. (2014). GlobalLeaks. Retrieved from http://www.youtube.com/watch?v=lWvQHpQ12Ws

Russia Radio. (2014, April 21). *Russian Su -24 scores off against the American "USS Donald Cook" in Black Sea*. Retrieved from http://indian.ruvr.ru/2014_04_21/Russian-Su-24-scores-off-against-the-American-USS-Donald-Cook-5786/

Russia Today. (2014a, March 3). *Russian Defense Ministry dismisses Ukraine ultimatum reports as 'total nonsense'*. Retrieved from http://rt.com/news/russia-dismiss-ultimatum-ukraine-644/

Russia Today. (2014b, March 16). *Ukrainian CyberBerkut takes down NATO websites*. Retrieved from http://rt.com/news/nato-websites-ddos-ukraine-146/

Russia Today. (2014c, March 16). *Crimean govt: Referendum website downed by cyber-attack from US*. Retrieved from http://rt.com/news/crimea-referendum-attack-website-194/

Russia Today. (2014d, March 14). *Russian media websites hit by 'massive' DDoS attack 'linked to Ukraine'*. Retrieved from http://rt.com/news/russian-media-ddos-ukraine-614/

Russia Today. (2014e, April 7). *Donetsk activists proclaim region's independence from Ukraine*. Retrieved from http://rt.com/news/donetsk-republic-protestukraine-841/

Russia wants a divided Ukraine, and despite the promise of the revolution it may well get one. (2014, March 22). *The Economist*. Retrieved from http://www.economist.com/news/briefing/21599413-russia-wants-divided-ukraine-and-despite-promise-revolution-it-may-well-get

Russon, M. (2014, March 4). Ukraine crisis: cyber war with Russia heating up, *International Business Times*. Retrieved from http://www.ibtimes.co.uk/ukraine-crisis-cyber-war-russia-heating-1438890

Ryan, M. (2005, June 8). The 'spider's web' of hacking, *BBC News*. Retrieved from http://news.bbc.co.uk/1/hi/uk/4072938.stm

Ryan, J. J. C. H., & Ryan, D. J. (2006). Expected benefits of information security investments. *Computers & Security*, *25*(8), 579–588. doi:10.1016/j.cose.2006.08.001

Saffire, W. (2004). The Farewell Dossier. *The New York Times*. Retrieved from http://www.nytimes.com/2004/02/02/opinion/the-farewell-dossier.html

Salik, N. A. (1998). CBMs –Past, Present and Future. *Pakistan Defense Review*. (pp. 3).

Salloum, R. (2014, April 16) Twitter post [Weblog]. Retrieved from https://twitter.com/Ranyah

Saltman, E. M., & Winter, C. (2014). *Islamic State: The Changing Face of Modern Jihadism*. London: Quilliam Foundation.

Saltzer, J. H., & Schroeder, M. (1973, October). The Protection of Information in Computer Systems. Fourth ACM Symposium on Operating System Principles. In *Communications of the ACM 17*, (1974, July 7). Retrieved from web.mit.edu/Saltzer/www/publications/protection/

Samaan, J.-L. (2008). Mythes et réalités des cyberguerres. *Politique Etrangere*, *4*(12), 829–841. doi:10.3917/pe.084.0829

Sanger, D. E. (2012). Obama Order Sped Up Wave of Cyberattacks Against Iran. *New York Times*. Retrieved from http://www.nytimes.com/2012/06/01/world/middleeast/obama-ordered-wave-of-cyberattacks-against-iran.html?pagewanted=all&_r=0

Sanger, D. E. (2013). Differences on Cybertheft Complicate China Talks. *The New York Times*.

Sanger, D. E. (2013). N.S.A. Leaks Make Plan for Cyber defense Unlikely. *The New York Times*.

Sanger, D. E. (2013, May 21). As Chinese leader's visit nears, U.S. is urged to allow counterattacks on hackers. *The New York Times*. Retrieved from http://www.nytimes.com/2013/05/22/world/asia/as-chinese-leaders-visit-nears-us-urged-to-allow-retaliation-for-cyberattacks.html?emc=tnt&tntemail0=y&_r=2&p%E2%80%A6&

Sanger, D. E. (2014, August 31). NATO set to ratify pledge on joint defense in case of major cyberattack. *The New York Times*. Retrieved from http://www.nytimes.com/2014/09/01/world/europe/nato-set-to-ratify-pledge-on-joint-defense-in-case-of-major-cyberattack.html?_r=1

Sanger, D. E., & Markoff, J. (2010, January 14). After Google's stand on China, U.S. treads lightly. *New York Times*. Retrieved from http://www.nytimes.com/2010/01/15/world/asia/15diplo.html?_r=0

Sanger, D. E., & Perlroth, N. (2013, May 19). Chinese Hackers Resume Attacks on U.S. Targets. *The New York Times*. Retrieved from http://www.nytimes.com/2013/05/20/world/asia/chinese-hackers-resume-attacks-on-us-targets.html?hp&_r=0

Sang-Hun, C. (2013). South Korea blames North for June Cyber Attacks. *The New York Times*.

Sarwar, B. (2013) *LOC Tensions: Need Facts not Hype.*

Satell, G. (2014, January 18). If you doubt that social media has changed the World, take a look at Ukraine. *Forbes*. Retrieved from http://www.forbes.com/sites/gregsatell/2014/01/18/if-you-doubt-that-social-media-has-changed-the-world-take-a-look-at-ukraine/

Saydjari, O. S. (2004). Cyber defense: Art to science. *Communications of the ACM, 47*(3), 52–57. doi:10.1145/971617.971645

Saydjari, O. S. (2008). Structuring for strategic cyber defense: A cyber Manhattan project blueprint. In *Proceedings of Computer Security Applications Conference (ACSAC)*, Anaheim, CA:IEEE. doi:10.1109/ACSAC.2008.53

Schaberreiter, T., Aubert, J., & Khadraoui, D. (2011a). Critical infrastructure security modelling and RESCI-MONITOR: A risk based critical infrastructure model. In P. Cunningham (Ed.), *Proceedings of the 2011 IST-Africa Conference, (2011, May 11-13)*, (pp. 1–8). Gaborone, Botswana.

Schaberreiter, T., Caldeira, F., Aubert, J., Monteiro, E., Khadraoui, D., & Simões, P. (2011b). Assurance and trust indicators to evaluate accuracy of on-line risk in critical infrastructures. In S. Bologna, & S. Wolthusen (Eds.), *Proceedings of the 6th International Workshop on Critical Information Infrastructures Security (CRITIS), (2011, September 8-9)*. Lucerne, Switzerland.

Scheier, B. (2003). *Beyond fear: Thinking sensibly about security in an uncertain world*. New York, NY: Springer-Verlag New York, Inc.

Schmidt, M. N. (Ed.). (2013). *Tallinn Manual on the International Law Applicable on Cyber Operations*. New York: Cambridge University Press.

Schmitt, M. N. (1998). Computer Network Attack and the Use of Force in International Law: Thoughts on a Normative Framework. *Columbia Journal of Transnational Law, 37*.

Schmitt, M. N. (Ed.). (2013). Tallinn Manual on the International Law Applicable to Cyber Warfare New York, Cambridge University Press.

Schmitt, M. (2012). Classification of cyber conflict. *Journal of Conflict and Security Law, 17*(2), 245–260. doi:10.1093/jcsl/krs018

Schmitt, M. N. (1999). Computer network attack and the use of force in international law: Thoughts on a normative framework. *Columbia Journal of Transnational Law, 37*(3), 885.

Schmitt, M. N. (2010). Cyber Operations in International Law: The Use of Force, Collective Security, Self-Defense, and Armed Conflicts," *Proceedings of a Workshop on Deterring Cyber Attacks: Informing Strategies and Developing Options for US Policy, National Research Council of the National Academies.* Washington D.C: 151.

Schmitt, M. N. (2012). International Law in Cyberspace: The Koh Speech and the Tallinn Manual Juxtaposed. *Harvard International Law Journal*, 54.

Schmitt, M. N. (Ed.). (2013). *The Tallinn Manual on the international law applicable to cyber warfare.* Cambridge: Cambridge University Press. doi:10.1017/CBO9781139169288

Schölkopf, B., Platt, J. C., Shawe-Taylor, J. C., Smola, A. J., & Williamson, R. C. (2001). Estimating the Support of a High-Dimensional Distribution. *Neural Computation Journal*, *13*(7), 1443–1471. doi:10.1162/089976601750264965 PMID:11440593

Sciences, N. U. C. E. (n.d). "FAST-NU for Computer and Emerging Sciences." Retrieved August 7, 2013, from http://nu.edu.pk/

SCO. (2013). "SCO – Cooperation on Security." Retrieved February 14, 2013, from http://www.infosco. eu/index.php/aboutsco/activities

SCO. (n.d). "SCO official website." Retrieved September 19, 2012, from http://www.sectsco.org/

SEA-ME-WE. (n.d). "SEA-ME-WE." Retrieved July 10, 2013, from http://www.seamewe4.com/

Secretary-General, D. o. P. a. S. C. A. U. C. f. D. R. o. t. (1982) Comprehensive Study on CBMs.

Secretary-General, D. o. P. a. S. C. A. U. N. C. f. D. R. o. t. (1982) Relationship between Disarmament and International Security.

SecureList. (2013). "Red October" diplomatic cyber attacks investigation. *Kaspersky Lab.* Retrieved from http://www.securelist.com/en/analysis/204792262/Red_October_Diplomatic_Cyber_Attacks_Investigation

Security, C. (n.d). "Cyber Security, OAS." Retrieved August 20, 2013, from http://www.oas.org/en/topics/cyber_security.asp

Security, S. (n.d). "PKI (Public Key Infrastructure). " Retrieved July 4, 2013, from http://searchsecurity.techtarget.com/definition/PKI

Security, U. H. "US Homeland Security: Cyber Laws & Regulations." Retrieved July 4, 2013, from http://www.dhs.gov/cybersecurity-laws-regulations

Security, W. F. o. S. P. M. P. P. o. I. (2003) Toward a Universal Order of Cyberspace: Managing Threats from Cybercrime to Cyberwar - Report & Recommendations.

SEECS. N. (n.d). "NUST SEECS." Retrieved August 7, 2013, from http://seecs.nust.edu.pk/

Segal, A. (2012) What to read on Cyber Security.

Segal, A. (2013) Defending an Open, Global, Secure and Resilient Internet. CFR Independent Task Force Report No. 70, 1

Segal, A. (2011). *US-China Cyber Hotline.* The Diplomat, The Diplomat.

Sengupta, N. P. S. (2013). U.S. Says Ring Stole 160 Million Credit Card Numbers. New York Times. New York.

Service, A. F. P. (2013). *Obama, Xi Discuss Military-to-Military Relations.* Cybersecurity.

Services, P. I. o. P. (n.d). "Pakistan Institute of Parliamentary Services ". Retrieved August 7, 2013, from http://www.pips.org. pk

Shackelford, S. J. (2009). "From Nuclear War to Net War: Analogizing Cyber Attacks in International Law." Berkley Journal of International Law: 192.

Shafritz, R. (2001). A survey of cyberstalking legislation. *UWLA Law Review, 32*, 323.

Shane, S. (2014, August 30). ISIS Displaying a Deft Command of Varied Media. *New York Times*. Retrieved from http://www.nytimes.com/2014/08/31/world/middleeast/isis-displaying-a-deft-command-of-varied-media.html?hp&action=click&pgtype=Homepage&version=LedeSum&module=first-column-region&region=top-news&WT.nav=top-news&_r=2

Shane, S., & Moynihan, C. (2013, September 1). Drug Agents Use Vast Phone Trove, Eclipsing N.S.A.'s. *The New York Times*.

Shane, J. (1996). Information superhighway: An overview of technology challenges U.S. general accounting office. *Journal of Government Information, 23*(1), 78–80. doi:10.1016/S1352-0237(96)90313-5

Shanker, E. B. T. (2012). Panetta Warns of Dire Threat of Cyberattack on U.S. New York Times. New York New York Times.

Shanker, T. (2013). Pentagon is Updating Conflict Rules in Cyberspace. New York Times, New York

Shanker, T., & Sanger, D. E. (2013, June 8). U.S. Helps Allies Trying to Battle Iranian Hackers. *The New York Times*. Retrieved from http://www.nytimes.com/2013/06/09/world/middleeast/us-helps-allies-trying-to-battle-iranian-hackers.html?pagewanted=1&_r=2

Shashank, J. (2014, August 22). Islamic State: Biggest threat to United States? *BBC News*. Retrieved from http://www.bbc.co.uk/news/world-middle-east-28896348

Shearer, J. (2013). *W32.Stuxnet*. Symantec.

Sheldon, F. T., Abercrombie, R. K., & Mili, A. (2009, January). Methodology for evaluating security controls based on key performance indicators and stakeholder mission. In *System Sciences, 2009. HICSS'09 42nd Hawaii International Conference*, (pp. 1-10). IEEE.

Sheldon, J. B. (2012). *Cyber Incident Information Sharing: A First Step towards Confidence Building? Cyber Security Conference 2012: The Role of Confidence-Building Measures in Assuring Cyber Stability*. Geneva, Switzerland: UNIDIR.

Shelley, L. (2004, September 27). Organized crime, cybercrime and terrorism. *Computer Crime Research Center*. Retrieved from http://www.crimeresearch.org/articles/Terrorism_Cybercrime/

Shevchenko, I. (2014). Femen on protests in Kiev: 'Now, it's fight or die.' *Dazed Digital*. Retrieved from http://www.dazeddigital.com/artsandculture/article/18966/1/femen-on-kiev-protests-now-its-fight-or-die

Shinn, D. (2011). Al Shabaab's foreign threat to Somalia. *Orbis, 55*(2), 203–215. doi:10.1016/j.orbis.2011.01.003

Shishko, R. (1995). NASA Systems Engineering Handbook, Special Publication (SP) SP-6105.

Shiwen, Z., Yangtao, Y., & Xinshan, W. (2001). *Xin shiqi sixiang zhengzhi gongzuo yanjiu lunwen ji*. Wuhan, China: Wuhan Daxue Chubanshe.

Shorrock, T. (2008). *Spies for Hire: The Secret World of Intelligence Outsourcing*. New York: Simon and Schuster.

Shubber, K. (2013, June 24). A simple guide to GCHQ's internet surveillance program Tempora. *Wired*. Retrieved from http://www.wired.co.uk/news/archive/2013-06/24/gchq-tempora-101

Shuster, S. (2014, March 24). Putin's fear of texting kept U.S. spymasters in the dark. *Time Magazine Online*. Retrieved from http://time.com/35932/ukraine-russia-putin-spies-kgb/

Siddique, A. (2013) Pakistan Demands Filters Before Lifting YouTube Ban.

Siman-Tov, S. E. a. D. (2012) Cyber Warfare: Concepts and Strategic Trends.

Simões, P., Cruz, T., Gomes, J., & Monteiro, E. (2013). On the use of Honeypots for detecting cyber attacks on Industrial Control Networks, *Proceedings of 12th European Conference on Information Warfare and Security*, eds. R Kuusisto & E Kurkinen, (pp 264–270). ACPI International.

Simões, P., Curado, M., Panzieri, S., Oliva, G., Minichino, M., Ciancamerla, E., et al. (2009). Common Ontology and Risk Prediction Algorithms – Preliminary Version. Panzieri, S., (Ed.). MICIE Project Deliverable D3.2.1. European Commission FP7.

Simões, P., Capodieci, P., Minicino, M., Panzieri, S., Castrucci, M., & Lev, L. (2010). An Alerting System for Interdependent Critical Infrastructures. In J. Demergis (Ed.), *Proceedings of the 9th European Conference on Information Warfare and Security (ECIW), (2010, July 1-2)*, (pp. 275–283). Thessaloniki, Greece.

Simon, H. (1962). The architecture of complexity. *Proceedings of the American Philosophical Society, 106*(6), 67–482.

Simonite, T. (2014, June 10). Digital summit: Microsoft's quantum search for the "next transistor". *MIT Technology Review*. Retrieved from http://www.technologyreview.com/news/528256/digital-summit-microsofts-quantum-search-for-the-next-transistor/

Simons, K. W. (2008). Self-defense: Reasonable beliefs or reasonable self-control? *New Criminal Law Review: An International and Interdisciplinary Journal, 11*(1), 51–90.

Simson, E. (2013). The U.S.–Russia Cybersecurity Pact: Just Paper. 2013.

Singer, P., & Friedman, A. (2014). *Cybersecurity and cyberwar: what everyone needs to know*. London: Oxford University Press.

Skoudis, E. (2004). *Malware: Fighting malicious code*. Prentice Hall Professional.

sKyWIper: CrySyS Lab. (2012). Budapest University of Technology and Economics Department of Telecommunications.

Smith, P. (2008, May). Network Operations Groups[Berlin.]. *Power Point Presentation for RIPE, 56*, 5–9.

Snake campaign & cyber espionage toolkit. (2014). *B. A. E.Systems*. Retrieved from http://www.baesystems.com/marketoform/snake_whitepaper.pdf

Social Mention. (2014) *Search results*. Retrieved from http://socialmention.com/

Softpedia (n.d). "India Japan to Expand Cyber Security Cooperation." Retrieved August 21, 2013, from http://news.softpedia. com/news/India-and-Japan-to-Expand-Cyber-Security-Cooperation-301524 .shtml

Sohail, H. (2013). *Information Technology Ministry: A Chaos so far*. The News, The News.

Sokolowski, J., Turnitsa, C., & Diallo, S. (2008). A Conceptual Modeling Method for Critical Infrastructure Modeling. In T. F. Znati, & H. D. Karatza (Eds.), *Proceedings of the 41st Annual Simulation Symposium (ANSS), (2008, April 14-16)*, (pp. 203–211). Ottawa, Canada. doi:10.1109/ANSS-41.2008.31

Sommestad, T., Ekstedt, M., & Johnson, P. (2009, January). Cyber security risks assessment with bayesian defense graphs and architectural models. In *System Sciences, 2009. HICSS'09. 42nd Hawaii International Conference*, (pp. 1-10). IEEE.

Sommestad, T., Ekstedt, M., & Johnson, P. (2010). A probabilistic relational model for security risk analysis. *Computers & Security, 29*(6), 659–679. doi:10.1016/j.cose.2010.02.002

Sorcher, S. (2015, April 1). Influencers: Companies should not be allowed to hack back. *The Christian Science Monitor.* Retrieved from http://www.csmonitor.com/World/Passcode/Passcode-Influencers/2015/0401/Influencers-Companies-should-not-be-allowed-to-hack-back

South Asia Confidence-Building Measures Timeline. (n. d.). *Stimson.org.* Retrieved from http://www.stimson.org/data-sets /south-asia-confidence-building-measures-cbm-timeline

Spence-Diehl, E. (2003). Stalking and technology: The double-edged sword. *Journal of Technology in Human Services, 22*(1), 5–18. doi:10.1300/J017v22n01_02

Spencer, R. (2007, August16). China launches 'big brother' surveillance program. *Vancouver Sun*, A11.

Spitzner, L. (2003). Honeytokens: The other honeypot.

Spitzner, L. (2002). *Honeypots: Tracking hackers.* Addison-Wesley Professional.

Spitzner, L. (2003). The honeynet project: Trapping the hackers. *IEEE Security and Privacy, 1*(2), 15–23. doi:10.1109/MSECP.2003.1193207

Stallings, W. (1998). *SNMP, SNMPv2, SNMPv3, and RMON 1 and 2.* Boston, MA: Addison-Wesley Longman Publishing Co., Inc.

Standage, T. (2007). *The Victorian Internet: The Remarkable Story of the Telegraph and the Nineteenth Century On-line Pioneers.* New York: Walker & Company.

Standifer, C. (2014, April 17). Ukraine's last ship, *US Naval Institute.* Retrieved from http://news.usni.org/2014/04/11/ukraines-last-ship

Starr, B. (2011). *Drone that crashed in Iran was on CIA recon mission.* CNN.

State Planning Organization. (2006). *Ninth development plan (2007-2013).*

State, T. U. D. o. (n.d). "Agreement between the United States of America and the Union of Soviet Socialist Republics on the Establishment of Nuclear Risk Reduction Centers (and Protocols Thereto)." Retrieved June 15, 2013, from http://www.state.gov/t/isn/5179

State, U. D. o. (2011). "Office of the Coordinator for Cyber Issues." Retrieved June 13, 2013, from http://www.state.gov/s/cyberissues/

State, U. D. o. (2013). "The ASEAN-U.S. Ministerial Meeting: Fact Sheet, Office of the Spokesperson, Washington, DC." Retrieved July 1, 2013, from http://www.state.gov/r/pa /prs/ps/2013/07/211389.htm

State, U. D. o. (n.d). "Welcome to the Nuclear Risk Reduction Center (NRRC): Confidence Building through Information Exchange." Retrieved July 4, 2013, from http://www.state.gov/t/avc/nrrc/

States, C. o. I. (n.d). "Commonwealth of Independent States." Retrieved January 12, 2013, from http://www.cisstat.com/eng/cis.htm

Statute of the International Court of Justice (1945).

stefanomele (n.d). "Cyber-security. The vexed question of global rules." Retrieved July 4, 2013, from http://www.stefanomele.it/news/dettaglio.asp?id=285

Sterner, E. (2011, Spring). Retaliatory deterrence in cyberspace. *Strategic Studies Quarterly, 62–80.*

Stilts, S. o. (2013). "Testifying before Senate Judiciary on Attribution and Cybersecurity." Retrieved July 30, 2013.

Stojanovski, D. (2013) Preventing a U.S.-China Cyber War.

Stokes, J., & Weedon, J. (2015, May 14). Security in an era of coercive attacks. *FireEye Blogs*. Retrieved from https://www.fireeye.com/blog/executive-perspective/2015/05/security_in_an_erao.html

Stoll, C. (1989). *The cuckoo's egg: tracking a spy through the maze of computer espionage.* New York: Doubleday.

Stoneburner, G., Goguen, A., & Feringa, A. (2002). Risk management guide for information technology systems. Nist special publication, 800(30), 800-30.

Stonesoft Security. (2014). *Cyberstrategy*. Retrieved from http://www.stonesoft-security.co.uk/solutions/cyber-strategy/

Strauss, L., & Cropsey, J. (1987). Introduction. In L. Strauss & J. Cropsey (Eds.), *History of Political Philosophy* (3rd Ed.), (pp. 1–6). Chicago, USA: The University of Chicago Press. doi:10.7208/chicago/9780226924717.001.0001

Strengthening law enforcement cooperation in the EU: the European Information Exchange Model. (2012). EIXM.

Studies, C. f. N. (n.d) Inventory of International Nonproliferation Organizations and Regimes.

Suciu, P. (2014, December 21). Why cyber warfare is so attractive to small nations. *Fortune*. Retrieved from http://fortune.com/2014/12/21/why-cyber-warfare-is-so-attractive-to-small-nations/

Summit, S. (2012). "Official Website of the Beijing SCO Summit 2012." Retrieved April 25, 2013, from http://www.scosummit2012.org/english/2012-04/28/c_131558560.htm

Sun Tzu. (2005). *Sunzi: the art of war and Sun Bin: the art of war.*(R. Wu, X. Wu, & W. Lin Trans. & Eds.). Beijing, China: Foreign Languages Press.

Szidarovszky, F., Gershon, M., & Duckstein, L. (1993). *Techniques for Multi-objective Decision Making in Systems.* Boca Raton, FL: CRC Press.

Taddeo, M. (2012). An analysis for a just cyber warfare. In *Proceedings of the 4h International Conference on Cyber Conflict (CYCON)*, Tallinn: IEEE.

Tashkent Declaration. (1966, October 1). *United Nations Peacekeeper*. Retrieved from http://peacemaker.un.org/india-pakistan-tashkent-declaration66

Technet (n.d). "Defining Malware." Retrieved August 14, 2013, from http://technet.microsoft.com/en-us/library / dd632948.aspx

Technical Details Behind a 400Gbps NTP Amplification DDoS Attack. (2014CloudFlare. Retrieved from.

Telang, R., & Wattal, S. (2007, August). An Empirical Analysis of the Impact of Software Vulnerability Announcements on Firm Stock Price. *IEEE Transactions on Software Engineering, 33*(8), 544–557. Retrieved from www.heinz.cmu.edu/~rtelang/tse_published.pdf. doi:10.1109/TSE.2007.70712

Telecommunication Regulatory Authority of India. (n. d.). Government of India. Retrieved from http://www.trai.gov.in/

Telecontrol equipment and systems - Part 5-104: Transmission protocols. (2006). International Electrotechnical Commission.

Temnycky, P. (2014, February 9). Unrest in Ukraine: Summarizing the Euromaidan. *Fordham Political Review*. Retrieved from http://fordhampoliticalreview.org/unrest-in-ukraine-summarizing-the-euromaidan/

Ten Chee-Wooi, Chen-Ching Liu, & Manimaran, G. (2008). Vulnerability Assessment of Cybersecurity for SCADA Systems. *Power Systems, IEEE Transactions on, 23*(4), 1836–1846.

Tenth development plan. (2013). Ministry of Development.

Terrorisme et Internet: le Hezbollah recourt largement à Internet pour diffuser sa haine anti-israélienne, anti-juive et anti-américaine dans le cadre de sa guerre psychologique. (2006). *Centres d'Etudes SpécialesInformation Center on Intelligence and Terrorism*. Retrieved from http://www.terrorism-info.org.il/data/pdf/PDF_18674_3.pdf

The Blue Helmets. (1996). *A Review of the UN Peacekeeping*. UN Department of Public Information.

The European Programme for Critical Infrastructure Protection (EPCIP) (No. MEMO/06/477). (2006). Commission of The European Communities. Brussels.

The grid 5000 project web site. (2013). *Grid5000*. Retrieved from http://www. grid5000.fr

The Guardian. (2013, June 28). Former US general James Cartwright named in Stuxnet leak inquiry. *The Guardian*. Retrieved from http://www.guardian.co.uk/world/2013/jun/28/general-cartwright-investigated-stuxnet-leak?CMP=twt_gu

The IP Commission Report. (2013). *Commission on the Theft of American Intellectual Property*. Retrieved from http://ipcommission.org/report/IP_Commission_Report_052213.pdf

The Law of Armed Conflict. (n. d.). *The International Red Cross Association*.

The London Conference. (n. d.). London: Chatham House.

The National Military Strategy for Cyberspace Operations (U). (2006). US JS Publication.

The Netherlands Country Report. (2011).

The North Atlantic Treaty (1949).

The Promotion of a Culture of Security for Information Systems and Networks in OECD Countries JT00196105. (2005, December 16). Retrieved from http://www.oecd.org/internet/ieconomy/35884541.pdf

The Swift Codes. (n. d.). *Theswiftcodes.com*. Retrieved from http://www.theswiftcodes.com/

The UK Cyber Security Strategy Protecting and promoting the UK in a digital world. (2011). *UK Cabinet*.

The White House. (2009). *Cyberspace Policy Review*. Washington, D.C.

The White House. (2013a). *Administration Strategy on Mitigating the Theft of U.S. Trade Secrets* Washington, DC: The White House. (pp. 141).

The White House. (2013b, August 30). Government Assessment of the Syrian Government's Use of Chemical Weapons on August 21, 2013. *The White House*.

The World Factbook. (2014). *CIA*. Retrieved from https://www.cia.gov/library/publications/the-world-factbook/geos/ae.html

Theiler, O. (2011). New threats: the cyber-dimension, Retrieved from http://www.nato.int/docu/review/2011/11-september/Cyber-Threads/EN/index.htm

Thomas, T. L. (2011). Nation-state Cyber Strategies: Examples from China and Russia. In F.D. Kramer, S.H. Starr, L.K. Wentz (Eds.), Cyberpower and National Security (465-488). National Defense University Press: Washington, D.C.

Thomas, T. L. (2004). *Cyber Bytes. Fort Leavenworth*. Foreign Military Studies Office.

Thomas, T. L. (2005). *Cyber Silhouettes: Shadows over Information Operations Fort Leavenworth*. Foreign Military Studies.

Thomas, T. L. (2007). *Decoding the Virtual Dragon. Fort Leavenworth*. Foreign Military Studies Office.

Thomas, T. L. (2009). *The Dragon's Quantum Leap: Transforming from a Mechanized to an Informatized Force Ft Leavenworth*. KS: FMSO.

Thompson, C. (2014, May 20). The revolutionary quantum computer that may not be quantum at all. *Wired*. Retrieved from http://www.wired.com/2014/05/quantum-computing/

Thomson Reuters. (2014, March 30). *Ukraine crisis: Russia downplays sanctions ahead of Paris talks*. Retrieved from http://www.cbc.ca/news/world/ukraine-crisis-russia-downplays-sanctions-ahead-of-paris-talks-1.2591839

Thonnard, O. (2010). *Vers un regroupement multicritères comme outil d'aide à l'attribution d'attaque dans le cyber-espace. (PhD)*. Paris: Ecole Nationale Supérieure des Télécommunications.

Thonnard, O., Mees, W., & Dacier, M. (2010). On a Multi-criteria Clustering Approach for Attack Attribution. *ACM Special Interest Group on Knowledge Discovery and Data Mining Explorations, 12*(1), 11–21.

Tibbs, H. (2013). *The Global Cyber Game*. London: Defence Academy of the United Kingdom.

Tikk, E., & Kaska, K. (2010). *Legal Cooperation to Investigate Cyber Incidents: Estonian Case Study and Lessons*. Paper presented at the 9th European Conference on Information Warfare and Security, Thessaloniki.

Tikk, E. (2011, June-July). Ten Rules for Cyber Security. *Survival, 53*(3), 119–132. doi:10.1080/00396338.2011.571016

Tikk, E., Kaska, K., Rünnimeri, K., Kert, M., Talihärm, A.-M., & Vihul, L. (2008). *Cyber Attacks Against Georgia: Legal Lessons Identified*. Tallinn, Estonia: CCDCOE.

Times, E. (2008). "Hoax call pushed Pakistan to brink of war with India." Retrieved October 3, 2012, from http://articles.economictimes.indiatimes.com/2008-12-06/news /28394766_1_india-and-pakistan-mumbai-attacks-mumbai-killings

Timlin, J. A. L. a. K. (2011) Cybersecurity and Cyberwarfare: Preliminary Assessment of National Doctrine and Organization.

Touré, D. H. I. (2011) The Quest for Cyber Peace.

Tracking GhostNet: Investigating a Cyber Espionage Network: The Information Warfare (2009). *Citizen Lab, & Group, T. S. Monitor*.

Tracy, J. (2000, January 13). Police get window of access to e-mail. *The Moscow Times*. Retrieved from http://www.themoscowtimes.com/sitemap/free/2000/1/article/police-get-window-of-access-to-e-mail/268089.html

Trist, E. (1980, April). *The evolution of socio-technical systems: A conceptual framework and an action research program*. Centre for the Study of Organizational Innovation, Wharton School, University of Pennsylvania, Philadelphia, PA.

Trope, K. L. (2014). US government eavesdropping on electronic communications: Where are we going? *Scitech Lawyer, 10*(2), 4–9.

Trusted Computing Base. (2015, May 16). *Wikimedia.org*. Retrieved from en.wikipedia.org/wiki/Trusted_computing_base

Trusted Information Sharing Network (TISN) for Critical Infrastructure Resilience. (2011). *TISN*. Retrieved from http://www.tisn.gov.au

Tschechien: Neuer Anlauf zur Wiedereinführung der Vorratsdatenspeicherung [Czech Republic: New attempt to reintroduce the data retention]. (2012). *U.N. Watched*. Retrieved from https://http://www.unwatched.org/EDRigram_10.11_Tschechien_Neuer_Anlauf_zur_Wiedereinfuehrung_der_Vorratsdatenspeicherung?pk_campaign=edri&pk_kwd=20120606

Tsiakis, T., & Stephanides, G. (2005). The economic approach of information security. *Computers & Security, 24*(2), 105–108. doi:10.1016/j.cose.2005.02.001

Tsvetkova, M., & Bush, J. (2014, March 15). Ukraine crisis triggers Russia's biggest anti-Putin protest in two years. *Reuters*. Retrieved from http://www.reuters.com/article/2014/03/15/ukraine-crisis-russia-rallies-idUSL6N0MC0JC20140315

TubeLeaks. (2014). Crimea Crisis - Russian Mi-35 combat helicopters flying over Sevastopol Ukraine [Video file]. Retrieved from http://www.youtube.com/watch?v=PfuCt0ZjzE0

Tucker, J. A., Metzger, M., & Barbera, P. (2014, February 28). *SMaPP Lab Data Report: Ukraine Protests 2013-2014*. Social Media and Political Participation Lab, New York University. Retrieved from http://smapp.nyu.edu/reports/Ukraine_Data_Report.pdf

Tucker, P. (2014, April 29). Why Ukraine has already lost the cyberwar, too. *Defence One*. Retrieved May 2, 2014, from http://www.defenseone.com/technology/2014/04/why-ukraine-has-already-lost-cyberwar-too/83350/

Turn the map around to prevent damage and loss from cyber attack. (2015, April 16). *Endgame* [White Paper]. Retrieved from http://pages.endgame.com/WC2015-04EnterpriseWhitepaper_WCYYYYMMDDWebContent.html

Twidle, K., Dulay, N., Lupu, E., & Sloman, M. (2009). Ponder2: A Policy System for Autonomous Pervasive Environments. In R. Calinescu, F. Liberal, M. Marin, L. Herrero, C. Turro, & M. Popescu (Eds.), *Proceedings of the Fifth International Conference on Autonomic and Autonomous Systems (ICAS), (2009, April 20-25)*, (pp. 330–335). Valencia, Spain. doi:10.1109/ICAS.2009.42

Twitter Case Study. (WMD). (2009). *World Movement for Democracy* Retrieved from http://www.wmd.org/resources/whats-being-done/information-and-communication-technologies/case-study-twitter

Twitter Status. (2010). *Ongoing denial-of-service attack*. Retrieved from http://status.twitter.com/post/157191978/ongoing-denial-of-service-attack

U.S. watching Russia for cyber attack tactics against Ukraine. (2014, March 1). *Flash Critic*. Retrieved from http://flashcritic.com/u-s-watching-russia-cyber-attack-tactics-ukraine/

UAE, Qatar have highest expat ratio in GCC. (2013, September 11). *Emirates 24/7*. Retrieved from: http://www.emirates247.com/news/emirates/uae-qatar-have-highest-expat-ratio-in-gcc-2013-09-11-1.520659

UK Ministry of Defence. (2014). Automating cyber defence responses. Retrieved from https://www.gov.uk/government/publications/cde-themed-competition-automation-of-cyber-defence-responses

Ukraine: pro-Russia activists proclaim independent republic in Donetsk. (2014, April 7). The Guardian. Retrieved from http://www.theguardian.com/world/2014/apr/07/ukraine-officer-shot-dead-russian-soldier-crimea

Ulanoff, L. (2014 May 13). Boko Haram won't stop Nigeria's mobile revolution. *Mashable*. Retrieved from http://mashable.com/2014/05/13/nigeria-internet-kidnapped-girls/

UN (1965). UNGA Resolution 2131 (XX), UN.

UN (1981). UNGA Resolution 36/103. G. Assemble, UN.

UN (2010). Report of the Group of Governmental Experts (GGE) on Developments in the Field of Information and Telecommunications in the Context of International Security, UN Document A/65/201 UN.

UN (n.d). "Group of Governmental Experts on Developments in the Field of Information and Telecommunications in the Context of International Security."

UN Development Group. (n. d.).

UN. (1988). "Special Report of the Disarmament Commission to the UNGA at its 3rd Special Session devoted to Disarmament, UN Document A/S/-15/3 (May 28, 1988)." from http://www.un.org/ga/search/view_doc.asp?symbol=A/S-15/3(SUPP) &Lang=E.

UN. (1999). UNGA Resolutions adopted in the 53rd session. G. Assembly, UN.

UN. (2000). "Optional Protocol to the Convention on the Rights of the Child on the Sale of Children, Child Prostitution and Child Pornography." Retrieved May 1, 2013, from http://treaties.un.org/doc/source/RecentTexts/iv-11c_eng.htm

UN. (n.d). "International Day against Nuclear Testing." Retrieved July 4, 2013, from http://www.un.org /en/events/ againstnucleartestsday/history.shtml

UNGA (1986). UNGA Resolution 41/60C, Considerations of Guidelines for Confidence-Building Measures

UNGA (2002). UNGA Resolution 57/53 UNGA.

UNGA (2003). UNGA Resolution 58/32 UNGA.

UNGA (2005). UNGA Resolution 60/45 UNGA.

UNGA (2006). UNGA Resolution 61/54 UNGA.

UNGA (2008). UNGA Resolution 62/17 UNGA.

UNGA (n.d). UNGA: Economic and Financial – The Second Committee. UNGA, UN.

UNGA (n.d). United Nations General Assembly, UN.

UNGA. (2002). *UNGA Resolution 63/37*. UNGA.

UNGA. (2003). *UNGA Resolution 58/199, UN Documentation Research Guide. UNGA.* UNGA.

UNGA. (2004). *UNGA Resolution 59/61*. UNGA.

UNGA. (2006). *UNGA Resolution 60/252*. UNGA.

UNGA. (2010). *UNGA Resolution 64/211*. UNGA.

UNGA. (2010). *UNGA Resolution 64/25*. UNGA.

UNGA. (2011). *UNGA 66/24, Developments in the Field of Information and Telecommunications in the Context of International Security*. UNGA.

UNIDIR. (2012). Cyber Security Conference 2012 (CS12).

Union, I. T. (2005). "World Summit on the Information Society Geneva 2003. " Retrieved June 19, 2013, from http:// www.itu.int/wsis/docs/geneva /official/dop.html

Union, I. T. (n.d). "What was the UN ICT Task Force?". Retrieved September 25, 2013, from https://www.itu.int/wsis/ basic/faqs_answer.asp?lang=en&faq_id=88

United Nations General Assembly. (2011, September 14). Letter dated 12 September 2011 from the Permanent Representatives of China, the Russian Federation, Tajikistan and Uzbekistan to the United Nations addressed to the Secretary-General. Retrieved from https://ccdcoe.org/sites/default/files/documents/UN-110912-CodeOfConduct_0.pdf

United Nations Office on Drugs and Crime. (2013). *The comprehensive study on cybercrime.* Retrieved from http://www.unodc.org/documents/organized-crime/cybercrime/CYBERCRIME_STUDY_210213.pdf

United Stated of America v. Jeffrey Lee Parson, No. 03-457M (United States District Court, Western District of Washington 2003).

United States and India Sign Cybersecurity Agreement. Department of Homeland Security. (2011). *Dhs.gov.* Retrieved from http://www.dhs.gov/news/2011/07 /19 /united-states-and-india-sign-cybersecurity-agreement

United States Army Cyberspace Operations Concept Capability Plan 2016-2028. (2010). *Tradoc Pamphlet, 525-7-8,* 8. Retrieved from http://fas.org/irp/doddir/army/pam525-7-8.pdf

United States Department of Defense. (2011). *Department of Defense strategy for operating in cyberspace.* Retrieved from http://www.defense.gov/news/d20110714cyber.pdf

United States Department of Defense. (2013). *Air-sea battle.* Retrieved http://www.defense.gov/pubs/ASB-ConceptImplementation-Summary-May-2013.pdf

University, B. (n.d) 66th Session of the UN.

UNODA (2013). Fact Sheet: Developments in the Field of Information and Telecommunications in the Context of International Security.

UNODA (n.d). "Confidence Building."

UNODA (n.d). Developments in the Field of Information and Telecommunications in the Context of International Security, UNDA.

UNODA (n.d). Developments in the Field of Information and Telecommunications in the Context of International Security. UNODA, UNODA.

UNODC (2013). Comprehensive Study on Cybercrime, Draft February 2013. New York, UN.

US allies Mexico, Chile and Brazil seek spying answers. (2013, July 11). *BBC News.*

US Army Cyber Command/2nd Army. (n. d.). *Arcyber.army.mil.* Retrieved from http://www.arcyber.army.mil/

US Department of Defense. (2015, April 17). *The DoD cyber strategy.* Retrieved from http://www.defense.gov/home/features/2015/0415_cyber-strategy/Final_2015_DoD_CYBER_STRATEGY_for_web.pdf

US Department of Justice Computer Crime and Intellectual Property Section Criminal Division. (2012). *Prosecuting computer crimes.* Retrieved from http://www.justice.gov/criminal/cybercrime/docs/ccmanual.pdf

US Department of State. (2015, May 18). An open and secure Internet: We must have both. Remarks made by John Kerry Secretary of State at *Korea University,* Seoul, South Korea. Retrieved from http://origin.www.uscc.gov/sites/default/files/annual_reports/Complete%202013%20Annual%20Report.PDF

US House of representatives. (2012). The Iranian Cyber Threat to the United States. *Homeland Security Policy Institute.* Retrieved from http://www2.gwu.edu/~nsarchiv/NSAEBB/NSAEBB424/docs/Cyber-071c.pdf

US NSC's Comprehensive National Cybersecurity Initiative. (n. d.). The White House. *Whitehouse.gov.* Retrieved from http://www.whitehouse.gov/cybersecurity/comprehensive-national-cybersecurity-initiative

US State Department. (n. d.). *Foreign Terrorist Organisations*. Retrieved from http://www.state.gov/j/ct/rls/other/des/123085.htm

US-CERT. (2013). "Security Tip (ST05-007): Risks of File-Sharing Technology." Retrieved February 14, 2013, from http://www.us-cert.gov/ncas/tips/ST05-007

USIP (n.d) Lahore Declaration, USIP Peace Agreements Digital Collection.

USS Donald Cook – Ship Characteristics. (2014). *U. S.Navy*. Retrieved from http://www.cook.navy.mil/

Valentino-Devries, J., & Gorman, S. (2013, August 20). What You Need to Know on New Details of NSA Spying, *The Wall Street Journal*. Retrieved from http://online.wsj.com/news/articles/SB10001424127887324108204579025222244858490

Vallone, R. P., Ross, L., & Lepper, M. R. (1985). The Hostile Media Phenomenon: Biased Perception and Perceptions of Media Bias in Coverage of the Beirut Massacre. In *Journal of Personality and Social Psychology, 49*(3), 8.

Vamosi, R. (2014, March 4). DDoS Attacks Silence Ukraine Cell Phones [Weblog comment]. Retrieved from https://mocana.com/blog/2014/03/04/ddos-attacks-hit-ukraine-cell-phones/

van Niekerk, B., & Maharaj, M. (2011). The IW Life Cycle Model, *South African Journal of Information Management, 13*. Available from http://www.sajim.co.za/index.php/SAJIM/article/view/476

van Niekerk, B., & Maharaj, M. (2012). Mobile devices and the military: useful tool or significant threat? In *Proceedings of the 4th Workshop on ICT Uses in Warfare and the Safeguarding of Peace* (IWSP 2012), Pretoria: CSIR and UKZN.

van Niekerk, B., & Maharaj, M. (2013). Social Media and Information Conflict. *International Journal of Communication, 7*, 1162–1184.

van Niekerk, B., Pillay, K., & Maharaj, M. (2011). Analysing the Role of ICTs in the Tunisian and Egyptian Unrest from an Information Warfare Perspective. *International Journal of Communication, 5*, 1406–1416.

van Vuuren, J. J., Phahlamohlaka, J., & Brazzoli, M. S. (2010). The impact of increase in braodband access on South African national security and the average citizen. *Journal of Information Warfare, 9*(3), 9–13.

Vanguard - Nigeria: Boko Haram leader vows to kill elder statesmen, others in new video. (2014). *Allafrica.com*. Retrieved from http://allafrica.com/stories/201402210294.html

Vatis, M. A. (2010) The Council of Europe Convention on Cybercrime. 207-224

Vautrinot, S. (2012, July 25). *Improving Military Capabilities for Cyber Operations*. [Statement to the House Armed Services Committee Subcommittee].

Velleman, J. D. (2000). *The Possibility of Practical Reason*. New York: Clarendon Press.

Verissimo, P., Neves, N., & Correia, M. (2008). The CRUTIAL reference critical information infrastructure architecture: a blueprint. In A. Gheorghe (Ed.), International Journal of System of Systems Engineering, 1/2, 78–95. doi:10.1504/IJSSE.2008.018132

Verissimo, P., Neves, N., Correia, M., Deswarte, Y., Kalam, A., Bondavalli, A., & Daidone, A. (2008b). The CRUTIAL Architecture for Critical Information Infrastructures. In R. Lemos, F. Giandomenico, C. Gacek, H. Muccini, & M. Vieira (Eds.), *Architecting Dependable Systems V*, 5135, 1–27). Springer Berlin Heidelberg. doi:10.1007/978-3-540-85571-2_1

Verton, D., & Brandt, A. (2012). Biography of a Worm. *PC World*. Retrieved from http://pcworld.about.net/magazine/2211p115id117808.htm

VICE. (2014, August 15). *The Islamic State (Full Length). VICE News*. Retrieved from https://news.vice.com/video/the-islamic-state-full-length

Vienna Document of the Negotiations on Confidence- and Security-Building. Proceedings of the 269th Plenary Meeting the OSCE Forum for Security Co-operation. (1999, November 16). OSCE. Istanbul. Retrieved from http://www.osce.org/fsc/41276

Vignard, K. (2011). Confronting Cyberconflict, UNIDIR Disarmament Forum.

Vijayan, J. (2013a, April 6). U.S. urged to let companies 'hack-back' at IP cyber thieves. *Computerworld*. Retrieved from http://www.computerworld.com/s/article/9239503/U.S._urged_to_let_companies_hack_back_at_IP_cyber_thieves

Vijayan, J. (2013b, May 29). Private retaliation in cyberspace a 'remarkably bad idea'. *Computerworld*. Retrieved from http://www.computerworld.com/s/article/9239606/Private_retaliation_in_cyberspace_a_remarkably_bad_idea_

Vijayan, J. (2014, July 2). Hackers hit more businesses through remote access accounts. *IT News*. Retrieved July 3, 2014, from http://itnews.com/security/80848/hackers-hit-more-businesses-through-remote-access-accounts?page=0,0

Virtual Global Task Force. (n. d.). Retrievedfrom http://www.virtualglobaltaskforce.com/

Von Behr, I., Reding, A., Edwards, C., & Gribbon, L. (2013). *Radicalization in the Digital Era: The Use of the Internet in 15 Cases of Terrorism and Extremism*. Cambridge: RAND.

Vural, Y., & Sağıroğlu, Ş. (2008). A Review on Enterprise Information Security and Standards. *Journal of the Faculty of Engineering and Architecture of Gazi University, 23*(2), 507–522.

Wadhwa, V. (2015, May 11). Quantum computing is about to overturn cybersecurity's balance of power. *The Washington Post*. Retrieved from http://www.washingtonpost.com/blogs/innovations/wp/2015/05/11/quantum-computing-is-about-to-overturn-cybersecuritys-balance-of-power/

Walden, I. (2003). Computer crime. In C. Reed & J. Angel (Eds.), *Computer Law*. London: Oxford University Press.

Walden, I. (2005). Crime and security in cyberspace. *Cambridge Review of International Affairs, 18*(1), 51–68. doi:10.1080/09557570500059563

Walker, B. B. (n.d) Transparency and Confidence Building Measures in Cyber Space: Towards Norms and Behaviors. 31-40

Walker, S. (2014, March 4). Russian propaganda and Ukrainian rumour fuel anger and hate in Crimea. *The Guardian*. Retrieved from http://www.theguardian.com/world/2014/mar/04/russian-propaganda-ukrainian-rumours-anger-hate-crimea

Wang, H. J., Guo, C., Simon, D. R., & Zugenmaier, A. (2004, August). Shield: Vulnerability-driven network filters for preventing known vulnerability exploits.[ACM.]. *Computer Communication Review, 34*(4), 193–204. doi:10.1145/1030194.1015489

Wang, Y., Wong, J., & Miner, A. (2004). Anomaly intrusion detection using one class SVM.*Information Assurance Workshop, 2004. Proceedings from the Fifth Annual IEEE SMC*, 358–364. doi:10.1109/IAW.2004.1437839

Warfield, M. H. (2003). Security implications of IPv6. *Internet Security Systems, 4*(1), 2–5.

Wasim, A. (2010). *Placing lapsed ordinance in Senate: Law ministry apologises to committee*. Dawn.

Waxman, M. C. (2011). Cyber-Attacks and the Use of Force: Back to the Future of Article 2(4). *Yale Journal of International Law, 36*(2), 421–459.

Web site of Russia Today hacked and defaced over Ukraine conflict. (2014, March 3). *Bitdefender*. Retrieved from http://www.bitdefender.com/security/web-site-of-russia-today-hacked-and-defaced-over-ukraine-conflict.html

Webb, J. P. (2012, June 26). The illegality of striking back against hackers. *Cybercrime Review*. Retrieved from http://www.cybercrimereview.com/2012/06/illegality-of-striking-back-against.html

Wegener, H. (2007) Harnessing the Perils in Cyberspace: Who is in Charge? 45-52

Wegener, H. (n.d) Regulating Cyber Behaviour: Some Initial Reflections on Codes of Conduct and Confidence-Building Measures.

Weimann, G. (2005). Cyberterrorism: The sum of all fears? *Studies in Conflict and Terrorism, 28*(2), 129–149. doi:10.1080/10576100590905110

Westby, J. (2012, November 29). Caution: Active response to cyber attacks has high risk. *Forbes*. Retrieved from http://www.forbes.com/sites/jodywestby/2012/11/29/caution-active-response-to-cyber-attacks-has-high-risk/

Westby, J. R. (Ed.). (2004). *International Guide to Cyber Security Chicago*. American Bar Association.

West, Z. (2012). Young fella, if you're looking for trouble I'll accommodate you: Deputizing private companies for the use of hackback. *Syracuse Law Review, 63*(1), 119–146.

What is Islamic State? (2014b, September 26). *BBC News*. Retrieved from http://www.bbc.co.uk/news/world-middle-east-29052144

What we investigate. (n. d.). Federal Bureau of Investigation, Albuquerque Division. Retrieved from http://www.fbi.gov/albuquerque/about-us/what-we-investigate

Wheeler, D. A., & Larsen, G. N. (2003). Techniques for cyber attack attribution. Retrieved from http://www.dtic.mil/cgi-bin/GetTRDoc?AD=ADA468859

Wheeler, D. A., & Larsen, G. N. (2003). *Techniques for Cyber Attack Attribution*. Alexandria, Virginia: Institute for Defense Analyses.

Whitehouse (n.d). "Cyber Security." Retrieved July 10, 2013, from http://www.whitehouse.gov/cybersecurity

Whitehouse (n.d). "Cyber Space Policy Review: Assuring a Trusted and Resilient Information and Communications Infrastructure." from http://www.whitehouse.gov/assets /documents/Cyberspace_Policy_Review_final.pdf

Whitehouse.gov. "The Sequester." Retrieved April 25, 2013, from http://www.whitehouse.gov/issues/sequester

White, J. (2013). The anti-surveillance state: New products that are challenging law enforcement. *The Journal of the Australian Institute of Professional Intelligence Officers, 21*(2), 17–36.

Whitman, M. E., & Mattord, H. J. (2004). *Principles of information security*. Boston, MA: Publisher Course Technology Press.

Wiki, I. L. (n.d). "APEC Cybersecurity Strategy." Retrieved June 15, 2013, from http://itlaw.wikia.com/wiki/APEC_Cybersecurity_Strategy.

William, A. Owens, K. W. D. a. H. S. L. e. (2009). Technology, Policy Law and Ethics regarding U.S. Acquisition and use of Cyberattack Capabilities. Washington DC, The National Academies.

Williams, M. (1999). Hacker Discovers Antigravity File in Military Computer. Retrieved from http://www.bibliotecapleyades.net/ciencia/secret_projects/project159.htm

Williams, M. (2009, July 14). U.K. not North Korea, source of DDoS attacks, research says. *Computer World*. Retrieved http://www.computerworld.com/s/article/9135492/U.K._not_North_Korea_source_of_DDOS_attacks_researcher_says

Willson, D. (2009). "A Global Problem: Cyberspace Threats Demand an International Approach." ISSA Journal August 2009.

Wilson, C. (2006, September 14). *Information operations and cyberwar: Capabilities and related policy issues*. CRS Report for Congress, RL31787. Retrieved from http://fas.org/irp/crs/RL31787.pdf

Wilson, W. (2008). *Botnets, cybercrime, and cyberterrorism: vulnerabilities and policy issues for congress*. Washington: Congressional Research Service.

Winkler, C., & Dauber, C. E. (Eds.). (2014). *Visual Propaganda and E-extremism in the Online Environment*. US Army War College Press & Strategic Studies Institute. Retrieved from http://permanent.access.gpo.gov/gpo51688/pub1213.pdf

Wireless News. (2013, June 29). CrowdStrike Unveils Big Data Active Defense Platform. *Wireless News*.

Wolf, J. B. (2000). War games meets the internet: Chasing 21st century cybercriminals with old laws and little money. *American Journal of Criminal Law*, *28*(1), 95–117.

Wolpert, S. (2006). *Shameful Flight: The Last Years of the British Empire in India*. USA: Oxford University Press.

Wolter, D. D. (2012). Looking towards the future of cyber security: what does a stable cyber environment look like?" UNIDIR Cyber Security Conference 2012: The Role of Confidence Building Measures in Assuring Cyber Stability. Cyber Security Conference 2012: The Role of Confidence-Building Measures in Assuring Cyber Stability, Geneva, Switzerland, UNIDIR.

Woodward, J. L., Jr., LGEN, USAF, Director for Command, Control, Communications and Computer Systems (February 2000). *Cybersecurity through Defense-in-Depth*. Washington, DC: The Joint Staff, Pentagon.

World Federation of Scientists Permanent Monitoring Panel on Information Security.(2003).

World Internet Users and Population Stats. (2014). *Internet World Stats*. Retrieved from http://www.internetworldstats.com/stats.htm

Wright, C., Monrose, F., & Masson, G. (2006). On inferring application protocol behaviors in encrypted network traffic. *Journal of Machine Learning Research*, *7*, 2745–2769.

Wustrow, E., Karir, M., Bailey, M., Jahanian, F., & Huston, G. (2010, November). Internet background radiation revisited. In *Proceedings of the 10th ACM SIGCOMM conference on Internet measurement* (pp. 62-74). ACM.

Wu, T. (1999). Application-centered internet analysis. *Virginia Law Review*, *85*(6), 1163–1204. doi:10.2307/1073968

Wu, T. (2006). The world trade law of censorship and internet filtering. *Chicago Journal of International Law*, *7*(1), 263–287.

Wymore, W. (1993). *Model-Based Systems Engineering*. Boca Raton: CRC Press.

X.1205, U. I.-T. (2011) Cybersecurity Information Exchange (CYBEX).

Xinghuanet (n.d). The Internet in China,. P. Han.

Yadron, D. (2015, January 8). Snowden: Don't hack back. *The Wall Street Journal*. Retrieved January 10, 2015, from http://blogs.wsj.com/digits/2015/01/08/snowden-dont-hack-back/

Yamin, T. (2012). "Nuclear Risk Reduction in South Asia." Journal of Contemporary Studies.

Yasin, R. (1998). Think twice before becoming a hacker attacker. *InternetWeek*, *745*, 30.

Yekaterinburg Declaration of the Heads of the Member States of the Shanghai Cooperation Organisation. (n. d.). Ministry of Foreign Affairs of the People's Republic of China. Retrieved from http://www.fmprc.gov.cn/eng/

Yin, J., & Taylor, P. M. (2008). Information operations from an Asian perspective: A comparative analysis. *Journal of Information Warfare*, *7*(1), 1–23.

Yu, L., Schwier, J. M., Craven, R. M., Brooks, R. R., & Griffin, C. (2013, July). Inferring statistically significant hidden markov models. *IEEE Transactions on Knowledge and Data Engineering*, *25*(7), 1548–1558. doi:10.1109/TKDE.2012.93

Yurcik, W. (1997). Information Warfare: Legal and Ethical Challenges of the Next Global Battleground," 2nd Annual Ethics and Technology Conference

Yusha, M. (2010). India - Pakistan's Cyber War: CBI Website Still Not Restored. Pakistan Spectator: Candid Blog, Pakistan Spectator: Candid Blog. 2013.

Zafar, K. (n.d). Cyber-crime: Two arrested for forgery, credit card fraud. Express Tribune, Express Tribune.

Zavrsnik, A. (2010). Towards an overregulated cyberspace. *Masaryk University Journal of Law & Technology*, *4*(2), 185–188.

Zemanek, K. (1987). Responsibility of states: General principles. In Encyclopaedia of Public International Law (Vol. 10, pp. 362-372).

Zetter, K. (2014, July 3). The NSA is targeting users of privacy services, leaked code shows. *Wired*. Retrieved July 3, 2014, from http://www.wired.com/2014/07/nsa-targets-users-of-privacy-services/

Zhu, B., Joseph, A., & Sastry, S. (2011). A Taxonomy of Cyber Attacks on SCADA Systems. In *Proceedings of the 2011 International Conference on Internet of Things and 4th International Conference on Cyber, Physical and Social Computing,* (pp. 380–388). doi:10.1109/iThings/CPSCom.2011.34

Zimmt, R. (2012). Spotlight on Iran. *The Meir Amit Intelligence and Terrorism Information Center*. Retrieved from http://www.terrorism-info.org.il/en/article/20370

Zoller, E. (1984). *Peacetime unilateral remedies: An analysis of countermeasures. Dobbs Ferry*. Transnational Publishers.

Zulfqar, S. (2013). Efficacy of Confidence Building Measures (CBMs) in India-Pakistan Relations. *IPRI Journal*, *XIII*(1), 10.

About the Contributors

Jean-Loup Richet is information systems service manager at Orange and a research fellow at ESSEC Business School - Institute for Strategic Innovation & Services. He graduated from the French National Institute of Telecommunications, Telecom Business School, and holds a Master of Research from IAE/HEC Paris. He is an expert in information systems security and has presented at several national and international conferences. He has published articles in academic and trade journals. Jean-Loup is currently a lecturer in Information Systems at Sorbonne Graduate Business School (MBA) and guest lecturer at HEC Paris, ESSEC and INT, focusing on cybersecurity, cyberwarfare, risk and crisis management.

***

Faruk Aydin is a captain in the Turkish Air Force. He has served various section of IT departments including administrative role. He has experience on software development, network management and information security.

Professor Paul Baines is Professor of Political Marketing at Cranfield School of Management and Course Director, MSc Management and Director, Baines Associates Limited. Paul was Managing Editor, Europe of the Journal of Political Marketing from 2010-2013. He is author/co-author of more than a hundred published articles, book chapters and books on marketing and political marketing issues. He holds bachelors, masters and doctoral degrees from The University of Manchester and a Postgraduate Certificate in Higher Education from Middlesex University. Paul is (co-)editor and co-author of numerous marketing texts, including: Political Marketing (Sage Publications, 2011), with Sir Robert Worcester, Roger Mortimore and Mark Gill, Explaining Cameron's Coalition (Biteback Publishing, 2011), Essentials of Marketing with Chris Fill and Kelly Page (Oxford University Press, 2013) and a 4 volume book set on Propaganda with Nicholas O'Shaughnessy (Sage Publications, 2013). Paul's marketing research consultancy experience includes studies on various communication research projects for the UK Foreign and Commonwealth Office, Home Office, and Ministry of Defence.

Cameron Brown is an Endeavour Executive Fellow. He graduated in law and psychology from the University of Melbourne and holds combined Masters level degrees from Macquarie University in international security, policing, intelligence and counter terrorism. He has also attained technical certifications in computer crime investigation, cyber-security, data recovery, and digital and network forensics. Cameron is affiliated with the Australian National University Cybercrime Observatory where he conducts in-depth research into emerging trends in forensic science, terrorism prevention, corruption, and modes of cyber-conflict. Internationally, he has worked with Transparency International and the United Nations. In the field he has served with police task-forces, government agencies, and the private sector where his responsibilities extend to provision of technical advice, investigative guidance, forensic analysis, and expert testimony. Cameron also practices as an international lawyer with professional pursuits related to strategic cyber defense, public policy engagement, data privacy, regulatory compliance, transactional risk, incident response, crisis management, and authentication of electronically stored information.

Filipe Caldeira is Adjunct Professor at the Informatics Department of the Polytechnic Institute of Viseu, Portugal. He obtained his doctoral degree in Informatics Engineering in 2014 from the Faculty of Sciences and Technology of the University of Coimbra. He is also a researcher at the Centre for Informatics and Systems of the University of Coimbra where he recently has been involved in European research project FP7 MICIE. His main research interests include ICT security, namely, policy-based management, trust and reputation systems, Security and Critical Infrastructure Protection.

Douglas Campbell Ph.D., was born on May 9, 1954 in Portsmouth, Virginia, and is an American citizen. He graduated from Kenitra American High School, Kenitra, Morocco, in 1972. He received his Bachelor of Science degree in Journalism from the University of Kansas in 1976 and was immediately commissioned as an Ensign in the United States Navy. He joined the U.S. Naval Reserve Program as an Intelligence Officer in 1980 and was transferred to the Retired Reserves as a Lieutenant Commander on 1 June 1999. Dr. Campbell received his Master of Science degree from the University of Southern California in Computer Systems Management in 1986 and his Doctor of Philosophy degree in Computer Security from Southwest University in New Orleans, Louisiana, in 1990. Dr. Campbell is president and CEO of Syneca Research Group, Inc., a veteran-owned small business. His clients include the U.S. Federal Aviation Administration and Department of Homeland Security (including Federal Emergency Management Agency, Transportation Security Administration, and Secret Service). The majority of his recent consulting has been in physical and cybersecurity of airports (e.g., San Francisco International Airport) and seaports (e.g., Puerto Rico Ports Authority). He is the author of more than a dozen books on information assurance and U.S. Navy and U.S. Marine Corps aviation history.

Alan Chong is Associate Professor at the S. Rajaratnam School of International Studies in Singapore. He has published widely on the notion of soft power and the role of ideas in constructing the international relations of Singapore and Asia. His publications have appeared in The Pacific Review; International Relations of the Asia-Pacific; Asian Survey; East Asia: an International Quarterly; Politics, Religion and Ideology; the Review of International Studies; the Cambridge Review of International Affairs and Armed Forces and Society. He is also the author of Foreign Policy in Global Information Space: Actualizing Soft Power (Palgrave, 2007). He is currently working on several projects exploring the notion of 'Asian international theory'. His interest in soft power has also led to inquiry into the sociological and philosophical foundations of international communication. In the latter area, he is currently working on a manuscript titled 'The International Politics of Communication: Representing Community in a Globalizing World'. In tandem, he has pursued a fledgling interest in researching cyber security issues. He has frequently been interviewed in the Asian media and consulted in think-tank networks in the region. Alan Chong can be contacted at: iscschong@ntu.edu.sg.

Tiago Cruz is Invited Assistant Professor at the University of Coimbra (Portugal), from where he got his PhD in Informatics Engineering, in 2012. He is also a researcher at the Centre for Informatics and Systems of the University of Coimbra. His research interests include (but are not restricted to) Broadband Network Architectures, Systems, Network Management, Security and Embedded Systems Design and Critical Infrastructure Security, with over 30 journal and conference publications in these areas. He has been involved in several European- and industry-funded research projects, with both technical and management activities.

Raymond Curts, Ph.D., was born December 2, 1946 in Philadelphia, Pennsylvania and is an American citizen. He graduated from Vandalia Community High School, Vandalia, Illinois in 1965. He received his Bachelor of Science in Aeronautical and Astronautical Engineering from the University of Illinois in 1970 and was commissioned as an Ensign in the United States Navy. In December 1972 he earned his wings as a Naval Aviator and was assigned to the U.S. Naval Base at Guantanamo Bay, Cuba. Returning to the continental United States in 1976, he became an instructor pilot in the Navy's Advanced Jet Training Command in Beeville, Texas where he earned a Master of Arts degree in Management and Business Administration from Webster University of St. Louis, Missouri. After tours of duty in Norfolk, Virginia; Rota, Spain; and Key West, Florida, he was stationed at the Space and Naval Warfare Systems Command (SPAWAR) in Washington, DC where he spent five years as the Navy's first Electronic Warfare Architect. During this time he earned a Ph.D. in Information Technology from George Mason University. Since retirement from the Naval service in 1992, Dr. Curts has supported a wide variety of government agencies with several major corporations. Currently he is providing Cybersecurity and systems integration support to the DoD, Intelligence Community (IC) components, the U.S. Navy and several other government agencies.

Olivier Danino is a researcher at the French Institute for Strategic Analysis. Specialist of the Israeli-Palestinian conflict, he has received the Duroselle Price for his work on Jerusalem. His research field also deals with how cyber impacts the Middle East conflicts, and with the cyber strategies adopted by states and non-states actors in this region. He has published several books on the Middle East, was invited in Israel for a simulation game on security and defense issues and has participated to international conferences on cyber terrorism.

Chris Demchak With engineering, economics, and comparative complex organization theory/political science degrees, Dr. Chris C. Demchak is the RADM Grace M. Hopper Professor of Cyber Security and Co-Director, Center for Cyber Conflict Studies (C3S), Strategic Research Department, U.S. Naval War College. Her research and many publications address global cyberspace as globally shared, insecure 'substrate' penetrating throughout the critical organizations of digitized societies, creating 'cybered conflict', and resulting in a rising 'Cyber Westphalia' of sovereign competitive complex socio-technical-economic systems (STESs). Demchak takes a systemic approach in focusing on emergent structures, comparative institutional evolution, adversary/defensive use of systemic cybered tools, virtual worlds/gaming for operationalized organizational learning, and designing systemic resilience against normal or adversary imposed surprise. She has taught international security studies and management, comparative organization theory, enterprise information systems, and cybersecurity for international/national security issues. Recent works include Designing Resilience (2010, co-edited); Wars of Disruption and Resilience

(2011); and a manuscript in production tentatively entitled Cyber Westphalia: Redrawing International Economics, Conflict, and Global Structures.

Peter Dombrowski is a professor of strategy in the Strategic Research Department at the Naval War College. Previous positions include chair of the Strategic Research Department, director of the Naval War College Press, editor of the Naval War College Review, co-editor of International Studies Quarterly, Associate Professor of Political Science at Iowa State University and defense analyst at ANSER, Inc. He has also been affiliated with research institutions including the East-West Center, The Brookings Institution, the Friedrich Ebert Foundation, and the Watson Institute for International Studies at Brown University among others. Dr Dombrowski is the author of over fifty books, monographs, articles, book chapters and government reports. Awards include a Chancellor's Scholarship for Prospective Leaders from the Alexander von Humboldt Foundation, the Navy Meritorious Civilian Service Medal, and the Navy Superior Civilian Service Medal. He received his B.A. from Williams College and an M.A. and Ph.D. from the University of Maryland.

Claude Fachkha is a cyber security researcher. In 2008, he received his Bachelor of Engineering in computer and communication from Notre Dame University. Two years later, he received his Master of Engineering in information systems security from Concordia University, Canada, where he is currently pursuing his Ph.D. degree in the Faculty of Electrical and Computer Engineering. Claude is a recipient of the prestigious Fonds de recherche du Québec – Nature et technologies (FQRNT) award. His current research interests are in the areas of computer network traffic analysis and the investigation of large-scale cyber attacks such as Distributed Denial of Service (DDoS), malware and botnet threats.

Clement Guitton is a PhD candidate in the department of War Studies at King's College London currently working on the topic of cyber security. In parallel to his research, he also works as an intelligence analyst for Tempest Security Intelligence. He has previous experience at the International Telecommunication Union (United Nations), and as a software engineer.

Helge Janicke is a Reader in Computer Science and the Head of the Software Technology Research Laboratory and DMU's Cyber Security Centre. He obtained his PhD in Computer Security in 2007 and has worked within the field of Cyber Security over the past decade. His current research activities include formal approaches applied to safety and security of industrial control systems; Technologies and methods employed in cyber warfare and the protection of Critical National Infrastructures; as well as the verification and enforcement of policies in distributed software-based systems.He is active in the research community as a reviewer for journals, funding bodies and serves on the programme committees of several international conferences in Cyber Security. Janicke published over 60 peer reviewed papers and currently chairs the International Symposium for Industrial Control System Cyber Security Research.

Kevin Jones is the Head of Airbus Group Innovations Cyber Operations team and is responsible for research and state of the art cyber security solutions in support of the Airbus Group (Airbus, Airbus Helicopters, and Airbus Defence & Space). He holds a BSc in Computer Science and MSc in Distributed Systems Integration from De Montfort University, Leicester where he also obtained his PhD: A Trust Based Approach to Mobile Multi-Agent System Security in 2010. He is active in the cyber security research community and holds a number of patents within the domain. He has many years of experience in consultancy to aid organisations in achieving accreditation to ISO27001 standard on Information Security Management and currently acts as a senior expert consultant to the Airbus Group on matters of cyber (information) security across multiple domains and platforms. Kevin's current research activities include Risk Assessments, Security Architectures, and Cyber Operations in; ICS/SCADA systems and Critical National Infrastructure (CNI), Security Operations Centres, Mobile Security, and Cloud Security. He currently chairs the International Symposium for Industrial Control System Cyber Security Research and is an elected expert to the Engineering and Physical Sciences Research Council (EPSRC). He has worked closely with UK Government agencies on ICS/SCADA cyber security and on European funded programmes such as the European Control System Security Incident Analysis Network. He is a Member of the BCS, IEEE, and ISC2 and accredited as a Certified Information Systems Security Professional (CISSP) and ISO27001 Lead Auditor.

Nigel Jones is a Visiting Fellow in the Defence Studies Department of King's College London. He specialises in the people and informational dimensions of policy, strategy and plans, particularly in the security and conflict contexts. Until March 2015, he was Senior Lecturer in Cyber Defence and Information Operations at Cranfield University at the Defence Academy of the United Kingdom. Prior to joining Cranfield, he directed the UK's Cyber Security Knowledge Transfer Network, bringing academic, public and private stakeholders together to work on innovation in contemporary cyber security challenges. This he did whilst at QinetiQ PLC where he ran a research and consultancy team. His interest in communications in security and conflict stems from his previous 16 years in the Army, that saw operational deployments in which he ran communications campaigns or provided training in audience analysis and communications planning.

Mark Maybury is Vice President and Chief Technology Officer and directs The MITRE Corporation's independent research and development program, oversees technology transfer and commercialization, and develops the corporate technology strategy. He is a board member of the DSB, AF SAB and OMG. From 2010 to 2013, Dr. Maybury served as Chief Scientist of the Air Force, advising the Secretary and Chief of Staff on a wide range of scientific and technical issues affecting the Air Force mission. Previously, Mark was the Executive Director of MITRE's Information Technology Division. Mark has authored or edited 10 books, more than 60 refereed publications, and was awarded patents in broadcast news understanding and personal casting. An IEEE and AAAI Fellow, Mark has served on multiple national advisory committees. He was recognized for support to the World Trade Center rescue and recovery, to the Coalition Provisional Authority in Baghdad, Iraq, and to the Presidential Terrorism Information Sharing Environment. Dr. Maybury holds an MBA from RPI and doctorate from the University of Cambridge.

Edmundo Monteiro is Full Professor at the University of Coimbra (UC), Portugal, from where he got the PhD in Electrical Engineering and the Habilitation in Informatics Engineering in 1996 and 2007 respectively. His research interests are Computer Networks, Wireless Communications, Quality of Service and Experience, Service Oriented Infrastructures, and Security. He is author of over 200 publications in books, journals, book chapters, and international conferences. He is also co-author of 9 international patents. Edmundo Monteiro is the Portuguese representative in IFIP-TC6, and senior member of IEEE Communication Society, and ACM Special Interest Group on Communications.

Brett van Niekerk graduated with his PhD in 2012 from the University of KwaZulu-Natal, South Africa, and has completed two years of postdoctoral research into information operations, information warfare, and critical infrastructure protection. He is currently a Senior Security Analyst at Transnet and an Honorary Research Fellow at the University of KwaZulu-Natal. He is serving as secretary for the International Federation of Information Processing's Working Group 9.10 on ICT in Peace and War, and has contributed to the ISO/IEC information security standards. He has multiple presentations and papers in information security and information warfare to his name. He also holds a BSc and a MSc in electronic engineering.

Nickolas O'Shaughnessy is Professor of Communication at Queen Mary, University of London. Previously he was Professor at the Universities of Brunel and Keele and Director of the Centre for Consumer and Social Marketing at Brunel. Prior to this, he was a Fellow (now Quondam Fellow) of Hughes Hall in the University of Cambridge, where he was also University Lecturer in Marketing. He has degrees from London, Oxford and Columbia universities, and a PhD from Cambridge. Nicholas is the author and co-author of numerous journal articles, chapters and books on marketing, propaganda (including terrorism) and political communication, including The Phenomenon of Political Marketing (Macmillan, 1990), Persuasion in Advertising (Routledge,), The Marketing Power of Emotion (Oxford,), Propaganda and Politics: Weapons of Mass Seduction (Manchester/Michigan, 2003). He is on the editorial board of various journals and is a Senior Editor of the Journal of Political Marketing. He has also been a parliamentary candidate and an (informal) adviser to John Major when Prime Minister. As a student, he was President of the Oxford Union.

Tolga Pusatli is an IT academic in the Department of Mathematics and Computer Science at the Cankaya University, Turkey where he undertakes lecturing in data and information management, information system and software. His research scope includes software quality and IT usage in the industry.

Latifa Ben Arfa Rabai is a University Assistant Professor in the Department of Computer Science at the Tunis University in the Higher Institute of Management (ISG). She received the computer science Engineering diploma in 1989 from the sciences faculty of Tunis and the PhD, from the sciences faculty of Tunis in 1992. Her research interest includes software engineering trends quantification, software engineering education, quality assessment in education and e-learning, and security measurement and quantification. She has published in information sciences Journal, IEEE Technology and Engineering Education magazine. She has participated in several international conferences covering topics related to the computer science, E-learning, quality assessment in education, cyber security.

Neila Rjaibi is a University Common Core Professor of Computer Science at the Higher Institute of Commerce and Accountancy of Bizerte (ISCCB), Tunisia, since September 2008. In 2007, Neila has graduated from the University of Tunis, Higher Institute of Management (ISG). In 2010, she holds her Master Diploma. In present, she is pursuing the Ph.D. degree. Her research interests are: Software Engineering, Cyber Security Measurement and Quantification, Security Risk Management, E-learning Systems. She has participated in international conferences and served as a technical program committee member for some. Also, she has published several papers in international journals and served as a reviewer for some. And she has authored several book chapters.

Michael Robinson is a PhD student at De Montfort University's Software Technology Research Laboratory with an interest in cyber warfare research. He has a multi-disciplinary background with Bachelor degrees in both computer science and international relations. He received his Master's degree in computer security from De Montfort University in 2012.

Paulo Simoes is Assistant Professor at the Department of Informatics Engineering of the University of Coimbra, Portugal, from where he obtained his doctoral degree in 2002. He regularly collaborates with Instituto Pedro Nunes as senior consultant, leading technology transfer projects for industry partners such as telecommunications operators and energy utilities. His main research interests include Network and Infrastructure Management, Security and Critical Infrastructure Protection. He has over 150 publications in refereed journals and conferences, and he has also been involved in several European research projects in these fields. Further information can be found at his homepage: http://eden.dei.uc.pt/~psimoes.

Ian Tunnicliffe is a Director at Accordance Associates. Over the past few years Ian Tunnicliffe has worked on a range of communications research, and media projects in countries across Asia, Africa and the Middle East including Syria, Iran, Iraq, Libya, Afghanistan and Pakistan. In 2013, his research work led to an invitation to testify to the United Kingdom House of Commons Defence Select Committee on understanding and communicating in the Middle East. Prior to that he served for 20 years in the British Army, seeing service on a range of operations including the First Gulf War, the withdrawal from Hong Kong, and the liberation of Kosovo and Northern Ireland. His last few years of service were in the UK Ministry of Defence (MOD), where he helped develop United Kingdom cross-government strategic communications plans in response to a number of international crises in the Balkans, Africa, Asia and especially the Middle East, during the Iraq crisis and conflict.

Tughral Yamin is the founding member and associate dean of the Centre for International Peace & Stability (CIPS). He earned his PhD from the Department of Defence and Strategic Studies from Quaid-i-Azam University Islamabad. In 2013 he was awarded a research fellowship in the International Program of the Cooperative Monitoring Center (CMC), Sandia National Laboratories (SNL) Albuquerque NM, USA to write a paper on CBMs in Cyber Space between India and Pakistan. He is the author of two books; The Evolution of Military Deterrence in South Asia; and Cyber CBMs between Pakistan and India. He is currently writing a book on peacekeeping operations in Somalia.His academic qualifications include an MSc in War Studies, MA in International Relations, BSc (hons) in War Studies and a BA in military art and sciences. He was awarded the gold medal for earning the first position in BA. He is a qualified interpreter in German language from the National University of Modern Languages Islamabad and has a first class diploma in German military language from the Federal Bureau of Languages Cologne. During his military career Professor Yamin attended the German General Staff College, Pakistan Army Command & Staff College Quetta and Pakistan Armed Forces War College Islamabad. He has taught at the Pakistan Army Command and Staff College Quetta, the National Defence University Islamabad, and the National University of Modern Languages Islamabad. Professor Yamin has delivered lectures to international audiences at the National University of Singapore; Atlantic Council, Washington DC; George Mason University, Washington DC; and National Defense University, Washington DC; on subjects like regional and information security. He has also delivered keynote speeches on net-centric warfare in seminars held in Singapore. He has represented his country as the senior armed forces delegate in the ASEAN Regional Forum meeting in Laos in 2005. His academic interests include India-Pakistan relations; confidence building measures; regional security; peacekeeping; peace building; conflict resolution; nuclear stability; arms control & disarmament; net-centric warfare; strategic decision making; and information security. He and his wife run a charity school for poor children in the suburbs of Islamabad.

Index

A

active defense 8, 166-168, 170, 174, 182, 184, 293
adversary 3, 7, 9, 12, 16, 21, 36, 46, 67-69, 72-73, 77, 79, 82, 168-169, 178-181, 202, 207, 211, 316, 331, 339, 344, 356-357, 382
agility 7-9, 12
Al Qaeda 297-298, 341-345, 348, 350, 356, 359
Al Shabaab 341-342, 349-351, 353, 355
anonymous 38, 41, 166, 176-178, 217, 271, 294-296, 314, 322-323, 325, 327, 329, 389
antivirus 79, 82, 154, 272, 290
armed attack 171-173, 246
ARP 66, 82, 177
attribution 3, 21, 23, 32-33, 37-48, 50-51, 60, 166, 176, 178-180, 182, 202, 205, 217, 233, 321
authentication 87-88, 90, 134, 154, 158, 175-176, 202, 241

B

backscatter 66, 82
Boko Haram 341-342, 347-349, 352, 355-356

C

Coercion (Cybered) 381
cooperation 41, 181-182, 205-206, 209-212, 219-220, 222, 224, 226-232, 236-237, 241-242, 246, 248, 276-277, 287, 290-293
counteroffensive 167-168, 178-179
Counter-Terrorism 221, 341, 343, 356, 359
CPU 28, 65, 82, 150
Critical Infrastructure Protection 122, 124, 127
Cyber Army 209, 285, 288, 295-296
cyber attack 4, 16, 21-22, 27-30, 32, 36, 38, 60, 64, 82, 273, 275, 277, 285, 299
cyber-attack 167, 169, 172-174, 176, 178, 181, 205, 210-211, 215, 217, 245, 308, 310, 329-331, 339
cybercrime 2, 76, 174, 205, 209, 218, 221-222, 227-231, 233, 236, 242, 248, 277, 286, 290-291, 375, 377
cyber defence 20-21, 23, 32, 36, 242, 275
cyber deterrence 22-23, 36
Cyber Early Warning System 21, 36
cybered conflict 367-369, 373-376, 378, 381, 394
cyber power 367, 375, 377-379, 381
cyberpropaganda 341-342, 351-354
cybersecurity principles 1, 9
Cybersecurity Threat 202
Cyberspace Situational Awareness (CSA) 12
Cyberspace 'Substrate' 382
cyber-strategy 308, 316, 321, 325, 329-331, 339
cyber threat 63, 122, 271, 277, 285, 291, 322
cyber war 36, 45, 63, 215, 227, 275, 277, 302-303, 367-368, 381
cyber warfare 8, 13-19, 21-33, 36, 45, 172, 205-206, 209-210, 212, 217, 221, 246, 288, 294
cyber weapon 25-27, 29, 36, 276
Cyber Westphalia 375, 381

D

darknet 65-70, 72-74, 79
DDoS 64-68, 70, 74, 79, 82-83, 167, 171, 208, 272, 280, 294, 296-297, 299, 301, 303, 306, 322-325, 327, 329
deception 5, 12, 167, 178-180, 203, 207, 327, 374-375, 377-378, 381, 386
Defacement Attack 306
Denial of Service Attacks (DoS) 294, 306
Distributed Denial of Service Attacks (DDoS) 167, 294, 306
DNS Amplification 83, 179

E

electronic warfare 207, 292, 303, 319, 325, 327, 339
encryption 9, 63, 87, 111, 146, 175-176, 178, 180, 206, 208, 218, 368

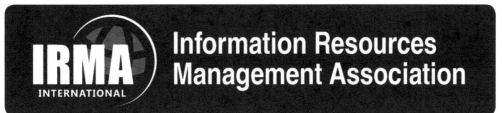

Information Resources Management Association

Become an IRMA Member

Members of the **Information Resources Management Association (IRMA)** understand the importance of community within their field of study. The Information Resources Management Association is an ideal venue through which professionals, students, and academicians can convene and share the latest industry innovations and scholarly research that is changing the field of information science and technology. Become a member today and enjoy the benefits of membership as well as the opportunity to collaborate and network with fellow experts in the field.

IRMA Membership Benefits:

- **One FREE Journal Subscription**

- **30% Off Additional Journal Subscriptions**

- **20% Off Book Purchases**

- Updates on the latest events and research on Information Resources Management through the IRMA-L listserv.

- Updates on new open access and downloadable content added to Research IRM.

- A copy of the Information Technology Management Newsletter twice a year.

- A certificate of membership.

IRMA Membership $195

Scan code to visit irma-international.org and begin by selecting your free journal subscription.

Membership is good for one full year.

Printed in the United States
By Bookmasters